P9-EDW-378

LIBRARY
ST. MICHAEL'S PREP SCHOOL
1042 STAR RD. - ORANGE, CA. 92667

(Continued on back endsheets)

Modern British Essayists, Second Series

Modern British Essayists, Second Series

8411

Edited by
Robert Beum

A Bruccoli Clark Layman Book
Gale Research Inc.
Detroit, New York, London

Advisory Board for
DICTIONARY OF LITERARY BIOGRAPHY

John Baker
William Cagle
Jane Christensen
Patrick O'Connor
Peter S. Prescott

Matthew J. Bruccoli and Richard Layman, *Editorial Directors*
C. E. Frazer Clark, Jr., *Managing Editor*

Printed in the United States of America

Published simultaneously in the United Kingdom
by Gale Research International Limited
(An affiliated company of Gale Research Inc.)

The paper used in this publication meets the minimum requirements
of American National Standard for Information Sciences—Permanence
Paper for Printed Library Materials, ANSI Z39.48-1984. ∞™

Copyright © 1990
Gale Research Inc.
835 Penobscot Bldg.
Detroit, MI 48226-4094

ISBN 0-8103-4580-3
90-43746 CIP

Contents

Plan of the Series

. . . Almost the most prodigious asset of a country, and perhaps its most precious possession, is its native literary product—when that product is fine and noble and enduring.

Mark Twain*

The advisory board, the editors, and the publisher of the *Dictionary of Literary Biography* are joined in endorsing Mark Twain's declaration. The literature of a nation provides an inexhaustible resource of permanent worth. We intend to make literature and its creators better understood and more accessible to students and the reading public, while satisfying the standards of teachers and scholars.

To meet these requirements, *literary biography* has been construed in terms of the author's achievement. The most important thing about a writer is his writing. Accordingly, the entries in *DLB* are career biographies, tracing the development of the author's canon and the evolution of his reputation.

The purpose of *DLB* is not only to provide reliable information in a convenient format but also to place the figures in the larger perspective of literary history and to offer appraisals of their accomplishments by qualified scholars.

The publication plan for *DLB* resulted from two years of preparation. The project was proposed to Bruccoli Clark by Frederick G. Ruffner, president of the Gale Research Company, in November 1975. After specimen entries were prepared and typeset, an advisory board was formed to refine the entry format and develop the series rationale. In meetings held during 1976, the publisher, series editors, and advisory board approved the scheme for a comprehensive biographical dictionary of persons who contributed to North American literature. Editorial work on the first volume began in January 1977, and it was published in 1978. In order to make *DLB* more than a reference tool and to compile volumes that individually have claim to status as literary history, it was decided to organize volumes by topic, period, or genre. Each of these freestanding volumes provides a biographical-bibliographical guide and overview for a particular area of literature. We are convinced that this organization—as opposed to a single alphabet method—constitutes a valuable innovation in the presentation of reference material. The volume plan necessarily requires many decisions for the placement and treatment of authors who might properly be included in two or three volumes. In some instances a major figure will be included in separate volumes, but with different entries emphasizing the aspect of his career appropriate to each volume. Ernest Hemingway, for example, is represented in *American Writers in Paris, 1920-1939* by an entry focusing on his expatriate apprenticeship; he is also in *American Novelists, 1910-1945* with an entry surveying his entire career. Each volume includes a cumulative index of subject authors and articles. Comprehensive indexes to the entire series are planned.

With volume ten in 1982 it was decided to enlarge the scope of *DLB*. By the end of 1986 twenty-one volumes treating British literature had been published, and volumes for Commonwealth and Modern European literature were in progress. The series has been further augmented by the *DLB Yearbooks* (since 1981) which update published entries and add new entries to keep the *DLB* current with contemporary activity. There have also been *DLB Documentary Series* volumes which provide biographical and critical source materials for figures whose work is judged to have particular interest for students. One of these companion volumes is entirely devoted to Tennessee Williams.

We define literature as the *intellectual commerce of a nation:* not merely as belles lettres but as that ample and complex process by which ideas are generated, shaped, and transmitted. *DLB* entries are not limited to "creative writers" but extend to other figures who in their time and in their way influenced the mind of a people. Thus the series encompasses historians, journalists, publishers, and screenwriters. By this means readers of *DLB* may be aided to perceive litera-

*From an unpublished section of Mark Twain's autobiography, copyright © by the Mark Twain Company.

ture not as cult scripture in the keeping of intellectual high priests but firmly positioned at the center of a nation's life.

DLB includes the major writers appropriate to each volume and those standing in the ranks immediately behind them. Scholarly and critical counsel has been sought in deciding which minor figures to include and how full their entries should be. Wherever possible, useful references are made to figures who do not warrant separate entries.

Each *DLB* volume has a volume editor responsible for planning the volume, selecting the figures for inclusion, and assigning the entries. Volume editors are also responsible for preparing, where appropriate, appendices surveying the major periodicals and literary and intellectual movements for their volumes, as well as lists of further readings. Work on the series as a whole is coordinated at the Bruccoli Clark Layman editorial center in Columbia, South Carolina, where the editorial staff is responsible for accuracy of the published volumes.

One feature that distinguishes *DLB* is the illustration policy–its concern with the iconography of literature. Just as an author is influenced by his surroundings, so is the reader's understanding of the author enhanced by a knowledge of his environment. Therefore *DLB* volumes include not only drawings, paintings, and photographs of authors, often depicting them at various stages in their careers, but also illustrations of their families and places where they lived. Title pages are regularly reproduced in facsimile along with dust jackets for modern authors. The dust jackets are a special feature of *DLB* because they often document better than anything else the way in which an author's work was perceived in its own time. Specimens of the writers' manuscripts are included when feasible.

Samuel Johnson rightly decreed that "The chief glory of every people arises from its authors." The purpose of the *Dictionary of Literary Biography* is to compile literary history in the surest way available to us–by accurate and comprehensive treatment of the lives and work of those who contributed to it.

The *DLB* Advisory Board

Foreword

No pages in our English literature give it more glory than those written by its essayists.

—James Milne

The facts justify a further assertion, somewhat bolder than Milne's: the informal essay has flourished better in the British Isles than anywhere else. There are more great and good essays than one can read, and there are always essayists one has not yet discovered. Except for a brief period of enfeeblement in the closing decades of the eighteenth century, the form remained vital for well over two centuries. It became popular in the Enlightenment and more popular still—and considerably more diversified—in the nineteenth century. Hard as it is to imagine in the post-verbal era, from the time of Charles Lamb to the outbreak of World War II new essays of every sort, many of them of outstanding merit, were constantly on hand in the newspapers and popular magazines as well as in literary journals. As late as the 1950s, schoolchildren, even in the United States, read "classic" essays rather than simplistic accounts of current events.

It seems natural enough that the informal essay should have prospered in the British Isles. Nothing is more definitive of British life than the paradox of individualism balanced by a profound if unobtrusive sociableness that manifests itself particularly in the desire to communicate—to speak and write and to do so articulately but also familiarly. Such a penchant—essentially a romantic one because its individualism is inclined more toward reverie and particularism than toward combative logic or ideology—is immensely propitious for all the verbal arts and drama and most obviously for the personal essay. The essay's main motive forces are, in fact, individualism and sociability: wonder and intellectual curiosity centering around one's own impressions, and at the same time the balancing desire to bring this subjective material into the public sphere, that is, to invite readers to recognize, compare, discover, respond.

Francis Bacon (*Essays*, 1597) is not really the progenitor of the type, even in England. Though informal, his essays are not personal or "famil-iar." In fact he is wary of the first person singular and writes in a way that appealed to many of the Augustan essayists, who, as J. B. Priestley observes, "never saw life from the angle of the individual—vain, humble, ridiculous, tragic—but always merely from the angle of a committee of sensible, well-intentioned persons." Bacon's essays are oxymoronic: informal and impersonal. Laconic and aphoristic but always generalizing, they reveal the man of intellectual speculation, the philosopher of prudence and worldly success, the pragmatic moralist. Humor, fancy, and poetry are in abeyance. The very fact that Bacon's performance, though much lauded in its time and later, established little enthusiasm for the essay as a genre seems further evidence for the innate romanticism of the Britons.

To catch on in the British Isles, the essay had to wait for a practitioner who harked farther back—to the personalism of Michel Eyquem de Montaigne—and who was, if not as philosophical as Bacon, not only homier and more amiable but also more willing to dwell within his own responses to congenial, humorous, tender, or beautiful things. Doing no more than what must have seemed perfectly natural to him, Abraham Cowley (*Several Discourses by Way of Essays*, 1668), that immensely approachable and affectionate human being, created the flavor that was just right to the native taste. Even though he was an admirer of Bacon, Cowley could not bring himself to adopt the glacial manner of his illustrious predecessor.

Yet it was the thing given impetus by Bacon—the rationalistic and scientific temper—that came to dominate Cowley's era and place its stamp on the essay as on everything else. Though it profited to some extent from the Cowleian model of light touch, geniality, and personal reference, the Enlightenment essay, following the canon that the general is nobler and more interesting than the particular or individual, developed as a vehicle for witty, amiable, or caustic comment on manners and morals and retained much of the impersonal tone of Lord Verulam. Within a manner infinitely chattier or sprightlier than Bacon's, the presence of the author remained, nevertheless, almost unfelt. Priestley is right again when he says that most of the Augustans "denied the essay the quickening breath of personality."

It was not till Romanticism's fascination with the particular and the subjective that the essay could become an instrument that answered, as fully as any prose can, to all the needs of the human spirit. Complement of Romantic poetry, the Romantic essay helped bring intellectual respectability to the highly specific and personal, including sensations and tonalities difficult to convey with complete lucidity or success. It was Lamb, an admirer of Cowley, who gave the essay its final freedom and created a new enthusiasm for it that was to last for well over a century.

Volumes 98 and 100 of the *Dictionary of Literary Biography, Modern British Essayists*, first and second series, cover essayists who wrote and published mainly between 1880 and 1960. To do justice to those who will have been active between 1960 and 2040 will likely prove to be a less formidable task: the informal essay, for reasons some of which are cogently stated by Joseph Wood Krutch ("No Essays, Please!," *Saturday Review*, 10 March 1951), has been in decline throughout the past several decades and shows no signs of regaining its vitality. One might think that the cults of casualness and "self-expression," which have grown continually in the twentieth century, would favor the development of the personal essay. But the opposite has happened, and one suspects that the climate creating and created by "self-expression" is in fact inimical to the essay. In any event, the younger writers of the English-speaking world—as of all the other worlds, it seems—show only a limited interest in the genre. They write, in one form or another, autobiography and semiautobiographical fantasy. Theirs is a freewheeling subjectivism based on unabashed self-absorption and self-projection. Some find clarities and demarcations actually abhorrent and write in such a way that no human face is indelibly drawn and no street's turnings are made a picture or a tale. The self becomes an all-devouring self-indulgence, and what constitutes, for most of us, the basis of reality—the "world . . . so full of a number of things"—is lost to view. The extreme example of such a writer is Jean Genet, who brings to radical development the subjectivism that was only a tendency in Jean-Jacques Rousseau. The accomplished essayists represented in these volumes, on the other hand, put one in the presence of something somehow deeper, more permanent, more universal, and even in some sense more useful than aberration or phantasmagoric reverie. To Cowley, Joseph Addison, Lamb, Holbrook Jackson, or Richard Church, the sense of meaningfulness and of enhanced vitality created or at least initiated by something outside the self is so welcome that the writer pays that other the homage of keeping it in view, of trying to limn it so that others will locate it. Many an essay offers delineations every bit as exact, vivid, and "objective" as those cropping up in fiction.

Aside from its immediate personal value as literature—as something aesthetically interesting and eminently rereadable—the familiar essay has made a steady, massive, but quiet contribution to the spirit of peace and the principle of individual freedom. The contemplative spirit on which the personal essay thrives is at the opposite pole from any sort of combativeness or aggression. The truth of personal experience, which is the form's inspiration, argues implicitly for individual freedom and against the politics—whether right, left, or center—of mindlessness, conformity, collectivity, and regimentation.

The present volumes offer biography and commentary on sixty-three writers; the number could well be expanded to a hundred or more. Resources being, as usual, limited, something less than the ideal of completeness and full justice has undoubtedly obtained. On the other hand, several fine essayists never well known and today almost unknown have at last found their biographers and may in time escape neglect. Among these are Holbrook Jackson, Elizabeth Wordsworth, and Dixon Scott.

Many practioners of the familiar essay also wrote literary criticism of the traditional type, and sometimes the two modes perform simultaneously, as in many of the highly personal and intellectually ambient prose pieces of William Butler Yeats. Several of the writers represented in these two volumes are primarily literary critics, but in every such case either the type of criticism they engage in or their extracritical pieces entitle them to representation. Essayists in "analytical" literary criticism have been excluded.

Finally, there seemed no good reason to exclude completely writers who favored the formal essay. In point of fact, a good many formal essays—even some purely scientific ones such as many of Max Planck's or Sir Humphry Davy's—have considerable literary merit and make their contribution to humanism because they can be read and re-read, just like the best pieces of William Hazlitt and Lamb, both for their largeness of vision and the charm of their performance. Nor are the lines always clearly drawn between the formal and the informal. In many of Michael Polanyi's essays, for example, a strong sense of personal involvement and even anecdotal and autobiographical elements accompany an analytical mode applied to a distinctly intellectual, sometimes even technical subject. There are further complica-tions. Chapters of books sometimes turn out to be self-contained essays. One discovers that there are book-length essays and that prefaces and introductions are often essays under other names. As usual, the empirical reality outstrips our desire for easy identifications and unexceptionable definitions and classifications. In doubtful or arguable cases I have opted for the principle that inclusion is usually healthier, fairer, and more useful than exclusion.

–Robert Beum

Acknowledgments

This book was produced by Bruccoli Clark Layman, Inc. Karen L. Rood is senior editor for the *Dictionary of Literary Biography* series. Philip B. Dematteis and Jack Turner were the in-house editors.

Production coordinator is James W. Hipp. Systems manager is Charles D. Brower. Photography editor is Susan Brennen Todd. Permissions editor is Jean W. Ross. Layout and graphics supervisor is Penney L. Haughton. Copyediting supervisor is Bill Adams. Typesetting supervisor is Kathleen M. Flanagan. Information systems analyst is George F. Dodge. Charles Lee Egleston is editorial associate. The production staff includes Rowena Betts, Anne L. M. Bowman, Polly Brown, Teresa Chaney, Patricia Coate, Marie Creed, Allison Deal, Holly L. Deal, Sarah A. Estes, Mary L. Goodwin, Cynthia Hallman, Susan C. Heath, David Marshall James, Kathy Lawler Merlette, Laura Garren Moore, John Myrick, Gina D. Peterman, Cathy J. Reese, Edward Scott, Laurrè Sinckler, Maxine K. Smalls, John C. Stone III, and Betsy L. Weinberg.

Walter W. Ross and Parris Boyd did the library research with the assistance of the following librarians at the Thomas Cooper Library of the University of South Carolina: Gwen Baxter, Daniel Boice, Faye Chadwell, Cathy Eckman, Gary Geer, Cathie Gottlieb, David L. Haggard, Jens Holley, Jackie Kinder, Thomas Marcil, Marcia Martin, Laurie Preston, Jean Rhyne, Carol Tobin, and Virginia Weathers.

Modern British Essayists, Second Series

Dictionary of Literary Biography

Richard Aldington

(8 July 1892 - 27 July 1962)

Charles Doyle
University of Victoria
and
Robert Beum

See also the Aldington entries in *DLB 20: British Poets, 1914-1945* and *DLB 36: British Novelists, 1890-1929: Modernists.*

SELECTED BOOKS: *Images (1910-1915)* (London: Poetry Bookshop, 1915); revised and enlarged as *Images Old and New* (Boston: Four Seas, 1916); enlarged again as *Images* (London: Egoist, 1919);

Reverie: A Little Book of Poems for H. D. (Cleveland: Clerk's Press, 1917):

The Love Poems of Myrrhine and Konallis, a Cycle of Prose Poems Written after the Greek Manner (Cleveland: Clerk's Press, 1917); enlarged as *The Love of Myrrhine and Konallis and Other Prose Poems* (Chicago: Covici, 1926);

Images of War: A Book of Poems (Westminster: C. W. Beaumont, 1919; enlarged edition, London: Allen & Unwin, 1919; Boston: Four Seas, 1920); enlarged as *War and Love (1915-1918)* (Boston: Four Seas, 1921);

Images of Desire (London: Elkin Mathews, 1919);

Exile and Other Poems (London: Allen & Unwin, 1923; Boston: Four Seas, 1924);

Literary Studies and Reviews (London: Allen & Unwin, 1924; New York: MacVeagh/Dial Press, 1924);

A Fool i' the Forest: A Phantasmagoria (London: Allen & Unwin, 1925; New York: MacVeagh/ Dial Press, 1925);

Voltaire (London: Routledge, 1925; London:

Routledge / New York: Dutton, 1925);

French Studies and Reviews (London: Allen & Unwin, 1926; New York: MacVeagh/Dial Press, 1926);

D. H. Lawrence: An Indiscretion (Seattle: University of Washington Book Store, 1927); republished as *D. H. Lawrence* (London: Chatto & Windus, 1930); revised and enlarged as *D. H. Lawrence: An Appreciation* (Harmondsworth: Penguin, 1950);

Remy de Gourmont: A Modern Man of Letters (Seattle: University of Washington Book Store, 1928);

Collected Poems (New York: Covici, Friede, 1928; London: Allen & Unwin, 1929);

Death of a Hero: A Novel (New York: Covici, Friede, 1929; London: Chatto & Windus, 1929; unexpurgated edition, 2 volumes, Paris: Babou & Kahane, 1930);

The Eaten Heart (Chapelle-Reanville: Hours Press, 1929; enlarged edition, London: Chatto & Windus, 1933);

At All Costs (London: Heinemann, 1930);

Last Straws (Paris: Hours Press, 1930);

Two Stories (London: Elkin Mathews & Marrot, 1930);

Love and the Luxembourg (New York: Covici, Friede, 1930); republished as *A Dream in the Luxembourg* (London: Chatto & Windus, 1930);

(By permission of Catherine Aldington Guillaume, Alister Kershaw, and Alan Bird)

Roads to Glory (London: Chatto & Windus, 1930; Garden City, N.Y.: Doubleday, Doran, 1931);

The Colonel's Daughter: A Novel (London: Chatto & Windus, 1931; Garden City, N.Y.: Doubleday, Doran, 1931);

Stepping Heavenward: A Record (Florence: Orioli, 1931; London: Chatto & Windus, 1931; Garden City, N.Y.: Doubleday, Doran, 1932);

Soft Answers: Five Stories (London: Chatto & Windus, 1932; Garden City, N.Y.: Doubleday, Doran, 1932);

All Men Are Enemies: A Romance (London: Chatto & Windus, 1933; Garden City, N.Y.: Doubleday, Doran, 1933);

The Poems of Richard Aldington (Garden City, N.Y.: Doubleday, Doran, 1934);

Women Must Work: A Novel (London: Chatto & Windus, 1934; Garden City, N.Y.: Doubleday, Doran, 1934);

D. H. Lawrence: A Complete List of His Works, Together with a Critical Appreciation (London:

Heinemann, 1935); republished as *D. H. Lawrence* (N.p.: Tobago, 1935);

Artifex: Sketches and Ideas (London: Chatto & Windus, 1935; Garden City, N.Y.: Doubleday, Doran, 1936);

Life Quest (London: Chatto & Windus, 1935; Garden City, N.Y.: Doubleday, Doran, 1935);

Life of a Lady: A Play, by Aldington and Derek Patmore (Garden City, N.Y.: Doubleday, Doran, 1936; London: Putnam's, 1936);

The Crystal World (London: Heinemann, 1937; Garden City, N.Y.: Doubleday, Doran, 1938);

Very Heaven (London & Toronto: Heinemann, 1937; Garden City, N.Y.: Doubleday, Doran, 1937);

Seven Against Reeves: A Comedy-Farce (London & Toronto: Heinemann, 1938: Garden City, N.Y.: Doubleday, Doran, 1938);

Rejected Guest: A Novel (New York: Viking, 1939; London & Toronto: Heinemann, 1939);

W. Somerset Maugham: An Appreciation (Garden City, N.Y.: Doubleday, Doran, 1939);

Life for Life's Sake: A Book of Reminiscences (New York: Viking, 1941; London: Cassell, 1968);

The Duke: Being an Account of the Life & Achievements of Arthur Wellesley, 1st Duke of Wellington (New York: Viking, 1943); republished as *Wellington: Being an Account of the Life & Achievements of Arthur Wellesley, 1st Duke of Wellington* (London & Toronto: Heinemann, 1946);

The Romance of Casanova: A Novel (New York: Duell, Sloan & Pearce, 1946; London & Toronto: Heinemann, 1947);

Four English Portraits, 1801-1851 (London: Evans, 1948);

The Complete Poems of Richard Aldington (London: Wingate, 1948);

Jane Austen (Pasadena: Ampersand Press, 1948);

The Strange Life of Charles Waterton, 1782-1865 (London: Evans, 1949; New York: Duell, Sloan & Pearce, 1949);

Portrait of a Genius But . . . The Life of D. H. Lawrence, 1885-1930 (London: Heinemann, 1950); republished as *D. H. Lawrence: Portrait of a Genius But . . .* (New York: Duell, Sloan & Pearce, 1950);

Pinorman: Personal Recollections of Norman Douglas, Pino Orioli, and Charles Prentice (London: Heinemann, 1954);

Ezra Pound and T. S. Eliot: A Lecture (Hurst, Berkshire: Peacocks Press, 1954);

Lawrence of Arabia: A Biographical Enquiry (London: Collins, 1955; Chicago: Regnery, 1955);

A. E. Housman and W. B. Yeats: Two Lectures (Hurst, Berkshire: Peacocks Press, 1955);

Introduction to Mistral (London: Heinemann, 1956; Carbondale: Southern Illinois University Press, 1960);

Frauds (London: Heinemann, 1957);

Portrait of a Rebel: The Life and Works of Robert Louis Stevenson (London: Evans, 1957);

Richard Aldington: Selected Critical Writings, 1928-1960, edited by Alister Kershaw (Carbondale: Southern Illinois University Press, 1970).

OTHER: *Letters of Madame De Sévigné to Her Daughter and Her Friends*, selected, with an introductory essay, by Aldington (London: Routledge, 1927; New York: Brentano's, 1927);

D. H. Lawrence, *Last Poems*, edited by Aldington and G. Orioli (New York: Viking, 1933; London: Secker, 1933);

D. H. Lawrence: Selected Poems, edited by Aldington (London: Secker, 1934);

The Spirit of Place: An Anthology Compiled from the Prose of D. H. Lawrence, edited, with an introduction, by Aldington (London: Heinemann, 1935);

The Viking Book of Poetry of the English-Speaking World, edited by Aldington (New York: Viking, 1941); republished as *Poetry of the English Speaking World* (London: Heinemann, 1947);

The Portable Oscar Wilde, edited by Aldington (New York: Viking, 1946); republished as *Oscar Wilde: Selected Works* (London: Heinemann, 1946);

Walter Pater: Selected Works, edited by Aldington (London: Heinemann, 1948; New York: Duell, Sloan & Pearce, 1948).

TRANSLATIONS: *The Poems of Anyte of Tegea* (London: Egoist Press, 1915; Cleveland: Clerk's Press, 1917);

Feodor Sogolub (Feodor Teternikov), *The Little Demon*, translated by Aldington and John Cournos (New York: Knopf, 1916);

Greek Songs in the Manner of Anacreon (London: Egoist Press, 1919);

Medallions in Clay (New York: Knopf, 1921); republished as *Medallions from Anyte of Tegea, Meleager of Gadara, the Anacreontea: Latin Poets of the Renaissance* (London: Chatto & Windus, 1930);

French Comedies of the XVIIIth Century (London: Routledge, 1923; London: Routledge / New York: Dutton, 1923);

Cyrano de Bergerac, *Voyages to the Moon and the Sun* (London: Routledge / New York: Dutton, 1923; London: Routledge, 1927);

Pierre Choderlos de Laclos, *Dangerous Acquaintances (Les Liaisons Dangereuses)* (London: Routledge, 1924; London: Routledge / New York: Dutton, 1924);

The Mystery of the Nativity, Translated from the Liégeois of the XVth Century (London: Allen & Unwin, 1924);

Pierre Custot, *Sturly* (London: Cape, 1924; Boston: Houghton Mifflin, 1924);

The Fifteen Joys of Marriage, Ascribed to Antoine De La Sale, c.1388-c.1462 (London: Routledge, 1926; London: Routledge / New York: Dutton, 1926);

Voltaire, *Candide and Other Romances* (London: Routledge, 1927; London: Routledge / New York: Dutton, 1927);

Letters of Voltaire and Frederick the Great (London: Routledge, 1927; New York: Brentano's, 1927);

Remy de Gourmont: Selections from All His Works (Chicago: Covici, 1928; London: Chatto & Windus, 1932);

Julien Benda, *The Treason of the Intellectuals (La Trahison des clercs)* (New York: W. Morrow, 1928);

Euripides, *Alcestis* (London: Chatto & Windus, 1930);

The Decameron of Giovanni Boccaccio (New York: Covici, Friede, 1930; London: Putnam's, 1930);

Larousse Encyclopedia of Mythology, translated by Aldington and Delano Ames (New York: Prometheus Press, 1959).

A writer of many talents and of some influence during the high period of Anglo-American literary modernism, Richard Aldington achieved distinction as a novelist, poet, biographer, translator, editor, reviewer, and essayist in cultural and literary criticism. His essays characteristically offer solid reasoning animated by personal intensity and tend to gather in a wealth of observation disciplined by a love of point and lucidity. After his death in 1962 Aldington was largely forgotten–except in the USSR–for almost a generation. Since the mid 1980s there have been signs of some degree of revival of his literary reputation.

The eldest son of Albert Edward Aldington, a law clerk, and Jessie May Godfrey Aldington, Edward Godfree Aldington was born on 8 July 1892 in Portsmouth, Hampshire, but spent most of his boyhood in Dover. Early on he adopted the first name Richard. A penchant for literature and languages was evident from his earliest school years; he found French particularly to his liking. In 1910 he entered University College in London, but because of his parents' lack of funds he left the following year.

It was in 1911 that Aldington found his way into London literary circles, where he met Ezra Pound at the salon of Mrs. Deighton (Brigit) Patmore; the following year he met Hilda Doolittle (H. D.). With these two American poets he was a founder in 1912 of the Imagist movement. It was later claimed, by Aldington and others, that his part in the movement was nominal and that it was in fact an invention of Pound's, chiefly to promote Doolittle's poetry. In the preface to *The Complete Poems of Richard Aldington* (1948) and elsewhere, Aldington declared that he had no

The American poet Hilda Doolittle (H. D.), who married Aldington in 1913. They separated in 1919 and were finally divorced in 1938.

intention of participating in a literary revolution; nevertheless, in some of his earliest criticism he is clearly an apologist for Imagism.

Up to the outbreak of World War I, Aldington was influenced by Pound and fellow Imagist F. S. Flint to steep himself in contemporary French poetry. In 1912 he traveled in Italy with Doolittle and did much translating of classical Italian poetry. After his marriage to Doolittle on 18 October 1913 he also translated classical Greek and Latin poetry. In 1914 he became assistant editor of the *Egoist* (formerly the *New Freewoman*), to which he contributed literary essays and reviews of modern poetry and French literature. He also contributed to the *New Age* and to the early numbers of the recently founded Chicago journal *Poetry*.

Aldington's earliest published criticism dealt almost exclusively with contemporary poetry. Among Aldington's *Egoist* contributions for 1914 were "Modern Poetry and the Imagists" on 1 June and "Free Verse in England" on 15 September. To the "Special Imagist Number" of the *Egoist* (1 May 1915) he contributed pieces on Pound and on the poetry of Flint. Two months later he wrote on Amy Lowell, who was to usurp Pound's place as self-appointed leader of the Imagists and convert the movement to what Pound called "Amygism."

From mid 1916 to November 1918 he served with the British army in France, surviving the grimmest trench fighting of those years. The war experience, which was to figure in much of his fiction, made him a bitter critic of English society and at the same time deepened his humanity. After his demobilization in February 1919 he separated from Doolittle and moved into a cottage in Berkshire. Commissions for articles came from the *Sphere*, *Poetry*, the *Living Age*, and the *Dial*, and the *Anglo-French Review* asked him for a series of articles on French literature. His main source of income, however, was the *Times Literary Supplement*, whose editor, Bruce Richmond, asked him in 1919 to become the journal's regular reviewer of French literature. He relates in his autobiography, *Life for Life's Sake* (1941), that he came to this task with what he considered insufficient background. When Richmond sent for a review of Victor Hugo's *Les Contemplations* (1856) Aldington felt daunted: "What troubled me at the moment was the perception of my incompetence to write with authority of Victor Hugo or indeed of any writer of more than temporary significance. I knew enough to know how little I knew." From 1919 to 1926 Aldington deepened his command of the French and Italian languages and literatures. He continued to write his own poetry as well as to translate, and twelve titles appeared between 1915 and 1924. Notwithstanding his later accomplishments in the novel and in biography, his obituary in the *Times* would say "he revealed his quality best as a critic, particularly of the minor classics and of French literature." Had Aldington's literary career ended in the late 1920s this judgment would have been entirely credible.

By the end of the war Imagism had ceased to exist as a movement, but, as William Pratt says in his anthology *The Imagist Poem* (1963), "it had become a tool which each poet could adapt to his own use." In "The Poetry of the Future" (*Poetry*, August 1919) Aldington issues an Imagist call for "the expression of distinguished minds in a distinguished manner," for live language, for technical competence, for a sense of tradition, and for a "personal flavour which is a guarantee of sincerity." Finally, he seeks a "more virile, more essentially artistic" deployment of vers libre. In "The Art of Poetry" (*Dial*, November 1920) Aldington

declares that bad style betrays a lack of sincerity. He develops this point at some length and in the process acknowledges a critical debt to his fellow Imagist Flint; but his ideas are equally indebted to various formulations by Pound, such as "I believe in technique as the test of a man's sincerity." Aldington's counterpart is "the precise expression of thoughts really thought, emotions really felt, perceptions really perceived."

Aldington continued to champion free verse as a flexible medium for true expression, but he was by no means a proponent of experimentalism for its own sake. For example, although he initially endorsed Wyndham Lewis's radically experimental magazine *Blast*, which began publication in June 1914, he soon backed away from it. A longtime foe of Victorian moralism and cant, Aldington nevertheless found suspect the postwar infatuation with artistic novelty for its own sake. In "The Disciples of Gertrude Stein" (*Poetry*, October 1920) he says that the Anglo-American modernists have in some respects misread current French writing: "Since 1912 there has been a revival of more or less humorous poetry in France. The *poètes futuristes*, the *poètes cubistes*, the *simultanéistes*, the *fantaisistes*, and lastly the *Dadaistes*, have contributed in varying degrees to the gaiety of nations. Obscurity of diction, extreme fragility of thought, a pleasing vacuum in place of a subject, and typographical excesses, are the hallmarks of genius in this new group." Early in his career Aldington had formed the ideal concept of "the good European" and he still held to it. He did not believe in the kind of experiment that entailed a repudiation of European cultural tradition.

In this stance he was close to Pound and to T. S. Eliot, both experimentalists and both, in their own ways, upholders of the European tradition. During the years when Aldington's strongest literary commitment was to a combination of poetry and criticism, his closest literary association was with Eliot, who in 1917 had succeeded to Aldington's former editorial position at the *Egoist*. In an article in the *New Statesman* in 1917 Eliot had attacked vers libre, but there and in *Ezra Pound: His Metric and Poetry* (1917) he praised Aldington's work in the medium. For his part, Aldington quickly recognized Eliot as an extraordinary critic. From the first, though, he had doubts about Eliot's poetry. In a letter to Eliot in July 1919 Aldington said that Eliot was "not the best but the only modern writer of prose criticism in English," but "I feel compelled to add

Aldington as a British infantryman, home on leave from France in 1916.
His experiences in World War I made him a bitter critic of English society.

that I dislike your poetry very much." Aldington persuaded Richmond to publish Eliot's critical work in the *Times Literary Supplement*; and shortly after Eliot started the *Criterion* in 1921 Aldington became, in effect, an assistant editor.

What Aldington and Eliot chiefly had in common was what Selwyn Kittredge in his 1976 dissertation calls "their sense of self-appointed guardianship over the great tradition of European letters." Kittredge observes of Pound, Eliot, and Aldington that "much of their work is concerned with questions of how and what to appreciate in poetry. They write more often than not from the vantage-point of teachers." As letters between Aldington and Eliot show, the two also instructed each other. One result of this mutuality is Eliot's landmark essay "Ulysses, Order and Myth" (*Dial*, November 1923), in which he outlines "the mythical method" of literary structure. This essay was a response to Aldington's "The Influence of Mr. James Joyce" (*English Review*, April 1921). Both

pieces are concerned with Joyce's experimental novel *Ulysses*, which was serialized in the *Little Review* from 1918 to 1920 (published in book form in 1922), as a portent for the future course of literature. Eliot perceives the novel's mythic substructure, its paralleling of "contemporaneity and antiquity," as an important method. Aldington is afraid that Joyce's "great undisciplined talent" will attract a "band of specious imitators." Pound found the curious mixture of common sense and obtuseness in Aldington's essay hilarious. Aldington had confessed to Eliot in a letter of 14 September 1920 that "I wrote it on an impulse, with no preliminary thought, without rereading or consulting a line of Joyce," but he had urged Eliot to reply to it and had thereby elicited one of Eliot's most influential essays. Whatever the limitations of Aldington's animadversions on *Ulysses*, his piece provided him with the occasion for a telling definition of literary naturalism—a school with which Aldington had limited sympathy because his own experience, including that in the war, had convinced him that human nature is not, on the whole, the despicable thing it is implied to be in most of the work of the thoroughgoing naturalists. All his life Aldington retained a strong, generous, but unsentimental humanitarianism and criticized all attempts to denigrate humankind.

Aldington's doubts about the value of Eliot's poetry culminated in the conviction that Eliot (and Pound) had sacrificed a great deal in the name of creating an interesting surface. Eliot was always uncomfortably aware of Aldington's misgivings. The main difficulty for the working relationship between the two men, though, lay in Eliot's failure to treat Aldington as an equal. Open conflict came in the mid 1920s. Aldington was working for the Routledge publishing firm on a series of volumes of translation and stood to be named editor or coeditor of the series; Eliot mounted what seemed to Aldington a rival series with Faber and Faber and interfered with Aldington's editorial prospects. By 1928, when Aldington left England to settle in France, he regarded Eliot both as an enemy and as a negative force in poetry. In a review in the *Sunday Referee* on 15 December 1929 Aldington contrasts what he sees as the life-affirmation of Aldous Huxley's essay collection *Do What You Will* with the negative worldview expressed in Eliot's poem "The Hollow Men" (1925)–"A greatly admired poem by the most admired poet of the day may be summarized in the following excerpted words: 'Hollow-dried - meaningless - dry - broken - dry - paralyzed-death's-hollow-I-dare-not-death's-broken-fading-death's - final - twilight - dead - cactus - stone - dead-fading-death's-broken-dying-broken-last-sightless-death.' The poet's genius is not in question, but I hate this exhibitionism of perpetual suicidal mania which never, never, comes to the point." Shortly afterward, Aldington complained in a *Sunday Referee* review of "Ash Wednesday" (1930) that since *The Waste Land* (1922) Eliot's poetry was all despair. At about the same time Aldington made Eliot an object of satire in his bestselling war novel *Death of a Hero* (1929), and Eliot and his wife were sharply lampooned in *Stepping Heavenward* (1931). Animus against Eliot continued throughout Aldington's life, with its latest printed expression in *Ezra Pound and T. S. Eliot: A Lecture* published in 1954 but written in the late 1930s, in which he treats Eliot's and Pound's techniques of extensive allusion as tantamount to plagiarism.

Aldington recognized that literature needs to change, to renew itself and avoid ossification. His tolerant attitude toward even the extremes of literary experiment in France as well as his own involvement in Imagism show his receptiveness to change plainly enough. Nevertheless, he was determined to remain a traditional literary critic rather than take up the new mode of minutely analytical explication. He regarded the majority of the "analytical" critics as essentially esoterists, and he thought that all artistic esoterism contributed to the atomization of culture–ultimately to the loneliness and frustration of individuals living in a world of limited, often inconsequential communication. He kept his own criticism–indeed, all his prose–highly accessible, and it remains so today. Virtually all of the essays in *Literary Studies and Reviews* (1924) and *French Studies and Reviews* (1926) are as interesting now as when they were coming out in the magazines of the 1920s; many have not become dated at all. To recognize their continuing vitality, one need only compare them with George Saintsbury's similar excursions into French and English letters. Most of the essays in the two books deal with French literature but often relate to English interests or developments. Aldington notes, for example, that Walter Pater had renewed the interest of English readers in the work of Joachim du Bellay, whose significance was that he was "one of the first introducers to France of the 'new Italian manner,' which was the manner of the Renaissance and the forerunner of so much of modern literature." Conversely, he discusses the influence of Sir Walter Scott on Alfred de Vigny's historical romance *Cinq-Mars* (1826).

In his adoption of what Herbert Read was to designate the "Plain style" of English prose, in his brevity and conciseness, in his ability to come quickly but courteously to the point, Aldington is modern in the best sense of the word. Both erudition–historical and philosophical as well as literary and linguistic–and poetic sensitivity obviate any tendency toward superficiality that might otherwise have resulted from an approach as commonsensical and no-nonsensical as Aldington's. In fact, much of the merit of these essays lies in Aldington's ability to isolate at once the more significant and widely interesting aspects of his topic and then to penetrate deeply into it with vigor but without undue haste. Piquant or salient details from the text or from the writer's life or milieu support and enliven Aldington's comments and conclusions. The overall effect is one of erudite, rich-minded, well-meaning exposition without pretension or idiosyncrasy.

Aldington seems to have been the first English critic to deal seriously with the implications of Victor Hugo's uncritical enthusiasm for *machinisme*; he was certainly the first to be amusingly forthright on the subject. His comments about Remy de Gourmont allow the reader spontaneously to see the universal application of the particulars. "An Approach to Marcel Proust" is one of the earliest English essays on Proust, and the essay on Nicolas Edmé Restif de la Bretonne was the first to call English readers' attention to Restif's literary value.

Despite his love of France and its literature, Aldington was by no means uncritically Francophile; he was always aware of the limitations of the French writers he dealt with. He says that the poet Signogne "constantly repeated himself. Few will wish for more than a few of his poems." Aldington's conclusion on Hugo—which may not be readily rebuttable—is that Hugo was "a poetic demagogue. It was therefore no more possible for him to be sincere than it is for other demagogues." Aldington maintained that France had produced no equal to Shakespeare and that, partly because England did have a Shakespeare, "the greatest English poets have a verbal richness and imagination almost unknown in French poetry."

"Landor's 'Hellenics'" in *Literary Studies and Reviews* was the first essay in English to come to grips with the most important critical problems presented by Walter Savage Landor's poetry and was the only such critique until the work of Donald Davie almost a quarter century later. A model of traditional literary analysis, it remains one of the most solid pieces ever written on Landor. Aldington's sympathies with "classicism," tempered by his sensitivity to Landor's characteristic defects, make him an excellent guide. The quotes from Landor's poems are well chosen, and Aldington's commentary on their diction is close without becoming overelaborated or pedantic. His remarks on the necessity of understanding the way Landor lived are particularly apt: "The peculiar circumstances of Landor's life and temperament easily allowed him to imagine himself now as Pericles, now as Epicurus, now as Sophocles, now as Diogenes. He lived so familiarly with great men that proud speech came naturally to him." To this day, there is no clearer explanation of the relationship between Landor's "Hellenism" and the inevitable "English" in his voice. In the

same essay Aldington expresses mistrust of coterie art and narrow scholarship, remarking that the "general reader" of poetry "is much more important than the literary 'Fossores' who exhume obscure and forgotten writers in their antiquarian zeal or bind on their brows a barren garland of praise for some wholly unnecessary researches."

In these essays, as generally in Aldington's writing, there is a certain attractive chasteness of style, despite the assertive element. Aldington never ornaments and seldom allows his expository prose anything even as showy as an epigram. At the same time, there are memorable bons mots, many of them provocative and bearing implications which modern thought has still not fully worked out: "There are few so bloodthirsty as your really tender humanitarian." "Perhaps one of the most useful things proved by [Proust's] books is that a mind steeped in tradition, a mind almost fastidiously respectful, has nevertheless created one of the most original novels of the time."

For his 1924 translation of Pierre Choderlos de Laclos's *Les Liaisons Dangereuses* (1782) Aldington wrote a substantial essay-introduction; its presentation of Laclos's life, character, and works shows Aldington's strength as an expository critic. The Laclos translation was part of Routledge's Library of Eighteenth-Century French Literature, for which Aldington served as translator and introducer. The introductions Aldington wrote for this series, such as the one for *French Comedies of the XVIIIth Century* (1923), though not intended as pioneering or original scholarship, are sound pedagogy. Aldington's major work of biographical criticism is *Voltaire* (1925); its achievement was widely recognized. Alyse Gregory, in a review in the *Dial* (1926), praised Aldington's "determined veracity" and his "critical sense, combined with historical perspective, personal intensity and literary craft."

From 1924 to 1927 Aldington provided reviews and articles for *Vogue*, most notably a series titled "Modern Free Verse." One of the articles in this series, on D. H. Lawrence's poetry, anticipates much that Aldington was to write about Lawrence up to and including the remarkable critical biography *Portrait of a Genius But . . .* (1950) and the many prefatory essays he wrote in the 1950s for Heinemann and Penguin editions of Lawrence's work. Far too modestly, Aldington considered the chapbook *D. H. Lawrence: An Indiscretion* (1927) "my first real bit of prose." This essay

Aldington in 1932

places Lawrence as one of the great English here-
tics, but, as its subject was quick to point out, "It's
more about you, my dear Richard, than about
me." It was, indeed, Aldington's declaration of independence from the British literary scene.
Shortly after its publication he, like Pound and
Lawrence, left England and returned only at
long intervals. Also in 1927 Aldington translated
Voltaire's *Candide*, and in 1928 he translated
Julien Benda's *La Trahison des clercs* (1927) as *The
Treason of the Intellectuals.*

In November 1929 the literary editor of the
Sunday Referee announced that "Mr. Richard Aldington, the distinguished poet, novelist, and
critic, will contribute a weekly critical causerie on
contemporary literature." In less than three years
Aldington turned out more than a hundred articles, promoting in many of them his lifelong
ideal of "the good European." Among his sub-

jects in these articles was Pound, who had long
since appointed himself (and been gratefully accepted as) Aldington's literary mentor. As late as
1930 Aldington praised Pound as being at the leading edge of American poetry, though by then he
had mixed feelings about Pound's work in both poetry and prose. He took no part in the international effort to have Pound released from his con-
finement at St. Elizabeth's Hospital, and while
Pound was still there Aldington published the attack *Ezra Pound and T. S. Eliot: A Lecture*. Even so,
after Pound returned to Italy he wrote to Aldington in August 1959, "This is to say I have for
you a lasting affection." In other *Referee* pieces Aldington sees Joyce's *Ulysses* as a demonstration of
"the barren misery of the pure intellect" and
praises Wyndham Lewis's satiric novel *The Apes of
God* (1930). He sums up his understanding of the
proper task of a reviewer as being "simply to give

an honest opinion on new books."

In 1935 Aldington moved to the United States. Most of his "familiar" or "personal" essays are collected in *Artifex*, which was published that year. In the preface to *Artifex*, Aldington says, "I call them articles, and not essays, because the essay is only an article in a high hat." Few had previously been published. Of the eighteen pieces, some are more narrative sketches than essays; at least one, "A Renaissance Aryan," is a literary pastiche based on the style and characteristic matter of the sixteenth-century Italian novella writer Matteo Bandello. The title essay is a lively rumination on diverse topics, all of them related in one way or another to the question of what the role of the genuine artist can and should be in the twentieth century. With no bitterness whatever, Aldington expresses his total disillusionment with the intellectual and artistic trends of the 1930s. His disaffection sounds much like that of Lawrence: "Certainly there is art now, but it is the art of hyperaesthesia, the art of exasperated neurasthenics. The latest aesthetic giggle, the newest *petit frisson*–anything, anything to seem original. The music of atonality, the painting and sculpture of super-realism, the literature of the stream of consciousness, the aestheticism of concrete and cocktails–neurasthenia and self-destruction. Intellectual snobbishness is the very essence of its appeal to the gangs and cliques of Paris and London. If it were not inaccessible to common sense they would not want it. . . . Why should we admire these self-conscious perversities, this feeble sodomizing of the Muses?" But the absurdity of pretentiousness has caught on with the commoners, too: in the half sketch, half essay "Jolly Girls" Aldington, unable to avoid the situation, is introduced to a "jolly girl," a peasant woman "gone podgy," a "whacking great lump of a woman in a bathing dress, with red arms and lumpy legs and a lumpy sort of face in spectacles. Aggressive. So that's her line–aggressive, not responsive jollity. . . . It is written, Blessed are the poor in spirit. If it means, to blazes with the pseudo-intellectuals, then I agree. But if it means, Blessed are the fatheads, I can't agree. Give me the rich, the abounding in spirit. There aren't so many of them." The first page of "Jolly Girls" presents the unexpected: a brief, cogent observation on the true nature of "stream of consciousness" writing. The flexibility of the informal essay genre allows such serendipities.

Aldington's contents are frequently better than his titles. The essay "Freedom of the Press" seems to promise the usual clichés of liberal/progressive rhetoric against censorship; as it turns out, Aldington is more interested in bringing himself (and the reader) to full astonishment at the sheer stupidity of most censorship than in defending "freedom of expression" per se. The typical censor is a commoner–or someone risen from commoners–with a too common mind: "What an Augean stable is the common mind!" As in "Jolly Girls" and "Artifex" Aldington divagates freely, and in some of his wanderings farthest away from the central topic he comes up with the most interesting points of all. "Freedom of the Press" is memorable partly because of its excursion into the subject of modern fascination with detective stories and partly because of some equally tangential meditations on the nature of artistic activity. "Art is a flowering of the life-impulse" sounds, again, like Lawrence but not unlike Oscar Wilde; and more Wildean yet is the next sentence: "It is as useless as a flower and as life itself."

One of the strongest pieces in *Artifex* is "Female Thinking Extravert," an essay-sketch on another pretender who once introduced herself to Aldington. This upper-class twenty-five-year-old does the worst kind of pretending–not just to others but to herself. Above all, she pretends to herself–Bloomsbury snobs had put the idea into her head–that she ought to want sex, despite the fact that "She wasn't in love with anyone. She wasn't in love with love. She wasn't a wanton. She hadn't any particular desires. Men didn't like her, and she didn't really like men." "Aggressively emancipated" and overwhelmed by what the Bloomsbury circle considered de rigueur, Anita "smoked lots of cigarettes and sprawled in one of my armchairs and talked about things she thought were highbrow." Her "body didn't want sexual experience, but Bloomsbury purlieus had put it into her not too well-furnished head that she ought to want it. And want it she did with a cold implacability of will which reminded me of the worst excesses of the Niebelungs. . . . [S]he had a bad attack of sex on the brain." Condescendingly, she "explained that 'one' had to have sexual experience of the right kind or 'one' developed complexes and couldn't admire the best modern poetry or be eligible for the communist party." Later Aldington happens to meet the girl again, and in response to his innocent "What have you been doing lately?" she responds, "I went to a divahn place–we all dance naked, you know."

"I didn't know. Isn't it rather cold and don't you stub your toes?"
"Sexual intercourse," she announced proudly, "took place–twice."
I laughed. I laughed loud in the way you musn't laugh among intellectuals. I went on laughing.

"Sea Travel" is the sort of highly personal essay that puts one closely in touch with aspects of the writer's temperament; but it is a fine essay in its own right, even if one has no particular interest in the man behind the writing. The title, once again, is hardly more than a tag cursorily chosen: the main subject is not sea travel in general but rather twentieth-century people's atrophied sense of wonder and their determination to take with them on their voyages all the sources of distraction they have on land. Aldington prefers "coming for a time into touch with essential truths and powers," the "naked perception of the great elements, their sacred play and happiness." The essay opens with an evocative sketch of English landscape "under a veiled sky, in February frost" as viewed from a train carrying Aldington toward a Channel port. The first two paragraphs are a microcosm of Aldington's perpetual ambivalence about his native land. For all his dissatisfaction with English life–including its physical aspects– Aldington remains conscious of being English ("I am not French") and is merely "glad," not overjoyed, to be leaving. The "dingy meanness" and the "philistinism" of England oppress him. At the same moment, though, he knows he is being "unfair," knows that "in sheltered nooks the long slender sallows would be furred with golden buds, and that though the hazel catkins would hang droopily in that dun air they would be golden too . . . that at least some of those sad-looking coppices concealed fragile white anemones . . . there would be early primroses, and perhaps part of a hillside whitened with snowdrops."

This passage illustrates the uncluttered descriptive writing characteristic of Aldington's essays and sketches. The descriptiveness is poetic but never "purple": the poetry of what is observed is really felt, never simply fabricated for effect, and is never sentimentally isolated from the awareness that life is brief and ridden with hardships. There is neither aesthetic swooning nor a mere resting in the surface pleasures of beauty. The focus remains on the things perceived, not on the response to them; and the reader experiences the warmth generated by the writer's faithful attention. This "objective" focus allows all the power of understatement to accumulate. A type

of chasteness or restraint, it shows again Aldington's affinities with "classicism" in attitude and style. In particular, of course, it shows the perceptual discipline he learned from Imagism, which was itself oriented essentially toward the classical. Worth noting too is that from hazel catkins, fragile white anemones, early primroses, "the gold-white sunlight, the blue-white air, the blue-green water dashed ceaselessly with foam" Aldington derives not so much an "aesthetic experience" as a profound sense of life speaking to life– or at least of nonhuman, cosmic vitality wakening vitality in the mortal frame, quickening it to joy in life, to a feeling of participating in the magnificent mysterious energy of the cosmos. Here is a sort of romantic element to balance the more strictly classical one. It is the same type of response one encounters so often in the work of Lawrence, and it would be surprising if Aldington's way of expressing perceptions and feelings had not gained in confidence from his long, close, and admiring association with Lawrence.

One of the incidental felicities of "Sea Travel" is a brief but pointed demurral on W. B. Yeats's attempt to revive the sense of wonder by bringing back the ancient Celtic heroes and beautiful ladies. Another is Aldington's momentary perception of a cosmic nightmare: "wonderful is the simple taken-for-granted fact that our sky is blue. It is such an incomparable background for the coloured earth, and stains the colourless sea with such variety of fluid blues and greens. How ghastly if our sky and sea were red–we could never exist in such a world–or if our sun glared like a white furnace mouth from a black sky. Yet there are such worlds." This passage is all the more effective for being sprung on the reader in an offhand way.

The closing essay of *Artifex*, "Mrs. Todgers," is a superbly written reminiscence of a cat that adopted Aldington even though she belonged to a nearby malt-house–one always nicely stocked with fresh mice. Why, Aldington wonders, was this cat so happy to switch households? "Doubtless, our fire, our shelter and our food? Not a bit of it. Mrs. Todgers was an exception to the economic interpretation of history. . . . [W]hat Mrs. Todgers wanted was not economic advantage, but a woman's life–a quiet home and a good steady man about the place." Aldington's good nature and humor are at their best in this essay-sketch, a blue-ribbon achievement–albeit little known–in the literature of pets.

Aldington en route from Trinidad to New York, 1935 (photograph by Robert Disraeli)

The writing of familiar essays and sketches (and in-betweens), forms that invite reverie and reminiscence, may have helped wean Aldington away from satire, a genre that easily revives the sense of one's actual frustrations and resentments and may thus create something of a psychological burden for the writer. In any event, after the ruminations and memories of *Artifex* Aldington wrote almost no satire, and none that was at all bitter.

Aldington and Doolittle were finally divorced in 1938; in the same year Aldington broke off with Brigit Patmore, with whom he had lived since 1928, and on 25 June he married Netta McCulloch. A week later she bore him a daughter, Catherine. From 1942 to 1946 he worked part of the time as a scriptwriter in Hollywood. During and after World War II he wrote several biographies that continue to be found attractive—when they are discovered. One of these, however—*Lawrence of Arabia* (1955)—was deeply critical of a popular hero and generated sufficient hostility to deal almost a death blow to Aldington's literary career.

The introductions and prefaces Aldington wrote for selections of the works of other writers, such as the lengthy introductions to Viking's *Portable Oscar Wilde* (1946) and *Walter Pater: Selected Works* (1948), and his biography *Introduction to Mistral* (1956) are large-minded and highly substantive essays. The Mistral book is, among other things, a stimulating and charming essay in the life and work of Frédéric Mistral as an example

of an alternative to what Matthew Arnold called the "sick hurry, the divided aims" of modern life.

The eight essays of *Frauds* (1957), published three years after Aldington exposed the fraudulent element in the T. E. Lawrence myth, show both that Aldington was not intimidated by the critics and that he could find imposture piquant and even amusing as well as deplorable. This sprightly work is one of Aldington's most appealing books, though the material is not of momentous importance and is certainly well out of the way of literary modernism. Maundy Gregory, General Cambronne, Titus Oates, Edward Kelley, George Psalmanzar, Thomas Chatterton, Thomas Griffiths Wainewright (the subject of Oscar Wilde's 1889 *Fortnightly Review* essay "Pen, Pencil, and Poison"), Roger Tichborne, and many other resolute deceivers emerge in all their ingloriousness. Aldington has no axe to grind, and his research is exemplary (for the essay on "Dr." Graham of "celestial bed" fame, Aldington had to learn a great deal about chemicals and pharmaceuticals of the late eighteenth century). His own honesty is sunny and sophisticated: it is never in danger of turning into aggressive righteousness. On the other hand, the mass-murderous careers of witch-hunters like Matthew Hopkins and of papist-hunters like Titus Oates cry out for comment, and Aldington meets the need. His judgments and the sympathy he expresses for the victims make the sordid material more endurable than it would be if Aldington had been a moral relativist. He is as interested in the milieu in which the impostor worked as in the fellow himself, and of course such a wide-ranging survey of human gullibility demonstrates that Aldington is no perfectionist or naive believer, à la Rousseau, in innate human goodness. The essays are replete with interesting out-of-the-way details, and in dealing with familiar figures or episodes Aldington usually creates a fresh focus (the treatment of Titus Oates is a fine example). As usual, Aldington's narrative skills give the material a charm it would not have had in the hands of a writer less practiced in the art of the story.

Acclaim from the Soviet Union in 1962 was a boost to Aldington's morale–but it came in the last year of his life. He died suddenly in his adopted village of Sury-en-Vaux on 27 July 1962.

A typical Aldington essay, whether familiar or critical, brings literary, social-historical, psychological, biographical, ethical, and philosophical considerations to bear upon the subject at hand. In the current age of specialization, many scholars and critics are unprepared to countenance such eclecticism and synthesis. The continuing prestige of specialization with a rationalist or positivist bias is no doubt one reason why Aldington's work remains relatively ignored or condescended to. But Aldington's rather old-fashioned love of wholeness and wisdom not only comes as a relief from specialization but results in writing that educates liberally, not least in its models of clean, flexible style.

Letters:

A Passionate Prodigality: Letters to Alan Bird from Richard Aldington, 1949-1962, edited by Miriam J. Benkovitz (New York: New York Public Library, 1976);

Literary Lifelines: the Richard Aldington-Lawrence Durrell Correspondence, edited by Ian S. MacNiven and Harry T. Moore (New York: Viking, 1981).

Bibliographies:

Alister Kershaw, *A Bibliography of the Works of Richard Aldington from 1915 to 1948* (Burlingame, Cal.: Wredon, 1950);

Norman T. Gates, "The Richard Aldington Collection at the Morris Library," *ICarbS*, 3 (1976): 61-68;

Gates, *A Checklist of the Letters of Richard Aldington* (Carbondale: Southern Illinois University Press, 1977).

Biography:

Charles Doyle, *Richard Aldington: A Biography* (London: Macmillan, 1989; Carbondale: Southern Illinois University Press, 1989).

References:

H. D. (Hilda Doolittle), *Bid Me to Live* (New York: Grove, 1960);

Keath Fraser, "A Note on Aldington and Free Verse," *Four Decades of Poetry,* 1 (January 1977): 222-225;

Norman T. Gates, "*Images of War* and *Death of a Hero:* Aldington's Twice-Used Images," *Modern British Literature,* 4 (Fall 1979): 120-127;

Gates, *The Poetry of Richard Aldington: A Critical Evaluation and an Anthology of Uncollected Poems* (University Park: Pennsylvania State University Press, 1974);

Gates, "Richard Aldington and the Clerk's Press," *Ohio Review,* 13 (Fall 1971): 21-27;

Alister Kershaw and Frédéric-Jacques Temple, eds., *Richard Aldington: An Intimate Portrait* (Carbondale: Southern Illinois University Press, 1965);

Selwyn Burnett Kittredge, "The Literary Career of Richard Aldington," Ph.D. dissertation, New York University, 1976;

Kittredge, "Richard Aldington's Challenge to T. S. Eliot: The Background of Their James Joyce Controversy," *James Joyce Quarterly,* 10 (Spring 1973): 339-341;

Phillip Knightley, "Aldington's Enquiry Concerning T. E. Lawrence," *Texas Quarterly,* 16 (Winter 1973): 98-105;

Thomas McGreevy, *Richard Aldington: An Englishman* (London: Chatto & Windus, 1931);

John Morris, "Richard Aldington and *Death of a Hero*–Or Life of an Anti-Hero?," in *The First World War in Fiction: A Collection of Critical Essays,* edited by Holger Klein (London: Macmillan, 1976), pp. 183-192;

Richard Eugene Smith, *Richard Aldington* (Boston: Twayne, 1977);

C. P. Snow, *Richard Aldington: An Appreciation* (London: Heinemann, 1938?).

Papers:

The library of Southern Illinois University at Carbondale holds an extensive collection of Richard Aldington's papers. Smaller collections are at the libraries of UCLA, the University of Texas, Yale, and Harvard.

Kingsley Amis

(16 April 1922 -   )

Bruce Stovel
University of Alberta

See also the Amis entries in *DLB 15: British Novelists, 1930-1959* and *DLB 27: Poets of Great Britain and Ireland, 1945-1960.*

BOOKS: *Bright November: Poems* (London: Fortune Press, 1947);

A Frame of Mind: Eighteen Poems (Reading, U.K.: School of Art, University of Reading, 1953);

Lucky Jim: A Novel (London: Gollancz, 1954; Garden City, N.Y.: Doubleday, 1954);

Kingsley Amis: Poems (Oxford: Fantasy Press, 1954);

That Uncertain Feeling: A Novel (London: Gollancz, 1955; New York: Harcourt, Brace, 1956);

A Case of Samples: Poems 1946-1956 (London: Gollancz, 1956; New York: Harcourt, Brace, 1957);

Socialism and the Intellectuals (London: Fabian Society, 1957);

I Like It Here: A Novel (London: Gollancz, 1958; New York: Harcourt, Brace, 1958);

Take a Girl Like You (London: Gollancz, 1960; New York: Harcourt, Brace & World, 1961);

New Maps of Hell: A Survey of Science Fiction (New York: Harcourt, Brace & World, 1960; London: Gollancz, 1961);

The Evans Country (Oxford: Fantasy Press, 1962);

My Enemy's Enemy (London: Gollancz, 1962; New York: Harcourt, Brace & World, 1963);

One Fat Englishman: A Novel (London: Gollancz, 1963; New York: Harcourt, Brace & World, 1964);

The Egyptologists: A Novel, by Amis and Robert Conquest (London: Cape, 1965; New York: Random House, 1966);

The James Bond Dossier (London: Cape, 1965; New York: New American Library, 1965);

The Book of Bond; Or Every Man His Own 007, as Lt.-Col. William ("Bill") Tanner (London: Cape, 1965; New York: Viking, 1965);

The Anti-Death League: A Novel (London: Gollancz, 1966; New York: Harcourt, Brace & World, 1966);

Kingsley Amis

A Look Round the Estate: Poems 1957-1967 (London: Cape, 1967; New York: Harcourt, Brace & World, 1968);

Colonel Sun: A James Bond Adventure, as Robert Markham (London: Cape, 1968; New York: Harper & Row, 1968);

Lucky Jim's Politics (London: Conservative Political Centre, 1968);

I Want It Now (London: Cape, 1968; New York: Harcourt, Brace & World, 1969);

The Green Man (London: Cape, 1969; New York: Harcourt, Brace & World, 1970);

What Became of Jane Austen? and Other Questions (London: Cape, 1970; New York: Harcourt Brace Jovanovich, 1971);

Girl, 20 (London: Cape, 1971; New York: Harcourt Brace Jovanovich, 1972);

Dear Illusion (London: Covent Garden Press, 1972);

On Drink (London: Cape, 1972; New York: Harcourt Brace Jovanovich, 1973);

The Riverside Villas Murder (London: Cape, 1973; New York: Harcourt Brace Jovanovich, 1973);

Ending Up (London: Cape, 1974; New York: Harcourt Brace Jovanovich, 1974);

Rudyard Kipling and His World (London: Thames & Hudson, 1975; New York: Scribners, 1975);

The Alteration (London: Cape, 1976; New York: Viking, 1977);

Jake's Thing (London: Hutchinson, 1978; New York: Viking, 1979);

The Darkwater Hall Mystery (Edinburgh: Tragara Press, 1978);

Collected Poems 1944-1979 (London: Hutchinson, 1979; New York: Viking, 1980);

An Arts Policy? (London: Centre for Policy Studies, 1979);

Collected Short Stories (London: Hutchinson, 1980);

Russian Hide-and-Seek: A Melodrama (London: Hutchinson, 1980);

Every Day Drinking (London: Hutchinson, 1983);

Stanley and the Women (London: Hutchinson, 1984; New York: Summit, 1985);

How's Your Glass? (London: Weidenfeld & Nicolson, 1984);

The Old Devils (London: Hutchinson, 1986).

OTHER: *Oxford Poetry, 1949*, edited by Amis and James Michie (Oxford: Blackwell, 1949);

Oscar Wilde: Poems and Essays, second edition, edited by Amis (London: Collins Classics, 1956);

"You That Love England; or, Limey, Stay Home," in *New World Writing*, edited by Stewart Richardson and Corlies M. Smith (Philadelphia: Lippincott, 1960), pp. 135-145;

Samuel Butler, *Erewhon, or Over the Range*, edited by Amis (New York: Signet Classic, 1961);

Spectrum: A Science Fiction Anthology, volumes 1-5, edited by Amis and Robert Conquest (London: Gollancz, 1961-1966; New York: Harcourt, Brace, 1962-1967);

"Communication and the Victorian Poet," in *British Victorian Literature: Recent Revaluations*, edited by S. K. Kumar (New York: New York University Press, 1969), pp. 39-52;

"Pernicious Participation," in *The Black Papers on Education* (London: Davis & Poynter, 1971), pp. 170-173;

"A Short Educational Dictionary," in *The Black Papers on Education* (London: Davis & Poynter, 1971), pp. 215-223;

Selected Stories of G. K. Chesterton, edited by Amis (London: Faber, 1972);

Tennyson, Selected by Kingsley Amis, edited by Amis (Harmondsworth, U.K.: Penguin, 1973);

"I.L.E.A. Confidential," by Amis and Conquest, in *Black Paper 1975: The Fight for Education*, edited by C. B. Cox and Rhodes Boyson (London: Dent, 1975), pp. 60-61;

Arthur Hutchings, *Mozart: The Man, the Music*, introduction by Amis (London: Schirmer, 1976);

Harold's Years: Impressions from the "New Statesman" and the "Spectator," edited by Amis (London: Quartet, 1977);

The New Oxford Book of Light Verse, edited, with an introduction, by Amis (London: Oxford University Press, 1978); republished as *The New Oxford Book of English Light Verse* (New York: Oxford University Press, 1978);

The Faber Popular Reciter, edited by Amis (London: Faber & Faber, 1978);

"Getting It Wrong," in *The State of the Language*, edited by Leonard Michaels and Christopher Ricks (Berkeley: University of California Press, 1980), pp. 24-33;

The Golden Age of Science Fiction, edited by Amis (London: Hutchinson, 1981);

"Oxford and After," in *Larkin at Sixty*, edited by Anthony Thwaite (London: Faber, 1982), pp. 23-30.

SELECTED PERIODICAL PUBLICATIONS–
UNCOLLECTED: "At the Jazz Band Ball," *Spectator*, 197 (28 September 1956): 409-411;

"Anglo-Saxon Platitudes," *Spectator*, 198 (5 April 1957): 285;

"Good, Brave Causes?," *Listener*, 65 (22 June 1961): 1087, 1092;

"What's Left for Patriotism?," *Observer*, 20 January 1963, p. 21;

"More Will Mean Worse," *Times* (London), 2 January 1967, p. 11; reprinted in *PMLA*, 82 (June 1967): 3;

"Involvement: Writers Reply," *London Magazine*, new series 5 (August 1968): 7;

"Real and Made-up People," *Times Literary Supplement*, 27 July 1973, pp. 847-848;

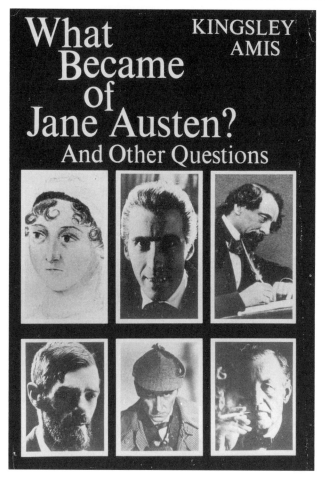

Dust jacket for the only collection of Amis's essays. Many of the essays have footnotes or postscripts that correct or even retract the original essay.

"Why Poetry?," *Observer Colour Magazine*, 30 September 1973, p. 7;

"The Art of the Impossible," *Times Literary Supplement*, 5 June 1981, p. 627;

"How I Lived in a Very Big House and Found God," *Times Literary Supplement*, 20 November 1981, p. 1352.

Although he is an accomplished poet and essayist, Kingsley Amis has always been best known as a novelist. In fact, his importance as an essayist is bound up with the astonishing success of his first novel, *Lucky Jim* (1954). Jim Dixon, lower-middle-class, secretly and inventively in revolt against the "cultivated" world in which he finds himself, quickly became a culture hero for a society which had suddenly lost most of its empire and world influence, where the old class system seemed discredited and a new social order was visibly in the making. In his *The Novel Now: A Student's Guide to Contemporary Fiction* (1967) An-

thony Burgess commented, "The most popular anti-hero of our time has been, without doubt, Jim Dixon of Kingsley Amis's *Lucky Jim*." Amis, in 1954 a young teacher of English literature at University College, Swansea, Wales, suddenly became one of the most listened-to voices in England. He would remain so for many years–an achievement due largely to his creation of a distinctive voice and persona. The stance was that of the ordinary man, *l'homme moyen sensuel*, as plain dealer: whenever high culture was boring and pretentious, Amis would say so; whenever lowbrow art had more to be said for it than the guardians of culture allowed, Amis would do the saying.

In this role Amis has written hundreds of essays, articles, book reviews, movie reviews, jazz reviews, and letters to the editor in prominent journals on both sides of the Atlantic; in the *Spectator* alone (Amis's favorite forum in his early years) he published more than 100 such items between 1953 and 1963. Jack Gohn's 1976 bibliography,

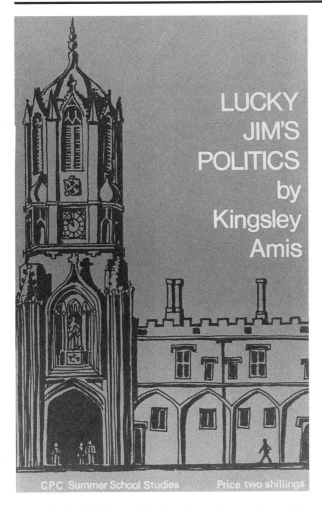

Cover for the 1968 pamphlet, based on a lecture given at Oxford in 1967, in which Amis attacks leftist political activism

tual life–a loss due mainly to his increasingly vehement conservatism in politics (Amis supported U.S. policy in Vietnam, for example) and his championing of such escapist forms of entertainment as science fiction, spy thrillers, detective stories, and horror movies. Lodge himself, for instance, said in a 1969 essay, "The Novelist at the Crossroads," that Amis's absorption with Ian Fleming's James Bond in the 1960s showed that he was no longer, as he had been in his novels and criticism of the 1950s, "a defender of a traditional kind of literary realism."

Amis was born in London in 1922, the only son of William Robert and Rosa Annie Amis. After serving in the signal corps from 1942 to 1945, rising to the rank of lieutenant, he came up to Oxford in 1945. Twice married and once divorced, the father of three children, Amis had been a full-time writer since 1963 (having taught English at the University of Swansea from 1949 to 1961 and at the University of Cambridge from 1961 to 1963). Amis's background and essential allegiances were implicit in the dedication of *Lucky Jim* to Philip Larkin. Amis and Larkin had been close friends since they were students together at St. John's College, Oxford, in the mid 1940s, and remained so until Larkin's death from cancer in 1985. Both were from humble backgrounds– Amis's father was a clerk in a mustard firm in London–and Larkin recalls in the introduction to the second edition of his *Jill: A Novel* (1964) that at Oxford he and Amis invented "the Yorkshire scholar," a character embodying in exaggerated form their own prejudices and disabilities, and conversed to each other "in his flat rapacious tones" (what chiefly distinguished the young Amis, according to Larkin, was his "genius for imaginative mimicry"). Larkin went on to become the major new poet of the 1950s, just as Amis was to be the decade's most exciting new novelist; and with their friend and fellow student at St. John's, John Wain, they formed the nucleus of "the Movement," a group of writers who became as central to the 1950s in Britain as W. H. Auden and his circle were to the 1930s. The Movement writers–the most notable of whom, apart from Larkin, Amis, and Wain, were Donald Davie and Thom Gunn–rejected the experimental methods and linguistic display of modernist writing, aiming instead at a more straightforward and lucid communication of shared experience with a larger audience. The title of Larkin's first widely successful volume of poetry, *The Less Deceived* (1955), sums up the Movement stance and that

which goes only to 1975 and is not exhaustive, lists 432 pieces of short nonfiction by Amis. Amis did gather 31 of his best and most distinctive essays into the collection *What Became of Jane Austen? and Other Questions* (1970), but he had his greatest impact as a writer of nonfiction before that date through the vast scattered body of his occasional writings. That impact is nicely defined by David Lodge in his essay "The Modern, The Contemporary, and the Importance of Being Amis": "The importance of being Amis . . . is in a sense greater than the sum of his works, individually considered as autotelic works of art. His novels, stories, poems, reviews, even *obiter dicta* reported in the newspapers, have focused in a very precise way a number of attitudes which a great many middle-class intellectuals find useful for purposes of self-definition." Ironically, by 1970, when his collection of essays appeared, Amis had already lost this central position in English intellec-

of Amis as critic and social commentator. In fact, Amis's attitude in his essays is essentially that of the speaker in "Church Going," the best-known poem in *The Less Deceived*: a bicycle-clipped visitor of cultural monuments, unpretentious, bored, irreverent, but also knowledgeable, curious, and "forever surprising / A hunger in himself to be more serious."

Amis the essayist can be seen at his best in his only collection, *What Became of Jane Austen? and Other Questions*. Eighteen of its thirty-one pieces were written in the 1950s; sixteen first appeared in the *Spectator*. The essays, which appear in roughly the order in which they were written, reflect Amis's range of interests and his changing public stance: the first two-thirds are on books and authors, beginning with pieces on classic authors such as Austen and John Keats and moving on to minor writers and lowbrow art forms; the final ten essays detail personal experiences or opinions. The last four essays, all relatively long and all written in the 1960s, are autobiographical and even confessional: "No More Parades," an account of why Amis resigned from his teaching position at Peterhouse College, Cambridge, in 1963; "A Memoir of My Father" and "Why Lucky Jim Turned Right," defenses of Amis's political about-face (the last title shows that Amis has been willing to identify his own opinions and attitudes with those of his most popular character); and "On Christ's Nature," which discusses how admiration of Christ can be consistent with disbelief in Christianity.

Amis speaks throughout as one who is "less deceived." Great authors are judged by Movement standards of truth to common experience, lack of pretentiousness, and clarity of expression and are found sadly lacking: Austen was corrupted in *Mansfield Park* (1814) by her own moral righteousness; Keats is "an often delightful, if often awkward, decorative poet" with a predilection for bookworn Greek mythology; Dickens is ruined by "ubiquitous, obsessive repetition, the inability to leave anything, good or bad, alone"; Lawrence is best left "on his pinnacle, inspiring, unapproachable, and unread." Amis takes exactly the opposite approach to lowbrow art: he devotes one essay each to detective stories, science fiction, spy thrillers, and horror films, and finds in them more enjoyment and more artistry than is generally allowed. Similarly, in "Why Lucky Jim Turned Right" Amis defends the Conservative party precisely because it disavows political idealism: "I have seen how many of the evils of life—

failure, loneliness, fear, boredom, inability to communicate—are ineradicable by political means, and that attempts so to eradicate them are disastrous."

One unusual feature of the volume is Amis's penchant for the palinode: twenty of the essays have postscripts or footnotes, added by Amis in 1970, that usually correct or even retract the original essay. After the Keats essay, first published in 1957, for instance, Amis adds a postscript in which he says, "This now strikes me as a rather clever undergraduate essay," praises Keats for having "democratized" poetry by making it personal, and ends with a grand, if double-edged, tribute: "no one who has never thought him the greatest poet in the world, no matter for how brief a period, has any real feeling for literature." One reviewer, Paul Theroux in *Book World*, objected: "This is haste. The postscripts should have occasioned a new article." One might argue, however, that these afterthoughts create just the intimate, candid, and informal relationship between writer and reader that Movement authors wanted.

What is most striking about these pieces is that Amis is not an essayist in the strict sense of the word—if an essay is understood to be an extended general argument. Amis's literary discussions tend to be short, provocative statements of opinion rather than arguments; his longer pieces are either old-fashioned "appreciations" (and so consist of affectionate description) or autobiographical narrations. As the title *What Became of Jane Austen? and Other Questions* suggests, Amis is concerned to air questions rather than to settle them. Theroux sums up this aspect of the volume in an elegant pun: "These are not essays, but responses, articles, often articles of faith." Another reviewer, Christopher Ricks in the *Listener*, made the same point: Amis the essayist, unlike Amis the novelist, "knows there are two sides to every question, the right side and the wrong side." The typical Amis "essay" is thus not an essay at all, but either an evocative appreciation or, more often, an ingenious invective. The writing tends to become memorable when Amis employs extended, novelistic narration—when, for instance, in "An Evening with Dylan Thomas" he describes how Thomas read the final line of Yeats's "Lapis Lazuli" with a ten-second, histrionic pause in the middle, or when he summarizes all he dislikes about Cambridge in "No More Parades" by depicting an upper-class undergraduate shattering the calm of a lunchtime pub

Illustration by Nicolas Bentley for On Drink, *one of three books on liquor that grew out of the columns Amis wrote for* Penthouse *magazine during the 1970s*

by bawling forth his callow opinions on the theater to his friends and relatives.

This absence of complex and connected argument keeps Amis from being a major essayist, and his essays have rarely been anthologized. Although he was widely read in the 1950s and 1960s, his essays are now mainly of interest for the light they throw on his writing in other genres, particularly his novels. As Theroux remarked in his review, *"What Became of Jane Austen?* is a chronicle of a writer's changing concerns rather than a detailed discussion of the concerns themselves." Even so, the nonspecialist will find the essays well worth reading for at least two reasons: Amis's ability to analyze his own thinking, and his wit and humor. As for the first point, if Amis airs his predilections and prejudices in his essays, he usually is also concerned to understand them, to isolate the literary or moral principle that explains and justifies his instinctive response. Essay after essay concludes with the enunciation of such a principle. "Pater and Old Chap," a caustic account of Warwick Deeping's snobbery-laden best-seller *Sorrell and Son* (1925), ends with the sentence, "It is the bad teaching of good lessons that

can be painful." "Who Needs No Introduction," a description of Jack Kerouac's egocentric exhibitionism at a panel discussion, builds to the reflection "that Mr. Kerouac's performance had acted as a useful supplement to his novels in demonstrating how little spontaneity has to do with talking off the top of the head." Amis analyzes the kind of response demanded by Dylan Thomas's prose in "Thomas the Rhymer" and concludes that "it is reading in this way which is really anti-poetic." In "In Slightly Different Form" Amis's embarrassment at reading Philip Roth's *Portnoy's Complaint* (1969) teaches him that "reading is a sort of social experience," since he finds that "I do not want to be told what I would not myself tell another person without feeling I was showing off— not about my sexual, but my social uninhibitedness."

On the second point: Amis will probably always be best known as a comic novelist, and anyone familiar with the novels will encounter many of the same comic devices in the essays. The reader is constantly surprised by inventive and precise analogies; for instance, in "Dracula, Frankenstein, Sons & Co.," his celebration of horror films, Amis finds the most recent offering from Hammer Films dull: "some of the minor people were oddly unattractive, as if the cast had been made up hastily from the sociology department of one of our new universities." Reviewing Arnold Wesker's plays in "Not Talking About Jerusalem," Amis says, "This air of being hastily translated from another language is endemic to Mr. Wesker's dialogue." Sometimes such an analogy forms a frame for an entire essay, as in "The Legion of the Lost," Amis's 1956 review of Colin Wilson's *The Outsider*—an influential book which popularized the concepts of alienation and absurdity. Amis takes the claim of alienation literally and imagines that Sartre, Camus, Kierkegaard, and others belong to a French Foreign Legion of the intellect; the book review becomes a military review which ends, "Right. Legion of the Lost . . . DIS-*MISS!*" These analogies are energized by striking colloquialisms; in the Wilson review he says, "All writers come alike to the ravening trend-hound" and admits that he states his own objections "at the risk of being written off as a spiritual wakey-wakey man." Amis also makes deft use of ironic dismissal. His review of Dylan Thomas's prose begins, "It can be asserted with utter finality that here is a volume which every admirer of Thomas's poems will want to possess, for most of the qualities found in the poems are to be found in it. In spite of this, the book seems to me to be worth having." Amis also employs more overt humor–the wisecrack, for instance, as in his comment on M. R. Ridley's *Keats' Craftsmanship* (1962): "surely a candidate for that old shortest-books series along with *Canadian Wit and Humour, Great Marxist Humanitarians,* and *The Vein of Humility in D. H. Lawrence.*"

Amis's reputation as an essayist is much slighter now than it was in its heyday in the 1950s and early 1960s. The reviews of *What Became of Jane Austen?* were mixed, and critics often expressed disappointment at the way Amis's career had developed. Richard Boston, for instance, reviewing the paperback edition in the *New Statesman* in 1972, remarked that as one reads through the book and follows Amis's evolution, the essays become increasingly predictable. The most carefully reasoned review, by Christopher Ricks, virtually dismissed the volume as consisting of "some good jokes, much bad reasoning, and a cheery peevishness."

Except for a handful of academic articles at the start of his career, Amis's literary criticism is devoted to defending genre fiction (escapist popular literature). This defense is made mainly in *New Maps of Hell: A Survey of Science Fiction* (1960), a book that derived from lectures that Amis gave in the Christian Gauss Seminars in Criticism at Princeton University during 1958-1959, and in *The James Bond Dossier* (1965), a handbook to Ian Fleming's spy thrillers. In 1968 Amis published under a pseudonym a continuation of the James Bond saga titled *Colonel Sun* (Fleming had died in 1964). Amis stresses two points about genre fiction. One is the childlike pleasure it offers to the imagination: "science fiction . . . provides a field which, while not actually repugnant to sense and decency, allows us to doff that mental and moral best behavior with which we feel we have to treat George Eliot and James and Faulkner, and frolic like badly brought-up children among the mobile jellyfishes and unstable atomic piles." The second point is that genre fiction, with its clear (if unspoken) rules, allows the author to display and the reader to enjoy virtuoso craftsmanship. Amis says in "A New James Bond," his account of how and why he wrote *Colonel Sun* (reprinted in *What Became of Jane Austen?*), that if "the best of serious fiction, so to call it, is better than anything any genre can offer," still, "this best is horribly rare, and a clumsy dissection of the heart is so much worse than boring as to be painful."

One piece of Amis's academic literary criticism is of special interest. "Communication and the Victorian Poet," an article in *Essays in Criticism* (October 1954; anthologized in *British Victorian Literature,* 1969), is a précis of Amis's rejected B. Litt. thesis at Oxford. It argues that Victorian poetry was at its most creative when its authors enjoyed direct and widespread communication with their audience and declined when that communication was lost. The argument reflects Amis's conception of his own art.

Amis is the author of three slender political pamphlets: *Socialism and the Intellectuals* (1957), *Lucky Jim's Politics* (1968), and *An Arts Policy?* (1979). The first two provoked a good deal of controversy on publication. The first, published by the Fabian Society, presents Amis as a moderate Labour supporter and ex-Marxist; the second, published by the Conservative party, presents him as an avowed Tory and former "Lefty." In fact, the two are strikingly consistent: Amis argues in both that pursuit of political ideology is a delusion–one especially dangerous to the artist, who is by definition a nonactivist. *Lucky Jim's Politics,* a recension of "Why Lucky Jim Turned Right" (first published in the *Sunday Telegraph* in 1967), defines the activist's fallacy: "the reason we are failing to get on, or simply not having a good enough time, is not because we are lazy and stupid, but because of the system. So now we oppose the system." *An Arts Policy?* argues that the Labour government's notions of culture show a misunderstanding of how culture is produced.

Amis's biography, *Rudyard Kipling and His World* (1975), is a handsome picture book in the Thames and Hudson series. Because of its format and intended audience it is not a work of scholarship, nor does it present an original thesis about its subject. Still, it is a shrewd, lucidly written account of Kipling's character and a vehement (and unfashionable) defense of his art. The book was widely and favorably reviewed.

Amis's three books on boozing, *On Drink* (1972), *Every Day Drinking* (1983), and *How's Your Glass?* (1984), are short, facetious, light in tone, and meant for a popular audience. They all grew out of Amis's fondness for wine and alcohol–and out of the column on drink that he produced every month, beginning in 1972 and continuing through the 1970s, for *Penthouse.* Such a column is the stuff of which Jim Dixon's dreams were made–but it no doubt helped form the general impression in the 1970s that Amis was no longer a serious artist, or at least no longer one of central

Amis, circa 1984 (photograph by Jerry Bauer)

importance. Amis wrote many jazz and movie reviews in the 1950s and 1960s, but he has not gathered his thoughts on these subjects into volume form.

Finally, there are Amis's individual, scattered essays and introductions to books he has edited. The post-1970 essays show that Amis is still witty, provocative, and an elegant stylist. Someone who wishes to sample the later prose might begin with "How I Lived in a Very Big House and Found God," Amis's "less deceived" *Times Literary Supplement* review of the 1981 television version of Evelyn Waugh's *Brideshead Revisited* (1945); or any of his contributions to the *Black Papers on Education*, a series of volumes that opposed current fashions in education; or his thoughtful and wide-ranging introduction to *The New Oxford Book of Light Verse* (1978); or his essay "Getting It Wrong" in the collection *The State of the Language* (1980), a witty analysis, with scores of examples, of why and how malapropism prevails in contemporary speech.

If his opinions and his stature have changed over the decades, Amis is still highly readable. In recent years, he is becoming recognized as a persistent and persisting figure on the English literary

scene: he was made an Honorary Fellow of St. John's College, Oxford, in 1976; in 1981 he was named a Commander, Order of the British Empire (C.B.E.); in 1986 his novel *The Old Devils* was awarded the prestigious Booker Prize; and he was knighted in 1990.

Interviews:

W. J. Weatherby, "Mr. Sellers and Mr. Amis: A Conversation Reported by W. J. Weatherby," *Guardian Weekly*, 84 (4 May 1961): 12;

Pat Williams, "My Kind of Comedy," *Twentieth Century*, 1970 (July 1961): 46-50;

John Silverlight, "Profile: Kingsley Amis," *Observer*, 14 January 1962, p. 13; reprinted as "Kingsley Amis: The Writer, The Symbol," *New York Herald Tribune Book Review*, 21 January 1962, p. 6;

Harry Fieldhouse, "Penthouse Interview: Kingsley Amis," *Penthouse*, 2 (October 1970): 35-39, 42;

James Gindin, "Kingsley Amis," in *Contemporary Novelists*, edited by James Vinson (New York: St. Martin's Press, 1972), pp. 44-48;

Pauline Peters, "Two on an Island," *Sunday Times Magazine* (London), 3 February 1974, pp. 64-66;

Peter Firchow, "Kingsley Amis," in his *The Writer's Place: Interviews on the Literary Situation in Contemporary England* (Minneapolis: University of Minnesota Press, 1974), pp. 15-38;

Clive James, "Kingsley Amis," *New Review*, 1 (July 1974): 21-28;

Melvyn Bragg, "Kingsley Amis Looks Back," *Listener*, 20 February 1975, pp. 240-241;

Michael Barber, "The Art of Fiction–LIX: Kingsley Amis," *Paris Review*, 16 (Winter 1975): 39-72;

Dale Salwak, "An Interview with Kingsley Amis," *Contemporary Literature*, 16 (Winter 1975): 1-18;

Auberon Waugh, "Amis: A Singular Man," *Sunday Telegraph Magazine*, 17 September 1978, pp. 33-36;

Jean W. Ross, "Interview With Kingsley Amis," in *Contemporary Authors*, new revision series 8, edited by Ann Evory and Linda Metzger (Detroit: Gale, 1983), pp. 32-34.

Bibliographies:

Rubin Rabinovitz, "Kingsley Amis Bibliography," in his *The Reaction against Experiment in the English Novel, 1950-60* (New York & London: Columbia University Press, 1967), pp. 174-178;

Jack Benoit Gohn, *Kingsley Amis: A Checklist* (Kent, Ohio: Kent State University Press, 1976);

Dale Salwak, *Kingsley Amis: A Reference Guide* (Boston: G. K. Hall, 1978).

References:

Bernard Bergonzi, "Kingsley Amis," in his *The Situation of the Novel* (London: Macmillan, 1970), pp. 161-174;

Anthony Burgess, "A Sort of Rebel," in his *The Novel Now: A Student's Guide to Contemporary Fiction* (New York: Norton, 1967), pp. 141-144;

Philip Gardner, *Kingsley Amis* (Boston: Twayne, 1981);

Martin Green, *Children of the Sun: A Narrative of "Decadence" in England after 1918* (New York: Basic Books, 1976), pp. 396-398, 417-426;

Philip Larkin, Introduction to his *Jill: A Novel*, second edition (London: Faber, 1964), pp.

11-19; reprinted in his *Required Writing: Miscellaneous Pieces 1955-1982* (London: Faber, 1983), pp. 17-26;

David Lodge, "The Modern, The Contemporary, and the Importance of Being Amis," *Critical Quarterly*, 5 (Winter 1963): 340-354; reprinted in his *Language of Fiction: Essays in Criticism and Verbal Analysis of the English Novel* (London: Routledge & Kegan Paul, 1966; New York: Columbia University Press, 1966), pp. 243-267;

Lodge, "The Novelist at the Crossroads," in his *The Novelist at the Crossroads and Other Essays on Fiction and Criticism* (New York: Cornell University Press, 1969), p. 20;

Neil McEwan, "Kingsley Amis," in his *The Survival of the Novel: British Fiction in the Later Twentieth Century* (London: Macmillan, 1981), pp. 78-97;

Blake Morrison, *The Movement: English Poetry and Fiction of the 1950s* (London: Oxford University Press, 1980);

William Van O'Connor, "Kingsley Amis: That Uncertain Feeling," in his *The New University Wits and the End of Modernism* (Carbondale: Southern Illinois University Press, 1963), pp. 75-102;

Rubin Rabinovitz, "Kingsley Amis," in his *The Reaction against Experiment in the English Novel, 1950-60* (New York & London: Columbia University Press, 1967), pp. 38-63;

Christopher Ricks, "I Was Like That Myself Once," *Listener*, 84 (26 November 1970): 739-740;

Paul Theroux, "Professional Writer," *Book World* (17 October 1971): 8;

John Wain, *Sprightly Running: Part of an Autobiography* (New York & London: Macmillan, 1962), pp. 167-169, 188, 202-205.

Papers:

The Harry Ransom Humanities Research Center at the University of Texas at Austin possesses some of Amis's letters, working materials for many of his novels (notably the manuscript, typescript, and notes for *Lucky Jim*), and the typescript of *The James Bond Dossier*. Manuscripts of several early poems are in the Lockwood Memorial Library, State University of New York at Buffalo.

Clifford Bax

(13 July 1886 - 18 November 1962)

J. P. Greenwood

See also the Bax entry in *DLB 10: Modern British Dramatists, 1900-1945.*

BOOKS: *Poems Dramatic and Lyrical* (London: Orpheus, 1911);

The Poetasters of Ispahan: A Verse-Comedy in One Act (London: Benmar, 1912; Boston: Baker International Play Bureau, 1929);

Friendship (London: Batsford, 1913; New York: Dutton, 1913);

Japanese Impromptus, by Bax and Gwendolen Daphne Bishop (Speen: Abbot's Hill, 1914);

The Rose and the Cross (London: Palmer, 1918);

Square Pegs: A Rhymed Fantasy for Two Girls (London: Hendersons, 1920); edited by Theodore Johnson, in his *Plays in Miniature, for Two or Three* (Boston: Baker, 1928);

A House of Words (Oxford: Blackwell, 1920);

Youth: Song, music by Arnold Bax (London: Murdoch, Murdoch, 1920);

Aspiration: Song, music by Arnold Bax (London: Murdoch, Murdoch, 1921);

Gleanings (Kensington: Printed for the author at the Favil Press, 1921);

The Traveller's Tale (Oxford: Blackwell, 1921);

Old King Cole (London: Daniel, 1921; London, New York & Los Angeles: French, 1935);

Shakespeare: A Play in Five Episodes, by Bax and H. F. Rubinstein (Boston: Houghton Mifflin, 1921; London: Benn, 1921);

Antique Pageantry: A Book of Verse-Plays (London: Hendersons, 1921)–comprises *The Poetasters of Ispahan, The Apricot Tree, The Summit*, and *Aucassin and Nicolette: A Verse Play*;

The Cloak (London: Palmer, 1921);

The Apricot Tree (London: Hendersons, 1921);

Up Stream: A Drama in Three Acts (Oxford: Blackwell, 1922; New York: Brentano's, 1923);

Polite Satires (London: Medici Society, 1922; Great Neck, N.Y.: Core Collection Books, 1976)–comprises *The Unknown Hand, The Volcanic Island*, and *Square Pegs*;

Midsummer Madness: A Play for Music (London:

Benn, 1923; New York: Stokes, 1923);

Prelude and Fugue: A Play in One Act (London: Palmer, 1923);

Nocturne in Palermo (London: Benn, 1924);

Studio Plays: Three Experiments in Dramatic Form (London: Palmer, 1924)–comprises *Prelude and Fugue, The Rose and the Cross*, and *The Cloak*;

Inland Far: A Book of Thoughts and Impressions (London: Heinemann, 1925);

Mr. Pepys: A Ballad-Opera (London: Heinemann, 1926; New York & London: French, 1927);

Bianca Cappello (London: Howe, 1927; New York: Viking, 1928);

Many a Green Isle (London: Heinemann, 1927);

Eight Poems, from Clifford Bax to Arnold Bennett, Christmas 1928 (London, 1928);

Aucassin and Nicolette: A Verse Play (Boston: Baker International Play Bureau, 1930);

Socrates: A Play in Six Scenes (London: Gollancz, 1930);

The Chronicles of Cupid: Being a Masque of Love throughout the Ages (London & New York: French, 1931);

The Immortal Lady: A Play in Three Acts (London: French, 1931); London & New York: French, 1932);

Valiant Ladies: Three New Plays (London: Mundanus/Gollancz, 1931)–comprises *The Venetian, The Rose Without a Thorn*, and *The Immortal Lady*;

The Venetian: A Play in Three Acts (London: French, 1931; New York: Farrar & Rinehart, 1931);

Twelve Short Plays: Serious and Comic (London: Gollancz, 1932)–comprises *Prelude and Fugue, The Summit, The Cloak, The Rose and the Cross, Aucassin and Nicolette, The Tale of the Wandering Scholar, The Unknown Hand, The Volcanic Island, Square Pegs, The Apricot Tree, Silly Willy*, and *The Poetasters of Ispahan*;

Leonardo da Vinci (London: Davies, 1932; New York: Appleton, 1932);

Farewell, My Muse (London: Dickson, 1932);

Clifford Bax

Pretty Witty Nell: An Account of Nell Gwyn and Her Environment (London: Chapman & Hall, 1932; New York: Morrow, 1933);

That Immortal Sea: A Meditation upon the Future of Religion and of Sexual Morality (London: Dickson, 1933);

The Rose Without a Thorn: A Play in Three Acts (London & New York: French, 1933);

April in August: A Play in Three Acts (London & New York: French, 1934);

The Quaker's 'Cello: A Play in One Act (London & New York: French, 1934);

Tragic Nesta: A Play in One Act (London & New York: French, 1934);

Ideas and People (London: Dickson, 1936);

The House of Borgia: A Play in Three Acts (London: Favil Press, 1937);

Highways and Biways in Essex (London: Macmillan, 1939);

The Life of the White Devil (London & Toronto: Cassell, 1940);

Evenings in Albany (London: Eyre & Spottiswoode, 1942);

Time with a Gift of Tears: A Modern Romance (London: Eyre & Spottiswoode, 1943);

Whither the Theatre . . . ? A Letter to a Young Playwright (London: Home & Van Thal, 1945);

The Beauty of Women (London: Muller, 1946);

Golden Eagle: A Drama (London: Home & Van Thal, 1946);

Hemlock for Eight: A Radio Play, by Bax and Leon M. Lion (London: Muller, 1946);

The Buddha: A Radio Version of His Life and Ideas (London: Gollancz, 1947);

The Play of St. Lawrence: A Pageant Play for Production in a Church (London: French, 1947);

Rosemary for Remembrance (London: Muller, 1948);

Circe: A Play in Three Acts (London: Muller, 1949);

Some I Knew Well (London: Phoenix House, 1951);

W. G. Grace, etc. (London: Phoenix House, 1952);

Who's Who in Heaven: A Sketch (Mortlocks, Meldreth [actually Royston, Hertfordshire]: Golden Head, 1954);

The Wandering Scholar: A Chamber Opera in One Act, music by Gustav Holst, edited by Benjamin Britten and Imogen Holst (London: Faber Music, 1968).

OTHER: *John Ruskin, The Crown of Wild Olive and The Cestus of Aglaia*, introduction by Bax (Everyman, 1908);

A. E. (George William Russell), *The Hero in Man*, edited by Bax (Ashdale, Hale & Cheshire: Dunlop / London: Bax 1909);

Rudolf Steiner, *Initiation and Its Results*, translated by Bax (New York: Macoy, 1909);

The Orpheus Series, edited by Bax and C. N. Dunlop (Hampstead: Orpheus, 1909-1912);

The New Mission of Art: A Study of Idealism in Art, by Jean Delville, translated by Francis Colmer, introductory notes by Bax and Edward Schuré (London: Francis Griffiths, 1910);

Twenty Chinese Poems, paraphrased by Bax (London: Budd, 1910); revised and enlarged as *Twenty-five Chinese Poems* (London: Hendersons, 1916);

Antonio Cippico, *The Night of the Kings: A Dramatic Poem*, translated by Bax (New York: Tower Bros. Stationery Co., 1919);

The Old Broughtonians Cricket Weeks, 6 volumes, compiled by Bax (Kensington: Favil, 1921-1938);

Carlo Goldoni, *Four Comedies*, edited and translated by Bax (London: Printed by the Curwen Press for C. Palmer, 1922);

The Golden Hind: A Quarterly Magazine of Art and Literature, 2 volumes, edited by Bax (London: Chapman & Hall, 1922-1924);

"A Queer Fellow," in *The Best British Short Stories, 1923*, pp. 41-46;

John Gay, *Polly, an Opera: Being the Sequel to The Beggar's Opera*, adapted by Bax (New York: Moffat Yard, 1923; London: Chapman & Hall, 1923);

Karel Capek, *"And So Ad Infinitum"* (*The Life of the Insects*), translated by Percy Selver, adapted by Bax and Nigel Playfair (London & New York: Oxford University Press, 1924);

Jacob Böhme, *The Signature of All Things, with Other Writings*, edited by Bax (London & Toronto: Dent / New York: Dutton, 1926);

Florence Farr, Bernard Shaw, W. B. Yeats; Letters, edited by Bax (Dublin: Cuala, 1941; New York: Dodd, Mead, 1942; London: Home & Van Thal, 1946);

The Noble Game of Cricket; Illustrated and Described from Pictures, Drawings, and Prints in the Collection of Sir Jeremiah Colman, introduction by Bax (London: Batsford, 1941);

Never Again!, edited by Bax (London: Hutchinson, 1942)–includes "Our Eternal Undergraduates," by Bax;

Torquato Tasso, *The Age of Gold: A Chorus Translated Out of Tasso's "L'Aminta,"* translated by Bax (Derby: Grasshopper Press, 1944);

Vintage Verse: An Anthology of Poetry in English, edited by Bax (London: Hollis & Carter, 1945; Great Neck, N.Y.: Granger, 1978);

All the World's a Stage: Theatrical Portraits, edited by Bax (London: Muller, 1946);

The Silver Casket: Being Love-Letters and Love-Poems Attributed to Mary Stuart, Queen of Scots, Now Modernised or Translated, edited by Bax (London: Home & Van Thal, 1946);

Letters and Poems by Mary Stuart, Queen of Scots, Now Modernised or Translated, edited by Bax (New York: Philosophical Library, 1947);

Robert Browning and Elizabeth Barrett Browning, *The Poetry of the Brownings*, compiled by Bax (London: Muller, 1947; Folcroft, Pa.: Folcroft Library Editions, 1973);

The Distaff Muse: An Anthology of Poetry Written by Women, compiled by Bax and Meum Stewart (London: Hollis & Carter, 1949);

"Test of Experience," in *Creators of the Modern Spirit: Towards a Philosophy of Faith, a Symposium*, edited by Barbara Waylen (London: Rockliff, 1951; New York: Macmillan, 1951), p. 111.

SELECTED PERIODICAL PUBLICATIONS–
UNCOLLECTED: "Stephen Phillips," *Poetry Review*, 7 (February 1916): 132;

"Style and Fashion in Literature," *Royal Society of Literature of the United Kingdom*, 21 (1944): 67-81.

A prolific playwright, poet, editor, and essayist, Clifford Bax considered himself an "ardent theosophist" at the age of twenty-three. His lifelong interest in the metaphysical is the basis for the common philosophical thread in much of his variegated output. Although Bax achieved modest success as a playwright, the subtle amalgam of Platonic, Christian, and Buddhist thought devel-

Bax (right) and Reginald Hine on the cricket field in 1909

oped in his essays seems sharply out of sympathy with the rationalistic materialism of his time. When working in an autobiographical mode, as in *Inland Far: A Book of Thoughts and Impressions* (1925), Bax conveys with admirable detachment his commitment to spiritualism. His impressionistic method is less suited to his biographical works, however, such as those on Leonardo da Vinci (1932) and Nell Gwyn (1932), which have, as a result, been less appreciated by reviewers. Also less successful is the more argumentative tone of *That Immortal Sea: A Meditation upon the Future of Religion and of Sexual Morality* (1933), where the author's lack of detachment detracts from his credibility. A balance is struck in his character sketches, such as those which comprise *Some I Knew Well* (1951); there, Bax, an enthusiastic student of personality, allows himself to meet his subjects comfortably at points of commonality. Bax's reputation as an essayist will ultimately rest on the constancy of his philosophical outlook and

the graceful, easy eloquence of his prose style.

Bax was born into an affluent London family on 13 July 1886 as the third son of Arthur Ridley and Charlotte Ellen Lea Bax. His uncle, Belfort Bax, was a noted philosopher; his brother Arnold became a composer.

A boyhood interest in cricket gave way quickly to literature when, at the age of fourteen, Bax read the works of John Keats in what he calls "an intense but hazy delight." From Keats he moved to Percy Bysshe Shelley, and by age fifteen, he says, he seemed to know both poets personally. A year later his literary enthusiasms led him to Alfred, Lord Tennyson, of whose *Idylls of the King* (1859-1885) Bax claimed to have memorized many a line before breakfast. His poetical grounding eventually extended itself to include Thomas Malory, the Elizabethans, Walt Whitman, and Leo Tolstoy, but found an apotheosis in the work of William Butler Yeats and Giosuè Carducci. Bax admired Yeats for resisting free verse; poetry, Bax felt, ought to go beyond the tinkle and jingle of rhyme. "The best poetry bears no date," Bax thought; instead, it reflects its timeless relation to human affairs–rather than to nature, in what Bax considered "the obsolete fashion of the nineteenth century." The key to the effectiveness of great poetry, according to Bax, is the "subtle enchantment" of rhythm, an aspect of verse which "builds a bridge between the conscious and the unconscious mind, thus effecting the great purpose of art."

Bax discovered Yeats at sixteen. On reading the latter's essay "Magic" in *Ideas of Good and Evil* (1903), he says, his "imagination went up in flames." Against his parents' wishes he abandoned plans to attend Cambridge and entered the Slade School of Art, where he "slaved for ten months without learning how to draw a pleasant line." Students at Slade nicknamed him "the Seer," and one afternoon when the class seemed to be busy drawing the model he discovered to his chagrin that they were all drawing caricatures of him. From there he moved to the Heatherly Art School, where he met Ernest Rhys and, through him, Yeats. Bax later remembered coming away from the "exaggerated chiaroscuro" of Yeats's "candlelit" room with a feeling of both elation and confusion. While Bax was still interested in writing poetry about conventionally erudite subjects, the great man advised him instead to "always write about what you know."

Determined to learn additional languages as an aid to poetic composition, in the spring of 1904 Bax went to Munich with two cousins via St. Mortiz, where the Swiss air ameliorated his asthma. He took with him *The History of the Rosicrucians*, Tolstoy's *Essays*, and works by "A. E." (George William Russell), the "poet of theosophy." In Munich Bax struck up an apparently platonic relationship with two girls, an American named Gabrielle and a Briton named Constantia. The girls, he says, "thawed his metaphysical snow": "every day, with the fire and faith of inexperience, we debated the riddles of life and the aims of art and the ideas of theosophy and the cult of heavenly Aphrodite."

In the winter of 1905, at Gabrielle's suggestion Bax set out on a journey around the world that took him to Naples; Aden; the Red Sea; Sydney, Australia; Auckland, Wellington, and the North Island of New Zealand; New Guinea; Hong Kong; Canton, China; Nagasaki, Kyoto, and Tokyo; Honolulu; San Francisco; Salt Lake City; Chicago; Niagara Falls; and New York City.

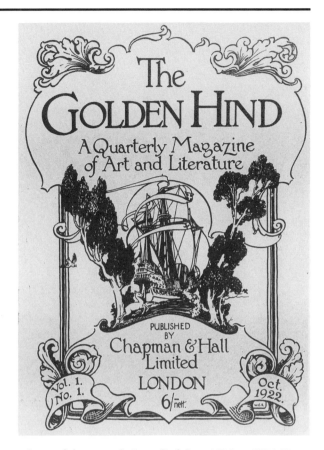

Cover of the quarterly Bax edited from 1922 to 1924 (Special Collections, Thomas Cooper Library, University of South Carolina)

Even as he traveled, Bax admits, he felt the influence on his perceptions of his bookish background: his view of life, he says, was "an intellectual fabric . . . tinged with mystical appreciation." He arrived in London in June 1906.

Upon his return, Bax shunned his contemporaries and the socialistic ideas for which they had become enthusiastic. He dabbled in astrology, a subject which "nourished my fancy." He developed his notion of the soul's entrapment in the body, and he "sojourned alone" on his "intellectual hill-top, enveloped by an inhospitable mist of metaphysics."

At twenty Bax discovered Plato; he later said that he had known "no joy, no joy of any kind to surpass the glory of delight" with which he experienced this philosopher's work. He found in the dialogues a "complete assuagement" of his "thirst" and felt the "Platonic view expanding my half-shaped thoughts with almost alarming speed." At about this time he decided to add French to his smattering of German, and arranged to study with a French girl named Odette. Their relationship, in Bax's words, was "like crystal, not clouded by sentimentality or influenced by desire." Odette called it "a little spiritual flirtation."

In August 1906 he went with his brother to Dublin, where he met Russell and discussed his idea of "starting a magazine that should revitalize the arts by attaching them to the deep thought of theosophy and should redeem theosophy by giving it aesthetic form." He called the magazine *Orpheus*, though he later admitted that he should have called it "*The Centaur*, for, with the characteristic zeal and misjudgement of youth, I was attempting to effect a bizarre alliance and to synthesize prematurely two equal but unrelated interests." The first issue of this "hole-and-corner production," as he called it, appeared in 1909 and was greeted warmly by Russell. He and Bax agreed that most English poetry moved "in a world of illusion because of its lack of fundamental ideas" and felt that the magazine would rectify this situation. The magazine, which continued publication until 1912, also allowed Bax to indulge his interest in translated versions of Chinese and Japanese poems.

In 1910 Bax married Gwendolen Daphne Bishop. In the summer of the following year he took possession of an old manor house in the village of Broughton-Gifford in Wiltshire. His three years there were spent at cricket, chess, and exchanges of wit among his masculine friends, with deeper contemplative discussions consuming the summer nights. The poet Edward Thomas broke long journeys on foot by staying with Bax for intervals of a month or more.

In the spring of 1913 Bax set out with his brother Arnold, the musician Gustav Holst, and Balfour Gardiner on a trip to Spain. Their itinerary included Gerona, Barcelona, a Benedictine monastery in Monistrol, and Majorca. Erudite conversationalists all, the four flew many a "speculative kite" on topics ranging from music and art to immortality.

In April 1916 Bax rented a studio in Edwardes Square, London, where he and his wife lived for the next eight years. By day he cultivated his writing–mostly plays–and his friendships; by night he worked at Whitehall as a news censor in the Press Bureau. During this time his life and philosophy were deeply affected by a Buddhist monk named Allan Bennett, whom he had first met in 1908 when Bennett had begun a self-declared mission to save the world from suffering. In the winter of 1919 Bennett read a series of papers on Buddhism to a group of friends at Bax's studio. The papers were published, a month before Bennett died in March 1923, under the title *The Wisdom of the Aryas*. In place of the doctrine of the Atman, or world soul, Bennett argued in favor of the anatta, or no-Atman doctrine, according to which the universe is impermanent and ever-changing, with no center, no eternal principle, and no immortal essence. For the Buddhist, suffering is unavoidable, and egoism is the first of all evils. If Buddhism were the tempting next step for the theosophist Bax, he seems not to have taken it; although he used it to buttress his arguments against egoism and separation. To Bax, constant change is itself "a form of immortality."

At Bennett's passing, Bax was struck by the insignificance of death. As he gazed at Bennett's spirit-departed body, he felt "the overwhelming sense that there was no connection between the extinct form at which I was gazing and the mind that had so often signalled to me through the brown eyes that were now closed. I had looked upon death, and after all I had seen nothing of any importance. . . . I had exposed the insignificance of an event that has overshadowed the minds of man from the dawn of the world."

Another periodical edited by Bax, *The Golden Hind*, appeared quarterly from 1922 to 1924; it was dedicated to presenting the work of new and established contributors in the fields of graphic and literary art. Bax contributed poetry and reviews; most of the latter dealt with translated works of poetry and drama.

In many ways his most attractive and important book, Bax's autobiographical *Inland Far* was published in 1925. In it Bax wished to convey "a sense that life is a romance, not bounded by birth and death." The "best chart of the universe," as Bax calls it, comprises the three main doctrines of theosophy: that there is "one spirit within all things," that this spirit is "for ever seeking to disengage itself from matter," and that through love the spirit "recovers its lost empire." Events in this life bear a karmic relation to those in the next. The most pressing and immediate task of modern man is to stem the rationalistic tide and recover the sense of ourselves as being "primarily spiritual and secondarily physical." Rather than a chronology, the book attempts to be "more like a volume of poems or an exhibition of pictures": "I look inward upon the flowing, the perturbed, the intricate pattern of thoughts and feelings and memories that I recognize as myself." Bax recounts carefully and exten-

CLIFFORD BAX

FAREWELL
MY MUSE

19 LD 32

LOVAT DICKSON LIMITED
38 BEDFORD STREET LONDON

Frontispiece and title page for the book in which Bax announced that he would write no more poetry

sively the "thoughts and impressions" of his developmental years, 1904 to 1914. *Inland Far* provides as clear and succinct a statement as can be found in Bax's work of the credo that infuses most of what he wrote: "Still believing in Absolute Truth, like an early Greek, and not supposing that a little physical science had devalued the metaphysics of the past, I conceived that a man might apprehend all truth if, continually aspiring to be more than himself, he should one day force a breach in the tough walls of his egoism . . . and, with the divine faculty of imagination, unite the impersonal essence of his being with the essence of all that, hitherto, had seemed outside him." Bax recounts conversations on ideas that preoccupy him, then elaborates on the matter from his own perspective. After relating the death of Bennett, the book closes with a statement of Bax's philosophical outlook and a plea for the importance of culture. Reviewing *Inland Far* in *Canadian Forum* when the book was republished in 1933, G. M. A. Grube found its "personal-

ities . . . full of life and significance"; he also remarked that "its gently flowing style carries us along many unexpectedly agreeable by-lanes of thought where we are glad to dally with the author, and here and there we cross a main road at a refreshingly unusual angle."

Bax's wife died in 1926; the following year he married Vera May Young. Also in 1927 he published *Many a Green Isle*, an account of a holiday at Cap d'Antibes. The book, Bax says on the first page, is not so much a collection of stories as an effort to "convey certain moods," impressions, or imaginative visions, rather like "verbal transcriptions of music." Disclaiming his own powers of invention, the author recounts, at a distance of more than five years, an all-night party in the garden of a chateau at which each guest told of "the happiest incident in his life." Various tales of love and adventure are recalled. Bax's own tale is a dream vision concerning a mythical meeting of Odysseus and the gods. The last guest to speak delivers an oraclelike discourse on the nature of happiness, which, she says, appears in life like a periodic oasis in a journey across a desert, a moment of contentment in a pilgrimage of pain and suffering. We should grow in understanding and sympathy, she argues, and outgrow egoism in order to become cognizant of our insignificance. The root of our contemporary restlessness, she says further, is our assumption that life is ephemeral and that death is extinction. In the end the book appears to be a dilatory work of picaresque fiction behind which the sometimes not so subtle guidance of the author's philosophical hand can be perceived. It closes with a restatement of the immortalist's creed and the author asking whether past, present, and future are not really simultaneous, whether "there is no straight line of history, so that bits of the 'future' may have appeared to us already as bits of the 'past'." A reviewer writing in *Punch* thought the book incorporated the weaknesses inherent in the borrowed form of the Italian *novellieri*, but said about the tales themselves that "for genial variety and fanciful grace the best are hard to beat." In 1929 Bax was elected chairman of the Incorporated Stage Society.

In his biography of Leonardo da Vinci, published in 1932, Bax claims that Leonardo was "one of the few painters to bequeath to the world an ideal type." "His work," says Bax, "was an attempt to escape from the obvious and the actual, . . . an escape from a mode of existence which he despised and loathed." The *Mona Lisa* is "a clear example of the feminine principle with which he had always been at war." The painter's intellect, Bax alleges, "caused him to loathe the origins of life and, almost as a corollary, the experience of living." Bax acknowledges his debt to Rachel Taylor's *Leonardo the Florentine* (1928) and, in the end, adds only a few impressionistic heresies to the body of scholarship on Leonardo. Reviewers tended to look on the book unkindly. Although Albert Guerard, writing in *Books*, noted "the evident sincerity of his heresies," the *Bookman* noted that the biography suffered "from roundness and balance." The *New York Times* mentioned Bax's "cynical estimate of the significance of the famous [Mona Lisa] smile," while Philip Henderson in the *Times Literary Supplement* thought that Bax "availed himself to a disproportionate extent of the inebriating prose of Mrs. Taylor's Leonardo the Florentine, and a great part of what he has to tell us had already been better told" elsewhere.

Also published in 1932 was a collection of poems entitled *Farewell, My Muse*. Discouraged by reviews in which, he says, his poetry was either "ignored or fiercely assailed," Bax admits in a valedictory note that he has not written any verse for eight years. People used to suggest, he says, that he was "meant by Nature to be an essayist." Bax bids farewell not only "to the earlier self who wrote this book" but to poetic expression in general. He thinks people now lack "the simplicity of mind" required to appreciate poetry at an intuitive level. "The world does not want poetry," he writes; "the contemplative mood is almost extinct," and "the future of poetry seems to me dark." Indeed, "poetry represents a bygone phase in the history of the human mind." Austin Clarke in *Life and Letters* thought that the valedictory note was "gracefully" written but predicted an "ungrateful" reception for Bax's view that the level of consciousness required to appreciate poetry was fast disappearing.

In *That Immortal Sea*, published in 1933, Bax predicts the future acceptance of the idea of the soul's immortality: "The aim of this book is to suggest that . . . men and women of the near future are likely to recover, though not in the old form, a belief that there is a God in the universe and an immortal spirit in man." The view of the world as one "watched over and directed by a benevolent Deity" is long past, he admits, and takes it upon himself to write "for those who are in search of a few ideas to which they may hold fast in the intellectual and moral confusion of our time." Bax sees himself as writing neither to the rationalists nor to the "medieval-minded" whose intellect "does not demand to be satisfied before they can be emotionally comfortable." He writes, rather, to the skeptics who are suspicious of science. Bax counters materialism, the theory of evolution, behaviorism, relativity theory, and Freudianism: "If I were a materialist," he writes, "I should be perpetually bothered by the evidence of pattern in the universe, by the apparent purposefulness of the evolutionary process, and most of all, by the difficulty of accounting for the existence of anything whatsoever." He attempts to develop a philosophy with which "we may face the apparent extinction of death," one which will spare us the fate of being the "spiritless victims of an age." Amid the "distraction" of modern life and the "domination of the scientific spirit" Bax posits the "fundamental unity of all things." He suggests that the individual soul is connected with a collective, immortal, and universal soul through acts of sympathy and love. Morally, therefore, "actions which make for union and harmony are good, and those which make for separation and discord are bad." Man's greatest enemy is egoism. As a result of the ultimate spiritual unity of all things, one may from time to time perceive partially the interweaving of past, present, and future: remembrances of past lives may occur to one in this life, and suggestions of future events may be glimpsed in the present. In addition to making sensible observations on the conduct of the sexes, he forecasts accurately the cult of health and the morality of personal taste. But in the end Bax sees history as the "slow and painful emergence of love . . . the full revelation of the immortal self within this world of mortality . . . the climax to which humanity, and perhaps all sentient creatures, are imperceptibly progressing." C. D. Burns, writing in the *International Journal of Ethics*, thought that the attitude expressed was "generous and hopeful" but found "no clear statement of the evidence upon which the standards of the author are based." G. M. A. Grube in *Canadian Forum* thought that the author's "conceptions of God and the soul are far too vague and indefinite" and that "his view of the future is a little jaundiced."

In 1945, with the bulk of his theatrical work behind him, Bax cast an essay entitled *Whither the Theatre. . . ?* in the form of a letter to a young playwright. Here Bax the essayist sounds as if Bax the playwright has felt the unhappy results of commercial pressures, managerial rewrites, and insensitive or uncomprehending audiences. He has harsh words for theater managers whose eyes are eagerly focused on the box office, for comedians who are ever ready to embellish the text, and especially for critics, whom he calls "morbid parasites," "vampires," and "monsters." Critics are "pompous," "brainless," "pretentious," "incapable of distinguishing between a play (if it is new) and the playing or production of it." He refers to actors, however, as "a pleasant race," and acting as "the original and essential art, the prototype of all the other arts." Advice to the young playwright includes a caution against directionless dialogue: "A play must be a growing organism" and "must progress" from one consciously designed point to another, as does a route on a road map. He calls Noël Coward's dialogue "glib" and George Bernard Shaw's drama "soulless." He argues for the liberties inherent in historical drama in which audiences will forgive a "modicum of eloquence," even poetry, in the dialogue; for the im-

portance of surprise; for the dignity and beauty of tragedy (theatrical tragedies, he says, are rehearsals for the tragedies of real life); and for the recovery of the religious play. E. O. D. Keown in *Punch* thought "much of what Bax says is sound sense and needs saying, though not enough people are likely to listen." He also felt the playwright's advice was "admirably free of the common fogs of art" but wondered, in the face of Bax's "baldheaded attack" on critics, where Bax himself would be without the critic James Agate's approval, and whether he would really prefer that "the Press ignore his work" altogether.

The Beauty of Women (1946) is an extended essay on archetypical female beauty through a brief consideration of historical types. Among the earthly exemplars of the ideal type are Nefertiti (Egypt), Phryne (Greece), Isabella d'Este (Renaissance), Frances Stewart (Stuart period), Emma Hamilton (eighteenth century), and Jane Burden (Victorian). Bax calls Burden a "Rossetti type" and suggests that the painter Dante Gabriel Rossetti "probably came into the world with his ideal woman already latent in his imagination; and, for all that we know about ourselves, that ideal may have been remembered from an earlier life." Bax mentions three "primordial images" of woman: "the serene, wide-bosomed Mother" (Demeter); "the tall, slender, exotic Paramour" (Calypso); and "the small, dainty, elfin King's-Daughter, the princess of the fairy tales" (Nell Gwyn). Noting that beauty is something far more subtle and mysterious than sex appeal, Bax concludes that "a true sense of beauty may, in fact, proclaim the immortality of the almost-forgotten soul." Reviewing the book for *Punch*, B. E. Bower found it "packed with pleasantries, lore, anecdote, quotation and infinite variety."

Rosemary for Remembrance (1948) is a collection of essays. The theme of "Design for Dying" is the interrelation of past and present through that bundle of mental images called the memory. In the narrative "M-Day" a group of friends reunite at Meum Stewart's home in the Hertfordshire fringe of Essex on Midsummer Day 1944. Though the war rumbles on in the background–the bombers hum overhead, the guns blaze forth in Hyde Park, the siren wails in Savile Row–the story fills with the "tender but melancholy perfume" of remembrance. In "Art and Aristocracy" Bax reveals his bias toward what he feels is an underlying strain of elitism in art. He laments "the flattening of society in the last forty years," "the triumph of Socialism," and the "decline in craftsmanship and taste." "Art is essentially aristocratic," he declares in his April 1943 lecture for the Royal Society of Literature, reprinted here. "It can never appeal to the majority because it requires a faculty of discrimination which most men never achieve." Bax bewails the "apotheosis" of "the Common Man" and the "seemingly interminable cult" of H. G. Wells and Shaw. Of his seven "principal ingredients" of prose style, Bax suggests that "Clarity," "Music," "Shapeliness," "Continuity," and "Variety" are learnable, while "Personality" and "Range" are gifts of the gods.

Some I Knew Well brings together brief biographical sketches and impressions of contemporary literateurs with Bax's own critical opinions of their work. Bax has his eye on the timeless, the durable, the work of interest to generations to come. Included are James Agate, Havelock Ellis, Allan Bennett, Gordon Bottomley, Stephen Phillips, Russell, Yeats, Aleister Crowley, Rhys, Gustav Holst, and Edward Thomas. The essay on Yeats, the "Chameleon Genius," is perhaps the most interesting. As a person, Yeats was "difficult (perhaps impossible) to know well," but "posterity will find that he is the bygone poet that they can know most intimately." Bax sensed at least six different personalities in the man: "poet," "storyteller," "public man," "uneager politician," "courteous gentleman," and "occultist." Though Bax thought Yeats a "negligible" playwright–Yeats, "like Bernard Shaw, does not give a different voice to each character"–he considered him "the poet-in-chief of those who used our language."

At its best, Bax's prose style reveals some of the marks of excellence he looked for in that of others and reflects the lifetime he spent trying to learn how to write "attractively and with distinction." The roundness of his periods together with the carefully crafted sound of his words give his voice dignity and beauty. Indeed, the prose of his essays has much the same "fastidiousness" and "gracefulness" that Allardyce Nicoll admired in Bax's drama–Nicoll calls Bax a "miniaturist," the theatrical equivalent of the painter Nicholas Hilliard–although the essays have more candor and directness than the plays. Bax's versatility and industry as a playwright, poet, and critic are inarguable, but it is only in the essays that one really meets the man and his unique philosophical outlook. The essay form seems the perfect vehicle for Bax's interweaving of impressionistic reminiscence and metaphysical musing.

Reference:

Allardyce Nicoll, *British Drama*, sixth edition, revised by J. C. Trewin (London: Harrap, 1978), p. 243.

Max Beerbohm
(24 August 1872 - 20 May 1956)

William Blissett
University of Toronto

See also the Beerbohm entry in *DLB 34: British Novelists, 1890-1929: Traditionalists.*

BOOKS: *Carmen Becceriense: Cum prolegomenis et commentario critico, edidit H.M.B* (Godalming, U.K., 1890);

The Works of Max Beerbohm, with a Bibliography by John Lane (London: Lane, 1896; New York: Scribners, 1896);

Caricatures of Twenty-five Gentlemen (London: Smithers, 1896);

The Happy Hypocrite: A Fairy Tale for Tired Men (New York & London: Lane, 1897);

More (London & New York: Lane, 1899);

Cartoons: "The Second Childhood of John Bull" (London: Swift, 1901);

The Poets' Corner (London: Heinemann, 1904; New York: Dodd, Mead, 1904);

A Book of Caricatures (London: Methuen, 1907);

Yet Again (London: Chapman & Hall, 1909; New York: Lane, 1910);

Zuleika Dobson; or, An Oxford Love Story (London: Heinemann, 1911; New York: Boni & Liveright, 1911);

Ballade tragique à double refrain (N.p., 1912);

A Christmas Garland, Woven by Max Beerbohm (London: Heinemann, 1912; New York: Dutton, 1912; enlarged, London: Heinemann, 1950);

Fifty Caricatures (London: Heinemann, 1913; New York: Dutton, 1913);

A Note on "Patience" (London: Miles, 1918);

Seven Men (London: Heinemann, 1919; New York: Knopf, 1920); enlarged as *Seven Men and Two Others* (London: Heinemann, 1950);

And Even Now (London: Heinemann, 1920; New York: Dutton, 1921);

A Survey (London: Heinemann, 1921; New York: Doubleday, Page, 1921);

Rossetti and His Circle (London: Heinemann, 1922);

The Works of Max Beerbohm, 10 volumes (London: Heinemann, 1922-1928);

A Peep into the Past (London: Privately printed, 1923; New York: Privately printed, 1923);

Douglas Glass

Things New and Old (London: Heinemann, 1923);

Around Theatres, 2 volumes (London: Heinemann, 1924; New York: Knopf, 1930);

The Guerdon (New York: Privately printed, 1925);

Observations (London: Heinemann, 1925);

Leaves from the Garland (New York: Privately printed, 1926);

The Dreadful Dragon of Hay Hill (London: Heinemann, 1928);

A Variety of Things (London: Heinemann, 1928; New York: Knopf, 1928);

Lytton Strachey (Cambridge: Cambridge University Press, 1943; New York: Knopf, 1943);

William Rothenstein: An Address Delivered by Max Beerbohm at the Memorial Service Held at Saint Martin-in-the-Fields Tuesday, March 6th 1945 (London: Privately printed, 1945);

The Mote in the Middle Distance: A Parody of Henry James (Berkeley, Cal.: Hart Press, 1946);

A Luncheon (Oxford, 1946);

Mainly on the Air (London: Heinemann, 1946; New York: Knopf, 1947; enlarged, 1957);

Sherlockiana: A Reminiscence of Sherlock Holmes (Tempe, Ariz.: Hill, 1948);

Dickens and Christmas, as George Moore Might Well Have Described Them (Berkeley, Cal.: Hart Press, 1955);

Caricatures by Max, from the Collection of the Ashmolean Museum (Oxford: Oxford University Press, 1958);

Max's Nineties: Drawings 1892-1899 (London: Hart-Davis, 1958; Philadelphia: Lippincott, 1958);

Selected Essays, edited by N. L. Clay (London: Heinemann, 1958);

The Incomparable Max (London: Heinemann, 1962; New York: Dodd, Mead, 1962);

Max in Verse: Rhymes and Parodies, edited by J. G. Riewald (Brattleboro, Vt.: Stephen Greene Press, 1963; London: Heinemann, 1964);

More Theatres 1898-1903 (London: Hart-Davis, 1969; New York: Taplinger, 1969);

The Bodley Head Max Beerbohm, edited by David Cecil (London: Bodley Head, 1970);

Last Theatres 1904-1910 (London: Hart-Davis, 1970; New York: Taplinger, 1970);

Selected Prose, edited by Cecil (Boston: Little, Brown, 1971);

A Peep into the Past, and Other Prose Pieces, edited by Rupert Hart-Davis (London: Heinemann, 1972; Brattleboro, Vt.: Stephen Greene Press, 1972);

Beerbohm's Literary Caricatures: From Homer to Huxley, edited by Riewald (Hamden, Conn.: Archon, 1977; London: Lane, 1977).

OTHER: *Herbert Beerbohm Tree: Some Memories of Him and of His Art*, edited by Beerbohm (New York: Dutton, 1917; London: Hutchinson, 1920);

Dixon Scott, *Men of Letters*, introduction by Beerbohm (London: Hodder & Stoughton, 1923).

Henry Maximilian Beerbohm, always known as Max, is a classic instance of the artist-writer with notable achievements in both fields—a spe-

Beerbohm in 1886

cialty, almost a monopoly, of English cultural history: other examples include William Blake, William Morris, Dante Gabriel Rossetti, James McNeill Whistler, Aubrey Beardsley, Wyndham Lewis, and David Jones. Some of Beerbohm's best literary criticism, expressed in the drawings of *The Poets' Corner* (1904) and *Rossetti and His Circle* (1922), is collected in *Beerbohm's Literary Caricatures* (1977), the captions often being as pointed and witty as the drawings.

In a radio talk ("London Revisited," in *Mainly on the Air*, 1946) he said with light irony, "I was born within sound of Bow Bells. I am in fact a genuine Cockney (as you will already have guessed by my accent)." His father, Julius Ewald Beerbohm, a prosperous grain merchant in the City of London, was a native of Memel on the Baltic and was of mixed Dutch, German, and Lithuanian stock. After the death of his first wife he had married her sister, Elizabeth Draper. Max Beerbohm, born on 24 August 1872, was the youngest of the second family–nineteen years younger than his half-brother, Herbert Beerbohm Tree (later Sir Herbert), who was already a famous actor-manager on the London stage when Beerbohm was in school. The two were always on good terms, although they were more like uncle and nephew than like brothers. Young Max once jokingly proposed a series of books titled "Brothers of Great Men," to begin with Herbert. Beerbohm enjoyed good health throughout his long life but could never proclaim, as his brother did, "I'm radiant."

"Even when I toddled prattling by my nurse's side I regretted the good old days when I had, and wasn't, a perambulator," Beerbohm wrote in "Going Out for a Walk" (*And Even Now*, 1920). In this artfully constructed sentence one observes the watchful and loving female presence and the tone of mild, consolable regret at the passage of time that were to continue all his life: it was his nature to be playful, articulate, composed, and protected. After leaving Oxford University Beerbohm lived mainly at home with his mother and sisters, of whom the one nearest in age and temperament to him, Dora, became an Anglican nun. At the age of thirty-eight he married the American actress Florence Kahn and went to live in Rapallo; after her death in 1951, and by her thoughtful provision, Elisabeth Jungmann, the devoted companion of Gerhart Hauptmann in his later years, became Beerbohm's devoted companion. They were married some weeks before he died on 20 May 1956.

One would suppose the school years of this small, unathletic, protected boy, in obedience to one of the deepest stereotypes of modern literature, to have been miserable; one would be mistaken. At Charterhouse (William Makepeace Thackeray's old school, described in *The Newcomes* [1855]) between 1885 and 1890 he achieved some proficiency in classical studies and mild fame and acceptance among the masters and the boys for the wit and bite of his earliest caricatures. He later recognized his "aptitude for Latin prose and Latin verse" as "essential to the making of a decent style," for "English is an immensely odd and irregular language" and "there are few who can so wield it as to make their meaning clear without prolixity–and among those few none who has not been well-grounded in Latin" ("Lytton Strachey," in *Mainly on the Air*). In *A Christmas Garland* (1912) he distinguishes himself from the schoolboy Robert Louis Stevenson, who "played the sedulous ape" to stylists like Mon-

taigne, Sir Thomas Browne, and William Hazlitt: "I, in my own very inferior boyhood, found it hard to revel in so much as a single page of any writer earlier than Thackeray"–a propensity that remained with him except for one great surge of expansion back to the Regency period, and a few other sorties, as in "A Clergyman" (*And Even Now*), back to the time of Samuel Johnson.

Beerbohm observes in the essay "Going Back to School" (published in *More* [1899]): "I was a modest, good-humoured boy. It was Oxford that has made me insufferable." True, he had gone up to Oxford already steeped in the works of the high priest of the aesthetic movement, Walter Pater, or so he would have the reader believe. "At school I had read *Marius the Epicurean* in bed and with a dark lantern. Indeed, I regarded it mainly as a tale of adventure, quite as fascinating as *Midshipman Easy*, and far less hard to understand, because there were no nautical terms in it." His disillusionment with Pater and with the distilled "insufferability" of his own early prose, carefully modeled on Pater, may be illustrated in the opening paragraphs of the mock-Paterian essay "Diminuendo" (published in *The Works of Max Beerbohm* [1896]):

> In the year of grace 1890, and in the beautiful autumn of that year, I was a freshman at Oxford. I remember how my tutor asked me what lectures I wished to attend, and how he laughed when I said that I wished to attend the lectures of Mr. Walter Pater. Also I remember how, one morning soon after, I went into Ryman's to order some foolish engraving for my room, and there saw, peering into a portfolio, a small, thick, rock-faced man, whose top-hat and gloves of *bright* dog-skin struck one of the many discords in that little city of learning or laughter. The serried bristles of his mustachio made for him a false-military air. I think I nearly went down when they told me that this was Pater.
>
> Not that even in those more decadent days of my childhood did I admire the man as a stylist. Even then I was angry that he should treat English as a dead language, bored by that sedulous ritual wherewith he laid out every sentence as in a shroud–hanging, like a widower, long over its marmoreal beauty or ever he could lay it at length in his book, its sepulchre. From that laden air, the so cadaverous murmur of that sanctuary, I would hook it at the beck of any jade.

Already in his Oxford years, 1890 to 1894, he began to attract notice by the exhibition and publication of caricatures and the appearance of

The Myrmidon Club, Merton College, Oxford, 1892; Beerbohm is seated on the ground at left (photograph courtesy of the Warden and Fellows of Merton College).

his first essays in the *Strand* magazine. It was then that he met his lifelong friends, the painter Will Rothenstein and the minor novelist and wit Reggie Turner. The prodigiously energetic young Rothenstein came to Oxford to draw the celebrities, among them Beerbohm, the only undergraduate; Turner became a faithful friend of Oscar Wilde in prosperity and in misery and attended him at his death. Vivid as was the impression Beerbohm made, his career as a scholar was unremarkable, and he left the university under no cloud but without a degree. He had been an active member of the Essay Society, and his first book of essays, titled with impudent finality *The Works of Max Beerbohm, with a Bibliography by John Lane* and largely written as an undergraduate, reveals both in content and style considerable reading about the Regency period, the lore of cosmetics, and the life and culture of the 1880s (about the latter he says, "to give an accurate and exhaustive account of that period would need a far less brilliant pen than mine").

With fellow undergraduates he attended the Tivoli and other London music halls, anticipat-

ing the vogue in intellectual circles of these hearty, rowdy, patriotic, and sentimental variety shows. This cult was shared by the painters Walter Sickert and Frederic Wedmore, the decadent writer Arthur Symons, and the popular humorist F. Anstey; its valediction was delivered in sepulchral tones by T. S. Eliot in his essay on Marie Lloyd (1923). Beerbohm recalls pursuing, amid the jolly din, conversations on Hesiod or Fra Angelico or John Henry Newman's conversion. "Were we after all, so very absurd?" he asks in "The Blight on the Music Halls" (published in *More*); "It was one of our aims to be absurd." He continues, "I shall be blushing, five years hence, at my present personality, in which I cannot now detect any flaw." It was part of the fun to think of these robust entertainments as already fading and blighted and to write elegiac spoof tributes to their memory: "I am glad to resuscitate their rhythm: bugle-notes to awake sleeping memories in some breasts; more melancholy for me, fainter, than scent of soever long-kept lavender." In 1942, in the depths of World War II, Beerbohm won the hearts of a vast radio audience by recalling the scene for the old and evoking it for the young in the talk "Music Halls of my Youth" (*Mainly on the Air*). He remembered seeing the Great MacDermott himself, whom he had heard in his childhood singing the Crimean War song, "We Don't Want to Fight, But, By Jingo, If We Do": "And here he was, in the flesh, in the grease-paint, surviving and thriving, to my delight; a huge old burly fellow, with a yellow wig and a vast expanse of crumpled shirt-front that had in the middle of it a very large, not *very* real diamond stud." Beerbohm remembered the words and music of another song, and gave over the air what he called "a croaking suggestion of it" in a clear, seventy-year-old voice.

"The gods have bestowed on Max the gift of perpetual old age," said Oscar Wilde of the young dandy fresh from Oxford, exercising his talents as caricaturist and essayist and establishing in countless social scenes his cameo role as wit and "mulierast." *Mulierast*, lover of women, a coinage of Beerbohm's or Robert Ross's on the model of *pederast*, distances him from Wilde and his circle, to which his own Oxford set and his brother's life in the theater had introduced him. Beerbohm's caricatures catch Wilde's vanity and grossness, and his sketch *A Peep into the Past*, written in the 1890s before Wilde's fall, privately printed in 1923, and generally inaccessible until 1972, imagines the affectionate but candid recollections of a young man in the far future who visits the aged Oscar. Wilde was a wit: he put his talent into his art, his genius into his life and speech. Beerbohm, though an amusing conversationalist, was most a wit with pen or pencil in hand. At its most brilliant, his writing achieves Wildean surprise without Wildean paradox: he is the master of the turn of phrase, not the inverted truism. He is closest to Wilde in his first collection (*The Works of Max Beerbohm*), when, in comparing the late Victorian age to the Regency, he remarks, "We are not strong enough to be wicked, and the Nonconformist Conscience makes cowards of us all" (in "King George the Fourth"); or when, in the essay on cosmetics that shocked some reviewers of the *Yellow Book*, in which it first appeared ("The Pervasion of Rouge," republished in *The Works of Max Beerbohm*), he hails the end of "the reign of terror of nature" and rejoices that "Artifice, that fair exile, has returned." A vigorous letter in his own defense (*Yellow Book*, July 1894) proclaims his satiric intent: "The qualities that I tried in my essay to travesty [were] paradox and mari-

vaudage, lassitude, a love of horror and all unusual things, a love of argot and archaism and the mysteries of style." The best thing in the letter, however, is a sentence containing surely the most sarcastic comma ever penned: "It is a pity that critics should show so little sympathy with writers, and curious when we consider that most of them tried to be writers themselves, once."

The familiar essayist has always been known for what Beerbohm calls "the obtrusion of his personality upon the reader" through tone of authorial voice, style of writing, even personal appearance and style of dress, whether slipshod and unbuttoned or neat and dandiacal. Beerbohm's appearance is well known to most of his readers, mainly through his own self-caricatures. The dandy is to the well-dressed man what the ballet dancer is to the man who dances well. If Beerbohm never achieved the total dedication, the labor-intensive fixation of the higher dandyism, he could understand and communicate its mystique, which is intensely self-regarding and yet, to be fully enjoyed, requires discerning spectators for its intricacies and studied simplicities. Beerbohm's style, whether he mentions clothes or not, is itself a costume consciously chosen for an occasion and never more deliberate than when he chooses to seem a little negligent, as in "Ouida" (in *More*): "For my own part, I am a dilettante, a *petit maître*. I love best in literature delicate and elaborate ingenuities of form and line." "[I am] a fidgety and uninspired person, unable to begin a piece of writing before I know just how it will end," he says in *Seven Men* (1919). Like Beau Brummell flicking a beautifully fitting sleeve, Beerbohm comments on a previous paragraph of his in "Royalty" (in *More*): "That, despite certain faults of exaggeration, is a piece of quite admirable prose." This sentence occurs appropriately in the essay on royalty, because it was a walk of life that never ceased to fascinate him as artist and writer, and in which appearance is, if not everything, very much indeed.

Beerbohm writes in a buttoned, not an unbuttoned style. His are familiar essays, but he does not make "the essayists' blatant bid for your love," as he calls it in "Dulcendo Judiciorum" (in *Yet Again*, 1909). He is not a cold writer, just a careful one: "Do not, reader, suspect that because I am choosing my words nicely, and playing with metaphor, and putting my commas in their proper places, my sorrow is not really and truly poignant. I write elaborately, for that is my habit, and habits are less easily broken than hearts"

Drawing of Beerbohm by his friend William Rothenstein, 1915 (Manchester City Art Galleries)

("Ichabod," in *Yet Again*). In "Diminuendo," the last of the essays in *The Works of Max Beerbohm* (he was then twenty-three; his friend Beardsley, an exact contemporary, had three years to live, Beerbohm sixty-one), he writes: "And I, who crave no knighthood, shall write no more. I shall write no more. Already I feel myself to be a trifle outmoded. I belong to the Beardsley period. Younger men, with months of activity before them, with fresher schemes and notions, with newer enthusiasm, have pressed forward since then. *Cedo junioribus*. Indeed, I stand aside with no regret. For to be outmoded is to be a classic, if one has written well. I have acceded to the hierarchy of good scribes and rather like my niche."

In spite of saying, twice, "I shall write no more," Beerbohm three years later brought out a new collection of twenty essays and called it, defiantly, *More*, to be followed by *Yet Again* with twenty-two essays and nine "Words for Pictures," and the last similarly titled collection, *And Even Now*, with twenty essays. Further essays are included in *A Variety of Things* (1928), *Mainly on the Air* (1946; enlarged, 1957), and the posthumous *A Peep into*

the *Past, and Other Prose Pieces* (1972). From 1898 to 1910 he wrote a weekly theatrical review; one hundred fifty-three of his articles were selected in 1924 as *Around Theatres*. Two posthumous collections of reviews complete the set–*More Theatres 1898-1903* (1969), with one hundred fifty-eight articles, and *Last Theatres 1904-1910* (1970), with one hundred fifty articles. Many of these theatrical reviews and comments can be considered essays, with all the marks of Beerbohm's style except the high polish that comes from long reworking.

The essays in *More*, if they make one think, make one think mainly about style. "An Infamous Brigade," if taken solemnly, might be mistaken for a panegyric of arson–and so some American journalists read, or pretended to read it–but its reason for existence is such a sentence as this: "Than the roaring of those great flames had I yet heard, than their red glory seen, nothing lovelier." Beerbohm is as playful and deft with syntax as E. E. Cummings with typography. The essay "Sign Boards" describes a jeweler's window with a marvelous metaphor, splendidly placed: "in the very middle of it, lay, like a bomb in a palace, one beautiful black pearl." If Beerbohm here plays with the language of the desperado and the arsonist, he can be trusted to play it safe. His writing is full of foregrounding, stylistic deviation, "baring the device," but these features do not contribute to any effect of "rough verbal surface"; rather, they are contained within a medium as smooth as Venetian glass. The full and methodical stylistic discussion by J. G. Riewald is essential for the serious student of these effects.

This smoothness, coolness, aloofness, and safety Beerbohm regards as "due mainly to a temperamental Toryism," and on another occasion he identifies himself as "a Tory anarchist." But he showed a cavalier indifference to political issues, with a few exceptions: he did write an article on Miss Christabel Pankhurst (1903; collected in *Last Theatres*) at the Bow Street police court as a courtroom drama which shows sympathy with the suffragettes, "excesses" and all; and, objecting to the distinction between "actor" and "actress," he consistently called them all "mimes." In "General Elections" (in *Yet Again*), however, he confesses a sporting interest in the personal contests; but "My mind is quite open on the subject of fiscal reform, and quite empty; and the void is not an aching one–I have no desire to fill it." He was also indifferent to intellectual issues; after a belated attempt to read the long-popular philosopher Henri Bergson on laughter, he wrote (in "Laughter," collected in *And Even Now*): "It distresses me, this failure to keep pace with the leaders of thought as they pass into oblivion." Beerbohm insists, however, that he is "not altogether fatuous": indeed, "I'll be hanged if I haven't a certain mellow wisdom." It would be difficult to find a writer with a less theoretical, less ideological mind.

For him, style is the clothing of thought; and he can convey firmly though lightheartedly what is wrong within by deft parody of the surface. In an early essay, "At Cowes" (1898; in *A Peep into the Past*), he shows what is amiss in the "fine writing" that commonly passes for style by almost falling into it: "I cannot imagine a place less provocative of sad or subtle thoughts. The smaller yachts, as they scud by, do not look at all like white butterflies, and the larger yachts, when their lamps are lighted at night and reflected on the dark waters, do not remind one in the least of jewelled arks upheld by slender, wavering columns of light." He can parody an old-fashioned editorial in "A Pathetic Imposture" (in *Yet Again*) or a fashionable playwright in "Mr. Pinero's Literary Style" (in *Around Theatres*), so that neither could be taken quite so seriously again. In "T. Fenning Dodworth" (*A Variety of Things*) and "Kolynatch" (*And Even Now*) he uses sharper two-edged instruments. The writer celebrating the career of Dodworth, like the many eminent men in politics, journalism, and the arts who have acclaimed Dodworth for his "pungency," cannot or will not admit that the plausible, articulate, right-thinking Dodworth is a nullity. In the second essay Beerbohm invents a foreign writer, Luntic Kolynatch (from Colney Hatch, an insane asylum), one of a "seemingly inexhaustible supply of anguished souls from the Continent–infantile wide-eyed Slavs, Titan Teutons, greatly blighted Scandinavians, all of them different, but all of them raving in a common darkness and with one common gesture plucking out their vitals for exportation." As the sketch proceeds, Beerbohm disappears and the writer of the essay emerges as a distinct personality with his way to make in literary journalism and Kolynatch as his chief investment. His subservient quotation of an established critic and his own assessment span the gamut of bad critical style: "As one of the critics avers, 'It is hardly too much to say that a time may or may not be not far distant, and may indeed be nearer than many of us suppose, when Luntic Kolynatch will, rightly or wrongly, be reckoned by some of

us as not the least of those writers who are especially symptomatic of the early twentieth century and are possibly "for all time" or for a more or less certainly not inconsiderable portion of time.' That is finely said. But I myself go somewhat farther. I say that Kolynatch's message has drowned out all previous messages and will drown any that may be uttered in the remotest future."

It may be said that Beerbohm's parodies have drowned out all previous parodies and will drown any that may be uttered in the remotest future. *A Christmas Garland, Woven by Max Beerbohm* consists of sixteen parodies of contemporary writers, all on Christmas themes, one of them ("A Sequelula to 'The Dynasts'" by "TH*M*SY H*RD") in verse, ten in the form of fiction, and five ("Some Damnable Errors about Christmas" by "G. K. CH*ST*RT*N," "Shakespeare and Christmas" by "FR*NK H*RR*S," "Christmas" by "G.S. STR**T," "A Straight Talk" by "G**RGE B*RN*RD SH*W," and "Dickens" by "G**RGE M**RE") in the form of essays. (An eleventh parody in fictional form, "All Roads" by "M**R*C* B*R*NG," was added to an enlarged edition of the book in 1950.) Beerbohm and G. K. Chesterton, who was two years younger than Beerbohm, found each other congenial opposites–slight and gigantic, slim and encompassing, reserved and exuberant, appraising and enthusiastic, tidy and untidy. "Max has every merit but democracy," Chesterton wrote in *All Things Considered* (1908), and crowned Beerbohm King Auberon in his fantastic novel *The Napoleon of Notting Hill* (1904)–the illustrations for which, by W. Graham Robertson, show the king with Beerbohm's features. Beerbohm, in the essay "A Morris for May Day" (*Yet Again*), refers to Chesterton's style as a "prance," as "dancing the Chesterton." The parody in *A Christmas Garland* catches this jolly girandole: "I look for the time when we shall wish one another a Merry Christmas every morning; when roast turkey and plum-pudding shall be the staple of our daily dinner, and the holly shall never be taken down from the walls, and every one will always be kissing every one else under the mistletoe." Nor does he hit only the brightly painted barn door of Chesterton's art and thought; he catches too Chesterton's sudden modulations to gravity: the thought of Christmas as merely a time of jubilation "never entered into the heads of the saints and scholars, the poets and painters, of the Middle Ages. Looking back across the years, they saw in that dark and ungarnished manger only a shrinking woman, a brooding man,

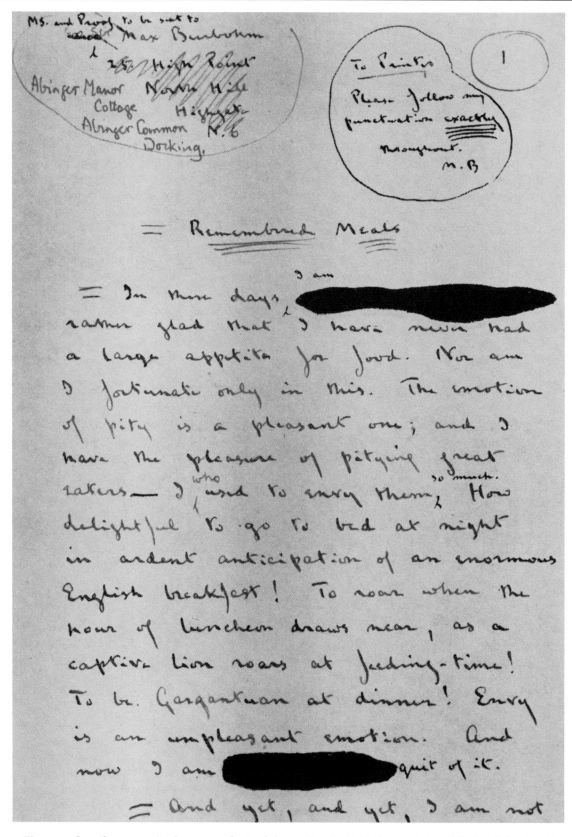

First page from the manuscript for an essay by Beerbohm, written in 1942 (by permission of the Beerbohm Estate)

and a child born to sorrow." It is Beerbohm's greatness as a parodist that he catches the inward elusive virtues of a writer as well as his foibles and tricks and vices of style.

Beerbohm's theatrical criticism is an important record of the London theater in the early twentieth century, a worthy successor to Bernard Shaw's *Our Theatres in the Nineties* (1931). In his last article for the *Saturday Review* (2 May 1898) Shaw recommended his successor with an echo, witty and incongruous, both of Beerbohm's "Diminuendo" and of Henrik Ibsen's *Master Builder* (1892), in a Beerbohm-like sentence ending in a carefully chosen—and as it proved, deathless—epithet: "The younger generation is knocking at the door, and as I open it there steps sprightly in the incomparable Max." Beerbohm's *Around Theatres* is more than a theatrical record: many of the articles could appear in a set of personal essays, the tone being set by the first, "Why I Ought Not to Have Become a Dramatic Critic." The article on a dramatization of Thomas Hardy's *Tess of the D'Urbervilles* (1891) is really an essay against the illustration of books. "Kipling's Entire" is part of Beerbohm's lifelong guerrilla tactics against the imperial hegemony of Rudyard Kipling; it argues, with outrageous aplomb, that Kipling, though "no lady," is "essentially feminine" in his glorification of toughness and violence: "For Mr. Kipling is nothing—never was anything—if not unsqueamish." Polemical articles include "The Invariable Badness of Amateur Acting" and "Agonising Samson." In "Soliloquies in Drama" he argues that it is easier "to accept soliloquy as a conventional substitute for silent thought than to accept confidence as an actual substitute." In "The Value of 'Sympathy' in Drama" (the quotation marks are a warning) he says: "If a man pursued by the Furies evoke from us nothing but a sporting interest as to which will win the race, Melpomene will disown him. Conversely, if he, sitting down on a basket of eggs or collapsing through a cucumber frame, wring from our hearts the tribute of pity and awe, the Muse of Farce—'Arriet,' or whatever her classic name may be—will none of him."

The end of Beerbohm's twelve years as a drama critic in 1910 was a turning point in his life. After a long engagement, he and Florence Kahn—whose acting as Rebecca in Ibsen's *Rosmersholm* (1866) he had reviewed in 1908, a review collected in *Around Theatres*—were married, left England, and settled in the Villino Chiaro in the north Italian coastal town of Rapallo. To his

friends in the world of art, literature, and the theater, it seemed a sad retirement into wedlock and expatriation. Beerbohm had for some time been aware of the waxing demands and waning pleasures of "social success," as is shown by his one-act play of that title (in *A Variety of Things*). His talent was a leisurely one, and he never got used to his weekly stint as a journalist. Rapallo was a pleasant place, and he could live there, well cared for by his wife, on little money. Certainly, there was no diminution of quality in his writing traceable to the move. His novel *Zuleika Dobson* (1911) could only be completed after his resignation as a reviewer; it contains embedded "essays" on Clio, on Oxford, and on death. The stories making up *Seven Men* (1919) were written in England when the Beerbohms retreated there during World War I; but perhaps the finest collection of essays, *And Even Now*, and certainly the finest collection of drawings, *Rossetti and His Circle*, belong to Rapallo.

The shock of World War I and the pace of change thereafter, coupled with contentment with a retired life and a sense that he had used the talents given him, combine to explain Beerbohm's inactivity in the last thirty years of his life. He was unable to complete the intricately conceived "Mirror of the Past" (the drafts and fragments were published by Lawrence Danson in *Max Beerbohm and the Act of Writing*, 1989). His later caricatures lack bite; not so the countless emendations, decorations, and desecrations that he laboriously inserted into his own books (often presentation copies), such as the appallingly vulgar "common reader" he drew as a frontispiece to his copy of Virginia Woolf's collection of essays— essays that he admired. His later writings are few and were mainly written for delivery on the radio. He was quite aware of the difference between addressing the eye and the ear, and a little of the syntactic intricacy and wit has been sacrificed; but the radio talks are a fine vintage from late-gathered grapes. If he had wished, he could have had a career in the broadcast media; but he was too leery of speed and modernity for that sort of employment. Asked if he was "traffic-conscious," he retorted (in "Speed," collected in *Mainly on the Air*), "How not be concussion-apprehensive, annihilation-evasive, and similar compound words?"

"I look forward to a crabbed and crusty old age. I mean to be a scourge of striplings," Beerbohm had written in 1903, at thirty-one, in a theater review titled "The Older and Better

Beerbohm and his wife, Florence Kahn Beerbohm, at their home in Abinger Common, England, in 1941
(photograph courtesy of Mrs. Noel Blakiston)

Music Hall" (*Around Theatres*); but the tone of the radio talk "Music Halls of My Youth" of 1942 is radiantly happy. In some of the other talks in *Mainly on the Air* a balance is struck: "London Revisited" (1935) celebrates the four or five districts he has always loved, but already in his boyhood "down by the docks, along the Mile End Road, throughout the arid reaches of South Kensington" London was "throwing out harsh hints of what the twentieth century had up its horrid sleeve." "From Bloomsbury to Bayswater" (1940) concedes that Bloomsbury may come to have a historic interest that it lacks for him—as the "focus of the intelligentsia . . . the mental underworld," a gloomy prophecy now fulfilled.

Max Beerbohm was never modern. One of his earliest essays, written in the mid 1890s, was a nostalgic evocation of the 1880s ("1880," in *The Works of Max Beerbohm*). He was at home in the Re-

gency period, the time of Rossetti and his circle, and his own earlier years. The very word *modern* he used in a sense hardly recognizable in the twentieth century: in his 1920 essay "Servants" (*And Even Now*) he writes: "To me F. M. Brown's 'Work' [a mid-Victorian picture that hangs in Manchester] is of all modern pictures the most delightful in composition and strongest in conception, the most alive and the most worthwhile." The sense of "modern art" as beginning with Paul Cézanne, who died in 1906, or with the Post-Impressionist exhibitions in London in 1910, 1911, and 1912, is quite absent here. (And yet, this same essay is startlingly modern in another respect: it would never have occurred to a Victorian to welcome, with humane, even almost democratic sentiments, the virtual disappearance of servants as a class.)

So too with modernity in literature. Lytton Strachey he recognized as a stylist in his own line and chose him as the subject of his Rede Lecture at Cambridge (1943), but he seems to have taken little interest in other writers of the high modern period: Beerbohm knew his Yeats, Hardy, Shaw, Wells, James, Conrad, and a host of smaller writers of the late-Victorian and Edwardian period, but his readers find it hard to realize that he outlived, and ignored, James Joyce and D. H. Lawrence. One maker of modern literature he knew as a neighbor in Rapallo, having probably first met him years before in London: Ezra Pound. (Shortly before World War II it was mooted that Pound should write the Life and Times of Max Beerbohm, but the book was never written.) Mauberley, Pound's persona in his poem "Hugh Selwyn Mauberley" (1920), recalls "Brennbaum, the Impeccable" and explains "The stiffness from spats to collar / Never relaxing into grace" (quite erroneously) by his being Jewish. Beerbohm had little to say about Pound except to observe that in referring to friends or acquaintances Pound became less and less appreciative and more sarcastic as he went on talking. Beerbohm never entered the Pound Era.

In England during the Italian-Abyssinian War in 1935-1936 and again from 1938 to 1947, Beerbohm received honorary doctorates from Edinburgh, Oxford, and Cambridge; an honorary fellowship in his old college, Merton; and a knighthood in 1939. The last honor had probably been delayed for many years not only by the ferocity of his caricatures of Edward VII but by his funny poem on King George V and Queen Mary (privately but widely circulated): its stanza endings alternate between "The King is duller than the Queen" and "The Queen is duller than the King." On his seventieth birthday, 24 August 1942, a Maximilian Society of seventy members was formed to honor him with a banquet and the gift of seventy bottles of wine. The BBC broadcasts of 1936 and especially of the darkest war years made him known to a far wider circle than ever before.

He returned to Rapallo in 1947 and remained there until his death in 1956. Friends old and new visited him at the Villino Chiaro; one of these, the American playwright S. N. Behrman, made notes of his conversations with Beerbohm and published them first in the *New Yorker* and then as a book (*Portrait of Max*, 1960). The *New Yorker* connection is altogether appropriate (in spite of Beerbohm's comical pretense of an aver-

sion to America), for the magazine annually has on its cover a dandy quizzing a butterfly, its cartoons and their captions are often Beerbohm-like, and "The Talk of the Town" column continues the stylish familiar essay in a manner that would be congenial to Beerbohm.

Few of his fervent modern admirers—Edmund Wilson, William Empson, Evelyn Waugh, Kingsley Amis, W. H. Auden—can be pictured as contentedly reading Charles Lamb or Thackeray or Stevenson, whose essays Beerbohm grew up on, or even (very much or very often) Pater or Wilde. It is as if Beerbohm had distilled the essences of those writers and relieved his readers of repeating the laborious process.

Writing the letter he allowed Bohun Lynch to use as the preface to *Max Beerbohm in Perspective* (1921), he said: "Years ago, G. B. S., in a light-hearted moment, called me 'the incomparable.' Note that I am *not* incomparable. Compare me. Compare me as essayist (for instance) with other essayists. Point out how much less human I am than Lamb, how much less intellectual than Hazlitt, and what an ignoramus beside Belloc; and how Chesterton's high spirits and abundance shame me; how unbalanced G. S. Street must think me, and how coarse too; and how much lighter E. V. Lucas's touch is than mine." To take up the challenge: in humanity and sentiment, his "William and Mary" (*And Even Now*) can rank with Lamb's nostalgic reveries; Hazlitt's account of coming to know the Romantic poets and Beerbohm's account of meeting Algernon Charles Swinburne in "No. 2, The Pines" (*And Even Now*) have nothing to fear from each other; Beerbohm is as playful as the Thackeray of the *Roundabout Papers* (1863) and much more exquisite; he is as exquisite as the Pater of *Appreciations* (1889) and much more playful. Hilaire Belloc had a various and capacious mind, but he wrote four hundred essays as a by-product of his more serious writing—sometimes as many as three a day—and so his standard is not up to Beerbohm's. Both Beerbohm and Chesterton are highly mannered and highly amusing writers; but beyond a point Chesterton can be almost a torment, whereas Beerbohm never approaches such a point. Street and Lucas, whom Beerbohm probably mentions for friendship's sake, have disappeared from view.

In the same letter to Lynch he begs, "Don't by dithyrambs hasten the reaction of critics against me."

Letters:

Max Beerbohm's Letters to Reggie Turner, edited by Rupert Hart-Davis (London: Hart-Davis, 1964; New York: Lippincott, 1965);

Max & Will: Max Beerbohm and William Rothenstein, Their Friendship and Letters, 1893-1945, edited by Mary M. Lago and Karl Beckson (London: Murray, 1975; Cambridge, Mass.: Harvard University Press, 1975);

Letters of Max Beerbohm 1892-1956, edited by Hart-Davis (London: Murray, 1988).

Bibliographies:

A. E. Gallatin, *Sir Max Beerbohm: Bibliographical Notes* (Cambridge, Mass.: Harvard University Press, 1944);

Gallatin and L. M. Oliver, *A Bibliography of the Works of Max Beerbohm* (Cambridge, Mass.: Harvard University Press, 1952);

Catalogue of the Library and Literary Manuscripts of the Late Sir Max Beerbohm (London: Sotheby, 1960).

Biographies:

S. N. Behrman, *Portrait of Max: An Intimate Memoir of Sir Max Beerbohm* (New York: Random House, 1960);

David Cecil, *Max: A Biography* (London: Constable, 1964).

References:

Lawrence Danson, *Max Beerbohm and the Act of Writing* (Oxford: Clarendon Press, 1989);

John Felstiner, *The Lies of Art: Max Beerbohm's Parody & Caricature* (London: Gollancz, 1973);

Bohun Lynch, *Max Beerbohm in Perspective* (London: Heinemann, 1921; New York: Knopf, 1922);

Bruce R. McElderry, *Max Beerbohm* (New York: Twayne, 1972);

Katherine Lyon Mix, *Max and the Americans* (Brattleboro, Vt.: Greene, 1974);

J. G. Riewald, *Sir Max Beerbohm, Man and Writer: A Critical Analysis with a Brief Life and a Bibliography* (The Hague: Nijhoff, 1953);

Riewald, ed., *The Surprise of Excellence: Modern Essays on Max Beerbohm* (Hamden, Conn.: Archon, 1974);

Robert Viscusi, *Max Beerbohm, or The Dandy Dante* (Baltimore: Johns Hopkins University Press, 1986);

A. C. Ward, *20th Century English Literature 1901-60* (London: Methuen, 1928), pp. 197-201.

Hilaire Belloc
(27 July 1870 - 16 July 1953)

Frank M. Tierney
University of Ottawa

See also the Belloc entry in *DLB 19: British Poets, 1880-1914.*

BOOKS: *Verses and Sonnets* (London: Ward & Downey, 1896);

The Bad Child's Book of Beasts (Oxford: Alden / London: Simpkin, Marshall, Hamilton, Kent, 1896; New York: Dutton, 1896);

Syllabus of a Course of Six Lectures on the French Revolution (Philadelphia: American Society for the Extension of University Teaching, 1896);

Syllabus of a Course of Six Lectures on the Crusades (Philadelphia: American Society for the Extension of University Teaching, 1896);

Syllabus of a Course of Six Lectures on Representative Frenchmen (Philadelphia: American Society for the Extension of University Teaching, 1896);

Syllabus of a Course of Six Lectures on Paris (Philadelphia: American Society for the Extension of University Teaching, 1897);

More Beasts (For Worse Children) (London & New York: Arnold, 1897; New York: Knopf, 1922);

The Modern Traveller (London: Arnold, 1898; New York: Knopf, 1923);

Danton: A Study (Oxford & London: Nisbet, 1899; New York: Scribners, 1899);

A Moral Alphabet (London: Arnold, 1899);

Lambkin's Remains, anonymous (Oxford: Proprietors of the J. R. C., 1900; New York: Mansfield, 1900);

Paris (London: Arnold, 1900; New York: Scribners, 1907);

Robespierre: A Study (London: Nisbet, 1901; New York: Scribners, 1901);

The Path to Rome (London: Allen, 1902; New York: Longmans, Green, 1902);

The Aftermath; or, Gleanings from a Busy Life . . . Caliban's Guide to Letters (London: Duckworth, 1903; New York: Dutton, 1903);

The Great Inquiry (Only Authorized Version) Faithfully Reported by H. B. . . . and Ornamented with

Hilaire Belloc in 1902

Sharp Cuts Drawn on the Spot by G. K. C., anonymous (London: Duckworth, 1903);

Avril: Being Essays on the Poetry of the French Renaissance (London: Duckworth, 1904; New York: Dutton, 1904);

Emmanuel Burden, Merchant, of Thames St., in the City of London: A Record of His Lineage, Speculations, Last Days and Death (London: Methuen, 1904; New York: Scribners, 1904);

The Old Road (London: Constable, 1904; Philadelphia: Lippincott, 1905);

Esto Perpetua: Algerian Studies and Impressions (London: Duckworth, 1906; New York: McBride, 1925);

47

Hills and the Sea (London: Methuen, 1906; New York: Scribners, 1906);

The Historic Thames (London: Dent / New York: Dutton, 1907);

Cautionary Tales for Children, Designed for the Admonition of Children between the Ages of Eight and Fourteen Years (London: Nash, 1908; New York: Knopf, 1922);

An Examination of Socialism (London: Catholic Truth Society, 1908);

On Nothing and Kindred Subjects (London: Methuen, 1908; New York: Dutton, 1909);

Mr. Clutterbuck's Election (London: Nash, 1908);

The Eye-Witness: Being a Series of Descriptions and Sketches in Which It Is Attempted to Reproduce Certain Incidents and Periods in History, as from the Testimony of a Person Present at Each (London: Nash, 1908; New York: Dutton, 1924);

The Pyrenees (London: Methuen, 1909; New York: Knopf, 1923);

A Change in the Cabinet (London: Methuen, 1909);

Marie Antoinette (London: Methuen, 1909; New York: Doubleday, Page, 1909);

On Everything (London: Methuen, 1909; New York: Dutton, 1910);

On Anything (London: Constable, 1910; New York: Dutton, 1910);

Pongo and the Bull (London: Constable, 1910);

On Something (London: Methuen, 1910; New York: Dutton, 1911);

Verses (London: Duckworth, 1910; New York: Gomme, 1916);

The Party System, by Belloc and Cecil Chesterton (London: Swift, 1911);

The French Revolution (London: Williams & Norgate, 1911; New York: Holt, 1911);

The Girondin (London & New York: Nelson, 1911; New York: Doubleday, Page, 1912);

More Peers: Verses (London: Swift, 1911; New York: Knopf, 1914);

First and Last (London: Methuen, 1911; New York: Dutton, 1912);

The Battle of Blenheim (London: Swift, 1911; Philadelphia & London: Lippincott, 1936);

Malplaquet (London: Swift, 1911);

Socialism and the Servile State: A Debate between Messrs. Hilaire Belloc and J. Ramsay MacDonald (London: South West London Federation of the Independent Labour Party, 1911);

Waterloo (London: Swift, 1912; revised edition, London: Rees, 1915);

The Four Men: A Farrago (London & New York: Nelson, 1912; Indianapolis: Bobbs-Merrill, 1912);

The Green Overcoat (Bristol: Arrowsmith, 1912; New York: McBride, Nast, 1912);

Tourcoing (London: Swift, 1912);

Warfare in England (London: Williams & Norgate, 1912);

This and That and the Other (London: Methuen, 1912; New York: Dodd, Mead, 1912);

The Servile State (London & Edinburgh: Foulis, 1912; Boston: Phillips, 1913);

The River of London (London & Edinburgh: Foulis, 1912);

Crécy (London: Swift, 1912);

The Stane Street: A Monograph (London: Constable, 1913; New York: Dutton, 1913);

The Book of the Bayeux Tapestry, Presenting the Complete Work in a Series of Colour Facsimiles: The Introduction and Narrative by Hilaire Belloc (London: Chatto & Windus, 1913; New York: Putnam's, 1914);

Poitiers (London: Rees, 1913);

The History of England from the First Invasion by the Romans to the Accession of King George the Fifth, volume 2 (London & Edinburgh: Sands / New York: Catholic Publication Society of America, 1915);

A General Sketch of the European War, 2 volumes (London, Edinburgh, Paris & New York: Nelson, 1915, 1916); republished as *The Elements of the Great War*, 2 volumes (New York: Hearst's International Library, 1915, 1916);

High Lights of the French Revolution (New York: Century, 1915);

Land and Water Map of the War and How to Use It: Drawn under the Direction of Hilaire Belloc (London: "Land & Water," 1915);

A Picked Company: Being a Selection from the Writings of H. Belloc (London: Methuen, 1915);

The Two Maps of Europe and Some Other Aspects of the Great War (London: Pearson, 1915);

At the Sign of the Lion, and Other Essays from the Books of Hilaire Belloc (Portland, Me.: Mosher, 1916);

The Second Year of the War (London: Burrup, Mathieson & Sprague, 1916);

The Last Days of the French Monarchy: With Many Illustrations from Paintings and Prints (London: Chapman & Hall, 1916);

Anti-Catholic History: How It Is Written (London: Catholic Truth Society, 1918);

The Free Press (London: Allen & Unwin, 1918);

Europe and the Faith (London: Constable, 1920; New York: Paulist Press, 1920);

The House of Commons and Monarchy (London: Allen & Unwin, 1920; New York: Harcourt, Brace, 1922);

Pascal's "Provincial Letters" (London: Catholic Truth Society, 1921);

The Jews (London, Bombay & Sydney: Constable, 1922; Boston: Houghton Mifflin, 1922; revised, 1937);

The Mercy of Allah (London: Chatto & Windus, 1922; New York: Appleton, 1922);

On (London: Methuen, 1923; New York: Doran, 1923);

Sonnets and Verse (London: Duckworth, 1923; New York: McBride, 1924; enlarged edition, London: Duckworth, 1938; New York: Sheed & Ward, 1939; enlarged again, London: Duckworth, 1954);

The Contrast (London: Arrowsmith, 1923; New York: McBride, 1924);

The Road (Manchester, U.K.: Printed & published for the British Reinforced Concrete Engineering Co. Ltd., by C. W. Hobson, 1923; New York: Harper, 1923);

The Campaign of 1812 and the Retreat from Moscow (London & New York: Nelson, 1924); republished as *Napoleon's Campaign of 1812 and the Retreat from Moscow* (New York & London: Harper, 1926);

Economics for Helen (London: Arrowsmith, 1924; New York & London: Putnam's, 1924); republished as *Economics for Young People: An Explanation of Capital, Labour, Wealth, Money, Production, Exchange, and Business, Domestic and International* (New York & London: Putnam's, 1925);

The Cruise of the "Nona" (London: Constable, 1925; Boston & New York: Houghton Mifflin, 1925);

A History of England, 4 volumes (London: Methuen, 1925-1931; New York & London: Putnam's, 1925-1931);

Mr. Petre: A Novel (London: Arrowsmith, 1925; New York: McBride, 1925);

Miniatures of French History (London, Edinburgh & New York: Nelson, 1925; New York & London: Harper, 1926);

Short Talks with the Dead and Others (Kensington: Cayme Press, 1926; New York: Harper, 1926);

The Emerald of Catherine the Great (London: Arrowsmith, 1926; New York & London: Harper, 1926);

A Companion to Mr. Wells's "Outline of History" (London: Sheed & Ward, 1926; San Francisco: Ecclesiastical Supply Association, 1927; revised edition, London: Sheed & Ward, 1929);

The Catholic Church and History (London: Burns, Oates & Washbourne, 1926; New York: Macmillan, 1926);

The Highway and Its Vehicles, edited by Geoffrey Holme (London: The Studio Limited, 1926);

Mr. Belloc Still Objects to Mr. Wells's "Outline of History" (London: Sheed & Ward, 1926; San Francisco: Ecclesiastical Supply Association, 1927);

Mrs. Markham's New History of England: Being an Introduction for Young People to the Current History and Institutions of Our Time (Kensington, U.K.: Cayme, 1926);

The Haunted House (London: Arrowsmith, 1927; New York & London: Harper, 1928);

Oliver Cromwell (London: Benn, 1927);

Towns of Destiny (New York: McBride, 1927); republished as *Many Cities* (London: Constable, 1928);

James the Second (London: Faber & Gwyer, 1928; Philadelphia: Lippincott, 1928);

How the Reformation Happened (London: Cape, 1928; New York: Dodd, Mead, 1928);

But Soft—We Are Observed! (London: Arrowsmith, 1928); republished as *Shadowed!* (New York & London: Harper, 1929);

A Conversation with an Angel and Other Essays (London: Cape, 1928; New York & London: Harper, 1929);

Belinda: A Tale of Affection in Youth and Age (London: Constable, 1928; New York & London: Harper, 1929);

The Chanty of the Nona (London: Faber & Gwyer, 1928);

Do We Agree? A Debate between G. K. Chesterton and Bernard Shaw, with Hilaire Belloc in the Chair (Hartford, Conn.: Mitchell, 1928);

Survivals and New Arrivals (London: Sheed & Ward, 1929; New York: Macmillan, 1929);

Joan of Arc (London, Toronto, Melbourne & Sydney: Cassell, 1929; Boston: Little, Brown, 1929);

The Missing Masterpiece: A Novel (London: Arrowsmith, 1929; New York & London: Harper, 1929);

Richelieu: A Study (Philadelphia & London: Lippincott, 1929; London: Benn, 1930);

Wolsey (London, Toronto, Melbourne & Sydney: Cassell, 1930; Philadelphia & London: Lippincott, 1930);

The Man Who Made Gold (London: Arrowsmith, 1930; New York & London: Harper, 1931);

New Cautionary Tales: Verses (London: Duckworth, 1930; New York: Harper, 1931);

Why I Am and Why I Am Not a Catholic, by Belloc and others (New York: Macmillan, 1930);

A Conversation with a Cat and Others (London, Toronto, Melbourne & Sydney: Cassell, 1931; New York & London: Harper, 1931);

Essays of a Catholic Layman in England (London: Sheed & Ward, 1931); republished as *Essays of a Catholic* (New York: Macmillan, 1931);

Cranmer (London, Toronto, Melbourne & Sydney: Cassell, 1931); republished as *Cranmer, Archbishop of Canterbury, 1533-1556* (Philadelphia & London: Lippincott, 1931);

Nine Nines; or, Novenas from a Chinese Litany of Odd Numbers (Oxford: Blackwell, 1931);

On Translation (Oxford: Clarendon Press, 1931);

Six British Battles (Bristol, U.K.: Arrowsmith, 1931);

Usury (London: Sheed & Ward, 1931);

An Heroic Poem in Praise of Wine (London: Davies, 1932);

Ladies and Gentlemen, for Adults Only and Mature at That (London: Duckworth, 1932);

The Question and the Answer (New York & Milwaukee: Bruce, 1932; London & New York: Longmans, Green, 1938);

Saulieu of the Morvan (New York: Ludowici-Celadon, 1932);

The Postmaster-General (London: Arrowsmith, 1932; Philadelphia: Lippincott, 1932);

Napoleon (London, Toronto, Melbourne & Sydney: Cassell, 1932; Philadelphia & London: Lippincott, 1932);

The Tactics and Strategy of the Great Duke of Marlborough (London: Arrowsmith, 1933);

Charles the First, King of England (London, Toronto, Melbourne & Sydney: Cassell, 1933; Philadelphia & London: Lippincott, 1933);

William the Conqueror (London: Davies, 1933; New York: Appleton-Century, 1934);

A Shorter History of England (London: Harrap, 1934; New York: Macmillan, 1934);

Cromwell (London, Toronto, Melbourne & Sydney: Cassell, 1934; Philadelphia & London: Lippincott, 1934);

Milton (London, Toronto, Melbourne & Sydney: Cassell, 1935; Philadelphia & London: Lippincott, 1935);

The Battle Ground (London, Toronto, Melbourne & Sydney: Cassell, 1936); republished as *The Battleground: Syria and Palestine, the*

Seedplot of Religion (Philadelphia & London: Lippincott, 1936);

Characters of the Reformation (London: Sheed & Ward, 1936; New York: Sheed & Ward, 1936);

The Hedge and the Horse (London, Toronto, Melbourne & Sydney: Cassell, 1936);

The County of Sussex: With Six Maps in the Text (London, Toronto, Melbourne & Sydney: Cassell, 1936);

An Essay on the Restoration of Property (London: Distributist League, 1936); republished as *The Restoration of Property* (New York: Sheed & Ward, 1936);

Selected Essays, compiled by John Edward Dineen (Philadelphia & London: Lippincott, 1936);

The Crusade: The World's Debate (London, Toronto, Melbourne & Sydney: Cassell, 1937); republished as *The Crusades: The World's Debate* (Milwaukee: Bruce, 1937);

The Crisis of Our Civilization (London, Toronto, Melbourne & Sydney: Cassell, 1937); republished as *The Crisis of Civilization* (New York: Fordham University Press, 1937);

An Essay on the Nature of Contemporary England (London: Constable, 1937; New York: Sheed & Ward, 1937);

The Issue (New York & London: Sheed & Ward, 1937);

The Case of Dr. Coulton (London: Sheed & Ward, 1938);

Stories, Essays, and Poems (London: Dent, 1938):

The Great Heresies (London: Sheed & Ward, 1938; New York: Sheed & Ward, 1938);

Return to the Baltic (London: Constable, 1938);

Monarchy: A Study of Louis XIV (London, Toronto, Melbourne & Sydney: Cassell, 1938; New York & London: Harper, 1938);

Cautionary Verses: The Collected Humorous Poems (London: Duckworth, 1939); republished as *Hilaire Belloc's Cautionary Verses: Illustrated Album Edition with the Original Pictures* (New York: Knopf, 1941);

On Sailing the Sea: A Collection of the Seagoing Writings of Hilaire Belloc, selected by W. N. Roughead (London: Methuen, 1939);

The Test Is Poland (London, 1939);

Charles II: The Last Rally (New York & London: Harper, 1939); republished as *The Last Rally: A Story of Charles II* (London, Toronto, Melbourne & Sydney: Cassell, 1940);

The Catholic and the War (London: Burns, Oates, 1940);

Belloc in Rome, 1901. The trip resulted in his spiritual autobiography in essay-travelogue form,
The Path to Rome *(1902).*

On the Place of Gilbert Chesterton in English Letters (London: Sheed & Ward, 1940; New York: Sheed & Ward, 1940);

The Silence of the Sea and Other Essays (New York: Sheed & Ward, 1940; London, Toronto, Melbourne & Sydney: Cassell, 1941);

Places (New York: Sheed & Ward, 1941; London, Toronto, Melbourne & Sydney: Cassell, 1942);

Elizabethan Commentary (London, Toronto, Melbourne & Sydney: Cassell, 1942); republished as *Elizabeth: Creature of Circumstance* (New York & London: Harper, 1942);

The Alternative: An Article Originally Written during Mr. Belloc's Parliamentary Days, for St. George's Review and Since Revised (London: Distributist Books, 1947);

Duncton Hill: Unaccompanied Part-song for S.A.T.B., music by David Moule-Evans (London:

Williams / Boston: B. F. Wood Music, 1947);

Selected Essays (London: Methuen, 1948);

Hilaire Belloc: An Anthology of His Prose and Verse, selected by Roughead (London: Hart-Davis, 1951; Philadelphia: Lippincott, 1951);

Songs of the South Country (London: Duckworth, 1951);

World Conflict (London: Catholic Truth Society, 1951);

The Verse of Hilaire Belloc, edited by Roughead (London: Nonesuch Press, 1954);

Essays, edited by Anthony Forster (London: Methuen, 1955);

One Thing and Another: A Miscellany from His Uncollected Essays, edited by Patrick Cahill (London: Hollis & Carter, 1955);

Collected Verses (Harmondsworth, U.K.: Penguin, 1958).

OTHER: Alvin Langdon Coburn, *London*, introduction by Belloc (London: Duckworth / New York: Brentano's, 1909);

"The Place of a Peasantry in Modern Civilisation," in *Co-operative Wholesale Societies Limited: Annual for 1910* (Manchester, 1910), pp. 279-298;

The Footpath Way: An Anthology for Walkers, introduction by Belloc (London: Sidgwick & Jackson, 1911);

Cecil Edward Chesterton, *The Perils of Peace*, introduction by Belloc (London: Laurie, 1916);

Ferdinand Foch, *The Principles of War*, translated by Belloc (New York: Holt, 1920);

Foch, *Precepts and Judgments: With a Sketch of the Military Career of Marshal Foch by Major A. Grasset*, translated by Belloc (New York: Holt, 1920);

"Mowing of a Field," in *Modern Essays*, edited by Christopher Morley (New York: Harcourt, Brace, 1921), pp. 113-127;

"On 'And,'" in *Essays by Present-day Writers*, edited by Raymond Woodbury Pence (New York: Macmillan, 1924);

"On an Unknown Country," in *A Book of Modern Essays*, edited by Bruce Walker McCullough and Edwin Berry Burgum (New York & Chicago: Scribners, 1926), pp. 163-168;

Clare Leighton, *Woodcuts*, introduction by Belloc (London & New York: Longmans, Green, 1930);

Joseph Bédier, *Tristan and Iseult*, translated by Belloc (New York: Boni, 1930).

In his time Hilaire Belloc enjoyed the same popularity with readers as George Bernard Shaw, H. G. Wells, and G. K. Chesterton. He wrote poetry, fiction, history, travel pieces, and works on topography, as well as articles and essays in a wide variety of modes including ridicule, parody, satire, and logical argumentation. Although his first love was poetry, the essay was his daily occupation. His themes are diverse: God, nature, society, culture, literature, politics, and history. His style is clear, concise, and profound whether he is being playful or charming, angry or bitter, humorous or funny.

Joseph Hilaire Pierre René Belloc was born in La Celle St. Cloud, near Paris, on 27 July 1870, a few days before the outbreak of the Franco-Prussian War. His grandfather Hilaire Belloc was a respected artist; his grandmother Louise Swanton Belloc was a writer of biographies and children's books. His father, Louis Swanton Belloc, was a lawyer; his mother, Elizabeth Parkes Belloc, an Englishwoman, was a prominent political activist and promoter of women's rights. Her father, Joseph Parkes, was a major figure in the passage of the Reform Bill of 1832, and her grandfather Joseph Priestley was one of the fathers of modern chemistry.

When Bismarck's forces conquered France on 4 September 1870, Belloc and his parents left for England. At the age of six, Belloc, already bilingual in French and English, was writing poetry and drawing excellent sketches and maps. At ten he was sent to the Oratory School at Birmingham, where he won many academic prizes. After leaving the Oratory he enrolled in the College Stanislas in Paris for one term, then lived for a short while on a farm in Sussex as a land agent before beginning work as a journalist. Drafted into the French army (he was still a French citizen), he served for a year in the Eighth Artillery Regiment as a driver. In 1893 he entered Balliol College, Oxford, graduating with first-class honors in history in 1895. He did not receive the fellowship that he had hoped for, nor was he able to live the life of an Oxford professor, which had been his goal. He did, however, receive exceptional distinctions in the university debating society. Upon graduation he began a career as a journalist and author. He married Elodie Agnes Hogan, of Napa, California, on 16 June 1896; they had three sons and two daughters.

Also in 1896 he published his first book, *Verses and Sonnets*. The revenue from the book was important, because Elodie and Belloc had their first child and his only other income was from university extension lectures, tutoring, and free-lance journalism. When *Verses and Sonnets* was scarcely noticed he turned to nonsense verse and prose, publishing *The Bad Child's Book of Beasts* (1896). In January 1897 the Bellocs toured America, where Belloc gave about a hundred lectures. By this time he had formed an adamant and aggressive position in favor of Roman Catholicism, and his relationships with those who held points of view different from his own tended to be hostile. His ungracious attitude, he admitted later in his life, was detrimental to his success. In 1899 he published his first work of history, *Danton*, which was enthusiastically received. That same year his militant Catholicism lost him a fellowship at Oxford and a professorship in history at Glasgow University. These losses were partly the motivation for his prose satire on a dull Oxford don, *Lambkin's Remains* (1900). It was at this time that Chesterton became his close friend and literary associate. In 1900, too, Belloc published *Paris*, which contains aspects of the personal essay and history; in 1901 his history *Robespierre* appeared; and in 1902 he published perhaps his greatest work, *The Path to Rome*, a spiritual autobiography in an essay-travelogue form based on a journey to Rome in 1901. By this time Belloc was well known as a journalist in the finest eighteenth-century tradition. He remained in great need of money, however, especially with the birth of a second child, a daughter; and so he published five books between June 1903 and November 1904, while still writing pamphlets for Catholic organizations and continuing his poetry, articles, and reviews. Still short of money, he studied briefly for the bar, withdrew, ran for election to Parliament as a Liberal, and won a seat on 13 January 1906. He soon became dissatisfied with the party system and disillusioned by the self-interest of those in power. He adopted a radical stance and finally resigned from Parliament in December 1909.

Belloc produced essays with ease, sometimes writing two or three in an afternoon to break the monotony of a more complex or difficult task—and because he needed the money. He produced more than four hundred essays: informal and almost casual, sometimes playful, more often serious, but always entertaining. His subjects are endless and his collections are seldom unified thematically. The essays evolved over the years from light enthusiasm to heavy seriousness, even to despondency in a few works. The essays in his first collection, *Hills and the Sea* (1906), had appeared in the *Speaker*, the *Pilot*, the *Morning Post*, the *Daily News*, the *Pall Mall Magazine*, the *Evening Standard*, the *Morning Leader*, and the *Westminster Gazette*. *Hills and the Sea* was published at a critical time in Belloc's life, coinciding with his decision to enter politics. The book, generally regarded as one of his best, places him in the company of the finest English essayists. Belloc's style is personal and open, quickly catching the reader's attention. The book is dedicated to himself and to Phil Kershaw, a friend and companion of Belloc's on his frequent trips to the Pyrenees. The opening essays describe two men traveling together at sea and in the mountains and experiencing joy and heroic action. These essays come close to the subject of metaphysics, a topic alien to Belloc's temperament: he deals with transcendental awareness, although he believed that the world could be experienced only through the senses. Such experiences as mountain climbing

and storms carry the two men closer to the mysterious and to "things not mortal."

From 1906 to 1910, including his turbulent years as a member of Parliament, Belloc published a biography of Marie Antoinette (1909), two books of travel and topography, two satirical novels, one volume of verse, four pamphlets, and five volumes of essays: *Hills and the Sea, On Nothing and Kindred Subjects* (1908), *On Everything* (1909), *On Anything* (1910), and *On Something* (1910). At the age of seventy-six Belloc reflected that he "wouldn't have written a word if I could have helped it. I only wrote for money. *The Path to Rome* is the only book I ever wrote for love." Belloc was strongly motivated to write essays for income, because he was able to sell each essay twice: first to a newspaper, then to a publisher for inclusion in a collection.

On Nothing and Kindred Subjects is a superb example of Belloc's humor. Satire is the dominant mode, and here as elsewhere it ranges widely, touching fashion, religion, morality, literature, and politics. Belloc explores the attitudes of James M. Barrie, Chesterton, and John Galsworthy on trivial subjects; satirizes politicians, churches, and spiritualists; and inveighs against pride of knowledge, concluding that "we are all ignorant of nearly everything there is to be known." The real meaning of "Nothing" is made clear in Belloc's preface: "Nothing is the reward of good men who alone can pretend to taste it in long easy sleep, it is the meditation of the wise and the charm of happy dreamers. So excellent and final is it that I would here and now declare to you that Nothing was the gate of eternity, that by passing through Nothing we reached our every object as passionate and happy beings." In the essay "Meditation" he points out that meditation requires detachment from the world of power, pride, and self-interest, in order to attain the spiritual and material harmony that results from doing God's Will. "On Jingals" summarizes his theory that the replacement of the monarchy by a weak republic is the cause of England's degeneration. "On a Man Who Was Protected by Another Man" charges that British imperialism is plundering natural resources, ignoring unique cultural habits, planting seeds of self-interest and capitalism, and causing hatred and violence. "On National Debts" points to the negative effect of imperialism on the English economy. Some of Belloc's political essays are angry, bitter, and scornful, but they are motivated by his love of his country and his determination to have it improve.

Belloc in 1910 (drawing by Eric Gill, published in Belloc's 1911 book The French Revolution*)*

On Everything, another collection of newspaper essays, has a cooler voice than *On Nothing*; Belloc seems more conscious of and concerned about his audience. The light, playful satire of *On Nothing* is replaced by a more biting satire that borders on cynicism. Belloc's mood now directly reflects his political experiences. His main strength as an essayist lies in his playful, charming melancholy, in his thoughts on the beautiful and the sad aspects of life; when he is topical, his fist is too tightly clenched. There are exceptions to his strong satire in *On Everything*, however, as in the beautiful essay "The Weald," his tribute to the unchanging countryside.

On Anything approximates the early essays in the variety of its subjects, its clarity, and its energetic style. The thirty-eight essays include such subjects as building castles in Spain, poetry, prophecy, methods of history, travel, Milton, Hans

Christian Andersen, and man's relationship with the devil. "On People in Books" reflects cynically on biographers who are not true to their subjects; "On Communications" explains that mass communications allow poor and ordinary people to see and know the world. The charm of the first three books is still evident, as are Belloc's intuition, intelligence, and adherence to Catholicism and tradition.

The last book of essays from his Parliamentary period, *On Something*, is dedicated "To Somebody." Some of the thirty "sketches," as Belloc calls them, appeared for the first time in this book; others were reprinted from the *Westminster Gazette*, the *Clarion*, the *English Review*, the *Morning Post*, and the *Manchester Guardian*. The satirical tone is largely replaced by an elegiac mode; in 1910 he was forty years old and in what he called "his middle years," and *On Something* reflects a pause in his reformist campaign, an attempt to reflect on larger issues. Belloc tended to be melancholy, because he was constantly aware of the tragedies of life. The beautiful, meditative essay "The Portrait of a Child" discusses the loss of innocence; "On Experience" expresses the realization of mutability, loss, and death. The year 1910 was a time of maturation for Belloc, a time when he was finally convinced that the political system, with its self-interested parties and leaders motivated by power and greed, was unchangeable. He withdrew with his family to King's Land in Sussex and devoted himself to writing.

First and Last (1911), the product of the first year of Belloc's withdrawal from public life, contains forty-one essays on many topics including politics (in "The Lunatic" a utopian democracy is proposed), social change ("The Old Gentleman's Opinions"), neglect of the past ("The Absence of the Past," "The Lost Things"), religion ("St. Patrick"), education ("Reality"), poetry ("José Maria de Heredia"), and literary criticism ("The Inheritance of Humour," "The Reward of Letters"). The dominant theme is history. He laments, in "On the Reading of History" and "On the Decline of the Book," that with the decline in reading the populace has become ignorant of history; "The Victory" analyzes an unnamed battle. Other historical essays include "Normandy and the Normans," "The Battle of Hastings," and "The Roman Roads in Picardy." Belloc's light humor and occasional satire are overwhelmed by a didactic tone that reflects his unpleasant experiences during his four years in Parliament, experiences that deepened his belief in the need for tradition, religious faith, unselfish politicians, and social enlightenment.

His seventh volume of essays, *This and That* (1912), reflects two years of tranquillity with Elodie and the children. Its forty short essays on various subjects show a controlled casualness that expresses Belloc's new relaxed mood. The book's preface projects the author at his playful, self-effacing best. He apologizes for writing so much "in very many different moods, and in so many different ways," and wonders how he can "introduce to the Reader the air in which the book that follows must be taken, but what air attaches in common to historical reconstructions, to abstract vagaries, to stories, to jests, to the impression of a storm, and to annoyance with a dead scientist?" He applies to the book the metaphor of a man with a "heap of rubbish in his cart": "you are not bound to buy, to borrow, or even to pick

up this book." Readers who do pick up *This and That* are still rewarded with deep insights, common sense, and concern for the refinement of humanity and of society. Belloc writes on diplomats, pedants, atheists, fame, rest, and the passing of the old inns of England. The final sentence of the essay on inns is a warning: "But when you have lost your Inns drown your empty selves, for you will have lost the last of England." The last essay in the book, "On Dropping Anchor," expresses the joy of returning home after a long and difficult voyage: "I shall tie up my canvas and fasten all for the night, and get ready for sleep. And that will be the end of my sailing."

In 1914 Elodie, who had always been of delicate health, died, and Belloc became despondent; he felt guilty that he had been unable to provide a stable home for Elodie and that he had not remained at home with her during their years of marriage. Through his constant faith he was able to regain the will to continue, although he mourned her for the rest of his life. He won fame and a substantial income during World War I through writing military analysis for the new journal *Land and Water* and through public speaking, giving at least one lecture every day. But these years were the most difficult time of his life. The war caused the loss of many close friends, including his best friend, Cecil Chesterton. Belloc's son Louis was gassed as an infantryman in France in 1917; he recovered and transferred to the flying corps, but his plane was lost on 26 August 1918 and his body was never found. Following these misfortunes, Belloc tended to focus on his religious writings, although he continued to attack such social evils as the misuse of power and money.

During the 1920s Belloc was not in the mainstream of literature because he had little sympathy for modern trends. His favorite authors were the comic novelist P. G. Wodehouse, the satirist Maurice Baring, and the little-remembered poet Ruth Pitter. The thirty essays in *On* (1923) deal with such topics as reform in education, footnotes, titles, bad verse, poets, technical words, sailing, the word *and*, and hatred of numbers. *Short Talks with the Dead and Others* (1926) contains twenty-nine essays, many of them dealing with literary criticism. Belloc was quick to admit his unfamiliarity with a wide range of contemporary literature and therefore his reluctance to write "serious" literary criticism; in fact, he believed that most literary criticism was pointless. Belloc's frame of reference for literature was classicism,

Daphne Pollen's lithograph of Belloc (1934)

and he believed that modernism fell short of that standard. *Short Talks with the Dead and Others* contains essays on Byron, Livy, good and bad poets, Wordsworth, and *Rasselas*. He holds Byron in high regard, but he seldom gives examples from Byron's work to justify his opinion. Wordsworth, he says, is not consistently a good poet. Livy is to be valued because, like Belloc, he produced an abundance of material, and like Belloc's, his histories were criticized for inaccuracies; such comments are really personal appreciation rather than literary criticism. His best critical essay, "On Rasselas," points to the truths expressed by Samuel Johnson, as well as to the work's artistic achievement, and gives many quotations from the novel. *A Conversation with an Angel and Other Essays* (1928) contains thirty-four humorous but not satiric essays on such topics as academic debates, the weakness of modern writers, the superficiality of book reviewers, and Lucifer. *A Conversation with a Cat and Others* (1931) returns to Belloc's serious mode. Many of its thirty-nine essays are on his-

torical subjects such as Charles Brandon, Duke of Suffolk; William Laud, Archbishop of Canterbury; Louis XIII of France; Charles II of England; Henry V; La Rochelle; and George Villiers, Duke of Buckingham. The essays are fine examples of Belloc's ability to restore historical characters to life with economy of language.

During the postwar years Belloc received an honorary doctor of law degree from Glasgow University, where he had been refused a teaching position early in his career. In 1931 he was invited to speak on translation in the Taylorian lecture series at Oxford University, where he had also been refused a position; the lecture was well received and was published the same year. Belloc also received recognition from several European governments for his writings on World War I.

The Silence of the Sea and Other Essays (1940) comprises forty-eight pieces that had previously appeared in the *Sunday Times*, *Truth*, the *Universe*, the *Weekly Review*, and the *Tablet*. Although there are essays on the joy of the sea, the security of permanence, and the value of controversy, the dominant genre is literary criticism. In "On Books" he writes, "Fear nothing. I do not propose to write on what is inside books. Nothing shall persuade me to do so! Of all the fatiguing, futile, empty trades, the worst, I suppose, is writing about writing." But he writes seriously about the high quality of the works of Sir Walter Scott, the superb visual imagination of John Bunyan, the importance of diaries, and the strengths of James Boswell, Jane Austen, and Shakespeare. He also discusses the English language in such essays as "On Euphemism" and "The Wisdom of the White Knight"; in "On the Future of English" he writes prophetically about the spread of English around the world and the corresponding weakening of its quality because of the rapidly increasing number of dialects. This book, like its predecessors, has an easy flowing style characterized by accuracy and charm.

Belloc wrote commentaries and analyses during World War II as he had during World War I; but his authority and influence had diminished, particularly because of his aggressive Catholicism. The collapse of France was devastating to him; even more so was the death of his son Peter on 2 April 1941, at age thirty-six. Peter had contracted pneumonia while serving as a marine in Scotland.

Belloc never regained his vitality after Peter's death. He suffered a slight stroke at the Reform Club on 30 January 1942. Although he continued to dictate articles, including an occasional one for the *Weekly Review*, his powers of concentration and expression began to fade. In 1943 Prime Minister Winston Churchill offered him the Companionship of Honour, but he gracefully declined it, as he did later when Oxford offered him an honorary fellowship at Balliol College. On 30 November 1950 his portrait by James Gunn was unveiled in the Debating Hall of the Oxford Union.

On 12 July 1953 his daughter found him lying on the floor of his study near the fireplace; his coat was smoldering. He suffered from burns and shock and was taken to the home of the Franciscan Missionaries at Guildford. He died on 16 July 1953 while his family recited the rosary by his bedside; nearby, a group of nuns sang a hymn he loved. The funeral was held at West Grinstead, and Belloc was buried beside Elodie and Peter. A solemn requiem was held a few days later at Westminster Cathedral; Father Ronald Knox preached the panegyric.

Belloc in 1939 (painting by James Gunn; collection of the Gunn family)

Belloc's thirteenth and final book of essays, *One Thing and Another*, was published in 1955; the thirty-eight essays from the period 1911 to 1941 were selected by Patrick Cahill, whose dedication reads, "In memory of one who spoke the truth, and called things by their right names." In "An Essay upon Essays upon Essays" Belloc points out the need for an abundance of essays to discuss all topics openly and frankly; he believes the essay to be a necessary platform in a healthy society. In "Tender Farewell to the World," Belloc, using the refrain "Must I leave you," addresses the countryside, towns, cities, history, human behavior, literature, and mountains, and concludes that he can leave them all without regret because they are "all spoilt beyond redemption." They have lost their dignity and become rubbish; they are "an offence." The modern world has destroyed the glories of the past, language is forgotten, and literature has degenerated from folly and obscenity to insanity. Belloc's tone is not bitter but angry and disgusted. He has tried all his life to change the direction of the world around him but has been overwhelmed by the forces of modernism. His hope lies in another world. In "Immortality," the final piece in the book, Belloc states the arguments for and against life after death; presents the Roman Catholic position as given by St. Thomas Aquinas; and concludes that there is a hereafter. The tone of the essay is controlled and confident and touched by Belloc's characteristic lightheartedness.

In his day Belloc's essays were received and reviewed with enthusiasm. Offering entertainment, charm, animated observation, and interpretation, they continue to live for readers who value masterful English prose and are concerned about the quality of material and spiritual life.

Bibliography:
Patrick Cahill, *The English First Editions of Hilaire Belloc* (London: Privately printed, 1953).

Biographies:
J. B. Morton, *Hilaire Belloc: A Memoir* (New York: Sheed & Ward, 1955);
Eleanor and Reginald Jebb, *Belloc, the Man* (Westminster, Md.: Newman Press, 1957);
Robert Speaight, *The Life of Hilaire Belloc* (London: Hollis & Carter, 1957).

References:
André Bordeaux, *Hilaire Belloc* (Lille: Service de Reproduction des Théses, Université de Lille, 1972);
Jay P. Corrin, *G. K. Chesterton and Hilaire Belloc: The Battle Against Modernity* (Athens: Ohio University Press, 1981);
Raymond Las Vergnas, *Chesterton, Belloc, Baring* (New York: Sheed & Ward, 1938);
John P. McCarthy, *Hilaire Belloc: Edwardian Radical* (Indianapolis: Liberty Press, 1973);
Frederick Wilhelmsen, *Hilaire Belloc: No Alienated Man* (New York: Sheed & Ward, 1953);
A. N. Wilson, *Hilaire Belloc* (London: Hamilton, 1984);
Douglas Woodruff, ed., *For Hilaire Belloc: Essays in Honor of His 71st Birthday* (New York: Sheed & Ward, 1942).

Papers:
A Belloc archive, containing some correspondence and literary manuscripts, is at the British Library.

Edmund Blunden
(1 November 1896 - 20 January 1974)

Nils Clausson
University of Regina

See also the Blunden entry in *DLB 20: British Poets, 1914-1945*.

BOOKS: *Poems 1913 and 1914* (Horsham, U.K.: Price, 1914);

The Barn (Uckfield, U.K.: Privately printed, 1916);

The Silver Bird of Herndyke Mill; Stane Street; The Gods of the World Beneath (Uckfield, U.K.: Privately printed, 1916);

The Harbingers (Uckfield, U.K.: Privately printed, 1916);

Pastorals: A Book of Verses (London: Macdonald, 1916);

The Waggoner and Other Poems (London: Sifgwick & Jackson, 1920; New York: Knopf, 1920);

The Appreciation of Literary Prose: Being One of the Special Courses of the Art of Life (London, 1921);

The Shepherd and Other Poems of Peace and War (London: Cobden-Sanderson, 1922; New York: Knopf, 1922);

Old Homes, A Poem (Clare, U.K.: Ward, 1922);

The Bonadventure: A Random Journal of an Atlantic Holiday (London: Cobden-Sanderson, 1922; New York: Putnam's, 1923);

Dead Letters (London: Printed for Holbrook Jackson at the Pelican Press, 1923);

To Nature (London: Beaumont Press, 1923);

Christ's Hospital: A Retrospect (London: Christophers, 1923);

Masks of Time (London: Beaumont Press, 1925);

The Augustan Books of Modern Poetry: Edmund Blunden (London: Benn, 1925);

English Poems (London: Cobden-Sanderson, 1926; New York: Knopf, 1926; revised edition, London: Duckworth, 1929);

More Footnotes to Literary History (Tokyo: Kenkyusha, 1926);

On Receiving from the Clarendon Press (Oxford: Clarendon Press, 1927);

On the Poems of Henry Vaughn: Characteristics and Imitations, with His Principal Latin Poems Carefully Translated into English Verse (London: Cobden-

Sanderson, 1927; Folcroft, Pa.: Folcroft Library Editions, 1974);

Lectures in English Literature (Tokyo: Kodowkan, 1927);

Retreat (London: Cobden-Sanderson, 1928; Garden City, N.Y.: Doubleday, Doran, 1928);

Japanese Garland (London: Beaumont, 1928);

Winter Nights (London: Faber & Gwyer, 1928);

Undertones of War (London: Cobden-Sanderson, 1928; Garden City, N.Y.: Doubleday, Doran, 1929; revised edition, London: Cobden-Sanderson, 1930; republished with a new introduction by the author, London: Collins, 1964);

Leigh Hunt's "Examiner" Examined (London: Cobden-Sanderson, 1928; New York & London: Harper, 1931);

Nature in English Literature (London: Hogarth Press, 1929; New York: Harcourt, Brace, 1929);

Shakespeare's Significances: A Paper Read before the Shakespeare Association (London: Oxford University Press, 1929; Folcroft, Pa.: Folcroft Library Editions, 1974);

Near and Far: New Poems (London: Cobden-Sanderson, 1929; New York & London: Harper, 1930);

Leigh Hunt: A Biography (London: Cobden-Sanderson, 1930; New York & London: Harper, 1932);

De Bello Germanico: A Fragment of Trench History (Hawstead, U.K.: G. A. Blunden, 1930);

A Summer's Fancy (London: Beaumont Press, 1930);

The Poems of Edmund Blunden (London: Cobden-Sanderson, 1930; New York & London: Harper, 1932);

Votive Tablets: Studies Chiefly Appreciative of English Authors and Books (London: Cobden-Sanderson, 1931; New York & London: Harper, 1932);

To Themis: Poems on Famous Trials with Other Pieces (London: Beaumont Press, 1931);

Edmund Blunden

Constantia and Francis: An Autumn Evening (Edinburgh: Privately printed, 1931);

In Summer: The Rotunda of the Bishop of Derry (London: Privately printed, 1931 [i.e. 1932]);

The Face of England in a Series of Occasional Sketches (London, New York & Toronto: Longmans, Green, 1932);

Fall In, Ghosts: An Essay on a Battalion Reunion (London: White Owl Press, 1932);

Halfway House: A Miscellany of New Poems (London: Cobden-Sanderson, 1932; New York: Macmillan, 1933);

We'll Shift Our Ground; or, Two on a Tour, by Blunden and Sylva Norman (London: Cobden-Sanderson, 1933);

The Epilogue for King John: Presented by the O.U.D.S. February 25th, 1933 on the Occasion of the Closing of the New Theatre Oxford (Oxford: Holywell Press, 1933);

Charles Lamb and His Contemporaries: Being the Clark Lectures Delivered at Trinity College, Cam-

bridge, 1932 (Cambridge: Cambridge University Press, 1933; New York: Macmillan, 1933);

The Mind's Eye: Essays (London: Cape, 1934);

Choice or Chance: New Poems (London: Cobden-Sanderson, 1934);

Edward Gibbon and His Age (Bristol: University of Bristol, 1935; Folcroft, Pa.: Folcroft Library Editions, 1975);

Keats's Publisher: A Memoir of John Taylor (1781-1864) (London: Cape, 1936; Clifton, N.J.: Kelley, 1975);

Verses to H.R.H. the Duke of Windsor (Oxford: Privately printed, 1936 [i.e. 1937]);

An Elegy and Other Poems (London: Cobden-Sanderson, 1937);

On Several Occasions (London: Corvius Press, 1939);

Poems 1930-1940 (London: Macmillan, 1940 [i.e. 1941]; New York: Macmillan, 1940 [i.e. 1941]);

English Villages (London: Collins, 1941; New York: Hastings House, 1941);

Thomas Hardy (London: Macmillan, 1941; New York: Macmillan, 1942);

Cricket Country (London: Collins, 1944);

Shells by a Stream: New Poems (London: Macmillan, 1944; New York: Macmillan, 1945);

Shelley: A Life Story (London: Collins, 1946; New York: Viking, 1947);

Shakespeare to Hardy: Short Studies of Characteristic English Authors Given in a Series of Lectures at Tokyo University (Tokyo: Kenkyusha, 1948; Folcroft, Pa.: Folcroft Library Editions, 1973);

Two Lectures on English Literature (Osaka: Kyoiku Tosho, 1948);

After the Bombing and Other Short Poems (London: Macmillan, 1949; New York: Macmillan, 1949);

Addresses on General Subjects Connected with English Literature Given at Tokyo University and Elsewhere in 1948 (Tokyo: Kenkyusha, 1949);

Sons of Light: A Series of Lectures on English Writers (Hosei: Hosei University Press, 1949; Folcroft, Pa.: Folcroft Library Editions, 1974);

Poetry and Science and Other Lectures (Osaka: Osaka Kyoiku Tosho, 1949);

Hamlet, and Other Studies (Tokyo: Yūhōdō, 1950);

Eastward: A Selection of Verses Original and Translated (Kyoto: Benrido, 1950);

Influential Books: Lectures Given at Waseda University in 1948 and 1949 (Tokyo: Hokuseido Press, 1950);

Favourite Studies in English Literature: Lecture Given at Keio University in 1948 and 1950 (Toyko: Hokuseido Press, 1950);

A Wanderer in Japan (Tokyo: Asahi-shimbun-sha, 1950);

Reprinted Papers, Partly Concerning Some English Romantic Poets: With a Few Postscripts (Tokyo: Kenkyusha, 1950; Norwood, Pa.: Norwood Editions, 1977);

Records of Friendship: Occasional and Epistolary Poems Written during Visits to Kyushu, edited by T. Nakayama (Kyushu: Kyushu University Press, 1950);

John Keats (London, New York & Toronto: Longmans, Green, 1950; revised, 1954; revised, 1959);

Edmund Blunden: A Selection of His Poetry and Prose, edited by Kenneth Hopkins (London: Hart-Davis, 1950; New York: Horizon Press, 1951);

Chaucer to "B.V.": With an Additional Paper on Herman Melville (Tokyo: Kenkyusha, 1950; Norwood, Pa.: Norwood Editions, 1977);

Sketches and Reflections (Tokyo: Eibunsha, 1951);

Essayists of the Romantic Period, edited by Ichiro Nishizaki (Tokyo: Kodokwan Press, 1952);

The Dede of Pittie: Dramatic Scenes Reflecting the History of Christ's Hospital and Offered in Celebration of the Quatercentenary 1953 at the Fortune Theatre (London: Christ's Hospital, 1953);

Charles Lamb (London, New York & Toronto: Longmans, Green, 1954; revised, 1964);

Poems of Many Years (London: Collins, 1957);

War Poets 1914-1918 (London: Longmans, Green, 1958; revised, 1964);

Three Young Poets: Critical Sketches of Byron, Shelley, and Keats (Tokyo: Kenkyusha, 1959; Folcroft, Pa.: Folcroft Press, 1970);

A Wessex Worthy: Thomas Russell (Beaminster, U.K.: Toucan Press, 1960);

English Scientists as Men of Letters (Hong Kong: Hong Kong University Press, 1961);

A Hong Kong House: Poems 1951-1961 (London: Collins, 1962);

William Crowe (1745-1829) (Beaminster, U.K.: Toucan Press, 1963);

A Corscambe Inhabitant (Beaminster, U.K.: Toucan Press, 1963);

Guest of Thomas Hardy (Beaminster, U.K.: Toucan Press, 1964);

A Brief Guide to the Great Church of the Holy Trinity, Long Melford (Ipswich, U.K.: East Anglian Magazine, 1965);

Eleven Poems (Cambridge: Golden Head Press, 1965 [i.e. 1966]);

A Selection of the Shorter Poems (Long Melford, U.K.: White, 1966);

Poems on Japan, Hitherto Uncollected and Mostly Unprinted: Compiled and Edited in Honour of His Seventieth Birthday, edited by Takeshi Saito (Tokyo: Kenkyusha Press, 1967);

A Few Not Quite Forgotten Writers? (London: English Association, 1967);

The Midnight Skaters: Poems for Young Children, edited by C. Day Lewis (London, Sydney & Toronto: Bodley Head, 1968);

A Selection from the Poems, edited by Jim White (Long Melford, U.K.: Restoration Fund Committee of the Great Church of the Holy Trinity, Long Melford, 1969);

John Clare: Beginner's Luck (Wateringbury, U.K.: Bridge Books, 1971).

OTHER: *John Clare: Poems Chiefly from Manuscript*, edited by Blunden and Alan Porter (London: Cobden-Sanderson, 1920; New York: Putnam's, 1921);

Christopher Smart, *A Song to David with Other Poems*, edited by Blunden (London: Cobden-Sanderson, 1924);

John Clare, *Madrigals and Chronicles*, edited by Blunden (London: Beaumont Press, 1924);

A Hundred English Poems from the Elizabethan Age to the Victorian: To Which Are Added Specimens of Sonnets, Ballads, Epigrams, &c.; and of the Principal American Poets, edited by Blunden (Tokyo: Kenkyusha, 1927; revised, 1949);

The Autobiography of Leigh Hunt, introduction by Blunden (Oxford: Oxford University Press, 1928);

Great Short Stories of the War, edited by Blunden (London: Eyre & Spottiswoode, 1930);

The Poems of Wilfred Owen, edited by Blunden (London: Chatto & Windus, 1931; New York: Viking Press, 1931);

Charles Lamb: His Life Recorded by His Contemporaries, compiled by Blunden (London: Hogarth Press, 1934);

Coleridge: Studies by Several Hands on the Hundredth Anniversary of His Death, edited by Blunden and Earl Leslie Griggs (London: Constable, 1934; Folcroft, Pa.: Folcroft Library Editions, 1973);

"Sussex," in *English Country: Fifteen Essays by Various Authors*, edited by H. J. Massingham (London: Wishart, 1934), pp. 43-60;

"Home Thoughts on Kent, 1844-1944," in *Eastes & Loud Ltd Centenary Souvenir* (Ashford, U.K.: Eastes & Loud, 1945 [dated 1944]), pp. 5-19;

"The Rural Tradition," in *The Natural Order: Essays in the Return to Husbandry*, edited by Massingham (London: Dent, 1945), pp. 21-30;

Christopher Smart, *Hymns for the Amusement of Children*, edited by Blunden (Oxford: Blackwell, 1948 [dated 1947]);

The Christ's Hospital Book, edited by Blunden and others (London: Hamilton, 1953; revised, 1958);

Ivor Gurney, *Poems Principally Selected from Unpublished Manuscripts*, edited by Blunden (London: Hutchinson, 1954);

Percy Bysshe Shelley, *Selected Poems*, edited by Blunden (London: Collins, 1954);

John Keats, *Selected Poems*, edited by Blunden (London & Glasgow: Collins, 1955);

Alfred, Lord Tennyson, *Selected Poems of Tennyson*, edited by Blunden (London, Melbourne & Toronto: Heinemann, 1960);

Wayside Poems of the Seventeenth Century: An Anthology, edited by Blunden and Bernard Mellor (Hong Kong: Hong Kong University Press, 1963);

Wayside Poems of the Early Eighteenth Century: An Anthology, edited by Blunden and Mellor (Hong Kong: Hong Kong University Press, 1964);

Wayside Sonnets, 1750-1850: An Anthology, edited by Blunden and Mellor (Hong Kong: Hong Kong University Press, 1971).

Edmund Charles Blunden was born in London on 1 November 1896 to Charles and Georgina Tyler Blunden but grew up in the rural village of Yalding, Kent, where his parents were schoolteachers from 1900 to 1912. The places of Blunden's birth and upbringing are symbolic of the two poles between which his adult life in England moved: the literary, intellectual, and scholarly circles centered in London and Oxford, and the English countryside which he celebrated in prose and verse throughout his career. It was writers in "the country tradition" (as Blunden called it) that drew his most memorable essays and books, and both as a scholar at Oxford and as a literary journalist in London Blunden tried to preserve and promote an awareness of England's rural tradition in a population becoming, to Blunden's distress, increasingly urbanized.

Blunden's link with England's southern countryside was further strengthened in 1913 when his parents left Yalding for teaching posts at the Framfield School in Sussex, a county rich in literary associations that worked their way into his writings. His father, who was a symbol of the rural values of Kent and Sussex, was a strong influence on Blunden. In the elegy "An Empty Chair (Chas. E. B.)," published in *A Hong Kong House: Poems 1951-1961*, Blunden idealized his father as a man "loving earth-skills (thought little of) / By which the whole's sustained." As Thomas Mallon points out, "Charles Blunden the cricketer, angler, kind and competent schoolmaster and churchman—this is the essential figure in the pre-1914 village landscape that Edmund Blunden was to celebrate as his ideal for half a century."

An early example of the congruence of Blunden's literary interests and his devotion to the countryside is his attendance at Christ's Hospital, which had moved from London to the Sussex Weald at about the time Blunden was born. Blunden later dedicated much of his criticism and scholarship to the famous men of letters who preceded him at the school, particularly Charles Lamb, Samuel Taylor Coleridge, and Leigh Hunt. Blunden's earliest poems, in the pastoral tradition, appeared in the school magazine, the *Blue*, and his connection with the school remained steadfast; at his death he was working on a biography of the school's most famous graduate, Coleridge.

In 1914, having won the senior classics scholarship, Blunden enrolled in Queen's College, Oxford. Then World War I intervened, spoiling forever the ideal world which the pastoral south, Christ's Hospital, and Oxford had combined to form in Blunden's mind. He served as a lieutenant in the Royal Sussex Regiment in France and Belgium, winning the Military Cross. The war was undoubtedly the greatest event in Blunden's life. The year before his death he wrote, "My experiences in the First World War have haunted me all my life and for many days I have, it seemed, lived in that world rather than this." The horror of the war probably accentuated the pastoral impulse in Blunden, for when he returned to England he clung even more firmly to the rural landscape of Kent and Sussex as the image of an ideal past, a paradise with which he was determined to prevent England from losing contact.

After his discharge in 1918 Blunden briefly resumed his studies at Oxford, but he soon moved with his bride, the former Mary Davies, to Boar's Hill, where the poets Robert Bridges and Robert Graves were living. There he began his serious career as a poet and a parallel one as a scholar. At Peterborough and Northampton he discovered collections of manuscripts by the nineteenth-century peasant poet John Clare, and with the help of his friend Alan Porter he produced in 1920 *John Clare: Poems Chiefly from Manuscript*. This first excursion into literary scholarship foreshadowed his later ones: Blunden regularly turned to neglected figures in English literature and history in an effort to give them the recognition he thought they deserved. For Blunden, criticism was almost always more a matter of expanding the literary canon than of further cultivating familiar fields. Clare was a "na-

ture poet," and throughout his life Blunden gave particular attention to figures who were connected with the "real" England of the countryside.

In 1920 Blunden moved to London to begin a career as a literary journalist. As John Middleton Murry's assistant on the *Athenaeum* he became a part of the London intellectual circle of the 1920s, including Philip and Ottoline Morrell, Leonard and Virginia Woolf, and Katherine Mansfield. He retained his position as subeditor when the *Athenaeum* was merged into the *Nation* in 1921. That year he traveled to South America aboard a cargo steamer to try to regain his health—he had not recovered from the nervous strain of the war, and his lungs had been permanently damaged by a gas attack. His major prose work of this period was *The Bonadventure* (1922), a travel book about the trip. Blunden continued to write travel literature throughout his career, especially about the Far East, and his travel essays show the same keen eye for detail, if not the same depth of feeling, as his writings on the English countryside.

Blunden was always dedicated to restoring the reputations of writers who had suffered neglect or misrepresentation. He tries, for example, to vindicate Clare from the misjudgments and falsifications of previous commentators and to give him his rightful place in English literature. Similarly, in his edition of Christopher Smart's *A Song to David with Other Poems* (1924) he expresses the hope that Smart's masterpiece will become "as familiar as 'L'Allegro.' "

In 1924 Blunden was invited to become Robert Nichols's successor as professor of English literature at Tokyo Imperial University; his marriage had become unhappy, and his wife remained in England. Blunden's influence on the study of English literature in Japan was immense. He trained a generation of Japanese scholars, helped found the English Reading Society, and encouraged aspiring poets among his students. Living in Japan provided Blunden with enough distance from his experience of the war that he was to write an account of it. *Undertones of War* (1928) became his most popular work and, in the opinion of many, his best. "In Japan," he wrote to his friend G. H. Grubb in 1930, "my sense of loss and eyelessness became stronger, the first year there being of course productive of long periods of loneliness, though later on I discovered many springs of hope and sympathy. I also had some *time* now &

Blunden in 1924, the year he first visited to Japan

then,–& so I began to picture the past as well as I could in words."

The keys to understanding *Undertones of War* are the connotations of *undertones* and the last sentence of the work, in which Blunden describes himself as "a harmless young shepherd in a soldier's coat." The tone throughout is modest, restrained, understated. Blunden for the most part stays in the background; he reveals little of his feelings and reactions. This short description of digging trenches is typical of Blunden's understatement throughout the work: "The process of thickening the trench walls meant working in the open, and the enemy laid his machine-guns accurately enough on the new job which could not be concealed from him, letting drive when he chose. So we lost men." Blunden shows characteristic restraint when recalling the theft of his walking-stick: "I . . . laid on my valise the ebony walking-stick which had been my grandfather's, and was

to be my pilgrim's staff. I went. I was away from it only a few minutes–it went." He cannot bring himself to accuse a fellow soldier of stealing.

Although *Undertones of War* proceeds more or less chronologically from Blunden's enlistment in 1915 ("I was not anxious to go," chapter 1 begins) to 1917 when he returned to a training center in England, the work is not an external narrative of battles and events. Rather it is a series of vignettes or episodes (one is tempted to call them idylls) that focus on seemingly unimportant things occurring in the day-to-day life of a platoon. In the introduction to a 1965 reprint of the work Blunden said, "I know that the experience to be sketched in it is very local, limited, incoherent. . . ." In chapter 18 he describes, and implicitly defends, his characteristic indirect, even at times tortured, method of writing; after recording a minor conversation with a brigade major about a trench tramway, he interrupts his narrative: "Do I loiter too long among little things? It may be so, but those whom I foresee as my readers will pardon the propensity. Each circumstance of the British experience that is still with me has ceased for me to be big or little, and now appeals to me more even than the highest exaltation of pain or scene in the 'Dynasts,' and than the heaven of adoration incarnadined with Desdemona's handkerchief. Was it nearer the soul of war to draw lines in coloured inks on vast maps at Montreuil or Whitehall, to hear of or to project colossal shocks in a sort of mathematical symbol, than to rub knees with some poor jaw-dropped resting sentry, under the dripping rubber sheet, balanced on the greasy firestep, a fragment of some rural newspaper or Mr. Bottomley's oracle beside him? . . . in this vicinity a peculiar difficulty would exist for the artist to select the sights, faces, words, incidents, which characterized the time. The art is rather to collect them, in their original form of incoherence. . . . Let the smoke of the German breakfast fires, yes, and the savour of their coffee, rise in these pages, and be kindly mused upon in our neighbouring saps of retrogression. Let my own curiosity have its little day, among the men of action and war-imagination."

Nevertheless, *Undertones of War* is not so incoherent as Blunden, with characteristic modesty, makes it out to be. The major unifying technique is Blunden's use of pastoral conventions, which he had already drawn upon for his poetry, to contrast with, and thus act as a criticism of, the horrors of war. Indeed, Paul Fussell in *The Great War and Modern Memory* (1975) calls *Undertones of War* "an extended pastoral elegy in prose. . . . Its distinction derives in large part from the delicacy with which it deploys the properties of traditional English literary pastoral in the service of the gentlest (though not always the gentlest) kind of irony." A typical strategy is to contrast a peaceful, innocent scene with the reality of war. "Jacob's Ladder was a long trench . . . requiring flights of stairs at one or two steep places. Leafy bushes and great green and yellow weeds looked into it as it dipped sharply into the green valley by Hamel, and hereabouts the aspect of peace and innocence was as yet prevailing. A cow with a crumpled horn, a harvest cart should have been visible here and there. The trenches ahead were curious, and not so pastoral. Ruined houses with rafters sticking out, with half-sloughed plaster and crazy window-frames, perched on a hillside, bleak and piteous that cloudy morning; dere-

lict trenches crept along below them by upheaved gardens, telling the story of savage bombardment." At a training session, "A Scottish expert . . . preached to us the beauty of the bayonet, though I fear he seemed to most of us more disgusting than inspiring in that peacefully ripening farmland." And in eighteenth-century style, Blunden apostrophizes a doomed farm cottage where he is briefly lodged: "Peaceful little one, standest thou yet? cool nook, earthly paradisal cupboard with leaf-green light to see poetry by, I fear much that 1918 was the ruin of thee." The archaic language here, as well as the pastoral setting, invokes an Edenic, preindustrial land free from the sins of modern technology and warfare.

With few exceptions the contemporary response to *Undertones of War* was highly favorable. Graves, however, reviewing it in the *Nation and Athenaeum* (15 December 1928), had mixed feelings; his "only complaint against this very worthwhile book," he wrote, was "that Blunden is too much of a gentleman. Loyalty keeps him from heaping the shames on the horrors. Almost everyone he mentions is more or less of a good fellow, or a stout fellow at least; the troops are seen in massacre, but never in stampede, with our own machine-guns rallying them." The first edition sold out in one day, and *Undertones of War* is Blunden's most reprinted work. In 1975 Fussell pronounced it, together with Siegfried Sassoon's and Graves's memoirs, "one of the permanent works engendered by memories of the war."

Blunden returned to England in 1927 and went back to work for the *Nation and Athenaeum*, then being edited by Leonard Woolf. Between 1927 and 1940, when he returned to military service as a staff member of the Oxford Training Corps, Blunden enjoyed his most productive period as an essayist and prose writer. His scholarly interests reasserted themselves in *On the Poems of Henry Vaughn* (1927), followed the next year by *Leigh Hunt's "Examiner" Examined*.

Less specialized is *Nature in English Literature* (1929), a volume in Leonard and Virginia Woolf's Hogarth Lectures on English Literature series. The book is much more than literary criticism; it is Blunden's lay sermon on nature, his affirmation of faith in the spirit of the English countryside, and his argument for the inseparability of English literature from the Englishman's love of nature. To Blunden, remarks Fussell, "the countryside is magical. It is as precious as English literature, with which indeed it is almost identical. . . . To Blunden, both the countryside and

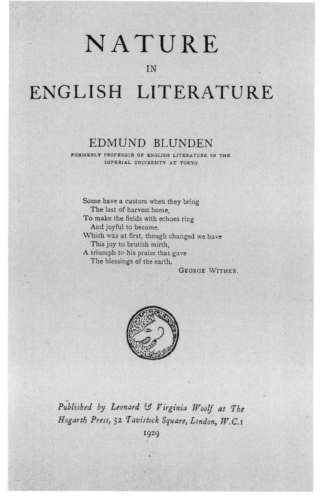

NATURE

IN

ENGLISH LITERATURE

EDMUND BLUNDEN

FORMERLY PROFESSOR OF ENGLISH LITERATURE IN THE
IMPERIAL UNIVERSITY AT TOKYO

Some have a custom when they bring
The last of harvest home,
To make the fields with echoes ring
And joyful to become.
Which was at first, though changed we have
This joy to brutish mirth,
A triumph to his praise that gave
The blessings of the earth.
GEORGE WITHER.

Published by Leonard & Virginia Woolf at The
Hogarth Press, 52 Tavistock Square, London, W.C.1
1929

Title page for the work in which Blunden demonstrates the inseparability of English literature from the Englishman's love of nature

English literature are 'alive,' and both have 'feelings.' " In Blunden's view, the Englishman–the "complete" Englishman, at any rate–enjoys a special relation with the countryside, despite the accelerating urbanization of England: "We see that times change, machines multiply, cities outrun the dreams of a century ago, agriculture declines; we lament the collapse of old and venerable parks into mere encampments of gracelessness, and the usurpation of old solitudes by despicable modern kraals, and hurtling landliners sweeping all before them in lanes where the partridge was safe with her brood all the sunny day. Old liberties are closed by new riches, peace broken by new noises, rusticity depraved into new urbanism. . . . But the catalogue of 'passing away' does not yet hinder this country from being, all points weighed, astonishingly beautiful, mellow with the pleasantest associations, the republic of birds and flowers, the earthly paradise of horse, sheep, heifer, and mongrel, the friendliest meeting-ground of Nature and man; and that this continuous astonishment for the affections and the senses is flourishing in 1929 is in part the highest tribute that the Englishman with all his achievements has ever won. Whether we approach him through his summer holiday or his inheritance of literature, we find him Nature's man."

Nature in English Literature is Blunden's effort to remind his countrymen just how much, through their inheritance of literature, they are Nature's men and women. To this end he greatly expands what most readers ordinarily think of as "English literature." The best parts of the book are those in which Blunden discusses writers and works that would scarcely warrant a footnote in a standard literary history. These include *The Farm-*

er's *Instructor*, William Ellis's 1747 book on sheep—"to me Ellis on Sheep is better than Ruskin on Sheepfolds"; Thomas Pennant's *History of Quadrupeds* (1781), beneath whose surface "there is a regard for Nature's family which Pennant might claim to be much more genuine a communion with the spirit of the universe than the more ambitious reveries of those who saw men as trees walking"; meteorological diaries from the *Gentleman's Magazine*; eighteenth-century guidebooks, which "often embodied the typical English liking (to use no more ambitious term) for the wind on the heath"; Harriet Martineau's *Complete Guide to the English Lakes* (1855), from which Blunden quotes "a page or two which, were not English literature as wealthy as it is, would be considered essential reading"; Thomas Gisborne's *Walks in a Forest* (1794); the anonymous *Episodes of Insect Life* (1849-1851), "a book which, from the standpoint of a peaceful patriot, I would as soon possess as the original edition of *In Memoriam*"; J. L. Knapp's *Journal of a Naturalist* (1829); Mary Roberts's *Annals of My Village* (1831); and Mary Mitford's *Our Village* (1824-1932). Such works, Blunden says, reveal "the quality of the English race, its contentment, its thoroughness, its way with Nature."

The book is by no means confined to such "minor" figures. In one chapter Blunden offers close readings of William Collins's "Ode to Evening" (1746), John Keats's "To Autumn" (1820) and Clare's "Autumn"—Clare, he says, is "in some lights the best poet of Nature that this country and for all I know any other country ever produced." In another he examines the philosophy of nature expressed in the poetry of Vaughan, William Wordsworth, Coleridge, and Percy Bysshe Shelley. His final chapter is devoted to Gilbert White—"the prose Virgil of England"—whose *Natural History and Antiquities of Selborne* (1789) he carefully examines in the context of White's predecessors and successors.

In 1931 Blunden became fellow and tutor in English literature at Merton College, Oxford. That same year he published *Votive Tablets: Studies Chiefly Appreciative of English Authors and Books*; this book and *The Mind's Eye* (1934) are his major collections of essays. As a literary critic, Blunden always had something of the votarist about him. Alec Hardie notes that "He is temperamentally unwilling to show other than sympathy; he makes a real attempt to meet an author on his own level, to know what he is trying to say, and not to force prejudices upon a victim. Rightly he has the repu-

tation of a kindly critic, preferring to find the authors's qualities and to gloss over faults." "If ever a man came to praise and not to bury," says Mallon, "it was he." (In *Keats's Publisher: A Memoir of John Taylor* [1936], Blunden quotes with approval Taylor's remark, "I think Praise should be given where it is due, and that Silence is sufficient Dispraise.") Blunden perhaps comes closest to describing his method and temperament as a critic at the beginning of the essay "The Country Tradition" in *Votive Tablets*, where he regrets the tendency of critics and scholars to avoid the unbeaten paths of literature: "The race of literary students, historians, selectors and interpreters has the tendency of soldiers in an attack, who often lose the orderly distribution in which they set out and become grouped and clustered round certain points and personalities. If we require a monograph on, or any kind of edition of, illustrious authors, or accounts of conspicuous types of literature, we find a superfluity: to him that hath is given with both hands; but if the subject is not popularly realised and extolled, then the forces of criticism are apt to fight shy of it altogether. Is it capricious to imagine that many useful or, as they used to be called, ingenious men of letters might have deserved better of their readers had they refrained from swelling the amount of printed matter concerning Byron or Browning, the Romantic period or the Ballad, and devoted themselves to some other question not already overwritten? For still, I think, the bewilderingly great assemblage of English books affords opportunities for valuable (though perhaps not enticingly lucrative) explorations and honest unassisted track-making."

Like so many of Blunden's essays, "The Country Tradition" is an act of piety, a tribute and memorial to those "unhonoured many ... who wrote the accounts of parishes and counties (even guide-books frequently transcending the mere programme of details to observe); those who kept journals of tours; theological ruralists who made their sermons of their natural history; the angling and other sporting writers, whose errors (as some consciences hold them to be) are not to be discussed apart from the virtues of their prevailing love of nature; the eulogists and biographers of the horse and dog (and other friends of man); the woodland haunters; the host of happy watchers of birds and butterflies, fishes and wild animals." The essay is a loving catalog of names and works which, although unfamiliar to most readers, are "akin to the distant profundities and spiritual seeings of Wordsworth": White, whose *Natural History and Antiquities of Selborne* ranks "among our imperishable books"; John Lawrence, who in *A Philosophical and Practical Treatise on Horses, and on the Moral Duties of Men towards the Brute Creation* (1798) pioneered the idea of animal rights; Jane Leapor, "the daughter of a Northamptonshire gardener, who died in 1745 in her twenty-fourth year" and who "makes her poems of the life she knows, and mostly avoids the stilted mannerisms of so many uneducated poets in her honest sense of a little heaven, under a cottage thatch"; Gisborne, whose *Walks in a Forest* may still be read "with placid enjoyment as the work of a generous spirit, a versifier well formed in general, particularly able in natural history, and studious of truth in observation and in word"; and Robert Bloomfield, whose *The Farmer's Boy* (1800) reveals "a humility free from meanness, and endurance without self-satisfaction, a devotion to duty capable of finding pleasure there, an innocence of view open to the sunbeams of idealism amid the dusty tracks of ignorance." Blunden's interest in these men and women is not just a narrow, antiquarian one; it is part of his lifelong effort to prevent a way of life that he valued from falling into desuetude. "The inspiration of nature and the country," he concludes the essay, "has been immensely fruitful year by year, and continues to arouse the heart, to summon the imagination and educate humanity." And although this inspiration has been "somewhat obscured by the commercialisation of its themes" and by "the clever improvisations of writers who chiefly gazed on nature through the windows of the Pullman car," there is still a need for "the natural and rural tradition in our prose and verse, warranted by strength of character, literary modesty and common sense." In summing up the virtues of this tradition–"strength of character, literary modesty and common sense"–Blunden is also summing up his own virtues as an essayist. Blunden does not just write *about* the country tradition; he writes *in* it.

Although Blunden wrote on the major Romantics (including a 1946 biography of Shelley) and on Hardy, his most characteristic criticism focuses on comparatively neglected figures such as Collins, Smart, Hunt, Henry Kirke White, William Cobbett, Henry Mackenzie, Robert Southey, Charles Churchill, Thomas Hood, and Michael Drayton. His works on Clare, the Northamptonshire "Peasant Poet" who went mad, and on Collins and Vaughan are typical. And as Hardie has

pointed out, nearly every author Blunden writes about has "some personal reason for deserving sympathy as a man: prolonged ill-health, madness, suicide, or some inability to deal with the circumstances of his time." These writers, like the English countryside so many of them wrote about, were often for Blunden a means of escape. Collins, for example, is praised because his poetry takes us "into a region unvisited by the shocks of event and injuries of society."

Sometimes there is a temperamental affinity between Blunden's subject and himself that explains his interest. This is certainly true of Charles Lamb, on whom Blunden delivered the 1932 Clark Lectures at Cambridge (published in 1933 as *Charles Lamb and His Contemporaries*). Both were Bluecoat boys, both good minor poets, both literary journalists. The familiar style of Lamb's essays (William Hazlitt and Hunt were also models) is strongly evident in Blunden's essays. Most of Lamb's "literary company," Blunden noted, "were devoted to English authors of a remoter time than their own century. . . ." Similarly, Blunden's poetry owes more to Collins and Clare than to T. S. Eliot and Ezra Pound. Lamb's particular scholarly passion was for Elizabethan drama, and his efforts to revive this literature struck a responsive chord in Blunden.

In 1933 Blunden married Sylva Norman, with whom he coauthored his only novel: *We'll Shift Our Ground; or, Two on a Tour* (1933). Like his first marriage, his second ended in divorce.

For Blunden, the English countryside usually meant the south, particularly Kent, Sussex, Hampshire, and Thomas Hardy's "Wessex." What these counties meant to him is clearly evident in "Sussex" (1934). The essay combines personal reminiscence with the partiality and enthusiasm of the local historian. As one would expect from the author of *Nature in English Literature*, Blunden perceives the rural landscape of Sussex through literary lenses. His recollection of Christ's Hospital, built in a "sleepy corner" of Sussex, immediately brings Shelley to his mind: "At our gates was Shelley Wood, and a half-lost moss-grown road led away from that green shade towards the home of Shelley. Indeed . . . our doctor's house was a home of Shelley, for it was his mother's in her early life." Sussex is like "a fairy wilderness" or a scene out of James Thomson's *The Seasons* (1726-1730): "Along the slopes [of Denne Park], I first caught the meaning of the Sussex poet who wrote of 'many a Nymph that wreathes her brows with sedge.' The avenue of

Caricature of Blunden by Ralph Hodgson (by permission of the National Portrait Gallery, London)

limes with the grey sleepy face of the mansion at the far, the sacred end, was like some half-real visions of eighteenth-century France. Beyond, and approached by circuits, there was a region of twilight thickets, like engravings from Thomson's 'Summer' by Woollett. . . ." Since Chichester was the birthplace of Collins, one of Blunden's favorite poets, he speculates on whether the "Ode to Evening" was "inspired . . . by some special memories of Up Park near Harting or of the Downs a few miles from his home." He quotes from Thomas Campbell's "Lines on the Camp Hill Near Hastings" (1831)–"a Sussex poem of the highest lustre," and he recalls that the man who perhaps suggested *The Rape of the Lock* (1714) to Alexander Pope, John Caryll, was from Sussex. The essay concludes, appropriately, with another reference to the county's greatest poet: "Above all I would see in some corner of Warnham Sir Timothy Shelley in Homeric word-combat with his son Percy Bysshe–the most celebrated instance of the Sussex man's 'won't be druv' doctrine as a game that could be played by two, and of the most startling importance to the literature of this country."

Blunden is also attracted to Sussex by the way its people "keep a good deal of their inherited views on man, nature and work." Sussex is for Blunden an image of the good society in which continuity balances–perhaps even outweighs–change. He reprimands the citizens of Chichester for allowing the house where Collins was born to "be supplanted, not unhandsomely, I grant, by a modern business building." But in spite of these concessions to modernity, Sussex still embodies for Blunden the essence of England and the English character: continuity, stability, and tranquillity.

By the 1940s Thomas Hardy had become something of a cult figure, especially among city dwellers longing to remake the English countryside into an image of what they thought they were losing. Blunden's celebration of the creator of Wessex in his biography *Thomas Hardy* (1941) was written partly in the same spirit as his essay on Sussex, as a paean of praise to a vanishing way of life. According to Blunden, Hardy's Tess is attractive "not so much for her personal tragedy as for the English country girl, a figure as beautiful as those in Keats's 'Ode to Autumn' and more distinctly related to these our tilled fields, our needs and our processes." He remarks that "so long as human beings are moved by the quality of the life of tree and wood, and find it a waking dream to step aside from their own affairs into the other world of forest branches, they will not be forgetful of Hardy . . . because he has seen the woodland and defined others' seeing in the bewildering lines and hues of its complexity." Blunden left Oxford in 1943 to join the staff of the *Times Literary Supplement* in London.

It is within the context of his writings on the countryside that Blunden's many essays on cricket and his book *Cricket Country* (1944) are perhaps best understood. As Mallon points out, "No activity better represented the village, Blunden thought, or was more fit for contented praise, than cricket." In his poem "Pride of the Village," published in *English Poems* (1926), Blunden elegizes a young cricketer, describing him as a poet who makes "his poems out of bat and ball"; cricket is "more than play"; it is "worship in the summer sun. . . ." In *Cricket Country* Blunden finds in Sassoon's successful captaincy of a country cricket team "a parallel to his poetry, that part of it at least which utters his sense of things natural and rural and their lasting pre-eminence." The date of *Cricket Country* is significant: writing during World War II, Blunden finds in cricket a set of lasting, pastoral values that can be set over against the war; thus the pastoralism of *Cricket Country* has much the same function as that of *Undertones of War* sixteen years before.

"Home Thoughts on Kent" (1945) was written for the centenary souvenir of Eastes and Loud, a firm of Ashford seed merchants; it was reprinted in *Edmund Blunden: A Selection of His Poetry and Prose* (1950). As he recalls "engined bombs" (Nazi rockets) falling on the Kent countryside during World War II, Blunden asks, "If men do these things in the green tree, what will they do in the dry? What will be the future course of the conflict between the patient wisdom of humanity, imaged in this lovely and beloved Weald round about me, and the evil fascination of 'new ideas' in applied sciences racing on without moral being?" In Kent—"a name with a conservative tone"—Blunden sees an emblem of the England that modern technology is trying, with some success, to destroy. The Kent countryside embodies the "moral being" that for Blunden is inseparable from nature and from true Englishness. He illustrates the character of the Kent resident from hop-growing, for which the county is famous: in 1578

Reynolds Scot, whose family lived near Ashford, published *A Perfite Platforme of a Hoppe Garden, and necessarie Instructions for the making and mayntenaunce thereof, with notes and rules for reformation of all abuses, commonly practised therein, very necessarie and expedient for all men to have, which in any wise have to doe with Hops*; when George Clinch published his *English Hops* (1919) he was able to say of Scot's work, " 'In many respects the information is as useful to-day as it was nearly three and a half centuries ago when it was published.' " As well as being largely free from change, Kent is also free from the class conflict that originated with the Industrial Revolution: "From the growing clash of capital and labour, of the privileged and the hapless, Kent was fortunately to a large extent free. . . . The yeoman was still [in the 1840s], as he remains now, the chief figure here, and it is not to Kent in the days of Charles Dickens that we look for instances of oppression and want, or the cold separation of class from class." But Kent is not all tradition; it is open to some change: "In Kent the traveller may certainly feel the security of tradition about him, and he may equally perceive the health of the experimental mind." As an example, Blunden points to the old Kent custom of introducing new species of orchard fruit and of selecting and improving old ones. He also acknowledges "two mighty developments, to which we are long accustomed": quarrying in the chalk for the lime needed by the farmer and "the vast Portland cement factories which have altered the appearance of some districts."

Blunden concludes the essay in characteristic fashion with two paragraphs on the literary associations of the county. He recalls Christopher Smart, who was born in Shipborne and, in 1752, memorialized the county's major industry in "The Hop Garden." The modern inheritors of Kent's "country tradition" include V. Sackville-West, whose long poem *The Land* (1926) "is remarkable not only as a reading of earth but as a garden of terms heard in Kentish speech"; Frank Kendon, C. Henry Warren, and F. J. Harvey Darton, whose works are "fragrant with our own scene and associations"; and finally Blunden's friends Sassoon, whose *The Old Century and Seven More Years* (1938) and *The Weald of Youth* (1942) "embody the secret of Kent," and Bridges, in whose poetry he finds "the frankness, the honour, the cheerfulness, the nature of the country community which he originally belonged to. . . ."

Blunden summed up his philosophy of the English countryside in "The Rural Tradition," written in 1945 for a collection of essays titled *The Natural Order: Essays in the Return to Husbandry*, edited by H. J. Massingham. The village community for Blunden embodies independence and continuity. He laments that a village, "suddenly cut off from its past, forced into some queer, new, uncertain way, by the violence of progress . . . should cease after so many years to bake its own bread, brew its beer, make its boots and shoes, shear its sheep, have its own grammar school. . . ." The blending of past and present in the countryside is perfectly caught in Blunden's description of Kentish hop workers: "A few weeks ago I was watching several of these Kentish men busy, as I have known them so many years, some hop-stringing and some with the dungcarts; what dexterity and diligence. . . . All was ancient, more ancient than the apple orchard with its crimson bloom in glorious multitude . . . and the cows and sheep among the lime-washed treetrunks; all was new with the new season, and the continued mastery of men brought up to know what will prosper in the long run and when to remember what had been the golden rule before." Blunden sees the permanence and change of nature–or, more accurately, the permanence of change: "All was ancient . . . all was new with the new season." For the farmer "to know what will prosper" in the future is a matter of remembering "what had been the golden rule before." This remembering Blunden calls the "country's wisdom," and it is of this wisdom that he wants to remind his readers.

In 1945 Blunden married Claire Margaret Poynting. He went to Japan in 1947 as the cultural liaison officer to the British mission, lecturing extensively on English literature. The essay "A Word for Kirke White," published in *Notes and Queries* (11 and 24 December 1948) and reprinted in *Edmund Blunden: A Selection of His Poetry and Prose*, is a good example of Blunden's modest attempts at giving minor writers recognition. "Little is remembered of his work except a few hymns," the fifth edition of *The Oxford Companion to English Literature* records, but Blunden feels differently. For in his short lifetime (he died at twenty-one), White, whom Blunden compares to Thomas Chatterton, was admired by such contemporaries as Southey (who edited his literary remains), Coleridge, Wordsworth, and Byron, and thus "has some permanent place in the story of Romantic poetry."

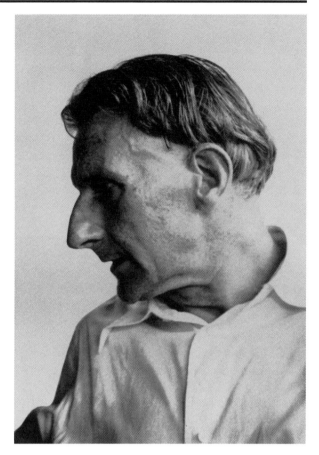

Blunden in 1955

Blunden returned to England in 1950 to work again for the *Times Literary Supplement*. In 1953 he became professor of English literature at the University of Hong Kong, where he taught for more than a decade. In 1964 he retired to Long Melford, Sudbury, Suffolk, but two years later he was appointed professor of poetry at Oxford. He resigned in 1968 due to ill health.

To the end of his life, Blunden's literary interests remained a continuation of his earlier ones. He wrote short studies of the Dorset poet Thomas Russell (1960), who, like Kirke White, died young, and of the scholar-poet William Crowe (1963), who edited Collins's works and whose topographical poem "Lewesdon Hill" (1788) makes him part of Blunden's "country tradition." The old interest in local county history resurfaces again in his *Brief Guide to the Great Church of the Holy Trinity, Long Melford* (1965). And it is highly appropriate that one of his last essays, *John Clare: Beginner's Luck* (1971), should be devoted to the poet on whom he wrote his first scholarly book more than half a century before. Blunden died on 20 January 1974.

Blunden's career as a critic and essayist shows not so much development and change as a continual circling around the same subjects and figures. What Mallon says about Blunden as a literary critic applies to him as an essayist in general: "The same subjects and the same names occur again and again in his lectures and books, and are recited almost in the manner of a lover. The sense of intimacy and regard between subject and explicator is unusual and impressive." As an inheritor of the nineteenth-century tradition of the familiar essay, Blunden exemplifies the virtues of modesty, sympathy, decency, intimacy, and loyalty.

Interviews:

Ichiro Nishizaki, Interview with Blunden, *Youth's Companion*, 7 (July 1949): 28-32;

Nishizaki, "On Life and Reading," *Study of English*, 52 (November 1963): 4-9;

Dom Moraes, "A Dream of Violence among the Spires: Edmund Blunden," *Nova* (London), (May 1966): 128-129, 131;

John Press, Interview with Blunden, in *The Poet Speaks*, edited by Peter Orr (London: Routledge & Kegan Paul, 1966), pp. 33-37.

Bibliography:

Brownlee Jean Kirkpatrick, *A Bibliography of Edmund Blunden* (Oxford: Clarendon Press, 1979).

References:

L. Aaronson, "Edmund Blunden," *Nineteenth Century and After*, 129 (June 1941): 580-585;

Bernard Bergonzi, *Heroes' Twilight: A Study of the Literature of the Great War* (London: Constable, 1965), pp. 68-72;

Chau Wah Ching, Lo King Man, and Yung Kai Kin, eds. *Edmund Blunden: Sixty-Five* (Hong Kong: Hong Kong Cultural Enterprise Co., 1965);

Paul Fussell, *The Great War and Modern Memory* (New York: Oxford University Press, 1975);

Alec M. Hardie, *Edmund Blunden*, revised edition (London: Longmans, Green, 1971);

Massao Hirai and Peter Milward, eds., *Edmund Blunden: A Tribute from Japan* (Tokyo: Kenkyusha, 1974);

Thomas Mallon, *Edmund Blunden* (Boston: Twayne, 1983);

J. E. Morpurgo, "Edmund Blunden: Poet of Community," *Contemporary Review*, 225 (October 1974): 192-198.

Papers:

The Humanities Research Center, University of Texas at Austin, has a collection of Edmund Blunden's letters, as well as the manuscripts of *Undertones of War* and poems; the Department of Manuscripts, British Library Reference Division, and the Berg Collection, New York Public Library, have manuscripts of poems.

Joyce Cary

(7 December 1888 - 29 March 1957)

Ronald Ayling
University of Alberta

See also the Cary entry in *DLB 15: British Novelists, 1930-1959.*

BOOKS: *Verse*, as Arthur Cary (Edinburgh: Grant, 1908);

Aissa Saved (London: Benn, 1932); republished, with new prefatory essay by Cary (London: Joseph, 1952; New York: Harper, 1962);

An American Visitor (London: Benn, 1933); republished, with new prefatory essay by Cary (London: Joseph, 1952; New York: Harper, 1961);

The African Witch (London: Gollancz, 1936; New York: Morrow, 1936); republished, with new prefatory essay by Cary (London: Joseph, 1951);

Castle Corner (London: Gollancz, 1938); republished, with new prefatory essay by Cary (London: Joseph, 1952; New York: Harper, 1963);

Mister Johnson (London: Gollancz, 1939; New York: Harper, 1951); republished, with new prefatory essay by Cary (London: Joseph, 1952);

Power in Men (London: Nicholson & Watson, 1939; Seattle: University of Washington Press, 1963);

Charley Is My Darling (London: Joseph, 1940; New York: Harper, 1960);

The Case for African Freedom (London: Secker & Warburg, 1941; revised and enlarged, 1944);

A House of Children (London: Joseph, 1941); republished, with new prefatory essay by Cary (London: Joseph, 1951; New York: Harper, 1956);

Herself Surprised (London: Joseph, 1941; New York: Harper, 1948); republished, with critical and biographical material by Andrew Wright (New York: Harper, 1961);

To Be a Pilgrim (London: Joseph, 1942; New York: Harper, 1942); republished, with new prefatory essay by Cary (London: Joseph, 1951);

Process of Real Freedom (London: Joseph, 1943);

The Horse's Mouth (London: Joseph, 1944; New York: Harper, 1950); republished, with new prefatory essay by Cary (London: Joseph, 1951);

Marching Soldier (London: Joseph, 1945);

The Moonlight (London: Joseph, 1946; New York: Harper, 1946); republished, with new prefatory essay by Cary (London: Joseph, 1952);

Britain and West Africa (London & New York: Longmans, Green, 1946; revised, 1947);

The Drunken Sailor: A Ballad-Epic (London: Joseph, 1947);

A Fearful Joy (London: Joseph, 1949; New York: Harper, 1949); republished, with new prefatory essay by Cary (London: Joseph, 1952);

Prisoner of Grace (London: Joseph, 1952; New York: Harper, 1952); republished, with new prefatory essay by Cary (London: Joseph, 1954);

Except the Lord: A Novel (New York: Harper, 1953; London: Joseph, 1953); republished, with commentary and notes by A. C. Ward (London: Longmans, 1966);

Not Honour More (London: Joseph, 1955; New York: Harper, 1955);

The Old Strife at Plant's, with Illustrations by the Author (Oxford: New Bodleian, 1956);

The Horse's Mouth, with a Self-Portrait and 8 Illustrations by the Author; and, The Old Strife at Plant's, a Discarded Chapter of The Horse's Mouth, edited by Wright (London: Rainbird, 1957);

Art and Reality (Cambridge: Cambridge University Press, 1958); republished as *Art and Reality: Ways of the Creative Process* (New York: Harper, 1958);

The Captive and the Free (New York: Harper, 1959; London: Joseph, 1959);

Spring Song and Other Stories (London: Joseph, 1960; New York: Harper, 1960);

Memoir of the Bobotes (Austin: University of Texas Press, 1960; London: Joseph, 1964);

The Case for African Freedom, and Other Writings on Africa (Austin: University of Texas Press, 1962);

Cock Jarvis: An Unfinished Novel, edited by A. G. Bishop (London: Joseph, 1974; New York: St. Martin's, 1975);

Selected Essays, edited by Bishop (London: Joseph, 1976; New York: St. Martin's, 1976).

Although he was primarily a novelist, and one whose artistic stature will probably increase with time, Joyce Cary's occasional prose writings are of considerable interest. Several of his autobiographical and travel impressions–reminiscent at times of William Golding's essays in a similar vein– are delightful sketches that reveal an admirably practical man and an integrated personality. Yet by his own testimony, such integrity came only as the result of a long and hard apprenticeship to life and art: in his training, he had to find his own way to self-expression; as with most artists, his formal education was of little practical help with either his writing or his painting. Having had to work on his own from a relatively early

age, whether as an inexperienced district officer administering a remote region of northern Nigeria or as a novelist attempting to encompass a vast social range in his fiction, Cary was forced to make up his mind for himself and to stand on his own feet. In both practical and aesthetic matters, therefore, he discovered early that he was cast in the role of an explorer; but he reveals in his early prose narrative *Memoir of the Bobotes* (1960) that his was an adventurous nature that relished self-reliant tasks.

Arthur Joyce Lunel Cary was born in Londonderry, Ireland, on 7 December 1888 to Arthur Pitt Chambers Cary, a consulting engineer, and Charlotte Louisa Joyce Cary. The family moved to London when Cary was a boy, but frequently returned to Ireland for visits. Cary's mother died in 1898; his father remarried in 1900, but his second wife died four years later. Cary attended Hurstleigh School in Tunbridge Wells from 1900 to 1903 and Clifton College in Bristol from 1903 to 1906. He studied art in Paris in 1906 and at the Board of Manufacturers School of Art in Edinburgh from 1907 to 1909, and read law at Trinity College, Oxford, between 1909 and 1912. In November 1912 he went to Montenegro to serve as a Red Cross medical orderly on the front lines of the First Balkan War between Montenegro and Turkey. "I wanted the experience of war," he told a literary critic more than forty years afterward, adding that at the time he had feared that there "would be no more wars." The statement reveals a profound ignorance of the mounting social dissensions within the Irish labor movement and among nationalist organizations in Cary's native land. Such discontent bubbled to the surface in the bitter Dublin Lockout of 1913 and the "terrible beauty" that W. B. Yeats was to celebrate in his poem on the 1916 Easter Rising. Unaware of these troubles– or, indeed, of the imminence of World War I– Cary experienced a mountain peasants' war in the Balkans that has been described by Walter Ernest Allen as "one of the last wars of its kind."

In the posthumously published *Memoir of the Bobotes*, which is partly based on diaries he kept in the Balkans, Cary likens the adventure to "a Maeterlinck tragedy"; but, although the casualties were high and the conditions harsh, he stresses the more lighthearted aspects (especially comedy at his own expense on various occasions) as well as the mundane and trivial incidents that loom large for men at the front. The book depicts the experiences of the twenty-four-year-old adven-

78

The only extant page from the manuscript draft for Memoirs of the Bobotes *(1960), Cary's account of his experiences as a Red Cross medical orderly during the First Balkan War (by permission of the Estate of Joyce Cary)*

turer in a style that is by turns laconic and facetious: "You object again that this history is all of meals, of stew and eggs. Anyone will tell you that a war is not made up of fighting, but just exactly of stew, and if you are lucky, eggs." As far as the fighting is concerned, there are several close calls and some affecting moments; notable among them is a vivid description of a tired stretcher party at night, with the fatigued narrator observing, "I fell several times, and my mind scarcely recorded the fact that I had been down and up again." Of a mountain redoubt glimpsed on one of these marches Cary writes: "The outpost was certainly an outpost; it might have been the last forward station of humanity on the rim of earth—wild men in sheepskins gazing from their crannies in the rocks, a little faint fire hidden here and there, nothing more than red embers, a cold hard wind, as steadily moving as a river, a sky of clouds below, shewing little triangles of the microscopic world between, and another close above—all about, rocks and splinters of rusty shell."

There seems little doubt that Cary was attracted to such conditions; it was probably the opportunity to make something of what he saw as primitive wilderness that led him to join the African Colonial Service in 1913. He was assigned to Nafada in northern Nigeria. In June 1916, while on leave, he married Gertrude (Trudy) Ogilvie, whom he had met at Oxford; they had four sons. During World War I he led troops of the Nigerian Regiment in the Cameroons Campaign, receiving a head wound at Mora Mountain. He was transferred to the remote district of Borgu in 1917 and remained there until 1919, when ill health forced him to leave government service. He settled in Oxford and tried to make a living as a writer, but had little success throughout the 1920s and 1930s; he was forced to take various jobs and to accept help from relatives and in-laws. During World War II he served for a while as head air raid warden in Oxford. He had his first best-seller with the novel *The Horse's Mouth* in 1944. Cary traveled to Africa in 1943 and to India in 1946, and—after his wife's death in 1949—made lecture tours of America in 1951 and 1953 and of Greece in 1955, although then he was already suffering from the paralytic illness that finally killed him on 29 March 1957.

Africa gave Cary a great deal in addition to the copious material it provided for five novels, some fine short stories, and occasional essays, several of book length. In "Travels in a Mind," published in *Selected Essays* (1976), he writes: "From Africa and India I brought unique experience of people who, with exactly the same fundamental characteristics as myself, had formed completely different ideas of law, of marriage, of religion; and, under the ruling of these ideas, realised their lives with dignity, order, and meaning. But also, and perhaps more importantly, I had a new revelation of the possibilities in life, of a new intensity and richness of living till then undiscovered to myself. In travelling abroad we learn to know not only our own country but ourselves in a new relation."

The future writer undoubtedly relished the many challenges offered by a job that carried with it considerable judicial power and heavy responsibilities, as well as the necessity to make immediate decisions and to live in enforced proximity to nature in a primitive state. He writes brilliantly of those days in "Christmas in Africa," published in *Selected Essays*; the concreteness of the image of a bathroom with a view is a typical touch of Cary pragmatism: "Just because Borgu was remote and cut off, just because I had no [telegraph] wire, I had been given free leave to make decisions, in fact to do what I liked. And there was always interesting and practical work at hand: mapping, road-making, bridge-building, the founding of markets and towns, the training of native staff; work I preferred very much to the endless minute-writing and form-filling of a big station in a rich province. Besides, when most of my colleagues were living in mud huts, I had a bungalow on a hill, a house of two storeys, with a broad balcony all around it. True, it was falling into ruin, and in one of my two upper rooms most of the floor was hole. But this too was an advantage. I could see from my bath right down into the office and know at once what I was in for that morning: a visit from old chiefs anxious to get up a war on the French frontier, hunters quarrelling about the correct division of a deer, one of my road gangs complaining of evil spirits who turned the edge of their best tools, or a witch murder with about twenty-five witnesses."

Subsequent philosophical and social essays, most of them written in the last fifteen years of Cary's life, drew sustenance from such firsthand experience. He says in an essay prefacing the 1952 edition of *An American Visitor* (originally published in 1933): "I was in a country full of social and tribal conflict where it was hard to devise even the elements of security and a reasonable life, especially for the masses. . . . The everlasting conflict between authority and freedom was not

Cary in the 1920s (courtesy of Tristram Cary)

an academic subject in Nigeria, it cropped up every day in a country where the traditional frame was in collapse and law had to be built while the queue waited." The philosophical essays—whose nature is apparent from their titles: *Power in Men* (1939), *The Case for African Freedom* (1941), *Process of Real Freedom* (1943), and *Britain and West Africa* (1946)–explore in more abstract terms many of the practical and metaphysical concerns in the novels. They are not merely intellectual exercises, however; the issues are always actual, contemporary, and immediately relevant.

"Because liberty is a certain kind of free power in men, governments and peoples must do certain things or be broken," Cary declares in *Power in Men*; the book was published three months before the outbreak of World War II, a conflict that was the inevitable culmination of two decades of increasing dictatorial government in Europe. *Process of Real Freedom* also explores immediate social issues. "Is there any cure for war?"

"What can prevent more and more terrible wars from destroying whole races and the very structure, even the memory, of freedom?" Confronting such questions in a situation that looked grim for the future of Western civilization, Cary gives reasoned expression to his faith in "the essence of democracy" and in mankind's capacity for creating and maintaining freedom. His arguments are nonetheless realistic, acknowledging the enlightened self-interest that invariably accompanies even the most idealistic of social programs and allowing for group as well as individual interests.

Outlining improvements that have characterized Western civilizations in modern times, he argues that the appearance of trade union organization has been a vital step forward in group democracy rather than "a chance event, which will vanish in its turn" and one that looks forward to a "balance of power" in a "new organised democracy"; that is why, he continues, "we dare to guess that group democracy, though

77

at present merely the shadow or first sketch of future states, may be a final kind of government." While acknowledging that "real democracies, where many groups have a great share of power, are still rare," Cary maintains a faith in the future that is primarily based on his observation that there is "a great deal of history to prove that co-operation and compromise are as frequent as the clash of wills." His essay remains a stimulating manifesto written with lucid conviction at a time of intense moral and intellectual crisis.

In *Process of Real Freedom* Cary asserted that nationalism was "the chief enemy of peace"; fourteen years later, in "Joyce Cary's Last Look at His Worlds," published in *Selected Essays*, he declared that as a government official in Nigeria he had witnessed "a primitive Africa, with no idea of racialism, or nationalism," and tribesmen who "knew neither nationalism, racialism nor that sense of inferiority which underlies so much racialism and makes it hysterical and psychotic.... But now this relation of trust between myself as an old-fashioned Nigerian political officer and the tribesmen would be described as paternalism, meaning by paternalism something disgraceful to both parties. It is replaced by what is called self-government, where these tribesmen would appeal to a Negro magistrate. And this is not disgraceful but admirable. Yet self-government is just as false a description of the actual situation as paternalism. In each case, the tribesman is under the law; the real change is simply in the colour of the magistrate and the idea that he represents, African nationalism. Nationalism is the idea that now dominates all political thinking and most propaganda. And it is tearing civilisation to pieces. It is, as I say, merely an idea, but it is based on feelings deep in human nature, of personal pride, ambition, and distrust of the stranger–feelings very easily worked up by a demagogue into arrogance and hatred, fear and revenge."

It is understandable that Cary's African writings have aroused hostility, especially from Third World critics. In neither his fiction nor his nonfiction is he hesitant to use words such as *primitive* or *savages* in relation to native societies and customs. Throughout his life he remained strongly antagonistic to nationalism; this attitude was presumably fostered by his Anglo-Irish background. His essays on African topics are perhaps best approached in the light of his lifelong preoccupation with problems of personal and social freedom and with the age-old dilemma of the conflicting demands of freedom and authority.

Cary's two major essays on Africa, despite the occasional historical inaccuracies shown by Christopher Fyfe in his introduction to *The Case for African Freedom, and Other Writings on Africa* (1962), are splendid, well-balanced studies of Africa in the 1940s and of the continent's future possibilities, given enlightened colonial policies and increased aid before and after independence. There is hard-hitting criticism of past and present European policies, including the occasional example of himself as a callow but self-confident district colonial officer ("a young and stupid officer"), a representative of ignorant colonial values that impede understanding of positive African values. Trenchant remarks on the still powerful reactionary force of tribalism, even though he believed that by the 1940s it was a dying force, and passionate arguments that "chiefs must learn to accommodate themselves to a rising democracy," show that twenty years after his retirement from the British colonial service Cary had strongly modified his original acquiescence to its policy of support for native tribal structures and government.

The Case for African Freedom was published in 1941 in the Searchlight Books series; edited by left-wing editors, including George Orwell, these books aimed at setting forth coherent policies on issues of contemporary importance. "If Mr Cary's book is more discursive and more detailed than the others" in the series, argues Orwell in the foreword, "it is because the problem of Africa is so vast and, in England, so little known that a preliminary survey is needed before any policy can be usefully stated.... It is because he so well understands the complexity of the situation that Mr Cary is especially fitted to plead for African freedom. He has an unusually independent mind, and many readers will feel a certain relief in reading a book on a political subject by a man who has thought deeply over the problems of our time, and has been above current political movements and their characteristic jargon."

The essay is a realistic document, boldly confronting the poverty of much of the continent and the imminent dangers of famine, economic enslavement, and racial war (especially in southern Africa). The need for a comprehensive plan for social and economic reform, with special emphasis on specific economic factors and on "small local units under native control" rather than grandiose schemes of reconstruction, as well as improved medical and educational facilities is argued with passionate lucidity. In keeping with the objectives of the series Cary outlines practical

Cary and his wife, Gertrude (Trudy) Ogilvie Cary, in the late 1940s (courtesy of Tristram Cary). Mrs. Cary died in 1949.

elements in such a plan, including cooperative group activity, adult education, and, in reaction to the utopian plans of many idealists who stressed rural development, the use of urban skills and labor. Cary argues that "it is only in towns that any development of the indigenous native civilization can be expected"; subsequent events have borne out the wisdom of this prophecy.

Britain and West Africa, published in 1946, was written as an introduction for British readers to the history, customs, trade, and future potential of this vast region. Fyfe has argued that in this work and *The Case for African Freedom* Cary "expounded his vision (the word 'blueprint' he explicitly repudiated) of West African development a rare example of the creative artist working in a political and economic field." Fyfe reminds the reader that Cary's "profoundest reflexions on Africa are contained in his novels," to which the two extended essays may be read as historical supplements; their political wisdom and vigorous polemical prose, however, entitle them to an honorable place in his nonfiction. Written more than a decade before the first of Britain's African colonies became independent, *Britain and West Africa*

concludes with an optimistic prophecy that was astonishingly prescient for 1945: "I think . . . that the new policy of a general all-round development is the only means in West Africa of keeping the social balance: of giving stability to a new set-up. . . . The new forms of society [in the Gold Coast] are still local and indigenous. They are full of that energy which, like the sap of the growing tree, springs from roots deep in their own native soil. The new Africa is no longer that of the primitive tribe, but neither is it an imitation culture taken from Europe. It is as racy and native as it has ever been. . . . There is no fear that tropical Africa will lose its local qualities when it is permitted to take its place in the world; rather it will bring to the world a new African civilization, new arts, new religion." The creator of this vision did not live to see its fulfillment in the contemporary artistry of Chinua Achebe, Wole Soyinka, Gabriel Okara, Ayi Kwei Armah, and many other West African writers whose rapid emergence could not have been envisaged in the mid 1940s. Even Cary could hardly have believed that the new African civilization would have blossomed so well so soon after independence.

Joyce Cary is not a great literary critic but his criticism–most of it written in the last decade of his life and reflecting a wide if undisciplined reading–is lively, scrupulous, and invariably down to earth; there is little of the sort of free-wheeling speculation that is to be found in, say, W. H. Auden's literary essays. In 1952 Cary was invited to give a series of three lectures at Oxford on "The Novel as Truth"; having thus been obliged, as he said, to examine his ideas on this subject, he enlarged upon these views in the six Clark Lectures that he prepared for delivery at Trinity College, Cambridge, in the fall of 1956. Too sick by this time to give them in person–they were read by his nephew–he nonetheless revised the talks for publication; they appeared in print in March 1958, a year after his death, as *Art and Reality*. The book offers a summation, in concise and straightforward terms, of the author's thinking toward the end of his career about certain technical as well as theoretical matters concerning the two artistic modes with which he had been preoccupied for most of his adult life: painting and the novel. Many of the ideas expressed in the Clark Lectures, and some illustrative examples, can be encountered in a less structured form in the critical writings included in *Selected Essays*.

A mature artist discussing the creative process can be a fascinating experience; the best parts of Cary's Clark Lectures and occasional literary essays are usually when he talks about technical matters in his own writing or that of others. "Unfinished Novels" and "The Way a Novel Gets Written" (in *Selected Essays*) offer highly personal accounts of his idiosyncratic creative methods. Judging from his descriptions, it is not at all strange that there are among his papers far more incomplete novels than finished ones; the only surprise, indeed, is that with such methods so much work did get into print, including sixteen novels, more than sixty essays, nine volumes of occasional prose writings, and two volumes of poetry. The reader learns from specific examples why there are among the Cary archives manuscripts in every stage of composition–some with a beginning and a conclusion, others with a middle and a beginning or a middle and an end; why there are some complete alternative drafts of published works; and how an opening chapter that set off a chain of creative explosions leading to a finished novel was eventually excluded from the final product. What the author regarded as "the best chapter" of *The Horse's Mouth* was cut out before publication; he says he intended to "enlarge it and

finish it" (he died before he could do so). A discussion of the many technical problems raised by a vast, overambitious novel reveals why he was unable to assemble the massive material into publishable form. (Alan Bishop was able to do it; and *Cock Jarvis* appeared in 1974, seventeen years after the novelist's death.)

A further fascinating revelation shows *The Moonlight* (1946) starting life as "a violent reaction" against Tolstoy's *Kreutzer Sonata* (1890), which was regarded by Cary as a great novel that is not only profoundly "unfair to women" but "stupid about them, and stupid about the world in which they had to create their lives." Among the more valuable aspects of these lectures are analyses of "technical failures" in novels and (as in an exceptional instance in Jane Austen, whose work Cary admired a great deal) the examination of cases where practical considerations of plot or narrative development intrude upon the artistic integrity of a novel. "Nothing is so illuminating as a great writer's mistakes," he argues, "and all of them make mistakes, for all of them are struggling to express an intuition of life which transcends any possible symbolic form." He continues: "All feel the limitations of language, of technique, and continually try to surpass them," instancing (rather astonishingly) James Joyce's *Finnegans Wake* (1939) as an experiment that in 1957 was just "beginning to be understood and, in time, will be common reading." Again and again he comes back to the moral dimension in art; indeed, if there is one common thread in the six lectures in *Art and Reality* it would perhaps be the intuitive moral sense that, for Cary, characterizes all great art. It is this sense that is most evident in Cary's practical-minded criticism.

Art and Reality includes a vehement attack on the behaviorist theory of art, making a strong case for reading as a highly imaginative critical exercise in "the use and meaning of a symbolic system." Although the reader may believe that he or she is, most of the time, being passively receptive, in truth the reader is continually "performing a highly active and complex creative act," albeit mostly at an intuitive, subconscious level.

Cary's criticism–tolerant, open-minded, and undogmatic–is written in an easygoing conversational style but without any sense of affected intimacy. His examples are usually taken from the great European classics: Tolstoy, Dickens, Proust, Flaubert, Dostoyevski, James, Hardy, and Conrad are prominent. Particularly notable is "The Tough World of Surtees" in *Selected Essays*: it is an illuminating and evenhanded appreciation of that neglected masterpiece, *Mr. Sponge's Sporting Tour* (1853). To read Robert Surtees, according to Cary, is "to escape for an hour or two from eyewash and cant into an atmosphere as brisk as one of his hunting mornings, sharp and raw, highly unflattering to everything in sight, faces, hedges, trees, nibbled pasture and greasy plough, but thoroughly bracing."

Published in 1976, Alan Bishop's *Selected Essays* assembled many of Cary's finest occasional prose works under three main headings: autobiographical and reflective writings, literary essays, and a group of primarily political, social, and historical pieces. If any body of nonfictional works is underrepresented here, it would be his meditations on the present and future of Africa. A fully comprehensive selection would also include several of his prefatory essays to individual works in the definitive Carfax Edition of his novels published in 1951 and 1952; these show him to be a perceptive critic of his own writings. An earlier posthumous publication, *Spring Song and Other Stories* (1960), includes several brief sketches that are as much finely etched impressionistic essays as they are stories: "Carmagnole," "A Glory of the Moon," and "A Hot Day," for instance, concern themselves with the everyday experiences of children. Here, as in his finest novels, Cary realizes with insightful delicacy various heightened states of mind and feeling.

Several of the most attractively written of the last essays are autobiographical; those that recall childhood–such as "Carrig Cnoc," "Barney Magonagel," and "Cromwell House"–are especially good, as one might expect from the author of that exquisite fictional creation *A House of Children* (1941). His portrait of the family retainer and jack-of-all-trades Magonagel is particularly memorable, and an early morning scene of Barney, with the young Cary, training greyhounds for racing is one of the finest passages in all of Cary's work, not least for its vivid evocation of the dogs' highly strung excitement. "Cromwell House" powerfully depicts the clash of cultures– Anglo-Irish and French–that Cary experienced within his family. His London experiences, no less than his Donegal memories, inspire passages of lyrical beauty. In "The Meaning of England" he says, "I was, like my family, sharply critical of the English and often of English policy, but my anger was that of a lover. I could not bear that England should be betrayed by her own children or by party politicians with narrow views and mean

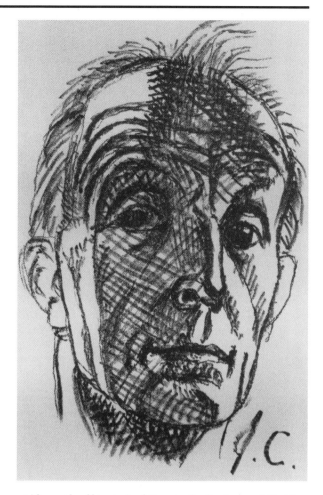

Lithograph self-portrait of Cary in the final year of his life

aims. I had, that is, a far more definite and romantic idea of England than the average born Englishman."

"The Heart of England" must be the best evocation of the quiet beauty of the Cotswolds that has ever been written (and it is a region that has been endlessly invoked in literature): "The Cotswold country is essentially a homeland; it has nothing grand, nothing to be called a mountain or a gorge; nothing like a big river or forest. Everything about it is delicate and gentle, it is full of small streams, as clear and pretty as their names, Windrush, Coln, Evenlode, which wind among small valleys with contours so subtly modulated that the eye is never startled but perpetually engaged. It is the chamber-music of landscape, a quartet where the brook sings to the two-acre field, the cottage above is a note that takes its meaning from both of them, and the whole is enclosed by a sky shaped by a stone roof, a smoking Cotswold chimney, a fan-shaped clump of beech, and the long curving lines of knolls that echo each other within this horizon like the counterpoint of a fugue." Here, as in his lovingly realized childhood memories or his impressions in "Westminster Abbey" and "Christmas in Africa," the reader is privileged to share as memorably as in his better-known fictional writings what Cary called "exalted occasions" (exalted in his memory, that is); as with D. H. Lawrence, whose writings he admired, the sense of place was indeed a constant inspiration to his artistry.

Interviews:

Stanley Parker, "Joyce Cary or What is Freedom?," *Oxford Mail*, 15 December 1942, p. 3;

Harvey Breit, "A Talk with Joyce Cary," *New York Times Book Review*, 18 February 1951, p. 14;

Graham Fisher, "A Great Author Faces up to Death," *Coronet*, 41 (January 1957): 41-44;

Nathan Cohen, "A Conversation with Joyce Cary," *Tamarack Review*, 3 (Spring 1957): 5-15;

"A Valedictory of a Great Writer," *Life* (25 March 1957): 105, 106, 108;

John Burrows and Alexander Hamilton, "An Interview with Joyce Cary," in *Writers at Work: The Paris Review Interviews*, edited by Malcolm Cowley (London: Secker & Warburg, 1958), pp. 47-62.

Biographies:

Malcolm Foster, *Joyce Cary: A Biography* (Boston: Houghton Mifflin, 1968);

Alan Bishop, *Gentleman Rider: A Life of Joyce Cary* (London: Joseph, 1988).

References:

Walter Ernest Allen, *Joyce Cary* (London: Longmans, Green, 1953);

Cornelia Cook, *Joyce Cary: Liberal Principles* (London: Vision, 1981);

Michael J. C. Echeruo, *Joyce Cary and the Dimensions of Order* (London: Macmillan, 1979);

Barbara Fisher, *Joyce Cary: The Writer and His Theme* (Gerrards Cross, U.K.: Smythe, 1980);

Fisher, ed., *Joyce Cary Remembered in Letters and Interviews by His Family and Others* (Gerrards Cross, U.K.: Smythe, 1988; Totowa, N.J.: Barnes & Noble, 1988);

Christopher Fyfe, Introduction to Cary's *The Case for African Freedom, and Other Writings on Africa* (Austin: University of Texas Press, 1962);

Dennis Hall, *Joyce Cary: A Reappraisal* (London: Macmillan, 1983);

Charles G. Hoffmann, *Joyce Cary: The Comedy of Freedom* (Pittsburgh: University of Pittsburgh Press, 1964);

S. H. Kanu, *A World of Everlasting Conflict: Joyce Cary's View of Man and Society* (Ibadan, Nigeria: Ibadan University Press, 1974);

M. M. Mahood, *Joyce Cary's Africa* (London: Camelot, 1964);

Andrew Wright, *Joyce Cary: A Preface to his Novels* (London: Chatto & Windus, 1958).

Papers:

The extensive James M. Osborn Collection of Joyce Cary's Manuscripts in the Bodleian Library, Oxford, includes many published writings that remain uncollected in book form as well as manuscripts of essays that have yet to appear in print.

Sir Winston Churchill

(30 November 1874 - 24 January 1965)

Laurence Kitzan

University of Saskatchewan

SELECTED BOOKS: *The Story of the Malakand Field Force: An Episode of Frontier War* (London & New York: Longmans, Green, 1898);

The River War: An Historical Account of the Reconquest of the Soudan, 2 volumes, edited by Col. Francis William Rhodes (London & New York: Longmans, Green, 1899; revised, 1 volume, 1902);

Savrola: A Tale of the Revolution in Laurania (New York: Longmans, Green, 1900; London: Longmans, Green, 1900);

London to Ladysmith via Pretoria (London & New York: Longmans, Green, 1900);

Ian Hamilton's March: Together with Extracts from the Diary of Lieutenant H. Frankland, a Prisoner of War at Pretoria (London & New York: Longmans, Green, 1900);

Mr. Brodrick's Army (London: Humphreys, 1903; Sacramento, Cal.: Churchilliana Co., 1977);

Why I Am a Free Trader (London: Stead, 1905);

Lord Randolph Churchill, 2 volumes (London & New York: Macmillan, 1906);

For Free Trade: A Collection of Speeches Delivered at Manchester or in the House of Commons during the Fiscal Controversy Preceding the Late General Election (London: Humphreys, 1906; Sacramento, Cal.: Churchilliana Co., 1977);

My African Journey (London: Hodder & Stoughton, 1908; New York: Doubleday, Doran, 1909);

Liberalism and the Social Problem (London: Hodder & Stoughton, 1909; New York: Doubleday, Doran, 1910);

The People's Rights (London: Hodder & Stoughton, 1910; New York: Taplinger, 1971);

Prison and Prisoners: A Speech Delivered in the House of Commons, 20th July, 1910 (London & New York: Cassell, 1910);

The World Crisis, 6 volumes (London: Butterworth, 1923-1931; New York: Scribners, 1923-1931); abridged and revised, 1 volume, London: Butterworth, 1931; New York: Scribners, 1931);

Sir Winston Churchill (Gale International Portrait Gallery)

Parliamentary Government and the Economic Problem: The Romanes Lecture Delivered in the Sheldonian Theatre, 19 June 1930 (Oxford: Clarendon Press, 1930);

My Early Life: A Roving Commission (London: Butterworth, 1930); republished as *A Roving Commission: My Early Life* (New York: Scribners, 1930);

India: Speeches and an Introduction (London: Butterworth, 1931);

Thoughts and Adventures (London: Butterworth, 1932); republished as *Amid These Storms: Thoughts and Adventures* (New York: Scribners, 1932);

Marlborough: His Life and Times, 4 volumes (London: Harrap, 1933-1938; New York: Scribners, 1933-1938);

Great Contemporaries (London: Butterworth, 1937; New York: Putnam's, 1937; revised and enlarged, London: Butterworth, 1938; revised, London: Macmillan, 1943; revised, London: Odhams, 1958);

Arms and the Covenant: Speeches, edited by Randolph S. Churchill (London: Harrap, 1938); republished as *While England Slept: A Survey of World Affairs* (New York: Putnam's, 1938);

Step by Step: 1936-1939 (London: Butterworth, 1939; New York: Putnam's, 1939);

Into Battle: Speeches, edited by Randolph S. Churchill (London: Cassell, 1941); republished as *Blood, Sweat and Tears* (New York: Putnam's, 1941);

The Unrelenting Struggle: War Speeches, edited by Charles Eade (London: Cassell, 1942; Boston: Little, Brown, 1942);

The End of the Beginning: War Speeches, edited by Eade (London: Cassell, 1943; Boston: Little, Brown, 1943);

Onwards to Victory: War Speeches, edited by Eade (London: Cassell, 1944; Boston: Little, Brown, 1944);

The Dawn of Liberation: War Speeches, edited by Eade (London: Cassell, 1945; Boston: Little, Brown, 1945);

Victory: War Speeches, edited by Eade (London: Cassell, 1946; Boston: Little, Brown, 1946);

War Speeches: 1940-1945 (London: Cassell, 1946);

Secret Session Speeches, edited by Eade (London: Cassell, 1946); republished as *Winston Churchill's Secret Session Speeches* (New York: Simon & Schuster, 1946);

The Sinews of Peace: Post-War Speeches, edited by Randolph S. Churchill (London: Cassell, 1948; Boston: Houghton Mifflin, 1949);

The Second World War, 6 volumes (Boston: Houghton Mifflin, 1948-1953; London: Cassell, 1948-1954)—comprises volume 1, *The Gathering Storm*; volume 2, *Their Finest Hour*; volume 3, *The Grand Alliance*; volume 4, *The Hinge of Fate*; volume 5, *Closing the Ring*; volume 6, *Triumph and Tragedy*;

Painting as a Pastime (London: Odham Press, Benn, 1948; New York: Whittlesey House, 1950);

Europe Unite: Speeches 1947 and 1948, edited by Randolph S. Churchill (London: Cassell, 1950; Boston: Houghton Mifflin, 1950);

Churchill in 1900, the year he was first elected to Parliament (Churchill Photograph Albums: Broadwater Collection)

In the Balance: Speeches 1949 and 1950, edited by Randolph S. Churchill (London: Cassell, 1951; Boston: Houghton Mifflin, 1952);

The War Speeches of the Rt. Hon. Winston S. Churchill, O.M., C.H., P.C., M.P., 3 volumes, edited by Eade (London: Cassell, 1952; Boston: Houghton Mifflin, 1953);

Stemming the Tide: Speeches 1951 and 1952, edited by Randolph S. Churchill (London: Cassell, 1953; Boston: Houghton Mifflin, 1954);

A History of the English-Speaking Peoples, 4 volumes (London: Cassell, 1956-1958; New York: Dodd Mead, 1956-1958)—comprises volume 1, *The Birth of Britain*; volume 2, *The New World*; volume 3, *The Age of Revolution*; volume 4, *The Great Democracies*;

The Unwritten Alliance: Speeches 1953 to 1959, edited by Randolph S. Churchill (London: Cassell, 1961);

Young Winston's Wars: The Original Despatches of Winston S. Churchill, War Correspondent, 1897-1900, edited by Frederick Woods (London: Cooper, 1972; New York: Viking Press, 1973);

The Collected Works of Sir Winston Churchill: Centenary Limited Edition, 34 volumes (London: Library of Imperial History, 1973-1976);

Winston S. Churchill: His Complete Speeches, 1897-1963, 8 volumes, edited by Robert Rhodes James (New York: Chelsea House, 1974);

The Collected Essays of Sir Winston Churchill, 4 volumes, edited by Michael Wolff (London: Library of Imperial History, 1976).

Sir Winston Churchill has become one of the legends of the twentieth century. A major and then an outstanding political figure in British and world history between 1905 and 1965, he was also a writer of substantial reputation and enormous output. A bibliographer, Frederick Woods, estimated in 1963 that "the total sales of his books in the English language alone are in the region of four million." In speech and written prose he has been noted as a master of the memorable phrase–"blood, toil, tears and sweat" caught the imagination of a generation. Although interest in his essays has been immeasurably enhanced by Churchill's status as statesman and historical writer, they have merit in their own right.

Winston Leonard Spencer Churchill was born at Blenheim Palace, the home of his grandfather, the seventh duke of Marlborough, on 30 November 1874. His parents were Lord Randolph Churchill, who was just beginning his erratically brilliant career as a Conservative member of Parliament, and the former Jennie Jerome, a socially prominent American from a wealthy family. Educated at private schools and at Harrow, Winston Churchill did not shine when exposed to the standard curriculum based on classics and to examiners who, as he noted in *My Early Life* (1930), "almost invariably" set questions "to which I was unable to suggest a satisfactory answer." A sensitive boy, Churchill suffered from his inability to establish a close relationship with his parents, especially his remote and much admired father. His educational deficiencies and his youthful interest in his battalions of toy soldiers convinced Lord Randolph that his son was destined for a military career, and he was duly enrolled at the Royal Military Academy, Sandhurst. He was commissioned in a cavalry regiment, the Fourth Hussars, in February 1895, shortly after the death of his father.

The various elements of Churchill's background were to have strong influences on his lengthy career. In his twenties Churchill began to show the same intense interest in politics that had characterized his father, and until almost the end of his life politics remained the passionate focus of his existence. A good deal of Churchill's determination in politics appears to stem from a continuing attempt to win, even posthumously, his father's approval. He idealized and attempted to realize Lord Randolph's political principles and initiatives–Tory democracy, social reform, and the reduction of military expenditure in times of peace. His outlook was always an aristocratic one, and his undoubtedly genuine reformist sentiments retained a strong element of paternalism. His experience in the military gave him a background different from that of most politicians: his martial expertise and his enthusiasm for making war were the despair of many of his colleagues during World War I but provided the makings of the Churchill legend in World War II.

The fact that his parents habitually lived beyond their income, as Lady Churchill continued to do throughout her widowhood, put into jeopardy Churchill's career as a cavalry officer–always an expensive proposition–and eventually helped push the young subaltern into a journalistic career. He attached himself to a North-West frontier punishment expedition in India in 1897 and sent reports to two newspapers. He had made a small amount of money by this means while serving with the Spanish forces during the Cuban revolt in 1895, but the publication of his revised reports from India as *The Story of the Malakand Field Force* (1898) brought him considerable notice in England as well as critical and financial success. In *The River War* (1899) he recounted his experiences in the Sudan campaign of 1898. During the Boer War he served as a war correspondent and was paid handsomely for his dispatches, which he then collected into two books, *London to Ladysmith via Pretoria* (1900) and *Ian Hamilton's March* (1900). The publicity surrounding Churchill's capture by the Boers in 1899 and his successful escape from a Pretoria prisoner-of-war camp helped sell his books and secure his election to Parliament as a Conservative in 1900. The profits from his publications and from a lecture tour in England and the United States recounting his South African experiences gave him the capital to operate in politics for many years without financial concern.

Churchill's dissatisfaction with the Conservative leaders and their lack of commitment to social reform, as well as frustrated ambition, led him to use the Conservative split over Joseph

Churchill, Secretary of State for War and Air, inspecting the British army of occupation in Cologne, August 1919
(Churchill Photograph Albums: Broadwater Collection)

Chamberlain's tariff reform campaign in 1904 as the occasion to move to the Liberal party, which was still committed to free trade. From 1905 to 1915 Churchill was continuously in office, first as under secretary for the colonies and then in the cabinet as president of the Board of Trade in 1908, home secretary in 1910, first lord of the Admiralty in 1911, and chancellor of the Duchy of Lancaster in 1915. His dedication to politics was so deep that on his honeymoon with the former Clementine Ogilvy Hozier in 1908 he carried on an extensive political correspondence. In the Board of Trade and as home secretary he was intimately involved with the social legislation of David Lloyd George but was also noted for an overenthusiastic deployment of troops in the railway strike of 1911. This action was indicative of his ability to switch rapidly from reasoned and moderate positions in times of peace to decisive action in what he perceived to be times of crisis. It

was a capacity that earned him a great deal of suspicion and hostility.

Churchill was one of the first cabinet ministers to be convinced of the necessity of British entry on the side of France in World War I; subsequently he made strong efforts to force upon the cabinet his ideas about methods for prosecuting the war. Despite this contribution–or perhaps because of it–Churchill, already naturally disliked by the Conservatives but also viewed with distrust by Liberals and Labour, was made the scapegoat for the Dardanelles fiasco and dropped from the Admiralty in 1915. He resigned from the cabinet a few months later, and for a brief period served as a field officer in the trenches of the western front. He then returned to politics and in June 1917 was appointed by Lloyd George as minister of munitions. He served as secretary of state for war and the air from 1918 to 1921 and as secretary of state for the colonies in 1921 and 1922. De-

Window display at Harrod's in London, January 1938, on the publication of Churchill's collection of biographical sketches

feated in the election of 1922, Churchill began a migration of allegiances through two more electoral defeats before he was elected as a Constitutionalist in 1924 and appointed to Stanley Baldwin's Conservative cabinet as chancellor of the exchequer, a position he held until the defeat of the government in 1929.

Despite long experience in office, a reputation as a brilliant speaker, and solid friendships in the political world, for the next ten years he was left out of Conservative-dominated governments. This fate reflected his isolation in politics and his reputation as a dangerous independent colleague; it also indicated a certain naïveté which belied his long political experience. During this period he vehemently attacked the leaders of the Conservative party for their stand on constitutional reform in India, which he believed was not ready for reform. With the emergence of Hitler he solemnly and often scathingly warned Conservative ministers of their lack of preparedness to meet a growing German military threat. Yet Churchill appeared surprised and hurt that neither Baldwin nor Neville Chamberlain felt his presence to be necessary in their cabinets of the 1930s.

Churchill's stand on the Nazi threat, though perhaps not as consistent as he later presented it in *The Gathering Storm* (1948), was sufficient to ensure his reintroduction to government as first lord of the Admiralty with the outbreak of war in 1939. He was evidently the man for a crisis situation, and when it became necessary to reorganize the government in 1940 Churchill succeeded almost by default to the position of prime minister. In the midst of military victory Churchill lost the prime ministry when the Conservatives were defeated in the election of 1945, but he regained the office in 1951. He was knighted by Queen Elizabeth on 24 April 1953. Plagued by the infirmities of age, including a series of strokes, he resigned as prime minister in 1955 and did not run for Parliament in the election of 1964. He died on 24 January 1965.

A survey of Churchill's career emphasizes the overwhelming preponderance of politics in his life. And yet throughout this period he had his living to make, a task he carried out successfully through his extensive writings. He made an excursion into melodramatic fiction with *Savrola* in 1900, but though the book sold well he did

Churchill meeting at Tehran with Soviet leader Joseph Stalin and President Franklin D. Roosevelt in 1943

not choose to repeat the experiment. Instead he concentrated on historical works. Some of these works describe events in which he himself was a participant: *The Story of the Malakand Field Force, The River War, London to Ladysmith via Pretoria, Ian Hamilton's March, The World Crisis* (1923-1931); and *The Second World War* (1948-1954); others deal with his family: *Lord Randolph Churchill* (1906) and *Marlborough: His Life and Times* (1933-1938); in still others, such as *A History of the English-Speaking Peoples* (1956-1958), he filters history through his own political experiences and comes up with an unabashed Whig interpretation. As a historian he is at his best in describing events with which he had an intimate connection, even given his biases and personal self-serving. Books more remote from Churchill's personal presence have serious weaknesses and illuminate his personality more than the period of which he is writing. Early in his political career he began the practice of publishing collections of his speeches with *Liberalism and the Social Problem* (1909). Two of his books are strictly autobiographi-

cal: *My African Journey* (1908) and *My Early Life*.

With the early establishment of his reputation as a vivid writer and political figure, Churchill was in considerable demand as a contributor to newspapers. His political eclipse between 1929 and 1939 did nothing to diminish this demand or his ability to profit by it. A collection of the best of his newspaper and journal articles, plus his Romanes Lecture delivered in 1930, was published in 1932 as *Thoughts and Adventures*. Biographical articles published between 1929 and 1936 were collected in 1937 as *Great Contemporaries*, which was republished several times with additions and deletions. It is mainly on these two books that Churchill's position as an essayist rests—though strictly speaking, almost all of his books can be viewed as collections of essays. Although the biographies and histories obviously have an overall unity, individual chapters tend to have an autonomy which turns them into set-piece essays. To a large extent this is a function of Churchill's method of composition. From early days, in fact from his years at Harrow when he dictated English essays to an older boy in return for Latin constructions, Churchill fell into the habit of dictating his works. By the 1930s the system was standardized; Maurice Ashley, one of his historical researchers, describes it in the 1974 biography of Churchill by Henry Pelling: "He would walk up and down the room (when I worked for him it was usually his bedroom) puffing at a cigar while a secretary patiently took it all down as best she could in Pitman. Occasionally he would say, 'Scrub that and start again.' At times he would stop . . . at others he would be entirely swept on by the stimulus of his imagination." The creation of these works, consequently, was similar to the creation of his speeches. Articles and books were the speaking of ideas that he had mulled over in his mind, in the same way as were both the impromptu speeches he made to dinner guests and acquaintances and the formally prepared speeches he gave on election platforms or to Parliament. But speeches by their nature are limited and self-contained, like essays. By "speechifying" his books, Churchill turned his chapters into essays.

As might be expected in an individual as single-minded and self-centered as Churchill, most of the essays included in the two collections are fragments of his autobiography. *Great Contemporaries* could have been subtitled "Great Men I Have Known, and Their Impact upon Me." These essays provide interesting viewpoints on many historical events and people. Churchill's "thoughts" in *Thoughts and Adventures* are often an amusing combination of shrewdness and naïveté. His musings in "A Second Choice" on being given the chance to live his life over again lead him to reject the desirability or usefulness of such a gift: "Life is a whole, and good and ill must be accepted together. The journey has been enjoyable and well worth making—once." Through its constantly growing capacity for destruction, science has made life potentially terrible, he points out in "Shall We All Commit Suicide?" It is science, too, that has created conditions in which heroes (Churchill was an inveterate hero-worshiper) and leaders are no longer relevant or possible, he says in "Mass Effects in Modern Life"; and by solving life's physical problems, without touching man's basic nature, he notes in "Fifty Years Hence," science had created dangers "out of all proportion to the growth of man's intellect, to the strength of his character or to the efficacy of his institutions." The Romanes Lecture, *Parliamentary Government and the Economic*

Problem, suggests the establishment of a parallel parliament of economic experts to offer advice to the elected Parliament–a proposal which indicates why Churchill has not been considered one of the great chancellors of the exchequer: he lacked understanding of both economics and economists.

Life for Churchill was an adventure to be recounted with relish. In "My Spy Story" he vivifies a spy scare in the Highlands of Scotland; in "A Day with Clemenceau" he tells about being under fire on the western front; "In the Air" presents him as pioneer aviator and air passenger. Joyous satisfaction is coupled with a dash of self-justification in "Consistency in Politics" and "The Battle of Sidney Street" and with a strong sense of the hand of fate that preserved his life in "With the Grenadiers" and " 'Plugstreet.' " The same sense of fatedness pervades his recounting of his political career in "Election Memories." He even adopted his hobbies in a dramatic fashion. In "Painting as a Pastime" he describes his desperation when he was removed from the Admiralty in 1915: "Like a sea-beast fished up from the depths, or a diver too suddenly hoisted, my veins threatened to burst from the fall in pressure. I had great anxiety and no means of relieving it; I had vehement convictions and small power to give effect to them." From this crisis he was rescued by experiments with his children's paint boxes, which turned him to the hobby of painting; the passionate pursuit of this hobby could distract his mind for periods of time even from politics.

Great Contemporaries deals with political figures, such as Archibald Philip Primrose, the Fifth Earl of Rosebery; Herbert Henry Asquith; Arthur James Balfour; and King George V, and military men, such as John French, Paul von Hindenburg, Ferdinand Foch, and Douglas Haig. The playwright George Bernard Shaw appears mainly as a writer of political ideas to which Churchill did not warm. In friend and foe he picks the qualities that he most admires; political and moral courage rank high, as do steadfast convictions, even when the principles upon which the convictions are based are wrong–herein lay Hitler's potential for both great good and great evil. Churchill admired intelligence, wit, and conversational sparkle, particularly as shown by his best friend, Lord Birkenhead. There is criticism in the essays but it is somewhat muted. Could anyone really expect the Kaiser, raised and existing in the florid atmosphere of the German Imperial Court, to behave other than as he did? Lord Curzon, with all his great gifts, lacked an essential quality: "In the House of Commons he met his match; and compared with the great Parliamentary figures of that time he was never regarded, even in his day, as an equal combatant or future rival." An ironic judgment, because without his great achievements as prime minister in World War II, the conclusion on Churchill might have been the same.

The enormous sales of Churchill's written works came after World War II and reflect the reputation that he won from that conflict. But even before the war he was a popular and well-read author. The essays help reveal why. They are simply written and easy to understand, with all the warm immediacy of a radio "chat." This style reflects Churchill's method of creation–the essays read as if they were spoken because they *were* spoken. Churchill appears to be constantly talking–to friends, to acquaintances, to cabinet colleagues, to Parliament, to the crowds at lectures and speeches. In his newspaper articles and essays he spoke to the people at large. From 1936 to 1939, for example, in a series of newspaper articles published in 1939 as *Step by Step*, he simply, directly, and confidentially took the British public into the heart of great matters. The result was that despite horrendous political errors, Churchill's political career was never destroyed. He was always near the front of the public and political mind. In 1940 he was not the politicians' first choice to succeed Chamberlain, nor that of the public–Anthony Eden ranked ahead of him in the polls. But he was in the running, and by a fortunate combination of circumstances he won the role that fulfilled his eagerly sought destiny.

Bibliography:
Frederick Woods, *A Bibliography of the Works of Sir Winston Churchill, KG, OM, CH* (London:

Vane, 1963; revised edition, London: Kaye & Ward, 1969).

Biographies:
Randolph S. Churchill and Martin Gilbert, *Winston S. Churchill*, 14 volumes to date (London: Heinemann, 1966- ; Boston: Houghton Mifflin, 1966-);
Henry Pelling, *Winston Churchill* (London: Macmillan, 1974);
William Manchester, *The Last Lion: Winston Spencer Churchill, Visions of Glory 1874-1932* (Boston & Toronto: Little, Brown, 1983).

References:
Raymond A. Callahan, *Churchill: Retreat from Empire* (Wilmington, Del.: Scholarly Resources, 1984);
John Freeman, "Mr. Winston Churchill as a Prose-Writer," *London Mercury* (April 1927): 626-634;
Martin Gilbert, *Churchill's Political Philosophy* (London: Oxford University Press, 1981);
Robert Rhodes James, *Churchill: A Study in Failure 1900-1939* (London: Weidenfeld & Nicolson, 1970);
Robin Prior, *Churchill's "World Crisis" as History* (London: Croom Helm, 1983);
A. J. P. Taylor and others, *Churchill Revised: A Critical Assessment* (New York: Dial Press, 1969);
Manfred Weidhorn, *Sir Winston Churchill* (Boston: Twayne, 1979).

Papers:
The private papers of Sir Winston Churchill are in the Chartwell Trust in the Public Records Office, London. They are presently reserved to the official biographer.

William Golding

(19 September 1911 -   )

Joyce T. Forbes
Lakehead University

See also the Golding entries in *DLB 15: British Novelists, 1930-1959* and *DLB Yearbook: 1983.*

BOOKS: *Poems* (London: Macmillan, 1934; New York: Macmillan, 1935);

Lord of the Flies (London: Faber & Faber, 1954; New York: Coward-McCann, 1955);

The Inheritors (London: Faber & Faber, 1955; New York: Harcourt, Brace & World, 1962);

Pincher Martin (London: Faber & Faber, 1956; New York: Capricorn, 1956); republished as *The Two Deaths of Christopher Martin* (New York: Harcourt, Brace & World, 1957);

Sometime, Never: Three Tales of Imagination, by Golding, John Wyndham, and Mervyn Peake (London: Eyre & Spottiswoode, 1956; New York: Ballantine, 1957);

The Brass Butterfly: A Play in Three Acts (London: Faber & Faber, 1958); republished with an introduction by Golding (London: Faber & Faber, 1963);

Free Fall (London: Faber & Faber, 1959; New York: Harcourt, Brace & World, 1960);

The Spire (London: Faber & Faber, 1964; New York: Harcourt, Brace & World, 1964);

The Hot Gates, and Other Occasional Pieces (London: Faber & Faber, 1965; New York: Harcourt, Brace & World, 1966);

The Pyramid (London: Faber & Faber, 1967; New York: Harcourt, Brace & World, 1967);

The Scorpion God: Three Short Novels (London: Faber & Faber, 1971; New York: Harcourt Brace Jovanovich, 1971);

Darkness Visible (London: Faber & Faber, 1979; New York: Farrar, Straus, Giroux, 1979);

Rites of Passage (London: Faber & Faber, 1980; New York: Farrar, Straus, Giroux, 1980);

A Moving Target (London: Faber & Faber, 1982; New York: Farrar, Straus, Giroux, 1982);

Nobel Lecture, 7 December 1983 (Leamington Spa, U.K.: Sixth Chamber, 1984);

The Paper Men (London: Faber & Faber, 1984; New York: Farrar, Straus, Giroux, 1984);

William Golding (photograph by Mark Gerson)

An Egyptian Journal (London & Boston: Faber & Faber, 1985);

Close Quarters (London: Faber & Faber, 1987; New York: Farrar, Straus, Giroux, 1987);

Fire Down Below (London: Faber & Faber, 1989; New York: Farrar, Straus, Giroux, 1989).

PLAY PRODUCTION: *The Brass Butterfly*, Oxford, New Theatre, April 1958.

MOTION PICTURE: *Lord of the Flies*, screenplay by Golding, British Lion Films, 1963.

RADIO: "Our Way of Life," *Third Programme*, BBC, 15 December 1956;

Miss Pulkinhorn, Third Programme, BBC, 20 April 1960;

Break My Heart, Third Programme, BBC, 3 February 1962.

OTHER: Jack Biles, *Talk: Conversations with William Golding,* foreword by Golding (New York: Harcourt Brace Jovanovich, 1970).

SELECTED PERIODICAL PUBLICATIONS–
UNCOLLECTED: "The Writer in His Age," *London Magazine,* 4 (May 1957): 45-46;

"Children's Books: Senior Bookshelf," *Listener,* 58 (December 1957): 953;

"In Retreat," review of *A Hermit Disclosed,* by Raleigh Trevelyan, *Spectator,* 204 (25 March 1960): 448-449;

"Raider," review of *John Paul Jones,* by Samuel Eliot Morrison, *Spectator,* 204 (20 May 1960): 741;

"Miss Pulkinhorn," *Encounter* (August 1960): 27-32;

"Man of God," review of *The Sabres of Paradise,* by Leslie Blanch, *Spectator,* 205 (7 October 1960): 530;

"Prospect of Eton," review of *Eton,* by Christopher Hollis, *Spectator,* 205 (25 November 1960): 856-857;

"Thin Partitions," review of *Some Reflections on Genius, and Other Essays,* by Russell Brain, *Spectator,* 206 (13 January 1961): 49;

"The Rise of Love," review of *The Characters of Love,* by John Bayley, *Spectator,* 206 (10 February 1961): 194;

"Androids All," review of *New Maps of Hell,* by Kingsley Amis, *Spectator,* 206 (24 February 1961): 263-264;

"All or Nothing," review of *The Faithful Thinker,* edited by A. C. Harwood, *Spectator,* 206 (24 March 1961): 410;

"Before the Beginning," review of *World Prehistory,* by Grahame Clark, *Spectator,* 206 (26 May 1961): 768;

"Thinking as a Hobby," *Holiday,* 31 (August 1961): 8, 10-13;

"Exile, Poverty, Homecoming," *Holiday,* 33 (April 1963): 10, 16-19;

"Advice to a Nervous Visitor," *Holiday,* 34 (July 1963): 42-43, 93-97, 125-126;

"The Best of Luck," *Holiday,* 35 (May 1964): 12, 14-17;

"The Condition of the Novel," *New Left Review* (January-February 1965): 34-35;

"Egypt and I," *Holiday,* 39 (April 1966): 32, 36, 38, 40, 42-44.

With the publication of *Lord of the Flies* in 1954, William Golding was recognized as an important modern novelist. As an essayist he is less well known. Golding has shied away from publicity, and even the interviews he has given provide sparse biographical information. His conversations with Jack Biles have added to this limited stock of information, and the shorter pieces he wrote from 1960 to 1962, during his brief career as a book reviewer for the *Spectator,* provide a complementary insight into Golding the man. In these essays he unbends freely and autobiographically. The first of Golding's essays published in the United States ("Thinking as a Hobby") appeared in the August 1961 issue of *Holiday* magazine. He continued to publish in this magazine until 1966. Other essays have appeared in *Esquire, Venture,* the *Kenyon Review,* and the *Times Literary Supplement.*

Golding's essays fall into three classes: travel pieces, humorous sketches, and philosophical observations, although these are not mutually exclusive. All are stylistically innovative, since in them he prunes his language to its bare essentials. The style of even the slightest pieces is brisk and economical. Equally characteristic are Golding's uncanny abilities to capture the spirit of place and project a wry sense of humor.

The travel pieces are largely descriptive, magazine-type essays; his recent book *An Egyptian Journal* (1985) also focuses on the excitements, irritations, and absurdities of the journey. Readers who know Golding only through *Lord of the Flies* would not guess at the abounding playfulness in much of his work. One of the nineteen pieces collected in Biles's *Talk: Conversations with William Golding* (1970), for example, reveals that Golding originally proposed the title "An Erection at Barchester" for *The Spire* (1964). Even in his philosophical essays, Golding's lighter side emerges. In an essay called "Fable" in *The Hot Gates* (1965), after talking about the writer of novels as a moralist, and man as producing evil as a bee produces honey, Golding ends his discussion of the novel as fable with this ironic statement: "It is in some ways a melancholy thought that I have become a school textbook before I am properly dead and buried. To go on being a schoolmaster so that I should have time to write novels was a tactic I employed in the struggle of life. But life, clever life, has got back at me."

Golding on his oyster smack, the Wild Rose *(photograph by John Miller)*

The son of Alec Golding, a distinguished British schoolmaster, Golding was born in St. Columb Minor, Cornwall, on 19 September 1911. As he reports in "Before the Beginning" (*Spectator*, 26 May 1961), his mother, Mildred Agatha Golding, confided to him that the sinking of the *Titanic* nine months after his birth taught her that the world is an "exhilarating but risky place." His perception that this catastrophe marked the end of innocence for his mother may have contributed to the critique of single-minded rationalism that runs throughout his novels and essays.

Golding's childhood, about which he talks in his essay "Billy the Kid" (1960; collected in *The Hot Gates*), was a relatively isolated one. Though he spent long holidays at the Cornish seaside, up to his first day at school he had known only his family. Such isolation probably contributed to the development of his love of books and his passion for words in themselves–which he collected as if they were "stamps or birds' eggs."

"Caught in the Bush" is the heading Golding uses in *The Hot Gates* for the two essays on his childhood. The bush in which the child Billy ("Billy the Kid") was caught was his own ego. It is in the other essay on his childhood, "The Ladder and the Tree" (also written in 1960), that Golding recalls his conscious decision to grow up. Fascinated in childhood by the mysterious, Golding was nurtured by the terror and darkness of his family's fourteenth-century home in Marlborough and the nearby graveyard. These feelings of the magical and irrational crystallized when he found and read *Edgar Allan Poe's Tales of Mystery and Imagination* (1908). The chestnut tree Golding discovered in a corner of his garden was his hidden ladder of escape from the fear created by his own obsessions. But the second and more important ladder he discovered was the inevitability of growth and change. To become the scientist he hoped to be, he had to climb this figurative ladder and also conquer his Latin verbs. Furthermore, his childhood experiences with the household servants indicated to him various complexities that were missing from his own life. He listened to the servants' letters that they read aloud. In addition, the young boy leafed through a subliterary magazine, *Peg's Paper*, which the servants enjoyed. At the age of twelve Golding began his first unpublished novel, which was to include as a background the rise of the trade union movement.

The young Golding's love of reading was not only based on children's classics by George Alfred Henty, Robert Michael Ballantyne, Jules Verne, and Edgar Rice Burroughs but included adult classics, especially the Greeks. Both groups exerted a permanent influence upon him. In a 1957 review in the *Listener* ("Children's Books: Senior Bookshelf") Golding asserts that worthwhile children's books fall into two categories: the great book and the good book. The former is great by any standard; the latter is a work of devoted craftsmanship. And of the many foreign children's books he received for reviewing, Golding found that few could be called even good. Most of the novels for children lacked imaginative intensity. A 1960 essay, "Islands" (collected in *The Hot Gates*), revisits scenes of his own childhood as Golding talks about the charm of children's stories such as Robert Louis Stevenson's *Treasure Island* (1883). On rereading it, the adult Golding concludes that this book remains as "sharp and swift" as the child Billy had found it. Johann Rudolf Wyss's *The Swiss Family Robinson* (1813; English translation, 1820) captures a child's sense of family as a whole world unto itself—contained, self-sufficient, and motionless. This feeling is, indeed, the charm of childhood, when "time is bright and uncomplicated as holidays spent by the seas."

Golding's other essays published in 1960 have little to do with his boyhood experiences or personality, but much to do with the nature of man. Having described himself as a citizen, a novelist, and a schoolmaster in "The Writer in His Age" (*London Magazine*, May 1957), Golding began to concern himself with social matters, particularly with the problems of proper instruction and appropriate forms of expression versus the use of raw power. His three review essays, "In Retreat," "Raider," and "Man of God" (all appearing in the *Spectator*), deal with citizens whose lives shed light upon the (often unfair) society of their times. The manipulative nature of man's use of power especially comes through in "In My Ark" (in *The Hot Gates*), a 1960 review essay on Gavin Maxwell's book *The Ring of Bright Water*; here

Golding claims that the modern love of animals and of "nature" is a manipulative force. The animal lover dotes on his pets yet manipulates horses. And even worse than this, he shows little loving kindness to people. Too often the declaration of Christian charity covers the dark destructiveness of a Miss Pulkinhorn, the fanatic churchgoer in Golding's radio play and short story of that name.

After two years at Brasenose College, Oxford, Golding had realized that his real interest was in what people said and did. He switched from science to English literature, specializing in Anglo-Saxon literature and language, receiving his B.A. in 1935. This change in interest reveals the tension between art and science in Golding. It was also this experience that made him suspicious of any discipline that develops only one aspect of the person. While still an undergraduate, Golding had published *Poems* (1934). When questioned later about this book, Golding replied that the poems are "poor, thin things" and that he would rather forget this early attempt at writing poetry. He believed that he turned to prose because he could not write poetry.

His involvement with small theater companies also began in the 1930s and grew to include work in radio and film. He was writer, actor, and producer for six years, from 1934 to 1940, and again from 1945 to 1954. His *Brass Butterfly: A Play in Three Acts* was performed at the New Theatre, Oxford, in 1958, and *Miss Pulkinhorn* was broadcast on 20 April 1960 by the BBC. The unpublished play *Break My Heart* appeared almost two years later on BBC in February 1962. The next year saw Golding's screenplay of *Lord of the Flies* produced by British Lion Films. During most of this period he was also a teacher and school administrator.

The year he married Ann Brookfield, 1939, was also the one in which he took up the position of schoolmaster of Bishop Wordsworth's School in Salisbury, Wiltshire. Golding held this position from 1939 to 1940 and again from 1945 to 1961. (It was during the second tenure that Golding was made a fellow of the Royal Society of Literature, in 1955.) Two 1960 review articles reflect Golding's experience at Salisbury. "Headmasters" (in *The Hot Gates*) is an important review of T. W. Bamford's book *Thomas Arnold*. Golding examines the power exerted by headmasters and in particular by Thomas Arnold. Described by Golding as a man of energy, self-esteem, and impatience, Arnold is best remembered for raising Rugby to the

Golding in 1955 (studio portrait by Howard Coster)

rank of a great public school. At its best, this power created the tradition that molded the imperial civil servants, the men who administered the government of the Sudan, for example. But at its worst, and seen in light of what Golding calls its "tempestuous kidnapping of the soul," this is the power that formulated the pattern of colonialism that brought about the tragedy of the Suez. Arnold's system could turn privileged young men into perpetual students, forever unable to grapple with the fundamental issue of the ethics of responsibility.

Another review article that analyzes the British educational system is "Prospect of Eton" (*Spectator*, 25 November 1960), occasioned by the publication of Christopher Hollis's *Eton*. Piqued by Hollis's great admiration for the quality of education at Eton, Golding states his sardonic conviction that England would not disappear if Eton ceased to exist. Noting the many contradictions implicit in the English character, Golding is concerned with the duplicity in the British educational system. By providing the prestigious, well-financed, public schools with competent masters and a favorable staff-student ratio, this system favors learning in the public schools to the disadvantage of the grammar schools. In "On the Crest of a Wave" (1960; in *The Hot Gates*) Golding is greatly concerned with the present trend of preparing young people to be mere wage earners and wonders what the future holds for novelists in England. In an intellectual climate in which genuine education is either being ignored or prostituted, is it possible to predict the nature of change? Heavily quoted by his critics is Golding's assertion about the state of mind in

Golding in 1965, the year The Hot Gates, *his first essay collection, was published (photograph by Conway Studios)*

which he wrote this essay: "I am by nature an optimist; but a defective logic–or a logic that I hope desperately is defective–makes a pessimist of me." Golding's pessimism surfaces in his observation that education should be closer to what H. G. Wells describes in *The History of Mr. Polly* (1910)–in which Wells's beautiful children are moving ahead–but education is actually going in a different direction, that of training for jobs. Golding sees the modern evil as technocracy, which, in focusing on current and strictly material problems, creates new dilemmas. Questions that take us beyond the present problems must be asked.

During World War II, from 1940 to 1945, Golding served in the Royal Navy, entering as an ordinary seaman but subsequently becoming an officer. In an interview with Biles entitled "Funny War Stories," Golding recalls how he expanded a two-sentence answer on the difference between a propellant and an explosive "into three pages with graphs and things." This feat resulted in his appointment to a highly secret research establishment controlled by Frederick Alexander Lindemann, who became Lord Cherwell and was Winston Churchill's scientific adviser. Evidently

Golding enjoyed the experience. Reminiscing amusingly over the quirks of fate, he recalled: "I was there for very nearly a year, right in the middle of England, all dressed up as a naval officer and trying to invent things that would sink submarines. It was fantastic. I enjoyed a lot of it, made immense bangs."

Golding worked on minesweepers, destroyers, and cruisers. He was lieutenant in command of a rocket-launching craft but also saw action against the *Bismarck*, with Atlantic convoys, during the D-Day landing, and in the attack on Walcheren. Behind his 1960 essay "The English Channel" (in *The Hot Gates*) is his experience of being adrift for three days in the channel. He describes his feelings on returning home and being overwhelmed by sudden excitement. He felt the keen need to study England closely but knew he must keep the traditional British stiff upper lip. After tracing the history of the channel through some of its highlights, Golding reminds himself that every story about the channel is someone else's tragedy.

Thus, in spite of the humorous war stories Golding recalls, for him the war was a crisis of faith that marked an awakening. During a 1962 interview with Maurice Dolbier (in Biles's *Talk*), Golding makes the following observation: "The basic point my generation discovered about man was that there was more evil in him than could be accounted for simply by social pressures. . . . We all saw a hell of a lot in the war that can't be accounted for except on the basis of original evil. Man is born to sin. Set him free, and he will be a sinner, not Rousseau's 'noble savage.' " The hero of Golding's novel *Free Fall* (1959) is literally and theologically in a state of free fall. *The Inheritors* (1955), his second novel, deals with Neanderthal characters living a wholly nonintellectual life. *Lord of the Flies* (rejected twenty-one times before its publication) traces the defects of society back to the individual. *Pincher Martin* (1956) is a work of visionary intensity concerned with archetypal opposites of good and evil, grace and damnation. Golding's war experience had a profound influence upon him. Henceforth, he questioned the neat rationalism and optimism of the historians of the past as he did that of the scientists of the present.

In "The Overriding Necessity," another of his conversations with Biles, Golding discusses what he perceives as the individual's need to bring all his experiences together. This deep need to form a whole out of trivial, discrete happenings and the deepest kind of experiences we have is, for Golding, the purpose behind man's life. Reminiscent of E. M. Forster's "Only Connect" (a major term used in *Howard's End*, 1910) is Golding's statement about unity: "If there is one faith I have it is that there is unity." A real-life hero for Golding was Rudolf Steiner, whose interests were diverse, yet who placed Christianity and the fate of man at the heart of all his interests and lived his life in head-on collision with the establishment. For Steiner, says Golding in "All or Nothing" (*Spectator*, 24 March 1961), "thinking itself was a spiritual activity, a kind of celestial dance that the sons of the morning are performing in the mind of man. Therefore philosophy and science, with their exercise of the strict forms of thought, are a direct way into communion with God."

History, too, was important to Golding–a way of unifying past and present. Two 1963 essays–"Digging for Pictures" and "Egypt from My Inside"–both now part of *The Hot Gates* collection, show how absorbed Golding was in history and prehistory. As an amateur archaeologist Golding sees archaeology as an impetus to the imagination. It makes one intimate with the experience of ordinary people and connects one with the past. Golding is an antiquarian at heart. In "Egypt from My Inside" he traces his fascination with Egypt back to the age of seven, when he abandoned writing a play about Egypt to learn hieroglyphics in which to write the play. He returns to this concern with history and prehistory in a later and longer version of "Egypt from My Inside" entitled "Egypt and I" (*Holiday*, April 1966). This essay incorporates material from the earlier essay, including the play-writing incident, the child Golding's visit to the museum, his note-taking from *The Book of the Dead*, and his introduction to Herodotus as first Egyptologist. It was Herodotus's method of experiment and common sense, writes Golding, that gave birth to "the lame giant we call civilization" and dissipated intellectual sloth. In the two Egypt essays as in "Digging for Pictures," Golding concerns himself with what he perceives as the painful yet triumphant capacity in man that makes intuitive leaps into the human situation. Another of Golding's well-known statements concerns his relationship with ancient Egypt: "Though I admire the Greeks I am not one of them, nor one of their intellectual children. . . . I am, in fact, an Ancient Egyptian with all their unreason, spiritual pragmatism and capacity for ambiguous belief."

The 1960s saw a growth in Golding's reputation. He obtained his M.A. from Oxford in 1961, and during the 1961-1962 school year was writer in residence at Hollins College, Virginia. In the 1961 essay "The Glass Door" (in *The Hot Gates*) Golding captures the virginlike somnolence and charm of a southern college, an enclave for the liberal education of young southern women. Yet, exotic foreign faces add color to the student body, and the demands of the technology of change will one day shatter this particular door on the privileged past.

Golding's American tour included Harvard, Vassar, Dartmouth, the Choate School, the University of Pennsylvania, and even television's *Today* show. It was also during this sojourn in the United States that "Thinking as a Hobby" was published in *Holiday*. A philosophical essay, it is an example of Golding's prose at its best. His style here has been described by Bernard F. Dick (in *William Golding*, 1967) as a mosaic, with each part delicately juxtaposing the other to produce a "dazzling configuration."

A hilarious essay that is mockingly austere in style and tone is "A Touch of Insomnia" (1961; in *The Hot Gates*). Aboard the luxury liner *Queen Elizabeth* and unable to sleep after a huge dinner, Golding uses the class distinctions of British society to spoof those aboard the ship–First Class, Middle Station, and Tourist Class. In this miniature world of high culture where entertainment is overeating, a six-course dinner ensures that the nannied, upper-class travelers will suffer from insomnia. And the professionals, frozen in their middle station, envy the dancing and frolicking of the tourist-class passengers.

The essay "Body and Soul" (1962; in *The Hot Gates*) reveals the harrowing nature of the lecture circuit in which Golding was then engaged. Scheduled to present three lectures in Los Angeles, he must fight the effects of jet lag and the feeling of disassociation it creates. Added to these discomforts are the attempts of his too-kind host to show him an entire city in one hour. The humor with which Golding handles the inconvenience of jet travel modulates into a style that captures the feeling of disassociation. His body does all the things it is supposed to do, including the delivery of the first lecture, before his soul arrives to join a body so tired it can no longer sleep.

"Through the Dutch Waterways" (1962; collected in *A Moving Target*, 1982) is a delightful and informative travelogue for tourists. Accompanied by his wife, Ann, their friend Viv, and their

Golding receiving his 1983 Nobel Prize from King Gustaf in Stockholm (photograph by Leif R. Jannson, Svenskt Pressfoto)

two children, David and Judith, Golding travels in an old boat, the *Wild Rose*, through the canals of Holland and across the old Zuider Zee. He claims that the greatness of Holland lies in her spirit and the quality of life her practical population leads. But even such a practical people as the Dutch overextend themselves with their expensive reclamation projects in their pastel land of "soft luminosities."

Golding's interest in places and the peculiar life they embody is also evident in another 1962 essay, "Shakespeare's Birthplace" (in *The Hot Gates*). As a child Golding lived only about fifty miles from Stratford-upon-Avon. But his interest in the bard was piqued only when images in Shakespeare's plays reflected the experience of the young Golding. It was only then that he undertook the journey on his bicycle to Stratford. Golding notes that Shakespeare's presence in the town of his birth continues to be enigmatic and elusive. The only means of experiencing the legacy of the bard is through the heart. One must be moved by his poetry. An experience of the heart

is like falling in love, taking a sacrament, or giving birth to a child. It cannot be bought as if it were a thing.

A spirited defense for translating, not transforming, Homer is the 1962 occasional essay "Surge and Thunder," which now appears in *A Moving Target*, Golding's second collection of essays. This essay is a review of Robert Fitzgerald's translation of *The Odyssey*. Though Golding praises the economy, speed, and excitement of Fitzgerald's verse, concluding that his translation is eminently readable, he laments that Fitzgerald falsifies the original. Golding's understanding of Greek literature comes through clearly in his assertion that Homeric poetry exemplifies "the art of the oral," which is different from the colloquial. And for Fitzgerald to tamper with the language–its epithets, repetitions, phrases, even contradictions–is for him to destroy the third hero (Odysseus and Homer being the others) of the epic: its oral technique.

Golding's ambivalence in being a visiting professor teaching a creative writing class at the university level is explored in "Gradus ad Parnassum" (1962; in *The Hot Gates*). Just being a writer in residence is itself a reward for an author. The position provides leisure, prestige, and adequate pay. However, the artist is also caught in a net, since he produces "fantasy work" and writes more slowly than he normally would. Golding believes that the literary world is being geared more and more to the academic world, and he fears that the result of this shift is a deepening of the gap between public and university consumption. Since the world of the university is not a replica of life outside the university, Golding affirms that the best place to learn creative writing is in the school of life.

In his foreword to Biles's *Talk*, Golding tells a story that illustrates his belief that modern technology is adversely influencing the thinking process of students. At the conclusion of a lecture and discussion at an American university, Golding saw a young man retrieve a secreted tape recorder from the room. On it was recorded Golding's conversation with students and faculty. Using Aesop's fable of the dog who gave up his bone for its reflection to illustrate the nature of the choice that student had made, Golding also saw the incident as illustrating a failure of modern assumptions. The recorded conversation is but a "fossilized impression" of a social occasion. Overcome by the convenience of modern technology, this student is satisfied with mere "leavings" and has given up the substance of an educational experience for its shadow.

Explaining, among other things, the crucial importance of what education or, to use Golding's term, "campus history" may achieve, is his essay "Fable" (in *The Hot Gates*). In an earlier form, "Fable" was a lecture given in 1962 at UCLA, where *Lord of the Flies*, with which this essay deals, was required reading. Like the Fool in Shakespeare's *King Lear* (1605-1606), Golding as fabulist is also a moralist who tells truth metaphorically. The human lesson that is tucked away inside *Lord of the Flies* is this: "The only enemy of man is inside him." Golding wants the student to understand that this enemy is manifest in the forces of "off-campus history," or the world outside. These forces include the "failure of human sympathy," "ignorance of facts," and the "objectivizing of our own inadequacies so as to make a scapegoat." Since they are not alive, they do not enhance life, yet they refuse to lie down. Death-bringing, they continue to threaten every child everywhere.

"Exile, Poverty, Homecoming" are the haunting themes of Irish poetry, writes Golding in this April 1963 essay (in *Holiday*). The Irish preoccupation with poverty and loss is found in James Joyce's great novels and in the works of other Irish writers, going back in time to Erse poetry. Golding states that as yet Ireland has not produced a "supremely great poet." Though it has neither a Homer, a Dante, nor a Shakespeare, he hopes that the true Irish voice, which surprised him in a thirteenth-century manuscript poem, will one day be heard.

Contrasted to the serious nature of his analysis of Irish literature, his "Advice to a Nervous Visitor" (*Holiday*, July 1963) is a comical travel guide about America. Yet it is not inaccurate in its assessment that the restless movement that distinguishes American culture is implicit in everything in the United States.

The year 1964 saw the publication of "Copernicus: A Universe Revealed" in *Holiday* (collected in *The Hot Gates*). This essay provided Golding with the opportunity to write a history lesson on the power of intuition as it operated in the life of the great astronomer, and to relate Copernicus's life to the period in which he lived. Golding posits the idea that religion, mathematics, and poetry met in Copernicus. But because he was a mathematician, Copernicus spent his life devoted to proving what he already believed. Golding reminds us that the Greeks took the first step toward a rational accounting of things, a course that dominated western thought up to the seventeenth century. The modern perception that Greek thinking was "the fairy tale of man's infancy"–because the Greeks perceived as cause and effect what many twentieth-century thinkers see as coincidence–is merely an expression of modern man's arrogance. Golding's position is reminiscent of that of Friedrich Max Müller, the great nineteenth-century orientalist and translator of the *Sacred Books of the East* (1875), whom Golding quotes as saying, "There never was a false god, nor was there really a false religion, unless you can call a child a false man."

"An Affection for Cathedrals," a December 1965 essay in *Holiday* (collected in *A Moving Target*), reveals that Winchester and Salisbury, old and not entirely beautiful cathedrals, still pull at Golding's heart. Only twenty-five miles from the town of Salisbury is Winchester, once England's capital. Kings and popes lie buried in the grounds of Winchester Cathedral, the site of three previous cathedrals; the present building is,

Golding with his wife, Ann (née Brookfield), and three Egyptian acquaintances (by permission of Faber and Faber)

in fact, an accretion of four hundred years of construction.

The 1960s, a productive decade for Golding, also brought additional awards. He received the James Tait Black Memorial Prize for *The Spire* and in 1966 was made honorary fellow of his alma mater, Brasenose College, and Commander, Order of the British Empire (CBE). Golding was later awarded honorary degrees by the University of Sussex (1970) and the University of Kent (1974).

The Scorpion God came out in 1971, consisting of three long novellas, one of which, "Envoy Extraordinary," had appeared some fifteen years before (in *Sometime, Never*, 1956). "The Scorpion God," the title novella, was written between *Free Fall* and *The Spire*, though it had remained unpublished. "Clonk Clonk," the third piece, was written just before its publication. Though the method used in each novella differs, there is a kind of thematic consistency in these works, all of which deal with crucial moments in history when consciousness changes.

Hailed as a major and important work by Golding critics is *Darkness Visible* (1979), a brilliant exploration of the weirdness of life presented through a chilling mystery story. The title recalls John Milton's description of the physical darkness of hell in *Paradise Lost* (1667). Golding examines the darkness that is visible in our times

and in the characters touched by the life of the hero, Matty. Golding's next book, *Rites of Passage* (1980), was awarded the Booker Prize, the highest literary award in Britain, in 1981. A masterly reconstruction of early-nineteenth-century prose styles and attitudes, this novel, more than any of the earlier Golding novels, comes closest to capturing the humorous Golding seen in so many of his essays.

Golding has continued to receive recognition from universities in the form of honorary degrees–in 1981 from the University of Warwick, and in 1983 from the universities of Oxford and Sorbonne. He was awarded the McConnell Prize for *A Moving Target* in 1982; then the Nobel Prize for Literature marked the high point in his career in 1983. The year 1984 saw the publication of a new novel, *The Paper Men*. It was also the year that Golding was made Companion of Literature, a Royal Society of Literature award.

In his preface to *A Moving Target* Golding notes that five of the sixteen pieces began as lectures. Inevitably modifications were introduced into the material as he worked on it for publication. Like the essays of *The Hot Gates* these are interesting stylistically as well as for their content. In addition to the essays first written for the lecturing circuit, *A Moving Target* is made up of book reviews and travel articles written for travel magazines. Grouped under the headings of "Places" and "Ideas," these essays tell about locales Golding has visited and loves, and discuss aspects of literature and life.

The essay entitled "Wiltshire" is a version of that published in *Venture* in 1966. It is neither the beauty, the flowers, nor the archaeological history of his native region that Golding loves; though obviously he finds delight in all these. Rather, it is the invisible character of Wiltshire, what Golding calls "a feeling of the heart." And this feeling he experiences as a desperate longing for home and hearth when he is away from the region.

"Egypt from My Outside," complementing the earlier essay "Egypt from My Inside," reaffirms Golding's abiding love for ancient Egypt. "Egypt from My Outside" was written in the winter of 1976 at the University of Kent at Canterbury. Well into his middle sixties, Golding realized then that he should no longer delay his actual physical journey to Egypt. Making his preparations for the voyage, eschewing the tourist routing that eliminates some of the hardships of travel in a foreign country, and accompanied only by his wife, Golding set out on a new adventure. It was, of course, an exhausting experience, both physically and emotionally, perhaps even spiritually. Golding learned that like other men, he was a prisoner of his own metaphors. He went to Egypt seeking a land of half a million dead; instead, he found that it was impossible to ignore the Egypt of the present—a country of forty million people.

The first section of *A Moving Target* ends, appropriately, with an essay that concerns itself not with one place but the earth itself. It is a review of Georg Gerster's *Grand Design: The Earth From Above* (1976). Rising beyond the demands of an occasional essay, Golding uses this opportunity to affirm his belief that man's trivial alterations to the earth's surface, seen from aerial photographs, will not outlive its natural features. "Gaia Lives: O. K.?" asks a partially optimistic Golding. Increasing knowledge of the microscopic and macroscopic nature of the earth, he hopes, will change sensibilities. And this, in turn, will enhance life on earth for all.

The article "Crabbed Youth and Age" (in the "Ideas" section) provides Golding with another forum and an opportunity to comment upon the influence of war on modern consciousness. It is a review of Paul Fussell's *The Great War and Modern Memory* (1975). Quite provocative, thinks Golding, is Fussell's acute and subtle per-

ception of the effects of the two world wars upon modern consciousness. At the level of consciousness, life continues to be frivolous, even cynical. However, our conceptual life manifests deep concerns of the soul. It is possible, opines Golding, that science discovered black holes in space because man had already invented them in inner space. If this is so, then black holes will probably be a part of the mythology of the future.

"The act of creation is a fierce, concentrated light that plays on a small area," writes Golding, and "though different from other capacities of the human spirit, is not to be set above them." This creative act he calls "Rough Magic," also the title of the essay that includes the sentence quoted. The essay was written in 1977 at the University of Kent. Because artists such as Jane Austen, John Steinbeck, Thomas Hardy, Charles Dickens, and Henry James were novelists, they observed, says Golding, a major convention of novel writing. They made their characters so alive that they seem to live on the page. Absorbed in the craft of writing, such novelists were generally too busy creating characters to write about how they wrote. Perhaps it is because Golding, like these other artists, has better things to offer in the form of his novels than in explanations of how he works that he has been so reticent about himself.

The first of the three final essays in *A Moving Target* gives its name to this book and was originally his May 1976 address to the group "Les Anglicistes" in Rouen. Golding discloses that as a writer he does not choose his themes; rather, the theme chooses him. Golding is the moving target. Having himself been a part of academe as college student and university writer in residence, and having written reviews, essays, and articles for magazines, periodicals, and newspapers, Golding knows, firsthand, of the cross-fertilization that occurs between the world of academe and that of journalism. For him, then, the story of the novel is in part the story of the mixture of creativity and analysis, of mythology and psychology.

It is not surprising that in a 1977 address to Les Anglicistes in Lille, Golding seems concerned that he is being identified as an anti-utopian novelist. It is in this address, entitled "Utopia and Antiutopia," that he identifies the varied types of analysis to which his novels have been subjected. Implicit in his criticism is his dislike of the pigeonholing tendency of academic criticism. Such an approach fails to make essential connections.

Golding with a copy of A Moving Target *(1982), his second collection of essays, for which he was awarded the McConnell Prize (photograph by Carole Latimer)*

Perhaps it is partly in response to his being so closely identified with the darker side of man portrayed in his novels that in "Belief and Creativity" Golding gives what may be seen as an affirmation of faith. And perhaps it is not accidental either that this 1980 essay was written in Hamburg. Looking back over the violence of the last thirty years, he states his belief that such violence was the expression of a revolt influenced by several things: man's exploitation of others; his sexual frustration; and the scientific process of natural selection operating in human society. However, beyond these explanations, and whether the revolutionary or terrorist knew it or not, man's revolt was against reductionism. Golding asserts that beyond such "transient horrors and beauties of our hell" lies hope. Such a revolt is a sign that human creativity will startle into new life, even in the midst of confusion and turmoil. Indeed, there is yet another reason for hope. For, concludes Golding, such a happening—ambivalent though it may be as an expression of human creativity—is only possible if there is a God that is ultimate and absolute.

As essayist and journalist, Golding is always accessible. As novelist, he is generally demanding. Most of his travel pieces are magazine-type essays and hence largely descriptive. However, the essays that make up his two collections are purged and expanded beyond the occasion out of which they arose and show Golding the essayist at his best. Wide-ranging and lucid, these essays are written on topics that remain alive, and even when they deal with deplorable human failings, good nature and humor lighten them. It is this side of Golding that has begun to filter through into the later novels.

Interviews:

Anonymous, "Portrait," *Time*, 70 (9 September 1957): 118;

Owen Webster, "Living with Chaos," *Books and Art* (March 1958): 15-16;

Frank Kermode, "The Meaning of It All," *Books and Bookmen* (October 1959): 9-10;

Owen Webster, "The Cosmic Outlook of an Original Novelist," *John O'London's* (28 January 1960): 7;

John W. Aldridge, "Mr. Golding's Own Story," *New York Times Book Review* (10 December 1961): 56-57;

"The Well Built House," in *Authors Talking* (London: BBC Broadwater Press, 1961);

Maurice Dolbier, "Running J. D. Salinger a Close Second," *New York Herald Tribune Books* (20 May 1962): 6, 15;

Douglas M. Davis, "Golding, the Optimist, Belies His Somber Pictures and Fiction," *National Observer*, 1 (7 September 1962): 4;

Anonymous, "*Lord of the Flies* Goes to College," *New Republic*, 148 (4 May 1963): 27-28, 29-30;

Davis, "A Conversation with William Golding," *New Republic*, 148 (4 May 1963): 28-30;

James Keating, "The Purdue Interview of William Golding," in the *Casebook Edition of William Golding's "Lord of the Flies,"* edited by James R. Baker and Arthur P. Ziegler, Jr. (New York: Putnam's, 1964);

Bernard F. Dick, "The Novelist Is a Displaced Person: An Interview with William Golding," *College English*, 26 (March 1965): 481-482;

Jack I. Biles, *Talk: Conversations with William Golding* (New York: Harcourt Brace Jovanovich, 1970).

Bibliographies:

James R. Baker, Bibliography, in *William Golding: A Critical Study* (New York: St. Martin's, 1965);

Jack I. Biles, "A William Golding Checklist," *Twentieth Century Literature*, 17 (April 1971): 107-122;

J. Don Vann, "William Golding: A Checklist of Criticism," *Serif*, 8 (June 1971): 21-26.

References:

Howard S. Babb, *The Novels of William Golding* (Columbus: Ohio State University Press, 1970);

James R. Baker, *William Golding: A Critical Study* (New York: St. Martin's, 1965);

Bernard F. Dick, *William Golding* (New York: Twayne, 1967);

Ian Gregor and Mark Kinkead-Weekes, *William Golding: A Critical Study* (London: Faber & Faber, 1967);

Arnold Johnston, *Of Earth and Darkness* (Columbia: University of Missouri Press, 1980);

R. Jones, "William Golding: Genius and Sublime Silly-Billy," *Virginia Quarterly Review*, 60 (Autumn 1984): 675-687;

Frank Kermode, *Puzzles and Epiphanies: Essays and Reviews 1958-1961* (London: Routledge & Kegan Paul, 1962);

Stephen Medcalf, *William Golding* (Essex, U.K.: Longmans, 1975);

William Nelson, *William Golding's "Lord of the Flies": A Source Book* (New York: Odyssey, 1963);

Bernard S. Oldsey and Stanley Weintraub, *The Art of William Golding* (New York: Harcourt, Brace & World, 1965);

Philip Redpath, *William Golding* (Totowa, N.J.: Barnes & Noble, 1986);

Virginia Tiger, *William Golding: The Dark Fields of Discovery* (London: Calder & Boyars, 1974).

Robert Graves

(24 July 1895 - 7 December 1985)

Angus Somerville
Brock University

See also the Graves entries in *DLB 20: British Poets, 1914-1945* and *DLB Yearbook: 1985*.

SELECTED BOOKS: *Over the Brazier* (London: Poetry Bookshop, 1916; New York: St. Martin's Press, 1975);

Goliath and David (London: Chiswick Press, 1916);

Fairies and Fusiliers (London: Heinemann, 1917; New York: Knopf, 1918);

Treasure Box (London: Chiswick Press, 1919);

Country Sentiment (London: Secker, 1920; New York: Knopf, 1920);

The Pier-Glass (London: Secker, 1921; New York: Knopf, 1921);

On English Poetry: Being an Irregular Approach to the Psychology of This Art, from Evidence Mainly Subjective (New York: Knopf, 1922; London: Heinemann, 1922);

Whipperginny (London: Heinemann, 1923; New York: Knopf, 1923);

The Feather Bed (Richmond, U.K.: Hogarth Press, 1923);

Mock Beggar Hall (London: Hogarth Press, 1924);

The Meaning of Dreams (London: Palmer, 1924; New York: Greenberg, 1925);

Poetic Unreason and Other Studies (London: Palmer, 1925; New York: Biblo & Tannen, 1968);

John Kemp's Wager: A Ballad Opera (Oxford: Blackwell, 1925; New York: French, 1925);

My Head! My Head!: Being the History of Elisha and the Shunamite Woman (London: Secker, 1925; New York: Knopf, 1925);

Contemporary Techniques of Poetry: A Political Analogy (London: Hogarth Press, 1925; Folcroft, Pa.: Folcroft Library Editions, 1971);

Welchman's Hose (London: Fleuron, 1925; Folcroft, Pa.: Folcroft Library Editions, 1971);

The Marmosite's Miscellany, as John Doyle (London: Hogarth Press, 1925);

Another Future of Poetry (London: Hogarth Press, 1926);

Impenetrability; or, The Proper Habit of English (London: Hogarth Press, 1926);

Robert Graves (photograph by Tom Blau)

Lars Porsena; or, The Future of Swearing and Improper Language (London: Paul, Trench, Trübner / New York: Dutton, 1927); revised as *The Future of Swearing and Improper Language* (London: Paul, Trench, Trübner, 1936);

Poems (1914-1926) (London: Heinemann, 1927; Garden City, N.Y.: Doubleday, Doran, 1929);

Poems (1914-1927) (London: Heinemann, 1927);

Lawrence and the Arabs (London: Cape, 1927); republished as *Lawrence and the Arabian Adventure* (Garden City, N.Y.: Doubleday, Doran, 1928); republished as *Lawrence and the Arabs: Concise Edition* (London & Toronto: Cape, 1934);

A Survey of Modernist Poetry, by Graves and Laura Riding (London: Heinemann, 1927; Garden City, N.Y.: Doubleday, Doran, 1928);

A Pamphlet against Anthologies, by Graves and Riding (London: Cape, 1928; Garden City, N.Y.: Doubleday, Doran, 1928);

Mrs. Fisher; or, The Future of Humour (London: Paul, Trench, Trübner / New York: Dutton, 1928);

The Shout (London: Mathews & Marrot, 1929; Folcroft, Pa.: Folcroft Library Editions, 1977);

Good-Bye to All That: An Autobiography (London: Cape, 1929; New York: Cape & Smith, 1930; revised edition, Garden City, N.Y.: Doubleday, 1957; London: Cassell, 1957);

Poems, 1929 (London: Seizin Press, 1929);

Ten Poems More (Paris: Hours Press, 1930);

But It Still Goes On: An Accumulation (London & Toronto: Cape, 1930; New York: Cape & Smith, 1931);

Poems, 1926-1930 (London: Heinemann, 1931);

To Whom Else? (Deyá, Majorca: Seizin Press, 1931; Folcroft, Pa.: Folcroft Library Editions, 1971);

No Decency Left, by Graves and Riding, as Barbara Rich (London: Cape, 1932);

Poems, 1930-1933 (London: Barker, 1933);

I, Claudius: From the Autobiography of Tiberius Claudius, Emperor of the Romans, Born B.C. 10, Murdered and Deified A.D. 54 (London: Barker, 1934; New York: Smith & Haas, 1934);

Claudius, the God and His Wife Messalina (London: Barker, 1934; New York: Smith & Haas, 1935);

"Antigua, Penny, Puce" (Deyá, Majorca: Seizin Press / London: Constable, 1936); republished as *The Antigua Stamp* (New York: Random House, 1937);

Count Belisarius (London, Toronto, Melbourne & Sydney: Cassell, 1938; New York: Random House, 1938);

Collected Poems (London, Toronto, Melbourne & Sydney: Cassell, 1938; New York: Random House, 1939);

No More Ghosts: Selected Poems (London: Faber & Faber, 1940);

Sergeant Lamb of the Ninth (London: Methuen, 1940); republished as *Sergeant Lamb's America* (New York: Random House, 1940);

The Long Week-End: A Social History of Great Britain, 1918-1939, by Graves and Alan Hodge (London: Faber & Faber, 1940; New York: Macmillan, 1941);

Pastel drawing by Eric Kennington of Graves in his World War I uniform

Proceed, Sergeant Lamb (London: Methuen, 1941; New York: Random House, 1941);

Work in Hand, by Graves, Hodge, and Norman Cameron (London: Hogarth Press, 1942);

The Story of Marie Powell, Wife to Mr. Milton (London, Toronto, Melbourne & Sydney: Cassell, 1943); republished as *Wife to Mr. Milton: The Story of Marie Powell* (New York: Creative Age Press, 1944);

The Reader over Your Shoulder: A Handbook for Writers of English Prose, by Graves and Hodge (London: Cape, 1943; New York: Macmillan, 1943; revised and abridged edition, London: Cape, 1947; New York: Vintage, 1979);

The Golden Fleece (London, Toronto, Melbourne & Sydney: Cassell, 1944); republished as *Hercules, My Shipmate: A Novel* (New York: Creative Age Press, 1945);

King Jesus (New York: Creative Age Press, 1946; London, Toronto, Melbourne & Sydney: Cassell, 1946);

Poems, 1938-1945 (London, Toronto, Melbourne & Sydney: Cassell, 1946; New York: Creative Age Press, 1946);

Collected Poems (1914-1947) (London, Toronto, Melbourne & Sydney: Cassell, 1948);

The White Goddess: A Historical Grammar of Poetic Myth (London: Faber & Faber, 1948; New York: Creative Age Press, 1948; revised and enlarged edition, London: Faber & Faber, 1952; New York: Vintage, 1958; revised and enlarged again, London: Faber & Faber, 1961);

Watch the North Wind Rise (New York: Creative Age Press, 1949); republished as *Seven Days in New Crete: A Novel* (London, Toronto, Melbourne, Sydney & Wellington: Cassell, 1949);

The Common Asphodel: Collected Essays on Poetry, 1922-1949 (London: Hamilton, 1949; Folcroft, Pa.: Folcroft Press, 1969);

The Islands of Unwisdom (Garden City, N.Y.: Doubleday, 1949); republished as *The Isles of Unwisdom* (London, Toronto, Melbourne, Sydney & Wellington: Cassell, 1950);

Occupation: Writer (New York: Creative Age Press, 1950; London: Cassell, 1951);

Poems and Satires, 1951 (London: Cassell, 1951);

Poems, 1953 (London: Cassell, 1953);

The Nazarene Gospel Restored, by Graves and Joshua Podro (London: Cassell, 1953; Garden City, N.Y.: Doubleday, 1954);

Homer's Daughter (London: Cassell, 1955; Garden City, N.Y.: Doubleday, 1955);

The Greek Myths, 2 volumes (Harmondsworth, U.K.: Penguin, 1955; Baltimore: Penguin, 1955);

Collected Poems 1955 (Garden City, N.Y.: Doubleday, 1955);

Adam's Rib and Other Anomalous Elements in the Hebrew Creation Myth: A New View (London: Trianon Press, 1955; New York: Yoseloff, 1958);

The Crowning Privilege: The Clark Lectures 1954-1955. Also Various Essays on Poetry and Sixteen New Poems (London: Cassell, 1955); revised as *The Crowning Privilege: Collected Essays on Poetry* (Garden City, N.Y.: Doubleday, 1956);

¡Catacrok!: Mostly Stories, Mostly Funny (London: Cassell, 1956);

Jesus in Rome: A Historical Conjecture, by Graves and Podro (London: Cassell, 1957);

They Hanged My Saintly Billy (London: Cassell, 1957; Garden City, N.Y.: Doubleday, 1957);

5 Pens in Hand (Garden City, N.Y.: Doubleday, 1958);

The Poems of Robert Graves Chosen by Himself (Garden City, N.Y.: Doubleday, 1958);

Steps: Stories, Talks, Essays, Poems, Studies in History (London: Cassell, 1958);

Collected Poems, 1959 (London: Cassell, 1959);

Food for Centaurs: Stories, Talks, Critical Studies, Poems (Garden City, N.Y.: Doubleday, 1960);

Greek Gods and Heroes (Garden City, N.Y.: Doubleday, 1960); republished as *Myths of Ancient Greece* (London: Cassell, 1961);

The Penny Fiddle: Poems for Children (London: Cassell, 1960; Garden City, N.Y.: Doubleday, 1961);

More Poems, 1961 (London: Cassell, 1961);

Collected Poems (Garden City, N.Y.: Doubleday, 1961);

Oxford Addresses on Poetry (London: Cassell, 1962; Garden City, N.Y.: Doubleday, 1962);

The Big Green Book (New York: Crowell-Collier, 1962; Harmondsworth, U.K.: Puffin, 1978);

New Poems, 1962 (London: Cassell, 1962; Garden City, N.Y.: Doubleday, 1963);

The More Deserving Cases: Eighteen Old Poems for Reconsideration (Marlborough, U.K.: Marlborough College Press, 1962; Folcroft, Pa.: Folcroft Press, 1969);

The Siege and Fall of Troy (London: Cassell, 1962; Garden City, N.Y.: Doubleday, 1963);

Nine Hundred Iron Chariots (Cambridge: Massachusetts Institute of Technology, 1963);

Hebrew Myths: The Book of Genesis, by Graves and Raphael Patai (Garden City, N.Y.: Doubleday, 1964; London: Cassell, 1964);

Collected Short Stories (Garden City, N.Y.: Doubleday, 1964; London: Cassell, 1965);

Man Does, Woman Is (London: Cassell, 1964; Garden City, N.Y.: Doubleday, 1964);

Ann at Highwood Hall: Poems for Children (London: Cassell, 1964; Garden City, N.Y.: Doubleday, 1966);

Love Respelt (London: Cassell, 1964; Garden City, N.Y.: Doubleday, 1966);

Mammon: Oration Delivered at the London School of Economics and Political Science on Friday, 6 December 1963 (London: London School of Economics and Political Science, 1964);

Mammon and the Black Goddess (London: Cassell, 1965; Garden City, N.Y.: Doubleday, 1965);

Majorca Observed, by Graves and Paul Hogarth (London: Cassell, 1965; Garden City, N.Y.: Doubleday, 1965);

Collected Poems, 1965 (London: Cassell, 1965; Garden City, N.Y.: Doubleday, 1966);

Two Wise Children (New York: Quist, 1966; London: Allen, 1967);

17 Poems Missing from Love Respelt (London: Rota, 1966);

Colophon to Love Respelt (London: Rota, 1967);

Poetic Craft and Principle: Lectures and Talks (London: Cassell, 1967);

Poems, 1965-1968 (London: Cassell, 1968; Garden City, N.Y.: Doubleday, 1969);

The Poor Boy Who Followed His Star (London: Cassell, 1968; Garden City, N.Y.: Doubleday, 1969);

The Crane Bag, and Other Disputed Subjects (London: Cassell, 1969);

On Poetry: Collected Talks and Essays (Garden City, N.Y.: Doubleday, 1969);

Beyond Giving: Poems (London: Rota, 1969);

Poems about Love (London: Cassell, 1969; Garden City, N.Y.: Doubleday, 1969);

Love Respelt Again (Garden City, N.Y.: Doubleday, 1969);

Poems, 1968-1970 (London: Cassell, 1970; Garden City, N.Y.: Doubleday, 1971);

The Green-Sailed Vessel: Poems (London: Rota, 1971);

Poems: Abridged for Dolls and Princes (London: Cassell, 1971; Garden City, N.Y.: Doubleday, 1971);

Poems, 1970-1972 (London: Cassell, 1972; Garden City, N.Y.: Doubleday, 1973);

Difficult Questions, Easy Answers (London: Cassell, 1972; Garden City, N.Y.: Doubleday, 1973);

Timeless Meeting: Poems (London: Rota, 1973);

At the Gate: Poems (London: Rota, 1974);

Collected Poems, 1975 (London: Cassell, 1975); republished as *New Collected Poems* (Garden City, N.Y.: Doubleday, 1977);

An Ancient Castle, edited by William David Thomas (London: Owen, 1980; New York: Kesend, 1981);

Eleven Songs (Deyá, Majorca: New Seizin Press, 1983).

OTHER: *Oxford Poetry 1921*, edited by Graves, Alan Porter, and Richard Hughes (Oxford: Blackwell, 1921);

The Winter Owl, edited by Graves (London: Palmer, 1923);

The English Ballad: A Short Critical Survey, edited by Graves (London: Benn, 1927); revised as *English and Scottish Ballads* (New York: Macmillan, 1957; London: Heinemann, 1957);

John Skelton (Laureate), edited by Graves (London: Benn, 1927);

The Less Familiar Nursery Rhymes, edited by Graves (London: Benn, 1927);

Charles Dickens, *The Real David Copperfield*, edited by Graves (London: Barker, 1933); republished as *David Copperfield, by Charles Dickens, Condensed by Robert Graves*, edited by Merrill P. Paine (New York & Chicago: Harcourt, Brace, 1934);

Frank Richards, *Old Soldiers Never Die*, rewritten by Graves (London: Faber & Faber, 1933);

Richards, *Old-Soldier Sahib*, rewritten by Graves (London: Faber & Faber, 1936; New York: Smith & Haas, 1936);

Thomas Edward Lawrence, *T. E. Lawrence to His Biographer, Robert Graves: Information about Himself in the Form of Letters, Notes and Answers to Questions, Edited with a Critical Commentary*, edited by Graves (New York: Doubleday, Doran, 1938);

Algernon Charles Swinburne, *An Old Saying: Poem*, foreword by Graves (Washington, D.C.: Mayfield, 1947);

The Comedies of Terence, edited by Graves (Garden City, N.Y.: Doubleday, 1962; London: Cassell, 1963).

TRANSLATIONS: Georg Schwarz, *Almost Forgotten Germany*, translated by Graves and Laura Riding (Deyá, Majorca: Seizin Press / London: Constable, 1936);

Lucius Apuleius, *The Transformations of Lucius, Otherwise Known as The Golden Ass* (Harmondsworth, U.K.: Penguin, 1950; New York: Farrar, Straus & Young, 1951);

Manuel de Jesús Galván, *The Cross and the Sword* (Bloomington: Indiana University Press, 1955; London: Gollancz, 1956);

Pedro Antonio de Alarcón, *The Infant with the Globe* (London: Trianon Press, 1955; New York & London: Yoseloff, 1955);

George Sand, *Winter in Majorca*, with José Quadrado's "Refutation of George Sand" (London: Cassell, 1956);

Lucan Pharsalia, *Dramatic Episodes of the Civil War* (Harmondsworth, U.K.: Penguin, 1956; Baltimore: Penguin, 1957);

Suetonius, *The Twelve Caesars* (Harmondsworth, U.K.: Penguin, 1956; Baltimore: Penguin, 1957);

Homer, *The Anger of Achilles: Homer's Iliad* (Garden City, N.Y.: Doubleday, 1959; London: Cassell, 1960);

Graves in 1923

The Rubáiyát of Omar Khayyám, translated by Graves and Omar Ali-Shah (London: Cassell, 1967);

The Song of Songs (New York: Potter, 1973; London: Collins, 1973).

Robert Graves's reputation must rest chiefly on his poetry and historical fiction; as an essayist he is extremely uneven. His essays are generally polemical, frequently eccentric. As a literary critic he is at times judicious, more often idiosyncratic, and sometimes prejudiced. Nonetheless, his critical essays provide a fascinating commentary on the forces which shaped him as a poet. His humorous and polemical essays add up to a coherent criticism of the "goddawfulness" of "all that"–the spiritual and moral poverty of the modern England which he abandoned for Majorca. His frequent adventures into anthropology and mythology in search of his White Goddess are to be seen not merely as a reflection of his complex relation-

ships with women but chiefly as an attempt to erect a personal poetic mythology over against the various mythologies, both religious and scientific, of the modern world. The joy and ecstasy of goddess worship are his defense against the rational and patriarchal myths of the present age. Much of Graves's occasional prose must be regarded as hackwork, produced to pay the bills. But everyone must pay bills, and the hackwork is never less than intelligent and witty, never other than obviously written by Robert Graves.

Robert von Ranke Graves was born in Wimbledon, England, on 24 July 1895 to Alfred Perceval and Amalie von Ranke Graves. After attending various preparatory schools he went to Charterhouse. Although an occasional master, such as George Mallory, won Graves's respect and affection, Charterhouse seemed to him a stultifying experience; it hardly made him eager to go up to Oxford, to which he won a scholarship in 1914, for more of the same. World War I intervened, and in August 1914 Graves enlisted as a junior officer in the Royal Welch Fusiliers. The war had a lasting effect on Graves, as his essays on the topic show. His autobiography, *Good-Bye to All That* (1929)–perhaps the best book to emerge from the war–and his war poems do not minimize the traumatic effect of the war upon him but avoid the Georgian nostalgias and the bitterness of many contemporary works dealing with similar experiences. In 1919 Graves was demobilized, neurasthenic, and having trouble with his lungs. He went to Oxford with his wife, the former Nancy Nicholson, whom he had married on 23 January 1918, and received a special dispensation to write a B.Litt. thesis instead of completing the usual B.A.

Graves's earliest published prose is largely literary criticism and may be divided into two groups: that published before his collaboration with Laura Riding and that written during the collaboration. The first group begins with *On English Poetry* (1922). Graves was powerfully influenced by W. H. R. Rivers, a neurologist he met in Edinburgh. The influence shows itself in the fact that the book is more concerned with the psychological processes of composition than with poetry itself. Graves must be among the earliest writers to apply Freudian theory to poetry, which he sees as originating in the fusion of ideas in the subconscious. Graves betrays his essentially romantic attitude to poetry in his suspicion of the analytical mind and of rational, classical poetry. *The Meaning of Dreams* (1924) is a misguided and unsuccessful attempt to popularize Freudian dream theory. In *Poetic Unreason and Other Studies* (1925), the published version of his B.Litt. thesis, Graves continues to extol the irrational, associative elements of romantic poetry at the expense of classical rationality. Romantic poetry, Graves argues, partakes of the nature of dream and is produced when the poet is in a trancelike state. Such poetry is best analyzed as the psychoanalyst approaches his investigations. Though Graves was never to relinquish his belief in the poetic trance and his championship of the irrational element in poetry, he later abandoned "scientific" Freudianism as an approach to poetry. *Contemporary Techniques of Poetry: A Political Analogy* (1925) carries on the distinction between classical and romantic poetry on the analogy of the political right and left, with the Georgians as a species of liberals. Graves sees himself as being somewhat left of center. *Another Future of Poetry* (1926) defends modern poetry against two charges: first, that since it

ceased to be oral, poetry has ceased to be powerful; second, that it has lost touch with the modern interest in science, which is better satisfied by prose. Graves argues that modern poetry appeals to all the senses, not merely hearing, and that prose, by its nature, cannot appeal to the feelings as poetry does. Graves also wonders whether modern man is seriously interested in science anyway. Other pieces from this period are *Impenetrability; or, The Proper Habit of English* (1926), which later grew into *The Reader over Your Shoulder* (1943), written in collaboration with Alan Hodge; and *The English Ballad* (1927), which reflects Graves's love of English folk song. One noncritical work deserves mention: in *Lars Porsena; or, The Future of Swearing and Improper Language* (1927) the real topic is the "goddawfulness" of "all that." Graves is less concerned with the future of obscenity than with the standards according to which people judge something to be obscene; it is in these standards that Graves finds the real obscenity. Ingenious euphemisms for the private parts, for instance, are for Graves truly obscene.

In 1926 Graves met Laura Riding, an American poet with whom he had already corresponded. Graves's wife was an independent woman, even something of a feminist; Riding was all of that to an extreme degree. She exercised a powerful influence on Graves; her sense of the meaning of her femininity and Graves's near adulation of her probably shaped some of the ideas which developed into *The White Goddess* (1948). The first fruit of Graves's collaboration with her was *A Survey of Modernist Poetry* (1927), which is close to being Graves's finest critical work. The book defends new poetry against the charge that it ignores the plain reader's rights by being obscure: the fault lies with the ordinary reader, who confuses simplicity and easy intelligibility with clarity and is unwilling to make the intellectual and imaginative effort demanded by great poetry. Perhaps the most significant point is the distinction made between modern poetry and modernist poetry. Modern poetry is desperately anxious to be contemporary and up-to-date, and it spawns "dead movements" such as Imagism. True modernist poetry, on the other hand, "should mean no more than fresh poetry, more poetry, poetry based on honest invention rather than on conscientious imitation of the time-spirit." Only two poets pass the Graves-Riding test with flying colors–Gerard Manley Hopkins and E. E. Cummings. The care with which Graves and Riding scrutinize text influenced the New Criticism. That care is not always evident in Graves's later criticism.

In the same year, 1927, Graves published *Lawrence and the Arabs*, which he had written in six weeks as a money-making venture. T. E. Lawrence himself gave Graves advice during the writing of the book, partly because he preferred that Graves produce the popular account of his life and partly because he wanted to help Graves earn some money. Perhaps understandably, adulation and potboiling predominate in the tone of the book.

In 1928 came *A Pamphlet against Anthologies*, written with Riding. The authors say that they have no objection to the private anthology; the published anthology, however, has a pernicious influence: the personal taste of the anthologist becomes, in the reader's perception, a judgment of the nature of English poetry. The taste or idiosyncrasy of the anthologist is certain to distort both the history of poetry and the reputation of individual poets. The *truth* about poetry and poets vanishes in anthologies. Worse, the shape of very popular anthologies, such as Francis Turner Palgrave's *Golden Treasury of the Best Songs and Lyrical Poems in the English Language* (1861; revised and enlarged, 1891), may subvert the nature of poetry by encouraging the writing of poems which seem designed to fit such an anthology. Anthologies may foster a corrupt taste in poetry even among poets. As an example of this taste Graves and Riding subject William Butler Yeats's "Lake Isle of Innisfree" to a devastating analysis. The pamphlet is savage and witty. Also in 1928 appeared *Mrs. Fisher; or, The Future of Humour*, which resembles *Lars Porsena* in being less concerned with the future than the awfulness of contemporary humor. The grotesquerie of what people find funny is the target of Graves's almost sociological analysis.

In 1929 Graves published *Good-Bye to All That*, his autobiography. Shortly afterward he departed to Majorca with Riding, fleeing England and a ruined marriage. Paul Fussell, in *The Great War and Modern Memory* (1975), sees *Good-Bye to All That* as less memoir than comedy of manners in the best Jonsonian tradition. As Fussell argues, Graves is less concerned with giving a factual account of his life than with depicting both school and war as stages admirably designed for the display of knaves and fools. The ironic and farcical elements of Graves's treatment of war, Fussell notes, had a strong influence on both Evelyn Waugh and Joseph Heller.

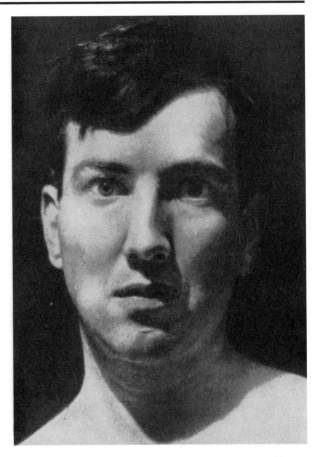

Graves in 1929, the year he moved to Majorca with Laura Riding

The Spanish civil war forced Graves to leave Majorca in 1939. During a brief trip to the United States that year his association with Laura Riding ended. During World War II Graves lived in England with Beryl Hodge, whom he married in May 1950. In collaboration with Beryl's husband, Alan Hodge, Graves wrote *The Long Week-End* (1940) and *The Reader over Your Shoulder*. The first is a social history of England between the wars; the second is an immensely readable handbook for writers of English prose.

The White Goddess is Graves's search for his muse through the mythology of Europe. The White Goddess is mother, lover, layer-out of the dead—gentle and destructive. She is the goddess of the matriarchy which, according to Graves, existed before the present patriarchy in both society and religion. All true poetry celebrates some aspect of what Graves calls "The Theme": "The Theme, briefly, is the antique story . . . of the birth, life, death, and resurrection of the God of the Waxing Year; the central chapters concern the God's losing battle with the God of the Waning Year for the love of the powerful threefold Goddess, their mother, bride and layer-out. The poet identifies himself with the God of the Waxing Year and his Muse with the Goddess; the rival is his blood-brother, his other self, his weird." But according to Graves, the Goddess was displaced by the coming of patriarchy with its male gods. At that point the Muses become "nine little departmental goddesses of inspiration" until Apollo "delegates their functions to male gods who are himself in multiplication.... With that, poetry becomes academic and decays until the Muse chooses to reassert her power in what are called Romantic Revivals." For Graves, true and romantic poetry is worship of the Muse by entranced poets. Keats, for instance, finds the Muse in "La Belle Dame sans Merci." Apollonian poets are academic, formal, rational. From our Apollonian world there is no lasting escape "until the industrial system breaks down for some reason or other . . . and nature reasserts herself with grass and trees among the ruins." A brief account cannot capture the erudition and dazzling eccentricity of this work. At the heart of it, however, is Graves's identification of his Goddess as the enemy of "all that." How faithful Graves remained to the anthropological sources of his work is debatable.

Graves's first collection of essays, *The Common Asphodel*, appeared in 1949. All the essays are literary criticism and represent what Graves wanted to preserve from his earlier critical work. He largely retained the practical observations on poetry but suppressed the Freudian theories, which he no longer accepted. There are a few essays from *Epilogue*, a miscellany edited by Graves and Riding between 1935 and 1937. "Coleridge and Wordsworth" recounts the pathetic fate of Coleridge at the hands of "friends" who were only too willing to use him. "Keats and Shelley" shows the influence of the ideas that are the mainstay of *The White Goddess*. For Keats, poetry was "a dominant female" in pursuit of "the shrinking, womanish poet with masculine lustfulness." Shelley, by attempting to combine philosophy with poetry, ended up as a spiritual hermaphrodite. "Poetry and Politics" argues that poetry is diminished if it attends to local, political causes. For instance, the Middle English poem *The Vision of William Concerning Piers Plowman*, attributed to William Langland, "was not a poem, but something between a work of philosophical speculation . . . and a diatribe." Chaucer, however, separated his political opinions from his poetic energies. As always the in-

dependence of poetry from the temporal and local is central to Graves's criticism.

Occupation: Writer (1950) is Graves's first large miscellany; it includes the occasional essays from the 1940s which Graves wished to preserve, short stories, and two plays. "Lars Porsena" and "Mrs. Fisher" appear in their final form. Several essays are explorations of Graves's determination to be himself, to judge for himself–some might say to be as eccentric as he chose. That determination underlies the whimsicality of "Charity Appeals," which presents the criteria according to which Graves responds to such appeals: "I always give to nuns because they have quiet melancholy voices; I never give to the Salvation Army because they have loud, happy ones." The concluding sentence is a perfect example of the tone and attitude of the essay: "I always give money to beggar-women with babies, because babies are very troublesome things to carry, even if they are borrowed." In "The Cult of Tolerance" Graves defends his right to be intolerant in defense of truth, saying that there "is no reason for regarding all truth as relative. To do so would make truth and fancy equivalent. Yet the relativity of truth is a fundamental tenet of modern liberal thought–the emergence of tolerance as a positive cult." Slightly bitter humor marks "Colonel Blimp's Ancestors," a historical survey of the persistence of incompetence in the British officer class from the Anglo-Saxon period until World War II. Graves's sympathy with feminism comes out in "-Ess," which concludes that employment of the feminine suffix has "a ring of male prejudice in it." "Pharaoh's Chariot Wheels" is a learned if idiosyncratic inquiry into the historical basis of the Exodus story. As so often, Graves finds traces of early goddess worship behind it. The essay reflects Graves's lasting fascination with the elucidation of biblical and other mythologies, which also informs such works as *King Jesus* (1946), *The White Goddess*, and *The Nazarene Gospel Restored* (1953).

The Crowning Privilege (1955) collects Graves's Clark Lectures of 1954-1955, some critical essays, and sixteen poems. The Clark Lectures are uneven and break little new critical ground. To be true to the Muse is the crowning privilege: Dryden and Pope, Apollonian poets, betrayed the Muse; Wordsworth postponed his treason until late in life. "These Be Your Gods, O Israel!" is a violent assault on "five living idols." Graves says of Yeats: "Instead of the Muse, he employed a ventriloquist's dummy called Crazy Jane. But

Graves at his home in Majorca (photograph by Baron)

he still had nothing to say." Ezra Pound is distinguished by a patchy education and barbarity. Of T. S. Eliot he says: "At any rate, what I like most about Eliot is that though one of his two hearts, the poetic one, has died . . . he continues to visit the grave wistfully and lay flowers on it." W. H. Auden is accused of plagiarizing from Riding. Dylan Thomas disguises insincerity beneath his rich, Welsh music. Some of the shots are cheap and carping, some of the criticism less than careful. "The Poet and His Public" is a succinct declaration of the poet's independence: "Frankly, honest Public, I am not professionally concerned with you, and expect nothing from you. Please give me no bouquets and I will give you no signed photographs."

Two miscellanies with overlapping contents, *Steps* and *5 Pens in Hand*, were published in 1958; the first appeared in Britain, the second in the United States. Both contain stories, talks, essays, and poems. "Pandora's Box and Eve's Apple" is a review of *Pandora's Box: The Changing Aspects of a Mythical Symbol* (1956) by Dora and Erwin Panof-

sky. In the course of the essay Graves learnedly argues that Pandora was a title of the triple Mother-Goddess Gaia or Rhea who was worshiped by the pre-Homeric inhabitants of Greece and says that the Church Fathers were right to see an analogy between Pandora and Eve. Reviewing *Wales and the Arthurian Legend* (1956) in "The Golden Roofs of Sinadon," Graves complains that the author, R. S. Loomis, has failed to recognize the matriarchal myth contained in the tenth-century Welsh poem *The Spoils of Annwn*. Sir Herbert Read is chastized in "An Eminent Collaborationist" for the use of psychoanalytical techniques in literary criticism. "The Fifth Column at Troy" suggests that the Palladium was surrendered to Ajax and Odysseus by a fifth column of Thracian priestesses in Troy who were anxious that it should not fall into Agamemnon's hands. Among the essays which appear in *Steps* alone, "Was Benedict Arnold a Traitor?" elegantly and persuasively rehabilitates its subject; "New Light on an Old Murder," based on Gordon Wasson's work on the role of mushroom cults in primitive religion, con-

Graves in later years (photograph by Cordelia Weedon)

cludes that the Roman emperor Claudius I was poisoned by *amanita phalloides*. In "What Food the Centaurs Ate" Graves argues that Dionysus was once a mushroom god in the service of the Great Goddess and that ambrosia was a hallucinogenic mushroom. Graves finds traces of the sacred mushroom in myths from all over Europe and the Middle East: for example, Samson's three hundred foxes, it is suggested, were actually hallucinogenic mushrooms consumed by his soldiers. The mushroom is regarded by Graves as an important element in the mysteries and frenzy associated with the worship of the Great Goddess. Of the strictly literary essays in *Steps*, "The Making and Marketing of Poetry" half-playfully but tellingly analyzes the intrusion of the standards of the consumer society into the writing of poetry in America. The "maker" makes because he wants to; the "producer" produces with an eye to the marketplace.

Food for Centaurs (1960) reprints much material from *Steps* and *5 Pens in Hand*. One new piece is "Two Studies of Scientific Atheism," a review of Bertrand Russell's *Why I Am Not a Christian* (1957) and Julian Huxley's *Religion without Revelation* (1957). Graves concludes: "As a boy, Russell invoked Apollo, the cold God of Science, to rescue him from the demons that oppressed

his childhood; Huxley in his turn, invoked Apollo to smother the social embarrassment caused by having privately felt awe for Our Lady of the Wild Things. Both now believe Apollo capable not only of superseding the senile Christian God but of initiating a new Golden Age of perfect naturalistic freedom." "The Butcher and the Cur" is a brief but chilling account of the slaughter perpetrated by Douglas Haig and David Lloyd George in World War I: "So Haig won his earldom, and Lloyd George his Khaki Election; but most of our friends had been killed and, of course, by 1938 the war had to be fought all over again."

Oxford Addresses on Poetry (1962) contains Graves's first series of lectures as professor of poetry at Oxford, a position to which he was elected in 1961. The lectures are a reworking of familiar material. The sixteenth-century English poet John Skelton is the type of the Muse poet, according to Graves. He winds up a virulent biography of Virgil, the Apollonian poet, by saying that "Virgil never consulted the Muse; he only borrowed Apollo's slide-rule." "Poetic Gold" is Graves's ironic account of his discovery that the "gold" medal he received as part of the Prince Alexander Droutzkoy Memorial Award in 1960 was, in fact, gold-plated. In "The Word Báraká" Graves takes the word to mean both divine rapture and, more domestically, the almost holy homeliness that resides in particular items, such as a cooking pot that has been used for years. Graves contrasts this quality with the calculated obsolescence of so many modern cultural and domestic products. "Poet's Paradise" tells of Graves's experience with psilocybin, a hallucinogenic mushroom extract.

In 1965 Graves published another collection of lectures and talks, *Mammon and the Black Goddess*; his 1962 Oxford lectures form a large part of the collection. In the first lecture Graves illustrates poetic vulgarity by scrutinizing some of the heartier passages of Robert Browning and Rudyard Kipling. The last two 1962 lectures recast the distinction between Apollonian and Muse poets in terms of technicians and craftsmen. In "Intimations of the Black Goddess," which combines the three Oxford Lectures of 1963, Graves says that he feels that the Black Goddess may be about to replace the White. She has neither the ferocity of Ishtar nor the complaisance of Vesta but has a new wisdom which combines the adventurousness of the one with the faith of the other and will lead the poet who has served his Muse back to "a sure instinct of love." "Mammon," an address to the London School of Economics, is Graves's personal history of money and usury. It records his ambivalent attitude to Mammon, who may be a good servant but is a bad master, one whose worship has the results that "there will always be more money tomorrow than yesterday and it will always be worth less . . . food will become progressively more insipid; goods progressively more expendable, which means less lovable." "Nine Hundred Iron Chariots" compares the mind of the scientist with that of the poet and argues typically that the truly original scientist "will see that the future of thought does not lie in the cosmical nonsense region of electronic computers but in the Paradisal region he will not be ashamed to call 'magic.' He must . . . allow full weight to the scientifically imponderable." The manner in which Graves's Goddess-worship and his attitude to women informed one another is revealed in "Real Women." A "real woman," sharing the sex of the Goddess, "neither despises nor worships man, but is proud not to have been born a man. . . . She is her own oracle of right and wrong."

Poetic Craft and Principle (1967) contains the Oxford lectures for 1964 and 1965. They add little to the picture of Graves as a critic. Marx and Mammon are the twin gods of the age, science and technology their instruments of control. *Difficult Questions, Easy Answers* (1972), Graves's last collection of essays, shows that all the old obsessions were still alive. There are accounts of soldiering and the Great War. "The Bible in Europe" is a rambling account of the historical basis of much biblical material, with St. Paul as the villain of the piece. "Goddesses and Obosoms" covers similar ground, paying particular attention to the Virgin Mary, who is described as an "obosom"–a visible manifestation of the vital force, the Great Goddess. Mary answers a need that patriarchal religion cannot satisfy. "The Universal Paradise," "Mushrooms and Religion," and "The Two Births of Dionysus" further explore the role of the mushroom in primitive ecstatic worship of the Goddess. "What Has Gone Wrong" sees the noble Olympians who displaced the Goddess as having themselves been ousted by the scum of Olympus: "namely, the pseudo-Apollo, god of uncontrolled science and technology, the pseudo-Ares . . . god of the secret police and the Khaki-Mafia and Plousios, the shameless god of Wealth who does nothing to distribute the food-surplus." Thus, "all that" is more "goddawful" than ever.

The major development in Graves's prose was from the Freudian approach of his early criticism to his discovery of the Goddess. But in both periods, the poet in his trance has a vision of a better world than the Apollonian, technological wasteland. That wasteland and those who make it are Graves's targets in all his nonfiction prose.

Letters:
In Broken Images: Selected Letters of Robert Graves, edited by Paul O'Prey (London: Hutchinson, 1982).

Bibliographies:
Fred H. Higginson, *A Bibliography of the Works of Robert Graves* (London: Vane, 1966; Hamden, Conn.: Archon, 1966);

John Woodrow Presley, "Addenda to F. H. Higginson's *Bibliography of the Works of Robert Graves*," *Papers of the Bibliographical Society of America*, 69 (1975): 568-569;

A. S. G. Edwards and Diane Tolomeo, "Robert Graves: A Check-List of His Publications, 1965-74," *Malahat Review*, 35 (1975): 168-179;

Anthony S. G. Edwards, "Further Addenda to Higginson: The Bibliography of Robert Graves," *Papers of the Bibliographical Society of America*, 71 (1977): 374-378; 75 (1981): 210-211;

Ellsworth Mason, "Emendations and Extensions of the Bibliography of Robert Graves," *Analytical and Enumerative Bibliography*, 2 (1978): 265-315.

Biography:
Martin Seymour-Smith, *Robert Graves: A Literary Biography* (London: Hutchinson, 1982); republished as *Robert Graves: His Life and Work* (New York: Holt, Rinehart & Winston, 1983).

References:
J. M. Cohen, *Robert Graves* (Edinburgh: Oliver & Boyd, 1960; New York: Grove, 1961);

Douglas Day, *Swifter than Reason: The Poetry and Criticism of Robert Graves* (Chapel Hill: University of North Carolina Press, 1963);

D. J. Enright, *Robert Graves and the Decline of Modernism* (Singapore: University of Malaya, 1960); republished in *Essays in Criticism*, 2 (1961): 319-336;

Paul Fussell, *The Great War and Modern Memory* (London & New York: Oxford University Press, 1975);

Randall Jarrell, "Graves and the White Goddess," in his *The Third Book of Criticism* (New York: Farrar, Straus & Giroux, 1966);

Patrick J. Keane, *A Wild Civility: Interactions in the Poetry and Thought of Robert Graves* (Columbia & London: University of Missouri Press, 1980);

Malahat Review, special Graves issue, edited by Robin Skelton and William David Thomas, 35 (1975);

James S. Mehoke, *Robert Graves: Peace-Weaver* (The Hague: Mouton, 1975);

Sydney Musgrove, *The Ancestry of "The White Goddess"* (Auckland, New Zealand: University of Auckland Press, 1962);

Martin Seymour-Smith, *Robert Graves* (London: Longmans, Green, 1956);

Seymour-Smith, "Robert Graves," in his *Guide to Modern World Literature* (New York: Funk & Wagnalls, 1973), pp. 244-247;

Shenandoah, special Graves issue, 13 (1962);

Katherine Snipes, *Robert Graves* (New York: Ungar, 1979);

Monroe K. Spears, "The Latest Graves: Poet and Private Eye," *Sewanee Review*, 73 (1965): 660-678;

George Stade, *Robert Graves* (New York: Columbia University Press, 1967);

George Steiner, "The Genius of Robert Graves," *Kenyon Review*, 22 (1960): 340-365;

John B. Vickery, *Robert Graves and the White Goddess* (Lincoln: University of Nebraska Press, 1972).

Papers:

An extensive collection of Robert Graves's papers is in the Graves Manuscript Collection at the University of Victoria, British Columbia. Other papers are in the Lockwood Memorial Library, State University of New York at Buffalo; the Berg Collection of the New York City Library; the Harry Ransom Humanities Research Center, University of Texas at Austin; and Southern Illinois University, at Carbondale.

Graham Greene

(2 October 1904 -)

Patrick J. Kelly
St. Thomas More College

See also the Greene entries in *DLB 13: British Dramatists Since World War II; DLB 15: British Novelists, 1930-1959; DLB 77: British Mystery Writers, 1920-1939;* and *DLB Yearbook: 1985.*

BOOKS: *Babbling April* (Oxford: Blackwell, 1925);

The Man Within (London: Heinemann, 1929; Garden City, N.Y.: Doubleday, Doran, 1929);

The Name of Action (London: Heinemann, 1930; Garden City, N.Y.: Doubleday, Doran, 1931);

Rumour at Nightfall (London: Heinemann, 1931; Garden City, N.Y.: Doubleday, Doran, 1932);

Stamboul Train (London: Heinemann, 1932; revised, 1932); republished as *Orient Express* (Garden City, N.Y.: Doubleday, Doran, 1933);

It's a Battlefield (London: Heinemann, 1934; Garden City, N.Y.: Doubleday, Doran, 1934);

England Made Me (London & Toronto: Heinemann, 1935; Garden City, N.Y.: Doubleday, Doran, 1935); republished as *The Shipwrecked* (New York: Viking, 1953);

The Bear Fell Free (London: Grayson & Grayson, 1935; Folcroft, Pa.: Folcroft, 1977);

The Basement Room, and Other Stories (London: Cresset, 1935);

Journey Without Maps (London & Toronto: Heinemann, 1936; Garden City, N.Y.: Doubleday, Doran, 1936);

A Gun for Sale: An Entertainment (London & Toronto: Heinemann, 1936); also published as *This Gun for Hire* (Garden City, N.Y.: Doubleday, Doran, 1936);

Brighton Rock (London & Toronto: Heinemann, 1938; New York: Viking, 1938);

The Lawless Roads (London, New York & Toronto: Longmans, Green, 1939); republished as *Another Mexico* (New York: Viking, 1939);

The Confidential Agent (London & Toronto: Heinemann, 1939; New York: Viking, 1939);

Graham Greene

Twenty-Four Short Stories, by Greene, James Laver, and Sylvia Townsend Warner (London: Cresset, 1939);

The Power and the Glory (London & Toronto: Heinemann, 1940); also published as *The Labyrinthine Ways* (New York: Viking, 1940);

British Dramatists (London: Collins, 1942);

The Ministry of Fear: An Entertainment (London & Toronto: Heinemann, 1943; New York: Viking, 1943);

The Little Train, anonymous (London: Eyre & Spottiswoode, 1946); as Greene (New York: Lothrop, Lee & Shepard, 1958);

Nineteen Stories (London & Toronto: Heinemann, 1947; New York: Viking, 1949); revised and enlarged as *Twenty-One Stories* (London, Mel-

116

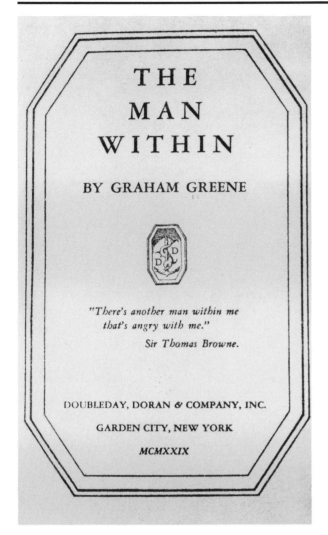

THE
MAN
WITHIN

BY GRAHAM GREENE

*"There's another man within me
that's angry with me."*

Sir Thomas Browne.

DOUBLEDAY, DORAN & COMPANY, INC.

GARDEN CITY, NEW YORK

MCMXXIX

Title page for the American edition of Greene's first published novel, in which he showed what Aldous Huxley called "a close physical contact with reality" (17 February 1930 letter to Robert Nichols), a quality also apparent in Greene's many essays

bourne & Toronto: Heinemann, 1954; New York: Viking, 1962);

The Heart of the Matter (Melbourne, London & Toronto: Heinemann, 1948; New York: Viking, 1948);

Why Do I Write?, by Greene, Elizabeth Bowen, and V. S. Pritchett (London: Marshall, 1948; Folcroft, Pa.: Folcroft, 1969);

The Third Man and The Fallen Idol (Melbourne, London & Toronto: Heinemann, 1950); abridged as *The Third Man* (New York: Viking, 1950);

The Little Fire Engine (London: Parrish, 1950); republished as *The Little Red Fire Engine* (New York: Lothrop, Lee & Shepard, 1952);

The Lost Childhood, and Other Essays (London: Eyre & Spottiswoode, 1951; New York: Viking, 1952);

The End of the Affair (Melbourne, London & Toronto: Heinemann, 1951; New York: Viking, 1951);

The Little Horse Bus (London: Parrish, 1952; New York: Lothrop, Lee & Shepard, 1954);

Essais Catholiques, translated (into French) by Marcelle Sibon (Paris: Editions du Seuil, 1953);

The Little Steamroller: A Story of Adventure, Mystery and Detection (London: Parrish, 1953; New York: Lothrop, Lee & Shepard, 1955);

The Living Room: A Play in Two Acts (Melbourne, London & Toronto: Heinemann, 1953; New York: Viking, 1954);

Loser Takes All (Melbourne, London & Toronto: Heinemann, 1955; New York: Viking, 1957);

The Quiet American (Melbourne, London & Toronto: Heinemann, 1955; New York: Viking, 1956);

The Potting Shed: A Play in Three Acts (New York: Viking, 1957; London, Melbourne & Toronto: Heinemann, 1958);

Our Man in Havana: An Entertainment (London, Melbourne & Toronto: Heinemann, 1958; New York: Viking, 1958);

The Complaisant Lover: A Comedy (London, Melbourne & Toronto: Heinemann, 1959; New York: Viking, 1961);

A Burnt-Out Case (London, Melbourne & Toronto: Heinemann, 1961; New York: Viking, 1961);

In Search of a Character: Two African Journals (London: Bodley Head, 1961; New York: Viking, 1961);

A Sense of Reality (London: Bodley Head, 1963; New York: Viking, 1963);

Carving a Statue: A Play (London: Bodley Head, 1964);

The Comedians (London: Bodley Head, 1966; New York: Viking, 1966);

Victorian Detective Fiction: A Catalogue of the Collection Made by Dorothy Glover & Graham Greene, by Greene and Dorothy Glover, edited by Eric Osborne (London, Sydney & Toronto: Bodley Head, 1966);

May We Borrow Your Husband? And Other Comedies of the Sexual Life (London, Sydney & Toronto: Bodley Head, 1967; New York: Viking, 1967);

Modern Film Scripts: The Third Man, by Greene and Carol Reed (London: Lorrimer, 1968; New York: Simon & Schuster, 1969);

Collected Essays (London, Sydney & Toronto: Bodley Head, 1969; New York: Viking, 1969);

Travels with My Aunt: A Novel (London, Sydney & Toronto: Bodley Head, 1969; New York: Viking, 1970);

A Sort of Life (London, Sydney & Toronto: Bodley Head, 1971; New York: Simon & Schuster, 1971);

The Pleasure-Dome: The Collected Film Criticism, 1935-40, edited by John Russell Taylor (London: Secker & Warburg, 1972); republished as *Graham Greene on Film: Collected Film Criticism, 1935-1940* (New York: Simon & Schuster, 1972);

Collected Stories (London: Bodley Head/Heinemann, 1972; New York: Viking, 1973);

The Honorary Consul (London, Sydney & Toronto: Bodley Head, 1973; New York: Simon & Schuster, 1973);

Lord Rochester's Monkey: Being the Life of John Wilmot, Second Earl of Rochester (London, Sydney & Toronto: Bodley Head, 1974; New York: Viking, 1974);

The Return of A. J. Raffles: An Edwardian Comedy in Three Acts Based Somewhat Loosely on E. W. Hornung's Characters in "The Amateur Cracksman" (London, Sydney & Toronto: Bodley Head, 1975; New York: Simon & Schuster, 1976);

The Human Factor (London, Sydney & Toronto: Bodley Head, 1978; New York: Simon & Schuster, 1978);

Doctor Fischer of Geneva, or the Bomb Party (London: Bodley Head, 1980; New York: Simon & Schuster, 1980);

Ways of Escape (London: Bodley Head, 1980; New York: Simon & Schuster, 1980);

Monsignor Quixote (London: Bodley Head, 1982; New York: Simon & Schuster, 1982);

Getting to Know the General: The Story of an Involvement (London: Bodley Head, 1984; New York: Simon & Schuster, 1984);

The Tenth Man (London: Bodley Head, 1985; New York: Simon & Schuster, 1985);

The Captain and the Enemy (New York & London: Viking Penguin, 1988);

Yours, Etc.: Letters to the Press, edited by Christopher Hawtree (New York: Viking Penguin, 1990);

The Last Word and Other Stories (London: Reinhardt, 1990).

Editions and Collections: *Three Plays* (London: Mercur, 1961);

Graham Greene: The Collected Edition, with introductions by Greene (London: Bodley Head/ Heinemann, 1970-);

The Portable Graham Greene, edited by Philip Stratford (New York: Viking, 1973; Harmondsworth, U.K.: Penguin, 1977);

Shades of Greene: The Televised Stories of Graham Greene (London: Bodley Head/Heinemann, 1975; New York: Penguin, 1977).

PLAY PRODUCTIONS: *The Living Room*, London, Wyndham's Theatre, 16 April 1953;

The Potting Shed, New York, Bijou Theatre, 29 January 1957; London, Globe Theatre, 5 February 1958;

The Complaisant Lover, London, Globe Theatre, 18 June 1959; New York, Ethel Barrymore Theatre, 1 November 1961;

Carving a Statue, London, Haymarket Theatre, 17 September 1964; New York, Gramercy Arts Theatre, 30 April 1968;

The Return of A. J. Raffles, London, Aldwych Theatre, 4 December 1975;

Yes and No and *For Whom the Bell Chimes*, Leicester, Haymarket Studio, 20 March 1980.

MOTION PICTURES: *Twenty-one Days*, screenplay by Greene and Basil Dean, Columbia, 1937; rereleased as *21 Days Together*, Columbia, 1940;

The Future's in the Air, commentary by Greene, Strand Film Unit, 1937;

The New Britain, commentary by Greene, Strand Film Unit, 1940;

Brighton Rock, screenplay by Greene and Terence Rattigan, Pathé, 1946; rereleased as *Young Scarface*, Mayer-Kingsley, 1952;

The Fallen Idol, screenplay by Greene, British Lion, 1948; rereleased, David O. Selznik, 1949;

The Third Man, screenplay by Greene, British Lion, 1949; rereleased, David O. Selznik, 1950;

The Stranger's Hand, produced by Greene and John Stafford, British Lion, 1954; rereleased, Distributors Corporation of America, 1955;

Loser Takes All, screenplay by Greene, British Lion, 1956; rereleased, Distributors Corporation of America, 1957;

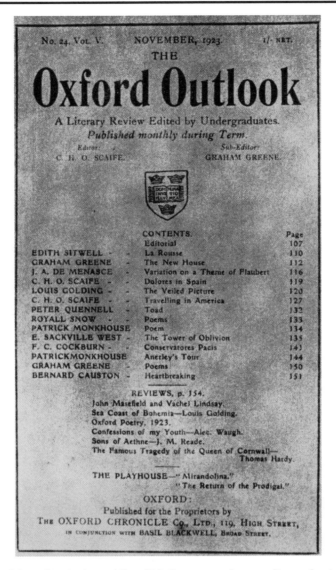

Title page for an issue of the university journal for which Greene served as an editor and writer from 1923 to 1925; his first book reviews appeared there in 1924.

Saint Joan, screenplay by Greene, United Artists, 1957;

Our Man in Havana, screenplay by Greene, Columbia, 1960;

The Comedians, screenplay by Greene, M-G-M, 1967.

OTHER: *The Old School: Essays by Divers Hands*, edited by Greene (London: Cape, 1934);

H. H. Munro, *The Best of Saki*, introduction by Greene (London: Lane, 1950; New York: Viking, 1961);

The Spy's Bedside Book: An Anthology, edited by Greene and Hugh Greene (London: Hart-Davis, 1957; New York: Carroll & Graf, 1985);

Ford Madox Ford, *The Bodley Head Ford Madox Ford*, volumes 1-4 edited by Greene (London: Bodley Head, 1962-1963);

An Impossible Woman: The Memoirs of Dottoressa Moor of Capri, edited by Greene (London, Sydney & Toronto: Bodley Head, 1975; New York: Viking, 1976);

Victorian Villainies, edited by Greene and Hugh Greene (Harmondsworth, U.K. & New York: Viking, 1984).

SELECTED PERIODICAL PUBLICATIONS– UNCOLLECTED:

FICTION

"The Lieutenant Died Last," *Collier's*, 105 (29 June 1940): 9-10;

"Men at Work," *New Yorker*, 17 (25 October 1941): 63-66;

"Proof Positive," *Harper's*, 195 (October 1947): 312-314;

"A Drive in the Country," *Harper's*, 195 (November 1947): 450-457;

"The Hint of an Exploration," *Commonweal*, 49 (11 February 1949): 438-442;

"The Third Man," *American Magazine*, 147 (March 1949): 142-160;

"Church Militant," *Commonweal*, 63 (6 January 1956): 350-352;

"Dear Dr. Falkenheim," *Vogue*, 141 (1 January 1963): 100-101;

"Dream of a Strange Land," *Saturday Evening Post* (19 January 1963): 44-47;

"Beauty," *Esquire*, 59 (April 1963): 60, 142;

"Root of All Evil," *Saturday Evening Post*, 237 (7 March 1964): 56-58;

"Invisible Japanese Gentlemen," *Saturday Evening Post*, 238 (20 November 1965): 60-61;

"Blessing," *Harper's*, 232 (March 1966): 91-94;

"Story," *Vogue*, 149 (1 January 1967): 94-95.

NONFICTION

"Middle-brow Film," *Fortnightly*, 145 (March 1936): 302-307;

"Ideas in the Cinema," *Spectator*, 159 (19 November 1937): 894-895;

"Self-Portrait," *Spectator*, 167 (18 July 1941): 66, 68;

"H. Sylvester," *Commonweal*, 33 (25 October 1949): 11-13;

"The Catholic Church's New Dogma: Assumption of Mary," *Life*, 29 (30 October 1950): 50-52;

"Malaya, The Forgotten War," *Life*, 31 (30 July 1951): 51-54;

"The Pope Who Remains a Priest," *Life*, 31 (24 September 1951): 146-148;

"The Return of Charlie Chaplin: An Open Letter," *New Statesman and Nation*, 45 (27 September 1952): 344;

"Indo-China," *New Republic*, 130 (5 April 1954): 13-15;

"Last Act in Indo-China," *New Republic*, 132 (9 May 1955): 9-11; (16 May 1955): 10-12;

"The Catholic Temper in Poland," *Atlantic Monthly*, 197 (March 1956): 39-41;

"In Search of a Character," *Harper's*, 224 (January 1962): 66-74;

"Return to Cuba," *New Republic*, 149 (2 November 1963): 16-18;

"Nightmare Republic," *New Republic*, 149 (16 November 1963): 18-20;

Greene in Liberia, 1935 (photograph courtesy of his cousin Countess Strachwitz, née Barbara Greene)

"Reflections on the Character of Kim Philby," *Esquire*, 70 (September 1968): 110-111.

Much of what is known of Graham Greene's life, character, and reading is found in his essays. As he himself points out, almost half of *Ways of Escape* (1980), the second volume of his autobiography, is made up of his introductions to the collected edition of his books being published by the Bodley Head. *A Sort of Life* (1971), Greene's account of his youth, is less indebted to the essays. However, the book's most compelling section—the story of his experiments with Russian roulette—first appeared twenty-five years earlier as the essay "The Revolver in the Corner Cupboard," and what is perhaps Greene's most famous essay, "The Lost Childhood," remains an essential supplement to *A Sort of Life* since it gives a fuller description of his childhood reading than he provides in the autobiography (both essays are collected in *The Lost Childhood, and Other Essays*, 1951).

Born in Berkhamsted, England, in 1904, Greene was as a child a passionate reader of books, and suggests in "The Lost Childhood" that "perhaps it is only in childhood that books have any deep influence on our lives." It is to H. Rider Haggard's *King Solomon's Mines* (1885) that Greene attributes his "odd African fixation." But it was Marjorie Bowen's *The Viper of Milan* (1906), read when he was fourteen, that instilled in him the desire to be a writer, provided him with a pattern of human nature, and at the same time it seems, confirmed his sense of a lost childhood. This last feeling is connected with the young Greene's horror of school–a revulsion made stronger by the divided loyalties instilled in the boy because his father was headmaster. Unable to bear the monotony of school life, he was driven at the age of sixteen to make a break for freedom by hiding out on Berkhamsted Common. This act led his parents (Charles and Marion Raymond Greene) to seek psychoanalysis for their son, and this period proved to be for Greene "perhaps the happiest six months of my life" (*A Sort of Life*).

In 1924 when he was a student at Oxford Greene wrote his first book reviews for the *Oxford Outlook*. But during the period between 1932 and 1942 he was most prolific as an essayist. At the beginning of 1932 Greene, who had been married for over four years (to Vivien Dayrell-Browning) and a convert to Catholicism for more than five, completed and published his first really impressive novel, *Stamboul Train* (published in the United States as *Orient Express*, 1933). By 1942 he had published an extraordinary number of essays and seven more novels, including *Brighton Rock* (1938) and *The Power and the Glory* (1940). Most of Greene's essays during this period were book reviews for the *Spectator*, a journal for which he was fiction editor between 1932 and 1935.

To evaluate Greene's achievement as an essayist, it is important to note the conditions under which the essays were first published. *Collected Essays* (1969) provides a useful cross section of his work in the genre. Although the title is a misnomer (hardly more than ten percent of Greene's essays are included), the book successfully reflects the variety of subjects encompassed in the uncollected as well as the collected essays.

Almost a third of *Collected Essays* consists of book reviews that appeared in the *Spectator* between 1932 and 1942. Some of these–such as the essays on Hans Christian Andersen, Dorothy Richardson, Conrad Aiken, and Arthur Conan Doyle–suffer from being excessively short (almost all are under one thousand words). Essays that appeared in other journals, such as the *New Statesman and Nation* and the *London Mercury*, are a more suitable length. In some cases Greene overcomes the problem of the brevity of the *Spectator* pieces by combining reviews on the same author. Thus the three essays on Frederick Rolfe are placed together, and three reviews on Somerset Maugham become the single essay "Some Notes on Somerset Maugham."

Greene's introductions and contributions to books also form a significant part of *Collected Essays*. "Fielding and Sterne," "The Young Dickens," and "Walter de la Mare's Short Stories" are among those essays that first appeared in books. The important series of six essays on Henry James is a particularly interesting case since the first three were originally published in books, the fourth and the sixth in the *New Statesman and Nation*, and the fifth in the *London Mercury*. By a judicious combination of essays from several sources Greene succeeds in giving unity and substance to *Collected Essays*.

The themes of the essays are, of course, as important as their forms and sources. By making the autobiographical essay "The Lost Childhood" his personal prologue to the collection, Greene signals his interest in those formative years of childhood and adolescence in the lives of the men and women whose accomplishments–or failures–he meditates on. Doggedly he pursues the secrets of those he writes of and, at least in the case of the creative writers he treats, the secrets of their work as well. His appraisal of James, the writer who has the foremost place in *Collected Essays*, is typical of this method. For Greene, James's public life was a facade; it is in the private universe that the true man is to be sought. It is here that Greene discovers that James possessed "a sense of evil religious in its intensity" that can only be ascribed to his "main fantasy, the idea of treachery" ("Henry James: The Private Universe").

Along with those who are obsessed–or even possessed–by their past, Greene deals with two other categories: those who are unsympathetic or petty, and those who have the special qualities needed for leadership. Examples of the former group, those whose hatred or egotism are for

Greene sitting for a 1937 sketch by Geoffrey Wylde (photograph by Nicholas Dennys); the drawing later appeared in the London Mercury, *which often published Greene's stories and essays.*

Greene essentially a failure of the sympathetic imagination, are Frederick Rolfe, Jessie Conrad, and Mrs. Cecil Chesterton. The leaders, on the other hand–the two Popes, Pius XII and John XXIII, and the Communists, Ho Chi Minh and Fidel Castro–have lost the sense of self in their love for their flock or people. They retain a remarkable humility: Pius XII and John XXIII still have the character of the parish priest in the confessional; Castro and Ho Chi Minh live as simply as peasants. Greene no doubt comes close to hero-worship in these portraits. Yet they must be evaluated in the context of the whole pantheon of those focused on, for they possess a stability that the obsessive figures lack, and a selflessness sadly absent in the petty or the rancorous.

During the same period (1932-1942) Greene also wrote most of his film reviews. In his introduction to *The Pleasure-Dome* (1972; published in the United States as *Graham Greene on Film*, also 1972), he gives an account of reviewing films for the *Spectator* from July 1935 to March 1940. The film reviews are even less satisfactory as essays than the book reviews in the same peri-

odical, for not only was Greene constrained by space and often by the necessity to deal with several films in a single article, but the requirement of summarizing plot allowed him even less space for evaluation than was provided by book reviews of the same length. Yet, taken as a whole, Greene's evaluations in these reviews are striking. His general perspective on the medium is consistently and brilliantly maintained: his awareness of how the camera can be used and of how film must follow different principles from the stage; his conviction that film must be a popular art, with the advantages that flow from this; his frequent assertion that the film must be true to life in a poetic rather than a naturalistic sense; and, finally, his belief that technique and content join in organic unity in the good film.

In 1942 Greene published *British Dramatists*, a short book that is really a long critical essay. The tone is more formal than in Greene's literary essays, no doubt because he is writing a commissioned work. Nonetheless, his penchant for the striking evaluative comment is evident–in this case, in comments that include not only ideas

Greene in 1939 (Bassano Studios; by permission of the National Portrait Gallery, London). During 1939, one of his most prolific years, Greene published three books and twenty-one periodical contributions, mostly reviews for the Spectator.

about individual writers (he dismisses George Bernard Shaw's drama of ideas as "the startling convolutions of a tumbler"), but also on whole periods in the history of English drama. The beginnings of English drama in religious ceremony provide Greene with a conception of ritual and abstract character that he applies as the test of both the dramatist and his age. William Shakespeare's greatness is not attributed to character as such but to the abstraction–Hamlet's revenge, Othello's jealousy, Macbeth's ambition–embodied in character. In the age of William Congreve, however, "the sense of ritual has been lost, for ritual is the representation of something real abstracted from any individual element," and the author's personality "has begun to shoulder his characters aside." In the modern period it is only John Millington Synge who has recaptured the power of the early stage through his seriousness, the scru-

pulous accuracy of his dialogue, and the exclusion of his own personality.

Why Do I Write? (1948) is another short book, which Greene wrote with Elizabeth Bowen and V. S. Pritchett. Ostensibly a series of letters in which the three authors interchange answers to the question posed by the title, the book is more accurately viewed as a series of essays since each author is intent on stating his personal credo as a writer and is only peripherally concerned with debating the question. In Greene's two essays we find an early statement of what has become a central theme in his later essays and interviews: the value of disloyalty. It is only by being disloyal that the artist can "roam experimentally through any human mind" and discover "the extra dimension of sympathy." To both the State and the Church the writer must be disloyal. The duty he owes to society is to accept no fa-

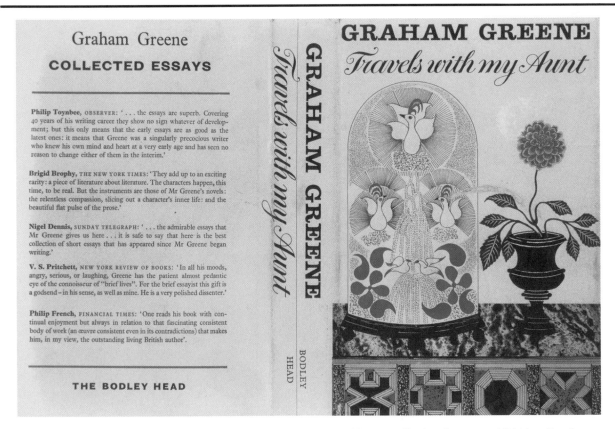

Dust jacket for Greene's 1969 comic novel, with reviewers' comments on his essay collection that was published earlier that year

vors, since gifts make for a forced loyalty that blights his integrity. With regard to his membership in the Catholic Church, Greene argues that "doubt and even denial must be given their chance of self-expression" if he is to remain true to the personal morality literature requires of him.

In the early 1950s Greene made his first attempts to collect groups of his essays in *The Lost Childhood, and Other Essays* and in *Essais Catholiques* (1953). The former work, now superseded by *Collected Essays*, was at the time clearly an attempt at a representative selection. *Collected Essays* is an expansion of this early selection for, although Greene omitted five essays from the 1951 book when he came to compile the later collection, only one of these–"The Revolver in the Corner Cupboard"–is significant. When *Collected Essays* appeared in 1969, reviewers bemoaned Greene's substituting "The Soupsweet Land," a rather light account of his experiences in Sierra Leone. But it seems now that Greene omitted his account of playing Russian roulette because he was to incorporate it as a central part of *A Sort of Life*.

Essais Catholiques, as the title implies, are essays written in French that deal directly with Catholic themes. Of the six essays, three first appeared in English and are translated into French by Marcelle Sibon: "The Paradox of a Pope," "Henry James: The Religious Aspect," and "Our Lady and Her Assumption." The other essays are speeches that Greene delivered in French and later published in the periodicals *Dieu Vivant* (1949 and 1951) and *La Table Ronde* (1948). He is concerned in these essays with several main assertions: that Christian civilization can be defined only by the Christian conscience; that sin exists because man is imperfect and that salvation can be achieved only through guilt and repentance; that there is a necessary tension between the Christian and the world; and that faith, rather than providing simple answers, plunges the believer into mystery and paradox.

By far the most interesting essays in Greene's later years began in 1970 with the preface to *Brighton Rock*, the first of a series of introductions to the novels in the Bodley Head *Collected Edition*. Unlike James in his prefaces, Greene provides little analysis of technique. A notable exception is the introduction to *The End of*

Graham Greene

the *Affair* (1951) in which Greene considers his decision to use the first-person perspective in that novel. More typically, Greene is concerned with the characters in his novels. He is often simply interested in whether they come alive. Thus, he finds life in Acky, the unfrocked clergyman in *A Gun for Sale* (1936; published in the United States as *This Gun for Hire*, also 1936), but finds that the industrialist Krogh in *England Made Me* (1935) refuses to come alive. At other times Greene speaks of how a character can take control of the author, having its source in a dream or some obscure unconscious force that Greene can only hint at. Such a character is the Anglo-Catholic Minty in *England Made Me*, whom the author simply could not keep down.

On the whole it is remarkable how little Greene comments in these introductions on the works themselves. At times he provides an elaborate evocation of the circumstances in which the novel was conceived and composed. (He is like James in this respect.) The larger part of the introduction to *The Ministry of Fear* (1943) is about Greene's years in Freetown, where he wrote the novel, even though the setting of the story is in London and touches on Greene's own experience

in the scenes of the blitz. In other introductions, such as that to *Our Man in Havana* (1958), Greene is more concerned with relating the setting of the novel to his own experience, in this case his several visits to Cuba. Yet even here Greene goes beyond his comic novel, for he sketches how his image of Cuba changed as he gradually became aware of Gen. Fulgencio Batista's cruelty. In the essay "Henry James: The Private Universe" Greene speaks of James's elusiveness as being like that of a conjuror's art. In his introductions Greene shows himself to be an adept conjuror as well, for he conceals as much about his novels as he discloses.

Greene's reputation as essayist cannot rival that of Greene as novelist, but it deserves to be ranked equally with that of Greene as short-story writer and playwright. Unfortunately, critics have seldom looked at the essays as literary works in their own right. With the exception of Elizabeth Davis's monograph on the essays (1984) and Philip Stratford's attempt, in chapter 5 of *Faith and Fiction: Creative Process in Greene and Mauriac* (1964), to trace Greene's growing awareness of his craft as reflected in the *Spectator* reviews, the essays have generally served as footnotes to the novels. This is perhaps not surprising. Since Greene's literary tastes, as well as his political and religious ideas, are reflected in the essays, it is inevitable that they be used as fodder by those who analyze the novels. When *Collected Essays* appeared, reviewers were prompt to underline the parallels between the essays and the novels, but evaluated the essays as impressionistic and idiosyncratic in themselves. Yet the frequency with which Greene's comments on other creative writers are quoted belies this view. Greene's evocative comment on Dickens's "secret prose" ("The Young Dickens," *Collected Essays*) has had a notable influence on those critics who have sought to account for Dickens's style. And Greene's emphasis on James's fascination with evil, overstated though it may be, nonetheless serves as a corrective to the imbalanced assessments of James as nothing more than a chronicler of manner and fine consciousness.

In the end Greene should be hailed as one of the small group of writers who have kept alive a much neglected genre in our century: the informal essay. In the account of his apprenticeship as a short-story writer he alludes to his discovery of how to write essays: "I was reminded of the kind of essays we were taught to write at school—you were told to make first a diagram which showed the development of the argument, rather as later a film producer would sometimes talk to me of the necessity of 'establishing' this or that and the imaginary value of 'continuity.' When school was safely behind me I began to write 'essays' again. I learned to trust the divagations of the mind. If you let the reins loose the horse will find its way home. The shape was something which grew of itself *inside* the essay, during the revision–you didn't have to think it out beforehand" (Introduction to the *Collected Stories*, 1972). This passage could serve not only as a description of the organic unity of many of Greene's essays, but also as an eloquent statement of why the informal essay at its best is a mode of creative writing.

Interviews:
Michael Mewshaw, "Greene in Antibes," *London Magazine*, 17 (June-July 1977): 33-45;

Marie-François Allain, *The Other Man: Conversations with Graham Greene* (New York: Simon & Schuster, 1981).

Bibliographies:
R. A. Wobbe, *Graham Greene: A Bibliography and Guide to Research* (New York & London: Garland, 1979);

A. F. Cassis, *Graham Greene: An Annotated Bibliography of Criticism* (Metuchen, N.J. & London: Scarecrow, 1981).

Biography:
Norman Sherry, *The Life of Graham Greene, Vol. 1: Nineteen Hundred Four to Nineteen Thirty-Nine* (New York: Viking Penguin, 1989).

References:
Kenneth and Miriam Farris Allott, *The Art of Graham Greene* (New York: Russell & Russell, 1951);

Harold Bloom, ed., *Graham Greene: Modern Critical Views* (New York: Chelsea House, 1987);

Elizabeth Davis, *Graham Greene: The Artist as Critic* (Fredericton, N.B.: York, 1984);

A. A. DeVitis, *Graham Greene* (New York: Twayne, 1964; revised, 1986);

Frank Kermode, "Mr. Greene's Eggs and Crosses," in his *Puzzles and Epiphanies* (New York: Chidmark, 1963), pp. 176-187;

B. P. Lamba, *Graham Greene: His Mind and Art* (New York: Apt Books, 1987);

François Mauriac, "Graham Greene," in his *Men I Hold Great* (New York: Philosophical Library, 1951), pp. 124-128;

Jeffrey Meyers, ed., *Graham Greene: A Revaluation* (New York: St. Martin's, 1989);

Paul O'Prey, *A Reader's Guide to Graham Greene* (New York: Thames & Hudson, 1988);

George Orwell, "The Sanctified Sinner," in *The Collected Essays, Journalism and Letters of George Orwell*, edited by Sonia Orwell and Ian Angus (New York: Harcourt, Brace & World, 1968);

Anne Salvatore, *Greene & Kierkegaard: The Discourse of Belief* (Tuscaloosa: University of Alabama Press, 1988);

Philip Stratford, *Faith and Fiction: Creative Process in Greene and Mauriac* (Notre Dame, Ind.: University of Notre Dame Press, 1964);

Stratford, ed., Introduction to *The Portable Graham Greene* (New York: Viking, 1973);

Evelyn Waugh, "Felix Culpa?," *Tablet*, 191 (5 June 1948): 352-354.

Papers:
There are working drafts and final manuscripts for some of Greene's essays, as well as for many of his books, at the Harry Ransom Humanities Research Center, University of Texas at Austin.

Aldous Huxley

(26 July 1894 - 22 November 1963)

George Woodcock

See also the Huxley entry in *DLB 36: British Novelists, 1890-1929: Modernists.*

BOOKS: *The Burning Wheel* (Oxford: Blackwell, 1916);

Jonah (Oxford: Holywell, 1917);

The Defeat of Youth and Other Poems (Oxford: Blackwell, 1918);

Limbo (London: Chatto & Windus, 1920; New York: Doran, 1920);

Leda (London: Chatto & Windus, 1920; New York: Doran, 1920);

Crome Yellow (London: Chatto & Windus, 1921; New York: Doran, 1922);

Mortal Coils (London: Chatto & Windus, 1922; New York: Doran, 1922);

On the Margin: Notes and Essays (London: Chatto & Windus, 1923; New York: Doran, 1923);

Antic Hay (London: Chatto & Windus, 1923; New York: Doran, 1923);

Little Mexican & Other Stories (London: Chatto & Windus, 1924); also published as *Young Archimedes and Other Stories* (New York: Doran, 1924);

Those Barren Leaves (London: Chatto & Windus, 1925; New York: Doran, 1925);

Along the Road: Notes and Essays of a Tourist (London: Chatto & Windus, 1925; New York: Doran, 1925);

Selected Poems (Oxford: Blackwell, 1925; New York: Appleton, 1925);

Two or Three Graces and Other Stories (London: Chatto & Windus, 1926; New York: Doran, 1926);

Jesting Pilate (London: Chatto & Windus, 1926; New York: Doran, 1926);

Essays New and Old (London: Chatto & Windus, 1926; New York: Doran, 1927);

Proper Studies (London: Chatto & Windus, 1927; Garden City, N.Y.: Doubleday, Doran, 1928);

Point Counter Point (London: Chatto & Windus, 1928; Garden City, N.Y.: Doubleday, Doran, 1928);

Aldous Huxley in 1958 (photograph by Wolf Suschitzky)

Arabia Infelix and Other Poems (London: Chatto & Windus / New York: Fountain, 1929);

Holy Face and Other Essays (London: Fleuron, 1929);

Do What You Will: Essays (London: Chatto & Windus, 1929; Garden City, N.Y.: Doubleday, Doran, 1929);

Brief Candles: Stories (London: Chatto & Windus, 1930; Garden City, N.Y.: Doubleday, Doran, 1930);

Vulgarity in Literature: Digressions from a Theme (London: Chatto & Windus, 1930);

Apennine (Gaylordsville, Conn.: Slide Mountain, 1930);

Music at Night and Other Essays (London: Chatto & Windus, 1931; Garden City, N.Y.: Doubleday, Doran, 1931);

The World of Light: A Comedy in Three Acts (London: Chatto & Windus, 1931; Garden City, N.Y.: Doubleday, Doran, 1931);

The Cicadas and Other Poems (London: Chatto & Windus, 1931; Garden City, N.Y.: Doubleday, Doran, 1931);

T. H. Huxley as a Man of Letters (London: Macmillan, 1932);

Brave New World (London: Chatto & Windus, 1932; Garden City, N.Y.: Doubleday, Doran, 1932);

Texts and Pretexts: An Anthology with Commentaries (London: Chatto & Windus, 1932; New York: Harper, 1933);

Beyond the Mexique Bay (London: Chatto & Windus, 1934; New York: Harper, 1934);

Eyeless in Gaza (London: Chatto & Windus, 1936; New York: Harper, 1936);

The Olive Tree and Other Essays (London: Chatto & Windus, 1936; New York: Harper, 1937);

What Are You Going to Do about It? The Case for Constructive Peace (London: Chatto & Windus, 1936; New York: Harper, 1936);

Ends and Means: An Enquiry into the Nature of Ideals and into the Methods Employed for Their Realization (London: Chatto & Windus, 1937; New York: Harper, 1937);

Stories, Essays, and Poems (London: Dent, 1937);

The Gioconda Smile (London: Chatto & Windus, 1938);

After Many a Summer (London: Chatto & Windus, 1939); republished as *After Many a Summer Dies the Swan* (New York: Harper, 1939);

Words and Their Meanings (Los Angeles: Ward Ritchie, 1940);

Grey Eminence: A Study in Religion and Politics (London: Chatto & Windus, 1941; New York: Harper, 1941);

The Art of Seeing (New York: Harper, 1942; London: Chatto & Windus, 1943);

Time Must Have a Stop (New York: Harper, 1944; London: Chatto & Windus, 1945);

Twice Seven: Fourteen Selected Stories (London: Reprint Society, 1944);

The Perennial Philosophy (New York: Harper, 1945; London: Chatto & Windus, 1946);

Science, Liberty, and Peace (New York: Harper, 1946; London: Chatto & Windus, 1947);

Verses and a Comedy (London: Chatto & Windus, 1946);

The World of Aldous Huxley: An Omnibus of His Fiction and Non-Fiction over Three Decades, edited by Charles J. Rolo (New York: Harper, 1947);

Ape and Essence (New York: Harper, 1948; London: Chatto & Windus, 1949);

The Gioconda Smile: A Play (London: Chatto & Windus, 1948; New York: Harper, 1948);

Prisons, with the "Carceri" Etchings by G. B. Piranesi (London: Trianon, 1949; Los Angeles: Zeitlin & Ver Brugge, 1949);

Themes and Variations (London: Chatto & Windus, 1950; New York: Harper, 1950);

The Devils of Loudun (London: Chatto & Windus, 1952; New York: Harper, 1952);

A Day in Windsor, by Huxley and J. A. Kings (London: Britannicus Liber, 1953);

The Doors of Perception (London: Chatto & Windus, 1954; New York: Harper, 1954);

The Genius and the Goddess (London: Chatto & Windus, 1955; New York: Harper, 1955);

Adonis and the Alphabet, and Other Essays (London: Chatto & Windus, 1956); also published as *Tomorrow and Tomorrow and Tomorrow, and Other Essays* (New York: Harper, 1956);

Heaven and Hell (London: Chatto & Windus, 1956; New York: Harper, 1956);

Collected Short Stories (London: Chatto & Windus, 1957; New York: Harper, 1957);

Brave New World Revisited (London: Chatto & Windus, 1958; New York: Harper, 1958);

Collected Essays (New York: Harper, 1959);

On Art and Artists, edited by Morris Philipson (London: Chatto & Windus, 1960; New York: Harper, 1960);

Island (London: Chatto & Windus, 1962; New York: Harper, 1962);

Literature and Science (London: Chatto & Windus, 1963; New York: Harper & Row, 1963);

The Crows of Pearlblossom (New York: Random House, 1967; London: Chatto & Windus, 1968).

Collections: *Rotunda: A Selection from the Works of Aldous Huxley* (London: Chatto & Windus, 1932);

Retrospect: An Omnibus of Aldous Huxley's Books (Garden City, N.Y.: Doubleday, Doran, 1933);

The Collected Poetry of Aldous Huxley, edited by Donald Watt (London: Chatto & Windus, 1971; New York: Harper & Row, 1971).

MOTION PICTURES: *Pride and Prejudice*, scenario by Huxley and Jane Murfin, M-G-M, 1940;

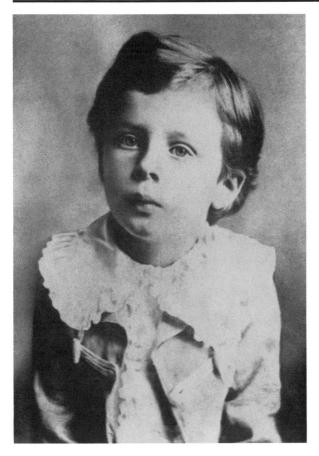

Huxley at about age five (courtesy of Matthew Huxley)

Madame Curie, treatment by Huxley, M-G-M, 1943;

Jane Eyre, scenario by Huxley, 20th Century-Fox, 1944;

A Woman's Vengeance, adaptation by Huxley from his play *The Gioconda Smile*, Universal-International, 1948.

OTHER: Thomas Humphry Ward, ed., *The English Poets: Selections with Critical Introductions*, includes introductions to the poetry of John Davidson, Ernest Dowson, and Richard Middleton by Huxley (London: Macmillan, 1918);

Rémy de Gourmont, *A Virgin Heart: A Novel*, translated by Huxley (New York: Brown, 1921; London: Allen & Unwin, 1926);

Frances Sheridan, *The Discovery: A Comedy in Five Acts*, adapted by Huxley (London: Chatto & Windus, 1924; New York: Doran, 1925);

Oliver Simon and Jules Rodenberg, *Printing of Today*, introduction by Huxley (London: Davies, 1928; New York: Harper, 1928);

Maurice A. Pink, *A Realist Looks at Democracy*, preface by Huxley (London: Benn, 1930; New York: Stokes, 1931);

Douglas Goldering, *The Fortune*, preface by Huxley (London: Harmsworth, 1931);

The Letters of D. H. Lawrence, edited with an introduction, by Huxley (London: Heinemann, 1932; New York: Viking, 1932);

Samuel Butler, *Erewhon*, introduction by Huxley (New York: Limited Editions Club, 1934);

Alfred H. Mendes, *Pitch Lake: A Story from Trinidad*, introduction by Huxley (London: Duckworth, 1934);

Norman Haire, *Birth-Control Methods (Contraception, Abortion, Sterilization)*, foreword by Huxley (London: Allen & Unwin, 1936);

An Encyclopedia of Pacifism, edited by Huxley (London: Chatto & Windus, 1937; New York: Harper, 1937);

Barthélemy de Ligt, *The Conquest of Violence: An Essay on War and Revolution*, introduction by Huxley (London: Routledge, 1938; New York: Dutton, 1938);

Knud Merrild, *Knud Merrild, a Poet and Two Painters: A Memoir of D. H. Lawrence*, preface by Huxley (London: Routledge, 1938; New York: Viking, 1939);

Maksim Gorky, *A Book of Short Stories*, edited by Avram Yarmolinsky and Baroness Moura Budberg, foreword by Huxley (London: Cape, 1939; New York: Holt, 1939);

Joseph Daniel Unwin, *Hopousia; or, The Sexual and Economic Foundations of a New Society*, introduction by Huxley (London: Allen & Unwin, 1940; New York: Piest, 1940);

Ashley Montagu, *Man's Most Dangerous Myth: The Fallacy of Race*, foreword by Huxley (London: Columbia University Press, 1942);

Bhagavadgita: The Song of God, translated by Swami Prabhavananda and Christopher Isherwood, introduction by Huxley (Hollywood, Cal.: Rodd, 1944; London: Phoenix House, 1947);

William Law, *Selected Mystical Writings*, edited by Stephen Hobhouse, foreword by Huxley (New York: Harper, 1948);

Ramakrishna, *Ramakrishna: Prophet of New India*, translated by Swami Nikhilananda, foreword by Huxley (New York: Harper, 1948; London: Rider, 1951);

Jiddu Krishnamurti, *The First and Last Freedom*, introduction by Huxley (New York: Harper, 1954; London: Gollancz, 1954);

Hubert Benoît, *The Supreme Doctrine: Psychological Studies in Zen Thought*, foreword by Huxley (London: Routledge & Kegan Paul, 1955; New York: Pantheon, 1955);

Frederick Mayer, *New Directions for the American University*, introduction by Huxley (Washington, D.C.: Public Affairs Press, 1957);

Alvah W. Sulloway, *Birth Control and Catholic Doctrine*, preface by Huxley (Boston: Beacon, 1959);

Danilo Dolci, *Report from Palermo*, introduction by Huxley (New York: Orion, 1959).

It has often been argued that even in his fiction Aldous Leonard Huxley never ceased to be the essayist. To the extent that, from *Crome Yellow* (1921) onward, he shared Thomas Love Peacock's interest in ideas as well as in manners, this is a just assessment. Huxley would have been the first to recognize its truth; he once said: "I am not a born novelist but some other kind of man of letters possessing enough ingenuity to be able to simulate a novelist's behaviour not too convincingly." It was not merely that, in a long life during which he wrote incessantly, despite times of near blindness and times of spiritual crisis, Huxley published a vast number of essays that appeared in periodicals and later were collected in books. His other nonfiction books–travel narratives such as *Jesting Pilate* (1926) and *Beyond the Mexique Bay* (1934) and studies in the more curious areas of history, as in *Grey Eminence* (1941) and *The Devils of Loudun* (1952)–tended to assume the form of interconnected reflections that resemble his essays. And even in his fiction, particularly as his original interest in manners began to decline after *Point Counter Point* (1928), the ideas became steadily more dominant so that the novels, from *Brave New World* (1932) onward, tended to become extended didactic essays in fiction, dominated by the burden of idea and argument, rather than novels in the ordinary sense.

For those who believe that the inclinations of writers are determined by heredity, or by a combination of heredity and early family background, Huxley might seem an almost perfect example. On both sides he came of distinguished Victorian intellectual lineages whose members had played crucial roles in that nineteenth-century movement of ideas that accompanied the shift from a religious to a scientific orientation among the British intelligentsia. Huxley was born on 26 July 1894 to Leonard and Judith Arnold Huxley.

His paternal grandfather was the well-known evolutionist Thomas Henry Huxley, but his father was not generously endowed with the Huxley talents, which seemed to leap from grandfathers to grandsons. However, Leonard Huxley sustained the family tradition of intellectual interests, retiring from a teaching post at Charterhouse to become a man of letters. In this role he was industrious rather than distinguished, but he must have kept in his children's minds an awareness of the campaigns of ideas in which his own father had been engaged, for during Aldous's childhood Leonard was engaged for years on a biography of Thomas Henry Huxley, followed by another of the great botanist Joseph Hooker, who had been his father's friend and companion in the evolutionary battles of the mid nineteenth century. The tradition of Thomas Henry Huxley led Aldous's brother Julian to become not merely a practical biologist but also a notable scientific popularizer in the years between the two World Wars, and Aldous himself was only prevented from starting on a scientific or medical career by the onset in his boyhood of eye diseases from which he never completely recovered.

This circumstance led him toward the other strain in his intellectual ancestry, that of the Arnolds. His maternal great-grandfather was Thomas Arnold of Rugby, the formidable reformer of the English public school system; Aldous's mother, Judith, was the daughter of Thomas's wayward namesake son who pioneered in New Zealand and Tasmania and returned to undergo tempests of faith and doubt that swept him into the Catholic church and out again, until a reconversion brought him to a final haven teaching in an Irish Catholic university as a colleague of Gerard Manley Hopkins. Arnold of Rugby's other son was Matthew Arnold, and though this famous great-uncle died six years before Aldous was born, his intellectual influence was considerable. The famous controversy in the 1880s between his two distinguished forebears, Thomas Henry Huxley and Matthew Arnold, reflected one of the great preoccupations of Aldous Huxley's later essays and novels, the question of whether, as the older Huxley put it, "man's moral nature be debased by the increase of his wisdom." Indeed, Aldous Huxley's *Literature and Science*, published in 1963 shortly before his death, opens with a reference to the Arnold-Huxley dispute and proceeds to review the whole question of the rivalry between literature and science, which had been given a new life during the

Huxley with his first son, Matthew, circa 1926 (courtesy of Matthew Huxley)

1960s by the equally famous dispute between C. P. Snow and F. R. Leavis. The literary as well as the scientific side of the controversy figured prominently in the childhoods of Aldous and Julian, for Judith Huxley was herself a notable bluestocking and an excellent teacher. Under her influence the Huxley interest in science was infused with a Wordsworthian poetry of nature. Thus the literary ambience in which Aldous Huxley grew up tended to be one in which the intellectual or moral content of writing was often more greatly valued than its aesthetic aspects.

Later, at Oxford, Huxley was attracted by the celebrated country house parties at Garsington Manor, where Lady Ottoline Morel presided like an Edwardian Circe over extraordinary gatherings of writers, painters, and radical intellectuals. There the directions Huxley had taken under the influence of his mother and his various forebears were strengthened. He met Bertrand Russell, T. S. Eliot, H. G. Wells, the three Sitwells, D. H. Lawrence, Arnold Bennett, Katherine Mansfield, and John Middleton Murry. Garsington Manor and its guests gave Huxley a setting and a cast of characters for his first novel, *Crome Yellow*, which reveals how much

more important to him were the ideas of his new acquaintances than their art.

Though he had already published some intellectual and jejune poetry while at Oxford, it was as an essayist that Huxley embarked on professional writing. He had briefly attempted teaching at Eton, where one of his students had been George Orwell. Then Murry engaged him as assistant editor of the *Atheneum*. Huxley became involved in a great deal of literary drudgery, including what he described as "the asininity of doing 'shorter notices' of bad books," but he also wrote, under the title of "Marginilia," a series of weekly pieces that would now be called "columns," but which then were called "middles" because of their position in the magazine, and which were eventually published, with some longer pieces, as Huxley's first book of essays, *On the Margin* (1923). It appeared in the same year as his second novel, *Antic Hay*, in which one of the more despicable characters, Mercaptan, is a writer of "middles." Huxley presented his own "middles" with an air of playful erudition; these little pieces, including "Bibliophily," "Modern Folk Poetry," and "Polite Conversation," rarely more than six or seven pages long, seem singularly dated in their remote archness. Yet some of them are first sketches of what would later become dominant preoccupations: a note on "Accidie" charts the beginning of Huxley's interest in Charles Baudelaire; an appreciation of Christopher Wren reflects his enduring admiration for the neoclassical in architecture. Two long pieces on Ben Jonson and Geoffrey Chaucer, signs of a wider literary ambition than the *Atheneum* could fulfill, close the volume. They anticipate Huxley's later writings by being more concerned with the social rather than with the aesthetic merits of the works he discusses. Huxley was indeed a critic, but from beginning to end a moral rather than a formal one.

Yet, as Huxley's joy in his growing literary craftsmanship displayed, the concern for form was not entirely absent, and in his second book of essays, *Along the Road: Notes and Essays of a Tourist* (1925), he argues the problem in an essay on Breughel the Elder, in which he defends the "great dramatic and reflective painters" against those who depreciate them in comparison with the formalists. The approach he displays is eclectic in the better sense of the word: "The contemporary insistence on form to the exclusion of everything else is an absurdity. So was the older insistence on exact imitation and sentiment to the exclusion of form. There need be no exclusions. In spite of the single name, there are many different kinds of painters and all of them, with the exception of those who cannot paint and those whose minds are trivial, vulgar and tedious, have a right to exist."

Along the Road represents the period of Huxley's liberation from journalistic drudgery. The success of his first two novels had enabled him to break away from the *Atheneum*, and from brief stints with other magazines, and to spend long periods living in Italy and later in France; this allowed him to travel farther afield than the Swiss holiday places of his Edwardian childhood: hence the title and subtitle of *Along the Road*. In fact it is by no means entirely a book about physical travel, and one is aware that, no longer limited by the constricting space of the "middle," Huxley is expanding his horizons mentally as well as territorially, and in the process developing a more discursive manner that enables him to pursue thoughts into their more elusive extremities.

There are indeed some excellent travel pieces, such as "Sabionetta," in which Huxley describes a small Italian town, once the capital of the tiny domain of a Renaissance princeling, with its miniature winter and summer palaces, its small theater, and its "noble Gallery of Antiques." Huxley is almost at his best as he discusses the quality of the neoclassical architecture and its rococo decorations, which echo an age that strove toward its own kind of excellence, and at the same time, he dips back into history and reconstructs the events of the time when the little town was built and the attitudes of the people who built it. There is a bit of art criticism, a bit of social history, a bit of biography, and the whole is brought together impressively under the control of a well-trained and civilized mind. Indeed, it is the splendid equipment of that mind that seems steadily more impressive. But Huxley, unlike most good travel writers, did not have a vivid visual imagination. A scene does not call up a whole panorama of personal pictorial memories as it might for Marcel Proust. It is more likely to call up a piece of anecdotal knowledge. A bitter night trapped in an inn in the blizzard-stricken Apennines reminds Huxley that Humphrey Davy and Michael Faraday once went there to inspect the gas jets burning out of the mountain; a trip along the Meuse from Namur to Dinant calls to mind his studies of the paintings of Joachim Patinir and leads him to the conclusion that painters are not so inventive as they often seem: there are things in nature that reflect art's most improbable fantasies. Or does Huxley mean, like Oscar Wilde, that painters–by shaping perceptions– enable us to see nature imitating their particular art?

Some essays in *Along the Road* are not on travel at all. A few anticipate Orwell by venturing into plebeian culture and discussing popular music and the cult of the amusing, though Huxley does it more flippantly and with less earnest sympathy than Orwell. A piece on "Work and Leisure" discusses with a great deal of foresight the problems of a technologically exploding culture and anticipates Huxley's later preoccupation with socioeconomic problems. And, on the whole, art is a more dominant preoccupation of this particular book than travel alone. Many of the journeys mentioned in *Along the Road* were taken to view works of art. Notable among them was a trip to Borgo San Sepulcro to see what Huxley called "The best picture in the world," Piero della Francesco's *Resurrection*. Huxley sees the painting not most significantly as a depiction of a Christian event, but as a "resurrection of the classical ideal, incredibly much grander and more beautiful than the classical reality." It is the "intellec-

Huxley and the English writer Gerald Heard, his close friend and traveling companion, at Black Mountain College in 1937 (courtesy of Matthew Huxley)

tual power" that appeals to him, and here the virtues and the defects of Huxley's view of the fine arts combine in the fact that he recognizes art as a matter of thought, whose "form" is Platonic and ideal rather than part of the actuality of the visible world. This is why, though he knew their work, the great modern masters such as Paul Cézanne and Georges Seurat are mere passing names in his books, and why Pablo Picasso appears in *Along the Road* merely so that the abstract designs on the banners used in the *palio* at Siena can be compared with his designs for the Russian ballet.

Huxley would return to one of the central themes of *Along the Road* in his travel books *Jesting Pilate* and *Beyond the Mexique Bay*, which seem to form a bridge between his essays and his fiction. Huxley was not a highly inventive novelist.

From *Crome Yellow* onward he developed his best characters out of people he had known, and when the settings of his youth were exhausted, he tended, as in *Those Barren Leaves* (1925), to use the Italian landscape that had temporarily become his home. Afterward, in *Point Counter Point* and *Eyeless in Gaza* (1936), he turned to a great extent to the sites of his more distant travels: Asia and Central America. But it was not merely a question of settings, for the travel books often assume the discrete form of brief essays on moral and aesthetic topics interspersed with scanty passages of description, and show Huxley working out the philosophical problems that attended his transformation from a novelist of manners, which he certainly was, up to *Point Counter Point*, to a didactic writer using fiction to propagate "true ideas," which he became in the last novels, from *Eyeless in Gaza* onward, concerned as he was with the propagation of his ideas of individual and collective salvation.

The parallel between Huxley and Leo Tolstoy is a striking one. Both men underwent a "conversion" that resulted in a profound change in the kinds of books they wrote, and in both there was an evident rejection of certain aspects of their past, which has led readers to see the lives of both novelists as sharply divided. Tolstoy encouraged this view by rejecting the novels that were triumphs in the art of fiction, such as *War and Peace* (1866) and *Anna Karenina* (1875-1877), and writing aggressively moralistic fictions such as *Resurrection* (1899-1900) and *The Kreutzer Sonata* (1889), which he justified in polemical works including *What is Art* (1896) and supplemented by religious and quasi-political tracts such as *The Kingdom of God is Within You* (1894) and *The Slavery of Our Times* (1900). But in fact the moralistic tendencies had been there in Tolstoy from the beginning, and what happened was merely the final triumph of a didactic urge that had already marred *War and Peace* with elaborate theoretical passages on the nature of war, history, and human greatness.

Similarly in Huxley the fascination with speculations on the destiny of mankind, which once had been relegated to pontificating elders like Scogan in *Crome Yellow* and Cardan in *Those Barren Leaves*, began to take control, and it was in his volumes of essays that the change in emphasis first became evident. The collections after *Along the Road–Proper Studies* (1927) and *Do What You Will* (1929)–mark a significant transition from the speculative to the didactic essay. Huxley is no longer recording his explorations of the world, either in terms of nature or of art. He is seeking means to change it, or at least to rationalize man's relation to it. *Proper Studies* is essentially an attempt–in a series of essays on such subjects as equality, education, and democracy, as religious dogmas and secular ideals–to establish a rational political system. *Do What You Will* is a book that attempts to combine the vitalism of D. H. Lawrence with the moderation of the classical Greeks. It is interesting mainly because Huxley is so clearly standing on the verge of the search for spiritual enlightenment and political methods conforming to it that would dominate the last decades of his life.

These books really mark a point of transition, when Huxley seemed not only to abandon the ambition to be a novelist in the full sense but

Huxley, circa 1950 (courtesy of Matthew Huxley)

also the desire to pursue the art of the essayist. His novels from *Eyeless in Gaza* onward seem directed toward exemplifying the spiritually oriented way of life that would reach its logical but aesthetically barren solution in the inane Utopia of his final novel, *Island* (1962); and his nonfictional writings tended to become tracts dedicated to teaching specific lessons. *Ends and Means* (1937) expounds nonviolent ways to deal with a violent world; *The Art of Seeing* (1942) advocates unorthodox methods of curing eye diseases; *The Doors of Perception* (1954) reveals the wonders of drug-induced visions; and *Brave New World Revisited* (1958) shows, by examining contemporary political and technological changes, how near the world had come in an amazingly short time to reproducing in real life the bad dream of his novel *Brave New World*.

Nevertheless, up to the time of his departure to California in 1937, Huxley did keep up to an extent the habit of writing essays, long and short, that was part of the customary routine of English men of letters during the 1920s and 1930s. It supplemented the royalties from novels that, after *Point Counter Point*, appeared at longer intervals than in the past, and it kept his name before the broad middlebrow audience who read the magazines. Two volumes of essays that may be compared with the earlier ones belong to this period: *Music at Night* (1931) and *The Olive Tree* (1936).

Music at Night consists partly of speculative pieces in the field of popular culture and partly of an interesting group of essays that seem to anticipate Huxley's own changing practices as a writer. The first group can perhaps be read most rewardingly as a kind of notebook for *Brave New World*; Huxley speculates in them rather neutrally on issues he would present with satirical force and ferocity in the novel. These pieces discuss a whole series of trends he saw as latent in the Anglo-American world of the late 1920s: the cult of perpetual youth; the problems of the increased leisure that technological developments would offer; the psychological perils of Fordism (the subjection of workers to mechanical processes); the possible development of eugenics as a means of shaping the man of the future; the implications of the attempt to make man primarily a consumer; and the perils to freedom of a dogmatic egalitarianism. A reading of these essays shows that, though *Brave New World* was projected onto the screen of the future, it was derived almost entirely from Huxley's alarmed observation of tendencies he saw in the world around him.

Of the literary essays, the most interesting are "Tragedy and the Whole Truth," "Art and the Obvious," and "Vulgarity in Literature," which seem to show Huxley developing a self-justificatory theory of literature. "Tragedy and the Whole Truth" has a late Tolstoyan ring as Huxley draws an opposition between two types of literature. One type, of which Shakespeare's tragedies are examples, acts quickly and intensely on audiences by isolating the dramatic elements of life. The "Wholly Truthful" literature, represented by the works of writers such as Proust, Dostoyevsky, and Lawrence, Huxley sees as "chemically impure" and mild in its catharsis because it is based on "the pattern of acceptance and resignation," on taking life as it is. Huxley grants that we need both types of literature, but it is clear that he is most attracted to a version of "Whole Truthism." In "Art and the Obvious" he argues that high art has retreated completely from certain areas of life because popular art has vulgarized them. But these aspects of life continue to exist: "And since they exist, they should be faced, fought with, and reduced to artistic order. By pretending that certain things are not there,

which in fact *are* there, much of the most accomplished modern art is condemning itself to incompleteness, to sterility, to premature decrepitude and death."

Vulgarity in literature, as Huxley points out in the essay which bears that title (and which he thought important enough to issue previously as a separate pamphlet in 1930), lies not in the nature of a book's content but in a pretentiousness unrelated to real life. He illustrates this with a comparison between the death of the child Ilusha in *The Brothers Karamazov* (1880) and the death of Charles Dickens's Little Nell (in *The Old Curiosity Shop*, 1841). Why is the first moving and the second not? It is, Huxley suggests, because Dickens isolates in a cloud of emotion the suffering and the innocence of Nell, while Dostoyevsky evokes vividly the factual details of everything that happens around Ilusha's deathbed, and so relates it constantly to "the actual realities of human life."

Indeed, Huxley himself would desert the fine art of fiction, though he preserved the craft, for a series of novels in which he sought "the actual realities" and in the process seemed often to abandon the resources of the imagination. Sometimes this shift of viewpoint involved strange new ways of looking at the visual arts he had written on so perceptively before; perhaps the most eccentric essay in *Music at Night* is "Meditation on El Greco," in which he presents the master of Toledo as an artistic Jonah imprisoned in an intestinal parody of the mystical experience, "the ecstasy that annihilates the personal soul, not by dissolving it out into universal infinity, but by drawing it down and drowning it in the warm, pulsating, tremulous darkness of the body."

At first sight *The Olive Tree*, published a few months after *Eyeless in Gaza*, seems a regression to an earlier past, for there are a pleasantly discursive travel essay, "In a Tunisian Oasis," articles on writers and a painter—Lawrence, Crébillon *fils*, and Benjamin Robert Haydon—and a piece on Huxley's grandfather, "T. H. Huxley as a Literary Man" (which had been separately published as *T. H. Huxley as a Man of Letters* in 1932). But appearances are deceptive. The travel essay and the piece on Crébillon were written in the early 1920s, and the Haydon essay was the introduction to an edition of the painter's autobiography published in 1926. The piece on T. H. Huxley and that on Lawrence were both written in 1931 and published originally in 1932, the second as the introduction to Aldous Huxley's edition of *The Letters of D. H. Lawrence*.

Huxley with his grandchildren Trevenen and Tessa, and his daughter-in-law Ellen Hovde Huxley at their home in Guilford, Connecticut, 1955 (courtesy of Matthew Huxley)

Huxley with his second wife, Laura (née Archera), at their Hollywood Hills home in 1959 (photograph copyright by Rosenys)

None of the later essays that complete the volume concerns a specific place or person. They discuss such varied subjects as the moral risks of a transcendental religion, and the olive tree as a symbol of peace and plenty, showing Huxley's growing involvement in pacifism and ecological concerns. Other essays anticipate Orwell by dwelling on the use of literature as propaganda and the distortion and impoverishment of the language for political purposes.

The irony, of course, it that from this time on Huxley himself began to use literature for something very close to propaganda. The burden of almost all his fiction thenceforth would be that the salvation of humanity from the plagues of war and ecological disaster could come about only through the creation of a nonacquisitive society, pacifist in politics, Kropotkinesque in economics, and personally oriented toward the mystical forms of religious experience that, in Huxley's view, prepared men and women for a life of practical sanity.

The same viewpoint permeates his collection of essays *Tomorrow and Tomorrow and Tomorrow* (printed in England as *Adonis and the Alphabet*), which appeared in 1956. Curiously it shows that while Huxley had not lost his critical interest in the other arts, he had ceased to apply it to literature. There are, indeed, two essays that remind one of the fine critical pieces of the 1920s and are no less excellent in Huxley's characteristic biographical-critical manner. "Doodles in a Dictionary," despite its misleading title, is one of the most sensitive descriptions ever written of Henri de Toulouse-Lautrec, and the essay on Carlo Gesualdo evokes with somber eloquence both the agonized personality of that murderer, masochist, and musical genius, and the setting of Renaissance Italy. The remaining essays of *Tomorrow and Tomorrow and Tomorrow* are concerned with issues, and in this direction Huxley wrote best in his self-contained tracts. His slow diminution as an essayist ran parallel to his decline as a novelist, and they both seem indissolubly linked to that longing for some ultimate "dissolving" of the personal soul "into universal infinity," which made him abandon that intense interest in personality and in the free perception of experience that inspires the best essayists and novelists alike.

Letters:

The Letters of Aldous Huxley, edited by Grover Smith (London: Chatto & Windus, 1969; New York: Harper & Row, 1969).

Interviews:

Hans Beerman, "An Interview with Aldous Huxley," *Midwest Quarterly*, 5 (April 1964): 223-230;

Writers at Work: The "Paris Review" Interviews, second series (New York, 1968), pp. 193-214.

Bibliographies:

Hanson R. Duval, *Aldous Huxley: A Bibliography* (New York: Arrow, 1939);

Clair Eschelbach and Joyce Lee Shober, *Aldous Huxley: A Bibliography, 1916-1959* (Berkeley: University of California Press, 1961);

Thomas D. Clareson and Carolyn S. Andrews, "Aldous Huxley: A Bibliography 1960-1964," *Extrapolation*, 6 (December 1964): 2-21;

Douglas Dennis Davis, "Aldous Huxley: A Bibliography, 1965-1973," *Bulletin of Bibliography and Magazine Notes*, 31 (1974): 67-70.

Biographies:

Ronald W. Clark, *The Huxleys* (New York: McGraw-Hill, 1968);

Laura Archera Huxley, *This Timeless Moment: A Personal View of Aldous Huxley* (London: Chatto & Windus, 1968; New York: Farrar, Straus & Giroux, 1968);

Sybille Bedford, *Aldous Huxley: A Biography*, 2 volumes (London: Chatto & Windus, 1973; London: Collins, 1974).

References:

John Atkins, *Aldous Huxley: A Literary Study* (London: Calder, 1956; New York: Roy, 1957);

Milton Birnbaum, *Aldous Huxley's Quest for Values* (New York: Library of Art & Social Science, 1971);

Peter Bowering, *Aldous Huxley: A Study of the Major Novels* (London: Athlone, 1968; New York: Oxford, 1969);

Laurence Brander, *Aldous Huxley: A Critical Study* (London: Hart-Davis, 1970; Lewisburg, Pa.: Bucknell University Press, 1970);

Jocelyn Brooke, *Aldous Huxley* (London: Longman's, Green, 1954);

Kishore Gandhi, *Aldous Huxley: The Search for Perennial Religion* (New Delhi: Arnold-Heinemann, 1980);

Alexander Henderson, *Aldous Huxley* (London: Chatto & Windus, 1935; New York: Harper, 1936);

Bede Hines, *The Social World of Aldous Huxley* (Loretto, Pa.: Seraphic, 1957);

Huxley in August 1963 at Saltwood Castle in England, the home of his friend Kenneth Clark
(courtesy of Matthew Huxley)

Charles M. Homes, *Aldous Huxley and the Way to Reality* (Bloomington: University of Indiana Press, 1970);

Julian Huxley, ed., *Aldous Huxley: A Memorial Volume* (London: Chatto & Windus, 1968; New York: Farrar, Straus & Giroux, 1968);

Keith M. May, *Aldous Huxley* (London: Elek, 1972);

Jerome Meckier, *Aldous Huxley: Satire and Structure* (London: Chatto & Windus, 1969; New York: Barnes & Noble, 1969);

Guinevera A. Nance, *Aldous Huxley* (New York: Continuum, 1988);

George Woodcock, *Dawn and the Darkest Hour: A Study of Aldous Huxley* (New York: Viking, 1972; London: Cape, 1972).

David Jones

(1 November 1895 - 28 October 1974)

Ian Ross
University of British Columbia

See also the Jones entry in *DLB 20: British Poets, 1914-1945*.

BOOKS: *In Parenthesis* (London: Faber & Faber, 1937; New York: Chilmark, 1962);

The Anathemata: Fragments of an Attempted Writing (London: Faber & Faber, 1952; New York: Chilmark, 1963);

Epoch and Artist: Selected Writings, edited by Harman Grisewood (London: Faber & Faber, 1959; New York: Chilmark, 1963);

The Fatigue (Cambridge: Rampant Lions, 1965);

The Tribune's Visitation (London: Fulcrum, 1969);

An Introduction to the Rime of the Ancient Mariner (London: Clover Hill, 1972);

The Sleeping Lord, and Other Fragments (London: Faber & Faber, 1974; New York: Chilmark, 1974);

The Kensington Mass (London: Agenda, 1975);

Use & Sign (Ispwich, U.K.: Golgonooza, 1975);

The Dying Gaul, and Other Writings, edited by Grisewood (London & Boston: Faber & Faber, 1978);

Introducing David Jones: A Selection of His Writings, edited by John Matthias (London & Boston: Faber & Faber, 1980);

The Roman Quarry and Other Sequences, edited by Grisewood and René Hague (London: Agenda, 1981; New York: Sheep Meadow, 1981);

The Narrows (Budleigh Salterton, Devon, U.K.: Interim, 1981).

RECORDING: *Readings from the Anathemata, In Parenthesis,* [and] *The Hunt*, Argo PLP 1093, 1967.

Walter David Jones was born on 1 November 1895 at Brockley, Kent, then becoming part of suburban London. Because of his affinity for Welsh culture, he subscribed the name David Jones to his artwork and writings, though occasionally he added Michael as a middle name after becoming a Roman Catholic in 1921. Site and local-ity meant a great deal to him, and for much of his career his home was in London or its vicinity. "For practically all my life," he wrote, "[I] have lived near where Thames runs softly" (*The Dying Gaul*, 1978). There were childhood holidays, however, with his grandparents in North Wales; war years in France (December 1915-February 1918) and Ireland (March-December 1918); prolonged stays in Wales connected with his training as a visual artist (1924-1926), at Capel-y-ffin among the Black Mountains on the Monmouth-Breconshire border and in a Benedictine monastery on Caldey Island, Pembrokeshire; a visit to Cairo and Jerusalem in 1934 undertaken for health reasons; and extensive stays at the Fort Hotel, Sidmouth, Devon (1933-1940), until he returned to London again shortly after the outbreak of World War II. In his teens it came to him that he was not to marry, though he did contract an engagement, broken off in 1927, to Petra Gill, daughter of the sculptor Eric Gill. Celibate and somewhat reclusive as he was, however, he made deep and lasting friendships with men and women, sustained with many detailed and extensive letters that provide a unique record of his feelings, ideas, and artistic projects; these letters have to be studied as clues to the matrix of his paintings, inscriptions, and writings both in prose and poetry. He moved in 1946 to a nursing home at Harrow-on-the-Hill, north of London, to receive treatment for the recurrence of a severe nervous disorder that first afflicted him in 1933. After recovery he remained in the Harrow area in rented single rooms he called his "dugouts," and he died on 28 October 1974 in the Calvary Nursing Home of the Blue Sisters on Sudbury Hill.

He once wrote of himself (in *The Dying Gaul*): "I am in no sense a scholar, but an artist, and it is paramount for any artist that he should use whatever happens to be to hand." From his earliest years he wanted to draw, an activity he felt came as naturally to him as wanting to stroke a cat, and his success in drawing made him, at the age of six, wish to be an artist when he grew

David Jones (photograph by Julian Sheppard)

up. His parents respected his wish and sent him to art school for the five years before World War I. But as he drew what was immediately and concretely at hand, the dancing bear he observed from his window in 1902, or the plaster cast of a figure identified as the Dying Gaul, which his teachers set before him in 1909 as a representative form of the antique, to be rendered before he was allowed to tackle a living model, Jones was storing up and becoming aware of the "deposits," to use his own word, essential for another side of the artist as he came to conceive that role: "a 'rememberer' . . . a sort of Boethius, who has been nick-named 'the Bridge,' because he carried forward into an altogether metamorphosed world certain of the fading oracles which had sustained antiquity" (*The Dying Gaul*).

Deposits of memory at first came to Jones principally from his parents. His father, James Jones, was born into a Welsh-speaking family living in Treffynnon (Holywell) but came to London seeking work as a compositor and rose to be the printer's overseer and later business manager of the *Christian Herald*. David's mother, Alice

Ann Bradshaw Jones, was the daughter of a master block- and mast-maker, whose trade was applied in the vicinity of the Pool of London. This grandfather, Ebenezer Bradshaw, is affectionately recalled and "re-presented" (another word favored by Jones) in the "Redriff " section of the long poem entitled *The Anathemata* (1952). Bradshaw's practice of a skilled trade illustrated for Jones definitions of aesthetic endeavor that he upheld steadfastly: "the virtue of art is to judge," and "art is a virtue of the practical intelligence" (*The Dying Gaul*). But Jones felt, as is made clear in *Epoch and Artist* (1959), that he belonged to his "father's people and their land," whose spirit touched him as his father sang "Mae hen wlad fy nhadau" and "Ar hyd y nos" effortlessly in perfect pitch in the "clear-vowelled Cymraeg [language]" and told stories from Gwynedd-is-Gonwy in the northwest corner of Wales. The "wonder," "pride," and "awe" David Jones felt in response to his father's heritage was reinforced by the holiday visits to North Wales, when he delighted in the unspoiled landscape of the Atlantic seacoast and high hills and once encountered his paternal grandfather, sitting by a fish weir of wattles and boulders near St. Trillos's chapel and resembling a figure (King Maelgwyn) from Welsh folklore.

Within these family circumstances lay the subject matter and the intellectual and imaginative challenges that David Jones contended with, extrapolated, and amplified as he developed into a visual artist and, later, a writer. Possibly there is an analogy with D. H. Lawrence, who believed his miner father was in touch with instinctive, intuitive animal life, while his schoolteacher mother, in his mind, was associated with refinement, ambition, and intellect. Paradoxically using his mother's legacy of refined consciousness and literary impulse, however, Lawrence sought to penetrate and reveal the lost father's world of animal sensation and contact with nature, at the same time excoriating the civilized world to which his mother wished to belong. Somewhat similarly, Jones, to a large extent imprisoned in the monoglot, urban, English culture of his mother, sought to realize in diverse artistic media a vision of an idealized Welsh past that was Catholic, aristocratic, pastoral, tradition-bound, and welcoming to the arts and their practitioners—a vision whose primary source seems to have been the stories and songs of his father.

Jones's essays account for the autobiographical basis of this vision of Wales, chart its extension through his inquiries into many disciplines—linguistic, archaeological, anthropological, sociological, literary, and historical—and explicate the theory of art and the artist developed to justify the whole enterprise. They also reveal how Jones in the thrall of this vision saw himself as an artist pitted against an epoch inimical to such a vision and deaf to, or at best impatient with, the theorizing that accompanied it.

Accordingly the essays are found to be mythopoeic and visionary in recreating the writer's life and the lost past of the father's race; they are polemical in validating his theories; and they are prophetic and denunciatory in reviewing the times and society he lived in, characterized, in his view, by "megalopolitan technocracy" (*Epoch and Artist*). Jones had a profoundly disturbing confrontation with the horrors of modern technological civilization during World War I, in which he fought as a private in the Royal Welsh Fusiliers. Even in this appalling time of conflict, however, he experienced a stage when the values he prized were uppermost. For him, as he reports in *Epoch and Artist*, the first six months of his time on the

Western Front were marked by the "intimate, continuing, domestic life of small contingents of men, within whose structure [one] could find [friends]." In these months, "there was a certain attractive amateurishness, and elbow room for idiosyncrasy that connected one with a less exacting past." But the bottom was knocked out of this life in July 1916 by the onset of the Battle of the Somme, in which he was wounded: "from then onward things hardened into a more relentless mechanical affair, took on a more sinister aspect." Nevertheless, during his service in the war, he did some sketching and attempted some writing, both forms handled in conventional ways but containing some seeds of his later development.

After the war he continued his art studies, became a convert to the Roman Catholic faith, and undertook an apprenticeship as an engraver and book illustrator under Eric Gill, first at Ditchling Common in Sussex and then at Capel-y-ffin. Through the Gill circle in the 1920s and through his association with the periodicals *Order* (1928-1929) and its successor, the *Colosseum* (beginning in 1934), based in Chelsea, Jones took part in discussions that furthered his intellectual maturity, helping to clarify his ideas about Catholic sacramental and liturgical thought and its relationship to art. In addition he was introduced to the congenial neo-Thomism of Jacques Maritain and the revisionist historical perspectives of Christopher Dawson, a member of the Chelsea circle. The attitudes of the group combined conservative social, political, and cultural sympathies with great interest in the contemporary, experimental creative work of Henri Matisse, Georges Braque, James Joyce, and T. S. Eliot. Jones came to know Eliot well through his Chelsea friends, and Eliot's *Notes towards the Definition of Culture* (begun in 1943, published in 1948) concerns the arguments of the Chelsea circle and, important to Jones, the need to defend the indigenous languages and cultures of the small nations of Europe, including the Welsh, if England and Europe were to retain any culture at all.

Through this period Jones was holding successful exhibitions of his watercolors and achieving a reputation for his engravings for book illustrations, as well as for his lettering. In 1928, about the time he accepted a commission to make copperplate engravings for an edition of Samuel Taylor Coleridge's *The Rime of the Ancient Mariner*, he began to write down "some sentences" that grew in the course of the next eight years or so into the long poem *In Parenthesis*, pub-

"Death and Life-in-Death," one of Jones's copper engravings for a 1929 edition of The Rime of the Ancient Mariner.
*The engravings were republished in a 1964 edition, with an introductory essay by Jones. In 1972 a
longer version of the essay was separately published.*

lished in 1937 by Faber and Faber, with which
Eliot was connected. Jones said of the poem (in
Epoch and Artist): "this writing has to do with
things I saw, felt, and was part of " between December 1915 and July 1916, the period before
the war "took on a more sinister aspect," reflecting the dire "civilizational situation" Jones believed he faced. The title arose because the poem
was "written . . . in a kind of space between . . .
[or] as you turn aside to do something," and because the war itself was a kind of parenthesis, as
is "our curious type of existence." It was in writing this poem that Jones made himself one of the
seiri cerdd ("carpenters of song") as the Welsh call
their bards. In addition he was drawn into being
an essay writer, for he was prevailed on to contribute a preface to *In Parenthesis* to introduce his
poem and himself to readers. Possibly this was
thought to be necessary because the poem was
strikingly avant-garde in language and effects,

sharing literary techniques with the work of
Joyce and Eliot: including shifting centers of consciousness; fragmented syntax; wide-ranging and
dense allusions to myth, legend, history, and
many other fields of human discourse; the rhythmic introduction of ideas and image-clusters as
unifying devices; and alternating lexical levels,
principally associated in Jones's case with the
Welsh and Cockney soldiers of his regiment,
whose humor and agony produced the layering
of the text.

Jones wrote in the preface that he did not intend *In Parenthesis* to be a "War Book," though it
happened to be concerned with war, and he expressed how sensitive men of his generation were
transformed by this particular war; "I think that
day by day in the Waste Land, the sudden vio-
lences and the long stillnesses, the sharp contours and unformed voids of that mysterious existence, profoundly affected the imagination of

142

those who suffered it. It was a place of enchantment. It is perhaps best described in Malory, book iv, chapter 15,–that landscape spoke 'with a grimly voice.' " The reference to "the Waste Land" makes one think of Eliot, and Jones acknowledged that reading *The Waste Land* (1922) had made a considerable impact on him. He also knew Eliot's sources, which were, in part at least, his, too: Jessie Weston's *From Ritual to Romance* (1920) and James G. Frazer's *The Golden Bough* (1890-1915). The only part of Joyce's work Jones seems to have known firsthand while writing *In Parenthesis* was the Anna Livia Plurabelle passage from *Finnegans Wake* (which he read in one of the "Work in Progress" installments in *transition* magazine, the book version being published in 1939).

It would be fair to say that the direction of these books by others converged with Jones's rather than influenced him. His invocation of Thomas Malory is perhaps more revealing, for it suggests that he could universalize his war experience by connecting it with *Le Morte d'Arthur* (1485), much as Joyce succeeds (in *Ulysses*, 1922) in expanding the significance of Leopold Bloom to a timeless level: Joyce links Bloom's wanderings in Dublin to those of the homeward journey of Odysseus and, more wickedly but characteristically, to Dante's descent into the underworld (represented by Dublin's nighttown), accompanied by Virgil (the character Stephen Dedalus), and final ascent to be with Beatrice in Heaven (Molly Bloom in the marriage bed). Like Joyce and Eliot, of course, Jones turns personal problems and dilemmas into opportunities to question human history and explore cultural phases as well as religious issues of importance, and these are the subjects of the essays by Jones that came to be gathered together with the preface to *In Parenthesis* and presented in *Epoch and Artist*.

The title *Epoch and Artist* focuses attention on a central concern of Jones, explicit or implicit in all his essays: what is it to be an artist in his times as contrasted with former times, when this figure had an acknowledged place in society because artistic aims were congruent with that society's aims. As the book's frontispiece there is a composite Welsh-English-Latin inscription by Jones, linking a "key line" from *Y Gododdin* (the earliest known Welsh poem), *"Beird byt barnant wyr o gallon,"* to an English version, "the bards of the world assess the men of valour," then continuing, "but *super sellam ivdicis non sedebvnt sed creatvram aevi confirmabvnt et deprecatio illorvm in operatione artis* and without these *non aedificatvr*

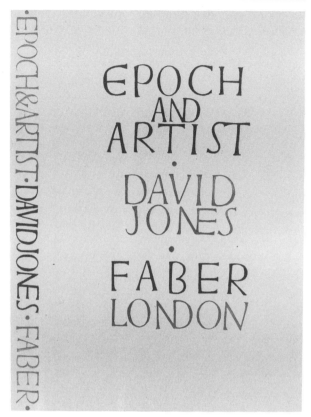

Dust jacket for Jones's 1959 essay collection, in which he discusses man, art, and history and their interrelationships

civitas." This theme of the bardic function extending to the function of all artists, also that of the city of man (and of God) not being built without the proper exercise of this function, guides the sequence of the essays. The arrangement seems to have been due to the percipience of the editor, Harman Grisewood, who was also responsible for the organization of *The Dying Gaul*, though he laments that in the latter case Jones was no longer alive to sanction the arrangement of the essays and offer advice about it.

As Jones's preface to *Epoch and Artist* makes clear, it was a religious insight arising from Catholic thought about the Eucharist that gave him a way of looking at man as a being in "his essential nature a *poeta*, one who makes things that are signs of something," and therefore a way of articulating criticism of the "technocracy in which we live," because it "conditions us all, [and] tends . . . in all sorts of contexts and at every level, to draw us away from [the] sign-world." It is true that Jones is imbued with notions drawn from Oswald Spengler about the "decline of the west" and the lateness of the times, but Jones found meaningful, and responded as essayist to, the claim Spengler made for all artists, that they show "things which tend to be impoverished, or misconceived, or altogether lost or willfully set aside in the preoccupations of our present intense technological phase, but which, none the less, belong to man." The "impoverished things" he shows in the essays include "site, place, locality, racial and cultural ties and all the rest of it" that for him were "very much involved in 'epoch.' " Never one to dwell at the abstract level for long, he was led by this concern to consider his Welsh background and his anxiety about the future of the Welsh heritage: "the actual land itself, its sites and rooted communities and all that has hitherto afforded a connection, however fragmented and attenuated with the foundational things." He sees as "one big contributory cause" to that anxiety the "actual nature of our megalopolitan technocracy and the kind of men it requires us to be," arising from his prevailing assumption that facts are empirical and have no other reference or validity. So, in this view, the "Welsh *res*," as well as "what is said to be done at the altar, and . . . what artists, under whatever mode, attempt all the day long" are all in the same category.

According to Grisewood, in his introduction to the book, the essays in *Epoch and Artist* seemed to fall naturally into four groups–a pattern repeated to a large extent in *The Dying Gaul*. The first group (made up of ten essays) is concerned with the " 'things of Wales,' considered on a personal level, but broaching Jones's deep concern for her relation with the rest of Britain and so with the whole Western World." There is no parallel to the stance of Hugh MacDiarmid's *Lucky Poet* (1943), which is a "self-study in literature and political ideas" by the contemporary Scottish poet, who shared Jones's concern for "Celticity itself." Jones is rueful, self-deprecatory about his knowledge of the Welsh language, at once serious about his art and ironic in outlook, perhaps taking a cue from the Chaucer of *The Canterbury Tales*. Jones's essays in this first group, by and large, are parts of a bildungsroman, and in some ways the most important sentences come at the end of the first essay, "Autobiographical Talk": "like the four figures in the *mabinogi* of Manawydan we may try our hands at different kinds of making; and we shall, I think, find that the same problems await us however variously disguised or metamorphosed." Through practicing the visual arts and reflecting on what he did, Jones had come to the view that a painting ought to be "a 'thing' having abstract qualities by which

it coheres and without which it cannot be said to exist. Further that it 'shows forth' something, is representational." He supposed that if this were true of one art, it would be true of others, but he considered that the "nice problems" of adjusting the balance of the "formal" and the "contential" could only be discovered through experience, and he offers accounts of the "making" of *In Parenthesis* and *The Anathemata* as a contribution to ongoing discussion of aesthetic questions. The range of subject matter and reference of all his work is summed up in what he notes about *The Anathemata*: "I was explicitly concerned with a recalling of certain things which I myself had received, things which are part of the complex deposits of this Island, so of course involving Wales and of course involving the central Christian rite and mythological historical, etc., data of all sorts." But that said, it occurred to him to add that he also considered the watercolor he had just painted of flowers in a glass calix to belong "*im*plicitly to the same world of remembering and celebrating as *The Anathemata*."

It is important to understand that for Jones the Welsh language had a magical quality, and that he knew more of it than he permitted himself to claim. He had to write about Wales and the "Welsh mythological element," for example, because he felt deeply this was an "*integral* part of our tradition," that is, the life-forming deposits of the island of Britain, and in similar manner he felt deeply about the "Catholic thing which has determined so much of our history and conditioned the thought of us all," leaving aside the truth or untruth of this religion itself.

The second group of essays is made up of the most abstract and difficult of them, offering comprehensive statements about the nature of man, art as the quintessentially human activity, and the tenor of the modern world as inimical to the artist and therefore to humanity. Jones was disappointed that this part of *Epoch and Artist*, so crucial to him, aroused so little response. Jones's position (stated in "Art and Democracy," the first essay in this group) is that man is a "prudential animal," that is, one differentiated by subscription to "faith and morals," not necessarily of a religious persuasion. Moreover, it is the nature of this animal "to practice an intransitive activity to which adheres a gratuitous quality." This is Jones's rephrasing of the dictum of Gill that "art is the sole intransitive activity of man." Other animals–bees, beavers, nuthatches–make beautiful things, for functional ends, but it is man's lot

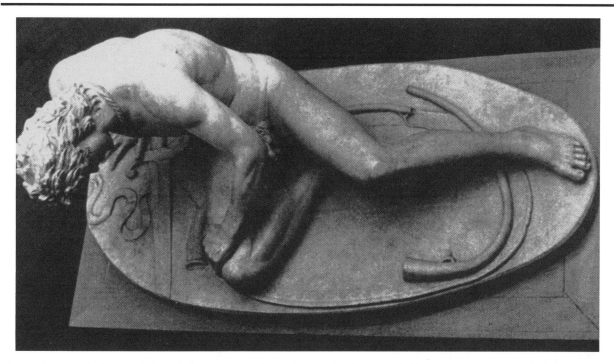

The Dying Gaul *(by permission of the Museum of Classical Archaeology, Cambridge). This ancient Greek bronze inspired Jones's 1959 essay of the same name, which was originally published in the* Listener, *then collected in* The Dying Gaul, and Other Writings *in 1978.*

alone to make things from free choice, gratuitously. Jones came to this way of thinking in 1919 (as he points out in an essay called "Art and Sacrament"), finding an analogy between Postimpressionist theory and Catholic teaching about the Eucharist: "I said, Well, the insistence that a painting must be a *thing* and not the impression of something has an affinity with what the Church said of the Mass, that what was oblated under the species of Bread and Wine at the Supper was the same *thing* as what was bloodily immolated on Calvary. Post-Impressionist theorists . . . were always loudly asserting that their aim was to make a 'thing'–let's say a mountain or a table or a girl that was one of these objects *under the form of paint*, and not an impression of 'mountain,' 'table,' or 'girl.' And that this idea was, *mutatis mutandis*, similar or analogous to what, I understood, the Church held with regard to Mass."

From "Art and Sacrament," and also from "Notes on the 1930s" and "The Utile," the reader sees why Jones asserts it is "axiomatic that all art is 'abstract' and that all art 're-presents.' " This latter term is the clue to Jones's notion that "man is unavoidably a sacramentalist and that his works are sacramental in character." By this he means man is given to making signs. An example is paleolithic man juxtaposing "marks on surfaces not with merely utile, but with significant intent; that

is to say a 're-presenting,' a 'showing again under other forms,' an 'effective recalling' of something was intended," as at the Lascaux caves ("The Utile"). Even more pertinent for Jones is Christ at the Last Supper saying, "Do this for a recalling of me," and so placing himself "in the order of Signs," to quote from the epigraph to *Epoch and Artist*. This formulation about Christ came from the Jesuit theologian, Maurice de la Taille, whose book *Mysterium Fidei* (1915) was known in outline to Gill's Ditchling community in the 1920s. It is in the light of this teaching about the Eucharist that Jones announces: "No artefacture no Christian religion," and "where artefacture is there is the muse." Hence arises the problem he considers again and again in different phrasings, that though man is intrinsically a sign-making animal, and the deepest religious truths are bound up with this activity, the present epoch–immersed in "megalopolitan technocracy"–is hostile to signs.

Among Jones's friends in the late 1920s and 1930s, there was discussion of a phenomenon called "The Break," meaning the division between the time when there was security about the world of sacrament and sign and the time when signs suffered a kind of invalidation. René Hague thought Hilaire Belloc had used the term to denote the break with Rome at the Reformation, and then Gill extended it to include the consequences of the Renaissance, the triumph of capitalism, and the dehumanization of the worker. Jones was particularly concerned about the fate of the artist as victim of "The Break," never sure if his choice of what was valid and available as signs would work. In his view the only solution was that the artist must "work within the limits of his love. There must be no mugging-up, no 'ought to know' or 'try to feel'; for only what is actually loved and known can be seen *sub specie aeternitatis*" (Preface to *The Anathemata*).

Jones conceived of the poet's role as that of the "rememberer," the lifter up of valid signs or, as he defined his comprehensive term "the anathemata": "the blessed things that have taken on what is cursed and the profane things that somehow are redeemed: the delights and also the 'ornaments' . . . things, or some aspect of them, that partake of the extra-utile and of the gratuitous; things that are the signs of something other, together with those signs that not only have the nature of a sign, but are themselves, under some mode, what they signify. Things set up, lifted up, or in whatever manner made over to the gods" (Preface to *The Anathemata*). Turn where he may in the modern world, however, Jones's man as artist finds a dichotomy between the utile and the "extra-utile," and a "divorce" between what he must be to suit the times and what he used to be, or perhaps ought to be, according to the true nature of his kind. The dilemma inescapably confronts him of either denying the sign world and thus negating his existence, or affirming the sign world and being increasingly puzzled by the dehumanized works characteristic of our society. Jones offers no way out of these difficulties, only the results of his own "reconnaissance." His perspective is that of the infantryman caught in trench warfare, and the only advice he can give is, "Soldier on!"

In the third group of essays, dealing with "epoch" and taking up the things of Britain and cognate subjects in a long perspective going back to the Roman Empire, there can be seen something of the congenial historical viewpoint of Christopher Dawson. His name heads the list acknowledged by Jones in the preface to *The Anathemata* of those who aided him to make his "artefacts," and Dawson's *The Age of the Gods* (1928) is specifically referred to in "The Dying Gaul" (reprinted in *The Dying Gaul, and Other Writings* in 1978). The associated essays by Jones generally reflect Dawson's analysis of the impact of imperialism on agrarian culture, what Christianity was like in the Dark Ages, and similar topics, though Jones has his own slant on these matters and brings in archaeological, linguistic, and other data from many sources.

Meditating on the Roman roads of Britain, for example (in "The Viae"), Jones is fascinated by the technical details of their making, which he assimilates to his memories of army fatigue parties and conjures up a picture of a Roman warrant officer in charge of a construction squad. This is done much in the manner of Kipling's historical evocations in *Puck of Pook's Hill* (1906); Eliot, to be sure, noticed affinities between Jones and Kipling. Characteristically, Jones brings in the Arthur of Welsh tradition as the "Director of Toil" who stands behind the Roman roads, also the mythological figure "Helen of the Hosts," who was the inspiration for the "poor buggers" who made the roads. And it is the figure of Arthur who dominates this whole group of essays. He is most substantially treated in "The Myth of Arthur": "[He] is the conveyer of order, even to the confines of chaos; he is the redeemer, in the strict sense of the word; he darkens the Lombard threshold only with his weapon; his potency is the instrument of redemption, the pawn-ticket that he presents is called Caledfwlch, Escalibur, Caliburn, with which he killed the black sorceress, the daughter of the white sorceress. Always the consolidator, the saviour and channel of power, the protector and life-giver, and more significantly for us 'the Director of Toil.' "

On another front Jones finds the "thread of frustration and betrayal" in Celtic literature "strangely congruent" with the fact that it was the Tudors of Môn who, in the sixteenth century, crushed the Irish and denied justice in their own language to their kinfolk in Wales. In the essay "Wales and Visual Form" Jones calls the Tudor policy of "ironing-out of what remained of the old order" a *Gleichsgeschaltung*, deliberately invoking a word associated with the Nazi form of "coordination" forced on the German people by terror following Hitler's accession to power in 1933. But for Jones the betrayed and dying "Gauls" also revive, through the persistence of the race and the tenacity of their art, and in this connection he instances James Joyce as the "most creative literary genius of this century" who manifested an "essential Celticity" in perfecting art that triumphed over the limitations of the current "megalopolitan civilization." But this is a topic best developed with reference to the fourth group of Jones's essays. This last group deals with the "artist," by taking up specific figures who illustrate or amplify Jones's viewpoint, and by deliberate intention *Epoch and Artist* culminates in an essay on Joyce.

In the first of these last pieces, Jones responds to a personal attack on a contemporary artist, Vincent Pasmore, for his subscription to "abstract art," by enunciating the principle "that it is an abstract *quality*, however hidden or devious, which determines the real worth of any work. . . . The one common factor implicit in all the arts of man resides in a certain juxtaposing of forms." In proof of his assertion, Jones employs a device that recurs in his prose writings, a list of items, in this case artifacts that reflect his wide range of aesthetic sympathies and keen eye for telling examples: Botticelli's *Primavera*, the White Horse of Uffington, the music of Monteverdi, Joyce's *Finnegans Wake* (1939), the "Alfred jewel," "the glass goblet I am now trying to draw," the shape of the liturgy, and the shape of a tea cup.

Long an admirer of Christopher Smart's *Song to David* (1924), Jones rejoiced in the discovery and publication in 1939 of the *Jubilato Agno* for its "feeling for, and unity with, the animal creation," also the "erratic, curious, difficult, sometimes jocular, occasionally very moving" association of ideas. Jones writes perceptively (in "Christopher Smart") of Smart's struggles with "stupefying and complicating elements," suggesting the problem of the poem arises from Smart's lack of "architectonic ability rather than his 'mental ill-health.' "

Also in this section are two pieces on Eric Gill, one a scrupulous assessment of his merits as a sculptor and the other an appreciative account of the man who carried on the intellectual and artistic tradition of John Ruskin and William Morris into the twentieth century, much to the benefit of Jones himself. Gill helped Jones's ideas to be clarified and his artistic skills to be honed.

The essay on Joyce is ostensibly a review of a picture book about his Dublin background, but in effect it is a hymn to this writer. Jones celebrates the dependence "on the particular, on place, site, locality" of this "most incarnational of artists," and his consequent ability "to make the universal shine out from the particular." The "accidents" and "conditioning factors" necessary for this achievement were, in part, access to English as the "lingua franca" of today; a comprehensive grasp of the Catholic mind, embracing everything from the school men to modern parochial practice, to gather in West European mythologi-

cal and cultural content; and knowledge of a "folk" in a Celtic hinterland, essential because they retained pre-Celtic "deposits" and had received Germanic-Latin infusions. Added to the foregoing was Joyce's understanding of an urban culture, juxtaposing seaport activities, the subculture of slums and pubs, and the world of learning–popular, humanistic, and scientific–ranging in origin from the eighteenth-century Enlightenment to the advanced "higher criticisms" that fashioned the twentieth-century mind. Accordingly, from these and other mixed data, Joyce fashioned "an art-form showing an essential Celticity as intricate, complex, flexible, exact, and abstract as anything from the visual arts of La Tène or Kells or the aural intricacies of medieval Welsh metric." This "hymn" to Joyce expresses the central concerns and highest ideals of Jones himself as artist.

The Celtic bards who were the progenitors of Joyce and Jones perfected their skills through long training and were assigned specific tasks. They remembered the noble deeds of their ancestors, incited their kinsmen to emulate them, and cursed their enemies. It is reported of the bardic schools in the Hebrides that those in training were required to lie in darkness in narrow booths, with stones on their bellies, and practice the discipline of mental composition. There is something of this ancient training and these formally assigned tasks in the essays of Jones. He curses the enemies of modern man under a thousand shapes: dehumanized working conditions, death-dealing technology, conurbations that swamp the individual, zeal for reformation and improvement that obliterates valid tradition, and adherence to dead words as well as denial of a living spirit. He remembers the deeds of valor from the past–above all, perhaps, that of the "young hero who stripped himself" and "mounted the high gallows in the sight of many" to redeem mankind, in *The Dream of the Road*; or, on the secular level, Owain Gwynedd in 1129 defeating his Welsh and English foes at Coleshill and ensuring thereafter that Holywell would be held by Welsh-speakers; or Adm. Horatio Nelson disclosing his Trafalgar battle plan that was "new," "singular," and "simple"; or Jones's fellow fusiliers in the Mametz Wood on the Somme in July 1916.

In *David Jones, Mythmaker* (1983) Elizabeth Ward condemns in Jones's essays the faults of "abstraction, repetitiveness, and eccentricity." There is some truth in these charges, and it should not be pretended that readers of "Art and Sacra-

Jones in the 1960s (photograph by Janet Stone)

ment," for example, will have an easy time. There are commensurate rewards, however, for those who persevere with Jones's prose. His passionately held convictions about history and art rivet one's attention. His abstractions from historical situations and artistic endeavors offer formal qualities to apprehend and test against current realities. His style, with its eccentricities of vocabulary, parenthetical syntax, and respectful awareness of the full meaning of words and culture is reminiscent of that of the grammarian Roger Ascham, part of the earliest tradition of the English essay. Jones's nearer contemporaries, G. K. Chesterton, Belloc, and Gill, taught him something about the handling of exposition and polemics congenial to his religious persuasion, but he reaches beyond this to touch common humanity. What he wrote about the "function of genuine myth" in *Epoch and Artist* appears to have been what he accepted for his own role as a "man detailed": "To conserve, to develop, to bring together, to make significant for the present what the past holds, without diminution or any deleting, but rather by transubstantiating the material,

. . . neither pedantic nor popularizing, not indifferent to scholarship, nor antiquarian, but saying always: 'of these thou hast given me have I lost none.' "

Letters:

Letters to Vernon Watkins, edited by Ruth Pryor (Cardiff: University of Wales Press, 1976);

List of Letters by David Jones, compiled by Charles J. Stoneburner (Granville, Ohio: Limekiln, 1977);

Letters to William Hayward, edited by Colin Wilcockson (London: Agenda, 1979);

Dai Greatcoat: A Self-Portrait of David Jones in His Letters, edited by René Hague (London & Boston: Faber & Faber, 1980);

Letters to a Friend, edited by Aneirin Talfan Davies (Swansea, U.K.: Triskele, 1980);

Inner Necessities: The Letters of David Jones to Desmond Chute, edited by Thomas Dilworth (Toronto: Anson-Cartwright, 1984).

Bibliography:

Samuel Rees, *David Jones: An Annotated Bibliogra-*

Samuel Rees, *David Jones: An Annotated Bibliography and Guide to Research* (New York & London: Garland, 1977).

Biography:

René Hague, *David Jones* (Cardiff: University of Wales Press & Welsh Arts Council, 1975);

William Blisset, *The Long Conversation: A Memoir of David Jones* (Oxford & New York: Oxford University Press, 1981).

References:

Agenda, special Jones issues, 5, nos. 1-3 (1967); 11, no. 4 (1973); 12, no. 1 (1974);

David Blamires, *David Jones: Artist and Writer* (Manchester: Manchester University Press, 1971; Toronto: University of Toronto Press, 1972);

David Jones Society Newsletter, 1 (March 1976);

Harman Grisewood, *David Jones: Writer and Artist* (London: BBC, 1966);

Jeremy Hooker, *David Jones: An Exploratory Study of the Writings* (London: Enitharmon, 1975);

Robin Ironside, *David Jones* (Harmondsworth, U.K.: Penguin, 1949);

Frank Kermode, *Puzzles and Epiphanies: Essays and Reviews, 1958-61* (London: Routledge & Kegan Paul, 1982), ch. 2;

Roland Mathias, ed., *David Jones: Eight Essays on His Work as Writer and Artist* (Llandysul, Wales: Gomer, 1976);

Philip Pacey, *David Jones and Other Wonder Voyagers* (Bridgend, Wales: Poetry Wales, 1982);

Samuel Rees, *David Jones* (Boston: Twayne, 1978);

Harold Rosenberg, *"Aesthetics of Crisis," New Yorker* (22 August 1964): 114-122;

Elizabeth Ward, *David Jones, Mythmaker* (Manchester: Manchester University Press, 1983).

Papers:

The National Library of Wales, Aberystwyth, Dyfed SY23 3BU, has the David Jones Archive, including manuscripts of all his major work and his library, also letters to Desmond Chute, Douglas Cleverdon, Saunders Lewis, and Kathleen Raine. Other papers are held by the Boston College Library; University of Essex Library, Wivenhoe Park, Colchester (letters to W. F. Jackson Knight); Fisher Rare Book Library, University of Toronto (letters to William Blissett and René Hague); Bodleian Library, Oxford (letters to Peter Levi); Merton College Library, Oxford (letters to William Hayward); University of Victoria Library, Victoria, British Columbia (letters to Herbert Read, Keidrych Rhys, and Meic Stephens–enclosing proofs of "The Wall"); and the Beinecke Rare Book Library, Yale University (letters to Harman Grisewood).

John Lehmann

(2 June 1907 - 7 April 1987)

Ralph Stewart
Acadia University

See also the Lehmann entry in *DLB 27: British Poets, 1914-1945.*

BOOKS: *A Garden Revisited, and Other Poems* (London: Woolf, 1931);

The Noise of History (London: Hogarth, 1934);

Prometheus and the Bolsheviks (London: Cresset, 1937; New York: Knopf, 1938);

Evil Was Abroad (London: Cresset, 1938);

New Writing in England (New York: Critics Group, 1939);

Down River: A Danubian Study (London: Cresset, 1939);

New Writing in Europe (Harmondsworth, U.K. & New York: Lane/Penguin, 1940);

Forty Poems (London: Hogarth, 1942);

The Sphere of Glass, and Other Poems (London: Hogarth, 1944);

The Age of the Dragon: Poems, 1930-1951 (London & New York: Longmans, Green, 1951);

The Open Night (London & New York: Longmans, Green, 1952);

Edith Sitwell (London & New York: Longmans, Green, 1952; revised, 1970);

The Whispering Gallery: Autobiography I (London & New York: Longmans, Green, 1955);

The Secret Messages (Stamford, Conn.: Overbrook, 1958);

I Am My Brother: Autobiography II (London: Longmans, Green 1960; New York: Reynal, 1960);

Ancestors and Friends (London: Eyre & Spottiswoode, 1962);

Collected Poems, 1930-1963 (London: Eyre & Spottiswoode, 1963);

Christ, the Hunter (London: Eyre & Spottiswoode, 1965);

The Ample Proposition: Autobiography 3 (London: Eyre & Spottiswoode, 1966);

A Nest of Tigers: Edith, Osbert and Sacheverell Sitwell in Their Times (London: Macmillan, 1968); republished as *A Nest of Tigers: The Sitwells in Their Times* (Boston: Little, Brown, 1968);

In My Own Time: Memoirs of a Literary Life (Boston: Little, Brown, 1969)–a revised and abridged version of *The Whispering Gallery, I Am My Brother,* and *The Ample Proposition;*

Holborn: An Historical Portrait of a London Borough (London: Macmillan, 1970);

The Reader at Night, and Other Poems (Toronto: Basilike, 1974);

Lewis Carroll and the Spirit of Nonsense (Nottingham: University of Nottingham, 1974);

Virginia Woolf and Her World (London: Thames & Hudson, 1975; New York: Harcourt Brace Jovanovich, 1975);

In the Purely Pagan Sense: A Novel (London: Blond & Briggs, 1976);

Edward Lear and His World (London: Thames & Hudson, 1977; New York: Scribners, 1977);

Thrown to the Woolfs: Leonard and Virginia Woolf and the Hogarth Press (London: Weidenfeld & Nicolson, 1978; New York: Holt, Rinehart & Winston, 1979);

Rupert Brooke: His Life and Legend (London: Weidenfeld & Nicolson, 1980); republished as *The Strange Destiny of Rupert Brooke* (New York: Holt, Rinehart & Winston, 1980);

The English Poets of the First World War (London: Thames & Hudson, 1981; New York: Thames & Hudson, 1982);

Three Literary Friendships (London: Quartet, 1983; New York: Holt, Rinehart & Winston, 1984);

New and Selected Poems (London: Enitharmon, 1985);

Christopher Isherwood (London: Weidenfeld & Nicolson, 1987; New York: Holt, 1988).

OTHER: *Folios of New Writing,* 12 volumes, edited by Lehmann (London: Hogarth, 1936-1941);

Ralph Fox, a Writer in Arms, edited by Lehmann, T. A. Jackson, and C. Day Lewis (London: Lawrence & Wishart, 1937);

Poems for Spain, edited by Lehmann & Stephen Spender (London: Hogarth, 1939);

150

John Lehmann at his desk in Carrington House, London, circa 1943 (photograph courtesy of Lehmann)

Poems from New Writing, 1936-1946, edited by Lehmann (London: Lehmann, 1946);

Shelley in Italy, edited by Lehmann (London: Lehmann, 1947);

French Stories from New Writing, edited by Lehmann (London: Lehmann, 1947); republished as *Modern French Stories* (New York: New Directions, 1948);

Demetrios Capetanakis: A Greek Poet in England, edited by Lehmann (London: Lehmann, 1947); republished as *Shores of Darkness: Poems and Essays* (New York: Devin-Adair, 1949);

English Stories from New Writing, edited by Lehmann (London: Lehmann, 1951); republished as *Best Stories from New Writing* (New York: Harcourt, Brace, 1951);

Pleasures of New Writing, edited by Lehmann (London: Lehmann, 1952);

The Craft of Letters in England: A Symposium, edited by Lehmann (London: Cresset, 1956; Boston: Houghton Mifflin, 1957);

Coming to London, edited by Lehmann (London: Phoenix House, 1957; Freeport, N.Y.: Books for Libraries, 1971);

Selected Poems of Edith Sitwell, edited by Lehmann (London: Macmillan, 1965);

Selected Letters of Edith Sitwell 1919-1964, edited by Lehmann and Derek Parker (London: Macmillan, 1970).

SELECTED PERIODICAL PUBLICATIONS–
UNCOLLECTED: "A Reader's Notebook–IV," *Penguin New Writing*, 16 (January-March 1943): 134-144;

"A Reader's Notebook–V," *Penguin New Writing*, 17 (April-June 1943): 155-165;

"The Heart of the Problem," *Penguin New Writing*, 18 (July-September 1943): 161-166;

"State Art and Scepticism," *Penguin New Writing*, 24 (January-March 1945): 157-166;

"In Daylight–I," *New Writing & Daylight*, 6 (September 1945): 7-15;

"In Daylight–II," *New Writing & Daylight*, 7 (September 1946): 7-13.

Lehmann at Eton in 1926, dressed for a Fourth of June boating party (photograph courtesy of Lehmann)

Highly regarded for his founding and talented editing of the vigorous, influential literary journals *New Writing*, *Penguin New Writing*, and the *London Magazine*, John Lehmann has had a long literary career, which began with a collection of poems in 1931 and now includes prose poetry, novels, travel books, histories, analyses of the contemporary scene, literary criticism, literary biography, autobiography, and essays. Lehmann is a creditable poet, and his early novel *Evil Was Abroad* (1938) continues to find readers, but it is nonfiction prose in which he has been notably prolific and impressive. One book, *The Open Night* (1952), is avowedly a collection of essays, and many other essays appear as chapters in travel books, histories, and autobiographies.

His father, Rudolph Chambers Lehmann, of German extraction, married Alice Marie Davis and settled at Fieldhead in Buckinghamshire; John was born to them on 2 June 1907 and spent his childhood at Fieldhead. At Eton from 1921 to 1927, he quickly acquired a reputation as scholarly and even brilliant; prefiguring his later career, he edited the school's magazine, *College Days*. He then went on to Trinity College, Cambridge, and was granted a B.A. in 1930.

Lehmann has written three volumes of autobiography, and also an account of his relationships with Leonard and Virginia Woolf, *Thrown to the Woolfs* (1978). These are interesting and not unimportant as accounts of the British (and sometimes European) intellectual and literary world but, beyond the description of his childhood, do not reveal much of Lehmann's personal feelings. Probably the main reason is his homosexuality, which he was unable to reveal in the 1950s and 1960s, and which makes him reticent about many of his relationships and actions. His later novel *In the Purely Pagan Sense* (1976) gives a detailed account of a homosexual's sex life up to later middle age and appears to be heavily autobiographical despite the customary disclaimer at the beginning. It is, therefore, a useful complement

Lehmann with his sisters Beatrix (left) and Rosamond (photograph by Howard Coster; courtesy of Lehmann)

to the official autobiographies, though it reads as a case study rather than a work of literature.

The first of Lehmann's autobiographies, *The Whispering Gallery* (1955), is the most interesting, and the part dealing with Lehmann's childhood in the Thames Valley is the most accomplished as literature. The absence of sexual complications is probably an advantage; but childhood is in any case amenable to literary treatment, because memories are incomplete and the writer must consciously select and fashion—the title of part 1, "Jewels in a Cave," suggests something of this process. Part 1 is made up of fifteen short essays, each built round a place, person, or type of activity. Lehmann describes the comprehensive world of his family's house and large garden. A school was provided there for the Lehmann children and their neighbors, and they had easy access to the Thames, "a magic highway

of the great world," which transformed the light around it. The nature of the child's world is conveyed especially through the brightness, subtlety, and pervasiveness of its light and color. Even in the library the books "in all the darkly glowing colours of their gold-printed leather bindings" seem to transmit their own light.

Lehmann peoples his world with parents, sisters, friends, and servants. Some of them have extrinsic interests: Lehmann's father, Rudolph, was a noted Liberal politician, journalist, and contributor to *Punch*, and his sister Beatrix became a famous actress while Rosamond, another sister, became a novelist. The servants are, however, equally important in the child's world, and indeed archetypal figures: the butler presides over the house and a fabulous treasure of silver; and the head gardener controls garden and river, like "some imperishable country god in humble disguise." The later essays in part 1 are concerned with school, pastimes, outings, and the annual holiday on the Isle of Wight, ending with the holiday transformed by news of war in August 1914. "Outside the enchanted garden, the world seemed to us on the whole rather ill-planned and unlovely." Something of the sense of a lost paradise lingers through the book.

The second part of *The Whispering Gallery* includes some vivid scenes of Lehmann's life at Eton but gives the impression that the author is gradually withdrawing to a distance. Lehmann moved from his family house ten miles down the Thames into Eton, and latterly about the same distance to London. He uses the river as a metaphor for growing up, with the "cities of the delta" representing the gaining of maturity. However, by the time he is at Cambridge and has more access to these cities, they appear "unsubstantial and disappointing," He seems to have gone through serious adolescent crises, but it is not clear what these were–though presumably, sexual problems were central. The remainder of *The Whispering Gallery* is still of considerable interest because of the descriptions of notable people and because Lehmann's own activities are often important. The most memorable sections are usually those that emerge as separate essays, such as the account of Julian Bell, a discourse on the political climate of the thirties, and the story of how Lehmann's influential journal *New Writing* was founded.

Lehmann's second volume of autobiography, *I Am My Brother* (1960), covers the war years and, Lehmann says in his introduction, aims to provide a personal account and also "contribute to the understanding of a crucial moment in the spiritual history of my countrymen." Neither of these aims is adequately achieved. Lehmann's personal reactions remain opaque: for example, he again writes of going through "a severe emotional and spiritual crisis" but does not explain its nature. As well, his statements about public behavior often sound platitudinous: "Nothing that had happened made us feel that we had been wrong to stand openly for the ideas of liberty and justice." Yet much of the book is valuable, for example the description of the Danube delta in part 1, and the energetic defense of wartime poets that makes up part 4, section 8.

The Ample Proposition (1966) covers the period from the end of war to the beginning of 1954, when Lehmann concluded his publishing career and became editor of the *London Magazine*.

It is a more satisfying work than its predecessor because it is less concerned with generalization and more with Lehmann's own achievements and personal observations. The longer reminiscences about literary people, such as T. S. Eliot, Stephen Spender, and Christopher Isherwood, are illuminating, and Lehmann's gift for vivid description of place often reappears.

Thrown to the Woolfs covers the period of Lehmann's often stormy association with Leonard and Virginia Woolf, as an employee and then partner in their Hogarth Press, between 1931 and 1946. It is informative, not only about the Woolfs but about Lehmann himself, and is in some respects more detailed and candid about these years of his life than his autobiography. The second section of the book covers the period from 1932 to 1938, when Lehmann was mainly in Vienna and had little contact with the Woolfs; here the literary figure discussed at greatest length is his friend Isherwood. Autobiography and biography are, of course, usually structured as narrative and not as a set of essays–*The Whispering Gallery* is an exception. *Thrown to the Woolfs* is basically narrative, as are Lehmann's various literary biographies.

Apart from his biographies, Lehmann has made two extended excursions into the past: a history of the London borough of Holborn, and an account of some "ancestors and friends" from the nineteenth century. Several sections of these books take the form of essays. Although *Holborn* (1970) makes clear Lehmann's affection for London, the most striking chapter (7) describes the slums near St. Giles Church as they were for about two centuries after the Great Fire of 1666. Lehmann brings out the misery of everyday life by a detailed examination of William Hogarth's picture of "Gin Lane" and, for later in the period, by focusing on "Rat's Castle" and the beggars who lodged in that dismal inn. He stresses the extreme overcrowding, squalor, and disease, while indirectly reminding the reader of the rural quiet and comparative prosperity that once characterized the area of St. Giles-in-the-Fields. Cows and pigs survived in some of the cellars till well into Victorian times, and the most notorious tavern was once named the "Beggars' Bush" and stood in open country. *Ancestors and Friends* (1962) is based on family letters and sometimes moves jerkily because of gaps in the evidence. But the account of Robert Chambers's youth–Chambers being a notable publisher, man of letters, and Lehmann's great-grandfather–does give

Lehmann with Virginia Woolf at Monk's House, the Woolfs' cottage at Rodmell, circa 1931

the flavor of early-nineteenth-century Edinburgh: the cramped lodgings of the old city, the Tolbooth prison at its center, and life in the taverns. And the stories of London literary figures of the 1860s, including Charles Dickens, Robert Browning, Edward Bulwer-Lytton, and now-forgotten characters, bring to life the milieu of Lehmann's grandparents.

Lehmann's two travel books are *Prometheus and the Bolsheviks* (1937) and *Down River* (1939), written as Europe moved toward war; both are much influenced by his left-wing political beliefs. *Prometheus*, the weaker of the two, describes Soviet Georgia, and to some extent the neighboring states of the Caucasus, under the rule of Russia, and is based on visits Lehmann made in 1935 and 1936. From the beginning there is a clash between Lehmann's aims–to describe a traditional

and distinctive part of the world, and to show how well non-Russian societies fare under the Soviet system. The latter theme predominates, but the evidence provided depends less on Lehmann's own observations than on uncritical summaries of official Soviet statements. "What the Bolsheviks plan they will achieve, unless entirely unforeseen circumstances intervene." Prometheus appears abruptly in the last chapter, in Lehmann's dreams, as an archetypal spokesman for human aspirations who is also an inhabitant of the region and applauds Soviet achievements in both preserving traditions and improving life; but this chapter does not do much to reconcile the two themes.

Yet the writer's intuition does quite frequently triumph over the political convert's beliefs, most completely in the descriptions of

Tbilisi, the capital city of Georgia, and of the remote tribes of the Caucasus mountains; these chapters (7 and 11) have the coherence of independent essays. Both contrast the old world and the new and show how rapidly the new is taking over. Lehmann's conscious position is that this is entirely a good thing, but his descriptions suggest the attraction of old Tbilisi and the beauty of mountains remote from good roads and five-year plans. The colors of the old world–silver cones of Byzantine churches against purple-brown hills; pale blue walls of old mosques; glinting copperware and silver–are more natural and subtle than the garish lights adorning the unfinished "Palace of the Soviets"; and the traditional crafts carried on in "little shops like rock caverns" are more varied and intriguing than activities in the new factories. Moreover, despite many confident statements, some of the images suggest that the future is uncertain. The massive new public buildings are still covered in scaffolding, and most building schemes have not even begun. The guide says brightly: "Formerly there was a 'caravanserai' here, a big untidy market. But it has all been cleared away, according to our plan, and we will make our own small 'Red Square' out of it." It is not clear when the small Red Square will materialize, or that it will be an improvement on the market.

Down River, written discontinuously over several years and completed in June 1939, is a historical and geographical examination of the countries bordering the Danube, from Austria to Romania. Austria is described in the greatest detail, and indeed the first half of the book is about Vienna, the incongruously large and sophisticated capital of a rather small and vulnerable country. The disintegration of the Austro-Hungarian empire left a power vacuum in the Danube basin, and the book considers whether this is likely to be filled by a German empire or by an independent federation of Danube states. It suggests that the latter is feasible because, though the people of the Danube are diverse in many respects, they also have a great deal in common. Lehmann lived in Vienna for much of the 1930s, traveled extensively in southeast Europe, and is able to convey "the sight, smell, sound, and feel" of the various countries and the economic and political forces at work in them. He moves smoothly between concrete and abstract. For example, he begins one chapter by describing the huge timber rafts on the upper river and the landscapes they travel through, goes on to explain the skills and hazards involved in assembling and navigating the rafts, turns to the relationship between lumbermen and farmers and the economic forces affecting their lives, and finally discusses the political implications of Austria's timber trade.

The most extended descriptions are of Vienna's architecture, of the Viennese relaxing at the Prater Fairground and Viennese Woods, and of the German invasion of March 1938. The theme of chapter 1 is expressed in the opening sentence: "No city in the world reveals the pattern of the past so clearly, nor provides so subtle a key to the character and spirits of its modern inhabitants, in the stones, the concrete and plaster of which it is built." Lehmann goes on to justify this claim, explaining Vienna's cosmopolitan nature and the major influences of Germany, France, Spain, and Italy. The city's most characteristic architecture is sensuous baroque, "a tumult of colour, a riot of movement instantaneously frozen." In contrast, there is the lonely gothic spire of St. Stephen's Cathedral, apparently an emblem of spirituality at the heart of pleasure-loving Vienna. It is an ambiguous symbol, however, changing color in different weathers and ultimately reinforcing the sense of a magic, insubstantial city.

The descriptions of the Prater and Vienna Woods also suggest a fairy-tale world of contrasts and the unexpected. In the Prater, "a mixture of Montmartre and Hampstead Heath, of Blackpool and Epsom Downs," illusion is the stock in trade of the entertainments and bars. In the Vienna Woods apparent monasteries, castles, and fortresses are never what they seem, and groups of revelers may actually be holding secret political meetings. The surrealist atmosphere is maintained in the last chapter of part 1 (reprinted in *The Whispering Gallery*), framed by Lehmann's train ride into Austria as the German invasion is beginning and, latterly, by the long queues of people trying unsuccessfully to leave by train. A passport official announces: "Everything is just as before.... Only a slight change in the regulations about those who wish to *leave* the country." The fall of Vienna seems almost magical, as if the Germans had only to mass their planes in the skies to annul the city's past and transform its citizens into Nazis. The smaller countries of the Danube then had to look elsewhere for help.

The approach of war naturally intensified Lehmann's feelings for his own country, and the Nazi-Soviet pact of August 1939 finally extin-

Covers for two of the journals Lehmann edited and wrote for during the 1940s (left: design by William Chappell; right: design by John Minton)

guished his support for Soviet Russia. Throughout World War II he was an influential promoter of literary culture, principally as an editor but also as a contributor to his own journals, notably *Penguin New Writing, Folios of New Writing, New Writing & Daylight,* and *Orpheus.* Most of his wartime essays are, not surprisingly, valuable mainly as records of their times, but a few have permanent interest. Some of the earlier essays defend Lehmann's literary generation against charges of meretriciousness in both life and art (George Orwell's description of W. H. Auden as a "gutless Kipling" shows how the charges may be combined). "Looking Back and Forward" (*Folios of New Writing,* 4, 1941) is the most convincing of these defenses and also a thoughtful study of the problems involved in tying literature to political action. Lehmann later returns to this theme, for example in "The Heart of the Problem" (*Penguin New Writing,* 18, July-September 1943), and expands on the attractions and dangers of state sponsorship of the arts, as well as discussing the mistake of straining to write socially valuable literature. This view is in direct contrast to the

opinions expressed in his prewar writings, which support the Soviet utilitarian, political view of art—but his praise of Russia was always rather tentative.

Lehmann values "a mind that can see the culture and life impulses of Europe as a whole, nourished from one central stem" ("The Heart of the Problem"), and his own critiques of European literature at the end of the war are wide-ranging and perceptive, notably on French existentialism ("In Daylight–I," *New Writing & Daylight,* 6, September 1945) and on contemporary Russian literature ("State Art and Scepticism," *Penguin New Writing,* 24, January-March 1945). Lehmann argues that both have made art subservient to another end, a philosophical view in one case and the dictates of the state in the other, and imagination has atrophied. He deals with Russian literature by satirically describing the basic social-realist plot, not forgetting the local commissar, "who always does prodigiously better than anyone else." Lehmann then examines the pronouncements of Soviet government spokesmen and brings out the absurdity of their attitudes by composing an enter-

Lehmann at Lake Cottage, his Sussex retreat, with his dog Carlotta in the early 1950s (photograph courtesy of Lehmann)

taining critique of various British writers according to Soviet standards; the British, of course, totally fail to achieve the correct political approach. However, other essays express the fear that, assisted by modern technology, British government and culture may become more like that of the Russians: "the secondary activities of cultural dissemination and exploitation may crowd out the primary, the only true life-giving activity of artistic creation" ("In Daylight–II," *New Writing & Daylight*, 7, September 1946).

Lehmann's fundamental attitudes to literary culture and society emerge clearly in his essays in *The Open Night*. Some of these are contemporary with the World War II group; the difference is that they deal with dead writers (though all modern). Lehmann can make detached judgments, and he is clear about his literary beliefs and standards. An essay on Marcel Proust's artistic credo ("The Most Austere School") begins with a quotation: "The idea of a popular art, like that of a patriotic art, even if it were not dangerous, seems to me absurd." Lehmann, awakened from the spell of the 1930s, delightedly agrees; he here sees art

as a mysterious force working independent of, and often in opposition to, ordinary emotions and abstract intelligence. The essays on the purpose of literature are, however, among the least successful, for Lehmann generalizes best when he is discussing a particular writer. For example, in "But For Beaumont Hamel" he examines the poetry of Rupert Brooke and Wilfred Owen in some detail, and considers the difference between writing about war before experiencing it and after doing so–the case of, respectively, Brooke and Owen. Lehmann argues that Brooke's poetry has a kind of "corrupting glibness," whereas Owen, in his verse, confronts death and suffering. Lehmann's essay becomes, then, a study of how to contend with the grimmest aspects of reality. In "Edward Thomas" he moves from the rhythms of Thomas's poetry to Thomas's perception of the world, especially his "passionate faith in the elemental things from which our civilization–with a kind of implacable yet helpless momentum–is exiling us."

Lehmann's essays on W. B. Yeats, James Joyce, and Virginia Woolf all start with a fragment of biography. With Yeats ("The Man Who Learned to Walk Naked") a description of the poet sleeping and apparently dreaming leads into a consideration of Yeats's dreams, independence, and vision. In the essay on Joyce ("Portrait of the Artist as an Escaper") the biographical element comes from analyzing a portrait by Augustus John, which suggests Joyce's intellectual power and determination, and also his blindness. Lehmann links Joyce's failing sight and his use of the weapons of "silence, exile and cunning" with the increasingly introverted nature of his works, and ultimately the production of "staggering examples of misdirected genius." Readers who disagree with this assessment will likely still find the essay an illuminating study of character and situation. Lehmann worked with Woolf, knew her well, and admired her; his essay makes use of this personal knowledge while maintaining detachment. He begins with two vivid and detailed word sketches of her: working "in the midst of an ever-encroaching forest of books" and partially relaxing in intense conversation; both suggest how literature sustained and yet exhausted her. He considers each of the novels as works in themselves and as part of a continuum, "successive expeditions towards the inexpressible" and

suggests how Woolf both reflected and changed modern sensibility.

This essay, like others in *The Open Night*, anticipates the method of Lehmann's later literary biographies: the fluid movement between literature and the writer's life, and between literature and society. Most of his work of the last twenty years is of this type, and his books are fine introductions to the Sitwells, Edward Lear, Rupert Brooke, and others.

Letters:

The Hogarth Letters (London: Chatto & Windus, 1985; Athens, Ga.: University of Georgia Press, 1986).

Reference:

Samuel Hynes, *The Auden Generation: Literature and Politics in England and the 1930s* (London: Bodley Head, 1976; New York: Viking, 1977).

Papers:

The Harry Ransom Humanities Research Center, University of Texas at Austin, holds a substantial collection of Lehmann's papers.

C. S. Lewis

(29 November 1898 - 22 November 1963)

Jonathan D. Evans
University of Georgia

See also the Lewis entry in *DLB 15: British Novelists, 1930-1959*.

BOOKS: *Spirits in Bondage*, as Clive Hamilton (London: Heinemann, 1919);

Dymer, as Hamilton (London: Dent, 1926; New York: Dutton, 1926);

The Pilgrim's Regress: An Allegorical Apology for Christianity, Reason and Romanticism (London: Dent, 1933; New York: Sheed & Ward, 1935);

The Allegory of Love: A Study in Medieval Tradition (Oxford: Clarendon, 1936; New York: Oxford University Press, 1958);

Out of the Silent Planet (London: Bodley Head, 1938; New York: Macmillan, 1943);

Rehabilitations and Other Essays (London & New York: Oxford University Press, 1939);

The Personal Heresy, by Lewis and E. M. W. Tillyard (London & New York: Oxford University Press, 1939);

The Problem of Pain (London: Bles, 1940; New York: Macmillan, 1943);

The Screwtape Letters (London: Bles, 1942; New York: Macmillan, 1943);

Broadcast Talks (London: Bles, 1942); republished as *The Case for Christianity* (New York: Macmillan, 1943);

A Preface to "Paradise Lost" (London & New York: Oxford University Press, 1942; revised and enlarged, 1959);

Christian Behaviour (London: Bles, 1943; New York: Macmillan, 1943);

Perelandra (London: Bodley Head, 1943; New York: Macmillan, 1944);

The Abolition of Man (London: Oxford University Press, 1943; New York: Macmillan, 1947);

Beyond Personality: The Christian Idea of God (London: Bles, 1944; New York: Macmillan, 1945);

That Hideous Strength (London: Bodley Head, 1945; New York: Macmillan, 1946);

The Great Divorce (London: Bles, 1945; New York: Macmillan, 1946);

C. S. Lewis (photograph by Wolf Suschitzky)

Miracles (New York: Macmillan, 1947; London: Bles, 1947);

Arthurian Torso, by Lewis and Charles Williams (London & New York: Oxford University Press, 1948);

Transposition (London: Bles, 1949); republished as *The Weight of Glory* (New York: Macmillan, 1949);

The Lion, The Witch and the Wardrobe (London: Bles, 1950; New York: Macmillan, 1950);

Prince Caspian (London: Bles, 1951; New York: Macmillan, 1951);

The Voyage of the "Dawn Treader" (London: Bles, 1952; New York: Macmillan, 1952);

Mere Christianity (London: Bles, 1952; New York: Macmillan, 1952);

The Silver Chair (London: Bles, 1953; New York: Macmillan, 1953);

The Horse and His Boy (London: Bles, 1954; New York: Macmillan, 1954);

English Literature in the Sixteenth Century, Excluding Drama (Oxford: Clarendon, 1954);

The Magician's Nephew (London: Bodley Head, 1955; New York: Macmillan, 1955);

Surprised by Joy: The Shape of My Early Life (London: Bles, 1955; New York: Harcourt, Brace & World, 1955);

The Last Battle (London: Bodley Head, 1956; New York: Macmillan, 1956);

Till We Have Faces (London: Bles, 1956; New York: Harcourt, Brace & World, 1957);

Reflections on the Psalms (London: Bles, 1958; New York: Harcourt, Brace & World, 1958);

Studies in Words (Cambridge: Cambridge University Press, 1960);

The Four Loves (London: Bles, 1960; New York: Harcourt, Brace & World, 1960);

The World's Last Night, and Other Essays (New York: Harcourt, Brace & World, 1960);

A Grief Observed (London: Faber & Faber, 1961; Greenwich, Conn.: Seabury Press, 1963);

An Experiment in Criticism (Cambridge: Cambridge University Press, 1961);

They Asked for a Paper (London: Bles, 1962);

The Discarded Image (Cambridge: Cambridge University Press, 1964);

Letters to Malcolm (London: Bles, 1964; New York: Harcourt, Brace & World, 1964);

Poems, edited by Walter Hooper (London: Bles, 1964; New York: Harcourt, Brace & World, 1965);

Screwtape Proposes a Toast (London: Collins, 1965);

Studies in Medieval and Renaissance Literature, edited by Hooper (Cambridge: Cambridge University Press, 1966);

Of Other Worlds: Essays and Stories, edited by Hooper (London: Bles, 1966; New York: Harcourt, Brace & World, 1967);

Spenser's Images of Life, edited by Alistair Fowler (Cambridge: Cambridge University Press, 1967);

Christian Reflections, edited by Hooper (Grand Rapids, Mich.: Eerdmans, 1967; London: Bles, 1967);

Narrative Poems, edited by Hooper (London: Bles, 1969; New York: Harcourt Brace Jovanovich, 1972);

Selected Literary Essays, edited by Hooper (Cambridge: Cambridge University Press, 1969);

God in the Dock, edited by Hooper (Grand Rapids, Mich.: Eerdmans, 1970); republished as *Undeceptions* (London: Bles, 1971);

Fernseed and Elephants, edited by Hooper (London: Fontana, 1975);

The Dark Tower, edited by Hooper (London: Collins, 1977; New York: Harcourt Brace Jovanovich, 1977);

On Stories and Other Essays, edited by Hooper (New York: Harcourt Brace Jovanovich, 1982);

Boxen: The Imaginary World of the Young, edited by Hooper (London: Collins, 1985);

Present Concerns (San Diego: Harcourt Brace Jovanovich, 1986).

Collections: *The Complete Chronicles of Narnia*, 7 volumes (Harmondsworth, U.K.: Penguin, 1965; New York: Macmillan, 1970);

A Mind Awake: An Anthology of C. S. Lewis, edited by Clyde S. Kilby (London: Bles, 1968; New York: Harcourt, Brace & World, 1969);

The Joyful Christian (New York: Macmillan, 1977);

Space Trilogy (New York: Macmillan, 1978);

The Essential C. S. Lewis (New York: Macmillan, 1988).

Clive Staples Lewis's importance as an essayist is identifiable with, and to a great extent owing to, his role as a popular apologist for the Christian faith. His emergence from a successful but nonetheless relatively obscure academic career into the limelight of popular acclaim was the result largely of four series of programs broadcast by the BBC in 1941 and 1942 in which Lewis responded to the invitation of James W. Welch to give "a series of talks on something like 'The Christian Faith As I See It–By A Layman.' " Lewis was a likely candidate for the job: *The Pilgrim's Regress* (1933), the autobiographical account of his conversion to Christianity, had been noticed earlier by Ashley Sampson of the Centenary Press and Geoffrey Bles Publishers; Sampson subsequently commissioned Lewis to write *The Problem of Pain* (1940). This book, which addresses in laymen's terms the theological problem of evil and related moral and ethical issues, had met with widespread success; Lewis's invitation to the BBC was prompted no doubt by the book's popularity but also in response to its demonstration of Lewis's ability to write engagingly on complex theological issues for a nonspecialist audience. The first

Lewis as a child in Belfast (by permission of the Estate of W. H. Lewis)

four successful fifteen-minute talks–"Right and Wrong: A Clue to the Meaning of the Universe?"– were broadcast in August 1941 and later published in *Broadcast Talks* (1942) and were followed in short order by three more series: "What Christians Believe," "Christian Behaviour," and "Beyond Personality," the last two separately published in 1943 and 1944. Lewis's status as a radio celebrity and as a writer and speaker in great demand was assured by the end of 1942. Throughout the remainder of World War II, he pursued an exhausting schedule of speaking engagements arranged by the chaplain-in-chief of the Royal Air Force, and he lectured at numerous churches, theological societies, and religious retreats from then until the end of his life. Indeed, the title of the collection of essays published in 1962, a year before his death, attests to the way in which his success as a speaker contributed to his career as an essayist: *They Asked for a Paper*.

The BBC broadcasts from the 1940s, all gathered later and revised for publication as *Mere Christianity* (1952), were significant to Lewis's essayistic endeavors in several ways. First, they furnished the general categories of thematic content that, alongside his professional writing as a literary scholar, would serve as the subject matter for the most popular of his essays throughout the remainder of his career: lay apologetics. Second, they set the rhetorical approach of stylistic clarity, even colloquial simplicity, that dominates his published essays. Lewis styled himself as a common man addressing concerns faced by all, including both the naive but honest skeptic and the unsophisticated Christian in an intellectually complex world; the title *Mere Christianity*, a phrase used by the seventeenth-century clergyman Richard Baxter, was meant to evoke the core of orthodox Christian beliefs and, as well, the common intellectual issues faced by everyday believers or inquirers into the Christian faith. Finally, the brevity of these talks established the format in which Lewis would flourish best: he is above all a master of the short form. Even his immensely popular *Screwtape Letters* (1942) adopts the fictive format of a series of brief epistles to treat religious themes developed elsewhere in Lewis's books and essays, and posthumously edited collections of his private letters have garnered an avid readership for many of the same reasons as his essays: their personal charm in the dispensing of advice and their wry, brief observations on common problems in Christian living make no excessive demands on the reader's patience or span of attention.

Many of Lewis's published essays were originally composed for oral presentation before a live audience. Some were given either as the headline address or in response to papers read before Oxford's Socratic Club, a forum for the public debate of intellectual problems with Christianity in which Lewis was instrumental both as a founding member and as president from 1941 to 1954. Other essays were delivered as sermons in churches and chapels around England and were among the "too numerous addresses," he says in the preface to *Transposition* (1949), "which I was induced to give during the late war and the years immediately following it." In preparing his oral texts for publication, Lewis was reluctant to make much substantive alteration, and so for this reason alone many of his essays adopt the characteristic first-person-singular rhetorical voice that is one of the memorable features of his essay style.

The relation between the spoken and the written word is one to which Lewis devoted conscious attention. In the preface to *Mere Christianity*, he commented that though he had removed contractions, recast sentences, and eliminated italics in his original broadcast texts, he hoped that he had done so "without altering . . . the 'popular' or 'familiar' tone which I had all along intended. A talk on the radio should, I think, be as like real talk as possible, and should not sound like an essay being read aloud. In my talks I had therefore used all the contractions and colloquialisms I ordinarily use in conversation." The talks to which Lewis referred really *were* essays read aloud, and the familiar tone he achieved in them remained a hallmark of his essay style throughout his career. Indeed, his essays often read like the written version of a one-sided conversation between Lewis and his audience, regardless of the communicative medium for which they were composed. This contributes much to the reader's sense of personal involvement with the author that helps to explain the enormous popularity of his essays.

Lewis was born in Belfast, Northern Ireland, on 29 November 1898, the son of Albert J. and Flora Hamilton Lewis; his mother died when he was still a boy. Lewis's early education was by private tutoring, at various public schools, and at Malvern College. In 1917 he entered University College, Oxford, but had to leave to serve as a soldier in World War I. After returning to Oxford and completing his studies, Lewis taught English literature there (at Magdalen College) until 1954, the year he accepted the chairmanship of Medieval and Renaissance Literature at Cambridge. In 1956 he married Joy Davidman Gresham, an American writer. Among Lewis's many awards was an honorary Doctor of Divinity degree from St. Andrew's University, an unusual honor for a layman to receive, in recognition of his career as a Christian apologist.

Lewis's essays have been described by Roger Lancelyn Green and Walter Hooper, his biographers, as characteristically manifesting a "love of clarity," with "striking metaphors" and "inexorable logic," demonstrating the "ability to incapsulate a great many facts into a few words." Nevill Coghill points to a "weight and clarity of argument, sudden turns of generalization and general paradox, the telling short sentence to sum a complex paragraph, and unexpected touches of personal approach to the reader. . . ." Lewis's appeal to the common humanity of his readers takes various forms, including the extensive and memorable use of analogy, a device in all likelihood derived from his knowledge of St. Thomas Aquinas, within whose theory of allegory the concept of analogy plays an important role. Lewis knew the allegorical mode quite well: his first autobiography (*The Pilgrim's Regress*) employs the genre, and one of his outstanding pieces of academic scholarship is *The Allegory of Love* (1936). In his usage of analogies he draws upon the simple and the homespun: in "Religion: Reality or Substitute" (1941; in *Christian Reflections*, 1967), for example, he proposes that people, sometimes mistaking substitutes for the reality they are supposed to replace, and vice versa, can ultimately come to prefer a substitute to the real thing. His central point is that true Christianity can sometimes appear less savory than the ersatz religiosity and false spirituality that often take its place, but along the way he draws analogies with several physical false substitutes and, by charming the

Lewis at age ten (right) with his father, Albert, and brother, Warren (by permission of the Estate of W. H. Lewis)

reader, manages to advance his argument. Examples include two boys stealing cigarettes and preferring them to cigars; wartime English households developing a preference for margarine rather than for butter; and Lewis's own childhood disappointment upon attending an orchestral performance because it did not sound enough like the gramophone recordings he was accustomed to hearing.

Lewis's deft handling of the "telling short sentence" likely derives from G. K. Chesterton, whose *Everlasting Man* (1925) was instrumental in Lewis's conversion and whose essays had much impressed him, earlier in life. During a hospital convalescence from trench fever in 1918, Lewis had read a volume of Chesterton's essays and later wrote of the experience: "I had never heard of him and had no idea of what he stood for; nor can I quite understand why he made such an immediate conquest of me.... His humor was of the kind which I like best–not 'jokes' imbedded

in the page like currants in a cake, still less (what I cannot endure), a general tone of flippancy and jocularity, but the humor which is not in any way separable from the argument but is rather ... the bloom on dialectic itself. The sword glitters not because the swordsman set out to make it glitter but because he is fighting for his life and therefore moving it very quickly" (*Surprised by Joy*, 1955). This appreciative description of Chesterton's work could serve almost identically to describe Lewis's own essays, in which wry comments and witty, aphoristic sentences, not out-and-out jokes, permeate the whole savory texture of his prose. Certainly the tone of Chestertonian humor is evident, as Lewis expresses in his prose an amused perspective that functions as a rhetorical analogue to the apparently detached, bemused facial expression that earned him his schoolmates' censure as a boy.

Lewis often effects in his essays the tone of the common man–and on at least one occasion,

Lewis in 1918 (by permission of the Estate of W. H. Lewis)

in 1948, he specifically identified his main audience as "the Intelligentsia of the Proletariat" (in "God in the Dock"). Sometimes he launches an essay by making the claim that he is an amateur in the subject he is about to address and therefore should not be taken too seriously. For example, he begins "On Church Music" (1949; in *Christian Reflections*) by saying, "I am a layman and one who can boast no musical education. I cannot even speak from the experience of a lifelong churchgoer. It follows that church music is a subject on which I cannot, even in the lowest degree, appear as a teacher." In "Modern Theology and Biblical Criticism" (*Christian Reflections*), he uses the same gesture of humility by reporting that he is "extremely ignorant" of the theological topic there addressed. This turns out to be a strategic move: Lewis goes on to suggest to his original audience of theological students that "you ought to know how a certain sort of theology strikes the outsider," and ultimately turns his humble rhetoric to an attack upon modern theological errors, which he was ever ready to expose—"I may have nothing but misunderstandings to lay before you [but] you ought to know that such misunderstand-

ings exist." The role of outsider, he suggests, may be especially prized as offering insight, a point he also makes in "Answers to Questions of Christianity" (1944; in *Undeceptions*, 1971–originally published as *God in the Dock*, 1970). In the latter essay the underlying motive for this affectation is developed at some length. Lewis believed that sophisticated theological language often conceals either unclear theology or, worse, unbelief. Lewis expresses in this essay and in others (such as "Christian Apologetics" in *Undeceptions*) the idea that clergymen and theologians must choose their words carefully, since the unsophisticated person is likely to misinterpret theological language—to his soul's confusion or even damnation.

More often, however, Lewis's essays address topics on which he genuinely does have the expertise to speak as an authority—or at least as an informed commentator—but he disguises his immensely literate background by cloaking his discourse in laymen's language. Lewis uses colloquialisms, homespun anecdotes, and the quoted speech of (sometimes real, sometimes fictive) everyday persons to gain his reader's emotional sympathy and, ultimately, intellectual allegiance. Lewis is given to using schoolboy slang, playing-field jargon, and colloquial phrases such as "dull dog" and "turkey-coxcomb"; exposing fallacious points with elegant rational proof, he will turn suddenly to dismiss faulty reasoning with such derisive colloquialisms as "bosh" or "poppycock"; and he uses such hyper-British lowbrow modifiers as "ruddy" and "bloody" to convey—and perhaps elicit—proletarian indignation.

Lewis is often credited with the use of unassailable logic, and careful dialectic was one of his important modes of operation. Lewis sets up straw men only to discard them, examines and then rejects red herrings, employs syllogism and enthymeme, deduces logical consequences, and reduces to absurdity fallacious inferences—sometimes pursuing them to the ultimate, often comical, degree. However, few readers can tolerate much really pure dialectic in popular essays, and more often than not Lewis wins his arguments through subtle identification with readers' preconceptions and common predilections rather than through pristine logic. Upon close analysis, Lewis's essays at times appear less strictly dialectical than they are generally thought to be, and it is not unfair to suggest that his readers are often distracted from the underlying structure of his arguments by the personalistic tone in which they are wrapped. The impression, fostered by his rhetoric, of a ruthlessly rational mind operating according to finely honed principles of inductive and deductive reasoning is to a great extent the result of careful structural organization, which includes clear signals reminding the reader what territory has been covered and announcing in advance where the essay intends to go.

Lewis's logic is not always unassailable. In fact, his apologetics are said to have suffered a stinging public defeat at a Socratic Club meeting early in 1947, at the hands of his debating opponent, the Catholic philosopher Elizabeth Anscombe. As Humphrey Carpenter recounts the event, Anscombe sharply criticized as "severely faulty" Lewis's proof that "the human reason is independent of the natural world." Though not all present were satisfied that Anscombe adequately supported her critique, "many who were at the meeting thought that a conclusive blow had been struck against one of [Lewis's] fundamental arguments," a blow from which he appears never to have fully recovered. Lewis is said to have been "in very low spirits" for some time after the debate, and when he fi-

Lewis walking at Oxford in 1938 (by permission of the Estate of W. H. Lewis)

nally returned to Christian apologetics a decade later in *Reflections on the Psalms* (1958), he appeared much less intellectually pugnacious. He never again employed strictly logical proof in rational defense of the Christian faith, and most of the apologetic essays published and republished late in his life and after his death date from the 1940s—that is, from before the Anscombe debate.

Carpenter indicates that Lewis's friends were well aware of his intellectual limitations: Charles Williams, for example, was suspicious of the heavy reliance on human reason as the "primary basis for belief in God." J. R. R. Tolkien, dubious about Lewis's "too close reliance on supposedly infallible dialectics," felt that he was "keen-witted rather than clear-sighted . . . logical within some given position, but in ranging argument neither lucid nor coherent. On the fallacies, verbal subterfuges, and false deductions of his opponents (and of his friends) he could dart like a hawk; yet he was himself often confused, failing to make essential distinctions, or seemingly unaware that his immediate contention had been already damaged by some 'point' that he had made elsewhere." Carpenter attributes Lewis's characteristic authorial voice not simply to dialectics but to several broad categories of mind: Lewisian subpersonae that Carpenter labels the Chestertonian, the boyish, the debater, and the poet.

Owen Barfield, an intellectual equal and sparring partner whom Lewis identified as a much-needed alter ego and whose friendship was based upon vigorous, healthy disagreement, also felt that the "real" Lewis concealed himself behind a variety of rhetorical poses. Barfield remarked that, upon reading Lewis's "An Open Letter to Dr. Tillyard" in *The Personal Heresy* (1939), he "slapped the book down and shouted: I don't believe it! It's *pastiche!*" Barfield was reacting primarily against the closing section of the essay, in which he perceived an excessively flowery and artificial pose of humility uncharacteristic of Lewis the lusty champion of hot debate. "It may of course have been deliberate *pastiche*, something that Lewis always enjoyed writing," said Barfield, but "all through the 'Personal Heresy' controversy there was something in his tone that seemed just subtly artificial." Lewis's statement, for example, castigating the self-avowed "heroism" of modern writers of poetry–"what meditation on human fate demands so much 'courage' as the act of stepping into a cold bath?"–seemed to Barfield (says Carpenter) to be "more appropriate to G. K. Chesterton than to Lewis.... But after his conversion this came more and more to be the kind of thing he said and the kind of attitude he took. Or rather, it was the kind of attitude he *thought* he took, or had decided to take. As Barfield expressed it, 'It left me with the impression not of "I say this," but of "this is the sort of thing a man might say." ' "

Although such excavations are fraught with the danger of excessive reductionism, such an analysis of Lewis's personality can be useful in the attempt to define his essay style. Carpenter says that "one can see much of Lewis's life as a series of masks or postures which he adopted, consciously or unconsciously, as his way of dealing with the world.... Indeed one can regard all Lewis's most successful literary work as pastiche. He chose a form from one source, an idea from another; he played at being (in turns) Bunyan, Chesterton, Tolkien, Williams, anybody he liked and admired. He was an impersonator, a mimic, a fine actor; but what lay at the heart of it all?" In the title essay of *The World's Last Night* (1960) Lewis himself likens the role of human personae to that of actors in a play whose final curtain

might fall at any moment–a metaphor born of his deeply held conviction of the inevitability of the next world and the high stakes inherent in living life in this one. One might answer Carpenter's query by saying that at the heart of Lewis's various writing personae lay the soul of a man thoroughly converted to Christianity. Lewis came to Christian faith from a strong and intellectually buttressed agnosticism, and the positions he later held were often adopted through religious obedience and reluctant but acquiescent intellectual assent rather than by simple habit, emotional disposition, or upbringing.

Lewis published about 125 essays during his lifetime, in a variety of publications including scholarly journals such as *Essays and Studies*, *Review of English Studies*, and *Essays in Criticism*; newspapers including the *Guardian*, *Time and Tide*, and the *Coventry Evening Telegraph*; church quarterlies and religious newspapers such as *Church Times*, *Christian Century*, *Christian Herald*, and the *Church of England Newspaper*; popular magazines including the *Saturday Evening Post*, *Atlantic Monthly*, and *Punch*; and smaller reviews, pamphlets, and newsletters, as well as writing prefaces to festschriften and other books. The variety of outlets is matched by the range of subject matter from which he was able to draw effectively for illustrative material, providing the similes, metaphors, and anecdotes with which his essays are liberally sprinkled.

Lewis's essays may be divided into two broad categories–literary criticism, mainly in his professional bailiwick of medieval and Renaissance literature; and religious essays, combining apologetics with other modes including the devotional, exegetical, meditative, and hortatory. As a literary scholar and critic, Lewis was unimpeachably professional; as a religious essayist, he may be said to have been a professional amateur. As to content, though a great many of his essays were occasional pieces designed for immediate presentation to a specific audience, Lewis returned again and again to a handful of main themes: the supernatural as an inescapable aspect of natural life; the uselessness of "culture" as a salvific enterprise; the error of reducing all human thought and perception to mere subjectivity; the fallacious developmentalism or progressivism inherent in modern thought; the Christian religion as the culmination of the mythic element in human culture–Christianity as "true myth." Collections of Lewis's literary-critical essays published during the author's lifetime include *Rehabili-*

Lewis at his Magdalen College desk in 1947 (photograph by A. P. Strong)

tations and Other Essays (1939) and *Studies in Words* (1960). Posthumously published volumes include *Studies in Medieval and Renaissance Literature* (1966), *Spenser's Images of Life* (1967), and *Selected Literary Essays* (1969).

But it is the religious essays that account principally for Lewis's achievement as an essayist. The 1940s were a period of incredible literary activity for Lewis, who published sixty-one essays in addition to the thirty-one newspaper installments of *The Screwtape Letters* and twenty-three of *The Great Divorce* (1945) in the *Guardian*, as well as the series of seven columns in the *Listener* that later were reprinted together as *Beyond Personality* in 1944.

Transposition–the first collection of essays to appear after the popular success of *The Problem of Pain, Miracles* (1947), and the printed versions of his BBC broadcasts–consists of three sermons and two addresses given earlier in the decade during the first period of his emerging reputation and includes some of his best work, in particular "The Weight of Glory" (the title essay of the U.S.

edition of the book), which has been called by his biographers "perhaps the most sublime piece of prose to come from his pen." Written in 1941, it develops a theme found again and again in his essays and fiction: the idea that, couched within the ordinary and mundane, there lie supernatural, everlasting spiritual realities. This world is not merely natural; it includes the supernatural. The concept applies most importantly to *people*: "It is a serious thing to live in a society of possible gods and goddesses, to remember that the dullest and most uninteresting person you talk to may one day be a creature which, if you saw it now, you would be strongly tempted to worship, or else a horror and a corruption such as you now meet, if at all, only in a nightmare. . . . There are no *ordinary* people. You have never talked to a mere mortal. Nations, cultures, arts, civilization–these are mortal. . . . But it is immortals whom we joke with, work with, marry, snub, and exploit–immortal horrors or everlasting splendors. . . . Next to the Blessed Sacrament itself, your neighbour is the holiest object presented to your senses. If he is your Christian neighbour he is holy in almost the same way, for in him also Christ *vere latitat*–the glorifier and the glorified, Glory Himself, is truly hidden." Lewis believed staunchly that the destiny of human souls involves an "absolutely unavoidable 'either-or' choice," ultimately, between heaven and hell: "We are not living in a world where all roads are radii of a circle and where all, if followed long enough, will therefore draw gradually nearer and finally meet at the centre: rather in a world where every road, after a few miles, forks into two, and each of these into two again, and at each fork you must make a decision."

Lewis is justly famous for his exploration, in fiction, of the hellish consequences of wrong choices in *The Screwtape Letters* and in *The Great Divorce*, from whose preface the latter passage above is quoted, as is the following: "I do not think that all who choose wrong roads perish; but their rescue consists in being put back on the right road. A wrong sum can be put right: but only by going back till you find the error and working it afresh from that point, never by simply *going on*. Evil can be undone, but it cannot 'develop' into good. . . . It is still 'either-or.' If we insist on keeping Hell (or even earth) we shall not see Heaven: if we accept Heaven we shall not be able to retain even the smallest and most intimate souvenir of Hell." "All day long," Lewis says in "The Weight of Glory," "we are, in some degree, helping each other to one or other of these destinations." All of Lewis's religious essays–indeed, all of his vast literary output–may be seen clearly as an attempt to point his readers in the direction of the right road. "The Weight of Glory" erects one of his most effective signposts.

Throughout the 1950s Lewis was engaged in writing his academic magnum opus, *English Literature in the Sixteenth Century, Excluding Drama (The Oxford History of English Literature, Vol. III*, 1954), his series of children's books *The Chronicles of Narnia* (collected in 1965), and other academic and fictional endeavors. Still, he published an average of three essays per year during this decade, about equally divided between academic criticism and theological subjects. In 1960 seven of the theological essays were gathered from their original venues and republished together as *The World's Last Night, and Other Essays*. The title of the main essay is borrowed from one of John Donne's Holy Sonnets (IX), and the subject is modern skepticism concerning the doctrine of the Second Coming of Christ. Lewis criticizes the inherent de-

velopmentalism of modern thought (another of his recurrent themes): "in my opinion, the modern conception of Progress or Evolution . . . is simply a myth, supported by no evidence whatever." He goes on to assert that "the myth arose earlier than the theorem" and that so-called scientific arguments against the eschatological teleology of Christian thought are unconvincing. As he does elsewhere, Lewis here uses apparent discrepancies between various Gospel writers' opinions concerning the imminence of Christ's return as evidence for the validity of the scriptural books as historical documents: "The evangelists have the first great characteristic of honest witnesses: they mention facts which are, at first sight, damaging to their main contention." The central idea of "The World's Last Night," though, is that the unpredictability of the return of Christ ought to have direct practical consequences for the way in which people live: "we do not and cannot know when the world drama will end. The curtain may be rung down at any moment: say, before you have finished reading this paragraph. . . . The doctrine of the Second Coming has failed, so far as we are concerned, if it does not make us realize that at every moment of every year in our lives, Donne's question 'What if this present were the world's last night?' is equally relevant." Lewis likens our position to that of actors in a play–actors who do not know when the play will end nor which act we are in: "We do not know who are the major characters and who the minor characters. The Author knows. . . . But we, never seeing the play from outside, never meeting any characters except the tiny minority who are 'on' in the same scenes as ourselves, wholly ignorant of the future and very imperfectly informed about the past, cannot tell at what moment the end ought to come." Christ might return at any moment; this awareness, says Lewis, ought to pervade our lives, causing us to view with skeptical humility all our successes, triumphs, and achievements and to pursue our activities in this world with sober diligence, obedient to our respective callings, knowing that we are destined for a greater realm.

They Asked for a Paper is the last collection of essays to be published before Lewis's death; it recycles four essays from two previous volumes and adds literary essays on *Hamlet*, Rudyard Kipling, Sir Walter Scott, "The Literary Impact of the Authorized Version" (1950), "Psycho-analysis and Literary Criticism" (1942), and "*De Descriptione Temporum*" (1954), originally a lecture inaugurat-

C. S. and W. H. (Warren) Lewis at Annogassan, Ireland, in 1949 (by permission of the Estate of W. H. Lewis)

ing the Cambridge University Chair of Medieval and Renaissance English, which was created for him and which he held from 1954 to 1963. Although it predated Lewis's death by nine years, the address reads more like a valedictory than an inaugural essay, the seasoned, almost elegiac reflections of an old scholar and teacher lamenting the passing of an old tradition and admonishing his young successors to recall a past into which he himself must inevitably retire. Lewis argues against "chronological snobbery," the idea that the new is necessarily better or even more advanced than the old. As his biographers point out, "Lewis was largely responsible for breaking down the artificial barrier . . . between the Middle Ages and the Renaissance," and the Cambridge chairmanship was one measure of his success in this regard. Coghill has alluded to a snatch of conversation–often requoted–between Lewis and himself. Lewis announced, enthusiastically: "I believe . . . I *believe* I have proved that

the Renaissance never happened in England. *Alternatively . . .* that if it did, *it had no importance.*" No medievalist could fail to delight in the idea of extending the Middle Ages beyond their traditional boundaries through the sixteenth and seventeenth centuries. Far greater changes in literature were recognized by Lewis as having occurred in the modern era, changes that rendered him and his generation, he thought, far closer to the old Western tradition than any of his students. "Speaking not only for myself but for all other Old Western men whom you may meet," Lewis charged his audience to use scholars of his generation wisely, for "There are not going to be many more dinosaurs" (*They Asked for a Paper*).

Lewis died on 22 November 1963. At the time, he was collecting the essays for another volume to be entitled "A Slip of the Tongue, And Other Pieces." With the exception of "A Slip of the Tongue," which was brand-new, and excluding an expansion of "Transposition," the volume

*Lewis on 21 December 1949 in his Oxford sitting room
(photograph by Norman Parkinson)*

tle children extended to literary/critical tastes as much as to anything else. All nine of the essays—to which three stories and an unfinished novel are appended—touch upon the juvenile wonder that Lewis championed both as a writer of literature and as a critic of it. In "On Stories," reprinted from a 1947 festschrift Lewis dedicated to his late friend Charles Williams, Lewis asserts that whatever is really enjoyable in stories partakes of a childlike wonder in narrative: "No book is really worth reading at the age of ten which is not equally (and often far more) worth reading at the age of fifty. . . ." In "On Juvenile Tastes" he says even more emphatically, "juvenile taste is simply human taste, going on from age to age," arguing against artificial distinctions between writing for children and writing for adults. Other essays in the book treat his approach in writing children's books and science fiction, and "On Criticism" is a hortatory piece in which he directs suggestions to professional reviewers of books concerning the ethics of their profession and to professional writers concerning how to read reviews of their work with humility and discernment. *On Stories* reprints this volume's essays, adding literary appraisals of Dorothy Sayers, E. R. Eddison, H. Rider Haggard, and George Orwell, and includes Lewis's original reviews of Tolkien's fantasy novels.

Christian Reflections contains some of Lewis's most important work in seeking a logical connection between his profession as a literary scholar and his vocation as a popular Christian apologist. The essay entitled "Christianity and Culture" combines three articles written by Lewis as part of a debate printed in the pages of *Theology* in 1940 and is said by his editor to represent "an early step in his spiritual pilgrimage—but certainly not his arrival." Lewis found both the New Testament and the doctors of the church, if not hostile toward sophisticated culture, at least skeptical of its efficacy in the Christian life. On the other hand, Lewis finds pragmatic and ethical justifications for the Christian who works in cultural affairs: one has to earn a living, and if one's talents run toward cultural production, then his labors in such fields are merely analogous to St. Paul's tent-making; secular abuse of culture toward harmful ends must be mitigated by a Christian counter-effect; the pleasures afforded through culture are not evil per se, but assume harmful function only when such pleasure is allowed to stand higher than spiritual values.

contains nothing that had not been printed at least twice earlier, some of the essays in fact appearing for the fourth time. In the end, the original preface and the title essay were dropped, and the volume appeared in 1965 as *Screwtape Proposes a Toast*.

Walter Hooper, Lewis's literary executor and posthumous editor, has been exceedingly productive in reprinting many of Lewis's essays—gathering them from sometimes obscure sources and, in some cases, publishing essays for the first time that survived only in manuscript among the late author's papers. More than half of Lewis's published essays are now available in the volumes edited and published by Hooper, including *Of Other Worlds: Essays and Stories* (1966), *Christian Reflections* (1967), *Undeceptions* (1971), *Fernseed and Elephants* (1975), *On Stories* (1982), and *Present Concerns* (1986).

In the essays in *Of Other Worlds*, Lewis gives expression to what Carpenter called the "boyishness" of his personality. Lewis believed that Christ's injunction that people must become as lit-

Lewis with his friend Owen Barfield, a literary critic, circa 1950 (by permission of Barfield)

In "Christianity and Literature," reprinted from *Rehabilitations*, Lewis comments that the Christian and the non-Christian will differ in their approaches to literature first of all insofar as modern secular criticism places higher value on creative "originality," whereas the Christian knows from the beginning that all human creativity is predicated upon the divine acts of creation and that none of the beauty man fashions, therefore, is truly original. For this reason, furthermore, "the Christian will take literature a little less seriously than the cultured Pagan: he will feel less uneasy with a purely hedonistic standard for at least many kinds of work. The unbeliever is always apt to make a kind of religion of his aesthetic experiences," whereas the Christian knows that "the salvation of a single soul is more important than the production or preservation of all the epics and tragedies in the whole world." As for cultural sophistication, he also knows that the vulgar are his spiritual superiors, since the whole tenor of the New Testament prefers the poor over the rich, the low over the high, and the hum-ble over the proud. Popular aesthetics, therefore, are not automatically to be despised. Much of what Lewis says here is fundamental to characteristically Lewisian positions developed elsewhere in his essays, criticism, and fiction: "We can play, as we can eat, to the glory of God. It thus may come about that the Christian views on literature will strike the world as shallow and flippant; but the world must not misunderstand. When Christian work is done on a serious subject there is no gravity and no sublimity it cannot attain. But they will belong to the theme. That is why they will be real and lasting—mighty nouns with which literature, an adjectival thing, is here united, far over-topping the fussy and ridiculous claims of literature that tries to be important simply as literature. And *a posteriori* it is not hard to argue that all the greatest poems have been made by men who valued something else much more than poetry—even if that something else were only cutting down enemies in a cattle-raid or tumbling a girl in a bed. The real frivolity, the solemn vacuity, is all with those who make literature a self-existent thing to be valued for its own sake."

Elsewhere in *Christian Reflections* Lewis deals with familiar themes: the corrosive effects of reductive subjectivism; the "scientific" myth of developmentalism; and a preference for humble rather than highbrow musical and linguistic tastes. Two essays presage later book-length treatments of prayer and the Psalms. Essays published for the first time in this volume include "De Futilitate," "The Funeral of a Great Myth," "The Psalms," "The Language of Religion," "Ethics," "Petitionary Prayer," and "Modern Theology and Biblical Criticism."

Undeceptions contains forty-eight essays: forty-seven republished from a variety of sometimes obscure sources and "Christian Apologetics," printed from a previously unpublished manuscript. This volume is not only the largest collection of Lewis's essays, it is also the most broadly representative of the spectrum of subjects upon which Lewis wrote. The essays are divided into three groupings: twenty-three essays with miracles as the central theme; sixteen loosely united around a general critique of various facets of modernism; and nine touching a variety of issues in which private morality and spirituality involve public policy—the ethics of capital punishment, for example, or domestic life, the observance of Christmas, and so on. The title for the American edition of the book, *God in the Dock*, is taken from the editor's title for an essay in the book's second section, originally published by Lewis in 1948 under the title "Difficulties in Presenting the Christian Faith to Modern Unbelievers." This important essay touches upon several themes close to Lewis's heart. He identifies three main barriers to popular acceptance of Christianity among the "Intelligentsia of the Proletariat," the audience he says he knows best: a fundamental skepticism about historiography; the failure of ecclesiastical authorities to translate theological language into vernacular idiom; and an insufficient awareness of personal sin. Inherent in modern unbelief, says Lewis, there is a high level of self-righteousness. While ancient man thought of God as a judge whom he must approach with all the self-abasement of the accused, modern man has taken a seat on the bench and put God in the dock: man "is quite a kindly judge," says Lewis, and "if God should have a reasonable defence ... he is ready to listen to it," ready, perhaps, even to acquit God, but nonetheless insisting that God owes man an accounting.

The same triad of modern prejudices is identified in another essay in the volume, "Christian Apologetics," written three years earlier. Lewis affects amateur status before his audience—"Some of you are priests and some are leaders of youth organizations. I have little right to address either. It is for priests to teach me, not for me to teach them." Nonetheless, Lewis admonishes them to defend Christian doctrine—what he elsewhere called "mere" Christianity—and to fix firmly in their minds the distinctions between heretical ("broad," "liberal," or "modern") doctrine and orthodoxy, between the major communions of the Christian church, and between official, ecclesiastical doctrine and clergymen's idiosyncratic theological opinions. He says, "Our business is to present that which is timeless in the particular language of our own age," as opposed to the "bad preacher," he says, who casts the ephemeral ideas of his own age in the language of traditional Christianity. Lewis's appeal for the use of the vernacular is followed by a list of eighteen common "religious" words with suggestions for avoiding their misuse or misinterpretation.

By his own admission Lewis's literary executor, Hooper, has been prodigious in his editorial capacities. *Fernseed and Elephants* contains eight essays, seven of them reprinted from earlier publications, with only one new one, "On Forgiveness," actually adding to Lewis's published oeuvre. In the preface to this volume, a book which—perhaps justifiably—has never been published in the United States, Hooper reports that Tolkien once teased him about "C. S. Lewis being the only one of his friends who had published more books *after* his death than before." The collection includes some of Lewis's best-known pieces, however, including "Membership," "The World's Last Night," and "The Efficacy of Prayer"; it includes, as well, "Learning in War-Time," "Historicism," and "Religion and Rocketry." The last essay in the volume, "Fernseed and Elephants," is a retitled republication of "Modern Theology and Biblical Criticism," originally published in *Christian Reflections*. Hooper calls it "the 'last word' in answer to the demythologizers." Austin Farrer expressed the thought that it was "the best thing Lewis ever wrote."

Of perhaps greater interest to Lewis's readers, however, is "On Forgiveness," written in 1947 and published from its sole manuscript source exclusively in this volume. In it Lewis articulates a distinction between *reasons* for failure and *excuses* for sin, saying that Christians often confuse the two and thereby fail to heed the command of Christ to forgive their neighbors' sins

Lewis at Cambridge in 1959 (by permission of the Estate of W. H. Lewis)

and—more dangerously—thus fail to receive the forgiveness of God. One must always *forgive* others' sins even when asked to *excuse* them, and one must never offer God *reasons* for behavior that He declares to be inexcusable but promises to forgive anyway. In characteristically good Lewisian humor, he points out the human tendency to accept other people's excuses much less generously than we expect others to accept our own; Lewis portrays a benevolent God who already knows all our best excuses for sins and probably knows some even better ones. But God is not fooled by them; nor does he fail to recognize sin as sin. When He forgives people, it is in full awareness of the "horror, dirt, meanness and malice" of their failures. "That, and only that," says Lewis, "is forgiveness; and that we can always have from God if we ask for it."

Present Concerns contains nineteen brief essays gathered primarily from articles Lewis published in such places as *Time and Tide*, the *Spectator*, and the *Sunday Times* in the 1940s and 1950s, as well as in more serious scholarly journals in the 1950s and 1960s. The book was designed by its editor (Hooper) to answer the question of

"what else was Lewis concerned about?" besides theology and literature, and to suggest how relevant Lewis's ideas remain. In it Lewis considers such subjects as the form and efficacy of modern-day chivalry, the teaching of English, private experiences of joy, recovery of childlike pleasure, and sexuality in literature—in other words, the same things that concern him in all his essays. Lewis's unfortunate experience of hazing and sadistic "fagging" at Malvern College—developed at some length in his biography and autobiography—is treated in a poignant piece titled "My First School"; Lewis's wartime preoccupation with the spiritual welfare of enlisted men and women is evident in three essays published originally in 1944; "Modern Man and His Categories of Thought," published for the first time in this volume, develops ideas introduced in "God in the Dock," "Christian Apologetics," and "The Language of Religion." And "Talking About Bicycles" whimsically treats the cycles of enchantment and disenchantment that afflict people in their efforts to achieve happiness. Lewis takes his examples from romantic love, wartime heroics, and political theory. But the essay begins with the rediscovery of a childlike joy in bicycling that recapitulates the original experience: "the mere fact of riding brings back a delicious whiff of memory," a taste of joy that is analogous in intensity to the experience of *Sehnsucht* that in his early life Lewis originally attached to the feeling of "Northernness" that he derived from the Norse sagas and Eddic poems. The piece is cast as an imaginary dialogue between a loquacious friend and the essay's reticent main persona.

Lewis's overall appeal as a writer combines his success in the divergent genres of fiction, literary history, poetry, devotional literature, letters, and children's stories with his importance and efficacy as a writer of essays. As to the latter, rigorous apologetics may define the core of his essayistic achievement, but in the end Lewis's impact as a popular essayist probably is due to the charming, personalistic style with which he undertook to defend, promote, and expound the implications of Christian faith in the whole fabric of life.

Letters:

Letters of C. S. Lewis, edited by W. H. Lewis (New York: Harcourt, Brace & World, 1966; London: Bles, 1966);

Letters to an American Lady, edited by Clyde S. Kilby (Grand Rapids, Mich.: Eerdmans,

1967; London: Hodder & Stoughton, 1969);

They Stand Together: The Letters of C. S. Lewis to Arthur Greeves, edited by Walter Hooper (New York: Macmillan, 1979; London: Collins, 1979);

Letters to Children (New York: Macmillan, 1985; London: Collins, 1985).

Bibliography:

Walter Hooper, "A Bibliography of the Writings of C. S. Lewis," in *Light on C. S. Lewis*, edited by Jocelyn Gibb (London: Bles, 1965; New York: Harcourt Brace Jovanovich, 1976), pp. 117-160.

Biography:

Roger Lancelyn Green and Walter Hooper, *C. S. Lewis: A Biography* (New York: Harcourt Brace Jovanovich, 1974; London: Collins, 1974).

References:

Owen Barfield, Introduction to *Light on C. S. Lewis*, edited by Jocelyn Gibb (London: Bles, 1965), pp. ix-xxi;

Humphrey Carpenter, *The Inklings: C. S. Lewis, J. R. R. Tolkien, Charles Williams, and Their Friends* (London: Allen & Unwin, 1978; Boston: Houghton Mifflin, 1979);

Nevill Coghill, "The Approach to English," in *Light on C. S. Lewis*, pp. 51-66;

James T. Como, ed., *"C. S. Lewis at the Breakfast Table" and Other Reminiscences* (New York: Macmillan, 1979);

Austin Farrer, "The Christian Apologist," in *Light on C. S. Lewis*, pp. 23-43;

Walter Hooper, *Past Watchful Dragons: The Narnian Chronicles of C. S. Lewis* (New York: Macmillan, 1974);

Peter J. Schakel, ed., *The Longing for a Form: Essays on the Fiction of C. S. Lewis* (Kent, Ohio: Kent State University Press, 1977);

Chad Walsh, *The Literary Legacy of C. S. Lewis* (New York: Harcourt Brace Jovanovich, 1979).

Papers:

Many of Lewis's papers are housed at Oxford's Bodleian Library and in the Marion E. Wade Collection at Wheaton College, Wheaton, Illinois.

Compton Mackenzie

(17 January 1883 - 30 November 1972)

Ian Ross
University of British Columbia

See also the Mackenzie entry in *DLB 34: British Novelists, 1890-1929: Traditionalists.*

BOOKS: *Poems* (Oxford: Blackwell / London: Simpkin, Marshall, Hamilton, Kent, 1907);

The Passionate Elopement (London: Secker, 1911; New York: Lane, 1911);

Carnival (London: Secker, 1912; New York: Appleton, 1912);

Kensington Rhymes (London: Secker, 1912);

Sinister Street, volume 1 (London: Secker, 1913); republished as *Youth's Encounter* (New York: Appleton, 1913);

Sinister Street, volume 2 (London: Secker, 1914; New York: Appleton, 1914);

Guy and Pauline (London: Secker, 1915); republished as *Plashers Mead* (New York & London: Harper, 1915);

The Early Life and Adventures of Sylvia Scarlett (London: Secker, 1918; New York & London: Harper, 1918);

Sylvia & Michael: The Later Adventures of Sylvia Scarlett (London: Secker, 1919; New York & London: Harper, 1919);

Poor Relations (London: Secker, 1919; New York & London: Harper, 1919);

The Vanity Girl (London & New York: Cassell, 1920; New York & London: Harper, 1920);

Rich Relatives (London: Secker, 1921; New York & London: Harper, 1921);

The Altar Steps (London & New York: Cassell, 1922; New York: Doran, 1922);

The Parson's Progress (London & New York: Cassell, 1923; New York: Doran, 1924);

Gramophone Nights, by Mackenzie and Archibald Marshall (London: Heinemann, 1923);

The Seven Ages of Woman (London: Secker, 1923; New York: Stokes, 1923);

The Heavenly Ladder (London & New York: Cassell, 1924; New York: Doran, 1924);

The Old Men of the Sea (London: Cassell, 1924; New York: Stokes, 1924); republished as *Paradise for Sale* (London: Macdonald, 1963);

Compton Mackenzie, circa 1954 (photograph by Robin Adler; by permission of the National Portrait Gallery, London)

Santa Claus in Summer (London: Constable, 1924; New York: Stokes, 1925);

Coral: A Sequel to "Carnival" (London & New York: Cassell, 1925; New York: Doran, 1925);

Fairy Gold (London & New York: Cassell, 1926; New York: Doran, 1926);

The Life and Adventures of Sylvia Scarlett (London: Secker, 1927);

Mabel in Queer Street (Oxford: Blackwell, 1927);

Rogues and Vagabonds (London: Cassell, 1927; New York: Doran, 1927);

176

Compton Mackenzie at twenty-four and Faith Stone Mackenzie at the time of their marriage in 1905

Vestal Fire (London: Cassell, 1927; New York: Doran, 1927);

Extraordinary Women: Theme and Variations (London: Secker, 1928; New York: Macy-Masius, 1928);

Extremes Meet (London & New York: Cassell, 1928; Garden City, N.Y.: Doubleday, Doran, 1928);

The Unpleasant Visitors (Oxford: Blackwell, 1928);

Gallipoli Memories (London, Toronto & New York: Cassell, 1929; Garden City, N.Y.: Doubleday, Doran, 1929);

The Adventures of Two Chairs (Oxford: Blackwell, 1929);

The Three Couriers (London: Cassell, 1929; Garden City, N.Y.: Doubleday, Doran, 1929);

April Fools (London: Cassell, 1930; Garden City, N.Y.: Doubleday, Doran, 1930);

The Enchanted Blanket (Oxford: Blackwell, 1930);

Told (Oxford: Blackwell, 1930; New York: Appleton, 1930);

First Athenian Memories (London: Cassell, 1931);

Buttercups and Daisies (London: Cassell, 1931); republished as *For Sale* (Garden City, N.Y.: Doubleday, Doran, 1931);

The Conceited Doll (Oxford: Blackwell, 1931);

Our Street (London: Cassell, 1931; Garden City, N.Y.: Doubleday, Doran, 1932);

The Fairy in the Window-Box (Oxford: Blackwell, 1932);

Greek Memories (London: Cassell, 1932);

Prince Charlie (de jure Charles III, King of Scotland, England, France and Ireland) (London: Davies, 1932; New York: Appleton, 1933);

Unconsidered Trifles (London: Secker, 1932);

The Dining-Room Battle (Oxford: Blackwell, 1933);

Literature in My Time (London: Rich & Cowan, 1933);

Water on the Brain (London: Cassell, 1933; Garden City, N.Y.: Doubleday, Doran, 1933);

The Lost Cause: A Jacobite Play (Edinburgh: Oliver & Boyd, 1933);

Reaped and Bound (London: Secker, 1933);

The Darkening Green (London: Cassell, 1934; Garden City, N.Y.: Doubleday, Doran, 1934);

The Enchanted Island (Oxford: Blackwell, 1934);

Marathon and Salamis (London: Davies, 1934);

Prince Charlie and His Ladies (London & Toronto: Cassell, 1934; New York: Knopf, 1935);

Figure of Eight (London: Cassell, 1936);

Catholicism and Scotland (London: Routledge, 1936);

The Naughtymobile (Oxford: Blackwell, 1936);

The East Wind of Love: Being Book One of "The Four Winds of Love" (London: Rich & Cowan, 1937); republished as *The East Wind* (New York: Dodd, Mead, 1937);

The South Wind of Love: Being Book Two of "The Four Winds of Love" (London: Rich & Cowan, 1937; New York: Dodd, Mead, 1937);

The Stairs that Kept on Going Down (Oxford: Blackwell, 1937);

Pericles (London: Hodder & Stoughton, 1937);

The Windsor Tapestry (London: Rich & Cowan, 1938; New York: Stokes, 1938);

A Musical Chair (London: Chatto & Windus, 1939);

The West Wind of Love: Being Book Three of "The Four Winds of Love" (London: Chatto & Windus, 1940; New York: Dodd, Mead, 1940);

West to North: Being Book Four of "The Four Winds of Love" (London: Chatto & Windus, 1940; New York: Dodd, Mead, 1941);

Aegean Memories (London: Chatto & Windus, 1940);

The Monarch of the Glen (London: Chatto & Windus, 1941; Boston: Houghton Mifflin, 1951);

The Red Tapeworm (London: Chatto & Windus, 1941);

Calvary, by Mackenzie and Faith Compton Mackenzie (London: Lane, 1942);

Keep the Home Guard Turning (London: Chatto & Windus, 1943);

Mr. Roosevelt (London: Harrap, 1943; New York: Dutton, 1944);

Wind of Freedom: The History of the Invasion of Greece by the Axis Powers, 1940-1941 (London: Chatto & Windus, 1943);

The North Wind of Love, Book One: Being Book V of "The Four Winds of Love" (London: Chatto & Windus, 1944; New York: Dodd, Mead, 1945);

The North Wind of Love, Book Two: Being Book VI of "The Four Winds of Love" (London: Chatto & Windus, 1945); republished as *Again to the North* (New York: Dodd, Mead, 1946);

Dr. Benes (London & Toronto: Harrap, 1946);

Whisky Galore (London: Chatto & Windus, 1947); republished as *Tight Little Island* (Boston: Houghton Mifflin, 1947);

The Vital Flame (London: Muller, 1947);

All Over the Place (London: Chatto & Windus, 1949);

Hunting the Fairies (London: Chatto & Windus, 1949);

Eastern Epic: Volume 1, Defence (London: Chatto & Windus, 1951);

The House of Coalport, 1750-1950 (London: Collins, 1951);

I Took a Journey: A Tour of National Trust Properties (London: Naldrett, 1951);

The Rival Monster (London: Chatto & Windus, 1952);

The Queen's House: A History of Buckingham Palace (London: Hutchinson, 1953);

The Savoy of London (London: Harrap, 1953);

Ben Nevis Goes East (London: Chatto & Windus, 1954);

Echoes (London: Chatto & Windus, 1954);

Realms of Silver: One Hundred Years of Banking in the East (London: Routledge & Kegan Paul, 1954);

My Record of Music (London: Hutchinson, 1955; New York: Putnam's, 1956);

Thin Ice (London: Chatto & Windus, 1956; New York: Putnam's, 1957);

Rockets Galore (London: Chatto & Windus, 1957);

Sublime Tobacco (London: Chatto & Windus, 1957; New York: Macmillan, 1958);

The Lunatic Republic (London: Chatto & Windus, 1959);

Cats' Company (London: Elek, 1960; New York: Taplinger, 1961);

Greece in My Life (London: Chatto & Windus, 1960);

Mezzotint (London: Chatto & Windus, 1961);

Catmint (London: Barrie & Rockliff, 1961; New York: Taplinger, 1962);

The Varsity Girl (London: Hamilton, 1962);

On Moral Courage (London: Collins, 1962); republished as *Certain Aspects of Moral Courage* (Garden City, N.Y.: Doubleday, 1962);

Look at Cats (London: Hamilton, 1963);

My Life and Times, 10 volumes (London: Chatto & Windus, 1963-1971);

Little Cat Lost (London: Barrie & Rockliff, 1965; New York: Macmillan, 1965);

The Stolen Soprano (London: Chatto & Windus, 1965);

Paper Lives (London: Chatto & Windus, 1966);

Frontispiece for Mackenzie's Greek Memories *(1932), showing the author in his World War I army uniform*

The Strongest Man on Earth (London: Chatto &
    Windus, 1968);
Robert Louis Stevenson (London: Morgan-
    Grampian, 1968; Cranbury, N.J.: Barnes,
    1969);
The Secret Island (London: Kaye & Ward, 1969);
Achilles (London: Aldus, 1972);
Jason (London: Aldus, 1972);
Perseus (London: Aldus, 1972);
Theseus (London: Aldus, 1972).
Collections: *The Four Winds of Love*, 6 volumes
    (London: Rich & Cowan, 1945);
The Adventures of Sylvia Scarlett (London: Macdon-
    ald, 1950)–comprises *Sylvia and Michael* and
    The Life and Adventures of Sylvia Scarlett;
The Compton Mackenzie Birthday Book, edited by
    Margery Weiner (London: Hutchinson,
    1951);
The Highland Omnibus (Harmondsworth, U.K.:
    Penguin, 1983).

PLAY PRODUCTION: *The Gentleman in Grey*,
    Edinburgh, Lyceum Theatre, March 1907.

As an essayist Compton Mackenzie cultivated a tradition going back to Michel de Montaigne and Francis Bacon, of flights of introspec-
tive and descriptive writing, often autobiographical in focus, with an application to princi-
pled conduct or at least a resolute attitude toward life and art. He digested experience in the
manner of Sir William Temple and could view
the metropolitan scene with detachment like the
"Mr. Spectator" created by Richard Steele and Joseph Addison, but was also accustomed to observing nature in the fashion of Gilbert White of
Selborne. Charles Lamb's whimsical humor was
not entirely foreign to Mackenzie; nor is the flow
of talk in his essays so very far removed from
that of William Hazlitt. Walter Pater was a star in
Mackenzie's intellectual firmament, but Mackenzie learned to view aestheticism through the
ironic eyes of Max Beerbohm. At the same time,
the example of Robert Louis Stevenson's debo-
nair romanticism attracted him, and his nearer
contemporaries G. K. Chesterton and Hilaire Belloc influenced him with their commitment to a
Catholic perspective. After an Anglican upbringing, he was received into the Roman Catholic
Church on Capri in April 1914, and yet he was
never the truculent religionist but always the
writer who went his own way and found his own
spiritual path.

Eldest son of a father of Scottish descent–
Edward Compton–and an American mother–
Virginia Bateman–both of whom were promi-
nent Victorian stage personalities, Anthony
Edward Montague Compton Mackenzie was born
on 17 January 1883 at West Hartlepool, Durham,
where his parents were on tour with the Comp-
ton Comedy Company, which they had founded
(Compton being an adopted stage name). D. H.
Lawrence remembered and caricatured him as
"The Man Who Loved Islands" (*Dial*, July 1927),
and he lived much of his full, varied life on
Capri, on the Channel Islands of Herm and
Jethou, on an islet on the Beauly in Inverness-
shire, and on Barra in the Outer Hebrides. But fittingly for the champion of Scottish nationalism
he became, Mackenzie died in Edinburgh on St.
Andrew's Day, 1972.

His lineage and his vagabond early years
may have endowed him with a slant on life often
at variance with English orthodoxies, a rebellious
feature of all his writings. Schooling in Latin and

Mackenzie with his dog, Hamlet, and secretary, James Eastwood, on the island of Herm, circa 1920

Greek at St. Paul's in London should have led to a classical scholarship to Balliol College, Oxford, or Trinity College, Cambridge, but in defiance of his headmaster he went up to Oxford to read history at Magdalen. Weekly essays for his tutors disciplined him as a writer, and he contributed to meetings of societies where papers were read and discussed by undergraduates sharpening their powers of criticism. There is an interesting account of this and other university activities conducive to the formation of Mackenzie as a writer in the Oxford section of his novel *Sinister Street* (1913, 1914). He did some acting, which was in his blood, and success as Gratiano in an Oxford University Dramatic Society production of William Shakespeare's *Merchant of Venice* brought him an offer of a contract at the Garrick Theatre in London, but he had also enjoyed founding and editing a periodical called the *Oxford Point of View*. The elegant Anglo-American essayist Logan Pearsall Smith noticed Mackenzie's talent and encouraged him to become a writer. In a cottage at Burford in the Cotswolds, near Oxford, preparing for his final examinations in 1904, he began his life's work as a writer, devoting himself to poetry.

His *Poems* was published at his expense by Blackwell in Oxford in 1907, but this proved to be a false start. There were to be others before he discovered his true métier. In the essay "My First Novel" (collected in *Echoes*, 1954) he says that he "always meant to be a playwright," and he gave vent to this ambition by writing a pastische of an eighteenth-century comedy, *The Gentleman in Grey*, which was successfully produced in March 1907 at the Lyceum Theatre in Edinburgh and remained in the repertoire of his parents' company for several years. Mackenzie was dissatisfied with the actual stage performance, however, and finding a refuge in Cornwall, he sat down to write the "ideal performance" in the form of a novel, *The Passionate Elopement* (eventually published in 1911). The manuscript was rejected by publisher after publisher, and Mackenzie turned to gardening in Cornwall to make a living, giving rein to an enthusiasm that was often the subject of his essays. One of them, "Gardening Once Upon a Time" (in *Unconsidered Trifles*, 1932), recounts how this commercial phase came to an end when "that pestilential brute, the daffodil fly" laid a fatal egg in a bulb of expensive Peter Barr daffodils. The resulting grub destroyed the bulb and Mackenzie's hopes of growing prizewinning daffodils. Immediately afterward a letter came from Martin Secker to say he wanted to publish *The Passionate Elopement*, which was a resounding success in 1911. Mackenzie found thereby a publisher and his role: not that of poet, nor playwright, nor daffodil grower, but novelist.

The forty novels he wrote among his hundred or so books include his most remarkable achievements. The early ones *Carnival* (1912) and *Sinister Street* attracted considerable acclaim, including that of Henry James, a family friend, whose efforts to turn himself into a dramatist with a version of *The American* (1877) had been furthered by the Compton Comedy Company. James reckoned Mackenzie to be one of the most promising of the "younger generation" of novelists of 1914. The overwhelming effect of World War I, however–during which Mackenzie served as a staff officer at Gallipoli and later as an intelligence officer in Athens and the Aegean–coupled with financial pressures, seemed to distract Mackenzie from his impulse to write the *comédie humaine* of his time, and he settled, or seemed to settle, for the self-description of "entertainer." To be sure, the American critic Edmund Wilson, who appreciated Mackenzie's unique slant on life, argued that his label did less than justice to the author whose many books, including collections of essays, couched in entertaining terms a serious defense of the rights of minorities with distinctive cultures who were threatened by obliterating forces directed by large centralizing powers.

Wilson made this point in connection with an assessment of *The Four Winds of Love* (1937-1945), a six-volume novel sequence whose interwoven life stories unfold a striking panorama of Europe during the first four decades of the twentieth century, when the wars involved not only the great powers but also the stubbornly irreducible little nations of the Continent–Greeks, Poles, and Czechs–as well as the Celtic fringe: the Cornish, Irish, Bretons, and Scots. There is a similar message in the most uproarious of Mackenzie's entertainments, *Whisky Galore* (1947). Its immense popular success as a novel, and later as a film, must derive from its deeply satisfying fable of the victory of the life spirit over all that is life-quenching, as little people resist the encroachment of the big and powerful. The novel tells of Hebridean islanders successfully rescuing from a wrecked ship, and preserving for social consumption, cases of their native whisky–

literally in Gaelic *uisge beatha* ("water of life")–when wartime British officialdom would have confiscated and destroyed this precious commodity.

A similar affirmation of the spirit of life and a willingness to satirize life-denial in many forms run through Mackenzie's nonfictional prose. The memoirs covering his service in Greece and the Aegean during World War I attack bureaucracy and bumbledom and brought him into court in 1932 on a trumped-up charge under the Official Secrets Act after *Greek Memories* was published that year. On legal advice, to avoid certain imprisonment arising from an in-camera hearing, he pleaded guilty when the matter reached final adjudication in 1933 and was fined one hundred pounds. Thereafter, he was strongly interested in conflicts between individuals and authority in legal frameworks, where principles of justice as well as the moral fiber of the parties involved are put to the test. This subject runs through the essays in his last collection, *On Moral Courage* (1962). In other collections–*Literature in My Time* (1933), *Reaped and Bound* (1933), *A Musical Chair* (1939), *Echoes*, and *My Record of Music* (1955)–one sees his enthusiasm for all that enhanced his life: animals, intriguing people, birds, plants, music, theater, literature, and the island settings that so delighted him. But there also surfaces his concern with the politics of survival for a small nation such as Scotland as being one form of the endless human struggle for adequate self-expression.

Another collection is *Unconsidered Trifles*, a selection made by the publisher Secker from Mackenzie's pieces published over twenty years (1912-1932) in such periodicals as the *English Review*, the *News Chronicle*, and the *Times*. The last essay in the volume, "Poetry and the Modern Novel," is perhaps the earliest to have been written and in origin was a talk given to the Poets' Club on 28 March 1912. It discusses a Baudelairean subject, the poetic nature of the modern city, a quality Mackenzie wished to incorporate in fiction: "I question whether the Tube [London underground train system] is not almost the finest adventure of travel which the world has known. For me, certainly, every journey is an Odyssey from the moment I enter the lift, with its subtle variations of mood–the subdued gaiety of expectation about half-past seven in contrast with the lassitude of the afternoon–the personalities of the liftmen, and the curious intimacy and relaxation of by-laws late at night."

Mackenzie with novelist Eric Linklater, whom he met in 1932

The first essay in the collection, "Memory," distinguishes neatly between two aspects of memory: "remembrance and reminiscence . . . meaning by the first the memory of vital experience, and by the second an ability to reproduce that and impress others." Mackenzie records and illustrates remarkable powers of remembrance, in his case stretching back to his eighth month, when he recalled being surprised by the difference in color between black-and-white rabbits and the ordinary variety. But understandably in view of his métier as novelist and essay writer, he cherished more deeply his power of reminiscence: "when that begins to fail I shall know I have written all I have to write, said all I have to say, and lived all I have to live." As matters turned out, this power was sustained all his life, and in his eighty-ninth year he was still writing, a tenth volume of autobiography behind him, though his virtual blindness made it necessary for him to guide his pen with wires tightly drawn across his sketch board. Even then he regarded himself with a touch of self-mockery, having in *Unconsidered Trifles* made clear his skepticism about "Grand Old Men of Literature." The essay so named evaluates claimants to this title and brings out its author's surprising, but just, estimate of the merit of Thomas Hardy's work over that of George Meredith.

Not surprising is Mackenzie's view of Esperanto: "I cannot see any future for a language in which the profoundest emotions that can sway humanity will be expressed by professorial agreement." He reckoned that Basque or "even Albanian" were worthier of study because of their "evidence of humanity's continuous life." Varying his style from logical discourse, he makes use of comic exaggeration in "What the Public Want" to illustrate the value of a "sense of theatre," which permits artists to enter into and appreciate their audience's reactions at the lowest level. In this essay he tells of attending a concert by the Irish tenor John McCormick in Dublin. At the interval, Mackenzie saw W. B. Yeats pacing up and

Compton and Faith Mackenzie outside the Old Bailey after his trial on Official Secrets Act charges in 1933. He was fined one hundred pounds, because of revelations in his Greek Memories.

down the circle promenade: "his whole distinguished appearance marked with such signs of suffering as the bound Prometheus may have shown under the assault of the vulture upon his liver. 'The dreadful clarity of all those words,' he was murmuring to himself with mellow groans. 'Every one of them could be heard.' I realized that McCormick's singing of *Kathleen Mavourneen* to a rapturous audience of his fellow-countrymen had been for the poet a genuine agony. He had risen from his seat with the evident intention of going down to Inisfree by the first train available."

A different kind of writing, again, is found in "Birds on My Island," where one encounters Mackenzie the naturalist. Keen of observation, he enters sympathetically into the life of the birds on the Channel Island of Jethou: "During the winter the oyster-catchers live decoratively in large groups like the birds in a Japanese painting; but as soon as they mate they forget all about the beautiful sweeping curves of black and white they traced across the winter sky, and become the fussiest and most undignified birds imaginable." Another of Mackenzie's enthusiasms was food, and recounting "Adventures" with it, he displays comic use of geographical and scientific imagery in reporting the result of ordering two dozen Lynnhaven oysters in a New York restaurant. After an hour or two, waiters appeared carrying "enormous bright metal dishes" and stopped at Mackenzie's table. The effect of setting down one of these dishes "was more of low tide on the Great Barrier Reef than of supper. The Great Barrier Reef, did I say? Nay, rather the imaginative reconstruction of a Mesozoic seascape, though I fancy those Lynnhaven oysters would have damned the neck of any plesiosaurus that tried to swallow them."

But places most of all arouse Mackenzie's powers of eloquence in this collection. His "Thoughts of Cornwall in Absence" are vivid evocations summoned by mention of names: "the ferry between Fowey and Poldruan in the starlight, Q[uiller-Couch]'s library at dusk with the windows blue as sapphires and the fire burning brightly and the half-covered sheet of paper on his desk where he has left off writing, gulls screaming and wheeling above the fishing-boats at Polperro, Godrevy lighthouse in a nor-westerly gale and the dark columbines on the cliff above Dead Man's Cove, the rich woods near Doublebois and the roundabouts at St. Just fair and the mighty swell booming in against Tol Pedn Penwith." Cornwall's beauty did not hold him forever, though, and his love for the Mediterranean and for islands drew him to Capri. He first went there after crossing from New York to Naples in 1913 with Faith Stone, whom he married in 1905. They found Sorrento dreary, and Mackenzie believed he understood why Henrick Ibsen had written *Ghosts* (1881) there, but Capri was different, as his essay about this island makes clear: "We knew that nothing could prevent our living for ever, if possible, in Capri. We knew it the moment we emerged from the funicular, which had brought us up five hundred feet through groves of lemons and figs, of vines and oranges and peaches, to the *piazza* of Capri. . . . Round us, in a jangle of bells and laughter and cracking whips, stood so many people, natives and foreigners, who from living in Capri had achieved such a brilliance of effect as butterflies and humming birds achieve from competing with the lights and colour of the tropics."

In 1933, the year following the publication of *Unconsidered Trifles*, Mackenzie was prevailed upon by his agent, Ralph Pinker, to write a book on contemporary literature for a series dealing with subjects "in my time," issued by Rich and Cowan, a new firm of London publishers. Mackenzie struggled on the island of Barra with *Literature in My Time*, far from detailed reference books and other literary people who might have been consulted. In consequence he was forced to draw on his own vivid memories of leading writers and literary tendencies from the 1890s to 1930, when it seemed to him that a classical culture had been abandoned and a barbaric age had arrived. In the essays that make up the book, Mackenzie again champions Hardy over Meredith, and he accounts for John Galsworthy's reputation on the Continent by suggesting that this novelist presents English people exactly as Europeans suppose them to be, a judgment confirmed by the renewed continental success of *The Forsyte Saga* (1922) when diffused as a television serial in the late 1960s. Taking issue with the antiromantic prejudice of the day, Mackenzie sees merit in Stevenson and Rupert Brooke. His most penetrating comments come in drawing a contrast between Lawrence, whom he had known in England and on Capri, and James Joyce, whose *Ulysses* (1922) Mackenzie considered to be the "major piece of literature this time has witnessed." He recollects that on Capri he gave Lawrence installments of *Ulysses* in the *Little Review*, and he suggests that *Lady Chatterley's Lover* (1928) was a misconceived answer to Joyce's treatment of sex, but he still pays tribute to the fire of original genius that burns in Lawrence's best prose.

Rooted in reminiscences also, the miscellaneous essays of *Reaped and Bound* range widely in subject matter: appreciation of music; recollections of such colorful characters as H. G. Pélissier, producer of the Follies at the Apollo Theatre in London, who prevailed on the author to write lyrics for a revue in 1910; Mackenzie's naturalist's vision of the life of garden and field; evocations of some of the smaller Scottish islands such as the Shiants in the Outer Hebrides, which he bought for five hundred pounds in 1925; and his concept of Scottish nationalism.

Writing on music, he tells in the first essay of his experience of finding pleasure in it after his student days, chiefly through his wife's piano playing and the chamber-music interests of her

family. When the Mackenzies moved in 1922 from Capri to Herm in the Channel Islands, he had thought of installing an Aeolian organ to provide music, but he found that musical comedies had replaced the symphonies formerly available on rolls for the instrument. He complained, and the Aeolian Company supplied him with a Hepplewhite model of an Aeolian Vocalion Gramophone. The next year, he founded and for many years edited a periodical called the *Gramophone*, providing information and criticism about available records and equipment. A book he published with the novelist Archibald Marshall, *Gramophone Nights* (1923), outlined a series of gramophone programs for every day of the month to introduce audiences to a wide range of classical and light music. In due course he published his editorials from the *Gramophone* in *A Musical Chair* and presented an expanded account of his interest in music and recordings in *My Record of Music*. The latter book incorporates the essay "Chamber Music and the Gramophone," also printed in *Reaped and Bound*. It was originally commissioned for the *Cyclopedic Survey of Chamber Music* (1929) by its editor and compiler, Walter Willson Cobbett. Cobbett had made a fortune in World War I promoting the British Belting and Asbestos Company and, a good amateur violinist himself and founder of a string quartet, he used his money to encourage knowledge and understanding of chamber music. It was this kind of music that Mackenzie principally loved, and he argued that the gramophone was in a way a "rival of the private string quartet," allowing for performance of personally chosen masterpieces when an owner wished. The recordings themselves were comparable to books in a library, and the recording companies were in the position of great publishing houses, likely to flourish by issuing great works that would last. Mackenzie's music criticism is vividly impressionistic, and he recognized its drawbacks, hoping that he did not offer "just the impressions of a literary temperament spoiling music with a pathetic fallacy," but he does reveal clearly how much recorded music meant to him. It was his habit to work at his writing far through the night to the accompaniment of chamber music on the gramophone, and he found constant refreshment in the mental associations brought about by music. Franz Peter Schubert's tunes, for example, best suited twilight, coming "in successive gusts of perfume as when one passes from border to border of the garden at the shutting-in of a long June day." Reflect-

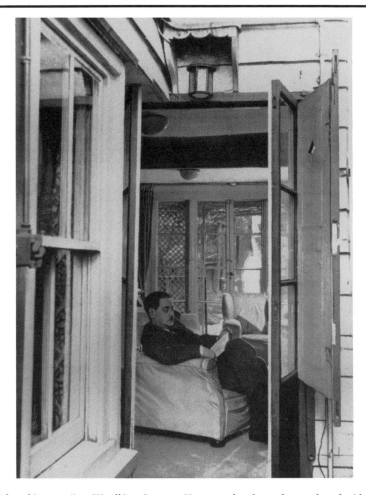

Mackenzie in "the white room" at Woodbine Cottage, Hampstead, a house he purchased with the profits from The Windsor Tapestry *(1938)*

ing on the magical effect of music, he wrote of "two trios of Mozart arranged for piano, violin and viola which make the very books on my shelves appear to dance" and claimed that "sweet peas in a bowl look more beautiful if looked at through an invisible web of sweet sounds."

The most impassioned and, at the same time, the most closely argued of the pieces in *Reaped and Bound* is the address Mackenzie gave on 29 January 1932, when he was installed as Lord Rector of Glasgow University. In defiance of the custom of electing prominent politicians, generally of the ruling party, who gave an address and took no further part in the life of the university, the Glasgow students elected Mackenzie as a Scottish nationalist who pledged to be a working rector and preside over meetings of the chief university administrative body, serving the interests of the students. Mackenzie opened the address with the topos of the assumed modesty of the speaker but pleaded that his presence be-

fore his audience was justified by the greatness of his cause. He then elevated his discussion to the plane of the ethics of nationalism rather than its politics. Surveying recent history, he concluded that the pretentions to a lasting empire had been shattered for Britain by the Boer War and World War I, and that a commercial age and relentless technological advance were bringing about improvement in physical conditions at the expense of the submergence of cultural, ethical, and spiritual values in the anonymity of a mass society. He recalled that 1932 was the centenary of Johann Wolfgang von Goethe's death and asked if "anybody here . . . believes that a universal man like Goethe could exist today? Why, a genius of ten times the demonic force of Goethe would evaporate in the conditions of modern life." But he also pointed out that 1832 was the year of Sir Walter Scott's death, and he described how at seven years of age he had been given Scott's *Tales of a Grandfather* (1827-1830). Reading and rereading its pages and, in his eighth year, crossing the border to Scotland for a first visit that led to many others inspired in him a love for his ancestral country linked to a vision of its turbulent history as well as a "dim, improbable" hope for the future. He had identified himself with the cause of the rebirth of Scotland, and he invited his young audience to do so also as a way of finding a way to live a nobler and saner life, resisting the degradations of modern mass society. His call was not couched in the terms of strident chauvinism then ringing in the beer halls of Munich, at Fascist rallies in Rome, and in the war party's broadcasts from Tokyo, but rather his words resembled those of Pericles addressing the Athenians during the crisis of their war with Sparta, seeking to imbue them with pride in their heritage and a desire to add further achievements to the renown of their city-state. The address concluded with a vision of Mackenzie gazing down on Glasgow from the Campsie Fells and finding that "her spires and chimneys . . . and towers and tenements and sparkling roofs" have something that he considered Athens and Rome, similarly observed from hills, could not give: "the glory and grandeur of the future, and the beating heart of a nation." History does not record that Mackenzie set the Clyde afire with nationalism, but perhaps his eloquent words helped to inspire those who cleansed the foul slums of Glasgow, endured the grueling years of the Depression and World War II, and are making the city again as commodious as its beautiful situation warrants.

Honoring his commitment to Scottish nationalism that had become pronounced in 1928, Mackenzie moved permanently to Scotland two years later, and Lord Lovat gave him as his home the shooting lodge on Eilean Aigas, an islet on the river Beauly in Inverness-shire. In the early 1930s the Mackenzies moved to Barra.

Early in the field as a patron and critic of gramophone recording, Mackenzie was also a pioneer broadcaster and commentator. His unflattering remark in the introductory essay to *Gramaphone Nights* about the "rubbish that is being buzzed into the ears of the public every day by the broadcasting companies" brought an invitation in 1923 from John Reith (later Lord Reith), managing director of the BBC, to come out to Savoy Hill to hear about company policy. A towering personality, Reith (as reported in *My Record of Music*) "spoke about the future of broadcasting with the fervid eloquence of a fanatic offering to his listeners the contemplations of eternal

life," and ended the interview by banging his desk with his fist and declaring "those who think they can impede what we are setting out to do will be smashed." Mackenzie assured Reith his views about broadcasting had been completely changed, whereupon he was invited to contribute to the recently begun *Radio Times*.

About the same time, he was called on by the BBC to play and comment on his choice of records for fifteen minutes each weekday at 1 P.M., there being no news at that hour. In *Echoes* Mackenzie presents some of his broadcasts as little essays, and in one of them, "Memories of Savoy Hill," he recounts the story of his first experience as the original BBC disc jockey. He had no script and the director of the broadcast stoically declared it would not matter if Mackenzie dried up, "because the only people listening at one o'clock will be the women washing up." Mackenzie allowed himself the hope that the "women washing up enjoyed those old records more than the men washing up today enjoy the one o'clock news." In other broadcast essays that appear in *Echoes*, Mackenzie describes his encounters with Edward Elgar, who once drummed out on his ribs the rhythm of the "March to the Guillotine" from Hector Berlioz's *Symphonie Fantastique*; with Ellen Terry, who had kissed him to seal a promise that she would come to hear his first sermon—Mackenzie, then being fifteen, having wanted to become a parson; with Henry James, who could not decide between a novel by H. G. Wells or one by Arnold Bennett as suitable entertainment for the visiting Mackenzie; and with that grandee of the Scottish nationalist movement, Robert Bontine Cunninghame Graham, who "looked at the future of Scotland with that logical Latin mind [he had a Spanish maternal grandmother], and faced up to the fact that unless Europe could preserve the independence of her small nations Europe was doomed." But strong though Mackenzie's memories were of people and places and things, he did not rely on nostalgic evocation alone, but allowed his mind to dart to the center of meaning in the fragments of his life he offered to listeners and readers. Thus he celebrates the rusticity of the London of his boyhood, where horses drew the omnibuses and the window boxes were to be found from May to the end of July, with "marguerites and geraniums, lobelias and calceolarias from top to bottom of every house from Kensington to Mayfair." At the same time, he notes that the fall of Oscar Wilde in 1895 and the savage sentence of imprisonment

Mackenzie crowning the May Queen at Denchworth Manor, where he had moved in April 1945

inflicted on him for homosexual practices shocked Europe, and led to "that outburst of Continental feeling against what was believed to be the foul hypocrisy of a country capable of such cynical greed as the acquisition of the two little Dutch republics in South Africa."

Mackenzie wrote in *Echoes* of the places that had greatly impressed him, and he described his "great fondness for small islands," thirty years of existence having been spent on them, including eight years on the Channel Island of Jethou, so small that its fifty acres only contained his household and himself as its inhabitants. His vindication was that "life on a small island restores human dignity: the individual is not overwhelmed by his own unimportance. This is particularly beneficent for the artist, who requires the solitude necessary to make him feel that the work he is producing today is not a futile drop in an ocean of human endeavour."

Into volume 7 of his autobiography, *My Life and Times* (1963-1971), he inserted the text of a broadcast he gave in autumn 1936 called "Living Off the Map." This can be discussed as perhaps the most fully realized of his island essays, describing Barra, where he built a house in 1935 and made his home until 1944, when he moved to England. (In 1952 he settled in Edinburgh for his last years.) Mackenzie begins his essay by stating that Barra is off the map like the other southern islands of the Outer Hebrides, because the thickened line of longitude that frames most maps of Britain obscures them, and they are consigned to the margin. He continues by claiming that he is reluctant to discuss life on Barra because he does not want to suggest that others living elsewhere would be challenged by it and presumably would want to come to the islands in crowds. The structure of the talk (or essay) then required him to give a physical description of Barra and its set-

Mackenzie (right) with his lifelong friend Gen. Ian Hamilton, Commander of the Mediterranean Expeditionary Force during World War I, who is featured in Mackenzie's Gallipoli Memories *(1929)*

ting, which he does with his usual attention to shapes and colors, employing the traditional device of boxing the compass: "Northward, an absolutely level square mile of beach composed of thousands of years of cockle-shells over which the tide flows sometimes sky-blue, sometimes dove-grey, sometimes pale green, the colour of a cowslip spathe." At the heart of the island is a "rolling moorland" rising to a hill of thirteen hundred feet, where a "miniature of the Highlands without the pines and birches" can "provide all the solitude a normal human being should want." But Mackenzie values the island more for its people than its solitude: "Barra is an extraordinarily happy place. Laughter is the keynote. There is always a good story going the rounds. Gaelic is a great language for wit, and with three-quarters of the population of Barra speaking both Gaelic and English, the native Gaelic wit salts the English." Mackenzie notes the cosmopolitan outlook of the Barra people, their good manners and savoir faire coupled with shy-

ness, and also their acceptance of his night-owl working habits. Like West Highland people generally, they did not accept the tyranny of time, but went to bed late and rose late to make the most of summer's late evening sunshine and avoid winter's prolonged morning twilight. When he wrote of the Islemen in *Whisky Galore* and other novels, Mackenzie was accused of producing caricatures, but in "Living Off the Map" he does not dwell on the idiosyncrasies of the Barra people but rather asserts of the island that "everybody in it is a real person; the way that life *on* the map is moving just now does make it more and more difficult for people to be themselves. Just as the life of the island as a whole is marked by a certain completeness and distinction, so are the lives of the individuals who make up this small community." Mackenzie instances the prevalence of nicknames on Barra and asks his audience to remember that at school the "award of a nickname always used to be a pledge of individuality." Mackenzie delighted in the individuality of the

Coddie, the Crookle, and other Barra personalities with whom he lived, and they responded to him with affection and interest in his work. At Mackenzie's funeral on Barra, an eighty-two-year-old piper, Calum Johnson, played the lament in the churchyard of St. Barr, Eoligarry, and then died at the graveside, having performed a last office for his friend.

Mackenzie endeared himself to the islanders of Barra by more than his personality. He actively championed their causes—for example, the right of crofter fishermen to a livelihood in an era when steam trawling was ruining local fishing. Such a cause drew Mackenzie into fights with governments local and central, part of his long-standing concern with the rights of little people and the exposure of the injustice perpetrated by authorities of various kinds. This concern lies behind the last volume of his essays, *On Moral Courage*. Searching for a definition of moral courage in the opening piece, Mackenzie turns to a declaration of James Fitzjames Stephen that it consisted of "readiness to expose oneself to suffering or inconvenience which does not affect the body. It arises from firmness of moral principle and is independent of the physical constitution." Mackenzie did not think that Stephen's career after he stood up to bullying at Eton was conspicuous for moral courage in this sense, but the separate essays inquire into some remarkable illustrations of this virtue. The second essay, for example, argues that Prime Minister Clement Attlee and Lord Louis Mountbatten possessed it notably at the time of the surrender of British power in India. Other essays laud as morally courageous those who stood by Wilde when he was tried, somewhat surprisingly juxtaposed by Mackenzie with Socrates and the Roman consul Regulus; the duke of Windsor; objectors to the British government's enactments and policies in World War II; Arthur Conan Doyle (creator of Sherlock Holmes, who fought against miscarriages of justice); heroes from the everyday world who appeared on the BBC television series *This Is Your Life*; and the German resisters to Nazi tyranny. Presenting these favorably viewed figures leads Mackenzie to contrast them with "politicians, judges, civil servants, chief constables and jacks-in-office," who are exposed for their moral cowardice. Two essays, "Memories of D. H. Lawrence" and "The Case of *Lady Chatterley's Lover*," promise to add further to Mackenzie's assessments of Lawrence as man and artist. However, he goes over ground already covered in *Literature in My Time*,

amplifying formerly expressed views by ridiculing the pundits summoned as defense witnesses in the prosecution of Penguin Books under the Obscene Publications Act of 1959 for publishing an unexpurgated version of Lawrence's last novel. Mackenzie believed that Lawrence was hagridden by sex and that this is what came out in *Lady Chatterley's Lover*; he did not think the defense witnesses were animated by moral courage. Mackenzie argues, however, that it would have been a true expression of moral courage to have defended *The Rainbow* when it was suppressed in 1915, an act that, Mackenzie believed, aroused paranoia in Lawrence and intensified the destructive nature of the *daimonion* that possessed him.

In the Lawrence essays and the others, Mackenzie narrates anecdotes with a sure touch and deftly characterizes people and describes settings. He rides his hobbyhorses: the pernicious effects of public school education, the vulgarization incident to modern translations of the Bible, and so on. He is as wittily and defiantly outrageous in his stands at eighty as he ever was. His style is pungent and serviceable, ranging from mastery of the stark epigram—"when war starts, reason departs"—to comic portraiture, as in the account of Lawrence and a young Roumanian competing on Capri as fanners of a charcoal stove and disputing about Plotinus: "Francis Brett Young and I once came upon them in the middle of an argument about Plotinus, both fanning away so hard that the room was full of the fumes of charcoal and neo-Platonism. Unless we had hurriedly opened the windows, both philosopher cooks might have been asphyxiated."

Opening windows—perhaps this is Mackenzie's greatest talent as a prose writer and essayist. For him there was a lifelong attraction in the Keatsian ideal of the beauty to be found in the play of sensuous language commensurate with the sensuousness of nature itself. In 1933 he launched a controversy among correspondents addressing themselves to the editor of the *Daily Mail*: he presented two lists of the ten most beautiful words in English. One list was phrased as blank verse: "Carnation, azure, peril, moon, forlorn, / Heart, silence, shadow, April, apricot," and the other as an Alexandrine couplet: "Damask and damson, doom and harlequin and fire, / Autumnal, vanity, flame, nectarine, desire." Writing about these lists in his autobiography in his eighty-fourth year, he confessed they had a "strange magic for me ... a sort of elixir of youth." But this Keatsian strain in his writing, possibly reinforced by his reading of Walter Pater and Charles Algernon Swinburne, was not overindulged. A corrective came from Mackenzie's own lively sense of the absurd and the farcical, together with the example of the deflating irony of Max Beerbohm, whom Mackenzie knew personally, and the sardonic humor of Stendhal, whose writing he encountered at a turning point in his career. In consequence, the windows that Mackenzie opens in his essays are truly revealing, and the breezes that he admits are refreshing and creative.

Bibliography:

Phillips V. Brooks, *A Bibliography Of and About the Works of Anthony Edward Montague Compton Mackenzie, Sir Compton Mackenzie, 1883-1972* (Norwood, Pa.: Norwood, 1984).

Biographies:

D. J. Dooley, *Compton Mackenzie* (New York: Twayne, 1974);

Andro Linklater, *Compton Mackenzie* (London: Chatto & Windus, 1987).

References:

Henry James, "The Younger Generation," *Times Literary Supplement*, 19 March and 2 April 1914; revised and expanded in *Henry James and H. G. Wells*, edited by Leon Edel and Gordon N. Ray (London: Hart-Davis, 1958);

D. H. Lawrence, "The Man Who Loved Islands," *Dial* (July 1927); republished in his *The Woman Who Rode Away* (New York: Knopf, 1928);

Edmund Wilson, *The Bit Between My Teeth: A Literary Chronicle of 1950-1965* (London: Allan, 1965; New York: Farrar, Straus & Giroux, 1965);

Kenneth Young, *Compton Mackenzie* (London: Longmans, Green, 1968).

Papers:

The primary location of Mackenzie's papers is the Harry Ransom Humanities Research Center, University of Texas at Austin, which also holds Mackenzie's personal library. There is a smaller collection of his papers at the Lilly Library, Indiana University, Bloomington. The National Library of Scotland, Edinburgh, also has some Mackenzie papers, and King's School, Canterbury, holds the manuscripts for the first volume of *Sinister Street*.

W. Somerset Maugham

(25 January 1874 - 16 December 1965)

Robert L. Calder

University of Saskatchewan

See also the Maugham entries in *DLB 10: Modern British Dramatists, 1900-1945* and *DLB 36: British Novelists, 1890-1929: Modernists.*

BOOKS: *Liza of Lambeth* (London: Unwin, 1897; revised, 1904; New York: Doran, 1921);

The Making of a Saint (London: Unwin, 1898; Boston: Page, 1898);

Orientations (London: Unwin, 1899);

The Hero (London: Hutchinson, 1901);

Mrs. Craddock (London: Heinemann, 1902; New York: Doran, 1920);

A Man of Honour: A Play in Four Acts (London: Chapman & Hall, 1903; Chicago: Dramatic Publishing, 1912);

The Merry-Go-Round (London: Heinemann, 1904);

The Land of the Blessed Virgin: Sketches and Impressions in Andalusia (London: Heinemann, 1905; New York: Knopf, 1920); republished as *Andalusia: Sketches and Impressions* (New York: Knopf, 1920);

The Bishop's Apron (London: Chapman & Hall, 1906);

The Explorer (London: Heinemann, 1908 [i.e., 1907]; New York: Baker & Taylor, 1909);

The Magician (London: Heinemann, 1908; New York: Doran, 1908);

Lady Frederick: A Comedy in Three Acts (London: Heinemann, 1912 [i.e., 1911]; Chicago: Dramatic Publishing, 1912?);

Jack Straw: A Farce in Three Acts (London: Heinemann, 1912 [i.e., 1911]; Chicago: Dramatic Publishing, 1912);

Mrs. Dot: A Farce in Three Acts (London: Heinemann, 1912; Chicago: Dramatic Publishing, 1912);

Penelope: A Comedy in Three Acts (London: Heinemann, 1912; Chicago: Dramatic Publishing, 1912);

The Explorer: A Melodrama in Four Acts (London: Heinemann, 1912; Chicago: Dramatic Publishing, 1912);

The Tenth Man: A Tragic Comedy in Three Acts (London: Heinemann, 1913; Chicago: Dramatic Publishing, 1913);

Landed Gentry: A Comedy in Four Acts (London: Heinemann, 1913; Chicago: Dramatic Publishing, 1913);

The Land of Promise: A Comedy in Four Acts (London: Bickers, 1913);

Smith: A Comedy in Four Acts (London: Heinemann, 1913; Chicago: Dramatic Publishing, 1913);

Of Human Bondage (London: Heinemann, 1915; New York: Doran, 1915; republished with an introduction by Maugham, London: Heinemann, 1934; abridged edition, New York: Pocket Books, 1950);

The Moon and Sixpence (London: Heinemann, 1919; New York: Doran, 1919);

The Unknown: A Play in Three Acts (London: Heinemann, 1920);

The Circle: A Comedy in Three Acts (London: Heinemann, 1921; New York: Doran, 1921);

The Trembling of a Leaf: Little Stories of the South Sea Islands (New York: Doran, 1921; London: Heinemann, 1921); republished as *Sadie Thompson: and Other Stories of the South Sea Islands* (London: Readers Library, 1928);

Caesar's Wife: A Comedy in Three Acts (London: Heinemann, 1922; New York: Doran, 1923);

East of Suez: A Play in Seven Scenes (London: Heinemann, 1922; New York: Doran, 1922);

The Land of Promise (London: Heinemann, 1922; New York: Doran, 1923);

On a Chinese Screen (London: Heinemann, 1922; New York: Doran, 1922);

Our Betters: A Comedy in Three Acts (London: Heinemann, 1923; New York: Doran, 1923);

Home and Beauty: A Farce in Three Acts (London: Heinemann, 1923);

The Unattainable: A Farce in Three Acts (London: Heinemann, 1924);

Loaves and Fishes: A Comedy in Four Acts (London: Heinemann, 1924);

W. Somerset Maugham in 1940 (BBC Hulton)

The Painted Veil (London: Heinemann, 1925; New York: Doran, 1925);

The Letter: A Play in Three Acts (New York: Doran, 1925; London: Heinemann, 1927);

The Casuarina Tree: Six Stories (London: Heinemann, 1926; New York: Doran, 1926);

The Constant Wife: A Comedy in Three Acts (New York: Doran, 1926; London: Heinemann, 1927);

Ashenden: or The British Agent (London: Heinemann, 1928; Garden City, N.Y.: Doubleday, Doran, 1928);

The Sacred Flame: A Play in Three Acts (Garden City, N.Y.: Doubleday, Doran, 1928; London: Heinemann, 1929);

The Gentleman in the Parlour: A Record of a Journey from Rangoon to Haiphong (London: Heinemann, 1930; Garden City, N.Y.: Doubleday, Doran, 1930);

Cakes and Ale: Or, The Skeleton in the Cupboard (London: Heinemann, 1930; Garden City, N.Y.: Doubleday, Doran, 1930);

The Bread-Winner: A Comedy in One Act (London: Heinemann, 1930; Garden City, N.Y.: Doubleday, Doran, 1931);

First Person Singular (Garden City, N.Y.: Doubleday, Doran, 1931; London: Heinemann, 1931);

The Book-Bag (Florence: Orioli, 1932);

The Narrow Corner (London: Heinemann, 1932; Garden City, N.Y.: Doubleday, Doran, 1932);

For Services Rendered: A Play in Three Acts (London: Heinemann, 1932; Garden City, N.Y.: Doubleday, Doran, 1933);

Ah King (Garden City, N.Y.: Doubleday, Doran, 1933; London: Heinemann, 1933);

Sheppey: A Play in Three Acts (London: Heinemann, 1933);

Don Fernando; or, Variations on Some Spanish Themes (London: Heinemann, 1935; Garden City, N.Y.: Doubleday, Doran, 1935; revised edition, London: Heinemann, 1950);

Cosmopolitans (Garden City, N.Y.: Doubleday, Doran, 1936; London: Heinemann, 1936);

Theatre: A Novel (Garden City, N.Y.: Doubleday, Doran, 1937; London & Toronto: Heinemann, 1937);

The Summing Up (London & Toronto: Heinemann, 1938; Garden City, N.Y.: Doubleday, Doran, 1938);

Christmas Holiday (London & Toronto: Heinemann, 1939; Garden City, N.Y.: Doubleday, Doran, 1939); republished as *Stranger in Paris* (New York: Bantam, 1949);

France at War (London: Heinemann, 1940; New York: Doubleday, Doran, 1940);

Books and You (London & Toronto: Heinemann, 1940; New York: Doubleday, Doran, 1940);

The Mixture as Before (London & Toronto: Heinemann, 1940; New York: Doubleday, Doran, 1940);

Up at the Villa (New York: Doubleday, Doran, 1941; London: Heinemann, 1941);

Strictly Personal (Garden City, N.Y.: Doubleday, Doran, 1941; London & Toronto: Heinemann, 1942);

The Hour Before the Dawn: A Novel (Garden City, N.Y.: Doubleday, Doran, 1942);

The Unconquered (New York: House of Books, 1944);

The Razor's Edge: A Novel (Garden City, N.Y.: Doubleday, Doran, 1944; London & Toronto: Heinemann, 1944);

Then and Now: A Novel (London & Toronto: Heinemann, 1946; Garden City, N.Y.: Doubleday, 1946); republished as *Fools and Their Folly* (New York: Avon, 1949);

Creatures of Circumstance (London: Heinemann, 1947; Garden City, N.Y.: Doubleday, 1947);

Catalina: A Romance (Melbourne, London & Toronto: Heinemann, 1948; Garden City, N.Y.: Doubleday, 1948);

Here and There: Short Stories (Melbourne, London & Toronto: Heinemann, 1948);

Great Novelists and Their Novels: Essays on the Ten Greatest Novels of the World and the Men and Women Who Wrote Them (Philadelphia & Toronto: Winston, 1948); revised and enlarged as *Ten Novels and Their Authors* (Melbourne, London & Toronto: Heinemann, 1954); republished as *The Art of Fiction: An Introduction to Ten Novels and Their Authors* (Garden City, N.Y.: Doubleday, 1955);

A Writer's Notebook (London: Heinemann, 1949; Garden City, N.Y.: Doubleday, 1949);

The Writer's Point of View (London: Cambridge University Press, 1951);

The Vagrant Mood: Six Essays (London: Heinemann, 1952; Garden City, N.Y.: Doubleday, 1953);

The World Over (Garden City, N.Y.: Doubleday, 1952);

The Noble Spániard: A Comedy in Three Acts, adapted from Ernest Grenet-Dancourt's *Les Gaîtés du veuvage* (London: Evans, 1953);

Points of View (London: Heinemann, 1958; Garden City, N.Y.: Doubleday, 1959);

Purely for My Pleasure (London: Heinemann, 1962; Garden City, N.Y.: Doubleday, 1962);

Selected Prefaces and Introductions (London: Heinemann, 1963);

Essays on Literature (London: New English Library/ Heinemann, 1967);

Seventeen Lost Stories, compiled by Craig V. Showalter (Garden City, N.Y.: Doubleday, 1969);

Marriages Are Made in Heaven: A Play in One Act (London: Blond, 1984);

A Traveller in Romance (London: Blond, 1984; New York: Potter, 1985).

Collections: *The Collected Plays*, 3 volumes (London: Heinemann, 1931);

The Collected Edition of the Works of W. Somerset Maugham, 35 volumes (London: Heinemann, 1931-1969);

East and West: The Collected Short Stories of W. Somerset Maugham (Garden City, N.Y.: Doubleday, Doran, 1934); republished as *Altogether* (London: Heinemann, 1934);

The Complete Short Stories of W. Somerset Maugham, 3 volumes (London: Heinemann, 1951);

The Travel Books of W. Somerset Maugham (London: Heinemann, 1955);

The Works of W. Somerset Maugham, 45 volumes (New York: Arno, 1977).

OTHER: *Traveller's Library*, compiled, with an introduction and notes, by Maugham (Garden City, N.Y.: Doubleday, Doran, 1933); republished as *Fifty Modern English Writers* (Garden City, N.Y.: Doubleday, Doran, 1933);

Tellers of Tales, compiled, with an introduction, by Maugham (New York: Doubleday, Doran, 1939);

Great Modern Reading, compiled by Maugham (Garden City, N.Y.: Doubleday, 1943);

A Choice of Kipling's Prose, compiled, with an introduction, by Maugham (London: Macmillan, 1952).

Few modern writers have been as prolific or as versatile as William Somerset Maugham. He wrote twenty novels–the best of which are *Of Human Bondage* (1915), *The Moon and Sixpence* (1919), *Cakes and Ale* (1930), and *The Razor's Edge* (1944). For nearly three decades he was one of

Cover for the American edition (1985) of a collection of character sketches and short essays by Maugham

the most popular dramatists in the English-speaking world, and among his twenty-five plays *The Circle* (1921) deserves a place in any history of theater. His more than one hundred short stories have made him one of the foremost English exponents of that genre in the twentieth century, and his spiritual and philosophical autobiography, *The Summing Up* (1938), is considered a classic. In addition, Maugham published travel books, collections of essays on various subjects, and prefaces, introductions, and critical essays on writers and the art of writing.

Maugham, the son of an English solicitor, was born in Paris and spent his first ten years in France. French thus became his first language, and for the remainder of his life he retained a love of France and a delicate, French quality in his prose. His mother, Edith Snell Maugham, died when he was eight, a trauma from which he never really recovered, and when his father, Robert Ormond Maugham, died two years later Som-

erset was sent to live with his aunt and uncle, Rev. and Mrs. Henry MacDonald Maugham, in a vicarage in Whitestable, Kent. After a miserable experience at King's School, Canterbury, which he graphically described in *Of Human Bondage*, he spent a year at Heidelberg University and then took a medical degree at St. Thomas's Hospital, London, though he never practiced, long having aspired to be a writer.

After a decade of struggle Maugham suddenly achieved unprecedented success as a dramatist in 1908, when he had four plays running simultaneously in London. On 26 May 1917 he married Syrie Barnardo Wellcome, and they had one child, Elizabeth Mary (later Lady Glendevon). Predominantly homosexual, however, Maugham was divorced in 1929, and spent the rest of his life with two successive secretary-companions, Gerald Haxton and Alan Searle. In 1928 he bought the Villa Mauresque, on Cap Ferrat in France, along the Côte d'Azur, and ex-

Maugham at King's School in Canterbury, which he attended from 1885 to 1889 (courtesy of the Estate of Lord Frederic Maugham)

cept for the years of World War II, lived there until his death. In 1954 he was awarded the Companion of Honour.

Much of Maugham's nonfiction defies strict classification, crossing the boundaries of autobiography, biography, essay, travelogue, and eulogy. Thus, though *The Summing Up* is frequently called an autobiography, it is in fact a series of essays on writing, drama, religion, philosophy, morality, and human nature. Similarly *A Writer's Notebook* (1949), his collection of observations from which he drew material for so much of his fiction, contains numerous critical comments on literature, art, philosophy, and religion. In both works the reader is in the company of an urbane and shrewd man of the world who reveals more about a variety of subjects than he does about himself.

One of the most itinerant of modern authors, Maugham traveled both to collect material for his fiction and to gain a sense of freedom from responsibility that he could never feel in England or at his villa. His first travel book, *The Land of the Blessed Virgin: Sketches and Impressions in Andalusia* (1905), describes his experiences in

the winter of 1897-1898 in southern Spain, where he had gone following five years of medical school and the publication of his first novel. Though now dated, and written in an elaborate style full of adjectives, the book conveys the excitement of the young author's discovery of the color, warmth, and vitality of Spain. He describes a bullfight, which he finds degrading but thrilling, the churches of Ronda, the cave in Manresa of Saint Ignatius Loyola, and the life and exuberance of Seville at night. The Spaniards, he concludes, possess a joy in living that escapes the English.

Much more mature, *On a Chinese Screen* (1922) is a collection of fifty-eight sketches made on a trip to China in the winter of 1919-1920. A series of word pictures, almost prose poems, they are precise and polished, many no more than a few paragraphs in length and only two taking up more than a dozen pages. Describing both the beauty and squalor of China, Maugham obtains his greatest effects from his evocation of the sense of place. His urbane and philosophical nature makes him especially sympathetic to the beliefs and manners inherent in Chinese civilization, though he admits that he can never fully understand the Chinese people he meets.

Like all of Maugham's writing, *On a Chinese Screen* reveals a greater interest in human beings than in places, and it contains some shrewd and gently critical sketches of westerners in China. These missionaries, consuls, company managers, and army officers are generally revealed to be narrow, intolerant, and insensitive to the culture and customs of the Chinese. One woman ignores the art around her and delights in re-creating the banality of Tunbridge Wells in her living room. A tobacco company official, blind to the spectacle of Chinese life, finds his only excitement in American adventure magazines. Among others are portraits of a missionary who hates the Chinese he has come to save, a liberal who abuses his rickshaw boy, and another missionary whose puritanism will not allow him to associate with a man who works for the tobacco company. Very nearly short stories, these sketches provide an interesting picture of pre-Communist China and explain some of the impetus behind the revolution.

The Gentleman in the Parlour (1930), which describes a journey Maugham took from Rangoon to Haiphong in 1922-1923, is a much different kind of travel book. Rather than a series of unconnected sketches, it is a chronological account of a trip that took him to Mandalay, Taunggyi, Keng

Page from Maugham's manuscript for Strictly Personal *(1941), his second autobiographical book (by permission of Yale University Library)*

Tung, Bangkok, Phnom Penh, Angkor Wat, Saigon, Hue, and Hanoi. Providing little practical information, the book is an impressionistic portrait by a sensitive traveler who enjoys a quiet hour on a turbid river as much as a tour through the ruins of a temple. *The Gentleman in the Parlour* is a book of warmth and gentle humor communicated in lucid, relaxed prose, and Maugham subtly interweaves his meditations with his descriptions of people and places so that he presents metaphysical conclusions as if they naturally arose from the environment. He spends several pages on the ruins of Angkor Wat, which he often said was the most impressive sight he had ever known. Nevertheless, he concludes that "the most awe-inspiring monument of antiquity is neither temple, nor citadel, nor great wall, but man," and his book contains sensitive portraits of people. Some of these sketches–"Mirage," "Mabel," "Masterson," and "A Marriage of Convenience"–were reprinted in his *Complete Short Stories* (1951). Another piece, "Princess September and the Nightingale," is an evocative fairy tale and an eloquent plea for personal freedom.

Considered by Graham Greene to be Maugham's best book, *Don Fernando* was first published in 1935 and then reissued with changes in 1950. More a work of intellectual and artistic history than a travel book, it deals with the Golden Age of Spain, reflecting that period's enormous creative energy. Maugham structured his book as a search for background material for a novel he proposed to write (and did years later, publishing it as *Catalina* in 1948). This structure gave him the pretext for examining the life of Saint Ignatius Loyola; the writings of Saint Teresa; the paintings of El Greco; Miguel de Cervantes's *Don Quixote* (1605, 1615); the playwright Lope de Vega; and other creative figures, such as Pedro Calderón, Diego Velázquez, Fray Luis de Leon, and Vicente Espinel. The best of these studies is the essay on El Greco, whom Maugham presents not as solitary, ascetic, and austere, but as a man who enjoyed music, luxury, and the company of others. *Don Fernando* is written in warm admiration for Spanish culture and civilization, but Maugham's conclusion is that of his study of the Far East: "It is not in art that they excelled, they excelled in what is greater than art–in man."

Maugham's two books of essays are a product of the final years of his writing career, when the creative urge gave way to the reflective mood. Both are eclectic, blending biography with criticism, and general observations with particular details. None of the essays is profound or strikingly original, but they are the urbane, seasoned view of a man who has known many of his subjects and is a practicing professional writer, and they are eminently readable. *The Vagrant Mood* (1952)–the first of the two collections–examines the minor nineteenth-century man-of-letters Augustus Hare, the seventeenth-century Spanish painter Francisco de Zurburan, the literary style of Edmund Burke, and Immanuel Kant's *Critique of Pure Reason* (1781; revised, 1787). Maugham also provides a surprising, serious study of mystery stories in "The Decline and Fall of the Detective Story." In "Some Novelists I Have Known" he gives useful and shrewd portraits of Henry James, H. G. Wells, Elizabeth Russell, Arnold Bennett, and Edith Wharton.

Except for one essay on an Indian mystic Maugham had met on his journey through India in 1936, *Points of View* (1958)–the second essay collection–is almost entirely concerned with writers and writing. Maugham discusses Johann Wolfgang von Goethe and his three novels, the prose style of the seventeenth-century churchman John Tillotson, and the careers of four French journalists: Jules Renard, Edmond and Jules Goncourt, and Paul Leauteaud. "The Short Story" is a final summation of all Maugham had written about the genre. Here he argues that James's stories are essentially trivial beneath the elaborate veneer, that Katherine Mansfield had a minor but worthwhile talent, that Kipling is underrated, and that Anton Chekhov is more skilled than Maugham had previously believed.

Both as an editor and an essayist Maugham produced a body of work that, taken as a whole, constitutes a substantial statement of a critical position. Like his fiction and drama, it is not innovative or particularly complex, but it carries the authority of a perceptive and cosmopolitan man who was widely read and who knew literature from the writer's point of view. His judgments are sound, albeit conventional, and readable.

Traveller's Library (1933) is Maugham's anthology of short stories, poems, and essays by fifty British writers ranging from Virginia Woolf to Michael Arlen, and he provides an introduction explaining the basis of their inclusion. *Tellers of Tales* (1939) is a collection of one hundred short stories from England, the United States, France, Russia, and Germany; his introduction traces the development of the short story from its nineteenth-century origins and anticipates his essay in *Points of View*. *Great Modern Reading* is a

wide-ranging anthology of American and English short stories, poems, letters, essays, and speeches compiled as part of the war effort in 1943, and it reveals the breadth of Maugham's reading.

Maugham's first major statement on the short story, the preface to his 1934 collection called *East and West* in the United States and *Altogether* in England, is the product of his prime and is the finest of his essays on the genre. Focusing on the writing of Chekhov and Guy de Maupassant as the best examples of opposing kinds of stories, he prefers the work of the French writer. In 1940 he turned to a more general discussion of literature in three magazine articles, which were published in book form later that year as *Books and You*. He treats poetry rather briefly, admitting a preference for anthologies, and he provides a sound guide to the fiction generally considered to be the best. Stendhal is his favorite novelist, with Marcel Proust and Leo Tolstoy close behind. Charles Dickens is the great English novelist, though Maugham himself finds more pleasure in Jane Austen. Though Walt Whitman and Edgar Allan Poe had genius, only Herman Melville among Americans can be considered a great and original author according to Maugham.

In 1948 Maugham published *Great Novelists and Their Novels*, revised and enlarged in 1954 as *Ten Novels and Their Authors*, which Laurence Brander has called one of "the two most useful books on the art of fiction in English." Following an introductory essay on the genre, in which he reiterates his belief in the novelist as storyteller and rejects the novel as platform, Maugham provides a discussion of the characters and best work of the "ten greatest" novelists: Henry Fielding, Austen, Stendhal, Honoré de Balzac, Dickens, Gustave Flaubert, Melville, Emily Brontë, Fyodor Dostoevski, and Tolstoy. Based on his thorough

Maugham with old schoolmate Charles Etheridge during a 1958 reunion at King's School, Canterbury (courtesy of King's School)

reading of authoritative biographies, Maugham's sketches are perceptive and lively, so that the effect ultimately is a concentration on the novelists rather than the novel.

The Writer's Point of View is a lecture Maugham gave to the National Book League in London in 1951 (published the same year), and it sums up his views on writing and professional authorship. He repeats his opinion that the purpose of literature is to entertain, though he is quick to point out that by entertainment he means that which interests, and thus books such as Tolstoy's *Anna Karenina* (1875-1877) and Stendhal's *Le Rouge et le Noir* (1831) are "entertaining." Arguing that the value of a work of art ultimately depends upon the personality of the artist, his prescription for authorship is exposure to the raw experience of life and the development of the skill to re-create it in language.

A Choice of Kipling's Prose (1952) includes an introduction by Maugham that is both a discus-

sion of the short-story form and a generous and warm treatment of the work of "the only writer of short stories our country has produced who can stand comparison with Guy de Maupassant and Chekhov." Believing that Kipling's best stories are those set in India, Maugham chose all but one of the sixteen tales from the period before the author's thirty-seventh year. Though acknowledging Kipling's faults, Maugham argued the case for his work at a time when serious critics and scholars ignored him.

The remainder of Maugham's nonfiction work is made up of a variety of material, most of which will be of value only to those with particular interests. *France at War*, written and published in 1940 as part of his propaganda work, sold in large numbers but soon proved to be an inaccurate analysis of the French situation at the beginning of World War II. Similarly a dozen articles published in American magazines in the early 1940s were designed to stress the common heritage of the British and the Americans. As well, over the sixty-five years of his writing career, Maugham produced prefaces to the works of friends such as Noël Coward, Gladys Cooper, Francis de Croisset, and Charles Hawtrey. He discussed art and artists in pieces on Gerald Kelly and Marie Laurencin; on paintings he liked; and on having his portrait painted in his book about his art collection, *Purely for My Pleasure* (1962). Various articles have sketched the famous and intriguing people he encountered: for example, the Aga Khan, Edward Marsh, Nelson Doubleday, and Boris Savinkov. These and several other small pieces were published in book form in *A Traveller in Romance* (1984).

Letters:
The Letters of William Somerset Maugham to Lady Juliet Duff (Pacific Palisades, Cal.: Rasselas, 1982).

Bibliographies:
Charles Sanders and others, *W. Somerset Maugham: An Annotated Bibliography of Writings About Him* (DeKalb: Northern Illinois University Press, 1970);
Raymond Toole Stott, *A Bibliography of the Works of W. Somerset Maugham* (London: Kaye & Ward, 1973).

Biographies:
Robin Maugham, *Somerset and All the Maughams* (New York: New American Library, 1966);
Frederic Raphael, *Somerset Maugham and His World* (London: Thames & Hudson, 1976);
Anthony Curtis, *Somerset Maugham* (London: Weidenfeld & Nicolson, 1977);
Ted Morgan, *Maugham* (New York: Simon & Schuster, 1980);
Robert L. Calder, *Willie: the Life of W. Somerset Maugham* (London: Heinemann, 1989).

References:
Laurence Brander, *Somerset Maugham: A Guide* (London: Oliver & Boyd, 1963);
Ivor Brown, *W. Somerset Maugham* (New York: Barnes, 1970);
Robert L. Calder, *W. Somerset Maugham and the Quest For Freedom* (London: Heinemann, 1972);
Richard Cordell, *Somerset Maugham: A Biographical and Critical Study* (London: Heinemann, 1961; revised, 1969);
Anthony Curtis, *The Pattern of Maugham* (London: Hamilton, 1974);
Joseph Dobrinsky, *La Jeunesse de Somerset Maugham (1874-1903)* (Paris: Etudes Anglaises, 1977);
M. K. Naik, *W. Somerset Maugham* (Norman: University of Oklahoma Press, 1966).

A. A. Milne

(18 January 1882 - 31 January 1956)

J. Kieran Kealy
University of British Columbia

See also the Milne entries in *DLB 10: Modern British Dramatists, 1900-1945* and *DLB 77: British Mystery Writers, 1920-1939.*

BOOKS: *Lovers in London* (London: Rivers, 1905);
The Day's Play (London: Methuen, 1910; New York: Dutton, 1925);
The Holiday Round (London: Methuen, 1912; New York: Dutton, 1925);
Once a Week (London: Methuen, 1914; New York: Dutton, 1925);
Happy Days (New York: Doran, 1915);
Once on a Time (London: Hodder & Stoughton, 1917; New York & London: Putnam's, 1922);
First Plays (London: Chatto & Windus, 1919; New York: Knopf, 1920)–comprises *Wurzel-Flummery, The Lucky One, The Boy Comes Home, Belinda: An April Folly,* and *The Red Feathers*;
Not That It Matters (London: Methuen, 1919; New York: Dutton, 1920);
If I May (London: Methuen, 1920; New York: Dutton, 1921);
Mr. Pim (London: Hodder & Stoughton, 1921; New York: Doran, 1922);
Second Plays (London: Chatto & Windus, 1921; New York: Knopf, 1922)–comprises *Make-Believe, Mr. Pim Passes By, The Camberley Triangle, The Romantic Age,* and *The Stepmother*;
The Sunny Side (London: Methuen, 1921; New York: Dutton, 1922);
The Red House Mystery (London: Methuen, 1922; New York: Dutton, 1922);
Three Plays (New York: Putnam's, 1922; London: Chatto & Windus, 1923)–comprises *The Dover Road, The Truth about Blayds,* and *The Great Broxopp*;
The Artist: A Duologue (London & New York: French, 1923);
The Man in the Bowler Hat: A Terribly Exciting Affair (London & New York: French, 1923);

A. A. Milne

Success (London: Chatto & Windus, 1923; New York: French, 1924);
When We Were Very Young (London: Methuen, 1924; New York: Dutton, 1924);
A Gallery of Children (London: Paul, 1925; Philadelphia: McKay, 1925);
Ariadne; or, Business First: A Comedy in Three Acts (London & New York: French, 1925);
For the Luncheon Interval: Cricket and Other Verses (London: Methuen, 1925; New York: Dutton, 1925);
To Have the Honour: A Comedy in Three Acts (London & New York: French, 1925);
Portrait of a Gentleman in Slippers: A Fairy Tale in One Act (London & New York: French, 1926);

Milne with his father, John Vine Milne, during the time the young Milne was a student at Westminster School (courtesy of the Milne family)

Winnie-the-Pooh (London: Methuen, 1926; New York: Dutton, 1926);

Now We Are Six (London: Methuen, 1927; New York: Dutton, 1927);

The Ascent of Man (London: Benn, 1928);

The House at Pooh Corner (London: Methuen, 1928; New York: Dutton, 1928);

The Ivory Door: A Legend in a Prologue and Three Acts (London & New York: Putnam's, 1928; London: Chatto & Windus, 1929);

Toad of Toad Hall: A Play from Kenneth Grahame's Book The Wind in the Willows (London: Methuen, 1929; New York: Scribners, 1929);

The Secret and Other Stories (New York: Fountain Press / London: Methuen, 1929);

By Way of Introduction (London: Methuen, 1929; New York: Dutton, 1929);

The Fourth Wall: Played in America under the Title of "The Perfect Alibi." A Detective Story in Three Acts (London & New York: French, 1929);

Michael and Mary: A Play in Three Acts (London: Chatto & Windus, 1930; London & New York: French, 1932);

When I Was Very Young (New York: Fountain Press / London: Methuen, 1930);

Two People (London: Methuen, 1931; New York: Dutton, 1931);

Four Days' Wonder (London: Methuen, 1933; New York: Dutton, 1933);

Peace with Honour (London: Methuen, 1934; New York: Dutton, 1934; revised, 1935);

More Plays (London: Chatto & Windus, 1935)–comprises *The Ivory Door, The Fourth Wall,* and *Other People's Lives;*

Miss Elizabeth Bennet: A Play from "Pride and Prejudice" (London: Chatto & Windus, 1936);

Miss Marlow at Play: A One-Act Comedy (London & New York: French, 1936);

The Magic Hill, and Other Stories (New York: Grosset & Dunlap, 1937);

The Princess and the Apple Tree, and Other Stories (New York: Grosset & Dunlap, 1937);

It's Too Late Now: The Autobiography of a Writer (London: Methuen, 1939); republished as *Autobiography* (New York: Dutton, 1939);

Behind the Lines: A Book of Poems (London: Methuen, 1940; New York: Dutton, 1940);

Sarah Simple: A Comedy in Three Acts (London & New York: French, 1940);

Why Steinbeck Wrote the Grapes of Wrath, by Joseph Henry Jackson; Did Shakespeare Translate the Decameron?, by Carter Meredith; Mr. Grahame, Mr. Roosevelt, and I, by A. A. Milne (New York: Limited Editions Club, 1940);

War with Honour (London: Macmillan, 1940);

War Aims Unlimited (London: Methuen, 1941);

The Ugly Duckling: A Play in One Act (London: French, 1941);

Chloe Marr (London: Methuen, 1946; New York: Dutton, 1946);

Books for Children, a Reader's Guide (London: Cambridge University Press, 1948);

Birthday Party, and Other Stories (New York: Dutton, 1948; London: Methuen, 1949);

The Norman Church (London: Methuen, 1948);

A Table near the Band, and Other Stories (London: Methuen, 1950; New York: Dutton, 1950);

Before the Flood: A Play in One Act (London & New York: French, 1951);

Year In, Year Out (London: Methuen, 1952; New York: Dutton, 1952);

Prince Rabbit and the Princess Who Could Not Laugh (London: Ward, 1966; New York: Dutton, 1966);

Five Minutes of Your Time (London: League of Nations Union, n.d.).

Editions and Collections: *Four Plays* (London: Chatto & Windus, 1926)–comprises *To Have the Honour; Ariadne, or Business First; Portrait of a Gentleman in Slippers;* and *Success;*

The Christopher Robin Story Book (London: Methuen, 1929); republished as *The Christopher Robin Reader* (New York: Dutton, 1929);

Those Were the Days (London: Methuen, 1929; New York: Dutton, 1929)–comprises *The Day's Play, The Holiday Round, Once a Week,* and *The Sunny Side;*

Very Young Verses, preface by Milne (London: Methuen, 1929)–includes selections from *When We Were Very Young* and *Now We Are Six;*

The Christopher Robin Birthday Book (London: Methuen, 1930; New York: Dutton, 1931);

Four Plays (New York: Putnam's, 1932)–comprises *Michael and Mary, To Have the Honour* as *Meet the Prince, The Fourth Wall* as *The Perfect Alibi,* and *Portrait of a Gentleman in Slippers;*

A. A. Milne, edited by E. V. Knox (London: Methuen, 1933);

The Pocket Milne (New York: Dutton, 1941; London: Methuen, 1942);

The Old Sailor, and Other Selections (New York: Dutton, 1947);

Sneezles, and Other Selections (New York: Dutton, 1947);

The King's Breakfast, and Other Selections (New York: Dutton, 1947);

Introducing Winnie-the-Pooh, and Other Selections (New York: Dutton, 1947);

Pooh's Birthday Book (New York: Dutton, 1963);

The Pooh Story Book (New York: Dutton, 1965; London: Methuen, 1967);

The Christopher Robin Book of Verse (New York: Dutton, 1967); republished as *The Christopher Robin Verse Book* (London: Methuen, 1969);

Winnie-the-Pooh, facsimile edition (London: Methuen, 1971; New York: Dutton, 1971).

SELECTED PERIODICAL PUBLICATIONS–
UNCOLLECTED: "The Rape of the Sherlock: Being the Only True Version of Holmes's Adventures," *Vanity Fair* (London), 70 (15 October 1903): 499;

"This England–According to Milne," *New York Times Magazine,* 25 July 1943, pp. 7, 17;

"New Explorations in Baker Street," *New York Times Magazine,* 9 March 1952, pp. 10ff;

"Always Time for a Rhyme," *New Herald Tribune Book Review,* 12 October 1952, p. 10.

A. A. Milne, father of Christopher Robin and creator of Winnie-the-Pooh, ended his career with a small verse in the *New York Herald Tribune Book Review* (12 October 1952) titled "Always Time for a Rhyme." The poem is the story of his life, in particular his literary life; it says in part:

Though a writer must confess his
Works aren't all of them successes,
Though his sermons fail to please,
Though his humor no one sees,
Yet he cannot help delighting
In the pleasure of the writing.

Throughout much of his career Milne's primary means of attaining such pleasure and delight was not the children's story nor the drama—the genres for which he is best known—but the light essay.

Alan Alexander Milne was born in London on 18 January 1882 to John Vine Milne, a schoolmaster at Henley House—a private boys' school—and Sarah Maria Heginbotham Milne. He attended Westminster School and then Trinity College, Cambridge, where he edited and contributed to the school magazine, the *Granta*. A series of dialogues Milne wrote for the *Granta* so impressed R. C. (Rudie) Lehmann, a staff member of *Punch*, that he asked Milne to submit a series of similar sketches to the humor magazine. Although these sketches were never published in *Punch*, Lehmann's interest convinced Milne to move to London after he graduated in 1903 with an honors degree in mathematics. There he began his career as a free-lance writer.

In his first year Milne was less than a complete success, earning only twenty pounds. By his third year he was making more than two hundred pounds and had published his first book. *Lovers in London* (1905) had been suggested by Barry Pain, a friend of Lehmann's, who persuaded Milne to expand a series of stories he had written for the *Saint James Gazette* on the escapades of an English boy and his vacuous American girlfriend. To the fewer than half-dozen pieces from the *Gazette* Milne added further tales until he finally had twenty-four more or less connected episodes chronicling the misadventures of his hero and heroine. The value of this initial publication was probably best assessed by Milne himself, who, upon rereading it, bought back all rights to the book for five pounds to keep it from being republished. Today it is highly valued by collectors—for its scarcity, not its literary value.

In February 1906 Milne was made an assistant editor of *Punch* and asked to submit a weekly essay. These essays are anthologized in four books: *The Day's Play* (1910), *The Holiday Round* (1912), *Once a Week* (1914), and *The Sunny Side* (1921). In 1929 all four collections were published together as *Those Were the Days*.

Daphne de Sélincourt Milne, circa 1925 (photograph by E. O. Hoppé); she had married Milne on 4 June 1913.

In *The Day's Play*—the title is a parody of Rudyard Kipling's *The Day's Work* (1898)—the first series of essays deals with the adventures of the Rabbits, a group of affluent young people whose world revolves around cricket matches, croquet, billiards, and endlessly witty conversation. The second section presents a series of letters to and from a recently born baby named Margery; the intense cuteness of the letters quickly becomes a bit overwhelming. In a group titled "Small Games" Milne introduces a figure who quickly became his favorite protagonist: the bumbling hero constantly at odds with the world about him. Here he is defeated successively by an exercise machine, progressive bridge, gardening, golf, and even the apparently safe task of shopping on Regent Street.

The title of *The Holiday Round* suggests much about the nature of the essays: Milne often seems to do little more than take his stock characters, such as the Rabbits, on their holidays. Still, there are occasional hints of a more mature Milne; these are nowhere more apparent than in his parodies of fairy tales. In "A Matter-of-fact Fairy Tale" Milne's frog-prince hero, Udo, finds his release from a seven-year bewitchment less than totally satisfying. It seems that he has aged during his forced hibernation and his beloved Beauty is no longer quite so certain that her prince is all that charming. In "A Modern Cinderella" the wisecracking heroine dutifully loses her slipper at the ball; but alas, it is found not by the prince but a footman, who decides to keep it as a souvenir.

There is also, even in this early collection, one example of Milne at his satiric best: "A Literary Light" is a wonderful parody of the literary tastes of his time. When the title character, Annesley Bupp, decides on a journalistic career, he immediately realizes that he must specialize. Unfortunately, only two possibilities come to mind: George Herbert and trams; he chooses the latter. In a description which clearly draws upon his experiences with literary lights of his time, Milne succinctly describes Bupp's meteoric rise up the literary ladder, culminating in his publication of "Some Curious Tram Accidents" and "Tram or Bus," articles which secure his position. Bupp soon graduates to work as a literary critic, where he becomes so renowned that he is recognized by his initials alone. One wonders if Milne, forced to write on a weekly basis, was beginning to see a bit of A. B. in A. A.

Once a Week is far more varied in its topics than earlier collections. A series titled "A Baker's Dozen," for example, illustrates the dilemma Milne faced in finding a new topic each week, for in it he resorts to writing of a Japanese dwarf tree named Sidney, a financier who speculates in a West African jaguar mine, and a pet show to which the narrator brings a pet blight named Hereward. Margery reappears in this series, a bit older but as cloyingly annoying as ever. She does, however, elicit one genuinely successful essay: in a lovely parody of the "third-son" type of fairy tale called "The King's Sons," the bumbling Prince Goldenlocks accidentally kills the fairy the king has enlisted to test his sons.

The essays that immediately follow this baker's dozen signal a significant change in focus, for in them the narrator, Ronald, marries Celia—an event no doubt inspired by Milne's own marriage to Dorothy (Daphne) de Sélincourt in 1913. Although the relationship between Ronald and Celia has a certain charm in the first stories in which they appear, it quickly becomes predictable as Milne chronicles the inept Ronald's experiences with doctors, income tax and insurance forms, leaky bathtubs, parrots that refuse to learn to talk, gardeners, and the difficulty of living in someone else's home. Although these accounts of his misadventures are often clever, Ronald—especially in the large doses provided by a collection of similar essays—becomes, as do many of Milne's essay characters, a bit predictable.

Once a Week also includes portraits of so-called successful men, such as Dr. Gordon Venables, who, in a moment of crisis, helps the patient of another practitioner. For his act of mercy Dr. Venables is censured by the British Medical Council. The story ends happily, however, for Dr. Venables's notoriety has ensured his success. He is last seen making a speech against the supertax. The best of the successful-men essays does not, however, appear in the section set aside for these luminaries but in a series called "Merely Players." Titled "The Renascence of Britain," it tells the uplifting tale of Peter Riley, who, after twelve years of intense training, wins the 1924 Olympic gold medal for "Pushing the Chisel (Free Style)." The conclusion of this tale displays Milne at his best: "And so England was herself again. There was only one discordant note in her triumph. Mr. P. A. Vaile pointed out in all the papers that Peter Riley, in the usual pig-headed English way, had been employing entirely the wrong grip. Mr. Vaile's book, *How to Push the Chisel*, illustrated with 50 fill plates of Mr. Vaile in knickerbockers pushing the Chisel, explained the correct method."

Milne's final collection of *Punch* essays, *The Sunny Side*, begins, appropriately enough, with yet another appearance of the ever-cheerful Rabbits, this time on vacation on the Riviera. Although there is an amusing account of the Rabbits' first confrontation with gaming tables, the stories are, for the most part, uninspired; the Rabbits themselves decide that the most exciting part of their vacation was sitting in the sun watching oranges grow. The section following the Rabbit stories, "Men of Letters," does, however, suggest a more mature Milne; here one finds, particularly in "The Complete Dramatist," Milne's initial efforts at establishing his dramatic criteria.

Some essays in this collection deal with Milne's experiences in World War I: he joined the army in 1915, was invalided in France in 1916, and returned to England to recuperate. These essays are an uneven lot at best, Milne's normal light tone and passion for celebrating the trivial being ill suited to the monstrosity that he saw war to be. Perhaps the most effective piece

Cotchford Farm, a retreat in Hartfield, Sussex, which Milne bought in 1925; the family often went there on weekends and holidays.

of the collection is the short verse that begins it, titled "O.B.E." In the last two stanzas Milne's attitude toward war becomes clear:

> I know a fellow of twenty-three,
> Who got a job with a fat M.P.–
> (Not caring much for the Infantry.)
> And he–thank God!–has the O.B.E.
> I had a friend; a friend, and he
> Just held the line for you and me,
> And kept the Germans from the sea,
> And died–without the O.B.E.
>   Thank God!
> He died without the O.B.E.

His later plea for pacifism, *Peace with Honour* (1934), may present his beliefs more elaborately but certainly not more eloquently.

The final essays in *The Sunny Side* are reminiscent of those in the earlier collections, as Ronald battles weighing machines and mailboxes, unsuccessfully attempts to have a ring engraved, and, in the delightful tale "A Warm Half-Hour," tries to get a block of ice home without being seen by

his neighbors. The majority of the Celia-Ronald stories are, however, little more than predictable one-act dramas, reminding one of television situation comedies. Frank Swinnerton calls them "the lightest of trifles." Milne does not disagree; he simply suggests that those were times when such trifles could be considered. As the title of the 1929 compilation of all four *Punch* collections puts it, those were the days. In his autobiography Milne affectionately remembers this early period: "The world was not then the damnable world which it is to-day; it was a world in which imaginative youth could be happy without feeling ashamed of its happiness. I was very young, very lighthearted, confident of myself, confident of the future. I loved my work."

Two anthologies collect essays from this period that were published not in *Punch* but in other British and American journals: *Not That It Matters* (1919) and *If I May* (1920). Actually, the two books are not very different from the four *Punch* collections. Once again one finds stories of games, of long country walks, of inept heroes and their inevitable conflicts with various bureaucracies, and of such trivial matters as owning an atlas, keeping a diary, or evaluating the difference between goldfish who inhabit lily-leaved ponds and those found in cheap fishbowls. But there are a few essays of genuine interest in the two collections, particularly those that provide early examples of Milne as a literary critic. *If I May*, for example, presents Milne's initial comments on children's literature, including his belief that children's books should never preach because children are particularly resistant to moralizing adults. There is also one genuinely memorable article. It appears in *Not That It Matters* and provides a vibrant example of Milne's meandering style at its best. "The Unfairness of Things" begins with a discussion of the *Shoe Manufacturers' Monthly* reports on squeaky shoes but turns quickly to the more socially important question of squeaky collars and then to a fairly elaborate examination of those few gifted individuals whose collars do not squeak. Milne decides that such men are the equivalent of those whom children or animals instinctively love, only in their case it is inanimate objects that love them. These men are truly blessed: windows open for them, clothes fit them, their luggage never gets lost, macaroni winds itself about their forks, and of course, their collars never squeak. But in a brilliant bit of rationalizing Milne decides that such men pay for their fortune by being fervently hated by all animate creatures; *he* certainly hates them. The essay concludes with the author moving to put on his collar, desperately hoping it will squeak.

The major limitation of *If I May*, *Not That It Matters*, and the four *Punch* collections is that the essays in them lack any real depth. A *Times Literary Supplement* review of *Not That It Matters* (27 November 1919) suggests that when dealing with Milne's essays one must distinguish between wit and humor: "In reading a humorist you are always conscious of the depths–about which the humorist himself may be exceedingly shy. A wit has no depths. It is his business, *qua* wit, to have none. He is to play for us on the surface; and the only thing that matters (not that even that, he would tell us, matters) is whether he can play prettily." Milne, the review concludes, is not a humorist; he is a wit who plays prettily.

Perhaps the kindest way of summarizing Milne's initial contributions as an essayist is to say that his sixteen years with *Punch* had at least served as a useful apprenticeship. Thomas Burnett Swann's judgment is less gentle; he sees the apprenticeship as faltering at best and dismisses

Milne's humor as superficial, contrived, and precious: "in his early essays, whimsy is not a mist but a cloud, as thick and finally as nauseating as a surfeit of cotton candy."

Milne must have realized it was time to move on to other things. When he was released from the army in 1918 he decided, despite Daphne's tears, not to return to *Punch* but to attempt a career in the theater. In 1920 he and Daphne had their only child, Christopher Robin.

Milne's next collection of essays, *By Way of Introduction*, did not appear until 1929; much had happened in the interim. Most critics consider the 1920s Milne's golden decade. During this period he had his most striking successes on the London stage, notably *Mr. Pim Passes By* (published, as *Mr. Pim*, in 1921) and *The Truth about Blayds* (published in 1922), and published the still well-respected mystery novel *The Red House Mystery* (1922). And between 1924 and 1928 he published the four wildly successful books about Christopher Robin and Winnie-the-Pooh. Thus, by 1929, Milne had established his reputation. He was a literary light who, like his own Mr. Bupp, was being asked to write introductions and reviews for other literary works.

By Way of Introduction is probably the most critically acclaimed of all of Milne's essay collections, in large part because Milne is at his best when talking of other literary works, even if they are his own. Many of Milne's introductions and reviews are little more than a series of anecdotes, stream-of-consciousness accounts of what the book under examination has evoked in his mind; but this curious approach often reveals a wise and discerning critic. Milne finds genius in the drawings of Ernest H. Shepard, the illustrator of the Pooh books; in the stories of Saki; and in Nigel Playfair's management of the Lyric Theatre, Hammersmith. Playfair's remarkable success, Milne says, resides in his ability to trust his own taste, a comment which reveals much about Milne's views on the conflicting aesthetic tastes of his time.

Milne's dramatic tastes are discussed in "Dramatic Art and Craft," in which he reviews George Jean Nathan's *The World in Falseface* (1923). Nathan condemns Milne's plays as strained and dull, calling him at best one of Britain's lesser playwrights. Milne's response is to compare Nathan's book to one recently written by Brander Matthews, which argues that one need not dismiss a play simply because it is commercially successful. Nathan, Milne asserts, en-

Of course as soon as Kanga unbuttoned her pocket, she saw what had happened. Just for a moment she thought she was frightened, and then she knew she wasn't; for she felt quite sure that Christopher Robin would never let any harm happen to Roo. So she said to herself, "If they are having a joke with me, I will have a joke with them."

"Now then, Roo dear," she said, as she took Piglet out of her pocket. "Bed-time."

"Aha!" said Piglet, as well as he could after his Terrifying Journey. But it wasn't a very good "Aha!" and Kanga didn't seem to understand what it meant.

"Bath first," said Kanga in a cheerful voice.

"Aha!" said Piglet again, looking anxiously for the others. But the others weren't there. Rabbit was playing with Baby Roo in his own house, and feeling more fond of him every minute, and Pooh, who had decided to be a Kanga, was still at the sandy place on the top of the Forest, practising jumps.

"I am not at all sure," said Kanga in a thoughtful voice, "that it wouldn't be a good idea to have a cold bath this evening. Are you like that, Roo, dear?"

Piglet, who had never been really fond of baths, shuddered a long indignant shudder, and said in as brave a voice as he could:

"Kanga, I see that the time has come to speak plainly."

"Funny little Roo," said Kanga, as she got the bath-water ready.

Page from Milne's manuscript for Winnie-the-Pooh *(by permission of the Master and Fellows of Trinity College, Cambridge)*

joys reading plays; Matthews enjoys seeing them. Nathan's attitude toward drama is flawed because he does not recognize the importance of the audience. Play writing, Milne contends, demands one who is not just an artist but a craftsman too, and it is this ability as a craftsman that creates the successful play. Such a craftsman must, above all, realize just how much is dictated to him by the true collaborators of his play, its audience.

Milne's criteria for the successful detective novel are to be found in the introduction to *The Red House Mystery*, reprinted in this collection. In the essay, "Introducing Crime," Milne establishes a firm set of rules for writing the detective story: it should be written in simple English; there must be no love interest; the detective must have a confidant with whom to discuss the case, clue by clue; most important, the detective must be an amateur. Milne detests the scientific detective with his microscope and fingerprinting kits: "What thrill do we get when the blood-spot on the missing man's handkerchief proves that he was recently bitten by a camel? Speaking for myself, none. The thing is so much too easy for the author, so much too difficult for his readers."

By Way of Introduction includes essays that remind one of Milne's earlier collections: descriptions of cricket matches, unlucky golfers, and bumbling heroes and their unsuccessful confrontations with matters as earthshaking as buying the proper present. But one also finds discussions of more weighty matters, such as spiritualism (he distrusts it) and love and marriage (he argues that marriages are successful only if one learns to see one's partner's point of view). The collection's most important essays are those on children's literature, a genre that Milne had begun to recognize as the area in which he would be. best remembered. In his introduction to E. S. Hartland's *The Science of Fairy Tales* (1891) he defends the value of the nursery tale and the Fairyland that it creates. It is in this world and perhaps only in this world, Milne argues, that one finds "that most tender of all virtues, simplicity." This is a world to be enchanted by, to be reverently enjoyed; it is certainly not one to be explained away by some scientific historian. His attitude toward those who seek to dismiss fantasy is even more obvious in the lovely little essay "Good King Wenceslas," in which he chronicles his childhood fantasies about this mystic ruler. First he imagined him as a brother of Santa Claus, one Wense Claus. Later he was told that Wenceslas was a "real king," and decided that he was a friend of Old King Cole.

Alas, however, he was finally convinced by a historian that Wenceslas was an actual monarch who was killed in Prague in 935 by a band of conspirators. The essay ends with Milne wondering about the value of such knowledge as he laments the loss of his boyhood friend; Santa Claus is now brotherless.

In "Children's Books" Milne sets forth his basic criteria for all books, whether they are intended for adults or children: they must be written well and they must be taken seriously, not just dashed off in the midst of some sleepless night. "The End of a Chapter" fittingly concludes Milne's collection. In it he bids adieu to his career as a children's writer. The fictional Christopher Robin, Milne says, was never meant to be confused with the real Christopher Robin; but (as the adult Christopher Robin Milne's books were sadly to relate) inevitably he was. And it is this confusion and ultimate exploitation that Milne wishes to put an end to: "I feel I have not exploited the legal Christopher Robin. All I have got from Christopher Robin is a name which he never uses, an introduction to his friends . . . and a gleam which I have tried to follow." And so Milne decided to leave the imaginary Christopher Robin behind to give the real Christopher Robin the freedom to make his own name on the basis of his own efforts. As Milne poignantly says, "I do not want C. R. Milne ever to wish that his names were Charles Robert." Though Milne discontinued his career as a children's writer to return to his beloved drama, perhaps the most important reason for his decision to leave Pooh and his friends behind is that the "gleam" was gone; and, as had not been the case with earlier creations like the Rabbits, Margery, and Ronald and Celia, this time he was wise enough to know when to leave.

By Way of Introduction, though as eclectic and chaotic as his earlier collections, presents Milne at his most thoughtful and most mature, a man at home with his own literary tastes. Ironically, the collection is best remembered for its comments on a genre that Milne hoped he was finally rid of. He was soon to find, however, that all else he did would be judged alongside of his four works of children's literature. As he said ten years later in his autobiography: "I wrote four 'Children's books,' containing altogether, I suppose, some 70,000 words–the number of words in the average-length novel. Having said goodbye to all that in 70,000 words, knowing that as far as I was concerned the mode was outmoded,

Milne and his son, Christopher, in 1934 (courtesy of the Milne family)

I gave up writing children's books. I wanted to escape from them as I had once wanted to escape from *Punch*; as I have always wanted to escape. In vain. England expects the writer, like the cobbler, to stick to his last. As Arnold Bennett pointed out: if you begin painting policemen, you must go on painting policemen, for then the public knows the answer–Policemen."

The next phase of Milne's career as an essayist has been called his philosophical period. In fact, Milne's utterances are more theological than philosophical, beginning with a thirty-two-page pamphlet, *The Ascent of Man* (1928), written as a contribution to the Affirmations: God in the Modern World series. Milne distinguishes his beliefs from those of orthodox Christianity, arguing that one should be concerned not with the next world but with this world. Similarly, one should see man's nature not as flawed but as one which aspires to divinity. In particular, he refuses to accept the orthodox belief that there is some innate fighting instinct within man that makes wars inevitable. Rather, he argues, wars occur because orthodox Christians seem to differentiate between private and public morality, believing that private killing is murder but killing in defense of one's state is not. Life, Milne asserts, should be seen as a constant struggle upward, "from Ugliness to Beauty, from the Beast to the God, from the Material to the Spiritual."

Milne's optimistic view of man's potentiality led him to question the justifiability of war, a question he began to ask during his experiences as a soldier in World War I and continued to examine, most eloquently, in what he considered his most important book, *Peace with Honour*, published in 1934. In this work Milne contends that all of the present problems in Europe could be solved if the politicians would simply realize the total absurdity of ever going to war again. Subsequent political events made much of what Milne says seem remarkably naive, and in the early 1940s he published two hastily written pamphlets denouncing his former ideas: *War with Honour* (1940) and *War Aims Unlimited* (1941). The latter, giving evidence of Milne's persistent belief that arbitration is a possible solution to war, calls for a League of Democracies which would expel those who abuse democratic principles. For the most part, however, the pamphlets are straightforward attacks on those who were then abusing democratic principles, be they fascist or communist. One can sense Milne's pain and even bewilderment throughout his two renunciations; his philosophic credo had never anticipated Hitler.

Milne's final collection of essays–in fact his final book of any kind published during his lifetime–appeared in 1952, three years before his death. Its title, *Year In, Year Out*, indicates its nostalgic nature. Although the collection has a kind of organization, the essays being somewhat arbitrarily grouped under months of the year, it is simply a collection of utterances written during the last thirty years of Milne's life.

The collection is illustrated by E. H. Shepard, Milne's collaborator on the Pooh books, and the drawing that precedes the January essays is of Pooh and his friends sitting down in a theater. Significantly, there is no Christopher Robin in the sketch; he has been replaced by a young girl who looks like Sir John Tenniel's Alice. The show these figures have come to watch is to be a "Variety Performance on the Author's Benefit Night." The author, of course, is Milne, who admits that the purpose of this collection is to give these thoughts some permanence, thereby fulfilling his yearning for immortality, even if only on dusty library shelves.

The collection, he also admits, is from a "drawer full of oddments" and thus should be regarded as a "calendar of disconnected thoughts and memories." As if to prove his point, the first two essays explore the price of sponges and the art of saying "thank you." The third essay, however, an homage to Charles Lutwidge Dodgson, assuages any fears that the collection will suffer from the same "lightness" that plagued his early *Punch* collections; for here one finds, once again, the mature critic who had been so effective in *By Way of Introduction*. It was something quite magi-

cal, Milne suggests, that transformed the mathematician and deacon Dodgson into Lewis Carroll. And Dodgson's success occurred precisely because he was wise enough to write "solely to amuse the strange Lewis Carroll, this childlike person whom he had suddenly discovered in himself." Nonetheless, Milne contends, one can still hear two voices in the Alice books, that of the stodgy Dodgson and that of the magical Carroll. It was the mathematics lecturer who unwisely decided to make Alice's adventures into dreams rather than realizing, as Milne does and Carroll did, that Alice was "a real little girl who, alone of all little girls, had had tea with the March Hare and the Mad Hatter, and played croquet with the Queen of Hearts." It is the absence of any dreamvision convention that makes *The Hunting of the Snark* (1876) Carroll's true masterpiece, "the most inspired nonsense in the language."

The February essays provide the same somewhat chaotic package that one finds in January, but there is a more serious tone. The initial discussion of central heating, for example, is interrupted when Milne points out what little value any heating is to a house after two flying bombs have hit it. This comment leads to a quite serious examination of the Korean War and a discussion of the oppressive nature of all Communist states. Englishmen, he argues, should never forget to assert their freedom, their right to choose a job and even to strike. They must remember that every restriction on liberty, however slight, "makes liberty less inevitable, its loss more natural and less worthy of dispute."

Succeeding months provide the same varied menu. In March one learns of the difficulty of naming horses, the charm of sundials, and Milne's theories on immortality, and then is asked to consider dropping the Old Testament from the Christian credo. The coming of April, not surprisingly, reminds Milne of gardens; but, not as obviously, it also reminds him of Sunday horoscopes, the absurdity of government subsidies, and even the difference between the novel and the play–a discussion which allows him once again to present his beliefs on the importance of *seeing* a play. The dramatist's awareness of his audience, Milne holds, makes him a craftsman as well as an artist. May's ramblings talk, quite properly, of May elections–but also of asparagus, cricket, income taxes, and modern art. The latter discussion betrays Milne's distrust for much of what he sees about him. Art has become too easy; there is no longer any regard for beauty. Most critics, he

A. A. Milne

suspects, agree but are afraid to say so.

The summer months turn Milne's thoughts to the countryside. He discusses pollution, the world's ugliest trees (sycamore and alder), and the world's silliest birds (ostrich and booby). He also provides lists of his ten favorite plants and ten most hated weeds, as well as brief discussions of bank holidays, wasps, and the nonsense one finds in idle conversation. The August collection, however, includes one essay worthy of note: a marvelous defense of escapist literature that deserves particular attention, touching as it does upon Milne's entire literary career. He asks his readers to be honest about their tastes and admit that a well-written detective story might well be as valuable and certainly as entertaining as some revered chronicle. He often dreams of a world where conventional literary values are turned up-side down, where romance and comedy are rated above realism and tragedy, a world "in which critics would not qualify so loftily Mr. Calverley's little book of light verse, but keep their condescension for the mausoleum of heavy verse by a Mr. Milton." This plea leads to a discussion of one of his favorite forms of so-called escapist literature, the detective story, which concludes that the dedicated reader often has distinct advantages over the detective when it comes to solving a crime: "To know beforehand that a Roman Catholic is safe from the rope in a Chesterton story; that no Labour Member will commit a murder for the sake of the Coles; that one can hardly expect Miss Dorothy Sayers to hang a real Oxford man: this gives us an unfair start on an inspector whose open mind only excludes suspicion of the local superintendent."

September's collection is dominated by Milne's rather moving reexamination of his pacifism. He distinguishes his beliefs as a pacifist from those of the conscientious objector, admitting that when a war breaks out, even pacifists must become a part of it. He still argues, however, that man must somehow reject even the possibility of war, and he sees the atomic bomb as the ultimate deterrent to all wars. Quoting Louis Pasteur, he says that war has now become so potentially devastating that even thinking of it is an impossibility. Thus he regards the atomic bomb not as a weapon of war but as a weapon of peace. Mercifully, Milne's quite graphic account of nuclear warfare is followed by a tribute to Oscar Wilde; but it is a tribute that ends with the realization that plays such as *The Importance of Being Earnest* (1899) can no longer be written in a world that has known two world wars. Novelists and playwrights today, he asserts, must write within a historic framework. The result is that the writer loses much of his power: "He is no longer a master of circumstances. He is no longer a god."

Milne's August and September declarations are the last serious notes in his somewhat cacophonous symphony; October, November, and December return to the light style and somewhat trivial topics of his first collections. The year and the collection end with Milne's admission that he is near the end of his day and that, when looking back on his literary career, he realizes that he wrote as he did because he knew no other way. He concludes by conceding that the brash American editor of the *Atlantic Monthly* who retitled the serialization of his autobiography "What Luck!" was probably correct after all.

Year In, Year Out provides a fitting final chapter to Milne's career as an essayist. As Swann says, it "is the self-portrait of a writer successful but not boastful—wise but not sententious, aging but not old—who for half a century, from his first adolescent trillings in *Punch* to this, his farewell without tears, has spoken his mind through the medium of essays."

In appraising Milne's contribution as an essayist, one must admit that most of his work is slight in impact. He is an author who thrives on chatting about trivialities—cricket matches, party conversations, trips to the country, asparagus, wasps, and the price of sponges. His naive view of how to solve the political problems of the mid 1930s shows how limited and perhaps sheltered a view of life Milne possessed. When, in his final collection, he mourns the loss of the godlike power

to create with no need to worry about the historicity of any of one's utterances, one senses how happy Milne was that, for so much of his career, he was freed from being relevant. Thus the faults one finds in Milne are faults he freely concedes. He is what he is. Swinnerton says that although Milne could create "delightful nonsense," he was "deficient in vulgarity, in energy, in largeness of thought, and in exuberance of action." But, Swinnerton reminds his readers, Milne simply wrote within his own capabilities: "those who judge Milne's work without knowledge of its spontaneity miss the fact that his is an easy and impulsive wit, just as those who judge it from a hostile viewpoint miss the fact that if he wrote as apparently they would have him write he would be egregiously false to his own experience."

A. A. Milne died on 31 January 1956 at the age of seventy-four, knowing that his contributions as a novelist, playwright, mystery writer, and certainly as an essayist would be forever eclipsed by what he called his "four trifles." In the short verse for the *New York Herald Tribune Book Review*, one of the last pieces he ever wrote, Milne accepts his fate:

> If a writer, why not write
> On whatever comes in sight?
> So—the Children's Books: a short
> Intermezzo of a sort:
> When I wrote them, little thinking
> All my years of pen-and-inking
> Would be almost lost among
> Those four trifles for the young.

Perhaps it was within the nursery world inhabited by Christopher Robin and his toys that Milne felt most secure, particularly when the real world was becoming more and more depressing. In *By Way of Introduction* Milne praises the simplicity of Fairyland, saying that it is not a place for the sophisticated or worldly wise. And yet it is an honest place, one in which good and evil are clearly defined: "Even in matters of high policy, when the King promises his daughter to the winner of a slippery-hill-climbing contest, no lawyers are called in afterwards to challenge the conditions. How blandly, one feels, would a modern Rumpelstilzkin announce that his name was really Robinson, and produce naturalization papers to prove it. But in Fairyland honesty was not the best policy, it was the only policy." Milne never found such honesty in a world of war and potential atomic devastation; perhaps that is the attraction of Pooh for all readers. James Hilton, in his review of *Year In, Year Out* (*New York Herald Tribune Book Review*, 15 November 1952), provides the most oft-quoted summary of Milne's accomplishments: "He has perfect vision out of a small window; and even when he looks through a bigger one the slight distortion can be very charming." To be fair to both Milne and Hilton, one should add Hilton's final comment: "fun and wit can hold their own at any age, and Goethe's 'Mehr Licht,' playfully misunderstood, might well be the motto of a writer who has given so much pleasure to so many." One might also add Swann's pronouncement on Pooh (and, by association, on Milne as well): "He underestimates himself." Milne does underestimate himself and, for the most part, critics underestimate his accomplishments. In the best of his essays and certainly in his children's books there is a compelling and attractive vision of what the world could be, if only it were inhabited by ever-understanding, quietly heroic, silly old bears.

Bibliography:
Tori Haring-Smith, *A. A. Milne: A Critical Bibliography* (New York & London: Garland, 1982).

Biography:
Ann Thwaite, *A. A. Milne: The Man Behind Winnie-the-Pooh* (New York: Random House, 1990); also published as *A. A. Milne—His Life* (London & Boston: Faber & Faber, 1990).

References:
James Hilton, "The Engaging Art of A. A. Milne: Perfect Vision out of a Small Window," *New York Herald Tribune Book Review*, 15 November 1952, pp. 1, 5;
Christopher Milne, *Enchanted Places* (London: Methuen, 1974);
Milne, *The Path through the Trees* (London: Methuen, 1979);
George Jean Nathan, *The World in Falseface* (New York: Knopf, 1923);
"Not That It Matters," Times Literary Supplement, 27 November 1919, p. 693;
Thomas Burnett Swann, *A. A. Milne* (New York: Twayne, 1971);
Frank Swinnerton, *The Georgian Scene: A Literary Panorama* (New York: Farrar & Rinehart, 1934), pp. 118-126.

Papers:
The manuscripts for A. A. Milne's Winnie-the-Pooh books are at Trinity College, Cambridge.

Charles Morgan
(22 January 1894 - 6 February 1958)

Charles E. May
California State University, Long Beach

See also the Morgan entry in *DLB 34: British Novelists, 1890-1929: Traditionalists.*

BOOKS: *The Gunroom* (London: Black, 1919);
My Name is Legion (London: Heinemann, 1925; New York: Knopf, 1925);
First Love (New York: Knopf, 1929);
Portrait in a Mirror (London: Macmillan, 1929; New York: Knopf, 1929);
The Fountain (London: Macmillan, 1932; New York: Knopf, 1932);
Epitaph on George Moore (London: Macmillan, 1935; New York: Macmillan, 1935);
Sparkenbroke (London: Macmillan, 1936; New York: Macmillan, 1936);
The Flashing Stream: A Play . . . with an Essay on Singleness of Mind (London: Macmillan, 1938; New York: Macmillan, 1938; revised, London: Macmillan, 1948);
The Voyage (London: Macmillan, 1940; New York: Macmillan, 1940);
The Empty Room (London: Macmillan, 1941; New York: Macmillan, 1941);
The House of Macmillan (1843-1943) (London: Macmillan, 1943; New York: Macmillan, 1944);
Reflections in a Mirror (London: Macmillan, 1944; New York: Macmillan, 1945);
The Artist in the Community (Glasgow: Jackson, 1945);
Reflections in a Mirror, Second Series (London: Macmillan, 1946; New York: Macmillan, 1947);
The Judge's Story (London: Macmillan, 1947; New York: Macmillan, 1947);
The Liberty of Thought and the Separation of Powers: A Modern Problem Considered in the Context of Montesquieu (Oxford: Clarendon Press, 1948);
The River Line (London: Macmillan, 1949; New York: Macmillan, 1949);
A Breeze of Morning (London: Macmillan, 1951; New York: Macmillan, 1951);
Liberties of the Mind (London: Macmillan, 1951; New York: Macmillan, 1951);

Charles Morgan (photograph by Roland d'Ursel, Brussels)

The River Line: A Play (London: Macmillan, 1952; New York: Macmillan, 1952);
The Burning Glass: A Play. With a Preface: On Power Over Nature (London: Macmillan/New York: St. Martin's, 1953);
Dialogue in Novels and Plays (Aldington, Kent: Hand & Flower, 1954);
On Learning to Write (London: Oxford University Press, 1954);
Challenge to Venus (London: Macmillan, 1957; New York: Macmillan, 1957);
The Writer and His World: Lectures and Essays (London: Macmillan, 1960);

Charles Morgan on Retrievers, edited by Ann Fowler and D. L. Walters (New York: Abercrombie & Fitch, 1968).

Although Charles Landbridge Morgan is better known as a novelist than as an essayist, having written eleven novels between the early 1920s and the late 1950s, most critics agree that his real talent lay in the essay form, for even in his novels he shows a predisposition for writing long and generalized philosophical arguments. Moreover, he was well known during World War II for his weekly series in the *Times Literary Supplement* entitled "Menander's Mirror"–short reflective essays that were welcome primarily for their leisurely and meditative prose, reminiscent of an older and more sedate era. As critic Albert Guerard said of Morgan's first essay collection, *Reflections in a Mirror* (1944), "The charm of [the] essays is their timely timelessness. London was blitzed and robot-bombed: but 'Menander' kept writing of 'Why Birds Sing,' of Ivan Turgenev, of 'Nausicaa and the Pelicans' " (*Nation*, September 1945).

Born on 22 January 1894, in Bromley, Kent, Morgan was the youngest of the four children of Mary Watkins Morgan and Charles Morgan, an engineer. The young Morgan entered the Royal Navy at age thirteen and later went to naval colleges at Osborne and Dartmouth. He served in China and the Atlantic between 1911 and 1913, at which time he left the navy to pursue a writing career. When World War I began, he rejoined the navy but was soon captured and held prisoner in Holland until 1917. Between 1918 and 1921 he studied at Brasenose College, Oxford, after which he worked for the *Times* of London as a drama critic until 1926, when he was made chief drama critic, a position he held until 1939, the year he became a naval official. He married Hilda Vaughan, another writer, in 1923. While serving at the Admiralty from 1939 to 1944 he had little time to work on his fiction and thus welcomed the opportunity to do the "Menander's Mirror" series in the *Times*. He lectured at the University of Glasgow and Oxford after the war and died in London in 1958.

Reflections in a Mirror and *Reflections in a Mirror, Second Series* (1946) contain more than forty brief essays, practically all of them from the "Menander's Mirror" series. They are primarily interesting to readers today for their presentation of the sedate and stoic British attitude during the bombing of England. In such essays as "In Search of Values" and "Ideas at War," Morgan ar-

Morgan as a Royal Navy cadet, 1911

gues, in the tradition of Matthew Arnold, for the relationship between art and religion as a source of value and the importance of aesthetic criticism–all concerns curiously Victorian in the midst of a world tainted by the Holocaust and threatened by Fascism.

Because art–literature in particular–is Morgan's primary interest, many of the pieces in the two *Reflections in a Mirror* collections are on such well-known nineteenth-century writers as Thomas Hardy, Emily Brontë, Leo Tolstoy, and Ivan Turgenev, all of whom embody Morgan's basically romantic point of view. However, because the war preoccupied him and his readers, quite a few more essays focus on issues of freedom and liberty, Germany's threat to Western culture, and the problem of coping with current anxieties. The rest deal with various English customs and val-

as from 16 Campden Hill Square
London W. 8

Tuesday, June 10
1941

Dear Eddie,

The Horace you sent me has March 18 on its flyleaf. Only your friendship can pardon so long a delay of my thanks for a book that has seldom, during three months, been out of reach of my hand. When it came I read it to myself & read it aloud at all times of the day and night and I wanted to send you a telegram of gratitude and excitement; but I didn't — wisely? foolishly? and planned a long letter, but I was forever finding new delights, the letter waited for them, day followed day and — well now, at last, I write about a book that has touched and stirred and enchanted me far more than any that

First page of a letter from Morgan to Edward Marsh regarding a book by the Roman poet Horace (copyright by J. C. Medley, Literary Executor of Charles Morgan; from Selected Letters of Charles Morgan, *edited by Eiluned Lewis, 1967)*

ues that serve as a bulwark against the barbarism of the Nazi threat. Both collections were praised by critics for their reflective quality and meditative mood, and both were seen as "war books," but only in terms of their lack of anger and their political topicality. They were admired primarily for their dignity and grace and their embodiment of the cultivated values of British democracy. Morgan thus came to represent during the war the very qualities that enabled England to withstand the onslaught, even as he represented the British values for which the war was being fought. Perhaps most typical of the responses to the essays was the view that it was remarkable that such quiet and cultured pieces could have been written at all in the midst of war and in the heart of a bomb-torn city.

Liberties of the Mind, Morgan's 1951 collection of essays, is made up of disparate pieces either written for or orally presented on various special occasions; they make a unified book because they represent Morgan's fears of what he calls "mind control" and because they are forced into the broad category of illustrations of "liberty." *The Liberty of Thought and the Separation of Powers* was previously published in a separate volume (1948), as was *The Artist in the Community* (1945), whereas the balance of the essays appeared in the *Times Literary Supplement*. The fact that many of them have been pressed into service to fit the general theme of liberty is indicated by added subtitles. For example, an essay on the Dark Ages is subtitled "The Liberty not to Despair," and an essay on the master and pupil relationship is subtitled "The Liberty of Teaching."

The major sections of the book are the essays that set forth Morgan's definition and affirmation of romanticism, including the introduction, entitled "Mind Control," and the essay "The Liberty of Thought." In the former, Morgan argues against the materialist view that romanticism is escapism focused on the unreal and urges instead that romanticism, which for him is the essence of art, seeks a spiritual reality beyond surface appearances. In the introductory essays he sounds the theme that obviously gave impetus to the creation of the book–his anxiety about the threat of what has since been called "brainwashing" (which Morgan here calls "switch control"), during which prisoners of the Russians, Morgan says, are transformed into gramophones into which a record has been inserted. He looks backward longingly to the Victorian era characterized by the romanticism of Alfred, Lord Tennyson and

Thomas Hardy, even as he despairs of the twentieth-century disease of what he calls "power" and "numerical thinking." He even associates brainwashing with the effect of habitual film watching and listening to the music of crooners. Anxiety about the "bomb," the iron curtain, and all the other elements of the cold war of the early fifties are given voice here. *Liberties of the Mind* was not as enthusiastically received as the two *Reflections in a Mirror* collections, perhaps because the dangers Morgan spells out are not so immediate as those he reflected upon during the war. Although the book was recognized for its Orwellian *1984* theme, the mannered rhetoric so typical of Morgan did not seem appropriate to the apocalyptic ideas.

The Writer and His World (1960) is made up of lectures and essays found after his death among his papers that largely had not appeared in book form before. The exceptions are *The Artist in the Community*, *Dialogue in Novels and Plays*, and *On Learning to Write*, the last two having been published separately in 1954. The most important of the previously unpublished pieces are the lectures "A Defence of Story-Telling" (1934) and "The Independence of Writers" (1948). The remainder are miscellaneous pieces, some of which, such as "The Word 'Serenity,' " "The Word 'Academic,' " and "Time Out," are reflective essays similar to the pieces published in "Menander's Mirror, "although there is no indication when and where they originally appeared.

Dialogue in Novels and Plays, a 1953 lecture to the P.E.N. Club in England, is an academic piece, although it is not rigorous criticism by any means. Morgan's major theory here, one that is consistent with the formalism and idealism he expresses elsewhere in his essays, is that dialogue is not a report, but rather a "formal means of penetrating to the essence of things." In *Learning to Write*, the presidential address to the English Association in 1954, he expresses his scorn for the amateur writer, his insistence on the hard-won technical skill required to be a professional writer, and his admiration for the Bible and the Prayer Book as the models of good writing. He also expresses an indication of his undying romanticism when he notes that Emily Brontë's *Wuthering Heights* (1848) is his favorite novel. Although delivered to other academics, this essay is general and argues that although one cannot be an artist merely by taking pains, one cannot be an artist without taking pains.

Morgan at Llangorse Lake, Breconshire, in 1940 (photograph by Rache Lovat Dickson)

"The Independence of Writers," a speech delivered in 1948 in Geneva, reiterates the arguments he made that same year in *The Liberty of Thought*–including his stand against all forms of propaganda, his insistence that all subjects are permissible in art, and his position that the artist's allegiance is never to the state. Based on his formalist and idealist notions, Morgan's argument is that art is never to persuade or instruct but rather to penetrate the appearance of things. Here as in other essays and in his novels, one can see why Morgan was a popular writer during the war but has not remained influential. Instead of understanding the spirit of his age, he rails against the collective vice of angst and tries to deny the age of anxiety that other English and American writers attempted to cope with. Morgan wanted to develop and preserve what he called a "Re-enlightenment" comparable to the Renaissance; however, what he mainly seems to

urge in his writing is a return to the Victorian age rather than to the Renaissance, a return to the more idealist elements of Keatsian romanticism, or to what he considers to be Hardy's romanticism.

In "Defence of Storytelling" he agrees with Percy Bysshe Shelley that the aim of storytelling is a penetration to the universal. Morgan's argument is a romantic defense of the imagination as a means to attain ideal beauty, which for him is absolute and universal, an aspect of God. Morgan says storytelling "fluidifies" the reader's imagination of the universals. In both the essay on storytelling and the essay on the independence of writers, Morgan argues that the supreme service of the writer is to get beyond appearances, to demonstrate that there is such a thing as vision, and to show that human love is its symbol. Morgan's preference is for what he calls pure storytelling, by which he often seems to mean romantic storytelling, both in the critical and in the popular sense, given that his examples are such works as *Tristan and Iseult, Manon Lescaut Abbé Prévost's* (1731), and Turgenev's *First Love* (1860). Morgan believes that what Shelley says of poetry also applies to aesthetic fiction, that it "lifts the veil from the hidden beauty of the world," enabling man to "imagine intensely and comprehensively." The value of storytelling is for Morgan the same as the value of love, poetry, and mystical apprehension; it provides a spiritual experience that sustains basic human values.

The criticisms that might be lodged against Morgan's essays are similar to those that have been lodged against his novels–they are too stiff and stifling. They are too generalized with philosophizing to succeed as personal essays, yet often too lacking in rigorous argument and scholarship to be of much interest as serious literary criticism. The main impression a modern reader is likely to have of the essays is simply that they are "old fashioned," both in their highly generalized and abstract style and in their nostalgia for the past, particularly the idealized romantic and Victorian past of English literature.

Because of his backward-looking views, Morgan seems completely out of step with other British writers of the first half of the twentieth century. He does not share in the awareness of the vast contemporary wasteland of values perceived by T. S. Eliot, Ezra Pound, W. H. Auden, and others; moreover he explicitly rejects such a perception. His essays may have been of some real practical value during the war–although he preached romanticism impractically–but this value was both immediate and short-lived. Morgan is a minor figure in twentieth-century British thought, and he is probably destined to remain so. One would have to look hard and long to find any of his influence on modern thought. Both in style and in content, his essays sound a retrospective note, a nostalgic longing for a world that perhaps never was and was never to be. Morgan may have fancied himself a misplaced romantic crying out in the wilderness, but he is now perceived only as a comfortable study-bound idealist, heard only briefly as a reassuring solace in the midst of the blitzkrieg.

Letters:

Selected Letters of Charles Morgan, edited by Eiluned Lewis (London & Melbourne: Macmillan, 1967).

Reference:

Henry Charles Duffin, *The Novels and Plays of Charles Morgan* (Cambridge: Bowes & Bowes, 1959).

Edwin Muir

(15 May 1887 - 3 January 1959)

W. Glenn Clever
University of Ottawa

See also the Muir entry in *DLB 20: British Poets, 1914-1945.*

BOOKS: *We Moderns: Enigmas and Guesses*, as Edward Moore (London: Allen & Unwin, 1918; republished under author's name, New York: Knopf, 1920);

Latitudes (London: Melrose, 1924; New York: Huebsch, 1924);

First Poems (London: Hogarth, 1925; New York: Huebsch, 1925);

Chorus of the Newly Dead (London: Hogarth, 1926);

Transition: Essays on Contemporary Literature (London: Hogarth, 1926; New York: Viking, 1926);

The Marionette (London: Hogarth, 1927; New York: Viking, 1927);

The Structure of the Novel (London: Hogarth, 1928; New York: Harcourt, Brace, 1929);

John Knox: Portrait of a Calvinist (London: Cape, 1929; New York: Viking, 1929);

The Three Brothers (London: Heinemann, 1931; New York: Doubleday, Doran, 1931);

Poor Tom (London: Dent, 1932);

Six Poems (Warlingham, Surrey: Samson, 1932);

Variations on a Time Theme (London: Dent, 1934);

Scottish Journey (London: Heinemann/Gollancz, 1935);

Social Credit and the Labour Party: An Appeal (London: Nott, 1935);

Scott and Scotland: The Predicament of the Scottish Writer (London: Routledge, 1936; New York: Speller, 1938);

Journeys and Places (London: Dent, 1937);

The Present Age from 1914, volume 5 of *Introductions to English Literature*, edited by Bonomy Dobrée (London: Cresset, 1939; New York: McBride, 1940);

The Story and the Fable: An Autobiography (London: Harrap, 1940); revised and enlarged as *An Autobiography* (London: Hogarth, 1954; New York: Sloane, 1954);

The Narrow Place (London: Faber & Faber, 1943);

Edwin Muir in London, July 1955 (photograph by Mark Gerson, FLIP)

The Voyage and Other Poems (London: Faber & Faber, 1946);

The Scots and Their Country (London: Longmans, Green, 1946?);

The Politics of King Lear (Glasgow: Jackson, 1947; New York: Haskell House, 1970);

Essays on Literature and Society (London: Hogarth, 1949; revised and enlarged, 1965; Cambridge, Mass.: Harvard University Press, 1965);

The Labyrinth (London: Faber & Faber, 1949; Folcroft, Pa.: Folcroft, 1977);

Collected Poems, 1921-1951, edited by J. C. Hall (London: Faber & Faber, 1952; New York: Grove, 1953);

Prometheus (London: Faber & Faber, 1954);

One Foot in Eden (London: Faber & Faber, 1956; New York: Grove, 1956);

Collected Poems, 1921-1958, edited by Hall and Willa Muir (London: Faber, 1960):

The Estate of Poetry (London: Hogarth, 1962; Cambridge, Mass.: Harvard University Press, 1962);

Selected Poems, edited by T. S. Eliot (London: Faber & Faber, 1965);

Edwin Muir: Uncollected Scottish Criticism, edited by Andrew Noble (London: Vision, 1982; Totawa, N.J.: Barnes & Noble, 1982).

SELECTED TRANSLATIONS: Lion Feuchtwanger, *Jud Süss*, translated by Edwin and Willa Muir (London, 1927);

Franz Kafka, *America*, translated by the Muirs (London: Routledge, 1938; New York: New Directions, 1946);

Kafka, *The Castle*, translated by the Muirs (London: Secker & Warburg, 1942);

Kafka, *The Trial*, translated by the Muirs (London: Secker & Warburg, 1945);

Kafka, *The Great Wall of China*, translated by the Muirs (New York: Schocken, 1946).

Edwin Muir made his mark as a poet, critic, novelist, journalist, translator, and a writer of evocative autobiography. His reputation grew slowly but steadily. In the 1920s and 1930s he was known mainly as a critic, particularly of the novel, and as the translator who introduced Franz Kafka to the English-reading public. Meanwhile as a poet he was mastering his medium with such effect that during the 1940s his poems began to reach an ever-increasing audience. By the 1950s critics of note were commenting that he was among the few major poets of the century and that a proper appreciation must rest on his whole canon for its singular poetic statement about man in the twentieth century.

Born on Pomona, one of the Orkney Islands of Scotland, Muir, the youngest of six children of James Muir, a small tenant farmer, and Elizabeth Cormack Muir, grew up in an agricultural community little changed since the Middle Ages; the peace and security of its natural cycles, customs, and beliefs, and the mysteries and won-

der of its legends, myths, ballads, and Bible stories provided Edenic roots for much of his poetry. "The Orkney I was born into," he says in *The Story and the Fable: An Autobiography* (1940), "was a place where there was no great distinction between the ordinary and the fabulous; the lives of living men turned into legend." But it was a hard life. At the age of fourteen, with his brothers away from home seeking work, his mother ill, and the family driven by their landlord to a farm that was poor and wet, Muir, always of delicate constitution and now emotionally as well as physically weakened, suffered the collapse of his peace and security as his father gave up farming and moved the family to Glasgow.

Muir found the transition total. In the slums and poverty of the city both his parents and two of his brothers were dead within five years, while he himself, supporting and nursing the family, worked at such jobs as were available to a youth whose schooling, at Kirkwall Burgh Grammar School, had ended with the move to Glasgow. But meanwhile he was beginning to read widely beyond the Bible, *Pilgrim's Progress*, and Robert Burns, to encompass William Morris, George Bernard Shaw, Henrik Ibsen, and especially Friedrich Nietzsche, whose style and philosophy of the superman Muir much admired. In his early twenties he attempted poetry in imitation of Heinrich Heine and had some accepted by the *New Age*. By 1916, rejected by the army, he had extended his studies to Molière and Stendhal. Also, having discovered socialism through authors such as Robert Blatchford, he had joined the National Guild League in Glasgow, where he lectured and helped publish the *Guildsman*. But Muir was always his own man and never fully accepted socialism, arguing against its utopian idealism, nor did he accept the communist enthusiasm of writers such as W. H. Auden and Stephen Spender.

He had also begun the series "We Moderns" (collected in 1918) in the *New Age*, modeled on Nietzsche's aphoristic style. It made no money, and the effort to produce it drained him emotionally. Written for rhetorical effect, the series was suited to the temper of the times, but Muir realized he was on the wrong path and by the 1950s was glad it was out of print. The series served only as a turning point in his journey away from the psychic stress that prompted it.

These Glasgow years provided the roots for later work. The transition from a close family and communal life in a world remote in time and

Muir in 1904 and Wilhelmina Anderson in 1910; they were married in 1919.

place to that of an orphan, without friends or communal support, in the worst slums of Britain devastated him. The sense of being trapped in a labyrinth of urban horror repeatedly surfaces in Muir's later work to the point where it functions in his poetry as a symbol of the plight of modern man. Moreover, his lifelong allegiance to his Scottish heritage surfaced later in *Scottish Journey* (1935) and other topographical and political works in which he sought to come to terms with the disparity between Scotland's "legendary past and its tawdry present."

In 1920 Muir turned to psychoanalysis for help for recurrent melancholia, a condition from which he was to suffer all his life. Somewhat of a mystic, he felt that the dreams and visions he had experienced from childhood, and those now revealed by analysis, were realities. This feeling eventually led to his rejection of Nietzchean philosophy as life-denying, and his acceptance of a more life-affirming faith, though it was 1952 before he fully accepted the essentially New Testament faith toward which he had been groping ever since he had lost touch with the strict Calvinis-

tic creed of his parents. His psychoanalytic treatment thus purged him of some of the bitterness reflected in *We Moderns*.

In 1919 he had married Wilhelmina (Willa) Anderson, a lecturer in a woman's college in London, an event he called the most important of his life for she encouraged him to move to London and become a full-time writer. In London Muir did reviews for the *Athenaeum*, dramatic criticism for the *Scotsman*, and regular articles for the *Freeman*. For years he lived by reviewing novels (more than a thousand) and as an occasional lecturer in English literature.

In 1921 the Muirs moved to Prague, where Muir became a journalist-essayist of considerable reputation in England and the United States, and the editor of the *European Quarterly* in 1934. The leisure time available, his first since leaving Orkney, released his inner energy, and he turned seriously to poetry, establishing himself as an English poet of note. Also he and Willa jointly began translating twentieth-century European authors. Although their most notable translations were of Kafka, that of Lion Feuchtwanger's *Jud Süss* was a

THE FREE LANCE BOOKS. IV

EDITED WITH INTRODUCTIONS BY H. L. MENCKEN

WE MODERNS:

ENIGMAS AND GUESSES

By EDWIN MUIR

NEW YORK ALFRED · A · KNOPF MCMXX

Title page for the American edition of Muir's first book, a collection of essays that originally appeared in The New Age

1927 best-seller (their share was only a £250 fee), and when they returned to England in 1927, Muir was acclaimed as the translator of *Jud Süss*.

Muir's popularity as a critic in Britain and the United States in the early 1920s had led him to collect some of his essays in *Latitudes* (1924). Though he realized that some of the pieces still bore the Nietzsche influence, he let them stand, noting in the preface his changed position. The collection, not especially noteworthy, has its good points: he expresses, especially in the essays on Dostoevsky, Ibsen, and Nietzsche, his awareness of a divinity which man, except momentarily, lacks the power to see, an awareness which informs and humanizes Muir's own early work. One of the best essays in the book, "A Note on the Scottish Ballads," is convincing criticism on the nature and power of poetry in the oral tradition. Muir also expresses a poetic that characterizes the work of "Shakespeare, Mozart, Homer, Goethe," as "the second book of revelation"; expects literature to have the "power of refreshing

us"; and views classical art as "so securely objective that whatever circumstances . . . it may describe, it . . . is entirely incapable of corrupting us." More generally, the book expresses his philosophy that life rests on a "fable," a reality one can never know except as myth, emblem, dream, and metaphor, but which informs all our lives and is the basis for our selves. To Muir such a reality was becoming less attainable under the stress of modern living, with the consequence of the bewilderment, cynicism, and despair of much of modern literature, a consequence all the more distressing because he believed that such a frame of mind blocks the possibility of therapeutic change.

In 1928, settled in Surrey, Muir published *The Structure of the Novel*, which is a model of prose style–simple, brief, and clear. Though some critics see it as flawed by its four arbitrary categories (novels of action and character, the dramatic novel, the chronicle, and the period novel), the argument is convincing and helps the reader to an appreciation of the genre. Largely this results from Muir's stance as an objective, clear-thinking critic of common sense and shrewdness, aware of the human implications of literature–a stance in the broad, humane tradition that preceded New Criticism. Muir shows that because so-called "flat" characters have a valid function in conveying one kind of vision of life, their presence in a novel is not a "fault" but a "quality" and since the imaginative world of the dramatic novel is in time, its values are universal, whereas the character novel, its world being in space, has social values.

After *The Structure of the Novel*, Muir published a biography of John Knox (1929). Though Peter H. Butter comments of this work that "his portrait of Knox as a sadistic religious fanatic is supported by a good deal of evidence . . . but is rather a one-sided one," (*Edwin Muir*, 1962), the book was well received in both Great Britain and the United States. Despite his own belief in the reality of dreams and visions, Muir assumes that Knox's certainty of prophetic power was illusory. But Muir's chief argument is against Knox's Calvinistic creed, as being morally and spiritually tyrannical. To Muir such a system, in its suppression of the creative imagination and of free human communication, was parallel to fascism or communism, the early course of which he had experienced in Europe.

The Muirs moved to St. Andrews, Scotland, in 1934, from where he toured Scotland and Orkney in preparation of *Scottish Journey*. Published in 1935, the book records the impact made on him when he arrived in Glasgow fresh from Orkney and found a century's gap between the traditional life of the islands and the industrial society of modern Glasgow. He was struck by the "generally sanctioned greed," the indifference to human life, and the spirit of compassion lost in the worship of material success. No sentimentalist, Muir reports with the authenticity of a reporter who knows his material firsthand, whose insights are informed. The book, which describes his tour of 1934, reports an inversion of traditional values, but an inversion "unselfconsciously celebrated as a triumph." He contrasts the urban wastelands with the natural landscapes of the Orkneys and describes the alienation, competitive struggle for gain, the squalor of daily life, and as in *John Knox* and his other works on Scotland, the decline in religion. He reports only what others were also reporting but differs in that the force of his insight and language gives his book a disturbing power.

In the 1935 pamphlet *Social Credit and the Labour Party* Muir argues that the best way to effect social improvement would be to put into practice Maj. C. H. Douglas's ideas that the state should control production, distribution, and exchange by nationalizing credit. That the pamphlet is no longer in print perhaps justifies Butter's opinion that on such a sociopolitical issue Muir was not a competent judge.

A year later came *Scott and Scotland* (1936). Muir's assertion that "Scotland can only create a national literature by writing in English," and his advice to its writers to forget Scots since it cannot encompass all of Scottish sensibility, led to a break in his limited association with the "Lallans" movement. This was followed by a long-sustained (unjustified) attack on him, mainly by Hugh MacDiarmid, as an anti-Scottish British hireling.

In *The Present Age from 1914* (1939) Muir again stresses the relationship of literature to life. By this time his reputation as critic and reviewer, which had grown rapidly and remained high in England while he lived in Scotland, was well established, though his own interests were turning more and more to poetry. In the next year came *The Story and the Fable*, an intense search for his own fable, a voyage of discovery of himself and his relationship to others, of the connection of his own life, as a unique individual, to the fabled exploits of mankind in myth and legend. It stemmed directly from his dreams and visions, especially those aroused by psychoanalysis, which

had given him an awareness of spiritual identity and helped confirm his feeling that such dreams and visions were as real as any other experience.

In 1941 Muir was invited to work for the British Council, first in Edinburgh, but from 1945 to 1948 in Prague, where he received an honorary doctorate from Charles University (1947). He had been delighted with Prague in 1921, but, by 1948, having seen firsthand the devastation caused by the ruthless Communist takeover, he felt life in the city a "calamity," its "vast image of impersonal power, the fearful shape of our modern inhumanity" (*An Autobiography*, 1954).

After the takeover, Muir and his wife moved to Cambridge, where the distress of his Prague experience culminated in the most severe depression of his life. In 1949 the council sent him to Rome, from where that same year he published his highly successful *Essays on Literature and Society*, as well as a book of poetry, *The Labyrinth*, which was widely acclaimed and reissued. The former has been called his best collection of critical essays, each concise and lucid, illuminating through forceful generalization rather than extended analysis–but then he was always impatient of intense textual analysis that ignores what to him were the vital questions. About authors who had influenced him he wrote as though seeking to teach himself about them. The essays show his power to make the moral judgments necessary in order to see and make clear the interconnections between one part of life and another. Again he takes up the theme that Western culture is curtailing the concept of what it is to be human by reducing man to a predator for material success. Thus his book of literary criticism is also implicitly a criticism of modern attitudes, especially those that devalue the imaginative experience and the mysteries of life embodied in traditional art. The essays range broadly. He asserts man's innate need for a spiritual identity, a need being atrophied by the trend to accept progress as a substitute religion. He feels that this intensifying trend leads in politics to the politician attempting to hold on to power by giving away what the country cannot afford, and in sexual morality leads to the promotion of sex as a substitute for happiness, and so to pornography.

In 1950 he was appointed warden of Newbattle Abbey College near Edinburgh, and a few years later published *An Autobiography*, a work praised widely for its human and aesthetic qualities, and for its remarkable similarity in archetypal patterns to those explored in the work of

Muir, his wife, Willa, and some of his students at Charles University in Prague on the occasion of his receiving an honorary doctorate. The ceremony was held on 15 May 1947, his sixtieth birthday.

Carl Jung. The book clearly expresses–even more so than *The Story and the Fable*, on which it is based–Muir's deep religious sensibility. He remained at the college until 1955, when he accepted the Charles Eliot Norton Chair of Poetry at Harvard for a year, following which he moved to Swaffham, near Cambridge.

The Estate of Poetry, published posthumously in 1962, is much concerned with the declining public capacity to understand the significance of archetypal figures, such as those in classical mythology, as they appear in art over the centuries, and with what Muir calls the "natural estate of poetry," by which he means "the actual response of a community to the poetry that is written for it . . . a natural thing: an exercise of the heart and imagination." Muir contends that whereas the oral tradition was able to sustain the peasantry for hundreds of years, poetry in modern times is irrelevant to most ordinary people because the

growing trend of better writers toward analysis and interpretation leaves the "helpful intermediary between literature and the reader" to the "bad critic who sees faults more clearly than virtues." Muir speaks of the need for critics like Charles Lamb, William Hazlitt, or Samuel Taylor Coleridge, who openly express their delight in works of imagination. He also admires Victorian critics such as George Saintsbury, Arthur Thomas Quiller-Couch, and Herbert Grierson, who through their own love for imaginative literature were able to kindle in students and general readers an interest that otherwise might not have developed.

As a critic Muir was a traditionalist, impatient of trendy methods (the New Critics, he said, gave him "claustrophobia"), and he was consistent in viewpoint, in the 1950s as in the 1920s, objecting to the writer displaying what Muir called an "attitude"–the ego asserting and presenting it-

Edwin Muir

self and so precluding objective vision. His own criticism shows the sharpness and clarity of a mind informed about the nature of art and about the writer's responsibility toward it to be sufficiently an artist that he can recognize beauty, then examine whether what he sees is truly beauty. Muir was as honest and frank in criticism of his own work as of the work of others, giving up Nietzsche as an ideal but retaining a respect for the impact of that artist-philosopher's work on European thought, and repudiating some of his own ideas as advanced in *Latitudes* just as he had some of those in *We Moderns*. Impatient of writing that served political ends, he reserved his respect for literature that transcended nationalist bounds.

Muir was known earlier as a critic chiefly through *The Structure of the Novel* and *Essays on Literature and Society*, but recent works such as Roger Knight's indicate a growing awareness that Muir's criticism generally is rewarding to read.

V. S. Pritchett judged Muir "the best novel reviewer between the wars . . . not merely [because] he wrote tersely, thoughtfully, and well. He was a wit," and unlike the "bitch-reviewers," had a "concern with the 'story' and the 'fable'" that "put him on the side of the creative imagination." Adverse criticism includes comments on the falling off of his critical productivity after the 1920s, but the number of his critical works still in print supports Herbert Read's view that Muir was "firm and profound, and of remarkable range."

Muir died on 3 January 1959 and is buried in Swaffham Prior churchyard near the tower dating back to the Battle of Maldon (991), one of the "church towers he loved to muse about as part of the human fable," according to Allie Corbin Hixon. Muir's epitaph is from "Milton," the first poem in his *One Foot in Eden* (1956): "His unblinded eyes / Saw far and near the fields of Paradise."

Selected Letters of Edwin Muir, edited by Peter H. Butter (London: Hogarth, 1974).

Bibliography:
Elgin W. Mellown, *Bibliography of the Writings of Edwin Muir* (Tuscaloosa: Alabama University Press, 1964; revised edition, London: Vane, 1966).

Biography:
Elgin W. Mellown, *Edwin Muir* (Boston: Twayne, 1979).

References:
Peter H. Butter, *Edwin Muir* (Edinburgh: Oliver & Boyd, 1962; New York: Grove, 1962);

Butter, *Edwin Muir: Man and Poet* (Edinburgh: Oliver & Boyd, 1966; New York: Barnes & Noble, 1967);

B. H. Fraser, *The Modern Writer and His World* (London: Penguin, 1964);

J. C. Hall, *Edwin Muir* (London: Longman's, Green, 1956);

Allie Corbin Hixon, *Edwin Muir: A Critical Study* (New York: Vantage, 1977);

Roger Knight, *Edwin Muir: An Introduction to His Work* (London & New York: Longman's, 1980);

Thomas Merton, "The True Legendary Sound: The Poetry and Criticism of Edwin Muir," *Sewanee Review*, 75 (Winter 1967): 317-324;

Willa Muir, *Belonging: A Memoir* (London: Hogarth, 1968);

Michael J. Phillips, *Edwin Muir: A Master of Modern Poetry* (Indianapolis: Hackett, 1978);

Herbert Read, *The Cult of Sincerity* (New York: Horizon, 1968), pp. 178-184;

Charles Tomlinson, "Poetry Today," in his *The Modern Age* (London: Penguin, 1961);

Christopher Wiseman, *Beyond the Labyrinth: A Study of Edwin Muir's Poetry* (Victoria, B.C.: Sono Nis, 1978).

Papers:
The National Library of Scotland holds the bulk of Muir's manuscripts, with some also in the BBC Archives, London.

Harold Nicolson
(21 November 1886 - 1 May 1968)

Christopher Kent
University of Saskatchewan

BOOKS: *Paul Verlaine* (London: Constable / Boston & New York: Houghton Mifflin, 1921);

Sweet Waters: A Novel (London: Constable, 1921; Boston & New York: Houghton Mifflin, 1922);

Tennyson: Aspects of His Life, Character and Poetry (London: Constable, 1923; Boston & New York: Houghton Mifflin, 1923);

Byron: The Last Journey, April 1823-April 1824 (London: Constable, 1924; Boston: Houghton Mifflin, 1924; enlarged edition, London: Constable, 1940; New York: Archon, 1969);

Swinburne (London & New York: Macmillan, 1926);

Some People (London: Constable, 1927; Boston & New York: Houghton Mifflin, 1927);

The Development of English Biography (London: Hogarth Press, 1927; New York: Harcourt, Brace, 1928);

Sir Arthur Nicolson, Bart., First Lord Carnock: A Study in the Old Diplomacy (London: Constable, 1930); republished as *Portrait of a Diplomatist: Being the Life of Sir Arthur Nicolson, First Lord Carnock, and a Study of the Origins of the Great War* (Boston & New York: Houghton Mifflin, 1930);

Swinburne and Baudelaire (Oxford: Clarendon Press, 1930; Folcroft, Pa.: Folcroft Press, 1969);

People and Things: Wireless Talks (London: Constable, 1931);

Public Faces: A Novel (London: Constable, 1932; Boston & New York: Houghton Mifflin, 1933);

Peacemaking, 1919 (London: Constable, 1933; Boston & New York: Houghton Mifflin, 1933);

Curzon: The Last Phase, 1919-1925. A Study in Post-War Diplomacy (London: Constable, 1934; Boston & New York: Houghton Mifflin, 1934);

Dwight Morrow (London: Constable, 1935; New York: Harcourt, Brace, 1935);

Politics in the Train (London: Constable, 1936);

Harold Nicolson in 1936 (photograph by Howard Coster; courtesy of Nigel Nicolson)

Helen's Tower (London: Constable, 1937; New York: Harcourt, Brace, 1938);

The Meaning of Prestige: The Rede Lecture Delivered before the University of Cambridge on 23 April, 1937 (Cambridge: University Press, 1937);

Small Talk (London: Constable, 1937; New York: Harcourt, Brace, 1937);

National Character and National Policy (Nottingham, U.K.: University College, 1938);

Diplomacy (London: Butterworth, 1939; New York: Harcourt, Brace, 1939);

Marginal Comment, January 6-August 4, 1939 (London: Constable, 1939);

Why Britain is at War (Harmondsworth, U.K.: Penguin, 1939);

Germany's Real War Aims (London, 1940);

229

*The Desire to Please: A Story of Hamilton Rowan
and the United Irishmen* (London: Constable,
1943; New York: Harcourt, Brace, 1943);

The Poetry of Byron (London: Oxford University
Press, 1943; Folcroft, Pa.: Folcroft Press,
1969);

Friday Mornings, 1941-1944 (London: Constable,
1944);

*The Congress of Vienna, a Study in Allied Unity:
1812-1822* (London: Constable, 1946; New
York: Harcourt, Brace, 1946);

The English Sense of Humour (London: Dropmore
Press, 1946);

Tennyson's Two Brothers (Cambridge: Cambridge
University Press, 1947; Folcroft, Pa.: Folcroft Library Editions, 1973);

Comments, 1944-1948 (London: Constable, 1948);

Benjamin Constant (London: Constable, 1949; Garden City, N.Y.: Doubleday, 1949);

The Future of the English-Speaking World (Glasgow:
Jackson, 1949);

King George the Fifth: His Life and Reign (London:
Constable, 1952; Garden City, N.Y.: Doubleday, 1953);

*The Evolution of Diplomatic Method: Being the
Chichele Lectures Delivered at the University of
Oxford in November 1953* (London: Consta-
ble, 1954; New York: Macmillan, 1954);

*Good Behaviour: Being a Study of Certain Types of
Civility* (London: Constable, 1955; Garden
City, N.Y.: Doubleday, 1956);

The English Sense of Humour, and Other Essays (London: Constable, 1956; New York: Funk &
Wagnalls, 1968);

Sainte-Beuve (London: Constable, 1957; Garden
City, N.Y.: Doubleday, 1957);

Journey to Java (London: Constable, 1957; Garden
City, N.Y.: Doubleday, 1958);

The Age of Reason: 1700-1789 (London: Consta-
ble, 1960); republished as *The Age of Reason:
The Eighteenth Century* (Garden City, N.Y.:
Doubleday, 1961);

The Old Diplomacy and the New (London: David Davies Memorial Institute of International Studies, 1961);

Monarchy (London: Weidenfeld & Nicolson, 1962);
republished as *Kings, Courts and Monarchy*
(New York: Simon & Schuster, 1962);

Diaries and Letters, 3 volumes, edited by Nigel Nicolson (London: Collins, 1966-1968; New
York: Atheneum, 1966-1968).

*Nicolson in 1912, at the time of his engagement to Vita
Sackville-West (courtesy of Nigel Nicolson)*

OTHER: Sir Horace G. M. Rumbold, *The War Crisis in Berlin, July-August 1914*, introduction
by Nicolson (London: Constable, 1944);

Another World than This: An Anthology, edited by Nicolson and Victoria Sackville-West (London:
Joseph, 1945);

Christopher B. Hobhouse, *Fox*, introduction by
Nicolson (London: Constable/Murray, 1947);

John R. Strick, *Poems*, memoir by Nicolson (London: Marshall, 1948);

Henri Benjamin Constant de Rebecque, *Adolphe;
and, The Red Note-Book*, introduction by Nicolson (London: Hamilton, 1948);

Peter Coats, *Great Gardens*, introduction by Nicolson (London: Weidenfeld & Nicolson,
1963).

Harold George Nicolson was born on 21 November 1886 in Tehran, where his father, Sir Arthur Nicolson, was a British diplomat; his mother
was the former Mary Katherine Rowan-Ham-
ilton. After a conventional upper-class education
at Wellington School and Balliol College, Oxford,

during which he drew little notice, he entered the diplomatic service in 1909 and began to rise rapidly. In 1913 he married the Hon. Victoria (Vita) Sackville-West, daughter of Lord Sackville, the owner of Knole, perhaps the most magnificent of all the English country houses. Apart from her aristocratic glamour Victoria was not the ideal diplomat's wife, as became evident after a year of embassy life in Constantinople. Far from being compliant to the demands of her husband's peripatetic, formality-laden profession, she was a strong-willed, independent woman who cared little for "society" or urban life. She had independent means and pursued an independent career as a poet and novelist. She also had a series of intensely passionate relationships with other women–the most notable and enduring being with Virginia Woolf–which initially put severe strains upon the marriage. Nicolson for his part had several homosexual liaisons, but these were more casual. Nonetheless, the couple had two children and achieved an accommodation which deepened into a remarkable relationship based on emotional dependence, intellectual sympathy, and physical independence. Exempted from military service during World War I because of his indispensability at the Foreign Office, Nicolson further distinguished himself in the intense diplomatic negotiations which reshaped postwar Europe. He was marked as a man who might in time rise to the top of his profession, as had his father, who was raised to the peerage as Lord Carnock in recognition of his services.

In the aftermath of the Versailles Peace Conference Nicolson, accustomed to being overworked, felt at loose ends. To fill up his free time he quickly and efficiently wrote his first book, *Paul Verlaine* (1921). As an author Nicolson found his métier early: he was above all a biographer and autobiographer. He was interested in lives and times, and in how the latter affected the former. He started with literary biography and was soon being bracketed with Lytton Strachey as one of the new school of biographers. This characterization did not please Strachey, who disliked Nicolson (the feeling was mutual) and regarded him as an inferior imitator–which he was not, although he failed to reach Strachey's level as a literary biographer. His best work would be his diplomatic biographies, in which his professional expertise and judgment came into play. But Nicolson's literary biographies, though based on secondary sources, were well received for their pol-

ished but unstrained style, apt quotation, and interesting if undemanding points of view. Thus Nicolson presents Verlaine as possessing a temperament that was "un-French" in many respects; and he rather cheerily undertakes, if not to rehabilitate the poet, at least to rescue his reputation from the opprobrium heaped upon him by the French in the hope that Verlaine might "find some honour, some fresh facet of forgiveness among us broader and less conventional Anglo-Saxons." Despite this remark Nicolson pussyfoots through Verlaine's affair with Rimbaud in a manner Edmund Wilson later attacked for its prudery.

Nicolson was ambivalent toward the Victorians; he was less inclined to mock them than were Strachey and some of the other Bloomsburyites because he admired many of their achievements, especially the British Empire. Loyalty, duty, and patriotism were in Nicolson's blood and prevented him from sharing the cynicism of the smart set. Yet in his short survey *The Development of English Biography* (1927) he denounces "the catastrophic failure of Victorian biography," in which earnest moralizing produced "impure biography," works written for some purpose other than conveying an accurate, truthful, and complete portrait of their subjects. Nicolson also speculates as to whether future developments in psychology will produce an utterly truthful method of biography, but one in which scientific techniques will expel the literary element altogether, leaving the "impure" biography as the only kind allowing the writer to exercise his art. Nicolson's *Tennyson* (1923) displays his ambivalence distinctly. It is again a defense, this time an attempt to rescue Tennyson, widely regarded as the epitome of Victorianism, from the scorn of Nicolson's contemporaries. His method is to present Tennyson as an anti-Victorian by emphasizing the late Tennyson, the gloomy, anguished bard of Aldworth, instead of the complacent sage of Farringford and celebrant of the high Victorian cult of progress. A central figure in Nicolson's literary biographies is the writer's public (that public, Nicolson might have argued, which prevented him from being perfectly frank about Verlaine). Nicolson was interested in the extent to which authors became prisoners, or pensioners, of public expectation. Thus it was part of Verlaine's "Anglo-Saxon sense of humour" both to resent, and to milk, the role of *poete maudit* during his last years. That Tennyson, at least in his middle years, became a victim of public expectation seems to be Nic-

HAROLD AND VITA NICOLSON decide that the Victorians were the only people who knew how to bring up their children. So they adopt the manner.

—

Drawing by Nicolson for his children, circa 1928 (by permission of Nigel Nicolson; courtesy of the Master and Fellows of Balliol College, Oxford)

olson's excuse for the "Victorian" Tennyson. He dismisses the Tennyson of *Idylls of the King* (1859-1885) and *Enoch Arden* (1864) with the comment that such poems must be left to the judgment of future generations, "since it is impossible for us to conquer the impression, doubtless an incorrect and transitory impression, that the poems of the Farringford period are for the most part intellectually insincere."

That Byron was quite literally the victim of his legend is the theme of *Byron: The Last Journey, April 1823-April 1824* (1924). It was written while Nicolson was wrestling with the diplomatic legacy of Missolonghi, the territorial disputes between Greece and Turkey that festered for a century after Greek independence. Though the book covers only the last year of Byron's life, its extreme detail testifies to Byron's achievement (and burden)

of being a legend in his own time. Practically all who knew him or even came into contact with him felt the need to record their impressions of a man who, according to Nicolson, sought in Greece the accomplishment that would justify his legend or the death that would free him from it. The book perhaps belongs more in the category of Nicolson's diplomatic biographies—his first, in fact—than the literary. Certainly one of its strengths is a deft exposition of the complex tangle of international issues surrounding Byron's mission to Missolonghi. One gains from the book some understanding of Nicolson's growing reputation in the Foreign Office as a writer of lucid and trenchant diplomatic memoranda and dispatches.

Less impressive is *Swinburne* (1926), commissioned for Macmillan's venerable "English Men of Letters" series, standby of generations of stu-

Nicolson and Sackville-West with their sons, Benedict (Ben) and Nigel, in 1929, just before Nicolson resigned from the diplomatic service (courtesy of Nigel Nicolson)

dents cramming for the English literature paper in the Civil Service examinations. In reading it one should bear in mind that it is a late product of the amateur era, before the rise of professional–that is, academic–literary criticism and history. As usual, Nicolson is free with the neat periodizations and bold generalizations beloved of examination candidates (and setters). Thus he pronounces Swinburne's poetry to be based on impressions and experiences gained before the age of twenty, after which the poet's development was arrested; hence the excessively personal character of his poetry: "Swinburne was not a universal, but a specialist poet." ("Discuss," one is tempted to add.)

Amid this spate of biographies Nicolson's professional career was ascending smoothly. In 1925 he was posted to Tehran as counselor to the British legation. "Vita-less" (she visited him briefly) and deprived of a library, Nicolson wrote what became the most popular of all his books, *Some People* (1927). This minor classic, which retains its somewhat Beerbohm-like nattiness, is a series of semifictional sketches of people who had

impinged on his life. It is, in fact, nine essays in oblique autobiography refracted through Miss Plimsoll, his governess; J. D. Marstock, his public-school hero; the snobs and aesthetes to whom he was drawn as an undergraduate; and others, each of whom stood at a critical juncture in Nicolson's development, each embodying a way of living or thinking that had to be reckoned with but ultimately resisted. Nicolson had already exhibited pronounced autobiographical tendencies, though even more veiled, in his novel *Sweet Waters* (1921), a heavily atmospheric story of diplomatic life and love in Constantinople in which he divides his own personality between the two main male characters, one "a little sodomitic cad," the other a resourceful, intelligent diplomat. *Some People* stirred a certain unease in diplomatic circles. Was it not somewhat improper, somewhat disloyal, for one of His Majesty's diplomats to exhibit the private and professional lives of himself and his colleagues? Sir Percy Lorraine, under whose ambassadorship in Persia Nicolson wrote the book, no doubt recognized the slightly mocking sketch of himself in it. He called it "a cad's book." The British ambassador to Italy rejected Nicolson's appointment to his embassy from fear of his pen. Nicolson became rather embarrassed by the book, and although he enjoyed its profits he disliked being reminded of it. Aspersions against his loyalty cut deep.

After a posting to Berlin from 1927 to 1929 which he did not enjoy, although it furthered his professional reputation and gave him a knowledge of German politics and character that he would draw upon heavily as a political observer during the next decade, Nicolson resigned from the diplomatic service. His wife's refusal to join him abroad was a powerful factor in this decision; another was that he would have greater freedom to pursue his literary and political interests. But he had doubts about the decision. He liked diplomacy and was good at it, and he could reasonably aspire to its summit: his father had once headed the profession. On the other hand, Sir Arthur's death in 1928 meant that Nicolson no longer needed to worry about disappointing his father's hopes.

Nicolson considered *Sir Arthur Nicolson, Bart., First Lord Carnock: A Study in the Old Diplomacy* (1930) his best book. It is indeed an excellent study: as biography and history it brilliantly fulfills the double promise of its title. As ambassador to Russia and then permanent undersecretary at the Foreign Office his father had been at the heart of Britain's pre–World War I foreign policy. Nicolson outlines the diplomatic origins of the war with a sympathy for Germany's position that is surprising, all the more so as his father had been regarded (unjustly, as Nicolson shows) as strongly anti-German. The biography was written in Berlin during the last, febrile years of the Weimar Republic by one who did not love the Germans as he did the French (and next to them, the Americans) but tried hard to understand them. His understanding was assisted by his early conviction that the Treaty of Versailles was unfairly, even dangerously vindictive toward Germany. The prewar power that Nicolson seemed most inclined to blame for World War I, on the evidence of *Sir Arthur Nicolson, Bart., First Lord Carnock*, was the defunct Austro-Hungarian Empire.

After leaving the diplomatic corps Nicolson spent eighteen months at Lord Beaverbrook's *Evening Standard* as a higher gossip columnist, commenting on the social, political, and literary scene. He also did a series of broadcast chats on the BBC, some of which were published as *People*

and Things (1931). He began to keep a full diary, which he maintained until his wife died in 1962. Some three million words in total, the diary was skillfully edited down by his son Nigel to about one-twentieth of its original length and published in three volumes between 1966 and 1968, along with some of the more than ten thousand letters Nicolson wrote during his life. The diary was perhaps written to be published: it is elegant and coherent. The discipline of diarist and correspondent contributed greatly to Nicolson's fluency as an essayist, journalist, and broadcaster. The diary also no doubt provided a useful source of information for his other writings. It may have contributed as well to Nicolson's greatest gift as an essayist, his ability to create in the reader the impression that he alone is being addressed. The feeling of intimacy imparted by Nicolson's conversational approach is heightened by the sense of personality he conveys: the sense that we know the author, and he wants us to know him even better. But Nicolson escapes the dangers of unpleasant egotism by his somewhat self-mocking manner. However well informed he is, he never sounds superior; however well connected, he never seems to be name-dropping. This engaging, somewhat self-effacing persona nevertheless persuades the reader that Nicolson's opinions are worth hearing. When he addresses political and diplomatic issues the ring of authority is unmistakable. When he talks about being measured for a shirt or going to a boxing match, about daydreams or the evocative power of smells (Nicolson was particularly conscious of the latter) he is a genial companion, just a bit more observant and articulate than the reader. Nicolson's BBC broadcasts were extremely popular, making him an early mass media "personality"; he also broadcast some successful conversations with his wife on such topics as marriage and sexual equality. The urbane, controlled, disembodied intimacy of radio proved to be Nicolson's forte. But he was conscious of the dangers of broadcasting. In the talk "Is the Broadcaster Sincere?" he discusses his fear of creating and becoming a victim of an artificial public persona. Happy to chat familiarly with two million anonymous BBC listeners, he had no wish to talk with the man in the street in the flesh. He was a gentleman and a snob, as he freely admitted–to himself and his close friends. When he entered politics his fastidious distaste for the "bedints" (meaning, in the private language he shared with his wife, all those who were beneath him) whose votes he sought made

Nicolson after his election to Parliament, 14 November 1935 (photograph from the Leicester Mail)

him a disastrous campaigner.

Nicolson's relationship with his wife probably owed a great deal of its famous success to the fact that much of it was epistolary. In his splendid letters Nicolson could be the kind of husband or father–passionate, candid, understanding, kind–that he wanted to be but found it harder to be face-to-face. He spent most of the week in London, where he had his flat, his clubs, and his friends. He was much more gregarious than his wife, who preferred the rural peace of Sissinghurst Castle, a ruin they acquired in 1930. Its renovation and especially the creation of its magnificent gardens, which Nicolson largely planned, became a close bond between them.

Politics seemed to offer a way of putting Nicolson's great expertise in foreign affairs to public use as a policymaker instead of a mere civil servant. There is a distinct element of wish fulfilment in his novel *Public Faces* (1932), a lighthearted description of an international crisis in which a bold young junior minister averts a world war by seizing the initiative from her fumbling seniors. A chilling note for the post-Hiroshima reader is Nicolson's prescient introduction of missiles and atomic bombs as causes of the crisis. But Nicolson's poor instincts as a politi-

cian were evident early in his support of Sir Oswald Mosley's New party. He resigned his newspaper and broadcasting work to edit the party journal *Action* and run for Parliament in the 1931 general election. As Mosley showed his increasingly fascist inclinations Nicolson drew back in dismay. (When Mosley talked about uniforms for his followers, Nicolson innocently suggested "grey flannel trousers and shirts.") In 1935 he finally entered Parliament as a member of Ramsay Macdonald's dwindling National Labour party, thereby reducing his claims to political preferment from the mainstream parties. He was able to stay in Parliament, which he loved dearly, for ten years because World War II postponed the next general election until 1945; he was then defeated, this time as an independent. Lacking any party clout, he never received the government office for which he thirsted–apart from a brief parliamentary secretaryship at the Ministry of Information–despite his ardent adulation of Prime Minister Winston Churchill. His biographer, James Lees-Milne, has attributed Nicolson's political failure to a lack of toughness and an intense desire to be liked–qualities that perhaps contributed to his success as an essayist. Nicolson eventually joined the Labour party in a vain at-

Nicolson at his typewriter (photograph by Derek Adkins; courtesy of Nigel Nicolson)

tempt to gain a peerage, but his socialism was very theoretical indeed.

If his political career failed, his literary career ran more smoothly. He drew from his diplomatic experience to write *Peacemaking, 1919* (1933), a memoir of his participation in the negotiation of the Treaty of Versailles–a treaty which Hitler was about to tear up. *Curzon: The Last Phase, 1919-1925* (1934) was a sort of pendant to his study of his father. Through an account of the great proconsul's last years Nicolson was able to describe and discuss the style and realities of postwar diplomacy. The title may intentionally echo that of his book on Byron, for Curzon, under whom Nicolson served, emerges as not unlike Byron in certain respects: a glamorous aristocrat who finally settled the century-old Turco-Greek issue with a Byronic flourish. *Dwight Morrow* (1935) tells of a newer style of diplomacy. The father-in-law of Charles Lindbergh, Morrow enjoyed a career of almost Horatio Alger-like simplicity–as Nicolson tells it, at least; there is a sort of American innocence to the book which gives it considerable charm and lightness, though

much of the innocence is doubtless Nicolson's own unfamiliarity with American politics. Morrow was an honest and much-loved man who rose from humble origins to become a leading figure in international finance (particularly the financing of World War I) and a successful ambassador to Mexico, only to die on the threshold of what might have been a major political career. *Diplomacy* (1939) is an extended discussion, aimed at the informed layman, of the history and practice of diplomacy. Like most of Nicolson's books, it is in many respects an extended essay in the sense that it retains a certain informality of manner. Nicolson's authorial self is unblushingly manifest in practically all of his books, as is his awareness of the reader, whom he often addresses directly. On diplomatic matters one is being lectured, rather than chatted to as on lighter topics, but the personal note is always there. Characteristic too is the absence of any reference to research or even authority other than the author's ipse dixit.

Apart from his books and his M.P.'s salary, Nicolson supported himself (though only just, as he lived on a generous scale and occasionally had to borrow from his wife) with higher journalism, essays, and reviews. He reviewed five books a week for the *Daily Telegraph*, for example–he was more an appreciative than a critical reviewer–and then moved to the *Observer*, where he was chief reviewer from 1948 to 1961, free to write spaciously on whatever he chose. From 1938 to 1952 he wrote a weekly page in the *Spectator* under the heading "Marginal Comment." Three of his books are selections of these essays, which are sometimes political, sometimes literary, and sometimes social, but usually on matters of public concern. The *Spectator* became Nicolson's platform and parliamentary surrogate. Even while he was in Parliament his essays were often those of an informed backbencher trying to amplify his voice. The voice, however, was not that of a partisan politician but of a highly civilized, sensible, middle-of-the-road commentator. Nicolson also wrote fortnightly for the Paris *Figaro* from 1946 to 1948. In 1947 he received the Legion of Honor as a great friend of France, particularly for his championship of free France during the Vichy regime. Nicolson's last two literary biographies, *Benjamin Constant* (1949) and *Sainte-Beuve* (1957), testify to his love and knowledge of French literature–especially of Sainte-Beuve, the patron saint of so many literary essayists, from Matthew Arnold and Augustine Birrell to Nic-

Nicolson and Sackville-West with their dog, Rollo, at their home, Sissinghurst, in 1959 (photograph by Philip Turner; courtesy of Nigel Nicolson)

olson, who were sympathetic literary conversationalists interested above all in the authorial psychology. Nicolson's literary biographies are in a sense extended essays in the manner of Sainte-Beuve.

Nicolson was influential in forming the niche for literary and intellectual chat for which the BBC, with its significantly titled "Talks Department" and its rather highbrow Third Programme, became famous. His broadcasting career was interrupted in 1931 when he canceled a series of ten radio talks titled "The New Spirit in Modern Literature" in protest against the censorship of John Reith, the BBC's notoriously puritanical director general, who forbade him to mention James Joyce's *Ulysses* (1922). He returned to the air in July 1938 with a series of influential and outspoken current affairs talks titled "The Last Week," in which he voiced some criticism of his government's policy of appeasing Germany, though official pressure forced him to moderate his opinions. In 1942 he became a member of the BBC's board of governors, where he was a

force for maintaining the corporation's independence of government control. In 1945 he gave a series of prime-time radio broadcasts in English and French on the Paris Peace talks. He appeared frequently on "Brains Trust," a popular intellectual talk program, where his informal essayist style served him well. His wife was one of the earliest owners of a television set, and he first appeared on television in 1939.

Nicolson published six books of collected broadcast and periodical essays; he perhaps reckoned these to be as much as the market would bear, although he could have published many more of equally high quality. But he would probably not have wished to be remembered as an essayist. During the 1930s he nourished a much larger literary ambition. He was fascinated by his family (as his wife was by hers)–by its role in history, by its contribution to his identity, by the presentness of the past, and by the thickness and twistedness of time's skein. Perhaps writing his father's life triggered the idea, but it was in a series with the provocatively Proustian title "In Search of the Past"

Nicolson in 1967 (photograph by Ian Graham; courtesy of Nigel Nicolson)

that he decided to test his literary powers to the fullest with an evocation of the historical roots of his world through the lens of certain figures in his family's past. This magnum opus, as vaguely sketched out in a few letters, is reminiscent of the semi-autobiographical roman-fleuve genre so popular especially in France early in the twentieth century (although Nicolson emphasized that his work was not to be fiction). Only two volumes in the series appeared. *Helen's Tower* (1937) is a biography of his maternal uncle, the Marquess of Dufferin, a paragon of Whig virtue whose Irish country house Clandeboye was a surrogate home to Nicolson when, as a boy, he bounced from one foreign capital to another in the wake of his father's career. It was a significant moment when he discovered that in Clandeboye, too, he was an alien, a member of the English upper class in a largely hostile Ireland. Yet he did have authentic Irish blood, as is evident from the only other book in the series. *The Desire to Please* (1943), a study of his mother's ascendancy family, focuses on his great-great-grandfather, Hamilton Rowan, a hot-blooded Irish rebel and patriot. Nicolson

was especially fascinated by his maternal ancestry (he was always very much his mother's son–he was sixty-five by the time she died), which was more exciting and aristocratic than his father's somewhat dour Scottish heritage. Such considerations, added to his cosmopolitan childhood, his diplomatic experience, and his marriage to a woman with the oldest English aristocratic blood on one side and Spanish gypsy blood on the other, may help to explain Nicolson's intense preoccupation with the phenomenon of Englishness. The self-referential quality of this preoccupation may have indicated a certain anxiety, but it gave him an excellent essay-writing and lecturing persona and endless grist for his mill. *Good Behaviour* (1955) and *The English Sense of Humour* (1956) are extended treatments of recurring themes in Nicolson's work. Good taste, politeness, manners–gentlemanliness in general–were all subjects on which Nicolson could expatiate with ease and charm, embroidering them with anecdotes appropriate to a well-read, well-traveled man.

Nicolson's reputation as a biographer was tested when he was commissioned to write *King*

238

George the Fifth: His Life and Reign (1952). It is the best of the official royal biographies, a difficult genre requiring skill and tact. For it he received a knighthood. At the height of his reputation, Nicolson was acclaimed by Somerset Maugham for his ability to capture personal appearance in words, and by John Betjeman as the greatest master of English prose. With his close friend Raymond Mortimer and Cyril Connolly he was the most important literary tastemaker of the 1940s and 1950s, and was dismissed by many "Angry Young Men" of the 1950s as the embodiment of the snobbery and insipidity of the Establishment. Yet in *Journey to Java* (1957), the diary of a sea voyage he took the year after the Suez crisis (which marked the close of his political and diplomatic generation), he was still in touch, still full of curiosity, still highly observant, and still capable of effortless, charming conversation with his readers. Only in his last two books, *The Age of Reason* (1960) and *Monarchy* (1962), both coffee-table

history, did he lose his powers and go slack. He was quite unstrung by his wife's death in 1962. He lived to witness, dimly, the great success of his diaries and to remark how odd it was to publish three books that he did not realize he had written. Happily, they belonged to his best period, showing a skilled essayist in the act of turning his life into literature. Nicolson died on 1 May 1968.

Biography:

James Lees-Milne, *Harold Nicolson: A Biography*, 2 volumes (London: Chatto & Windus, 1980-1981).

References:

Victoria Glendinning, *Vita: A Biography of V. Sackville-West* (New York: Knopf, 1983);

Nigel Nicolson, *Portrait of a Marriage* (London: Weidenfeld & Nicolson, 1973; New York: Atheneum, 1973);

Edmund Wilson, "Through the Embassy Window," *New Yorker*, 1 January 1944.

Michael Polanyi

(11 March 1891 - 22 February 1976)

Angus Somerville
Brock University

BOOKS: *Atomic Reactions* (London: Williams & Norgate, 1932);

U.S.S.R. Economics: Fundamental Data, System and Spirit (Manchester, U.K.: Manchester University Press, 1935);

The Contempt of Freedom: The Russian Experiment and After (London: Watts, 1940; New York: Arno Press, 1975);

Full Employment and Free Trade (Cambridge: Cambridge University Press, 1945; New York: Macmillan, 1948);

Rights and Duties of Science (Oxford: Society for Freedom in Science, 1945);

The Planning of Science (Oxford: Society for Freedom in Science, 1946);

Science, Faith and Society (Chicago: University of Chicago Press, 1946; London: Oxford University Press, 1946);

The Foundations of Academic Freedom (Oxford: Society for Freedom in Science, 1947);

The Logic of Liberty: Reflections and Rejoinders (Chicago: University of Chicago Press, 1951; London: Routledge & Kegan Paul, 1951);

Pure and Applied Science and Their Appropriate Forms of Organization (Oxford: Society for Freedom in Science, 1953);

The Magic of Marxism and the Next Stage of History (Manchester, U.K.: Committee on Science and Freedom, 1956);

Personal Knowledge: Towards a Post-Critical Philosophy (Chicago: University of Chicago Press, 1958; London: Routledge & Kegan Paul, 1958);

The Study of Man (Chicago: University of Chicago Press, 1959; London: Routledge & Kegan Paul, 1959);

Beyond Nihilism (Cambridge: Cambridge University Press, 1960);

History and Hope: An Analysis of Our Age (Charlottesville: University of Virginia, 1961);

The Republic of Science, Its Political and Economic Theory: A Lecture Delivered at Roosevelt University, January 11, 1962 (Chicago: Roosevelt University, 1962);

Michael Polanyi (Department of Special Collections, University of Chicago Library)

The Tacit Dimension (Garden City, N.Y.: Doubleday, 1966; London: Routledge & Kegan Paul, 1967);

Knowing and Being: Essays, edited by Marjorie Grene (Chicago: University of Chicago Press, 1969; London: Routledge & Kegan Paul, 1969);

Scientific Thought and Social Reality: Essays, edited by Fred Schwartz, Psychological Issues, volume 8, no. 4, monograph 32 (New York: International Universities Press, 1974);

Meaning, by Polanyi and Harry Prosch (Chicago & London: University of Chicago Press, 1975 [i.e. 1976]).

SELECTED PERIODICAL PUBLICATION—
UNCOLLECTED: "What is a Painting?," *American Scholar*, 39 (Autumn 1970): 655-669.

A question that runs through much of Michael Polanyi's writing is: "Why did we destroy Europe?" Why did the nineteenth century with its reforming zeal, with its immensely high ambitions for the improvement of the human condition produce a modern age of unparalleled destructiveness? As Richard L. Gelwick points out in chapter 1 of *The Way of Discovery* (1977), for Polanyi the answer lies in the fusion of the moral intensity of the great reformers with a false notion of scientific objectivity. Marxism, for example, claims scientific objectivity for its theories: disagreement with it is thus a deviation from "objective" scientific truth. But the driving force behind Marxism is moral and reforming zeal. This coupling of a submerged moral zeal with objectivism is for Polanyi the dynamism which produced the Marxist and fascist revolutions of the twentieth century. The coupling lends a quasi-scientific authority to the cruelty and oppressiveness of all fanatical movements which can claim to rest upon the objective inevitability of the operation of "scientific" laws. Moral intensity thus deprived of moral restraint is the great threat to civilization and freedom in the modern world. In Polanyi's view, the problem is at bottom a mistaken notion of scientific objectivity, a confused theory of knowledge. He regarded scientism and positivism as fatally reductive epistemologies. Much of his writing is the exposition of a sane and humane theory—the theory of tacit knowing. The rest is concerned with the dangers to liberty of life and thought presented by the "dynamo-coupling" of moral zeal with scientism. He abandoned an extraordinary career in physical chemistry to produce a long series of essays which form an exceptionally coherent and lucid attack on what he regarded as the fundamental errors of the twentieth century.

From the beginning, Polanyi's career was marked by his refusal to be limited by traditional disciplinary divisions. He was born in Budapest, Hungary, on 11 March 1891. His father, also named Michael, was a wealthy civil engineer who financed and built railroads; he lost most of his money when Polanyi was eight and died six years

later, leaving his widow and five children in straitened circumstances and forcing Polanyi to earn money tutoring rich schoolboys. Polanyi's mother, Cecile Wohl Polanyi, became the center of a circle of young artists, writers, and scholars. Polanyi's first degree was in medicine at the University of Budapest in 1913; by that time he had already published his first scientific paper, "Chemistry of the Hydrocephalic Liquid" (1910). In 1913 and 1914 he studied chemistry at Karlsruhe University in Germany and published papers on the application of quantum theory to the third law of thermodynamics and on adsorption.

With the outbreak of World War I Polanyi became a medical officer in the Austro-Hungarian army. Nonetheless, he managed to continue his work on thermodynamics, work in which he was assisted by an extensive correspondence with Albert Einstein. A period of convalescence from diphtheria gave Polanyi the leisure to complete his dissertation on adsorption, which he submitted for a doctorate in chemistry at Budapest University in 1917.

After serving briefly in the Hungarian Ministry of Health and spending a year as a lecturer at Karlsruhe University, Polanyi moved to Berlin in 1920 to assume a post at the Kaiser Wilhelm Institute of Fiber Research. He married Magda Elizabeth Kemeny, a chemical engineer, in February 1921; they had two sons. In Berlin his research interests changed direction again. He did important work on the X-ray diffraction pattern of natural plant fibers and on the plasticity and strength of solid material. Yet another shift in direction occurred in 1925, when Polanyi transferred to the Kaiser Wilhelm Institute for Physical Chemistry, where he was engaged in the investigation of reaction kinetics. In 1929 he became a life member of the institute. Most of his work on reaction kinetics, however, was carried out at Manchester University in England, where, after resigning his post at the Kaiser Wilhelm Institute in 1933 in protest against the Nazi government, he took the chair of physical chemistry.

The move to England brought philosophical and social concerns closer to the center of Polanyi's attention—a process which was accelerated by a growing appreciation of the implications of communism as practiced in the Soviet Union. In *The Tacit Dimension* (1966) he gives an account of how a visit to Russia in 1935 impressed upon him a recognition of the destructiveness of the twentieth century's fusion of misconstrued scientific rationalism with moral fervor:

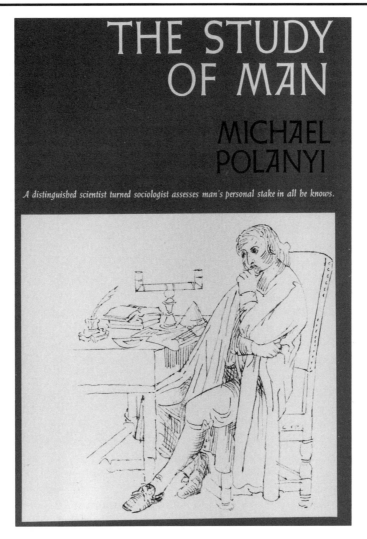

Cover for Polanyi's 1959 philosophical investigation into epistemology, in which he continues to discuss ideas put forth in Personal Knowledge *(1958) and in his Gifford Lectures of 1951-1952 (courtesy of the University of Chicago Press)*

I first met questions of philosophy when I came up against the Soviet ideology under Stalin which denied justification to the pursuit of science. I remember a conversation I had with Bukharin in Moscow in 1935. . . . he said that pure science was a morbid symptom of a class society; under socialism the conception of science pursued for its own sake would disappear, for the interests of scientists would spontaneously turn to problems of the current Five-Year Plan.

I was struck by the fact that this denial of the very existence of independent scientific thought came from a socialist theory which derived its tremendous persuasive power from its claim to scientific certainty. The scientific outlook appeared to have produced a mechanical conception of man and history in which there was no place for science itself. This conception denied altogether any intrinsic power to thought and thus denied any grounds for claiming freedom of thought.

I saw also that this self-immolation of the mind was actuated by powerful moral motives. The mechanical course of history was to bring universal justice. Scientific skepticism would trust only material necessity for achieving universal brotherhood. Skepticism and utopianism had thus fused into a new skeptical fanaticism.

The immediate result of this conversation with Nikolay Bukharin was a flurry of perceptive writing on the effects of Soviet scientism upon both the pursuit of science and the liberty of the individual. *U.S.S.R. Economics* (1935) argues that the Communist effort to stimulate and control economic activity was bound to fail because of the flawed objective view of science on which communism itself was founded. This view could not allow sufficiently for the personal element in social and economic relationships.

The Contempt of Freedom (1940) gathers together social and economic essays written between 1935 and 1940. In the preface Polanyi remarks that "progressive minds were so fascinated by the prospects of the revolution in Russia that they had little interest left for the fate of the traditional liberties.... Progress had become antagonistic to liberty." The divorce between progress and liberty is the major theme of these diverse and admirably articulated essays.

The earliest essay, "Soviet Economics–Fact and Theory," covers substantially the same ground as *U.S.S.R. Economics.* Polanyi recognizes that the Soviet system gives the worker a new and greater degree of security. He sums up the "collectivist" view of the worker's situation: "State management by a bureaucracy linked to the working class is a new and valid expression of economic consciousness for the workers: once more it gives meaning to their labours." But Polanyi points out that collectivism by its nature ignores "the value of individual independence and attacks at every point the ideas and institutions which would set limits to public authority."

Other essays in the collection adopt larger perspectives on the divorce between progress and liberty. "Truth and Propaganda" illustrates the fascination of "progressive minds" in the West with the revolution in Russia. The minds in question are those of Sidney and Beatrice Webb, whose book *Soviet Communism: A New Civilisation?* (1935) Polanyi subjects to a scathing analysis in which a controlled anger is evident. The Webbs' great error, for Polanyi, is to write as though the Soviet legal system and institutions represented the actuality of the Soviet state and the reality of life in that state. Polanyi points out that great and cruel dictatorships like Hitler's or Stalin's may rely on democratic institutions controlled by the use of "secret terror." Such dictatorships frequently obtain overwhelming mandates by producing massive turnouts of voters in "free" elections. Only intellectual self-deception permits the Webbs to maintain their wildly rosy picture of life under an oppressive socialist regime. For example, Polanyi is gently ironic about the Webbs' attempt to represent the struggle between Stalin and Trotsky as an example of the freedom of thought and speech which prevailed in the Soviet Union under Stalin. "The result is a presentation which . . . conveys nothing else but a monumental apologia of Soviet institutions and of the free-

Polanyi in 1968 (photograph by Ted Shreshinsky)

dom enjoyed under them, while on closer examination it proves to be so full of nicely adjusted reservations . . . that the careful student finds it impossible to form any picture whatsoever of the political system of the country." He ends the essay with a politely contemptuous assessment of the significance of apologetics such as were produced by the Webbs: "Many thinkers do not believe in truth; of those who do, few consider it to be right to tell the truth regardless of political consequences. . . . Unless intellectuals make a new departure, inspired by unflinching veracity, truth will remain powerless against propaganda."

"The Rights and Duties of Science," a review of J. D. Bernal's *The Social Function of Science*

(1939), takes up the issues raised by Bukharin's belief that scientists would "spontaneously turn to problems of the current Five-Year Plan." Bernal was, like the Webbs, seduced by the "progressivism" of the Soviet Union and failed to recognize or admit the disastrous effects of the political direction of scientific research. Bernal's optimistic view of the Soviet scientist's freedom to take "a conscious and determinate part in a common enterprise" is, for Polanyi, a travesty of the true situation of the Soviet scientist, who is "Dragooned into the lip service of a preposterous ideology, harried by the crazy suspicions of omnipotent officials; arbitrarily imprisoned or in constant danger of such imprisonment." The frequently benevolent attempt to coerce science into "socially useful" paths is a topic to which Polanyi returned again and again. The Soviet attempt in this direction depended on central planning; the stultifying effects of such planning on all human activity are the theme of the last-written essay in the collection, "Collectivist Planning," which concludes: "General planning is the wholesale destruction of freedom; cultural planning would be the end of all inspired enquiry, of every creative effort, and planned economy would make life into something between a universal monastery and a forced labour camp."

Several essays first published in 1945 and reprinted in *Scientific Thought and Social Reality* (1974) advance considerably Polanyi's defense of the freedom of science and develop his alternative to positivist theories of scientific knowledge. These essays explore the active and personal participation of the knower in knowing. "The Autonomy of Science" emphasizes the intuitive creativity of the good scientist working within and responsible to scientific standards which are transmitted from teacher to student in the great centers of scientific inquiry. The informed opinion of the scientific community and adherence to traditionally accepted standards prevent research from "running wild in the absence of any proper directive influence." The traditional values of the scientific community accommodate the individual scientist's exercise of his art, which—like the exercise of any other art or profession—relies heavily on intuition and skill: "The individual scientists take the initiative in choosing their problems and conducting their investigations; the body of scientists controls each of its members by imposing the standards of science; and finally, the people decide in public discussion whether or not to accept science as the true explanation of nature." Sci-

ence, then, rests on the freedom of the individual to follow his intuitions and to investigate what he sees as problems: this freedom is prevented from developing into wild subjectivity by what Polanyi later called the "conviviality" of the scientific community. The remainder of the essay is an account of "two recent instances on record of attempts to break the autonomy of scientific life and to subordinate it to state direction." The Nazi attempt is dismissed briefly as "crude and cynical"; but the effects of Trofim Lysenko on Soviet science are regarded as more serious and receive lengthy attention. Polanyi finds an irony in the corruption of a branch of science by Lysenko and his Russian followers: "There is no doubt at all about the unwavering desire of the Soviet government to advance the progress of science.... Yet [its] subsidies ... benefited science only so long as they flowed into channels controlled by independent scientific opinion, whereas as soon as their allocation was accompanied by attempts at establishing governmental direction they exercised a violently destructive influence." The dangers to science presented by the Nazi and Soviet governments are clear enough, according to Polanyi; more insidious is the tendency among scientists in the free world to weaken the principles of scientific autonomy by urging the adjustment of science to social ends: "Fired by misguided generosity, these scientists would sacrifice science—forgetting that it is theirs only in trust for the purpose of cultivation, not theirs to give away and allow to perish." Perhaps as important as the defense of scientific freedom in this essay is the location of scientific knowledge in the community of knowers and in the intuitions and skill of the individual scientist. Objective scientific knowledge cannot be detached from the human knower. The implications of this view of scientific knowledge were pursued later in Polanyi's career.

In "Science and the Modern Crisis" Polanyi attempts a brief historical account of the origin not merely of the threat to scientific autonomy discussed in the preceding essay but also of the curious marriage of a "hardheaded materialist conception of politics" with intolerance and fanaticism. Through Thomas Hobbes and Jean-Jacques Rousseau, Polanyi traces the development of the notion that the sovereign must be absolute. The moral standards of humanity "were still on guard against the advance of the Hobbesian Leviathan" until the scientific materialism of the nineteenth century denied the reality of moral aspirations: "To understand the position we must realize that

Cover for the 1969 collection that includes essays from the 1960s, such as "Beyond Nihilism" and "The Republic of Science" (courtesy of the University of Chicago Press)

Marx—in spite of his denial of morality as an independent force—was passionately dominated by moral motives.... Here lies the origin of modern fanaticism. It is the force of moral aspirations driven underground, and giving their support to a supposed scientific theory which promises social salvation by the mere force of violence." For Polanyi, fascism differs from Marxism only in the fascist use of the sentiment of patriotism, "a much narrower aspiration than the desire for universal justice which underlies Marxism."

These papers from 1945 argue that modern positivist scientism coupled with a political philosophy which denies moral aspirations is fatal to the freedom of science and of society; what it means to be a free scientist and what it means to be a free individual cannot be discussed separately. This point is argued in "The Social Message of Pure Science," a 1945 address to the British Associ-

ation for the Advancement of Science that is reprinted in *The Logic of Liberty* (1951). Polanyi asks what purpose pure science has; his answer is that the free pursuit of science is the paradigm of the life of a free society: "And where ... universities have allowed themselves to be cajoled or terrorized into compromising their standards, we feel that the very roots of our civilization have been marred.... The world needs science to-day above all as an example of the good life. Spread out over the planet scientists form even to-day, though submerged by disaster, the body of a great and good society." "Science and Welfare," also from 1945 and also reprinted in *The Logic of Liberty*, takes up the interrelationship of science and society. The essay develops Polanyi's assault on utilitarian views of science by showing that the discoveries of pure science with the most far-reaching practical effects (for example, those of

Copernicus, Galileo, or Kepler) were pursued without regard for utilitarian considerations. The essay ends by placing the perils of science in a wider social and intellectual context: "The extravagant idea of subordinating science to the planning of welfare has formed but one part of a general attack on the status of intellectual and moral life. There are a number of important movements to-day denying the ultimate reality of rational and moral processes. A vast force of naturalistic prejudice is relentlessly attacking the conception of man as an essentially rational being." Polanyi argues that materialist scientism with its false notion of an objectivity detached from the knower does not simply reduce scientific knowledge but also diminishes the reasoning, moral individual to a manifestation of impersonal natural processes and laws.

Clearly, Polanyi's interests were taking him ever further from pure science. A major step toward a new career as social thinker and philosopher was the appearance in 1946 of *Science, Faith and Society*, the published version of the Riddell Lectures delivered at Durham University in 1945. These lectures are in part a determined attack on the notion of scientific objectivity as the impersonal application of virtually mechanical scientific procedures. Polanyi begins his first lecture by emphasizing the degree to which the successful scientist relies for his discoveries upon his intuitive and often inexplicable integration of what may be widely dispersed data. Next, he argues that a purely procedural approach to science is inadequate on the grounds that "just as there is no proof of a proposition in natural science which cannot conceivably turn out to be incomplete, so also there is no refutation which cannot conceivably turn out to have been unfounded. There is a residue of personal judgment required in deciding–as the scientist eventually must–what weight to attach to any particular set of evidence in regard to the validity of a particular proposition. The propositions of science thus appear to be in the nature of guesses." Near the end of the first lecture Polanyi underscores the degree to which the scientist is personally and morally responsible for his guesses: "The scientist's task is not to observe any allegedly correct procedure but to get right results. He has to establish contact, by whatever means, with the hidden reality of which he is predicating. His conscience must therefore give its ultimate assent always from a sense of having established that contact. . . . This indicates the presence of a moral element in the

foundations of science." Thus, the scientific knowledge of reality is a function of the intellectual and moral being of the individual knower.

The remaining two lectures turn to the scientist as a member of the scientific and larger communities. The leading idea of the second lecture is that "science can exist and continue to exist only because its premises can be embodied in a tradition which can be held in common by a community." In Polanyi's view, the life of science rests on a traditional foundation of ideals analogous to the traditions which inform law or a living religion. The traditions of science and law operate, according to Polanyi, under a "General Authority" which "leaves the decisions for interpreting general rules in the hands of numerous independent individuals." The necessary freedom of the scientist and the scientific community is likely to survive only in a free society. In the third lecture Polanyi argues that the myth of an impersonal and detached objective science destroys the free society by reducing the individual scientist's urge to follow his own intuitions and aims to "a selfish desire for his own amusement."

As the number and extent of Polanyi's social and philosophical works increased, the quantity of his scientific publications diminished. Polanyi recognized the change in his commitments by resigning his chair of physical chemistry at Manchester in 1948 to occupy a specially created chair of social studies at the same university. He held this chair until his retirement in 1958, when he moved to Merton College, Oxford, as a senior research fellow in philosophy. He served as a visiting professor at the University of Chicago in 1950 and again in 1954.

Science, Faith and Society dwelt much upon matters of epistemology. Clearly, the rejoinder to positivism and objectivism required the development of Polanyi's view of how men–not scientists alone–know and discover. Epistemology is the chief topic of "On the Introduction of Science into Moral Subjects," published first in 1954 and reprinted in *Scientific Thought and Social Reality*. Polanyi attacks the reductivism inherent in behaviorism and certain types of scientific anthropology. Such reductivism is "the logical terminus of looking at man in a completely detached manner, in accordance with the accepted ideal of the scientific method." Another target is logical positivism, which attempts "to judge our mental activities according to the criteria which scientific statements must fulfill, or which they are, at any rate, currently believed to fulfill. . . . Hence to

MICHAEL POLANYI and HARRY PROSCH

MEANING

Cover for Polanyi's last book (1976), a collection of his lectures on aesthetics, which Harry Prosch helped him prepare for publication (courtesy of the University of Chicago Press)

call something immoral, unjust, or evil has no verifiable meaning." Polanyi's program is that "we should try to mend the break between science and our understanding of ourselves as sentient and responsible beings by incorporating into our conception of scientific knowledge the part which we ourselves necessarily contribute to such knowledge."

Polanyi explains his view of the observer's participation in the act of knowing by distinguishing between what he calls "subsidiary awareness" and "focal awareness." The user of a hammer, for example, has a subsidiary awareness of the feelings in the palm of his hand, while he attends to or has a focal awareness of driving in the nail. Polanyi further clarifies the distinction:

> We may think of the hammer replaced by a probe, used for exploring the interior of a hidden cavity. Think how a blind man feels his way by use of a stick, which involves transposing the shocks transmitted to his hand and the muscles

holding the stick into an awareness of the things touched by the stick. . . .

> Our subsidiary awareness of tools and probes can be regarded, therefore, as a condition in which they come to form part of our body. . . . While we rely on a tool or a probe, these things cannot be deliberately handled in themselves or critically examined as external objects. Instead, we pour ourselves into them and assimilate them as part of our own existence, uncritically.

That is, we attend *from* the physical clues provided by the tools, in which we "indwell," but attend *to* the object of focal awareness. For Polanyi our use of the "formalism of a science" is continuous with our use of tools and probes: "We may generalize this process so as to include the acceptance and use of intellectual tools such as are offered by an interpretative framework and in particular by the formalism of a science. While we rely on such a formalism it is not an object under examination but a tool of observation." That is, as we "dwell in" physical clues in using probes, so do we dwell in the framework of the formalism of a science when conducting scientific investigation. Tools, intellectual or physical, become part of the persons we are. Polanyi concludes: "Science does not require that we study man and society in a detached manner. On the contrary, the part played by personal knowledge in science suggests that the science of man should rely on greatly extended uses of personal knowing."

This essay grew in part from Polanyi's Gifford Lectures of 1951-1952 at the University of Aberdeen. The ideas both of the lectures and the paper were given expanded and definitive form in the massive *Personal Knowledge* (1958), the substance of which is repeated in *The Study of Man* (1959). These developments in Polanyi's thought were, however, given their most succinct expression in 1966 in *The Tacit Dimension*, the published version of the Terry Lectures delivered at Yale University in 1962. In *The Tacit Dimension* Polanyi indicates that the initial hint for his idea that in knowing we assimilate or integrate subsidiary clues came from Gestalt psychology, but Gestalt with a difference: "Gestalt psychology has assumed that perception of a physiognomy takes place through the spontaneous equilibration of its particulars impressed on the retina or on the brain. However, I am looking at Gestalt, on the contrary, as the outcome of an active shaping of experience performed in the pursuit of knowledge. This shaping or integrating I hold to be the great and indispensable tacit power by which all knowledge is discovered, and, once discovered, is held to be true." Subsidiary clues–the tacit dimension–may remain inexplicit; thus, "we can know more than we can tell." In tacit knowing we rely on our awareness of subsidiary clues as a means of attending to the focus of our thought or scrutiny: "In the case of human physiognomy, I would now say that we rely on our awareness of its features for attending to the characteristic appearance of a face. We are attending *from* the features to the face, and thus may be unable to specify the features." Thus, tacit awareness may exist below the level of consciousness. It is only through tacit knowing that one can "account (1) for a valid knowledge of a problem, (2) for the scientist's capacity to pursue it, guided by his sense of approaching its solution, and (3) for a valid anticipation of the yet indeterminate implications of the discovery arrived at in the end." Polanyi illustrates these points by citing Plato's statement in the *Meno* that if all knowledge were explicit there could be no knowledge of problems, the early Copernicans' anticipatory sense that their theory was true rather than simply useful, and the construction of mathematical theory.

The effect of all this is to place the knower squarely in the midst of knowing. But does this not open the way to unchecked subjectivism? Polanyi answers that question in the final essay in *The Tacit Dimension*, "A Society of Explorers." He argues that the scientist's acts and choices are indeed his own but that "his acts stand under the judgment of the hidden reality he seeks to uncover. . . . His acts are personal judgments exercised responsibly with a view to a reality with which he is seeking to establish contact . . . he expects that others–if similarly equipped–will also recognize the presence that guided him. . . . he will claim that his results are universally valid. . . . I speak not of an *established* universality, but of a universal *intent*, for the scientist cannot know whether his claims will be accepted." Thus the scientist works under the final correction of reality, knowledge of which is modified and deepened as science uncovers more of its inexhaustible nature. One paragraph toward the end of the essay not merely sums up much of the argument but also points to some wider philosophical implications of the theory of tacit knowing: "My account of scientific discovery describes an existential choice. We start the pursuit of discovery by pouring ourselves into the subsidiary elements of a problem and we continue to spill ourselves into

further clues as we advance further, so that we arrive at discovery fully committed to it as an aspect of reality. These choices create in us a new existence, which challenges others to transform themselves in its image. To this extent, then, 'existence precedes essence,' that is, it comes before the truth that we establish and make our own."

Polanyi left Oxford University in 1961. He was a distinguished research fellow at the University of Virginia that year; a visiting professor at Duke University in 1964; a senior fellow at the Center of Advanced Studies, Wesleyan University, in 1965; and a visiting professor at the University of Chicago from 1967 to 1969. *Knowing and Being* (1969) contains an excellent selection of essays written by Polanyi during the 1960s. They reveal that all of his earlier social, philosophical, and scientific concerns were still active. "Beyond Nihilism," the final form of a paper published separately in 1960, deepens his analysis of the historical origins of scientism, Marxism, and fascism and ends rather hopefully with the view that we have gone beyond the period of nihilistic violence and arrived at a point where a new civility may prevail. "The Message of the Hungarian Revolution" closes with the hope that "Once the disasters of the past fifty years are clearly seen to have been pointless, Europeans may turn once more to cultivate their own garden." Papers such as these attempt to make sense of and find hope in the apparently senseless and hopeless. Other essays in the collection, such as "The Republic of Science" and "The Growth of Science in Society," continue Polanyi's long-standing defense of science. Articles on tacit knowing cover substantially the same ground as *The Tacit Dimension*. The last essay in *Knowing and Being*, "Life's Irreducible Structure," argues powerfully against psychological, scientific, and philosophical reductivism by making brilliant use of the notion of "boundary conditions" from physics. Just as the function and operation of a machine cannot be described reductively in terms of the physical laws which it harnesses (that is, to which it sets boundary conditions), so the mental activities of human beings cannot be understood in purely neurophysiological terms: "Mechanisms, whether man-made or morphological, are boundary conditions harnessing the laws of inanimate nature, being themselves irreducible to those laws. The pattern of organic bases in DNA which functions as a genetic code is a boundary condition irreducible to physics and chemistry. Further controlling principles of life may be represented as a hierarchy of bound-

Michael Polanyi (Department of Special Collections, University of Chicago Library)

ary conditions extending, in the case of man, to consciousness and responsibility."

Late in his life Polanyi turned to consideration of aesthetic matters, especially to an examination of how tacit powers of integration operate in understanding the arts. In "What Is a Painting?" (1970) he argues that one's subsidiary awareness of the flat canvas of a painting prevents distortion of its perspective when it is viewed from an angle. This argument leads to a larger statement of the role of subsidiary awareness of the "frame" or artificial form in the arts in general: "The normal painting of all times belongs to the same class as poetry and drama, for it possesses an artificial frame that contradicts its subject and yet is so closely fused with this subject that the union of the two acquires a quality of its own, a quality unexampled in nature.... In this artifi-

cial estrangement of its subject lies the power of all painting to represent matters drawn from experience in terms that transcend all natural experience. And therein lies equally the power of *all* representative art."

Most of Polanyi's important work on aesthetics was delivered as lectures at the universities of Chicago and Texas between 1969 and 1971. These lectures were collected in 1976 as *Meaning.* Because of his advanced age, Polanyi was assisted in preparing the book for publication by Harry Prosch; Polanyi died on 22 February 1976. Chapters 10 and 11 of *Meaning* are most interesting in their revelation of the daring with which Polanyi was still capable of striking out in new directions. In chapter 10, "Acceptance of Religion," he remarks: "Visionary art has shown us that, even when the story content of a work of art quite obviously has no plausibility, it is nevertheless possible for our imagination to integrate these incompatible elements into a meaning." Polanyi suggests that religion may be accepted on similar terms. What makes acceptance of religion more difficult than acceptance of visionary art is that "the contents of a religion will have as their import the story of a fundamentally *meaningful* world, whereas the import of a work of visual art is rather that the world is a *meaningless* heap of inchoate things." Polanyi then turns to a consideration of "whether the materialistic and scientistic commitments of twentieth-century man irrevocably bar his acceptance of such a possibility." Chapter 11, "Order," answers the question, rehabilitating the notions of "teleology" and "ends" by means of an extremely elegant examination of laws of motion, quantum mechanics, and the development of an embryo. Polanyi concludes that "We might justifiably claim, therefore, that everything we know is *full* of meaning, is not absurd at all" and that "modern science cannot properly be understood to tell us that the world is meaningless and pointless, that it is absurd. The supposition that it is absurd is a modern myth, created imaginatively from the clues produced by a profound misunderstanding of what science and knowledge are and what they require, a misunderstanding spawned by positivistic leftovers in our thinking and long allegiance to the false ideal of objectivity from which we have been unable to shake ourselves quite free. These are the stoppages in our ears that we must pull out if we are ever once more to experience the full range of meanings possible to man." Among those meanings is God.

The journey from hydrocephalic liquid to *Meaning* is a long but coherent one. The coherence is the broad intellect and humane intelligence of a complete man. Michael Polanyi charted deep and difficult waters. He never popularized, but he always remained absolutely lucid and readily intelligible. He wrote in a language which was not his native tongue with ease and great power. His career testifies that philosophy need not be written in the arcane dialect of the professional philosopher. Most impressive is his telling use of material from a vast range of experience and knowledge. All was written with the urgency of a man who felt deeply the moral and spiritual shocks of the twentieth century.

In England, Polanyi's ideas never had the influence for which he hoped. His major influence has been among American thinkers who have always seemed more willing to emulate his adventurousness in leaping over traditional disciplinary barriers and boundaries. In chapter 5 of *The Way of Discovery* Gelwick discusses Polanyi's impact at length, drawing attention to *Intellect and Hope* (1968), which brings together a variety of thinkers from many areas of thought in testimony to Polanyi's influence in North America. Helmuth Kuhn argues that Polanyi has made metaphysics possible once more. Cahall Daly draws parallels between Ludwig Wittgenstein and Polanyi in their attacks on the reductive tendency of positivism. Arthur Koestler's *The Act of Creation* (1964) is clearly indebted to Polanyi. Finally, the conferences of the Study Group on Foundations of Cultural Unity, organized by Marjorie Grene, are evidence of the wide attraction of Polanyi's thought. The growing attack on scientism and positivism in the latter years of the twentieth century owes much to Michael Polanyi.

References:

Richard L. Gelwick, *The Way of Discovery: An Introduction to the Thought of Michael Polanyi* (New York: Oxford University Press, 1977);

Thomas A. Langford and William H. Potent, eds., *Intellect and Hope: Essays in the Thought of Michael Polanyi* (Durham, N.C.: Duke University Press, 1968);

Harry Prosch, *Michael Polanyi: A Critical Exposition* (Albany: State University of New York Press, 1986);

E. P. Wigner and R. A. Hodgkin, "Michael Polanyi," *Biographical Memoirs of Fellows of the Royal Society*, 23 (1977): 413-448.

Papers:

The Department of Special Collections, University of Chicago Library, has a large collection of Polanyi's papers, including letters, manuscripts, research notes, and photographs of Polanyi, his family, and his friends.

J. B. Priestley

(13 September 1894 - 14 August 1984)

R. D. Schell
Laurentian University

See also the Priestley entries in *DLB 10: Modern British Dramatists, 1900-1945; DLB 34: British Novelists, 1890-1929: Traditionalists; DLB 77: British Mystery Writers, 1920-1939;* and *DLB Yearbook 1984.*

SELECTED BOOKS: *The Chapman of Rhymes* (London: Moring, 1918);

Brief Diversions: Being Tales, Travesties, and Epigrams (Cambridge: Bowes & Bowes, 1922);

Papers from Lilliput (Cambridge: Bowes & Bowes, 1922);

I for One (London: Lane, 1923; New York: Dodd, Mead, 1924);

Figures in Modern Literature (London: Lane, 1924; New York: Dodd, Mead, 1924);

The English Comic Characters (London: Lane, 1925; New York: Dodd, Mead, 1925);

George Meredith (London: Macmillan, 1926; New York: Macmillan, 1926);

Talking (London: Jarrolds, 1926; New York & London: Harper, 1926);

Essays of Today and Yesterday (London: Harrap, 1926);

Open House: A Book of Essays (London: Heinemann, 1927; New York & London: Harper, 1927);

Thomas Love Peacock (London: Macmillan, 1927; New York: Macmillan, 1927);

The English Novel (London: Benn, 1927; revised edition, London & New York: Nelson, 1935);

Adam in Moonshine (London: Heinemann, 1927; New York: Harper, 1927);

Benighted (London: Heinemann, 1927); republished as *The Old Dark House* (New York: Harper, 1928);

Apes and Angels: A Book of Essays (London: Methuen, 1928); republished as *Too Many People, and Other Reflections* (New York: Harper, 1928);

The Balconinny, and Other Essays (London: Methuen, 1929); republished as *The Balconinny* (New York & London: Harper, 1930);

J. B. Priestley (photograph copyright by Reynolds News)

English Humour (London & New York: Longmans, Green, 1929; Folcroft, Pa.: Folcroft Library Editions, 1973; revised edition, London: Heinemann, 1976);

The Good Companions (London: Heinemann, 1929; New York: Harper, 1929);

Farthing Hall, by Priestley and Hugh Walpole (London: Macmillan, 1929; Garden City, N.Y.: Doubleday, Doran, 1929);

The Town Major of Miraucourt (London: Heinemann, 1930);

Angel Pavement (London: Heinemann, 1930; New York & London: Harper, 1930);

Dangerous Corner: A Play in Three Acts (London: Heinemann, 1932; New York, Los Angeles & London: French, 1932);

251

Faraway (London: Heinemann, 1932; New York: Harper, 1932);

The Lost Generation: An Armistice Day Article (London: Peace Committee of the Society of Friends, 1932);

Self-Selected Essays (London: Heinemann, 1932; New York & London: Harper, 1933);

Dangerous Corner: A Novel by Priestley and Ruth Holland (London: Hamilton, 1932);

I'll Tell You Everything, by Priestley and Gerald Bullett (New York: Macmillan, 1932); republished as *I'll Tell You Everything: A Frolic* (London: Heinemann, 1933);

The Roundabout: A Comedy in Three Acts (London: Heinemann, 1933; New York: French, 1933);

Albert Goes Through (London: Heinemann, 1933; New York & London: Harper, 1933);

Wonder Hero (London: Heinemann, 1933; New York & London: Harper, 1933);

Eden End: A Play in Three Acts (London: Heinemann, 1934; New York & Los Angeles: French, 1935);

English Journey: Being a Rambling but Truthful Account of What One Man Saw and Heard and Felt and Thought during a Journey through England during the Autumn of the Year 1933 (London: Heinemann/Gollancz, 1934; New York & London: Harper, 1934);

Laburnum Grove: An Immoral Comedy in Three Acts (London: Heinemann, 1934; New York & Los Angeles: French, 1935);

Four-in-Hand (London: Heinemann, 1934)—comprises *Adam in Moonshine*, *Laburnum Grove*, *The Roundabout*, short stories, and essays;

You and Me and War (London: National Peace Council, 1935);

The Good Companions: A Play in Two Acts, dramatized by Priestley and Edward Knoblock (London, New York & Los Angeles: French, 1935);

Cornelius: A Business Affair in Three Transactions (London & Toronto: Heinemann, 1935; New York & Los Angeles: French, 1936);

Three Plays and a Preface (London: Heinemann, 1935; New York & London: Harper, 1935)—comprises "Preface," *Dangerous Corner: A Play in Three Acts*, *Eden End: A Play in Three Acts*, and *Cornelius: A Business Affair in Three Transactions*;

Duet in Floodlight: A Comedy (London & Toronto: Heinemann, 1935);

Spring Tide, by Priestley (as Peter Goldsmith) and George Billiam (London: Heinemann, 1936);

Bees on the Boatdeck: A Farcical Tragedy in Two Acts (London: Heinemann, 1936);

They Walk in the City: The Lovers in the Stone Forest (London: Heinemann, 1936; New York & London: Harper, 1936);

Time and the Conways: A Play in Three Acts (London: Heinemann, 1937; New York & London: Harper, 1938);

People at Sea: A Play in Three Acts (London: Heinemann, 1937);

Mystery at Greenfingers: A Comedy of Detection (London: French, 1937);

Midnight on the Desert: A Chapter of Autobiography (London & Toronto: Heinemann, 1937); republished as *Midnight on the Desert: Being an Excursion into Autobiography during a Winter in America, 1935-36* (New York & London: Harper, 1937);

I Have Been Here Before: A Play in Three Acts (London: Heinemann, 1937; New York & London: Harper, 1938);

When We are Married: A Yorkshire Farcical Comedy (London: Heinemann, 1938; London & New York: French, 1938);

The Doomsday Men: An Adventure (London: Heinemann, 1938; New York & London: Harper, 1938);

Johnson over Jordan: The Play; and All about It (an Essay) (London & Toronto: Heinemann, 1939; New York & London: Harper, 1939);

Rain upon Godshill: A Further Chapter of Autobiography (London: Heinemann, 1939; New York & London: Harper, 1939);

Let the People Sing (London & Toronto: Heinemann, 1939; New York & London: Harper, 1940);

Postscripts (London & Toronto: Heinemann, 1940); republished as *All England Listened: The Wartime Broadcasts of J. B. Priestley* (New York: Chilmark Press, 1968);

Britain Speaks (New York & London: Harper, 1940);

The Book Crisis, by Priestley, Walpole, Geoffrey Faber, and others, edited by Gilbert McAllister (London: Faber & Faber, 1940);

Out of the People (London: Collins/Heinemann, 1941; New York & London: Harper, 1941);

Britain at War (New York & London: Harper, 1942);

Black-out in Gretley: A Story of and for Wartime (London & Toronto: Heinemann, 1942; New York & London: Harper, 1942);

Daylight on Saturday: A Novel about an Aircraft Factory (London & Toronto: Heinemann, 1943; New York & London: Harper, 1943);

British Women Go to War (London: Collins, 1943);

Three Plays (London: Heinemann, 1943)–comprises *Music at Night, The Long Mirror,* and *They Came to a City*;

The New Citizen (London: Council for Education in World Citizenship, 1944);

Manpower: The Story of Britain's Mobilization for War (London: His Majesty's Stationery Office, 1944);

Desert Highway: A Play in Two Acts and One Interlude (London: Heinemann, 1944);

Here Are Your Answers (London: Common Wealth Popular Library, 1944);

Letter to a Returning Serviceman (London: Home & Van Thal, 1945);

Three Comedies (London: Heinemann, 1945)–comprises *Good Night Children, The Golden Fleece,* and *How Are They at Home?*;

Three Men in New Suits (London & Toronto: Heinemann, 1945; New York & London: Harper, 1945);

Bright Day (London & Toronto: Heinemann, 1946; New York & London: Harper, 1946);

Russian Journey (London: Society for Cultural Relations with the U.S.S.R., 1946);

The Secret Dream: An Essay on Britain, America, and Russia (London: Turnstile Press, 1946);

H. G. Wells (London: Chiswick Press, 1946);

Ever since Paradise: An Entertainment Chiefly Referring to Love and Marriage (London: French, 1946);

The Arts under Socialism: A Lecture Given to the Fabian Society, with a Postscript on What the Government Should Do for the Arts Here and Now (London: Turnstile Press, 1947);

Jenny Villiers: A Story of the Theatre (London & Toronto: Heinemann, 1947; New York: Harper, 1947);

Theatre Outlook (London: Nicholson & Watson, 1947);

An Inspector Calls: A Play in Three Acts (London & Toronto: Heinemann, 1947; London & New York: French, 1948);

The Rose and Crown: A Play in One Act (London: French, 1947);

The High Toby: A Play for the Toy Theatre (Harmondsworth, U.K.: Penguin, 1948);

The Linden Tree: A Play in Two Acts and Four Scenes (London: Heinemann, 1948); republished with *An Inspector Calls* (New York: Harper, 1948);

Plays, 3 volumes (London: Heinemann, 1948-1950; New York: Harper, 1950-1952);

Delight (London: Heinemann, 1949; New York: Harper, 1949);

Home Is Tomorrow: A Play in Two Acts (London: Heinemann, 1949);

The Olympians: Opera in Three Acts, music by Arthur Bliss (London: Novello, 1949);

Bright Shadow: A Play of Detection in Three Acts (London: French, 1950);

Summer Day's Dream: A Play in Two Acts (London: French, 1950);

Going Up: Stories and Sketches (London: Pan, 1950);

Festival at Farbridge (London: Heinemann, 1951); republished as *Festival* (New York: Harper, 1951);

Dragon's Mouth: A Dramatic Quartet in Two Parts, by Priestley and Jacquetta Hawkes (London: Heinemann, 1952; New York: Harper, 1952);

Private Rooms: A One Act Comedy in the Viennese Style (London: French, 1953);

Try It Again: A One Act Play (London: French, 1953);

Mother's Day: A Comedy in One Act (London: French, 1953);

Treasure on Pelican: A Play in Three Acts (London: Evans, 1953);

The Other Place, and Other Stories of the Same Sort (London: Heinemann, 1953; New York: Harper, 1953);

The Magicians (London: Heinemann, 1954; New York: Harper, 1954);

Low Notes on a High Level: A Frolic (London: Heinemann, 1954; New York: Harper, 1954);

A Glass of Bitter: A Play in One Act (London: French, 1954);

Journey down a Rainbow, by Priestley and Hawkes (London: Heinemann/Cresset, 1955; New York: Harper, 1955);

The Scandalous Affair of Mr. Kettle and Mrs. Moon: A Comedy in Three Acts (London: French, 1956);

The Writer in a Changing Society (Aldington, U.K.: Hand and Flower Press, 1956);

All about Ourselves, and Other Essays, edited by Eric Gillett (London: Heinemann, 1956);

Thoughts in the Wilderness (London: Heinemann, 1957; New York: Harper, 1957);

The Art of the Dramatist (London: Heinemann, 1957);

The house at 34 Mannheim Road, Bradford, Yorkshire, where Priestley was born on 13 September 1894

Topside; or The Future of England: A Dialogue (London: Heinemann, 1958);

The Glass Cage: A Play in Two Acts (London: French, 1958);

The Story of Theatre (London: Rathbone, 1959); republished as *The Wonderful World of the Theatre* (Garden City, N.Y.: Garden City Books, 1959); revised and enlarged as *The Wonderful World of the Theatre* (London: Macdonald, 1969; Garden City, N.Y.: Doubleday, 1969);

Literature and Western Man (London: Heinemann, 1960; New York: Harper, 1960);

William Hazlitt (London: Longmans, Green, 1960);

Charles Dickens: A Pictorial Biography (London: Thames & Hudson, 1961; New York: Viking, 1962); republished as *Charles Dickens and His World* (London: Thames & Hudson, 1969; New York: Viking, 1969);

Saturn over the Water: An Account of His Adventures in London, New York, South America, and Australia, by Tim Bedford, Painter; edited, with Some Preliminary and Concluding Remarks, by

Henry Sulgrave; and Here Presented to the Reading Public* (London: Heinemann, 1961; Garden City, N.Y.: Doubleday, 1961);

The Thirty-First of June: A Tale of True Love, Enterprise, and Progress, in the Arthurian and Adatomic Ages (London: Heinemann, 1961; Garden City, N.Y.: Doubleday, 1962);

The Shapes of Sleep: A Topical Tale (London: Heinemann, 1962; Garden City, N.Y.: Doubleday, 1962);

Margin Released: A Writer's Reminiscences and Reflections (London: Heinemann, 1962; New York: Harper & Row, 1962);

Sir Michael and Sir George: A Tale of COSMA and DISCUS and the New Elizabethans (London: Heinemann, 1964); republished as *Sir Michael and Sir George: A Comedy of the New Elizabethans* (Boston: Little, Brown, 1965);

A Severed Head, by Priestley and Iris Murdoch (London: Chatto & Windus, 1964);

Man and Time (London: Aldus, 1964; Garden City, N.Y.: Doubleday, 1964);

Lost Empires: Being Richard Herncastle's Account of His Life on the Variety Stage from November 1913 to August 1914, Together with a Prologue and Epilogue (London: Heinemann, 1965; Boston: Little, Brown, 1965);

Salt Is Leaving (London: Pan, 1966; New York: Harper & Row, 1966);

The Moments, and Other Pieces (London: Heinemann, 1966);

It's an Old Country (London: Heinemann, 1967; Boston: Little, Brown, 1967);

Trumpets over the Sea: Being a Rambling and Egotistical Account of the London Symphony Orchestra's Engagement at Daytona Beach, Florida, in July-August 1967 (London: Heinemann, 1968);

Essays of Five Decades, edited by Susan Cooper (Boston: Little, Brown, 1968; London: Heinemann, 1969);

The Image Men, 2 volumes (London: Heinemann, 1968-1969)—comprises volume 1, *Out of Town*; volume 2, *London End*; republished in 1 volume (Boston: Little, Brown, 1969);

The Prince of Pleasure and His Regency, 1811-20 (London: Heinemann, 1969; New York: Harper & Row, 1969);

The Edwardians (London: Heinemann, 1970; New York: Harper & Row, 1970);

Anton Chekhov (London: International Textbook, 1970);

Snoggle: A Story for Anybody Between 9 and 90 (London: Heinemann, 1971; New York: Harcourt Brace Jovanovich, 1972);

Over the Long High Wall: Some Reflections and Speculations on Life, Death, and Time (London: Heinemann, 1972);

Victoria's Heyday (London: Heinemann, 1972; New York: Harper & Row, 1972);

The English (London: Heinemann, 1973; New York: Viking, 1973);

Outcries and Asides (London: Heinemann, 1974);

A Visit to New Zealand (London: Heinemann, 1974);

Particular Pleasures: Being a Personal Record of Some Varied Arts and Many Different Artists (London: Heinemann, 1975; New York: Stein & Day, 1975);

The Carfitt Crisis, and Two Other Stories (London: Heinemann, 1975; New York: Stein & Day, 1976)–comprises "The Carfitt Crisis," "Underground," and "The Pavilion of Masks";

Found, Lost, Found; or, The English Way of Life (London: Heinemann, 1976; Boston: G. K. Hall, 1976);

The Happy Dream: An Essay (Andoversford, U.K.: Whittington, 1976);

Instead of the Trees: A Final Chapter of Autobiography (London: Heinemann, 1977; New York: Stein & Day, 1977);

Seeing Stratford (Stratford-upon-Avon: Celandine Press, 1982);

If I Ran the B.B.C. (Washington, D.C.: National Association of Broadcasters, n.d.).

OTHER: *Essayists Past and Present*, edited, with an introduction, by Priestley (London: Jenkins, 1925; New York: Dial, 1925);

Fools and Philosophers: A Gallery of Comic Figures from English Literature, edited by Priestley (London: Lane, 1925; New York: Dodd, Mead, 1925);

Thomas Moore, *Tom Moore's Diary*, edited by Priestley (Cambridge: Cambridge University Press, 1925);

The Book of Bodley Head Verse: Being a Selection of Poetry Published at the Bodley Head, edited by Priestley (London: Lane / New York: Dodd, Mead, 1926);

Henry Fielding, *The History of the Adventures of Joseph Andrews and His Friend Mr. Abraham Adams*, introduction by Priestley (London: Lane / New York: Dodd, Mead, 1926);

Fielding, *Tom Jones: The History of a Foundling*, introduction by Priestley (New York: Limited Editions Club, 1931);

Our Nation's Heritage, edited by Priestley (London: Dent, 1939);

Home from Dunkirk: A Photographic Record in Aid of the British Red Cross and St. John, introduction by Priestley (London: Murray, 1940);

Charles Dickens, *Scenes of London Life, from "Sketches by Boz,"* edited by Priestley (London: Pan, 1947);

Stephen Leacock, *The Bodley Head Leacock*, edited by Priestley (London: Bodley Head, 1957);

Four English Novels, edited by Priestley and O. B. Davis (New York: Harcourt, Brace, 1960);

4 English Biographies, edited by Priestley and Davis (New York: Harcourt, Brace & World, 1961);

Adventures in English Literature, edited by Priestley (New York: Harcourt, Brace & World, 1963).

J. B. Priestley's writing career spanned more than seventy years and covered many genres. After war service and Cambridge he became a prolific literary journalist, throughout the 1920s collecting his essays in more or less annual volumes; established himself after two years of more modest novelistic successes with the runaway best-seller *The Good Companions* in 1929; and began a long theatrical career, which included producing as well as writing, with a dramatization of the same novel in 1931. He subsequently wrote some thirty novels, nearly fifty plays, and several screenplays. In wartime his broadcasts helped to strengthen resolve both in England and America, and his concerns became more overtly social and socialist. While the popularity of his dramas and fiction was declining somewhat in the 1950s and after, he turned to writing for more serious journals of social concern and diversified still further into travel writing, social history, and loosely philosophical speculation. An article he wrote for the *New Statesman* was instrumental in the founding of the Campaign for Nuclear Disarmament. He served as a delegate to UNESCO and on the board of the National Theatre; declined a knighthood and a peerage but, in 1977, accepted nomination to the Order of Merit (to which members are named by the monarch rather than the government) and, very belatedly, to the Freedom of the City of Bradford.

John Priestley (he added the middle name Boynton in adult life) was born on 13 September 1894 in the Yorkshire wool-processing and marketing town of Bradford, whose new wealth produced the self-assured millionaires of T. S. Eliot's *The Waste Land* (1922). He said that his mother,

Priestley in 1925 (drawing by Austin; from John Atkins, J. B. Priestley: The Last of the Sages, *1981)*

who died during his infancy, was probably a mill girl; his father, Jonathan Priestley, was also of a working-class family, a background he transcended by becoming a schoolteacher. As well as an impetus for Victorian-style self-improvement, his father provided Priestley with a rigorously moral Baptist religion, which Priestley abandoned in his youth, and a socialist political allegiance that owed little to Marx and much to English nonconformity and working-class independence of spirit and which remained part of his outlook for the rest of his life. North-of-England textile towns in the nineteenth century were breeding grounds of a fierce civic pride which produced a new non-London kind of cultural milieu. Of this milieu Priestley was in some ways the ideal product. Leaving school to work as a clerk in the wool trade, he found relief from the tedium of the office in the improving culture provided by good public libraries, intermittently high-quality theater, and rambunctious music halls. The frequent company of an older man, a poet of minor note, also provided important nurture.

An early start at serious writing, part-time and probably unpaid, for the *Bradford Pioneer,* a Labour party weekly, was interrupted by the outbreak of World War I. Priestley enlisted almost immediately, doubtless in the almost universally shared belief that hostilities would be over in a few weeks. Sent to the front in France in the opening weeks of the war, he endured the mud and boredom and carnage of the trenches before being wounded. A long period of convalescence ended with his elevation to lieutenant and a return to the front, where mustard gas eventually rendered him unfit for further combat. The final phase of his military service was administrative: first he was made a letter censor, then an arranger of entertainments, and finally, on the basis of his slight knowledge of German, he was placed in charge of a prisoner-of-war camp. In the latter role a characteristic insubordination against instructions that would have submitted his charges to needless misery went unpunished.

The war over, Priestley declined his regulation medals and was sent to Cambridge on an educational rehabilitation grant. He did not fit in well because of his class background and northern manner and accent. He quickly dropped out of English literature–he later said some scathing things about university English courses, which were then new at Cambridge–and emerged in 1921, without (he said) having worked particularly hard, with a degree in history. On finishing his degree, he went to work as a university extension lecturer and as a publisher's reader for John Lane. Also in 1921 he married Pat Tempest, an old Bradford friend. With the strain of supporting a new family, Priestley did what writing for money he could.

Priestley's marriage produced two daughters and ended with his wife's death from cancer in 1925. The following year he married Jane Wyndham Lewis, the former wife of the writer D. B. Wyndham Lewis; Priestley had sought solace with her during his first wife's illness, and she had already borne his child. But suspicions that he was unfaithful put great strain on the marriage, which was finally dissolved in 1952, and it seems to have brought Priestley little joy and considerable guilt. For much of his life his relations with women remained complex and unsatisfactory.

Apart from an unexceptional collection of verse, published in 1918 while he was still in uniform and citing his regimental affiliation on the title page, Priestley's first volume was *Brief Diversions* (1922); it was published in Cambridge by Bowes and Bowes, which was more a bookstore than a serious publisher. It contains parodies, of a kind that do not really transcend the standard level of undergraduate humor, of such public figures as William Butler Yeats, A. E. Housman, the flamboyant poet Alfred Noyes, and the popular Cambridge English teacher Sir Arthur Quiller-Couch. Little mercy is shown. On an only slightly higher level, there is a parable of deliberately biblical orotundity: "A certain rich man, having discovered a new method of adulterating milk for babies, determined to celebrate. . . ." Priestley was never to tire of taking such potshots at the rich, the privileged, and the self-important.

He wrote frequently (and anonymously, as was then the practice) for the *Times Literary Supplement* and also for many stylish periodicals of the day: the *London Mercury*, the *Outlook*, the *Cambridge Review*, and the *Challenge*. He wrote for the *Yorkshire Observer* as "Peter of Pomfret," the first of many stock fictional self-characterizations of his own personality. Throughout his long writing career Priestley was an inveterate collector and reprinter of his own essays. The first collection, *Papers from Lilliput*, came in 1922; and the steady stream continued, one every year or two, until more financially rewarding successes with fiction and the theater overtook him.

The informal essay, since much fallen in favor, was at that time still in considerable vogue and had a two-hundred-year ancestry reaching back through Charles Lamb and William Hazlitt to Dr. Johnson, Joseph Addison, Richard Steele, and Jonathan Swift. By Priestley's time the essay could be about anything (or nothing) at all and was the supremely personal genre of writing. Priestley's essays are also a projection of the peculiar qualities of his Englishness and, indeed, frequently feature the enterprise, which lasted his whole life, of giving form to the imponderables that constitute the English character. Priestley's life gave him a strong awareness of cultural variety and diversity–he speaks often of how the Cambridge establishment of his student days saw in him a "northern lout of uncertain temperament"– and much of his literary personality exists at the point of tension that came from being deeply hurt by this sort of thing (while never consciously admitting it) and simultaneously thriving on it. Central to Priestley's sense of Englishness is thus a high valuation–a celebration, almost–of diversity and especially eccentricity.

The pastoral energy of Priestley's essays resides in this enthusiasm for the positive eccentricities of the English, the satirical energy in his attacks on anything and everything that threatens them. Experience of the trenches broke down the conviction that supported many of the traditional social hierarchies of English society, as a whole generation learned to see through the lying, the pomposity, the self-importance, and the organizational incompetence that frequently characterized their superiors. Much of the punch of Priestley's writing comes from this kind of clarity of understanding of the nature of human relations and power structures, and doubtless the social changes the war brought about did much to enlarge the company of those ready to respond eagerly to the peculiar social qualities of his wit. He could write equally well of English quirkiness, of hating strangers, of the merits of dull company, of Humpty-Dumpty or Mr. Micawber, and of the merits of listening to bad pianists. He repeatedly emphasizes the function of humor in the maintenance of a free people: "Were I a despot, I would take care that my country's *Punch* were on my side."

Talking (1926), a single long essay, presents Priestley at his early essay-writing best, showing off just a tad too cleverly (as the British aphorism has it) his broad cultural literacy, pontificating breezily for his own delight and for that of the "knowing" reader–speaking, for example, of Dr. Johnson's "judicial habit of mind: the conclusiveness of his talk. He settled everything too quickly." Priestley's was a milder and more genial version, perhaps, of the kind of criticism as character assassination for the diversion of the sporting public that characterized much nineteenth-century reviewing. Often just a hint of something darker and mildly sinful adds to the reader's delight: "It has been said that there is in all friendship between the sexes, no matter how cool it may appear, a faint erotic element, the ghost of a flirtation." That "there is something like intoxication in the best talk" suggests the spirit in which Priestley wrote–and was read.

Some light is shed on Priestley's essay-writing skills by his book on Hazlitt (1960), which declares Hazlitt the "supreme essayist for young men, bent on writing themselves, to study and devour" and adds, "He was my favorite, my model author, and the only one who directly influenced my writing." Like Priestley, Hazlitt had come from a background of religious nonconformity, was something of a rebel in politics, and had a complex love life: he was "a man who knew what he had to be angry about . . . who celebrated with gratitude and joy every intense moment that pierced the heart and irradiated the spirit."

The 1920s was also the period of a spate of critical books by Priestley: general studies of modern literature (1924), of comic characters (1925), and of the English novel (1927), and works on George Meredith (1926) and Thomas Love Peacock (1927). This part of Priestley's output has to be seen in the context of a now-vanished tradition in which literary criticism held a quasi-literary status, a genre to be read almost for its own sake, and therefore a serious book-publishing money-maker, long before the postwar proliferation of university places made undergraduate casebooks a profitable genre. (Biography is achieving a somewhat similar status today.) The obvious mentor for this genre was its

principal academic practitioner, George Saintsbury, holder of the land's most magnificently endowed chair of English at Edinburgh University and an object of Priestley's fun-poking in *Brief Diversions*.

Priestley's literary allegiances at this point are to a conservative canon of safe literary classics. To echo the title of one book, *the* English comic characters are Touchstone, Falstaff, Parson Adams, the Shandy brothers, Mr. Collins, and Mr. Micawber. To echo another, *the* figures of modern literature are Arnold Bennett, Walter de la Mare, Housman, Saintsbury (significantly, Priestley admires the "sheer bulk of his work"), and Robert Lynd and J. C. Squire (the last two were pillars of the influential literary weekly the *Nation*). There is no budding awareness (at least not in print) at this time of the work of Eliot, of D. H. Lawrence, of James Joyce, or of Virginia Woolf, and this lack of awareness is perhaps indicative of the reason for Priestley's own low status on English literature curricula.

This period of Priestley's life saw him considering and turning down university teaching posts in favor of further work reading for publishers. It also saw his almost meteoric rise as a novelist. *Adam in Moonshine* (1927), his first novel, was followed the same year by *Benighted*, which achieved the bonus of good American sales (so essential to really lucrative writing) and, in 1932, the distinction of a film version under its 1928 American title, *The Old Dark House*. Cooperation with Hugh Walpole, who saw Priestley as "a North Country no-nonsense-about-me-I-know-my-mind kind of man," produced *Farthing Hall* (1929) and earned an advance that gave Priestley the free time to write novels seriously. With *The Good Companions*, a long book about traveling theatrical performers, he achieved real fame and fortune at the age of thirty-five. Sales rose near Christmas to five thousand a day and helped land Priestley a twenty-pounds-a-time book column for the *Evening News* of London. Producing more than sixteen thousand pounds in income in its first two years (roughly one million 1990 dollars in purchasing power), the book was eventually translated into more than twenty languages and was filmed twice. The following year brought the publication of *Angel Pavement*, which perhaps benefited from a relaxation of pressure facilitated by material success and which is often taken to be Priestley's most successful novel. Thirty-odd more novels followed, at regular intervals, down to the late 1960s.

Priestley with his second wife, the former Jane Wyndham Lewis, and their children in 1933 (BBC Hulton)

Priestley's long association with the theater began unpropitiously in 1931 with a stage version of *The Good Companions* (published, 1935) for which Priestley used the services of a collaborator. When the production threatened to close after a few days for want of attendance, Priestley characteristically gambled some of his own resources to keep it running until it effected the turnaround upon which he built his subsequent long run of theatrical successes.

English Journey (1934) is an account of a selective yet systematic tour undertaken to determine the impact of the economic ills of the early 1930s on the common people of different parts of England. The success of the book derives less from its subject than from its relaxed, laid-back style. It is a decidedly odd book, an exercise in a kind of love/hate relationship between the writer and his country and fellow countrymen. It is, on the one hand, pervaded by the eternal optimism that characterizes so much of Priestley's writing. On the other hand, there is something just a touch nasty about it. Again and again one feels that Priestley has gotten the genuine, down-to-earth flavor of the place where he is and the people he has met; but at the same time, so many of the peo-

ple who fall into his company are so pathetic that their dissection at his hands seems cruel and condescending.

Priestley's commercial success was frequently offset by critical ambivalence: Virginia Woolf, for example, caustically called Priestley and Bennett "the tradesmen of letters." This lack of critical acclaim seems to have bothered him enormously; while he frequently claimed that he did not really care, his raising the issue so often demonstrates that he did. The fact is that Priestley, attached as he was to the Victorian tradition of the novel as entertainment, lacked much sense of the dynamics of literary change. Literary experiment in a Priestley novel or play is often limited to problems of storytelling or relationships. The radicalness of Woolf, Joyce, or Eliot is of an altogether different order. Priestley countered critical suggestions that he was second-rate by ostensibly agreeing and going on to describe himself as an honest craftsman making the best of what he was.

In June 1940 a motley of some eight hundred-odd vessels–pleasure boats, river ferries, and fishing smacks–evacuated a third of a million stranded troops from Dunkirk on the north

Priestley delivering one of his "Postscripts" talks over the BBC in 1940 (BBC Hulton)

coast of Nazi-occupied France. The spirit of England tensed and strengthened at the physical defeat and emotional victory implicit in the event. Two days later Priestley was heard after the evening news on the BBC in the first of nineteen talks he gave in the "Postscripts" series (published in book form, 1940), celebrating the "folly and the grandeur of the English people" and speaking in homely terms of the part played by the little pleasure steamers. Priestley had a knack for articulating the subliminal feelings of the ordinary man and for giving a human face to the problems of surviving the tribulations of war; his voice on the radio was, for a while, perhaps second only to Winston Churchill's as a booster of public morale. The contrast between the two could not have been greater. Though the more traditional rhetoric of Churchill's upper-class voice gave shape to the fighting spirit of the nation, Priestley's second broadcast could begin in almost lulling tones: "I don't think there has ever been a lovelier English summer than this last one." The down-to-earth quality of his Yorkshire accent, proverbially a serious social liability in the class-stratified England of the day, would have stood out against the uniform "fixed" southern ac-

cent then enforced on professional radio announcers; its "unofficial" ring may well have done much to help him achieve something like compulsory-listening status for an estimated third of the adult population of the land. He spoke of ordinary experiences, such as going to the cinema or working as a local defense volunteer, and of increasingly all-too-ordinary experiences–of hearing the fire of antiaircraft guns and even of being away, in response to a last-minute speaking request, from a hotel room whose bombing would otherwise have killed him. Always it is the heroism of the unheroic that comes to the fore: "men also have their hour of greatness when weakness suddenly towers into strength; when ordinary easy-going tolerant men rise in their anger and strike down evil like the angels of the wrath of God." Recurrently, the war is conceived as a struggle between despair and hope, power is seen as a substitute for the joy of creation, and the Nazi grasp for dynastic greatness is vilified as "the most violent expression of the despair of the modern world." Priestley shares with his audience what he describes as the open secret of the free: "British spirits rise–to the bewilderment and secret concern of the Nazis."

Priestley's wartime services also included a series of broadcasts for an American audience over the BBC overseas service, published as *Britain Speaks* (1940); readings from his fiction (some specifically composed for oral delivery); and several official publications which could only be called war propaganda materials. The latter group includes the expensively produced *British Women Go to War* (1943), featuring many glossy colored photographs of young ladies, with spotless coveralls and overneat hair, standing serious-faced in the midst of machinery previously touched (and even seen) only by men. The commentary offers, as do all of Priestley's writings of the day, the vision of a transformed future that places the war effort in a wider and more positive context–a context that subsequent events so sadly failed to match up to.

Priestley said in his final "Postscript" that the decision to terminate the highly successful series was solely his; but there is known to have been some official dissatisfaction with his talks, and there likely was, at least later in the war, some proscription or unacceptable attaching of conditions to his broadcasting services. Popular legend that Churchill was instrumental, either through jealousy of Priestley's success or from a sense that the values implied differed too far from his own, remains unproven. Priestley later claimed to have possessed two letters, one from the BBC and one from the ministry of information, each ascribing his dismissal to the other.

One factor in establishment dissatisfaction was undoubtedly the increasingly socialist tone of Priestley's talks and writing. Priestley's humor had always derived from a willingness to turn the classes against each other, to "see through" the trappings of privilege and the pomposity of high position from the perspective of the ordinary man. Socialist concern was implicit in his upbringing and in his youthful writing for the *Bradford Pioneer*; something in the early course of the war seems to have reawakened this somewhat dormant side of his complex personality.

In the 1945 general election Priestley stood as an independent progressive candidate for the anachronistic and since-abolished Cambridge University constituency. That he should run independently while working hard for the Labour cause generally was perhaps due to a desire not to make so absolute a party identification; or perhaps he wished the satisfaction of gaining votes on the prestige of his own name alone. He was, in any case, badly defeated: although he knew all along that the Cambridge seat was so Conservative as to be impossible for him to win, that the successful Tory outpolled him more than ten to one was a bitter blow to his ego.

After the war Priestley wrote several "reconstructionist" pamphlets, generally hortatory and homiletic in tone. *Letter to a Returning Serviceman* (1945) invokes the authority of the author's own trench experience in World War I. Priestley distinguishes in vaguely Marxist terms between the essential nature of man's labor and the shadow-nature of money, and expresses an innocent hope that the war may yet serve a worthwhile purpose if its aftermath brings about at least some hints of a new social order: "Western man now finds himself linked to his fellows." On the other hand, *The Arts under Socialism* (1947) is almost a party piece in its implicit assumption that socialism will be the shape of the future; indeed, the book even begs for protection of the arts from socialism's possible excesses. Priestley is at pains to point out that the state exists for art, not art for the state; that art is integral to society, not an icing on the cake; and that the state cannot bring art about by committee decision or official sponsorship but that it can help art to thrive by creating a climate that cherishes it.

Priestley remained a public figure, connected with what he saw as the causes of the nation. He brags of doing at no cost to the exchequer the work of cultural embassy for which the British Council receives millions of pounds of public money, and of bringing in pounds for England to boot. In the early 1950s he became a director of, and frequent writer for, the *New Statesman*, Britain's premier weekly journal of moderate political dissent. He was an odd choice for such a position: many at the *New Statesman* considered him intellectually somewhat less than completely respectable, and he had attempted to secure the dismissal of the paper's drama critic. He brought to the paper a new note, described in its semiofficial history as "a note of something like a weary contempt for all politicians whatever their party." He helped to restore the tradition of radicalism, somewhat harder for the left-wing paper to maintain after the postwar Labour party electoral landslide replaced its former principal target with a government of moderate socialist persuasion. He also helped the paper to articulate the country's position in a world polarized between two conflicting powers, neither of them England. The Campaign for Nuclear Disarmament began with a Priestley article (2 November 1957) responding to what he saw as the folly of Britain's determination to have the hydrogen bomb: "Our bargaining power is slight; the force of our example might be great."

If his journalism of the period was powerful in its logic and cogent in its topicality, his attempt in *Topside; or The Future of England* (1958) to systematize his vision of what was wrong with society somehow fails to make nearly as much of an appeal to the imagination. Taking a cue from the claim of the *Times* to be read by the top people, Priestley coined the word *topside* to designate the "giant human polyp" of mindless, impersonal forces that direct society in an absence of any kind of vision or leadership. Topside is what prevents society from advancing along the socialist lines Priestley favors; it is a "reaction against a revolution that never happened," a subliminal conspiracy against change or progress that transcends party politics. Ramsay MacDonald, to so many the underminer of the higher purpose of the early Labour governments of which he was the leader, is seen as a man who represented everything and stood for nothing, who gave England a stability it did not need; Stanley Baldwin, in fomenting the Edward VIII abdication crisis, destroyed a king seen by Priestley as capable of releasing energies in the people that topside's miasmal stupidity could not tolerate. Topside, with its emptiness of any belief that might bring positive conversion to itself, is the opposite of the wartime Churchill, to whom the people could respond with everything they were and had.

During a 1935-1936 visit to Hollywood and the Arizona desert Priestley had encountered the unorthodox work of the Russian philosopher-mystic P. D. Ouspensky. The speculative melding of western rationality and eastern intuitionism and the cyclical multidimensional theories of time in Ouspensky's *A New Model of the Universe* (1931) had an immediate influence on Priestley's play *I Have Been Here Before* (1937). The almost-simultaneous *Time and the Conways* (1937), on the other hand, reflected theories about precognitive dreams found in the early aircraft designer J. W. Dunne's *An Experiment with Time* and *The Serial Universe* (1934), the first of which Priestley had reviewed when it appeared in 1927. Late in life Priestley returned more overtly to arcane ideas of time in *Man and Time* (1964), an attempt to correct what he saw as common misconceptions through an examination of time as succession and as a mode of inner evolutionary development. Ostensibly a lavishly illustrated and encyclo-

pedic examination of time, surveying the history of its measurement, its mythology, its science, and man's understanding of it, the book seems to exist for the purpose of lending weight to its speculative final section. This part of the book presents itself as a serious if somewhat amateur attempt to elucidate more adequately our sense of time through the examination of some of Priestley's personal experiences and through an enormous correspondence which resulted from public requests for accounts of "time experiences." The ideas of Dunne, Ouspensky, and Georges Ivanovitch Gurdjieff figure prominently, but the book's aim, at least, is the admirable one of trying to find some pointers to an understanding of time that will help save mankind from its tyranny.

Over the Long High Wall (1972) seems intended as a brief philosophical last will and testament, an attempt to synthesize a systematic approach to the meaning of life and the nature of man's existence in society. Here again the world of dreams and of time is important, culminating in a rather secular sense of immortality as consciousness surviving death. An optimistic view of the individual is matched, as so often in Priestley's advancing years, by a cynical and pessimistic view of society, here spoken of as "a society that appears to dislike itself." Then-current social phenomena, the hippie and women's liberation movements, are discussed in a way that seems to sympathize with the motivations of the movements but not with the social manifestations that resulted. The term "cyanide society," derived from the practice of the suicide-pill-carrying Nazis, is coined to designate the self-destructive tendencies of modern society.

As Priestley's position as a best-selling novelist with a couple of new plays each year waned, his critical perspectives began to do some catching up. *Literature and Western Man* (1960) makes some amends, but there is still some nagging special pleading. Joyce, he says, is "deservedly recognized as one of the masters of the modern movement," but adding that he "created his own magnificent cul-de-sac" suggests that the perpetuation of older traditions of fiction—as practiced by Priestley himself—is still the way forward. And asking if we really need as much of Dublin as Joyce gives us misses something essential in the nature of artistic creation that one perhaps cannot expect from a writer who takes so much of his tone from the environment of the moment. His citing of Woolf's novels as exquisite examples of the

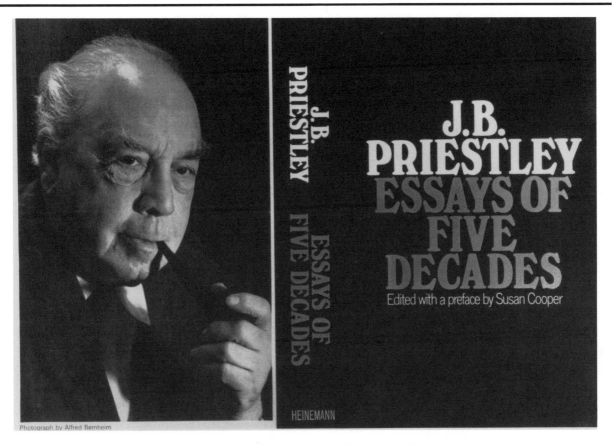

Dust jacket for the 1969 British edition of Priestley's collected essays

deeply subjective method of fiction is still yoked to seeing her rejection of H. G. Wells and Bennett as "arrogantly narrow." He is clearly more interested in Eliot as a man than as a writer. Eliot's prose is seen as the product of a persona which suggests "behind its chilly didacticism an intolerance and arrogance from which Eliot as a man seems quite free." Priestley was at least wise enough to know instinctively that he could never abandon his own roots, and he saw Eliot as imaginatively boxed in by the impossibility of playing a rebel role in his adopted country: he "turned to drama, perhaps to avoid direct and personal speech." In the end Priestley is more at ease with an uncontested classic of long-standing status, such as Alexander Pope, whom he can comfortably pronounce a master "within the strict limits of manner, style, and range of feeling." An article from the 1950s on F. R. Leavis shows some gallantry in its protest against Leavis's faint praise of Woolf as a "slender talent." But Leavis had also told his undergraduates that "no time need be wasted on Priestley." Although Priestley claims to be fully aware that his own literary status is not of the highest order, he is clearly hurt and, in retaliation, declares Leavis not really a literary critic at all but a "sort of Calvinist theologian of popular culture." As far as his own abilities are concerned, Priestley says that culture is a democracy of many talents in which all honest effort counts, not least his own. The Leavisite cultural aristocracy of the very few who can stand up to a rigorous and selective scrutiny is a value that is impenetrable to him. *Anton Chekhov* (1970) makes it clear that Priestley ended as he began–happiest with writers whose work could most easily be subsumed to an examination of their lives.

None of Priestley's accounts of his foreign trips can be counted as travel literature in any conventional sense. *Russian Journey* (1946) can, with hindsight, easily be seen as a preconditioned attempt to see the nation that had been England's rather odd World War II ally in the most positive possible light. Not that the book is at all (at least in the worst 1950s American sense) procommunist; it is not really political at all. Nor does it reward the reader with any sense of Priestley's reactions to the attractions of the cities he visits; they remain largely undescribed and unreacted to. The whole aim is to produce a persuasive picture–

Priestley in 1970

which now seems quite hollow–of a nation of human values and harmony of purpose. "The Russian is," Priestley believes with breathtaking naïveté and innocence, "a born collectivist." *The Secret Dream* (1946), sermonlike and more than a trifle simplistic, finds a Gallic triad of virtues in the three allied nations: British liberty, American equality, and Russian fraternity.

Journey down a Rainbow (1955) was written in collaboration with his third wife, Jacquetta Hawkes, an archaeologist he married in 1953. On one level an account of a visit to New Mexico and Texas, the book is on another an attempt at a diagnosis of an American society caught in a vor-

tex of transition. Priestley's prescriptive analysis is implied in his coining of the pejorative word "admass," by which he designates the spiral of increasing productivity, inflation, and an ever-rising material standard of living. This spiral he sees as the product of high-pressure advertising and salesmanship, accompanied by mass communications and a "cultural democracy" that fails to recognize any real creative achievement. It may be preferable to live in an admass culture than in a state of unemployment, poverty, suffering, and hunger, "but that is about all that can be said in favour of it." Some of the particular detail of Priestley's observation is telling, but more often than not it is vitiated by categorical dislikes: American academics and American girls are recurrent targets. There is too much readiness to put the seal of finality on the judgment that American society is doomed by some inexplicable lethargic torpor: for Priestley, far too much is summed up by a young woman who, while possessing everything that a materialist society values, asks in an unguarded momentary lapse of confidence, "What's the use of all this?"

Priestley's attempts at social analysis seem always to backfire when his subject is not England. *A Visit to New Zealand* (1974), an account of a government junket to generate goodwill, fares even worse than the others. Priestley is trying desperately to be nice, going out of his way above all to find New Zealand preferable to Australia; yet his enthusiasm is weak, and the best he can do is praise the above-average arts subsidies and the perceived absence of criminal riffraff. The overall impression is that although the first day there might be novel and even interesting, on the second or third day one would start to be bored out of one's mind.

In the late 1930s Priestley had written two quasi-autobiographical volumes. Each of these, *Midnight on the Desert* (1937) and *Rain upon Godshill* (1939), was written within the framing device of the place of its composition–a hut in the Arizona desert and the study of his home on the Isle of Wight, respectively. Paying scant attention to chronology and introducing their most interesting revelations in the form of flashback scraps of background detail interspersed into the much-less-relevant present, both depend on the vagaries of memory and dream. Priestley called them "chapters of autobiography," but they are not autobiography in any usual sense. They are, in essence, loose essays about the author thinking about his own past, glimpses into the process of his coming to terms with himself. A third "chapter" appeared in 1977 as *Instead of the Trees*. It follows something of the same time-disjunctive pattern, not so much covering the later part of Priestley's life as providing the medium for a more concerted series of forays back to his early life. Much shorter than the earlier volumes, it is extended in length by the reprinting from the previous year's private-press edition of *The Happy Dream*, a literary birthday present to his wife that sees her, more than a trifle sentimentally, as the answer to all his dreams and desires. *Instead of the Trees* is further extended by a series of typically opinionated "afterthoughts" about topical issues. His one

other autobiographical work, *Margin Released* (1962), is basically a reprint of recollections written for serialization in the *Sunday Times*.

Priestley had two periods of activity producing extended essays for what are usually called coffee-table books, although it must be stressed that his preparation was always thorough and the writing never less than lively and evocative of the spirit of the subject. *The Story of Theatre* (1959) was followed by *Charles Dickens: A Pictorial Biography* (1961), on an author he had always found among the most congenial, and *Man and Time*. His last concerted writing project was a trilogy of social-history books: *The Prince of Pleasure and His Regency, 1811-20* (1969), *The Edwardians* (1970), and *Victoria's Heyday* (1972). The second is perhaps the most interesting in that it charts a period of transition seen from the inside, and with the advantage of half-a-century's hindsight. Priestley sees the Edwardian era as a richly creative decade; he obviously feels deep nostalgia for what the war destroyed, the more so since it was the formative time of his own life. His personal social history is a sidelight in the book: there is, for example, a picture of the house he was born in. *The English* (1973) is an attempt at one of the broadest possible topics, the definition of a nation and its people. *Particular Pleasures* (1975) is perhaps the best of the lot, an anthology of reproduced paintings and of portraits of stage actors and movie stars, each followed by a brief sketch suggesting why Priestley values the work or person depicted. It is a very personal book: the actors section begins with Peggy Ashcroft, for whom Priestley long felt affection and unrequited desire.

A writer who learned early to work quickly and without much revision, Priestley came to wonder whether he had perhaps written too much. Having risen from a humble background through the cultural nourishment of north-of-England culture, he was no natural for acceptance by a south-based establishment; he claimed not to notice or to mind his frequent exclusion, but he obviously did. One of the most materially rewarded writers of any real merit in the twentieth century, he nevertheless craved as well the critical acclaim that the "quality" press reviewers and academia usually withheld or doled out grudgingly. Although he was invited around the world to lecture, it grated on him that no American university of the first rank ever invited him. True to the socialistic spirit of his upbringing, he believed to his dying day in the more equitable distribution of wealth–though he was always sure that his own should not be included in the redistribution– and caustic words about the swingeing level of British taxation were frequently forthcoming. Watching his artistic contemporaries vote against such rake-offs with their feet by immigrating to an appropriate tax haven, he stayed in England until his death on 14 August 1984, well aware of the importance of his roots and of the creative strangulation that would have come from abandoning them. But the England to which he felt allegiance had long since ceased to exist; hence he perpetuated a role that both comforted and distressed him: that of professional grumbler and rebel against a culture and a country he could not live without.

Priestley's devotion to the essay was lifelong, and the prolific novelist published more essay collections than novels. The familiar essay held a special place in his affection; he became an expert on the English familiar essay, and his introduction to the 1925 anthology *Essayists Past and Present* is perhaps the finest of all brief commentaries on the genre. Although the personal essay as it is recognized today began with Montaigne, British writers took it up (after the example of Abraham Cowley) with enthusiasm and gave it a development and a prestige it was never to acquire in France. Obviously the form suited some peculiarly British predilection in expression; in any event, it came to seem indigenously English. It is not surprising that a writer as thoroughly British as Priestley, whose deepest response came when something quickened his sense of his own roots in the long tradition of England's green and pleasant land, should have found the English-adopted personal essay congenial. It suited, as well, his own bent for sociableness and spontaneity, and its accessibility made it all the more welcome for a writer possessed of both multiple interests and a relentless creative drive. In the novel Priestley preferred a *story*, a chronology unfolding from earlier events through later ones toward a prepared-for conclusion. Yet he found the traditional storytelling novel quite difficult, almost too challenging. His many successes owed more to hard crafting and persistence than to narrative facility; by his own admission he often found it excruciatingly difficult to keep a story moving ahead, and even when he turns the trick his novels are, like those of his master, Dickens, more impressive for character, description, humor, and "wisdom" than for neat and exciting narrative technique. The less demanding structure of the

personal essay seemed an immense relief after the challenge of serious fiction.

One of the mainstays of Priestley's fiction is its persistent comedy–Priestley is a worthy successor to Henry Fielding and Dickens; but even if he had written no fiction his essays would entitle him to a place within the first rank of British humorists. In fact, the early essays actually establish him as a fine humorist, not as a master essayist, and even in the earliest essays (for example, "On a Mouth-Organ" or "An Apology for Bad Pianists" in *Papers from Lilliput*) the comedy is often of the same high quality that is to be found in the best of his later work. Reasonably honest and accurate in self-assessment, Priestley nevertheless is not to be accepted uncritically when he evaluates his own work. He frequently errs on the side of modesty and self-deprecation. From the following remarks in *Margin Released* one would neither be tempted to read the early essays nor suspect the thoughtful hilarity they frequently offer: "The early essays I wrote . . . were mostly literary exercises. There was nothing much I really wanted to say, but for some years I took great pains with these pieces, like a man learning to play an instrument. Though I kept right on into the thirties writing weekly essays, for . . . the *Saturday Review* . . . and then . . . the *Week End Review* . . . I knew that this kind of essay, personal in tone but elaborately composed, was already almost an anachronism. It had had an Indian summer in the period 1900-1914, when newspapers still published essays."

"There was nothing much I really wanted to say . . .": here Priestley not only leaves unmentioned his early achievement in laughter of a type that implies humanistic wisdom, but he refrains from claiming what could legitimately be claimed: that in these early pieces the "anachronistic" element–the Edwardian/early Georgian tonality–is itself something to say, a faithful evocation of a vanishing world of unhurriedness, gracefulness, and personal touch. For all his fascination with "ideas"–social, cultural, political, economic, psychological, aesthetic–Priestley well knew that all deeper "Edwardianism" is worth saying, being directly relevant to humane values of personal and social well-being. On its lighter and more ephemeral side, Priestley's Edwardianism is another of his contributions to comedy, understood in the older sense of that which is pleasant rather than the reverse. The anachronistic streak in Priestley persisted and at least held its own against his more forward-looking tendencies. Explicit as well as implicit celebration of vanished eras (*Lost Empires* is the title of a 1965 novel) is a constantly recurring motif in his later work. Much of the literature on Priestley has been written by people far more modernist and progressivist and dry-eyed than the loyalist of the Yorkshire sheep country; their portraits often need to be corrected. It is impossible to conceal Priestley the nostalgist, the poet of the past; it is not going too far to say that all of his social criticism is characterized by a constant awareness that "character" has been going rapidly out of modern man and that politics, on all sides of the spectrum, seems bound to a consumerist and trivialist mentality that contrasts with the social and political idealism of the nineteenth century and with the inspiriting personalism that persisted even into the 1920s and 1930s.

Priestley is one of the few writers who continued to produce distinguished familiar essays after World War II had created both a mood and an economy inimical to the belletristic tradition. Even Priestley's own periodical essays show a certain change after 1940: they reflect the new era's preference for addressing "serious" (meaning topical) issues, particularly social and political ones. More than a few essays Priestley published in the 1950s and 1960s are, in the main, polemics for British radicalism, not familiar essays in the tradition of Montaigne and Lamb. But this reflection of the latter twentieth century's politicizing of life and letters is only a tendency in Priestley; many of the later essays are as charmingly and intensely personal and as apolitical as any in *Apes and Angels* or *Papers from Lilliput*. *Delight* (1949) is a book-length essay subdivided into 114 smaller essays on people, places, and things that at one time or another had brought Priestley that most apolitical of emotions. *Particular Pleasures* is domi-

nated by a similar spirit. In between the two is *Outcries and Asides* (1974), 200 pieces of table talk of which many are miniature essays, and all are full of spirited good sense–Priestley is nowhere more stimulating or more essayistic in the sense of taking an informal and unpretentious "try" at a subject.

Bibliography:

Alan Edwin Day, *J. B. Priestley: An Annotated Bibliography* (New York: Garland, 1980).

Biography:

Vincent Brome, *J. B. Priestley* (London: Hamilton, 1988).

References:

John Atkins, *J. B. Priestley: The Last of the Sages* (London: Calder, 1981; New York: Riverrun Press, 1981);

John Braine, *J. B. Priestley* (London: Weidenfeld & Nicolson, 1978);

Asa Briggs, *The History of Broadcasting in the United Kingdom*, volume 3 (London: Oxford University Press, 1970);

Susan Cooper, *J. B. Priestley: Portrait of an Author* (London: Heinemann, 1970);

A. A. DeVitis and Albert E. Kalson, *J. B. Priestley* (Boston: G. K. Hall, 1980);

David Hughes, *J. B. Priestley: An Informal Study of His Work* (London: Hart-Davis, 1958);

Edward Hyams, *The New Statesman: The History of the First Fifty Years 1913-1963* (London: Longmans, Green, 1963);

Evelyn Waugh, "Anything Wrong with Priestley?," in *A Little Order: A Selection of his Journalism*, edited by Donat Gallagher (London: Eyre Methuen, 1977);

Kenneth Young, *J. B. Priestley*, Writers and Their Work, no. 257 (London: Longmans Group for the British Council, 1977).

Bertrand Russell
(18 May 1872 - 2 February 1970)

Ralph Stewart
Acadia University

SELECTED BOOKS: *German Social Democracy* (London, New York & Bombay: Longmans, Green, 1896; New York: Simon & Schuster, 1965);

An Essay on the Foundations of Geometry (Cambridge: Cambridge University Press, 1897; New York: Dover, 1956);

A Critical Exposition of the Philosophy of Leibniz: With an Appendix of Leading Passages (Cambridge: Cambridge University Press, 1900); republished as *The Philosophy of Leibniz* (New York: Macmillan, 1937);

The Principles of Mathematics (Cambridge: Cambridge University Press, 1903; New York: Norton, 1937);

Philosophical Essays (London: Allen & Unwin, 1910; revised, 1966; New York: Simon & Schuster, 1966);

Principia Mathematica, 3 volumes, by Russell and Alfred North Whitehead (Cambridge: Cambridge University Press, 1910-1913);

The Problems of Philosophy (London: Williams & Norgate, 1912; New York: Holt, 1912);

War, the Offspring of War (London: Union of Democratic Control, 1914);

Our Knowledge of the External World as a Field for Scientific Method in Philosophy (London: Allen & Unwin, 1914; Chicago: Open Court, 1914);

The Philosophy of Pacifism (London: League of Peace and Freedom, 1915);

Justice in War-Time (Chicago & London: Open Court, 1916; London: Allen & Unwin, 1916);

Principles of Social Reconstruction (London: Allen & Unwin, 1916); republished as *Why Men Fight; A Method of Abolishing the International Duel* (New York: Century, 1917);

Political Ideals (New York: Century, 1917; London: Allen & Unwin, 1963);

Mysticism and Logic, and Other Essays (London: Allen & Unwin, 1917; Garden City, N.Y.: Doubleday, 1917);

Roads to Freedom: Socialism, Anarchism and Syndicalism (London: Allen & Unwin, 1918); repub-

Bertrand Russell (Gale International Portrait Gallery)

lished as *Proposed Roads to Freedom: Socialism, Anarchism and Syndicalism* (New York: Holt, 1919);

Introduction to Mathematical Philosophy (London: Allen & Unwin, 1919; New York: Macmillan, 1919);

The Practice and Theory of Bolshevism (London: Allen & Unwin, 1920); republished as *Bolshevism: Practice and Theory* (New York: Harcourt, Brace & Howe, 1920);

The Analysis of Mind (London: Allen & Unwin, 1921; New York: Macmillan, 1921);

Free Thought and Official Propaganda (New York: Huebsch, 1922; London: Allen & Unwin, 1922);

The Problem of China (London: Allen & Unwin, 1922; New York: Century, 1922);

The Prospects of Industrial Civilization, by Russell and Dora Russell (New York: Century, 1923; London: Allen & Unwin, 1923);

The ABC of Atoms (New York: Dutton, 1923; London: Paul, 1923);

Icarus; or, The Future of Science (New York: Dutton, 1924; London: Kegan Paul, 1924);

How to Be Free and Happy (New York: Rand School of Social Science, 1924);

Bolshevism and the West, by Russell and Scott Nearing (London: Allen & Unwin, 1924);

What I Believe (New York: Dutton, 1925; London: Kegan Paul, 1925);

The ABC of Relativity (New York & London: Harper, 1925; London: Kegan Paul, 1925);

On Education, Especially in Early Childhood (London: Allen & Unwin, 1926); republished as *Education and the Good Life* (New York: Boni & Liveright, 1926);

Why I Am Not a Christian (London: Watts, 1927; Girard, Kans.: Haldeman-Julius, 1929);

The Analysis of Matter (New York: Harcourt, Brace, 1927; London: Kegan Paul, Trench, Trubner, 1927);

An Outline of Philosophy (London: Allen & Unwin, 1927); republished as *Philosophy* (New York: Norton, 1927);

Selected Papers of Bertrand Russell (New York: Modern Library, 1927);

Sceptical Essays (New York: Norton, 1928; London: Allen & Unwin, 1928);

Marriage and Morals (New York: Liveright, 1929; London: Allen & Unwin, 1929);

Has Religion Made Useful Contributions to Civilization?: An Examination and a Criticism (London: Watts, 1930; Girard, Kans.: Haldeman-Julius, n.d.);

The Conquest of Happiness (New York: Liveright, 1930; London: Allen & Unwin, 1930);

The Scientific Outlook (New York: Norton, 1931; London: Allen & Unwin, 1931);

Education and the Social Order (London: Allen & Unwin, 1932); republished as *Education and the Modern World* (New York: Norton, 1932);

Freedom and Organization 1814-1914 (London: Allen & Unwin, 1934); republished as *Freedom versus Organization 1812-1914* (New York: Norton, 1934);

Religion and Science (New York: Holt, 1935; London: Butterworth-Nelson, 1935);

In Praise of Idleness and Other Essays (New York: Norton, 1935; London: Allen & Unwin, 1935);

Which Way to Peace? (London: Joseph, 1936);

Alys Pearsall Smith Russell in 1897; she had married Russell in 1894

Power: A New Social Analysis (New York: Norton, 1938; London: Allen & Unwin, 1938);

An Inquiry into Meaning and Truth (New York: Norton, 1940; London: Allen & Unwin, 1940);

How to Become a Philosopher: The Art of Rational Conjecture (Girard, Kans.: Haldeman-Julius, 1942);

How to Become a Logician: The Art of Drawing Inferences (Girard, Kans.: Haldeman-Julius, 1942);

How to Become a Mathematician: The Art of Reckoning (Girard, Kans.: Haldeman-Julius, 1942);

How to Read and Understand History: The Past as the Key to the Future (Girard, Kans.: Haldeman-Julius, 1943);

An Outline of Intellectual Rubbish: A Hilarious Catalogue of Organized and Individual Stupidity (Girard, Kans.: Haldeman-Julius, 1943);

A History of Western Philosophy: Its Connection with Political and Social Circumstances from the Earliest Times to the Present Day (New York: Simon & Schuster, 1945; London: Allen & Unwin, 1946);

Ideas That Have Helped Mankind (Girard, Kans.: Haldeman-Julius, 1946);

Ideas That Have Harmed Mankind (Girard, Kans.: Haldeman-Julius, 1946);

Physics and Experience (London: Cambridge University Press, 1946; New York: Macmillan, 1946);

Philosophy and Politics (London: Cambridge University Press, 1947);

Human Knowledge: Its Scope and Limits (London: Allen & Unwin, 1948; New York: Simon & Schuster, 1948);

Values in the Atomic Age (London: Allen & Unwin, 1949);

Authority and the Individual (London: Allen & Unwin, 1949; New York: Simon & Schuster, 1949);

Unpopular Essays (London: Allen & Unwin, 1950; New York: Simon & Schuster, 1950);

New Hopes for a Changing World (London: Allen & Unwin, 1951; New York: Simon & Schuster, 1951);

The Impact of Science on Society (London: Allen & Unwin, 1952; New York: Simon & Schuster, 1953);

How Near Is War? (London: Ridgway, 1952);

Dictionary of Mind, Matter, and Morals (New York: Philosophical Library, 1952);

What Is Freedom? (London: Batchworth Press, 1952);

What Is Democracy? (London: Batchworth Press, 1953);

The Good Citizens Alphabet (London: Gaberbocchus Press, 1953; New York: Philosophical Library, 1958);

Satan in the Suburbs and Other Stories (New York: Simon & Schuster, 1953; London: Lane, 1953);

History as an Art (Aldington, U.K.: Hand and Flower Press, 1954);

Nightmares of Eminent Persons and Other Stories (London: Lane, 1954; New York: Simon & Schuster, 1954);

Human Society in Ethics and Politics (London: Allen & Unwin, 1954; New York: Simon & Schuster, 1955);

Logic and Knowledge (London: Allen & Unwin, 1956; New York: Macmillan, 1956);

Portraits from Memory and Other Essays (London: Allen & Unwin, 1956; New York: Simon & Schuster, 1956);

Understanding History and Other Essays (New York: Philosophical Library, 1957);

Why I Am Not a Christian and Other Essays on Religion and Related Subjects (London: Allen & Unwin, 1957; New York: Simon & Schuster, 1957);

The Will to Doubt (New York: Philosophical Library, 1958; London: Allen & Unwin, 1958);

Bertrand Russell's Best: Silhouettes in Satire (London: Allen & Unwin, 1958; New York: New American Library, 1958);

Common Sense and Nuclear Warfare (London: Allen & Unwin, 1959; New York: Simon & Schuster, 1960);

My Philosophical Development (London: Allen & Unwin, 1959; New York: Simon & Schuster, 1959);

Wisdom of the West: A Historical Survey of Western Philosophy in Its Social and Political Setting, edited by Paul Foulkes (London: Macdonald, 1959; Garden City, N.Y.: Doubleday, 1959);

Bertrand Russell Speaks His Mind (Cleveland & New York: World, 1960; London: Barker, 1960);

The Basic Writings of Bertrand Russell, edited by Robert E. Egner and Lester E. Denonn (London: Allen & Unwin, 1961; New York: Simon & Schuster, 1961);

Fact and Fiction (London: Allen & Unwin, 1961; New York: Simon & Schuster, 1962);

Has Man a Future? (London: Allen & Unwin, 1961; New York: Simon & Schuster, 1962);

History of the World in Epitome (London: Gaberbocchus Press, 1962);

Unarmed Victory (London: Allen & Unwin, 1963; New York: Simon & Schuster, 1963);

War and Atrocity in Vietnam (London: Bertrand Russell Peace Foundation, 1965);

War Crimes in Vietnam (London: Allen & Unwin, 1967; New York: Monthly Review Press, 1967);

The Autobiography of Bertrand Russell, 3 volumes (volume 1, London: Allen & Unwin, 1967; Boston: Little, Brown, 1967; volume 2, London: Allen & Unwin, 1968; Boston: Little, Brown, 1968; volume 3, London: Allen & Unwin, 1969; New York: Simon & Schuster, 1969);

The Art of Philosophizing and Other Essays (New York: Philosophical Library, 1968);

Russell's Logical Atomism, edited by David Pears (London: Fontana, 1972);

The Life of Bertrand Russell in Pictures and His Own Words, edited by Christopher Farley and David Hodgson (Nottingham, U.K.: Bertrand Russell Peace Foundation, 1972);

The Free Man's Worship.

To Dr Faustus in his study Mephistopheles told the history of the Creation, saying:

"The endless praises of the choirs of angels had begun to grow wearisome; for, after all, did he not deserve their praise? Had he not given them endless joy? Would it not be more amusing to obtain undeserved praise, to be worshipped by beings whom he tortured? He smiled inwardly, & resolved that the great drama should be performed.

"For countless ages the hot nebula whirled aimlessly through space. At length it began to take shape, the central mass threw off planets, the planets cooled, boiling seas & burning mountains heaved & tossed, from black masses of cloud hot sheets of rain deluged the barely solid crust. And now the first germ of life grew in the depths of the ocean, & developed rapidly, in the fructifying warmth, into vast forest trees, huge ferns springing from the damp mould, sea-monsters breeding, fighting, devouring, & passing away. And from the monsters, as the play unfolded itself, man was born, with the power of thought, the knowledge of good & evil, & the cruel thirst for worship. And man saw that all is passing in this mad monstrous world, that all is struggling to snatch, at any cost, a few brief moments of life before Death's inexorable decree. And man said: "There is a hidden

First page of the manuscript for Russell's best-known essay, which has usually been published with the title "A Free Man's Worship" (Bertrand Russell Archives at McMaster University)

My Own Philosophy (Hamilton, Ont.: McMaster University Library Press, 1972);

Atheism (New York: Arno Press, 1972);

The Collected Stories of Bertrand Russell, edited by Barry Feinberg (London: Allen & Unwin, 1972; New York: Simon & Schuster, 1973);

Essays in Analysis, edited by Douglas Lackey (London: Allen & Unwin, 1973; New York: Braziller, 1973);

Mortals and Others: Bertrand Russell's American Essays 1931-1935, edited by Harry Ruja (London: Allen & Unwin, 1975);

The Collected Papers of Bertrand Russell, McMaster University Edition, edited by Kenneth Blackwell and others, 3 volumes to date (London: Allen & Unwin, 1983-   ).

SELECTED PERIODICAL PUBLICATIONS—
UNCOLLECTED: "The Russell Memorandum: Relationship with Ralph Schoenman," *New Statesman*, 80 (11 September 1970): 292-296;

"How Russell Wrote," *Russell: The Journal of the Bertrand Russell Archives*, 8 (1972-1973): 13-15.

Bertrand Russell is best known to the general public as a political writer and activist, and to the learned world as a mathematician and philosopher. In the former role he was famous, or perhaps notorious; in the latter he was one of the most distinguished men of the twentieth century. It is not at all surprising that Russell's more specialized works in mathematics, philosophy, and politics have overshadowed what is of general interest and may be considered as literature. He was, however, one of the best essayists of his period.

Russell's career was abnormally long. Few writers have the opportunity to write a new preface for a book composed seventy years before, as Russell did for *German Social Democracy* (published in 1896 and 1965), and presumably no other critic of the Vietnam War of the late 1960s was able to approach it with memories of the British-Afghan war of 1878. Russell's immediate awareness of the past was extended further backward by family connections. He was brought up in the house of his grandfather, Lord John Russell, who was a member of Parliament at the time of Waterloo and was afterward twice prime minister of Britain. Lord John Russell was also a writer and appears in the *Oxford Companion to English Literature* (his grandson was not included until the 1967 edition). At his grandfather's

house Russell met many notable people; his earliest debating triumph, and not his least, was silencing the poet Robert Browning. "I exclaimed in a piercing voice, 'I wish that man would stop talking.' And he did." Dining at the house of his maternal grandmother must also have been useful preparation for his controversial career. His four uncles—an Anglican, an agnostic, a Catholic priest, and a Mohammedan—argued with one another incessantly.

Bertrand Arthur William Russell was born on 18 May 1872 at Ravenscroft, the home of his parents, Lord and Lady Amberley, in south Wales. His maternal grandfather was Lord Stanley of Alderney. The Russells and Stanleys have been distinguished for about five hundred years, and Russell himself was to succeed to an earldom. Family expectations were high, and as a child Russell was disappointed in his great-uncle, the Honorable Sir Charles Elliot, K.C.B. "I was told that he was Rear Admiral and that there is a grander sort of admiral called Admiral of the Fleet. This rather pained me and I felt he should have done something about it." One's ancestors and family are presumably important if one is aware of them and reacts to the traditions they established—as Russell says in *Marriage and Morals* (1929), people called Darwin will tend to make the most of whatever scientific ability they possess. It is significant that both Lord John and Bertrand Russell were less proud of the many successful men of war, commerce, state administration, and diplomacy in the family than of the William Russell who was executed in 1683 as rebel to the king. Russell was also made aware that he was descended from Scotch Covenanters on his father's side and Irish Jacobites on his mother's—both groups with a strong preference for martyrdom rather than compromise.

Russell's distinguished family background could not save him from a tragic early childhood and unhappy adolescence. When he was two his mother and sister died of diphtheria, and eighteen months later his father also died. The two atheists whom Russell's parents had appointed as guardians were set aside, and Bertrand and his brother Frank went to stay with Lord and Lady Russell at their house in Richmond Park, near London. Frank, who was seven years older, was sent to school, but Bertrand lived with his grandmother (Lord John died in 1878) and a succession of tutors until shortly before going to Cambridge University. Many of Lady Russell's family and friends were dead, and she tended to live in

Campaign photograph of Russell taken during his unsuccessful attempt at winning a seat in Parliament, 1907
(Bertrand Russell Archives at McMaster University)

the past. She was a Scotch Presbyterian, and breakfast was preceded by prayers, piano practice, and a cold bath. On the positive side, she helped Russell to acquire a deep feeling for history–almost as strong a passion with him as mathematics and philosophy–and strengthened his independence. Her favorite biblical text, "Thou shalt not follow a multitude to do evil," might also stand as her grandson's motto.

Initially, Russell had difficulty learning multiplication tables, and in algebra he thought his tutor was refusing to divulge what "x" and "y" stood for out of sheer perversity. Geometry was also disappointing, because it was based on unproven axioms. In his teens, however, mathematics became an absorbing interest; indeed, he later believed that only the desire to learn more of it prevented him from committing suicide. His depression appears to have stemmed from sexual

frustration and guilt, combined with religious doubts which culminated in atheism. There are moving passages in his diary of the period, where he records the penalties of seeking truth at all costs. But he concludes: "One ought perhaps to look upon all these things as a martyrdom, since very often truth attained by one man may lead to the increase in the happiness of many others though not to his own. On the whole I am inclined to continue to pursue truth. . . ." By the time he went to Cambridge in 1890 his mind was more settled. He studied mathematics for three years and philosophy for one, and greatly enjoyed the new intellectual challenges and opportunities for friendship. On graduating, he proposed to Alys Pearsall Smith, the daughter of Philadelphia Quakers who had settled in England; he had been in love with her for two years. Russell's family bitterly opposed the match, but they were married in December 1894.

273

The couple then spent three months in Berlin. "I remember," he says in his autobiography (1967-1969), "a cold, bright day in early spring when I walked by myself in the Tiergarten, and made projects of future work. I thought that I would write one series of books on the philosophy of the sciences from pure mathematics to physiology, and another series of books on social questions. I hoped that the two series might ultimately meet in a synthesis at once scientific and practical." This projection is, in fact, an approximate guide to Russell's career; although the ultimate synthesis never materialized, his ability to combine historical knowledge, political observation, and theoretical analysis is apparent from the beginning in *German Social Democracy*. Apart from innumerable articles, he was to publish eighty or ninety books (depending on what one counts as a book). About one-third of the books are technical–on mathematics, philosophy, or specific scientific ideas–although admittedly Russell has a knack of making abstruse subjects interesting to the layman. About half are political and social, giving the reasons for the existing state of society and the ways it should be reorganized. The technical work tended to come earlier in Russell's career and the political writings later, although as late as *Human Knowledge: Its Scope and Limits* (1948) Russell was still developing new ideas in philosophy. Setting aside the more technical and social books leaves about a dozen that are approximately literary in form–the autobiographies, fiction, and perhaps seven books made up of essays of general interest: *Mysticism and Logic, and Other Essays* (1917), *Sceptical Essays* (1928), *In Praise of Idleness and Other Essays* (1935), *Unpopular Essays* (1950), *Portraits from Memory and Other Essays* (1956), *Why I Am Not a Christian and Other Essays on Religion and Related Subjects* (1957), and *Fact and Fiction* (1961). As the publication dates suggest, each book represents several years' accumulation. (*Why I Am Not a Christian* spans more than fifty years.) Such essays were written infrequently, by Russell's standards, and may be seen as by-products of his central interests.

Russell was happily married until 1902, when, according to his own account, he suddenly realized that he no longer loved Alys and did not wish to stay with her. They lived together miserably for nine more years, however, until Russell left and began an affair with Lady Ottoline Morrell. In the unhappy years of his marriage he devoted himself mainly to his greatest mathematical work. *Principia Mathematica* (1910-1913), writ-ten in collaboration with Alfred North Whitehead, attempts to give a logical justification for all the basic mathematical axioms. Russell points out, not without pride, that the book was an even greater financial flop than Milton's *Paradise Lost*.

Most of his writings of this period are too technical to appeal to the general reader. Admittedly the distinction between specialized work and literature–always vague with expository prose–is especially so in many of Russell's essays, for he is as clear and readable as the subject allows. In *Philosophical Essays* (1910), for example, he considers the theory of pragmatism, that a belief is true if it is useful, and imagines a pragmatist in action in the British Museum: "We can imagine some person long engaged in a comparative study of libraries, and having, in the process, naturally lost all taste for reading, declaring that the catalogue is the only important thing–as for the books, they are useless lumber; no one ever wants them, and the principle of economy should lead us to be content with the catalogue. Indeed, if you consider the matter with an open mind, you will see that the catalogue *is* the library, for it tells you everything you can possibly wish to know about the library. Let us, then, save the taxpayers' money by destroying the books: allow free access to the catalogue, but condemn the desire to read as involving an exploded dogmatic realism." This passage might well be from a literary essay. Analogy and irony are literary devices (and may be extended into the literary forms of allegory or satire), and the irony here is consistent. The pragmatist, who considers himself sensible, advanced, and open-minded, is parodied as a self-righteous bigot. This example may suggest that Russell is most literary when most insulting, which is at least partly true; irony is his natural mode.

Such passages are, however, atypical of the essays they appear in, where the writing is generally more abstract and specialized and constitutes well-written philosophy rather than literature. The only exceptions are the first four essays in *Mysticism and Logic*, written between 1903 and 1914, and perhaps the short essay "On History" in the second edition of *Philosophical Essays* (1966). The title essay of *Mysticism and Logic* is more wide-ranging than most of Russell's work because it discusses mystic (intuitive) apprehension of reality as well as rational analysis. Russell naturally considers the latter paramount, but he is sympathetic to mysticism because it represents the claims of human emotion, and in particular the

Lady Ottoline Morrell, with whom Russell had an affair that lasted from 1911 until 1916
(Bertrand Russell Archives at McMaster University)

sense of good and evil. Throughout much of his career Russell tried–ultimately without success–to integrate mysticism and logic so as to give ethics a solid intellectual-philosophical base. Here he skirts the problem by suggesting that a purely rational or scientific approach to reality automatically incorporates a higher ethical standpoint. He was to change his mind on this point. "The Study of Mathematics" and "The Place of Science in a Liberal Education" argue for the value of math and science in shaping generally desirable habits of mind, quite apart from their usefulness in developing technology. In style, they are as clear, precise, and persuasive as Russell's later essays, but they differ in conveying serenity rather than tension. They celebrate the world of pure intellect as opposed to the compromises of ordinary life; this world is associated with vaguely classical images, such as a Greek temple and an Italian palace.

"On History" in *Philosophical Essays* also praises the kind of abstract learning that enlarges the imagination. In the second half of the essay, however, Russell moves into an entirely different style, heavy in alliteration, rhythm, and imagery: "Through unnumbered generations, forgotten sons worshipped at the tombs of forgotten fathers, forgotten mothers bore warriors whose bones whitened the silent steppes of Asia." Some of the purple passages are moving, but the overall effect is rather incomplete and unsatisfactory. Russell often seems to assume that a statement becomes true if it is loaded with enough emotion. "The past alone is truly real. . . . Only the dead exist fully."

The best known of Russell's essays in this romantic-rhetorical style, and the most accomplished, is the atheist's sermon "A Free Man's Worship" in *Mysticism and Logic, and Other Essays*. The ideas running through it are that life is a tragedy

Lady Constance Malleson (usually known by her stage name, Colette O'Niel), who was Russell's mistress from 1916 to 1920 (Bertrand Russell Archives at McMaster University)

but we should play out our parts, that we should worship truth and not power (for the latter leads to cruelty), and that there are some absolutes in the life of the mind–truth, beauty, and the world of the past. In this consistent and unified essay the extended descriptions and metaphors–such as sacrificing to Moloch, the cavern of despair, the citadel of Tragedy, the march of life–convey intense feeling. The language is strained and the images derivative; the cavern of despair, for example, owes a lot to Plato's metaphor of the cave. Russell has said that at this period he was influenced by the late-Victorian essayist Walter Pater, and also by seventeenth-century authors such as Milton, Thomas Browne, and Jeremy Taylor. Pater's influence helps to explain the rather self-conscious aestheticism. As regards the seventeenth-century authors, Russell does reproduce some of their cadences and syntax, and his

themes and metaphors would be familiar to them, but his writing is much less concrete and controlled. Russell himself later eschewed the style as too rhetorical, but it continues to appear, somewhat diluted, in the conclusions of many of his books.

World War I was the most political period of Russell's life until old age. He had already campaigned strongly for women's suffrage, stood for Parliament in 1907, and supported the Liberals in the election of 1910 against the power of the House of Lords (he never changed his mind on this issue), but these campaigns did not absorb him in the same way as his pacifist activities did: "when the war came I felt as if I heard the voice of God. I knew that it was my business to protest, however futile protest might be. My whole nature was involved." He opposed going to war with Germany in the first place, and then worked for an early peace treaty and against compulsory military service (he was himself too old to be conscripted). In 1916 he was convicted of writing a leaflet protesting the imprisonment of a conscientious objector and, as a consequence, dismissed from the lectureship at Trinity College, Cambridge, which he had held since 1910. This was a considerable blow, as Cambridge had become his home in every sense. The government then prevented him from leaving Britain to lecture at Harvard. Russell later felt that his pacifist speeches and articles were becoming ineffectual, and he devoted more time to philosophy. Ironically, he was then jailed for six months for writing, as he recalled in his autobiography, that the American army, "whether or not they will prove efficient against the Germans, will no doubt be capable of intimidating strikers, an occupation to which the American Army is accustomed when at home." He did get permission to read and write in prison, and there he composed *Introduction to Mathematical Philosophy* (1919) and part of *The Analysis of Mind* (1921).

In the decade from 1911 to 1921 his personal life was confused but less unhappy. Lady Ottoline would not leave her husband for Russell, and their affair lapsed, though they remained close friends. In 1916 Russell met Lady Constance Malleson, usually known by her stage name of Colette O'Niel, and they had a stormy relationship for the next four years. Their main reason for not marrying was, perhaps, that Russell badly wanted children and Colette did not. He then became involved in an up-and-down affair with Dora Black. They visited Russia and quarreled bitterly over the Communist government, which Russell detested; but then they set out for a year in China together—although, according to their daughter, the invitation came from a gentleman with the unpromising name of Fu Ling Yu. Russell wanted marriage and children, Dora children only. Russell finally got his way, and they were married in September 1921, seven weeks before the birth of John Conrad Russell.

It is curious that Russell named both his sons after the same man (Conrad Sebastian was born in 1937) and even more curious that the man was Joseph Conrad, the novelist. Conrad was a Pole with no faith in political movements, and one would not expect him to have much in common with Russell beyond hatred of Russia. Yet Russell admired Conrad greatly; he seems to have shared, at least much of the time, Conrad's deeply pessimistic view of human life, above all

his sense of the isolation and loneliness of each individual. In a brief essay on Conrad in *Portraits from Memory and Other Essays* Russell recounts Conrad's story "Amy Foster" (1901), in which a foreigner is abandoned in England: "He dies alone and hopeless. I have wondered at times how much of this man's loneliness Conrad had felt among the English." Despite his family background, Russell must often have felt similarly isolated. He never wavered from the Puritan tenet, held by Lady Russell, that one should follow one's own light and distrust the multitude's; but, especially during World War I, when he was widely considered a traitor, he paid a heavy price. This tenet, which colors many of his beliefs and attitudes, can be associated with his temperamental preference for anarchism. Perhaps the most fundamental assumption of his many books on political ideas, beginning with *Principles of Social Reconstruction* (published in the United States as *Why Men Fight*) in 1916, is that society is little more than a disagreeable necessity. In *Power: A New Social Analysis* (1938) he says that "The organized life of the community is necessary, but it is necessary as mechanism, not something to be valued on its own account." In Russell's view, social problems arise mainly from the conflicting claims of the individual and society, and he tends to ignore other factors. Yet his record as a social analyst and prophet is surprisingly good—and better than he usually gets credit for—as most readers of *German Social Democracy* and *The Practice and Theory of Bolshevism* (1920) will agree.

For six years after his second marriage Russell settled down as a hardworking intellectual journalist, ostracized by the establishment but financially successful and able to relax every summer with his family at their house in Cornwall. Katharine Jane was born in December 1923. Russell wrote several books of popular science—explaining, for example, Einstein's theory of relativity to the public—and continued to write on philosophy and politics. The short book *Icarus* (1924) makes clear his change of attitude to science and scientists. He had believed that the scientific outlook was, in itself, ethically positive; but now he sees it as amoral or even negative because it ignores basic human values and may lead to facile overconfidence. He fears three separate possibilities: a trivial society like that later described in Aldous Huxley's *Brave New World* (1932), a totalitarian society as in George Orwell's *Nineteen Eighty-Four* (1949), and worldwide devastation through atomic warfare. Russell develops these themes in considerably more detail in later books (he complained, not without reason, that most of the ideas in *Brave New World* were taken from his book *The Scientific Outlook* [1931]), and the third one came to dominate his thought in the 1950s and 1960s.

In 1927 Russell and his wife opened Beacon Hill School on the estate belonging to Russell's brother Frank. As a school it seems to have been quite successful, but its effect on the family was disastrous. John and Katharine had to be treated like the other children during term time, and both parents tried to do several potentially full-time jobs at once–teaching, administering, and earning money through lecture tours and journalism to support the school. Their marriage did not survive the strains; in the early 1930s Dora had two children by another man, and Russell entered into an affair with Patricia (Peter) Spence, who had been the children's governess. The family finally broke up in 1934, with John and Kate going to Dartington school and splitting their vacations between parents. Russell and Peter Spence were married in January 1936, and Conrad was born the following year.

At an age when most people have retired, Russell found himself with two families to support and no means of his own. He had given away his inherited money in a manner that he explained in a letter to Ottoline Morrell in 1912: "But just when I am thinking of getting a new great coat, I get a letter from some young man, educated but penniless, who will be all right in a few years if he can just get enough food to keep alive till he gets work–and so on. I don't as a rule help weak people–I help strong people who will soon need no more help." He seems defensive about being charitable. Russell had become an earl on Frank's death in 1931, but the title carried no financial benefits–indeed, it brought the obligation to provide Frank's widow with a sizable allowance. He wanted money, security, and time to spend on philosophy but had great difficulty finding a university position that would provide these things; Cambridge, Princeton, and Harvard turned him down. He finally arranged a year's appointment at the University of Chicago, and he sailed for the United States in September 1938.

The majority of Russell's best-known essays were written in the interwar period, including all those in *Sceptical Essays* and *In Praise of Idleness*, and many in *Unpopular Essays* and *Why I Am Not a Christian*. In a 1925 note on his writing (pub-

lished in *Russell: The Journal of the Bertrand Russell Archives*, 1972-1973) he describes his earlier style, now abandoned, as "too rhetorical" and says that he has come to favor the eighteenth century rather than the seventeenth. With the qualification that the plain style he refers to is as characteristic of the late seventeenth century as the early eighteenth–and indeed the writers he names, Swift and Defoe, were born in the 1660s–this comment does suggest some of the qualities of Russell's new style, which became his distinctive one: forthright, irreverent, frequently expressing extreme positions through antithesis and irony. Like Sherlock Holmes, Russell believed that all problems can be solved by intellectual power, and he required less evidence to work with than did the great detective. Indeed, he had not much interest in detail, and the corroborative evidence for his ideas is rather sparse. His interest was in abstract patterns, such as the historical development of liberalism or the effect of conventional beliefs about virtue.

Patterns of this type seem unpromising as the bases for literary essays; one expects them to be limited in initial appeal and predictable in development. Russell, however, makes his propositions seem striking and important and, as he develops them, maintains the atmosphere of a debate where new ideas are always appearing. His analogies are piquant and often surprising, like the comparison in *Sceptical Essays* of mankind to a society whose only function is to act the part of the First Sailor in *Hamlet*. Arguments can take unexpected twists even within paragraphs; for example, a theoretical definition of work can turn into a satire on politicians. Russell is fond of stating a paradoxical or outrageous proposition and then backing it up ingeniously–this is often the pattern for a complete essay: "I regard [religion] as a disease born of fear and as a source of untold misery to the human race" (*Why I Am Not a Christian*); "Our age is the most parochial since Homer" (*Unpopular Essays*); "Immense harm is caused by the belief that work is virtuous" (*In Praise of Idleness*). The reader immediately knows Russell's conclusion, but not how he will get there.

Some readers object that Russell deals in gross oversimplifications. He is, of course, prepared to defend any of his positions, but some allowance should be made for deliberate overstatement. Hyperbole is a traditional literary device, especially in debate. "That Plato's *Republic* should have been admired, on its political side, by decent people is perhaps the most astonishing

Russell with his second wife, Dora Black Russell—whom he married in 1921—and some students at their Beacon Hill School. The Russells started the school in 1927; the strain of running it, together with their other responsibilities, broke up the marriage in 1934.

example of literary snobbery in all history," he says in *Unpopular Essays*. Here, as frequently, Russell is trying to sweep aside traditional judgments with calculated irreverence, so as to allow a fresh look. Understatement can emphasize more subtly, and is more recognizably a literary device. "In some circles in Paris, men are admired for their artistic or literary excellence, strange as it may seem. In a German university, a man may actually be admired for his learning," he says in *Sceptical Essays*. Sometimes irony is sustained for most of an essay, as in "Nice People" (*Why I Am Not a Christian*), "The Harm That Good Men Do" (*Sceptical Essays*), and "Obituary" (*Unpopular Essays*), though usually it is intermittent. Much of it arises from tensions in Russell's own attitudes: he has strong convictions and seeks absolute proofs but is intellectually persuaded that emotion must be controlled by reason and that very few things are certain. Hence his justified reputation as a passionate skeptic. One result is that his many arguments against dogmatism tend to be presented dogmatically:

I wish to propose for the reader's favourable consideration a doctrine which may, I fear, appear wildly paradoxical and subversive. The doctrine in question is this: that it is undesirable to believe a proposition when there is no ground whatever for supposing it true.

[Reacting to the suggestion that his previous book was not, as Russell had said, accessible to the general educated public] I will therefore confess that there are several sentences in the present volume which some unusually stupid children of ten might find a little puzzling.

The first quotation is the opening of *Sceptical Essays*, and the second is from the introduction to *Unpopular Essays*. The first is an appeal for open-mindedness, and the second asserts (indirectly) that the ordinary person is perfectly capable of understanding complex ideas. These are both moderate liberal sentiments, but they are expressed, characteristically, by attacking the opposite positions; the first of these positions is represented as

Russell; his third wife, Patricia (Peter) Spence Russell, whom he married in 1936; and their son Conrad, 1940
(Associated Press)

credulous and the second as foolish and snobbish.

Not surprisingly, Russell made enemies; and he continued to have difficulty finding employment during his six years in America. He was also unhappy because he was in exile—ironically, during a war that he supported—and his new marriage was foundering. After a year at Chicago he went to the University of California, but he disliked the regime of the president there and resigned when he was offered a post at City College, New York. He then found that the New York position had not been confirmed, and it was refused him on various grounds—that he was not an American, that he was not of proven competence, and that his books showed him to be immoral. He was saved from a financial crisis when, at the end of 1940, Dr. Albert Barnes offered him well-paid work as a lecturer with the Barnes

Foundation. Two years later Russell had quarreled with Barnes and was again looking for work. He supported himself through a series of lectures at Bryn Mawr and Princeton, a publisher's advance for what was to become *A History of Western Philosophy* (1945), and ultimately a judicial settlement from Barnes for breaking a five-year contract. In the summer of 1944 he was offered a fellowship at Trinity, his old college in Cambridge, and was delighted to accept.

A History of Western Philosophy became a bestseller, but its current reputation is mixed. Maurice Cranston, a political philosopher, has described it as "in part inexcusably bad"; Wayne Booth, a literary critic, calls it "largely worthless." Much depends on the reader's expectations, and anyone wanting an uncritical summary of philosophers' ideas will not find it in Russell's book; but *A History of Western Philosophy* is lively, informative, catholic in sympathy, and thought-provoking. Russell describes his own mode of procedure thus: "In studying a philosopher, the right attitude is neither reverence nor contempt, but first a kind of hypothetical sympathy, until it is possible to know what it feels like to believe in his theories, and only then a revival of the critical attitude, which should resemble, as far as possible, the state of mind of a person abandoning opinions which he has hitherto held. Contempt interferes with the first part of this process, and reverence with the second." Russell assumes, surely correctly, that an account of a philosopher's ideas should include critical examination, and when he wishes to censure he is not, of course, impeded by reverence for the great: "I conclude that the Aristotelian doctrines with which we have been concerned in this chapter are wholly false." Yet Russell does follow his own doctrine of first trying to understand a philosopher sympathetically, as is most evident in his discussions of Hegel and Nietzsche, for whom he has strong antipathy. His accounts of their ideas are sufficiently complete and balanced to show why they are usually considered major philosophers; these accounts are quite different from his entertaining attack on Hegel in the essay "Politics and Philosophy" in *Unpopular Essays*.

In another of the pieces in *Unpopular Essays*, "An Outline of Intellectual Rubbish," Russell recommends having "imaginary dialogues" with people of different cultures and beliefs from other countries and historical periods. Much of *A History of Western Philosophy* consists of such dialogues, in the form of combative debate. One often has the sense of Russell calling up ghosts to defend themselves. Plato is challenged as an advocate of totalitarianism, Aristotle as an obstacle to intellectual progress; Francis Bacon's philosophy is "in many ways unsatisfactory," and Hobbes's has "grave defects." The debate is heightened by Russell's fondness for making moral judgments, which sometimes seem to take precedence over intellectual ones: "Spinoza (1632-77) is the noblest and most lovable of the great philosophers"; "Leibnitz (1646-1716) was one of the supreme intellects of all time, but as a man he was not admirable." The two kinds of judgment are often combined in discussions of ethical systems and political theories, for Russell believes that "a man's ethic usually reflects his character." His criticisms are therefore often couched in personal terms: Aristotle's ethics will be "useful to comfortable men of weak passions"; Hegel has twisted his meta-physics to justify "cruelty and international brigandage." But although the most memorable parts of *A History of Western Philosophy* are the assaults on what Russell regards as sacred cows, his sympathies are wide and not easily predictable; for example, his accounts of Catholic philosophers are surprisingly positive.

Russell was happy to return from America to Trinity College, but his personal life continued to be troubled. In 1949 he separated from his wife and was for some time estranged from their son, Conrad. He married Edith Finch, an American, in 1952, and this fourth marriage was happy. But his elder son, John, became seriously ill, and Russell, at eighty-one, assumed the responsibility of bringing up John's three young daughters. Throughout this period he gained steadily in public respectability, perhaps because his political views, especially his anticommunism, were then fashionable; the authorities may also have assumed that he was too near death, or at least senility, to be much of a threat. In 1948 he gave the first of the BBC's Reith Lectures series, in 1949 he was awarded the British Order of Merit, and in 1950 he received the Nobel Prize for literature. The period of respectability lasted until about 1955, when he launched a manifesto on nuclear disarmament.

In his eighties Russell branched out into a new area of literature and published two collections of short stories, *Satan in the Suburbs and Other Stories* (1953) and *Nightmares of Eminent Persons and Other Stories* (1954). These books are interesting in themselves and throw new light on Russell, but they also suggest the limitations of his imagination. In 1925 he had commended a passage in his book *The Problem of China* (1922). Curiously, this passage is entirely different from Russell's other writing, as even a sentence may indicate: "One night, very late, our boat stopped in a desolate spot where there were no houses, but only a great sandbank, and beyond it a row of poplars with the rising moon behind them." This—otherwise unremarkable—visual imagery makes one realize the almost complete absence of visualization elsewhere in Russell's books. When he does use metaphors, they are generally conventional and moribund, such as "the temple of reason." He seems, therefore, to lack one of the basic abilities for imaginative writing. Yet Russell had in his youth hoped to write a novel, and he made a sustained attempt in 1912; the result was the unsatisfactory story "The Perplexities of John Forstice," published posthumously in *The Collected*

Russell in 1962 with his fourth wife, the former Edith Finch, whom he married in 1952, and his secretary, Ralph Schoenman (Sport & General)

Stories of Bertrand Russell (1972). It consists mainly of long abstract speeches, and this is the kind of novel one can envisage Russell writing successfully; but he does not manage to convey a setting, show interaction between the characters, or make them speak distinctively. In the later short stories, however, Russell circumvents many of his limitations. The characters are sketched in just enough to have shape and be fairly believable; the main interest is in plot and, especially, the development of ideas. Russell says in the introduction to *Satan in the Suburbs and Other Stories* that his stories are not meant to "point a moral or illustrate a doctrine," but in fact much of their appeal comes from a resemblance to parable. Most of them are concerned with the nature of evil, and the devil appears frequently.

Russell moved to a remote house in north Wales in 1955, but this physical isolation did not curtail his public activities. Most of the activities were dictated by his fear of nuclear war. He established an annual conference of eminent scientists to work toward disarmament, which first met at Pugwash, Nova Scotia, in 1957. He became the first president of the British Campaign for Nuclear Disarmament; later he launched a parallel movement, the Committee of 100, that advocated nonviolent civil disobedience to oppose nuclear bases in Britain. As a consequence, he and his wife were sentenced to two months in prison; but after doctors' representations the sentence was reduced to a week (Russell was then eighty-nine). In 1963 he resigned from the Committee of 100 and set up two "Peace Foundations" through which he propagated his views. The switches of organization arose partly from personal disagreements but also from Russell's idea that each set of tactics could only be effective for a limited time. He frequently sent letters and cables to political leaders, most notably in 1962 during the

Cuban missile crisis between the United States and the Soviet Union and the border clashes between India and China; both events are described in his *Unarmed Victory* (1963). He has sometimes been ridiculed for believing that world affairs could be influenced in this way, but he did get serious replies from the heads of state and at least provided an extra diplomatic channel. The Russian leader Nikita Khrushchev replied on radio and in the press to Russell's cable on the missile crisis. Moreover, as Russell argued, if an action is even remotely likely to lessen the chance of nuclear war, one should take it.

Russell's *Wisdom of the West* (1959) is, in general, a condensed, illustrated, somewhat toned-down version of *A History of Western Philosophy*, but with new material on several modern philosophers. *Portraits from Memory and Other Essays* and, to a lesser extent, *Fact and Fiction* include valuable autobiographical sketches. *Portraits from Memory* is half autobiography and half general essays. *Fact and Fiction* has a section of autobiography, another of fiction, and many political essays. The autobiographical sections of both books were written by 1957 and reflect Russell's period of mellow respectability. They are a better introduction to his life than his official autobiography–the essay form gives him the space needed to fill in an episode or character and also sharpens the effect. The section "Six Autobiographical Essays" in *Portraits from Memory and Other Essays* is both personal and historical, describing the Victorian hopes and expectations that Russell shared and what became of them. The "Portraits" blend reminiscences of Russell's experiences of various people–such as Bernard Shaw, H. G. Wells, and Conrad–with a cogent description of their personalities. A sketch of Lord John Russell maintains the same balance, for it is based on a memory of crowds assembling in 1878 to cheer Lord John on the fiftieth anniversary of the repeal of the Test Act (which had discriminated heavily against anyone not a member of the Church of England). As elsewhere, Russell sees himself as a Rip Van Winkle unnaturally preserved from an earlier world. In *Fact and Fiction* he discusses books that influenced him. He explains his continued pleasure in Shelley's poetry–with its "extraordinary quality of light, like sunshine after a storm"–what he learned from Turgenev about revolutionaries, and his later disillusionment with Ibsen. It is a pity that Russell did not have more time for literary criticism. Most of the other essays in *Fact and Fiction* are political and concerned with persuading the reader of a few specific points. They are well written but, like Russell's other writing of the 1960s, rather limited, tending to reduce every situation to an either-or position.

Apart from nuclear disarmament, Russell's main preoccupation in his last years was the American involvement in Vietnam. He denounced the government for sending in troops and the army for war crimes such as torture and the deliberate killing of civilians. As a result he was, more than ever before, disliked by American authorities and reviled in the press. In 1966 he established an "International War Crimes Tribunal" to try the Americans, on the analogy of the Nuremberg Trials of alleged German war criminals; but he left the organization of it to Ralph Schoenman, who was his secretary and assistant from 1960 to 1966. Schoenman was an unfortunate choice as "Secretary General," and the Tribunal was not well organized and not very effective politically. At the end of 1967 Russell became ill with pneumonia, and thereafter was frail and often confined to a wheelchair. He continued to make public statements–for example, on the Soviet invasion of Czechoslovakia–but wrote little else. His autobiography, parts of which had been written much earlier, was published in three volumes from 1967 to 1969. On 31 January 1970 he dictated his last public message, condemning Israeli air raids on Egypt, and two days later he died.

Russell remains a controversial figure who can arouse strong loyalties and antagonisms. As with any good expository writer, his style conveys much of his personality, but interpretations of this personality vary. Even hostile critics will grant him intellectual power and precision and, for better or worse, idealism and a combative temperament. Most readers will also find him genial, witty, open-minded, and candid. Both groups will be aware, at least after reading widely in Russell's essays, of strong emotions crackling under the intellectual surface of his prose, and of serious purposes despite the wit and flippancy. It comes as no surprise when he compares his pacifist convictions during the 1914-1918 war to the Voice of God; he believed in absolutes and despised compromise. One of the "Maxims for Revolutionists" appended to Shaw's *Man and Superman* (1905) reads, "The reasonable man adapts himself to the world: the unreasonable one persists in trying to adapt the world to himself. Therefore all progress depends on the unreasonable man." In this sense, Russell was fundamentally unreasonable.

Bibliography:

Martin Werner, *Bertrand Russell: A Bibliography of His Writing 1895-1976* (Munich, New York, London & Paris: Saur / Hamden, Conn.: Linnet Books, 1981).

Biography:

Ronald W. Clark, *The Life of Bertrand Russell* (New York: Knopf, 1976).

References:

Wayne C. Booth, *Modern Dogma and the Rhetoric of Assent* (Chicago & London: Chicago University Press, 1974);

Andrew Brink and Richard Kenpel, "The Importance of the Essayist on Social Issues," *Russell*, 33-34 (1979): 13-29;

Ronald W. Clark, *Bertrand Russell and His World* (London: Thames & Hudson, 1981);

Maurice Cranston, "Bertrand Russell: Towards a Complete Portrait," *Encounter*, 46 (1976): 65-79;

Rupert Crawshay-Williams, *Russell Remembered* (London: Oxford University Press, 1970);

Margaret Moran, "Bertrand Russell's Early Approaches to Literature," *University of Toronto Quarterly*, 54 (1984): 56-78;

Dora Russell, *The Tamarisk Tree: My Quest for Liberty and Love* (New York: Putnam's, 1975);

Ralph Schoenman, ed., *Bertrand Russell: Philosopher of the Century: Essays in His Honour* (London: Allen & Unwin, 1967);

John G. Slater, "One Hundred Years of Bertrand Russell: An Appraisal," *Russell*, 23-24 (1976): 4-25;

Katharine Tait, *My Father Bertrand Russell* (New York: Harcourt, Brace & World, 1975);

J. E. Thomas and Kenneth Blackwell, eds., *Russell in Review: The Bertrand Russell Century Celebrations* (Toronto: Stevens, 1976);

Alan Wood, *Bertrand Russell: The Passionate Sceptic* (London: Allen & Unwin, 1957).

Papers:

The Bertrand Russell Archives at McMaster University, Hamilton, Ontario, contain most of Russell's extant papers.

Dorothy L. Sayers

(13 June 1893 - 17 December 1957)

R. D. Stock
University of Nebraska at Lincoln

See also the Sayers entries in *DLB 10: Modern British Dramatists, 1900-1945; DLB 36: British Novelists, 1890-1929: Modernists*; and *DLB 77: British Mystery Writers, 1920-1939.*

BOOKS: *Op. I* (Oxford: Blackwell, 1916);

Catholic Tales and Christian Songs (Oxford: Blackwell, 1918);

Whose Body? (New York: Boni & Liveright, 1923; London: Unwin, 1923);

Clouds of Witness (London: Unwin, 1926); republished as *Clouds of Witnesses* (New York: Dial, 1927);

Unnatural Death (London: Benn, 1927); republished as *The Dawson Pedigree* (New York: Dial, 1928);

The Unpleasantness at the Bellona Club (London: Benn, 1928; New York: Payson & Clarke, 1928);

Lord Peter Views the Body (London: Gollancz, 1928; New York: Payson & Clarke, 1929);

The Documents in the Case, by Sayers and Robert Eustace (Dr. Eustace Robert Barton) (London: Benn, 1930; New York: Brewer & Warren, 1930);

Strong Poison (London: Gollancz, 1930; New York: Brewer & Warren, 1930);

The Five Red Herrings (London: Gollancz, 1931); republished as *Suspicious Characters* (New York: Brewer, Warren & Putnam, 1931);

The Floating Admiral, by Sayers and others (London: Hodder & Stoughton, 1931; New York: Doubleday, Doran, 1932);

Have His Carcase (London: Gollancz, 1932; New York: Brewer, Warren & Putnam, 1932);

Murder Must Advertise: A Detective Story (London: Gollancz, 1933; New York: Harcourt, Brace, 1933);

Ask a Policeman, by Sayers and others (London: Barker, 1933; New York: Morrow, 1933);

Hangman's Holiday (London: Gollancz, 1933; New York: Harcourt, Brace, 1933);

The Nine Tailors: Changes Rung on an Old Theme in Two Short Touches and Two Full Peals (London: Gollancz, 1934; New York: Harcourt, Brace, 1934);

Gaudy Night (London: Gollancz, 1935; New York: Harcourt, Brace, 1936);

Papers Relating to the Family of Wimsey, by Sayers and others, as Matthew Wimsey (London: Privately printed, 1936);

Busman's Honeymoon: A Detective Comedy in Three Acts, by Sayers and Muriel St. Clare Byrne (London: Gollancz, 1937; New York: Dramatists' Play Service, 1939);

Busman's Honeymoon: A Love Story with Detective Interruptions (New York: Harcourt, Brace, 1937; London: Gollancz, 1937);

The Zeal of Thy House (London: Gollancz, 1937; New York: Harcourt, Brace, 1937);

An Account of Lord Mortimer Wimsey, Hermit of the Marsh (Oxford: Privately printed, 1937);

The Greatest Drama Ever Staged (London: Hodder & Stoughton, 1938);

Double Death: A Murder Story, by Sayers and others (London: Gollancz, 1939);

Strong Meat (London: Hodder & Stoughton, 1939);

The Devil to Pay: Being the Famous History of John Faustus, the Conjurer of Wittenberg in Germany; How He Sold His Immortal Soul to the Enemy of Mankind, and Was Served XXIV Years by Mephistopheles, and Obtained Helen of Troy to His Paramour, with Many Other Marvels; and How God Dealt with Him at the Last: A Stage-Play (London: Gollancz, 1939; New York: Harcourt, Brace, 1939);

In the Teeth of the Evidence and Other Stories (London: Gollancz, 1939; New York: Harcourt, Brace, 1940);

He That Should Come: A Nativity Play in One Act (London: Gollancz, 1939);

Begin Here: A War-Time Essay (London: Gollancz, 1940; New York: Harcourt, Brace, 1941);

Creed or Chaos?: Address Delivered at the Biennial Festival of the Church Tutorial Classes Association in Derby, May 4th, 1940 (London: Hodder & Stoughton, 1940);

Dorothy L. Sayers (photograph by Howard Coster)

The Mysterious English (London: Macmillan, 1941);

The Mind of the Maker (London: Methuen, 1941; New York: Harcourt, Brace, 1941);

Why Work?: An Address Delivered at Eastbourne, April 23rd, 1942 (London: Methuen, 1942);

The Other Six Deadly Sins: An Address Given to the Public Morality Council at Caxton Hall, Westminster, on October 23rd, 1941 (London: Methuen, 1943);

The Man Born to Be King: A Play-Cycle on the Life of Our Lord and Saviour Jesus Christ, Written for Broadcasting (London: Gollancz, 1943; New York: Harper, 1949);

Even the Parrot: Exemplary Conversations for Enlightened Children (London: Methuen, 1944);

The Just Vengeance: The Lichfield Festival Play for 1946 (London: Gollancz, 1946);

Unpopular Opinions (London: Gollancz, 1946; New York: Harcourt, Brace, 1947);

Making Sense of the Universe: An Address Given at the Kingsway Hall on Ash Wednesday, March 6th, 1946 (London: St. Anne's Church House, 1946);

Creed or Chaos? and Other Essays in Popular Theology (London: Methuen, 1947; New York: Harcourt, Brace, 1949);

The Lost Tools of Learning: Paper Read at a Vacation Course in Education, Oxford 1947 (London: Methuen, 1948);

The Emperor Constantine: A Chronicle (London: Gollancz, 1951; New York: Harper, 1951);

Introductory Papers on Dante (London: Methuen, 1954; New York: Harper, 1955);

Further Papers on Dante (London: Methuen, 1957; New York: Harper, 1957);

The Poetry of Search and the Poetry of Statement and Other Posthumous Essays on Literature, Religion and Language (London: Gollancz, 1963);

Christian Letters to a Post-Christian World: A Selection of Essays, edited by Roderick Jellema (Grand Rapids, Mich.: Eerdmans, 1969); republished as *The Whimsical Christian: 18 Essays* (New York: Macmillan, 1978);

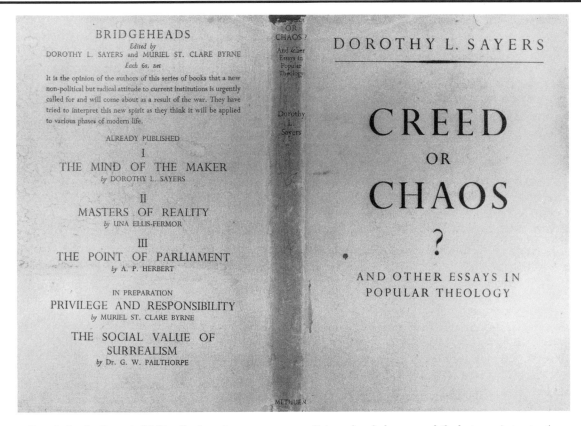

Dust jacket for Sayers's 1947 collection of seven essays on religion, church dogma, and the layperson's perspective

Talboys (New York, Evanston, San Francisco & London: Harper, 1972);

Striding Folly, Including Three Final Lord Peter Wimsey Stories (London: New English Library, 1973);

Wilkie Collins: A Critical and Biographical Study, edited by E. R. Gregory (Toledo, Ohio: Friends of the University of Toledo Libraries, 1977).

OTHER: *Great Short Stories of Detection, Mystery and Horror*, edited, with an introduction, by Sayers (London: Gollancz, 1928); republished as *The Omnibus of Crime* (New York: Payson & Clarke, 1929);

Tristan in Brittany: Being Fragments of the Romance of Tristan, Written in the XII Century, by Thomas the Anglo-Norman, translated by Sayers (London: Benn, 1929; New York: Payson & Clarke, 1929);

Great Short Stories of Detection, Mystery and Horror, Second Series, edited, with an introduction, by Sayers (London: Gollancz, 1931); republished as *The Second Omnibus of Crime* (New York: Coward-McCann, 1932);

Great Short Stories of Detection, Mystery and Horror,

Third Series, edited, with an introduction, by Sayers (London: Gollancz, 1934); republished as *The Third Omnibus of Crime* (New York: Coward-McCann, 1935);

"The Murder of Julia Wallace," in *Great Unsolved Crimes* (London: Hutchinson, 1935), pp. 111-122; revised in *The Anatomy of Murder: Famous Crimes Critically Considered by Members of the Detection Club* (London: Lane, 1936; New York: Macmillan, 1937), pp. 157-211;

"Blood Sacrifice," in *Six against the Yard*, by Sayers and others (London: Selwyn & Blount, 1936), pp. 197-233; republished as *Six against Scotland Yard* (New York: Doubleday, Doran, 1936), pp. 197-233;

Tales of Detection, edited by Sayers (London: Dent, 1936);

Wilkie Collins, *The Moonstone*, introduction by Sayers (London: Dent / New York: Dutton, 1944);

Garet Garrett, *A Time Is Born*, introduction by Sayers (Oxford: Blackwell, 1945);

The Comedy of Dante Alighieri the Florentine, Cantica I: Hell, translated by Sayers (Harmondsworth, U.K.: Penguin, 1949);

The Comedy of Dante Alighieri the Florentine, Cantica II: Purgatory, translated by Sayers (Harmondsworth, U.K.: Penguin, 1955);

The Song of Roland, translated by Sayers (Harmondsworth, U.K.: Penguin, 1957);

The Comedy of Dante Alighieri the Florentine, Cantica III: Paradise, translated by Sayers, completed by Barbara Reynolds (Harmondsworth, U.K.: Penguin, 1962).

Although Dorothy L. Sayers is known chiefly for her detective fiction and somewhat less well for her translation of Dante's *Divine Comedy*, she was also a prolific and controversial essayist and lecturer. She is among the more significant modern British Christian apologists; if she is not so well known as G. K. Chesterton or C. S. Lewis, for example, it is partly because her other work has overshadowed her expository prose.

Dorothy Leigh Sayers was born in Oxford on 13 June 1893 to the Reverend Henry Sayers and Helen May Leigh Sayers. After being graduated from Somerville College, Oxford, in 1915, she worked as a teacher of modern languages and as a reader for the Blackwell publishing firm, then, from 1922 until 1929, as a copywriter for a London advertising firm. In 1926 she married Capt. Oswald Atherton Fleming, who was then a successful journalist; within two years his health broke down, and he remained unemployed until his death in 1950. Sayers introduced her popular detective, Lord Peter Wimsey, in her first novel, *Whose Body?* (1923), and published her major mysteries over the next fourteen years. During that time Sayers wrote some essays, most of them concerned with the art of the detective story. Her introduction to *Great Short Stories of Detection, Mystery and Horror* (1928) speedily achieved the status of a classic. She distinguishes there between the "Romantic" or "purely sensational" and the "Classical" or "purely intellectual" lines of mystery writing, tracing both back to Poe. In this essay and in her introduction to *Great Short Stories of Detection, Mystery and Horror, Second Series* (1931) Sayers notes and approves of a tendency to combine the detective and the psychological novel–a propensity of her own fiction as it developed through the 1930s. She also wrote reviews of mystery novels for the *Sunday Times* from 1933 to 1935.

By the end of the 1930s Sayers had tired of writing mysteries and was turning to other genres, primarily the drama and the essay-lecture. She had always been interested in many more things than detective stories, but her growing sense of vocation as a Christian writer and the exigencies of World War II were developing her into a trenchant and provocative commentator on public affairs. The first substantial result of this development was *Begin Here: A War-Time Essay* (1940), where Sayers is no longer the professional mystery writer discoursing on her craft but an interpreter of global issues. She sees war–any war–"not as an end, but a beginning," and she calls for some "creative line of action" to restore coherence to Western, Christian civilization. Concisely and sweepingly she describes the emergence of the modern world out of the Middle Ages and the Renaissance.

Her next book-length essay was *The Mind of the Maker* (1941), which she considered an important continuation of her effort in *Begin Here* to give guidance to a dismayed, demoralized generation. It is also the most elaborate development of a subject that had long interested her and to which she would return in later essays and lectures: man as *homo faber*, the image of God the Creator. *The Mind of the Maker*–indisputably her greatest and most influential nonfiction book–develops an intricate analogy between the Trinity and the threefold activity of the creative writer. There is the initial Idea (the Father), the Energy (the Son) needed to be aware of and to contemplate the Idea, and the Power (the Holy Spirit) to execute the work, to communicate it to others. The theology and the analogy have been found faulty by some, but the book was admired by C. S. Lewis and other discriminating critics. It stands as an important modern work of Christian aesthetics, shedding light on the psychology as well as the theology of creativity.

Unpopular Opinions (1946) brings together twenty-one essays composed between 1935 and 1945. These pieces address contemporary issues of morality, aesthetics, and politics from a Christian perspective and include sharp polemics, witty discussions of the use and abuse of English, and playful, mock-scholarly studies of the Sherlock Holmes canon. One of the best-known essays in the book is "The Mysterious English," which explores the whimsy, inconsistency, and horror of abstraction or systematic theory that typify English law, language, and culture. Another essay, which has often been reprinted, is the 1938 address "Are Women Human?" Sayers deals wittily with what is now called male chauvinism but castigates ideologues and particularly assails

Sayers in 1937

the "error of insisting that there is an aggressively feminist 'point of view' about everything."

The seven essays in *Creed or Chaos? and Other Essays in Popular Theology* (1947), written in the early to mid 1940s, are more homogeneous. The title essay argues that dogmas–especially the doctrines of the Incarnation and Redemption–are important bases of thought and action, and it advises the Church of England to hold on to doctrinal and theological coherence and to resist nebulousness and sentimentality. The other essays also take up aspects of church doctrine and policy, emphasizing the excitement of dogma, the challenging aspects of Christ (who is depicted as decidedly *not* "Jesus meek and mild"), and the imperative need of making doctrines and dogmas meaningful to the modern layman.

Sayers's last intellectual interest, and one of her strongest, was Dante. She translated the *Inferno* and *Purgatorio* and had just gotten into the *Paradiso* when she died, apparently of a stroke,

on 17 December 1957. Her introductions to *Hell* (1949) and *Purgatory* (1955) have become influential and popular treatments of Dante and his theological-political milieu. Somewhat more scholarly are her two collections of essays, *Introductory Papers on Dante* (1954) and *Further Papers on Dante* (1957), where she canvasses such subjects as Dante's humor, techniques, and worldview. A posthumous anthology, *The Poetry of Search and the Poetry of Statement* (1963), has further material on Dante but also contains a significant piece on the novels of Charles Williams and an influential essay on educational reform, "The Lost Tools of Learning." Sayers's career as an essayist can be sorted into three phases: the introductions and reviews of the late 1920s and early 1930s dealing with detective fiction; the book-length essays and collections of the late 1930s and the 1940s on a variety of contemporary topics and on theology; and the Dante introductions and essays of the 1950s. Her work on Dante is a natural progression from the first two phases: she writes about him as a master of narrative (she found him an "incomparable story-teller"), as an energetic and incisive commentator on his times, and as a profound Christian writer.

Sayers's pieces on Dante have been criticized as too superficial, sketchy, and polemical, and indeed she may have overstressed Dante's comical side in her campaign to make him popular. But she was no dilettante. Soundly trained as a scholar, she studied the Dante literature intensely and had a good grasp of Dante's milieu. She succeeded in arousing a wider interest in his great poem; and her translations of the *Divine Comedy*, with her introductions and extensive commentaries, have continued to be influential in their paperbound editions.

Sayers was a scholar and critic whose essays are aimed at a nonprofessional, nonacademic audience, and they have the strengths and weaknesses characteristic of such an approach. Her prose is lively—even racy—and almost always pungent. Some of her essays have naturally become dated, but her discussions of detective fiction, Christian theology, aesthetics, and Dante must still be reckoned with in any thorough account of those subjects.

Bibliographies:

Robert B. Harmon and Margaret A. Burger, *An Annotated Guide to the Works of Dorothy L. Sayers* (New York: Garland, 1977);

Colleen B. Gilbert, *A Bibliography of the Works of Dorothy L. Sayers* (London: Macmillan, 1977; Hamden, Conn.: Archon, 1978);

Ruth T. Youngberg, *Dorothy L. Sayers: A Reference Guide* (Boston: Hall, 1982).

Biographies:

Janet Hitchman, *Such a Strange Lady: An Introduction to Dorothy L. Sayers, 1893-1957* (New York: Harper & Row, 1975);

Ralph E. Hone, *Dorothy L. Sayers: A Literary Biography* (Kent, Ohio: Kent State University Press, 1979);

James Brabazon, *Dorothy L. Sayers: A Biography* (New York: Scribners, 1981).

References:

Margaret Hannay, ed., *As Her Whimsey Took Her: Critical Essays on the Work of Dorothy L. Sayers* (Kent, Ohio: Kent State University Press, 1979);

Barbara Reynolds, *The Passionate Intellect: Dorothy L. Sayers' Encounter with Dante* (Kent, Ohio & London: Kent State University Press, 1989).

Papers:

The Dorothy L. Sayers Literary and Historical Society in Witham, Essex, England, has manuscripts, memorabilia, and source materials. The Marion E. Wade Collection at Wheaton College in Wheaton, Illinois, has the bulk of Sayers's manuscripts, first editions, and secondary materials.

Osbert Sitwell

(6 December 1892 - 4 May 1969)

Thomas A. Kuhlman
Creighton University

BOOKS: *Twentieth Century Harlequinade, and Other Poems*, by Sitwell and Edith Sitwell (Oxford: Blackwell, 1916);

The Winstonburg Line: Three Satires (London: Hendersons, 1919);

Argonaut and Juggernaut (London: Chatto & Windus, 1919; New York: Knopf, 1920);

At the House of Mrs. Kinfoot: Consisting of Four Satires (Kensington: Favil Press, 1921);

Who Killed Cock-Robin?: Remarks on Poetry, on Its Criticism, and, as a Sad Warning, the Story of Eunuch Arden (London: Daniel, 1921);

Out of the Flame (London: Richards, 1923; New York: Doran, 1925);

Triple Fugue (London: Richards, 1924; New York: Doran, 1925);

Brighton, by Sitwell and Margaret Barton (London: Faber & Faber, 1925; Boston & New York: Houghton Mifflin, 1935);

C. R. W. Nevinson, as O. S. (London: Benn, 1925; New York: Scribners, 1925);

Discursions on Travel, Art and Life (London: Richards, 1925; New York: Doran, 1925);

Poor Young People, by Sitwell, Edith Sitwell, and Sacheverell Sitwell (London: The Fleuron, 1925);

Before the Bombardment (London: Duckworth, 1926; New York: Doran, 1926);

All at Sea: A Social Tragedy in Three Acts for First-class Passengers Only, by Osbert and Sacheverell Sitwell, with a Preface Entitled A Few Days in an Author's Life, by Osbert Sitwell (London: Duckworth, 1927; Garden City, N.Y.: Doubleday, Doran, 1928);

England Reclaimed: A Book of Eclogues (London: Duckworth, 1927; Garden City, N.Y.: Doubleday, Doran, 1928);

The People's Album of London Statues (London: Duckworth, 1928);

Miss Mew (Stanford Dingley, U.K.: Mill House Press, 1929);

The Man Who Lost Himself (London: Duckworth, 1929; New York: Coward-McCann, 1930);

Osbert Sitwell in 1942

Dumb-Animal, and Other Stories (London: Duckworth, 1930; Philadelphia: Lippincott, 1931);

Three-quarter Length Portrait of Michael Arlen. With a Preface: The History of a Portrait, by the Author (London: Heinemann / New York: Doubleday, Doran, 1930);

The Collected Satires and Poems of Osbert Sitwell (London: Duckworth, 1931; New York: AMS Press, 1976);

291

Sitwell, age eighteen

A Three-quarter Length Portrait of the Viscountess Wimborne (Cambridge: Cambridge University Press, 1931);

Dickens (London: Chatto & Windus, 1932; Folcroft, Pa.: Folcroft Press, 1969);

Miracle on Sinai: A Satirical Novel (London: Duckworth, 1933; New York: Holt, 1934);

Penny Foolish: A Book of Tirades and Panegyrics (London: Macmillan, 1935; Freeport, N.Y.: Books for Libraries Press, 1967);

Mrs. Kimber (London: Macmillan, 1937; Folcroft, Pa.: Folcroft Library Editions, 1971);

Those Were the Days: Panorama with Figures (London: Macmillan, 1938);

Trio: Dissertations on Some Aspects of National Genius, Delivered as the Northcliffe Lectures at the University of London in 1937, by Sitwell, Edith Sitwell, and Sacheverell Sitwell (London: Macmillan, 1938; Freeport, N.Y.: Books for Libraries Press, 1970);

Escape with Me!: An Oriental Sketch-book (London: Macmillan, 1939; New York: Harrison-Hilton, 1940);

Open the Door!: A Volume of Stories (London: Macmillan, 1941; New York: Smith & Durrell, 1941);

A Place of One's Own (London: Macmillan, 1941);

Gentle Caesar: A Play in Three Acts, by Sitwell and Rubeigh James Minney (London: Macmillan, 1942);

Selected Poems, Old and New (London: Duckworth, 1943; New York: AMS Press, 1976);

Left Hand, Right Hand! (Boston: Little, Brown, 1944; London: Macmillan, 1945);

A Letter to My Son (London: Home & Van Thal, 1944);

Sing High! Sing Low!: A Book of Essays (London: Macmillan, 1944);

The True Story of Dick Whittington: A Christmas Story for Cat-Lovers (London: Home & Van Thal, 1945);

The Scarlet Tree (Boston: Little, Brown, 1946; London: Macmillan, 1946);

Alive—Alive Oh! and Other Stories (London: Pan, 1947);

Great Morning! (Boston: Little, Brown, 1947; London: Macmillan, 1948);

The Novels of George Meredith and Some Notes on the English Novel (London: Oxford University Press, 1947; Folcroft, Pa.: Folcroft Press, 1969);

Four Songs of the Italian Earth (Pawlet, Vt.: Banyan Press, 1948);

Laughter in the Next Room (Boston: Little, Brown, 1948; London: Macmillan, 1948);

Death of a God, and Other Stories (London: Macmillan, 1949);

Demos the Emperor: A Secular Oratorio (London: Macmillan, 1949; Folcroft, Pa.: Folcroft Library Editions, 1977);

England Reclaimed, and Other Poems (Boston: Little, Brown, 1949);

Introduction to the Catalogue of the Frick Collection: Published on the Founder's Centenary, 19 December 1949 (New York: Ram Press, 1949);

Noble Essences: A Book of Characters (Boston: Little, Brown, 1950); republished as *Noble Essences; or, Courteous Revelations: Being a Book of Char-*

acters and the Fifth and Last Volume of Left Hand, Right Hand, an Autobiography (London: Macmillan, 1950);

Winters of Content, and Other Discursions on Mediterranean Art and Travel (London: Duckworth, 1950; Philadelphia: Lippincott, 1952);

Wrack at Tidesend, a Book of Balnearics: Being the Second Volume of England Reclaimed (London: Macmillan, 1952; New York: Caedmon, 1953);

Collected Stories (London: Duckworth, 1953; New York: Harper, 1953);

The Four Continents: Being More Discursions on Travel, Art, and Life (London: Macmillan, 1954; New York: Harper, 1954);

On the Continent: A Book of Inquilinics. Being the Third Volume of England Reclaimed (London: Macmillan, 1958);

Fee Fi Fo Fum!: A Book of Fairy Stories (London: Macmillan, 1959);

A Place of One's Own, and Other Stories (London: Icon, 1961);

Tales My Father Taught Me: An Evocation of Extravagant Episodes (Boston: Little, Brown, 1962; London: Hutchinson, 1962);

Pound Wise (London: Hutchinson, 1963; Boston: Little, Brown, 1963);

Queen Mary and Others (London: Joseph, 1974; New York: Day, 1975).

OTHER: *Victoriana: A Symposium of Victorian Wisdom*, edited by Sitwell and Margaret Barton (London: Duckworth, 1931);

Ifan Kyrle Fletcher, *Ronald Firbank: A Memoir*, contribution by Sitwell (New York: Brentano's, 1932);

Two Generations, edited by Sitwell (London: Macmillan, 1940);

Sober Truth: A Collection of Nineteenth-Century Episodes, Fantastic, Grotesque and Mysterious, edited by Sitwell and Barton (London: MacDonald, 1944);

Walter Sickert, *A Free House! Or, The Artist as Craftsman*, edited by Sitwell (London: Macmillan, 1947).

In his critical essay on Osbert Sitwell (1951) Roger Fulford tells of his subject's being disparaged for wasting too much time with the aristocratic society to which, by birth, he belonged. The charge, in short, was that Sitwell was lazy. One of Sitwell's friends, the novelist Arnold Bennett, was present to hear the remark, and after considerable laughter responded, "The truth

with Osbert is that he has seven professions, not one, and a life devoted to each." Fulford lists among these professions those of "writer, traveler, politician, pamphleteer, editor, and organizer of picture exhibitions."

Most of Sitwell's essays were written, as he notes in the introduction to the collection *Pound Wise* (1963), "before the dissolution of the British Empire." The fact is significant, because for good or ill, they all exhibit the ironic attitude of the self-aware imperialist. His nonfiction prose is characterized by extreme worldliness and erudition, by a self-assurance verging upon arrogance; but if mockery pervades his paragraphs, it is mixed with the sincerity of one who has little to gain and much less to fear because of the stand he takes. Sitwell could well have chosen Horace's phrase *Odi profanum vulgus* for his motto; and yet however frequently his essays demonstrate that their author "despises the vulgar herd," so accurate is the skewering of contemporary folly among all social classes, and so genuine is his passionate approval of the truly creative, honest, and beautiful that Sitwell ultimately must be judged innocent of snobbery. Beneath the surface of poisonous mirth is a reservoir of decency and goodwill to all but the most essential of enemies. In style, the essays show a superlative command of diction and rhythm, and can be read as much for the pleasure to be derived from leisured complexity of syntax as for the enjoyment of precise observation, sensual imagery, and unfailing wit.

Although he first won notice and praise through his poetry and then earned moderate success as a novelist and short-story writer, Sitwell's five volumes of autobiographical essays, begun in 1943 and completed in 1950, are generally considered to be his masterpiece–an achievement, indeed, not far behind Proust's *Remembrance of Things Past* (1913-1927) as a compendium of the author's detailed impressions of a fashionable milieu. Other essays–on places exotic and familiar, on customs momentous or trivial, and on institutions to be admired or despised–merit similar respect for the author's mastery of the genre.

The author was born on 6 December 1892 at Renishaw, his family's ancestral seat in Derbyshire, and was christened Francis Osbert Sacheverell Sitwell. His father, Sir George, had become a baronet at the age of two–the youngest in England; and by living to the age of eighty-three, he held his baronetcy longer than any other Englishman since the early Middle Ages. Osbert's

Sitwell with his sister, Dame Edith Sitwell (photograph by Hans Wild)

mother's descent was a source of particular pride both to her husband and to her children. Lady Ida Denison was the daughter of Lord Londesborough and the granddaughter of the Duke of Beaufort, who was a direct descendant of the Plantagenets–a fact Osbert and his siblings used for their own comfort and, it must be admitted, occasionally to put others in their place in a world which was becoming, from the Sitwells' point of view, excessively democratized.

Five years older than Osbert was his sister, Edith, who grew up to become a well-known poet. Two years younger than Osbert was his brother Sacheverell, who would become best known for his studies on baroque art, architecture, and opera. While Edith felt deprived of affection from her father, and unquestionably was denied, because of her sex, the educational opportunities afforded her brothers, all three children early recognized in each other a commonality of interests and talents which seemed to stand (if it actually did not wholly do so) in opposition to the tastes and opinions of their parents, and for the rest of their lives there existed a bond among them which caused them to be looked upon as a trio.

Sitwell first attended a day school in Scarborough, the Yorkshire seaside resort where his maternal grandfather maintained a residence. He hated this school for the bullying he received as a nobleman's son at the mercy of the sons of the bourgeoisie. At Ludgrove School at New Barnet, a boarding school preparatory for Eton, he discovered at least equal hostility directed against him by the sons of aristocrats; and at Eton from 1903 to 1911 he had a more disillusioning experience yet. Two essays in *Pound Wise* are devoted to the subject of English schools for boys, and two others to his detestation of sports and games as part of education. "On Private Schools" projects his bitterness: boys at such schools, he says, "are whisked off to places of dreary internment . . .

Sitwell at his family's castle, Montegufoni, near Florence, Italy (photograph by Reresby Sitwell)

where the most extraordinary tribal values and standards prevail: and though these, as it were, labour camps are varied according to their years, they remain in one or another of them (unless they have the good fortune to be expelled with ignominy) until such time as their characters have been formed in the same hard, dense and unpleasant mould as that of those who teach them."

Sitwell's attitude toward the British public school (which corresponds roughly to an American *private* school) was even harsher. His essay on this institution begins, "Public schools are to private schools as lunatic asylums to mental homes; larger and less comfortable" and, he charges, "since the beginning of the nineteenth century have injured incalculably the English governing classes." Finding the popularity of the public school to have its source in the values of the industrial revolution, values all three Sitwells consistently found deficient if not completely false, Sitwell criticizes the famous Dr. Arnold of Rugby for his innovation of compulsory games. He re-

lated that when he, as a former student, was asked by the provost of Eton for a contribution to a fund to buy more land for playing fields, he promised a check on the condition that the money not be used for "the odious habit of compulsory games, which had ruined the minds of so many of the most intelligent of my contemporaries." The irony with which the essay concludes is characteristic of Sitwell's work in the genre:

Public schools constitute, in fact, no longer factories of gentlemen, but, instead, so many corpse factories. Their methods are antiquated to such a degree that it is almost impossible to remedy them. From the class-conscious point of view of those who dread government by the workers, the most desirable thing in the world would be democratization of the public schools. If miners and mill hands could only be educated at Eton, there would never be any strikes, or if there were, these would be unsuccessful; would mean no more than an Eton or Harrow match. Always teach people of whom you are afraid "to play the game": in other words to be hoodwinked through-

Sitwell at the family estate, Renishaw, in Derbyshire in the late 1950s (photograph by Hans Wild)

out life, and to be contented with conditions with which they have no right to allow themselves to be contented.

The titles of the next two essays in *Pound Wise* summarize their contents: "Games (1) as a Menace to the Country" and "Games (2) as a Pernicious Influence on the Individual." Especially in the latter, however, whimsy overrules sourness, and these essays show the author more as a clever humorist than as a somber social critic: "As to qualities of leadership: was a particular devotion to golf or cricket ever recorded–to take a few great English names at random–of Raleigh, Marlborough, Henry V, Peterborough, the Black Prince, Fox or Nelson; any more than of such negligible highbrows as Shakespeare, Milton, Pope, Keats or Blake?"

From Eton, Sitwell wanted and expected to go on to Christ Church College, Oxford, but his father had different plans. In 1912 he was sent as

a "military crammer" to Camberley, as preparation for Sandhurst, and then even Sandhurst was denied him; Sir George arranged for his son a second lieutenant's position in the yeomanry, and Sitwell went to Aldershot. So generally unsuitable was this posting that he soon suffered a nervous breakdown, was granted a compassionate leave, and went to Italy to recover his health. On his return he was made an officer in the fashionable Grenadier Guards, and until the outbreak of World War I he was stationed at the Wellington Barracks in London.

At that time began Sitwell's regular association with the leaders of British society. His friends included Mrs. George Keppel and her daughter Violet; Margot Asquith, wife of the prime minister; and Lady Sackville, mistress of the great country house Knole. He joined the Marlborough Club and began a lifelong involvement in the world of creative artists, meeting

Sitwell at his desk (photograph by Bill Brandt)

such figures as the composers Debussy and Delius and the novelist George Moore. He quickly became an expert on ballet and put together a first-rate collection of books on the subject.

In the summer of 1914 his term as a Grenadier expired, and he reluctantly went north to accept the job in the Scarborough town clerk's office that his father had, with his traditional high-handedness, arranged for him. Then the Great War broke out, and Sitwell was spared the tedium of duty in the provincial bureaucracy. The alternative, combat in Flanders, provided direct experience of the folly and carnage he considered the older generation had callously allowed to overcome the European continent. After the harrowing battle of Loos, he managed a leave during which he spent some time with the diplomat and writer Harold Nicolson; they talked, as he later wrote, of nothing but "pictures, Palladio, and palaces." The subjects were, of course, typical Sitwell family interests. Blood poisoning and complications from a foot injury he had sustained at the front rendered him unfit for further combat. By 1916 he was publishing satirical pacifist verse in *Wheels*, a magazine conceived by Nancy Cunard and directed by Edith Sitwell. At

the end of the war he was living in Swan Walk, Chelsea; on Armistice night he gave a dinner for Sergey Diaghilev of the Ballet Russe. He began publishing satirical poems in the *Nation* under the name "*Miles*." Although he never grew enthusiastic about the virtues of "the Common Man" as did so many intellectuals of the period, at Eton he had admired communism and Trotsky. In the 1918 general election he stood for Parliament as a Liberal but was defeated. In 1919 he was contributing poems to the Labour party's *Daily Herald*, and he became a lifelong critic of Winston Churchill.

The arts, however, were his primary interest. His friends included Ezra Pound, T. S. Eliot, Cyril Connolly, Cecil Beaton, Evelyn Waugh, Peter Quennell, and Kenneth Clark. Sharing with Edith and Sacheverell old grudges against their parents, whose eccentricities and occasional meanness had proved a continuing source of embarrassment to them, he declared himself the absolute enemy of what they called "the Squirearchy" or "the Golden Horde," by which the trio meant the majority of the aristocracy and landed gentry, whose interests seemed confined to drinking, card playing, and fox hunting. The three young Sitwells equally condemned as philistine most of the Georgian and Edwardian poets.

On 12 June 1923 at the Aeolian Hall in London, Sitwell produced a performance by his sister of *Facade*, a series of her poems read to music composed by his friend and protégé, William Walton. When the event proved a failure with audience and critics alike, the Sitwells' sense of alienation from popular taste increased. Noel Coward lampooned the work and the family in a revue called *London Calling!*, resulting in a feud between himself and the Sitwells that was resolved only many years later. When *Facade* was performed again in April 1926 in Chelsea, however, it was a success. As a boy of ten Sitwell had been to Italy, where his father had purchased the castle Montegufoni near Florence; and the first thing he had done at the end of the war was to travel to Spain with his brother for some passionate sightseeing. He would continue his enthusiastic traveling for the rest of his life. In April 1925 he published his first collection of essays about these experiences, *Discursions on Travel, Art and Life*. Of "these leisurely, Beckfordian pieces on Catania and Lecce, his travels in Sicily and his researches on the Bourbon kings of Naples," his biographer John Pearson writes, "he managed to convey a tone of voice, an easiness of style and

Sitwell shortly before his death in 1969 (photograph by Frank Magro)

learning that guarantee their place in the travel literature of Italy."

Among the professions Sitwell was judged by Arnold Bennett to have followed were organizer of exhibitions of paintings and politician. The chief example of the former occurred in 1924 when he and his brother founded the Magnasco Society, named after a neglected seventeenth-century painter they admired. Each year the society held a splendid dinner at the Savoy Hotel, surrounded by borrowed baroque paintings and presided over by such figures as a future Duke of Wellington. Both brothers, Pearson notes, believed in the baroque as "a world before the Fall–the Fall in the Sitwells' case being the multitudinous disasters of the 19th century–industrialization, the Reform Acts, total war and the decay of taste and manners." Yet despite the reactionary attitude inferred by Pearson's comment, at least once Osbert chose not to remain aloof from the rough-and-tumble of major national events. When the great General Strike broke out in 1926 he persuaded his friend Lady Alice Wimborne, one of the many grand and rich society ladies who doted upon him, to bring together at a lunch the major figures from the government, the trade unions, and the press in an attempt to work out a solution. In an essay in *Laughter in the Next Room* (1948), the fourth volume in his autobiography, Sitwell discusses at length his part in "certain negotiations which helped to end the strike." Although it is doubtful that Sitwell should be credited with directly influencing the outcome, certainly no other occasion in his life provided him with such direct access to power; and he clearly relished the image of an aristocrat working behind the scenes to effect harmony between labor and capital.

Essentially, however, despite a never-ending delight in publicity almost for its own sake, Sitwell enjoyed the privilege of living outside the realm of public affairs while still escaping the pressures, chiefly economic, known by most who live only private lives. In 1926-1927 he made the first of his many trips to the United States, and in Manhattan he met Marianne Moore and Alexander Woollcott, toured Harlem with its most notable literateur/tour guide, Carl Van Vechten, and immensely enjoyed the European art collection of Henry Clay Frick on Fifth Avenue. Trips to the Italian Riviera, North Africa, and the Orient soon followed. With his young friend David Horner he visited Angkor Wat in 1933, and he spent New Year's 1934 with Harold Acton in Peking.

From 1934 until the beginning of World War II Sitwell contributed weekly columns to the *Sunday Referee*; in 1935 a collection of these essays appeared under the title *Penny Foolish*. Pearson writes of them: "they provide a wonderfully readable self-portrait of the author. There are descriptions of his travels . . . , his views on privacy and snobbery, on friends and enemies and ghosts and gardening, on . . . prigs and progress. Altogether the impression . . . is of a garrulous, immensely civilized original, a high-brow eccentric who insists upon the luxury of saying and doing exactly what he wants."

In the 1930s Sitwell formed a close friendship with Queen Mary and the Duke and Duchess of York; he developed a dislike for the Prince of Wales and Mrs. Simpson. His last novel, *Those Were the Days*, appeared in 1938, and then he was off to Guatemala with Horner, chiefly staying in the colonial city of Antigua while writing the book *Escape with Me!* (1939) about his visit to China.

The years of World War II he spent mostly at Renishaw, living the quiet life of a country squire. On 8 July 1943, upon the death of his father at the castle in Tuscany, he became the fifth baronet. Ironically, although with his anti-Churchill, pacifist, and antidemocratic leanings he felt little enthusiasm for the war, his family was making an inadvertent contribution to the cause of civilized Western values during the conflict: the Italian government had used Montegufoni to hide many important Renaissance paintings.

The *Sunday Times* awarded Sitwell one thousand pounds and a gold medal for the first two volumes of his autobiography. Despite coming down with Parkinson's disease, he traveled frequently to America, often in the company of his sister, who in the 1950s was negotiating in Hollywood concerning a movie to be made from her biography of Queen Elizabeth I.

The subtitle of Sitwell's final travel book, *The Four Continents: Being More Discursions on Travel, Art, and Life* (1954), is a reference, of course, to his collected essays of nearly thirty years earlier. Here, as always, he is relaxed and philosophical. Each essay rambles on in graceful, most unjournalistic periods, often wandering within a single paragraph across a variety of places and subjects. Pessimism concerning "progress," especially after the first use of the atomic bomb, is pervasive in these essays, but he can still find romance in the towers of Manhattan or the quiet waters off Sarasota. A significant device in the collection is his extended reflection on the four "elements," earth, air, water, and fire.

His final collection of essays was *Tales My Father Taught Me* (1962), dealing mostly with details and anecdotes of life at Renishaw House. Sit-well's last years were spent at the castle in Italy, where he died on 4 May 1969. His ashes were buried in the Protestant cemetery at Allori, near Florence.

Bibliography:

Richard Fifoot, *A Bibliography of Edith, Osbert and Sacheverell Sitwell*, revised edition (Hamden, Conn.: Archon, 1971).

Biographies:

Rodolphe Louis Mégroz, *The Three Sitwells: A Biographical and Critical Study* (London: Richards, 1927; Port Washington, N.Y.: Kennikat, 1969);

John Lehmann, *A Nest of Tigers: Edith, Osbert and Sacheverell Sitwell in Their Times* (London: Macmillan, 1968);

John Pearson, *Facades: Edith, Osbert and Sacheverell Sitwell* (London: Macmillan, 1979); republished as *The Sitwells: A Family Biography* (New York: Harcourt Brace Jovanovich, 1979).

Reference:

Roger Fulford, *Osbert Sitwell* (London: Longmans, Green, 1951).

Papers:

Osbert Sitwell's papers are at the Harry Ransom Humanities Research Center, University of Texas at Austin.

H. M. Tomlinson

(21 June 1873 - 5 February 1958)

John Lingard
University of Western Ontario

See also the Tomlinson entry in *DLB 36: British Novelists, 1890-1929: Modernists.*

BOOKS: *The Sea and the Jungle* (London: Duckworth, 1912; New York: Dutton, 1913);

Old Junk (London: Melrose, 1918; New York: Knopf, 1920; revised edition, London: Cape, 1933);

London River (London & New York: Cassell, 1921; enlarged and revised, 1951);

Waiting for Daylight (London & New York: Cassell, 1922);

Tidemarks: Some Records of a Journey to the Beaches of the Moluccas and the Forest of Malaya, in 1923 (London & New York: Cassell, 1924); republished as *Tide Marks, Being Some Records of a Journey to the Beaches of the Moluccas and the Forest of Malaya in 1923* (New York & London: Harper, 1924);

Under the Red Ensign (London: Williams & Norgate, 1926; revised edition, London: Faber & Faber, 1932); republished as *The Foreshore of England: Or, Under the Red Ensign* (New York & London: Harper, 1927);

Gifts of Fortune and Hints for Those About to Travel (New York & London: Harper, 1926); republished as *Gifts of Fortune; With Some Hints for Those About to Travel* (London: Heinemann, 1926);

Gallion's Reach: A Romance (London: Heinemann, 1927; New York & London: Harper, 1927);

A Brown Owl (Garden City, N.Y.: Henry & Longwell, 1928);

Illusion, 1915 (New York: Harper, 1928; London: Heinemann, 1929);

Thomas Hardy (New York: Gaige, 1929);

Côte d'Or (London: Faber & Faber, 1929);

All Our Yesterdays (London: Heinemann, 1930; New York & London: Harper, 1930);

Between the Lines (Cambridge, Mass.: Harvard University Press, 1930);

War Books (Cleveland, Ohio: Rowfant Club, 1930);

H. M. Tomlinson in 1949 (photograph by H. Charles Tomlinson)

Norman Douglas (London: Chatto & Windus, 1931; New York & London: Harper, 1931; revised and enlarged edition, London: Hutchinson, 1952);

Out of Soundings (New York & London: Harper, 1931; London: Heinemann, 1931);

The Snows of Helicon (New York & London: Harper, 1933; London: Heinemann, 1933);

Below London Bridge (London: Cassell, 1934; New York & London: Harper, 1935);

South to Cadiz (New York & London: Harper, 1934; London: Heinemann, 1934);

Mars His Idiot (New York & London: Harper, 1935; London: Heinemann, 1935);

Pipe All Hands (New York & London: Harper, 1937); republished as *All Hands!* (London: Heinemann, 1937);

The Day Before: A Romantic Chronicle (New York: Putnam's, 1939; London: Heinemann, 1940);

The Wind Is Rising (London: Hodder & Stoughton, 1941; Boston: Little, Brown, 1942);

Ports of Call (London: Corvinus, 1942);

The Turn of the Tide (London: Hodder & Stoughton, 1945; New York: Macmillan, 1947);

Morning Light: The Islanders in the Days of Oak and Hemp (London: Hodder & Stoughton, 1946; New York: Macmillan, 1947);

The Face of the Earth, With Some Hints for Those About to Travel (London: Duckworth, 1950; Indianapolis: Bobbs-Merrill, 1950);

Malay Waters: The Story of Little Ships Coasting Out of Singapore and Penang in Peace and War (London: Hodder & Stoughton, 1950);

The Haunted Forest (London: Hodder & Stoughton, 1951);

H. M. Tomlinson: A Selection From His Writings, edited by Kenneth Hopkins (London: Hutchinson, 1953);

A Mingled Yarn: Autobiographical Sketches (London: Duckworth, 1953; Indianapolis: Bobbs-Merrill, 1953);

The Trumpet Shall Sound (London: Hodder & Stoughton, 1957; New York: Random House, 1957).

OTHER: Edmund Blunden, *The Bonaventure: A Random Journal of an Atlantic Holiday*, introduction by Tomlinson (New York: Putnam's, 1923);

"Adelphi Terrace," in *H. W. M.: A Selection from the Writings of H. W. Massingham*, edited by Massingham (New York: Harcourt, Brace, 1925);

Christopher Morley, *Safety Pins and Other Essays*, introduction by Tomlinson (London: Cape, 1925);

"Robert Louis Stevenson," in *Great Names, Being an Anthology of English & American Literature From Chaucer to Francis Thompson*, edited by Walter J. Turner (New York: Dial, 1926);

Herman Melville, *Pierre; or, The Ambiguities*, preface by Tomlinson (New York: Dutton, 1929);

Great Sea Stories of All Nations, edited, with an introduction, by Tomlinson (Garden City, N.Y.:

Doubleday, Doran, 1930; London: Harrap, 1930);

Samuel Butler, *Erewhon; or, Over the Range*, introduction by Tomlinson (New York: Chelsea House, 1931);

H. Cotton Minchin, ed., *Best Short Stories of the War*, introduction by Tomlinson (New York & London: Harper, 1931);

An Anthology of Modern Travel Writing, edited by Tomlinson (London & New York: Nelson, 1936).

During his lifetime, H. M. Tomlinson was popularly known as a writer of the sea in the Joseph Conrad tradition and as the author of travel books. It is possible, however, that his literary reputation will rest on his essays, which cover a wide variety of subjects and are distinguished by a natural elegance of style and a mastery of form. Addressing the Harvard Union in 1927 (in a lecture published as *Between the Lines*, 1930), Tomlinson humorously dismissed the idea that he was a "second Conrad" and claimed that his true teachers were Ralph Waldo Emerson and Henry David Thoreau. It is to this American tradition, and to the reflective English school of Thomas Browne's *Hydriotaphia: Urne Buriall* (1658) and Charles Lamb's *Essays of Elia* (1823), that Tomlinson, the essayist, belongs.

Henry Major Tomlinson was born in Wanstead, Essex, on 21 June 1873; the eldest son of Henry and Emily Tomlinson, he grew up in Poplar, close to the docks and the waterway he was to describe with loving detail in *London River* (1921). After his father's death in 1886 Tomlinson was employed as a shipping clerk and in 1904 began his distinguished career as a journalist with the radical *Morning Leader*. His first three articles involved the sea, being about North Sea trawlers, naval maneuvers, and a voyage by tramp steamer up the Amazon to San Antonio Falls, a trip that became the basis for his first and best-known book, *The Sea and the Jungle* (1912).

Old Junk, the first evidence of Tomlinson's transition from journalism to essay writing, appeared in 1918. S. K. Ratcliffe, in his foreword to the American edition (1920), says that, compared with *The Sea and the Jungle*, "*Old Junk* is not, in the same organic sense, a book. The sketches and essays of which it is composed are of different years and . . . of a wide variety of theme." There is, however, a unifying fascination with the revelation of unexpected beauty, value, or even horror, in the apparently banal or every-

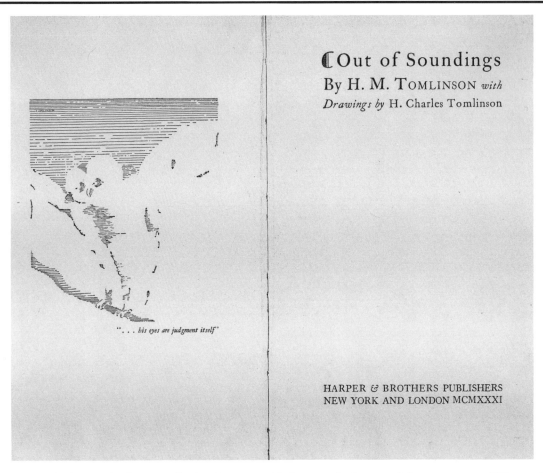

"... *his eyes are judgment itself*"

℃ Out of Soundings
By H. M. TOMLINSON *with*
Drawings by H. Charles Tomlinson

HARPER & BROTHERS PUBLISHERS
NEW YORK AND LONDON MCMXXXI

Frontispiece and title page for the essay collection that opens with the story of a brown owl that once outstared Thomas Hardy

day. In "Transfiguration" a coastal landscape is seen "as though joyous in the first dawn." In "The Pit Mouth" sacrificial heroism is shown by "a common miner." In "The Call" a supposedly simple village youth constructs a wireless set out of old junk. "The Voyage of the Mona" moves with masterly understatement from a quiet fishing village to the terrors of a storm at sea. At one point a lascar's walking stick seems to change into a serpent. Commenting on this collection in 1922, Robert Lynd wrote (in *Books and Authors*) that "As a recorder of the things he has seen [Tomlinson] has the three great gifts of imagery, style and humour," and Lynd singled out for special praise the haunting description of a derelict sailing ship: "She went astern of us fast, and a great comber ran at her, as if it had but just spied her, and thought she was escaping. There was a high white flash, and a concussion we heard. She had gone. But she appeared again, far away, forlorn on a summit in desolation, black against the sunset. The stump of her bowsprit, the accusatory finger of the dead, pointed at the sky." J. B. Priestley said of this passage, "There is the ring of genuine tragic feeling in this clean and strong prose, all the more moving because of its reticence" (*Saturday Review of Literature*, 1 January 1927).

The last seven essays in *Old Junk* stem from Tomlinson's experience as a *Daily News* war correspondent in France from August 1914 to 1917, when he was withdrawn by the Newspaper Proprietors' Association for being too "humanitarian," in other words, too antiwar. The best of these essays, "On Leave," defines with concision and insight the alienation experienced by soldiers temporarily returning from the trenches to a still-pastoral England: "Your revival at home, when on leave, is full of wonderful commonplaces, especially now, with summer ripening. The yellow-hammer is heard on the telegraph wire, and the voices of children in the wood, and the dust of white English country roads is smelled at evening. All that is a delight which is miraculous in its intensity. But it is very lonesome and far. It is curious to feel that you are really there, delighting in the vividness of this recollection of the past, and yet balked by the knowledge that you are, nevertheless, outside this world of home, though it looks and smells and sounds so close; and that you may never enter it again. It is like the landscape in a mirror, the luminous projection of what is behind you. But you are not there." Few other writers could hold in such delicate balance an Edwardian and a modern frame of mind. Edmund Blunden called *Old Junk* "a book for the lovers of Lamb, for in it one hears a century later that most strong, sweet, most immutable undersong which inspired Elia."

In his first postwar volume, *London River*, Tomlinson drew "eleven sketches of that mysterious and powerful influence–the river that has made London what it is." The sketches were acclaimed for their poetic beauty. Priestley found in "A Shipping Parish," for example, the power of "exact detail observed against a vague, glamorous background of dim horizons and lovely lost ships."

In *Waiting for Daylight* (1922) Tomlinson primarily writes of the war again. Each of the book's thirty-three sections is precisely dated, and the whole traces one man's reactions to war and its aftermath, from the trenches–"In Ypres" (July 1915)–to a renewal of hope in "Breaking the Spell" (8 April 1922). There is once more a great variety of topics, ranging from the war itself to islands, travel books, Thomas Carlyle, and ships' figureheads, but the central theme is that nothing can be viewed or discussed innocently again. This idea is expressed most memorably in "The Nobodies" (11 November 1918), in which Tomlinson sees the common soldier as "a gigantic legendary form charged with tragedy and drama . . . a shape forlorn against the alien light of the setting of a day of dread, the ghost of what was fair, but was broken, and is lost." Ashley Gibson wrote that such passages made the volume "one of the truest, freshest and wisest books" to have come out of World War I (*Bookman*, June 1922). A more recent commentator, Derek Severn, feels that Tomlinson "put more of his deepest self into his war writing than into any of his other work" (*London Magazine*, February 1979).

In the mid 1920s Tomlinson left journalism to become a free-lance writer and novelist. The first two books of this period–*Tidemarks* (1924) and *Under the Red Ensign* (1926)–have little more than historical interest today. In *Gifts of Fortune* (1926), however, he collected some of his finest and most characteristic prose. D. H. Lawrence

Drawing of Tomlinson by Irene Hawkins

felt that "the key to this book" was a repeated quest away from "our world of disillusion" to "coasts of illusion," where we "come into contact with other worlds" (in *Phoenix*, edited by Edward D. McDonald, 1936). An example of the visionary quality Lawrence found in *Gifts of Fortune* is the conclusion of "On the Chesil Bank," in which Tomlinson describes six herons, standing at sunrise "like immense figures of bronze. They were gigantic and ominous in that light. They stood in another world. They were like a warning of what once was, and could be again." At the end of his review, Lawrence expressed gratitude "to a man who sets new visions, new feelings sensitively quivering in us."

In 1927 Tomlinson achieved some popular success with his first novel, *Gallion's Reach: A Romance*, but his gifts would always be more suited to the essay form, which in Tomlinson's hands sometimes reads like a short story. In *Illusion, 1915* (1928), for example, Tomlinson shapes a possibly real encounter involving a servant named Whelan, himself, and a British officer named Upcott into a subtle but powerful parable. The re-

H. M. Tomlinson

ported dialogue is dryly accurate, as when the officer orders drinks:

> "Whelan!"
> "Sir!"
> "Whisky. I say, have you seen Major Weston today?"
> "No, sir. He was killed last night, sir."
> Upcott rose and stared at me. Then he sat down again. "Bring the drinks, Whelan," he said.

This classically British stiff-upper-lip response to loss is contrasted with the gallant eccentricity of a French colonel who, as Upcott narrates, punctuated a dinner party with fanfares on a hunting horn, and produced a pack of erotic postcards to demonstrate why France would fight "till not a German was this side of the Rhine; that or death." Tomlinson is able to discover a civilized pathos behind the element of caricature in both incidents. As he writes in his conclusion, any episode is "as meet and proper as another," when played against the background of a war that turns civilization itself into an illusion.

There is a similar subtlety about *Out of Soundings* (1931). In the opening piece (separately published in 1928) Tomlinson makes memorable a brown owl that once outstared Thomas Hardy. "The Changeling" is a story about the unknowability of other people and seems to anticipate Harold Pinter. The more polemical studies in this volume reflect Tomlinson's lifelong distrust of technological progress. "A Lost Wood," "Beauty and the Beast," and "All in a Night" recount the destructive effects on nature and the human spirit of the automobile, talking pictures, radio, and airplanes. Tomlinson's critique of progress is never reactionary, however, and his arguments are often quietly reasonable. *Out of Soundings* ends with a reflection on the death of Thomas Hardy, whose writing, for Tomlinson, preserved "more of the salt of English life in the talk of the characters . . . and more of the English land in his scenes, than in all Hansard, and in all the controversies and guide-books." Tomlinson's criticism is often too subjective and too generalized to be truly valuable, but in "One January Morning" (separately published as *Thomas Hardy* in 1929) he identifies what is permanent in Hardy with precision and feeling.

John Freeman once wrote that Tomlinson's writings too often presented the author "as a man exasperated by the wantonness of war" (*London Mercury*, August 1927). Certainly *Mars His Idiot* (1935), Tomlinson's longest antiwar tract, has found few admirers. It includes an uncharacteristic shrillness, and one American reviewer, William Harlan Hale, pointed to the work's "rather windy wandering that one associates with much modern British journalism" (*Saturday Review of Literature*, 30 November 1935). Far more successful were *The Wind Is Rising* (1941) and *The Turn of the Tide* (1945), two journals that provide an often moving chronicle of British life during World War II. Still convinced that war is "an obscene outrage on the intelligence," Tomlinson supports Britain's war effort on the grounds that an "abominable dominion has to be overcome" (*The Wind Is Rising*). The books were well received, not least for what R. Ellis Roberts (in the *Saturday Review of Literature*, 14 June 1947) called the "curious dignity" of their style.

Tomlinson's last self-edited essay collections, *The Face of the Earth* (1950) and *A Mingled Yarn* (1953), are mainly anthologies of previously published work. The most interesting new material can be found in four autobiographical essays from *A Mingled Yarn*, especially "After Fifty Years," a pleasant tribute from Tomlinson to his wife, Florence (née Hammond), whom he had married in 1898. His last publication was the novel *The Trumpet Shall Sound* (1957). He died on 5 February 1958 in London. Derek Severn remarks that, on reading Tomlinson again in 1979, "it is not difficult to believe the inscription on his gravestone at Abbotsbury in Dorset–an epitaph adapted from Hardy, whose work he loved: 'He was a good man, and did good things.'"

Almost all commentary on Tomlinson agrees on the excellence of his prose style. This is something he seems to have discovered quite early in his career and sustained rather than developed over the years. It is possible, though, to see an increasing mastery of the essay form, which reaches its peak in *Out of Soundings*. Once relatively popular, his work seems to have sunk into obscurity since his death. In 1979 Severn could write that Tomlinson's centenary in 1973 "passed without notice, and not one of his thirty books is now in print" in England. Most of his best essays have, however, been recently reprinted in America, and the first book-length study of Tomlinson (by Fred D. Crawford) appeared in 1981. Tomlinson's subtle, often visionary essays deserve a wide audience, as Severn says, because they are "records of the responses of a sensitive, wise and humane observer at a time when the world was being torn apart."

References:

John Alcorn, *The Nature Novel from Hardy to Lawrence* (New York: Columbia University Press, 1977), pp. 42-59;

Edmund Blunden, "H. M. Tomlinson," in *Edmund Blunden: A Selection of His Poetry and Prose*, edited by Kenneth Hopkins (New York: Horizon, 1961), pp. 303-308;

Fred D. Crawford, *H. M. Tomlinson* (Boston: Twayne, 1981);

John Freeman, "Mr. H. M. Tomlinson," *London Mercury*, 16 (August 1927): 400-408;

Alva A. Gay, "H. M. Tomlinson, Essayist and Traveller," in *Studies in Honour of John Wilcox by Members of the English Department, Wayne State University*, edited by A. Dayle Wallace and Woodburn O. Ross (Detroit: Wayne State University Press, 1958), pp. 209-217;

Ashley Gibson, "H. M. Tomlinson," *Bookman*, 62 (April 1922): 6-7;

Gibson, "Through Western Windows," *Bookman*, 62 (June 1922): 134;

John Gunther, "The Tomlinson Legend," *Bookman*, 62 (February 1926): 686-689;

William Harlan Hale, "Mr. Tomlinson on War and Youth," *Saturday Review of Literature*, 13 (30 November 1935): 6;

Kenneth Hopkins, Introduction to *H. M. Tomlinson: A Selection From His Writings*, edited by Hopkins (London: Hutchinson, 1953), pp. 11-19;

D. H. Lawrence, "*Gifts of Fortune*, by H. M. Tomlinson," in *Phoenix: The Posthumous Papers of D. H. Lawrence*, edited by Edward D. McDonald (New York: Viking, 1936), pp. 342-345;

Robert Lynd, "Mr. H. M. Tomlinson," in his *Books and Authors* (London: Cobden-Sanderson, 1922), pp. 226-232;

Frederick P. Mayer, "H. M. Tomlinson: The Eternal Youth," *Virginia Quarterly Review*, 4 (January 1928): 72-82;

J. B. Priestley, "H. M. Tomlinson," *Saturday Review of Literature*, 23 (1 January 1927): 477-478;

S. K. Ratcliffe, Foreword to Tomlinson's *Old Junk* (New York: Knopf, 1920);

Ratcliffe, "The Ultimate Ordeal," *Saturday Review of Literature*, 25 (21 March 1942): 7;

R. Ellis Roberts, "A Publicist With Keen Eyes," *Saturday Review of Literature*, 30 (14 June 1947): 10;

Derek Severn, "A Minor Master: H. M. Tomlinson," *London Magazine*, new series 18 (February 1979): 47-58;

Edward Weeks, "Authors and Aviators," *Atlantic Monthly*, 172 (November 1943): 58-59;

Patrick Edward White, "Varieties of Primitivism in the Travel Books of D. H. Lawrence, Norman Douglas and H. M. Tomlinson," Ph.D. dissertation, University of Iowa, 1980.

Alfred North Whitehead
(15 February 1861 - 30 December 1947)

R. C. Johnson
University of British Columbia

BOOKS: *A Treatise on Universal Algebra* (Cambridge: Cambridge University Press, 1898);

The Axioms of Projective Geometry (Cambridge: Cambridge University Press, 1906; New York: Hafner, 1971);

The Axioms of Descriptive Geometry (Cambridge: Cambridge University Press, 1907; New York: Hafner, 1971);

Principia Mathematica, 3 volumes by Whitehead and Bertrand Russell (Cambridge: Cambridge University Press, 1910-1913);

An Introduction to Mathematics (London: Williams & Norgate, 1911; New York: Holt, 1911);

The Organization of Thought, Educational and Scientific (London: Williams & Norgate, 1917; Philadelphia: Lippincott, 1917);

An Enquiry Concerning the Principles of Natural Knowledge (Cambridge: Cambridge University Press, 1919);

The Concept of Nature (Cambridge: Cambridge University Press, 1920);

The Principle of Relativity, with Applications to Physical Science (Cambridge: Cambridge University Press, 1922);

Science and the Modern World (New York: Macmillan, 1925; Cambridge: Cambridge University Press, 1926);

Religion in the Making (New York: Macmillan, 1926; Cambridge: Cambridge University Press, 1926);

Symbolism, Its Meaning and Effect (New York: Macmillan, 1927; Cambridge: Cambridge University Press, 1928);

The Aims of Education and Other Essays (New York: Macmillan, 1929; London: Williams & Norgate, 1929);

The Function of Reason (Princeton: Princeton University Press, 1929);

Process and Reality: An Essay in Cosmology (New York: Macmillan, 1929; Cambridge: Cambridge University Press, 1929);

Adventures of Ideas (New York: Macmillan, 1933; Cambridge: Cambridge University Press, 1933);

Alfred North Whitehead

Nature and Life (Chicago: University of Chicago Press, 1934; Cambridge: Cambridge University Press, 1934):

Modes of Thought (New York: Macmillan, 1938; Cambridge: Cambridge University Press, 1938);

Essays in Science and Philosophy (New York: Philosophical Library, 1947; London & New York: Rider, 1948);

Dialogues of Alfred North Whitehead, edited by Lucien Price (Boston: Little, Brown, 1954; London: Reinhardt, 1954);

The Interpretation of Science: Selected Essays, edited by A. H. Johnson (Indianapolis: Bobbs-Merrill, 1961).

Collection: *Alfred North Whitehead: An Anthology*, edited by F. S. C. Northrop and Mason W. Gross (New York: Macmillan, 1953).

OTHER: "Mathematics and the Good" and "Immortality," in *The Philosophy of Alfred North Whitehead*, edited by Paul Arthur Schilpp (New York: Tudor, 1941).

Alfred North Whitehead is best known as a philosopher and a mathematician. He achieved recognition as a mathematician in 1910 when he began collaborating with his student, Bertrand Russell, on the three-volume *Principia Mathematica* (1910-1913). His fame as a philosopher grew more slowly, but by 1925 his philosophy of "organism" was widely recognized as being an outstanding contribution to Western thought. During the period in which he was achieving his reputation as a philosopher, Whitehead was writing and speaking on several other topics, such as education, the history of science, and the history of Western culture. In the latter half of his life, these fields, along with metaphysics, formed his major interests. In educational theory he drew attention to errors in the commonly held views of child psychology, examined the ramifications of those errors, and gave a detailed plan of his own. His theory, applauded by John Dewey, affected the nature of education in Britain. With regard to the history of science, although at times he wrote quite technically, he explained and put into clear perspective the major turning points in the history of man's thought; and he showed the impact each stage had upon contemporary thought. His essays on culture divide into two streams: the major stream examines the past from a history-of-ideas perspective; the other stream examines and comments on the political realities of the contemporary world from the perspective of a political theorist.

Whitehead's primary mode of expressing his ideas was to lecture and then publish his lectures as books. Generally his books contain lectures that may be read separately as essays; the pieces are linked, however, by the common theme of the collection and any lecture may grow out of its predecessor. A lecture series may contain highly technical sections as well as lectures suitable for the general public. Whitehead showed that he was aware of this technical problem: for example, after several chapters tracing the development of scientific thought through the centuries in *Science and the Modern World* (1925), he inserted two highly complex chapters on metaphysics, but tells readers "who find metaphysics, even in two slight chapters, irksome . . . to proceed at once to the chapter on 'Religion and Science,' which resumes the topic of the impact of science on modern thought."

Alfred North Whitehead was born in Ramsgate, Isle of Thanet, Kent, on 15 February 1861. His father was Rev. Alfred Whitehead, a headmaster and priest of the Church of England; his mother, Sarah, was the daughter of the wealthy London businessman William Buckmaster. Whitehead spent the first fourteen years of his life in and around Ramsgate under the tutelage of his father, steeping himself in English history. Occasionally he visited his maternal grandmother in London, watching Queen Victoria pass in processionals from the apartment windows. At age fourteen he left home to spend five years at the public school of Sherborne in Dorset. While there he received a good classics education, one which showed its influence in his later years, and he excelled in mathematics. In 1880, with a Trinity College scholarship, Whitehead began his career at Cambridge. He later taught mathematics at Trinity College from 1885 until he resigned in 1910. From 1911 to 1914 he taught at University College, London, then at Imperial College in London from 1914 to 1924, and at Harvard from fall 1924 to May 1936. In 1890 he married Evelyn Wade, and they had four children: North, 1891; an unnamed boy who died at birth in 1892; Jessie, 1893; and Eric Alfred, 1898, who became a pilot and was killed in 1918 during World War I. By 1890 Whitehead had begun his fruitful association with Bertrand Russell. From the time of his marriage until late in his life Whitehead was active in community affairs, but as a committee member rather than as a politician. His publishing career began in 1898 with *A Treatise on Universal Algebra*. After leaving University College, Whitehead gave several series of lectures at British and American universities, most of them collected and published. He was elected a fellow of the British Academy in 1931 and awarded the Order of Merit in 1945. He died on 30 December 1947 in Cambridge, Massachusetts, at the age of eighty-six.

Whitehead's Tarner Lectures, given at Trinity College, were published in 1920 under the title *The Concept of Nature*. The lecture series had

Whitehead in 1939 after one of his many lectures at Harvard, where he was a full-time professor from 1924 to 1936 (photograph courtesy of Mrs. T. North Whitehead)

as its subject "the philosophy of the sciences, and the relations or want of relations between the different departments of knowledge." Whitehead was the first lecturer in the series. This book forms a companion to *An Enquiry Concerning the Principles of Natural Knowledge* (1919), which discusses the same subjects based on ideas drawn from mathematical physics. *The Concept of Nature* keeps closer to the techniques of philosophical speculation and excludes mathematical notation, which is the core of its companion. The task set forth in *The Concept of Nature* is to develop a philosophy of nature upon which a science investigating nature can be based. In order to clarify the picture, Whitehead spends two chapters tracing how scientific materialism has muddled the philosophical thinking about nature. Beginning with Plato's somewhat undefined concept of matter, made more concrete and rigid by Aristotle–that a basic,

unknowable material substance underlies all physical entities–Whitehead traces the career of that concept, known as scientific materialism, through the major scientific thinkers, such as Francis Bacon, Isaac Newton, and John Locke, to its final dissolution in the discoveries of Albert Einstein. Paralleling the notion of materialism is what Whitehead calls the bifurcation of nature, that dichotomy between the knower and the known that perplexed such thinkers as David Hume and René Descartes. In discussing the theories of perception that then became current, he emphasizes that the major stumbling block in developing an adequate philosophy of nature has been the confusion of the sensory evidence of the "fact" with the operation of the mind upon that evidence. The "fact" is the thing itself that somehow causes sensations in the first place; "factors" are those aspects by which one knows the "fact" (red, circular); an "entity" is that combination of "factors" identified as the "fact." How and why we perceive are interesting areas, but *what* we perceive is the only field for scientific study. Because what we perceive is real and created by the mind, a scientific study of it can produce valuable knowledge.

In discussing earlier philosophers and scientists, Whitehead shows how important to science the triumph of scientific materialism has been, but then shows the inadequacy of that materialism to explain recent discoveries in physics, and since his purpose is to develop a philosophy of nature that will support modern investigation, his attention necessarily turns to relativity theory and its philosophical ramifications. He first describes the principle of relativity as it applies to both time and space, and he points out the difference between his and Einstein's theories. He next gives a detailed definition of key terms such as "extension," "events," and "continuity," and offers an explanation of the method of extensive abstraction by which he is able to define a "moment." Although quite complex, these chapters demonstrate clearly the new philosophy of nature upon which a science can be constructed. In his summary, Whitehead presents several examples of new ways of thought: space has nothing to do with substances, but only with their attributes, so that space is the resultant of relations between bits of matter; time is expressible in terms of the relations of a bit of matter with itself; nature is known to us in our experience as a complex of passing events; and finally, space and time are merely ways of expressing certain truths about the relations between events: they are abstractions.

The publication of *Science and the Modern World* in 1925 established Whitehead as a major philosopher. The book consists mostly of a series of eight Lowell Lectures given at Harvard University, and it is probably the most widely read of Whitehead's books, receiving several reprintings and being published in paperback in 1948. The theme is the energizing of a state of mind in the modern world, the generalizations of that state of mind, and its impact upon the world's spiritual forces. One of Whitehead's major interests is to survey the development of the scientific mind through history. Beginning with Greek thought, he praises the Greeks' intuitive grasp of reality, citing Pythagoras, Archimedes, and Plato. Whitehead sees the idea of fate in Greek tragedy as the basis for the modern concept of order in nature.

Following the Greek period the great contribution of the Middle Ages to the formation of the scientific movement was the belief that every detailed occurrence can be correlated with its antecedents in a definite manner, thus exemplifying general principles. Although its assumptions were based on authorities such as the Bible, rather than on observations, thus being rational rather than empirical, the Middle Ages formed one long training period in the same sense of order. The seventeenth century for Whitehead marks the real beginning of the modern world. He outlines the remarkable intellectual advances made by Newton and Locke and shows their effects on the philosophy of the time. Scientific materialism proved useful for scientists working on the specific problems of eighteenth-century science, but it did not satisfy the intuitive perceptions of the Romantic poets, and a perceivable gap developed between the artists and spiritual thinkers on one hand, and the scientists on the other. In his discussion of the Romantic nature poets Whitehead outlines his own concept: "I would term the doctrine of these lectures, the theory of *organic mechanism*. In this theory, the molecules may blindly run in accordance with the general laws, but the molecules differ in their intrinsic characters according to the general organic plans of the situations in which they find themselves . . . [a] doctrine [that] involves the abandonment of the traditional scientific materialism, and the substitution of an alternate doctrine of organism." Whitehead learned a lot from the nature poets; a few pages later he echoes William Wordsworth when he says, "This is the solution of the problem which I gave in my last lecture. . . . In a certain sense, everything is everywhere at all times. For every location involves an aspect of itself in every other location. Thus every spatio-temporal standpoint mirrors the world." It is a short step from this notion to the notion of relativity, which he treats in subsequent chapters.

One other aspect of *Science and the Modern World* deserves mention. Throughout much of his life Whitehead was an agnostic, believing that God is unknowable rather than accepting the intellectually untenable position of either the Anglican or the Catholic Church. But much of Whitehead's thought centered on the puzzle of first causes. In this book, in *Process and Reality* (1929), and in *Adventures of Ideas* (1933), he comes to grips with the basic question. Much to the dismay of many of his contemporaries, Whitehead estab-

To my great regret bad health, culminating in a serious illness, has prevented study of the chapters in this book, ~~previous~~ before publication By taking my writings as a text for discussion, the authors of these chapters have done me an honour which I fully appreciate.

The absence of any direct expression of my reaction to these chapters is but a slight loss. The progress of philosophy does not primarily involve reactions of agreement or dissent. It essentially ~~depends~~ consists in the enlargement of thought, whereby contradictions and agreements are transformed into partial aspects of wider points of view. Thus my own reaction to this book should consist in devoting many years to rewriting my previous works. Unfortunately this is impossible.

The two chapters which follow were delivered as lectures in Harvard in the years 1940, 1941, respectively. They summarize

Facsimile of an introductory note by Whitehead included in The Philosophy of Alfred North Whitehead *(1941), edited by Paul Arthur Schilpp. The note precedes two of Whitehead's essays, "Mathematics and the Good" and "Immortality."*

2

basic ideas from which my philosophic thought has developed, and which became more clear in the course of that development.

Finally, I wish to ~~express~~ state my sense of the energy and zeal with which Professor Schilpp is editing a series of volumes, each volume expressing the points of view of a large group of writers. He is producing a display of contemporary thought, unified in each volume by its reference to ~~some~~ contemporary writer as providing a common text. In this enterprise the function of the text is to produce a unity in the thoughts of the authors of the chapters. Professor Schilpp deserves our gratitude for discovering a new mode of exhibiting contemporary thought.

My thanks are also due to Dr Victor Lowe and Dr Robert Baldwin for their unremitting zeal in discovering ~~~~ miscellaneous publications extending over sixty years.

Cambridge, Mass.   Alfred North Whitehead
September 20, 1941

lished both a metaphysical proof for the existence of God and an ethical principle linking the concept of deity to his process philosophy, which he discusses in *Adventures of Ideas*: "Some particular *how* is necessary, and some particularization in the *what* of matter of fact is necessary. The only alternative to this admission, is to deny the reality of actual occasions. Their apparent irrational limitation must be taken as a proof of illusion and we must look for reality behind the scene. If we reject this alternative behind the scene, we must provide a ground for limitation which stands among the attributes of the substantial activity. This attribute provides the limitation for which no reason can be given: for all reason flows from it. God is the ultimate limitation, and His existence is the ultimate irrationality. For no reason can be given for just that limitation which it stands in His nature to impose. God is not concrete, but he is the ground for concrete actuality. No reason can be given for the nature of God, because that nature is the ground of rationality." Whitehead's focus on the concept of God as the "ultimate limitation" demonstrates the influence mathematics had in the development of his metaphysics, which in turn influenced his career as a teacher.

The Aims of Education, first published in 1929, has as its primary idea, in Whitehead's words, that "students are alive, and the purpose of education is to stimulate and guide their self-development.... The whole book is a protest against dead knowledge, that is to say, inert ideas." The chapters were originally delivered as addresses at various conferences, but when bound together they form a statement of Whitehead's beliefs concerning educational topics, as seen in "The Rhythm of Education" and "The Rhythmic Claims of Freedom of Discipline." Other chapters examine the various curricula of the British school system–the literary, the scientific, the technical, and the classical–and endeavor to harmonize their purposes so that some aspect of all may be experienced by every student. Throughout his work on education, Whitehead emphasizes the necessity for a student to see the utility of what he is studying, to learn the principles firsthand, and to see that what he is studying is connected intimately to his life and generally to all existence. Whitehead recognizes that mankind is naturally specialist, and he is in favor of specialized learning, but learning must not be disconnected from life. He resolves the generalist-specialist problem in this way: "What education has to impart is an intimate sense for the power

of ideas, for the beauty for ideas, and for the structure of ideas, together with a particular body of knowledge which has peculiar reference to the life of the being possessing it."

In the chapters on rhythm in education, Whitehead takes issue with the conventional wisdom of his day. His first point is that a student should undertake subjects and modes of study when the student is ready for them; different students are ready at different times. Next, he says that the difficulty of a subject is not a factor in its order of precedence; a child who learns the alphabet and correlates visual shapes with sounds could just as easily be taught calculus. What is important is that the young students should be excited by the subject. There are, he proposes, three stages in the student's intellectual progress: the stage of romance or novelty; the stage of precision; and the stage of generalization. In the first stage, "knowledge is not dominated by systematic procedure." Rather, the student apprehends facts and becomes excited by the realization of the possibilities of unexplored relationships. Education in this first stage must concern itself with ordering the ferment already stirring in the student's mind. In the second stage, precision, the width of the relationships the student perceives is subordinated to exactness of formulation. The student must now learn how to analyze; he must learn discipline, technique, and classification. The final stage, generalization, is a synthesis of the first two. That is, the student returns to the first period of romance, but now he brings to it the tools learned in the second stage.

Although these stages recur many times throughout life as one becomes excited by ideas, Whitehead sees these stages also as defining one complete life cycle: novelty and romance lasting from birth to adolescence; precision from adolescence to early adulthood; and generalization from adulthood until death. Because of this larger learning cycle that Whitehead perceives in human beings, he proposes a course of education that, by taking into account, would produce students who are both more alive to and better able to investigate the world of ideas. Of course, various disciplines are presented to a student at different stages of his development and to some extent determine what curriculum that individual will study at any particular time. Thus, when language, including the study of foreign languages, enters the stage of precision, science usually begins its period of ferment, and they continue in the same relationship, language reaching its pe-

Alfred North Whitehead (photograph by Richard Carver Wood)

riod of generalization when science reaches the stage of precision. Whitehead would develop curricula that take into account both the student's stage of development and the type of study the student is ready for at that particular stage. Whitehead would have both language and mathematics taught very early in life, science much later, giving as his reason that children are observably much more interested in talking and counting than they are in seeing how things work.

Whitehead's view of twentieth-century education is rather pessimistic; he sees it as a descent from divine wisdom to textbook knowledge. Modern education has produced dull minds, according to him; the mind must be able to run freely among, and be excited by, its subjects. Knowledge may be the acquiring of ordered fact, but wisdom comes from being free in the presence of knowledge. To avoid textbook dullness, education must guide the individual toward a comprehension of the art of life, and the art of life is self-guidance in the adventure of existence. The ultimate motive power alike in science, morality, and religion is the sense of value and the sense

of importance it excites. Education must lead one, in wonder, curiosity, and reverence, to desire to merge the personality with something beyond itself–with the sense of beauty, of realized perfection.

Much of the book investigates the relationships between the various kinds of curricula. When discussing the relationship of technical training to science and literature, Whitehead claims that workers should see their work as play, much as the Benedictine monks saw themselves as fellow workers with Christ. For laborers to feel that their work is worthwhile, they must be taught culture, the effect being to divest labor from associations with aimless toil. However, the workers he is talking about are those who have received an establishment education. Thus, when he discusses the place of literature in a technical education, the usefulness of training in science, and the fact that technical education is training in the art of utilizing knowledge for the manufacture of material products, Whitehead seems to be combating both the prejudices of the working class against the more esoteric of university studies and the intellectual elitism that refuses to recognize the values inherent in a technical education. He goes on to point out that the liberal Greek education, which created science, encouraged art, and maintained freedom of thought, was possibly only because the culture used slave labor. Therefore, because England, a land without slaves, needs the same labor, the education that the laborer receives should be as satisfying to him, and more useful, than a liberal education. A liberal education, Whitehead says, is for the purpose of improving thought and aesthetic appreciation; "the field of acquirement is large, and the individual so fleeting and so fragmentary: classical scholars, scientists, headmasters are alike ignoramuses." For certain people, it is a good education, but the expression of the human spirit is not confined to literature, nor to a liberal education.

For Whitehead the preferred educational curriculum is the scientific curriculum focusing on mathematics, for he sees it as meeting both practical and ethical ends. His discussion of this point turns into a consideration of the principles involved in setting up a mathematical course of study: what the student should be expected to learn from a study of geometry, trigonometry, and so forth. Regarding the other curricula, Whitehead sees the classical curriculum as being in trouble in modern schools simply because "Classics" is no longer the road to career advancement. "Opportunity has now shifted its location, and Classics is in danger." Yet he points out many reasons why Classics should be studied: to discipline character and achieve culture; to learn the history of Europe; and to develop one's faculty of logic. In his discussion of the role of universities, he points out that the management of a university faculty is not analogous to managing a business, for the task of a university is to weld together knowledge and experience. The importance of universities is that they provide the place and the means for the final stage in the student's intellectual training; after this stage, growth and development come from within the individual.

Whitehead addresses his own development in *Essays in Science and Philosophy*, a small collection of lectures and essays spanning the period from 1912 to 1937. The pieces are organized into four sections: autobiography, philosophy, education, and science. The first section brings together essays about Whitehead's early years and early schooling; they show how his interest in history was prompted both by a strong classical education and by the provocative evidence of Roman occupation all around him. In the essays on education, he refers to these early experiences as being the proper kind of material to fertilize young minds. The section on philosophy introduces many of the key aspects in his concept of organism, which summarizes thus: "The misconception which has haunted philosophic literature throughout the centuries is the notion of 'independent existence.' There is no such mode of existence; every entity is only to be understood in terms of the way in which it is interwoven with the rest of the Universe." Also among the essays of the first three sections are several that give insight into his practical politics. In one essay he justifies giving up Czechoslovakia to Adolf Hitler; in another he supports the Balfour Declaration of 1917, which gave British support to the concept of a Jewish state in Palestine. In these essays he seems to rely on a Victorian worldview of politics rather than his own thought; he recognizes the great achievements, for example, of the Palestinian intellectual tradition, but seems not to grasp what it means to a Palestinian, to a Czech, or to anyone to have the nations of the world agree to give away one's homeland to a people one despises. Yet in the same collection, in "Immortality" (originally published in *The Philosophy of Alfred North Whitehead*, edited by Paul Arthur Schilpp, 1941), he denies the intellectual authority of the world by directly contradicting Plato and the theology derived from him: "Value refers to Fact, and Fact refers to Value." Whitehead goes on to say that value cannot be considered apart from activity, because there is no such thing as a self-contained abstraction. Later, when speaking about Communism, he negates the concept of the state as a religious entity, saying, "We have developed a moral individuality; and in that respect, we face the universe–alone."

Adventures of Ideas is Whitehead's summary statement about what constitutes civilization and how civilization arose. Although it includes some material from earlier lecture series and from previously published articles, the book presents coherent and well-integrated arguments and discussions about the energizing ideas that have brought the world to its present condition. The first section of the book, called "Sociological," traces one idea, the freedom of the human soul, from its inception in Greek thought, through its refinement under medieval Christian thinkers, past the contributions of the Methodists, the Quakers, the Freethinkers, and the scientists, into its codification in the laws of the great nations of the present. Whitehead suggests that the notion of freedom found its way through persuasion rather than force. He says, "But beyond these special activities a greater bond of sympathy has arisen. This bond is the growth of reverence for that power in virtue of which nature harbours ideal ends, and produces individual beings capable of conscious discrimination of such ends. This reverence is the foundation of the respect for man as man. It thereby secures that liberty of thought and action, required for the upward adventures of life on this Earth."

The next section discusses science, not precisely a history of science, but an examination of the effect of general scientific ideas on the changing culture of Europe–similar to the examination made in *Science and the Modern World*. The section called "Philosophical" provides a more accessible account of the metaphysics detailed in *Process and Reality*. It attempts to explain the metaphysical meanings of such terms as "mortality and immortality"; "the past, the present, and the future"; and "causation and memory." In the final section, "Civilization," he discusses the meaning and function for civilization of the concepts of truth, beauty, and peace. Even perfect civilizations exhibiting truth and beauty, he argues, have been and will be destroyed because of the tedium of infinite repetition; therefore, one is persuaded by a sense of tragedy and a sense of evil to go beyond achieved perfection. Although Whitehead's summation of beauty, art, and personality belong distinctly to a philosopher rather than to an artist, his final statement of the idea of the book is that of a poet: "At the heart of the nature of things, there are always the dream of youth and the harvest of tragedy. The Adventure of the Universe starts with the dream and reaps tragic Beauty. This is the secret of the union of Zest with Peace– That the suffering attains its end in a Harmony of Harmonies. The immediate experience of this Final Fact, with its union of Youth and Tragedy, is the sense of Peace. In this way the World receives its persuasion towards such perfections as are possible for its diverse individual occasions."

Although Whitehead began his professional career as a mathematician and collaborated with Russell on the important *Principia Mathematica*, he is better known popularly for his writings on education and on the history of Western culture. He is best known professionally as the man who developed the philosophy of organism into one of the most important contributions to Western thought, along with the work of Einstein, in the first half of the twentieth century. His essays stand as good examples of the clarity and persuasiveness of his ideas.

Bibliography:

Barry A. Woodbridge, ed., *Alfred North Whitehead: A Primary-Secondary Bibliography* (Bowling Green, Ohio: Philosophy Documentation Center, 1977).

Biography:

Victor Lowe, *Alfred North Whitehead: The Man and His Work*, 2 volumes (Baltimore: Johns Hopkins University Press, 1985, 1990).

References:

David L. Hall, *The Civilization of Experience: A Whiteheadian Theory of Culture* (New York: Fordham University Press, 1973);

Charles Hartshorne, *Whitehead's Philosophy: Selected Essays 1935-1970* (Lincoln: University of Nebraska Press, 1972);

Paul G. Kuntz, *Alfred North Whitehead* (Boston: Hall, 1984);

Victor Lowe, *Understanding Whitehead* (Baltimore: Johns Hopkins University Press, 1962);

Robert M. Palter, *Whitehead's Philosophy of Science* (Chicago: University of Chicago Press, 1960);

Paul Arthur Schilpp, ed., *The Philosophy of Alfred North Whitehead* (New York: Tudor, 1941).

Charles Williams
(20 September 1886 - 15 May 1945)

Nancy-Lou Patterson
University of Waterloo

BOOKS: *The Silver Stair* (London: Herbert & Daniel, 1912);

Poems of Conformity (London & New York: Oxford University Press, 1917);

Divorce (London & New York: Oxford University Press, 1920);

Windows of Night (London: Oxford University Press, 1924);

The Carol of Amen House, music by Hubert J. Foss (London, 1927);

The Masque of the Manuscript, music by Foss (London: Henderson & Spalding, 1927);

An Urbanity (London: Privately printed, 1927);

A Myth of Shakespeare (London: Oxford University Press, 1928);

The Masque of Perusal (London: Privately printed, 1929);

Heroes and Kings (London: Sylvan Press, 1930);

Poetry at Present (Oxford: Clarendon Press, 1930; Freeport, N.Y.: Books for Libraries Press, 1969);

War In Heaven (London: Faber & Faber, 1930; New York: Pellegrini & Cudahy, 1949);

Three Plays (London: Oxford University Press, 1931)—comprises *The Witch, The Chaste Wanton,* and *The Rite of the Passion;*

Many Dimensions (London: Gollancz, 1931; New York: Pellegrini & Cudahy, 1949);

The Place of the Lion: A New Novel (London: Mundanus/Gollancz, 1931; New York: Norton, 1932);

The Greater Trumps (London: Gollancz, 1932; New York: Pellegrini & Cudahy, 1950);

The English Poetic Mind (Oxford: Clarendon Press, 1932; New York: Russell & Russell, 1963);

Bacon (London: Barker, 1933; New York: Harper, 1933);

Reason and Beauty in the Poetic Mind (Oxford: Clarendon Press, 1933; Folcroft, Pa.: Folcroft Library Editions, 1974);

Shadows of Ecstasy (London: Gollancz, 1933; New York: Pellegrini & Cudahy, 1950);

James I (London: Barker, 1934; New York: Roy, 1953);

Charles Williams (photograph by Elliott & Fry)

Rochester (London: Barker, 1935; Folcroft, Pa.: Folcroft Library Editions, 1976);

Queen Elizabeth (London: Duckworth, 1936);

Thomas Cranmer of Canterbury (London: Oxford University Press, 1936);

Descent into Hell (London: Faber & Faber, 1937; Grand Rapids, Mich.: Eerdmans, 1947);

Henry VII (London: Barker, 1937);

Stories of Great Names (London: Oxford University Press, 1937);

He Came Down from Heaven (London: Heinemann, 1938);

Taliessin through Logres (London & New York: Oxford University Press, 1938);

The Descent of the Dove: A Short History of the Holy Spirit in the Church (London: Longmans, 1939; New York: Oxford University Press, 1939);

Judgement at Chelmsford: A Pageant Play Written by Charles Williams for Performance at the New Scala Theatre, London . . . from September 23rd to October 7th, 1939, in Celebration of the Twenty-fifth Anniversary of the Diocese at Chelmsford (London: Oxford University Press, 1939);

Religion and Love in Dante: The Theology of Romantic Love (Westminster, U.K.: Dacre Press, 1941; Norwood, Pa.: Norwood Editions, 1978);

The Way of Exchange (London: Clarke, 1941);

Witchcraft (London: Faber & Faber, 1941; Cleveland: World, 1959);

The Forgiveness of Sins (London: Bles, 1942);

The Figure of Beatrice (London: Faber & Faber, 1943; New York: Noonday Press, 1961);

The Region of the Summer Stars (London: Nicholson & Watson, 1944);

To Michal, after Marriage: A Poem (Derby, U.K.: Bacon & Hudson, 1944);

All Hallows' Eve (London: Faber & Faber, 1945; New York: Pellegrini & Cudahy, 1948);

The House of the Octopus (London: Edinburgh House Press, 1945);

Flecker of Dean Close (London & Edinburgh: Canterbury Press, 1946);

Arthurian Torso: Containing the Posthumous Fragment of The Figure of Arthur, by Charles Williams, and a Commentary on the Arthurian Poems of Charles Williams by C. S. Lewis (London & New York: Oxford University Press, 1948);

Seed of Adam, and Other Plays (London & New York: Oxford University Press, 1948);

Scorpion Reef (New York: Macmillan, 1953);

The Image of the City, and Other Essays, edited by Anne Ridler (London & New York: Oxford University Press, 1958);

Selected Writings, edited by Ridler (London: Oxford University Press, 1961);

Collected Plays (London & New York: Oxford University Press, 1963).

OTHER: *Poems of Home and Overseas*, edited by Williams and V. H. Collins (Oxford: Clarendon Press, 1921);

A Book of Victorian Narrative Verse, edited, with a preface, by Williams (Oxford: Clarendon Press, 1927);

"Notes on Possible Endings to *Edwin Drood*," in *The Mystery of Edwin Drood*, by Charles Dick-

Williams as a young man in St. Albans (photograph by Phyllis Jones)

ens (London: Oxford University Press, 1927), pp. 366-376;

Gerard Manley Hopkins, *Poems*, edited by Robert Bridges, second edition, introduction by Williams (London: Oxford University Press, 1931);

Sir Edmund Kerchever Chambers, *A Short Life of Shakespeare, with the Sources*, abridged by Williams (Oxford: Clarendon Press, 1933);

The New Book of English Verse, edited, with an introduction, by Williams (London: Gollancz, 1935; New York: Macmillan, 1936);

" 'Troilus and Cressida' and 'Hamlet,' " and "Henry V," in *Shakespeare Criticism, 1919-35*, edited by Anne Bradby (London: Oxford University Press, 1936), pp. 180-208;

"Queen Victoria," in *More Short Biographies*, edited by R. C. Goffin (London: Oxford University Press, 1938), pp. 29-49;

Søren Kierkegaard, *The Present Age*, translated by Alexander Dru and Walter Lowrie, introduction by Williams (London: Oxford University Press, 1940);

The English Poems of John Milton, edited, with an introduction, by Williams (London: Oxford University Press, 1940);

The New Christian Year, edited by Williams (London & New York: Oxford University Press, 1941);

The Letters of Evelyn Underhill, edited, with an introduction, by Williams (London: Longmans, Green, 1943);

"On the Poetry of *The Duchess of Malfi*," in *The Duchess of Malfi*, by John Webster (London: Sylvan Press, 1945), pp. xv-xxii;

Wilfrid Gibson, *Solway Ford, and Other Poems*, edited by Williams (London: Faber & Faber, 1945).

SELECTED PERIODICAL PUBLICATIONS–
UNCOLLECTED: "The Hero in English Verse," *Contemporary Review*, 118 (December 1920): 831-838;

"The Commonwealth in English Verse," *Contemporary Review*, 124 (August 1923): 228-236;

"The One-Eared Man," *Dominant*, 1 (April 1928): 11-12;

"The History of Critical Music," *Dominant*, 1 (April 1928): Supplement, iv-v;

"Notes on Religious Drama," *Chelmsford Diocesan Chronicle*, 23 (May 1937): 75-76;

"H. M. P.," *Lantern* (January 1938): 98-101;

"On Byron and Byronism," *Bulletin of the British Institute of the University of Paris* (April 1938): 13-19;

"Taste in Literature," *Listener*, 24 (26 December 1940): 913-914;

"The Recovery of Spiritual Initiative," *Christendom*, 19 (December 1940): 238-249;

"The War for Compassion," *Sword of the Spirit*, no. 20 (15 May 1941): 7;

"Notes on the Way," *Time and Tide*, 22 (13 September 1941): 769;

"Paracelsus," *Time and Tide*, 22 (27 September 1941): 820-821;

"Notes on the Way," *Time and Tide*, 23 (28 February 1942): 170-171;

"Notes on the Way," *Time and Tide*, 23 (7 March 1942): 194-195;

"St. John of the Cross," *Time and Tide*, 23 (27 June 1942): 522;

"A Dialogue on Mr. Eliot's Poem," *Dublin Review*, 212 (April 1943): 114-122;

"Hell," *St. Albans Diocesan Magazine* (April 1943);

"Tasso," *Time and Tide*, 25 (11 March 1944): 216.

Charles Williams thought of himself primarily as a poet; he published seven volumes of poetry between 1912 and 1944. He also wrote seven novels and fifteen plays. During his lifetime, however, his most frequently anthologized works were essays of literary criticism, chiefly about poetry, and his essays continued to be anthologized posthumously. In the late twentieth century Williams speaks as a significant and even prophetic voice of his own period, writing with intense awareness of the watershed in literary style and subject matter between the Edwardian era and the era dividing the two world wars.

Charles Walter Stansby Williams was born on 20 September 1886 in Holloway, North London, to Walter and Mary Wall Williams. His parents were devout members of the Church of England. He called himself an "irrevocable bourgeois . . . (though a Cockney bourgeois, let me add a little haughtily; there are degrees even in dust)." In 1894 the family moved to St. Albans, where Walter Williams, suffering from failing sight, opened a shop for artists' supplies. Williams attended St. Albans Grammar School, then began to commute daily to University College, London, where he studied Latin, French, and English history until a lack of family funds forced him to leave at eighteen. After four years assisting in the New Connexion Methodist Bookroom in London and attending classes at the Working Men's College on Crowndale Road, Williams became a proofreader at Oxford University Press in 1908. In the same year he met Florence Conway, the daughter of a St. Albans ironmonger. In the context of their falling in love, Williams was set to proofing a translation of *The Divine Comedy*: this coincidence of life and art was the germ of his great theme of the Beatrician vision.

With his first volume of poetry, *The Silver Stair* (1912), Williams's literary career began. In 1914 he was declared unfit for military service due to the persistent trembling of his hands; thus, in addition to missing the Oxbridge education of his literary peers, he also missed the profound initiation of the trenches. He married Florence (whom he dubbed "Michal") on 12 April 1917 in St. Albans Abbey. On 21 September he was installed into an offshoot of the Golden Dawn, an occult order much influenced by the Christian occultist A. E. Waite. Publication of his *Poems of Conformity* (1917) coincided with these events.

Williams (left) with William Butler Yeats, circa 1917 (Marion E. Wade Collection, Wheaton College, Wheaton, Illinois)

The year 1920 brought a third book of poetry, *Divorce*, and Williams's first essay in literary criticism, "The Hero in English Verse." He began as he was to continue: already poetry and theology appear hand in hand. The Hero, according to Williams, is "a poetic figure to symbolize Man," and the theme of "humanity undergoing its doom" is explored in the works of Milton, Tennyson, Browning, Wordsworth, and Patmore. Williams's peculiar vocabulary–"Omnipotence" as a title of God, for example–begins to appear, as does his intention to better the *Idylls of the King* (1859-1885) with Arthurian poems after his own heart.

A son, Michael, was born in 1922. The following year Williams began lecturing at the London County Council Literary Institute. In his second essay, "The Commonwealth in English Verse" (1923), he explores the "ideal commonwealth," a precursor of his major theme of "the City." Among Shelley, Patmore, Wordsworth, Swinburne, Robert Browning, and Tennyson, Williams finds that Browning has best recognized that "each happy family combines freedom with obedience, the individual with the Community." In the Oxford University Press, with its august

publisher, Henry Milford, Williams thought he saw "the Community" exemplified.

An eccentric but compelling lecturer, Williams had begun to acquire a following of students and admirers. He published his fourth volume of poetry, *Windows of Night*, in 1924. By this time an editor, he produced two introductions to literary works–"Notes on Possible Endings to *Edwin Drood*" (1927) and a "Prefatory Note" in *A Book of Longer Modern Verse* (1926)–and began to write the first of his occult novels, *Shadows of Ecstasy*, which was published in 1933. At forty, he fell in love with the Oxford University Press's new librarian, Phyllis Jones, whom he dubbed first "Phillida" and then "Celia." For her he wrote *An Urbanity* and *The Masque of the Manuscript*, both performed at Amen House in Warwick–where the Oxford University Press had moved in 1924–and privately published in 1927. Phyllis fell in love as well, but with someone else. During this intense period of unconsummated and unrequited love he wrote the preface to *A Book of Victorian Narrative Verse* (1927), which notes that in Victorian literature noble conduct was an end in itself and that "nobility cannot afford to be conscious of itself," lest, like Tenny-

POETRY AT
PRESENT

BY

CHARLES WILLIAMS

OXFORD
AT THE CLARENDON PRESS
1930

Title page for Williams's first book of literary criticism, in which each of sixteen essays on contemporary British poets is accompanied by a poem by Williams in the manner of that poet

son's Arthur, it risk "mere pomposity." He laments that nobility has become "unfashionable," while "subtlety, . . . irony, and bitterness" prevail.

Two slight comic essays preface a major development in Williams's critical career. In "The One-Eared Man" (1928) he comments upon the absence of images in music; music, he says, is "the resolution of all knowledge into its simplest form." To this abstract element he was to return. In "The History of Critical Music" (1928) he wittily imagines a music devoted to the criticism of other music. Williams carried out a similar exercise in his first volume of criticism, *Poetry at Present* (1930), in which each of sixteen essays on contemporary British poets is accompanied by a poem in the manner of that poet. The essays in *Poetry at Present* were seriously meant, however. Three of them were separately published; "John Masefield" preceded the book in the *Saturday Review of Literature*, probably because its subject had just been named Poet Laureate. In Masefield, Wil-

liams detects "a substitution of loveliness for intensity." In "T. S. Eliot" Williams comments wryly that "quite a number of [Eliot's] lines are his own creation." He pronounces *The Waste Land* (1922) a "Hell varied by intense poetry," and asks hopefully, "Can this hell be rather the place of purgation?" Williams became friends with Eliot in 1934. "Robert Bridges" praises Bridges's poetry as "beauty in restraint."

In 1931 Williams published an introduction to the *Poems* of Gerard Manley Hopkins; most critics think that Hopkins was the model for Williams's later poetic style. He praises Hopkins's "continued shocks of strength and beauty" and says the poet's theories are only ways of "explaining to himself his own poetic energy." The lectures Williams delivered to evening classes for the London City Council at the City Literary Institute and to many Evening Institutes in London formed the background for his second critical volume, *The English Poetic Mind* (1932). In 1933 appeared his first biography, *Bacon*, as well as a brief biographical essay, "Lord Macaulay."

Williams's most seminal critical essay, "The Ostentation of Poetry," appeared as the introductory chapter of his third book of literary criticism, *Reason and Beauty in the Poetic Mind* (1933). His ideas, like so many in the twentieth century, are presaged by the *Biographia Literaria* (1817) of Samuel Taylor Coleridge. Chapter 18, "Language of metrical composition, why and wherein essentially different from that of prose," calls attention to the peculiar "*order*" of verse when compared "with the language of ordinary men." Coleridge says that in poetry, as the "elements are formed into metre artificially, by a voluntary design . . . so the traces of present volition should throughout the metrical language be proportionately discernible." The poet, according to Coleridge, states boldly: "I write in metre, because I am about to use a language different from that of prose." In "The Ostentation of Verse" Williams observes that despite the trend away from strict patterns in poetry, patterns are still a "necessity." The difference between poetry and prose "is ostentatiously insisted upon by the verse itself"; indeed, "The ostentation is part of the verse." The poem exists "neither in the pattern nor the subject of which we are separately aware, but in the resultant whole." Williams calls attention to the "flagrancy" of the "pattern," that is, of the abstract elements in poetry. These elements are "the decision of the writer," a "personal choice among impersonal patterns." Williams follows Coleridge in saying that poetry is the willed and controlled use of metre and metaphor to create effects different from those of prose.

The ostentatious abstract element of poetry as defined by Williams appears again in F. W. Bateson's *English Poetry: A Critical Introduction* (1950), though without attribution: "It is only indeed by a process of abstraction that the poet can give meaning." In the twentieth century, consciousness of the abstract element in art is central to the practice as well as the criticism of art: Williams's essay of 1933 is an important manifestation of this consciousness in its historical context. (The concept of poetic "ostentation," adumbrated by Coleridge, developed by Williams, and then further elaborated by Bateson, is thoroughly explored in Robert Beum's *Poetic Art of William Butler Yeats* [1968], which sees ostentation or "verbal conspicuousness" as the touchstone, the definitive feature of all poetry.)

In his introduction to *The New Book of English Verse* (1935) Williams bases his choices upon an "effort to avoid Cant." This important essay introduces his view that for Milton "the Satanic rebellion was not only wicked but silly." Also included is an insight as profound as that of "The Ostentation of Poetry." Williams states of his era, "It is the moment of the close of the myths. English verse had carried in its tradition a continual use of the myths–of Achilles, Alexander, Arthur, of the fables and the religions, especially of that greatest of the myths, . . . Christianity." Now, the myths, "If they are ever used, . . . are recognized as states of awareness." This recognition arises, Williams says, from "the conscious knowledge of our consciousness." Consciousness of abstraction and consciousness of consciousness are the twin foci of twentieth-century criticism, and Williams contributed to the development of both concepts.

Two selections from *The English Poetic Mind* were anthologized in 1936 in *Shakespeare Criticism, 1919-35*, indicating the importance of Williams's criticism in his own period. In the first of these passages, which are somewhat awkwardly excised from their original context, *Troilus and Cressida* and *Hamlet* are seen as embodying Shakespeare's struggle to make his poetry match the human experience of deciding and acting in a world where what is may change to what ought not to be: Williams's experiences with Phyllis Jones underlie this interpretation. Also in *Shakespeare Criticism, 1919-35* is the essay "Henry V," which discusses "the sublime Fourth Chorus" ("Now entertain conjecture of a time").

REASON AND BEAUTY
IN THE
POETIC MIND

BY

CHARLES WILLIAMS

OXFORD
AT THE CLARENDON PRESS
1933

Title page for the book that includes Williams's seminal essay, "The Ostentation of Poetry"

In 1935 Williams received the highest compliment ever paid to his abilities as a playwright: he was invited to follow Eliot's masterpiece *Murder in the Cathedral*, performed that year at Canterbury Cathedral, with a play of his own. *Thomas Cranmer of Canterbury*, produced and published in 1936, is perhaps Williams's best play. In February of that year C. S. Lewis borrowed a copy of *The Place of the Lion* (1931) and wrote to a friend that it was "a really great book." In March Williams received a letter expressing Lewis's delight in his novel, and the next day he wrote to praise Lewis's *The Allegory of Love*, which he had proofread for the Oxford University Press. The two men soon met for lunch in London, and their friendship ensued.

An essay, "Notes on Religious Drama," followed Williams's Canterbury play in 1937. The major event of that year for Williams was the publication of *Descent into Hell*, his masterpiece, in which his theme of "Substitution" is embodied rather than argued. The ideas of "Co-inherence" (the oneness of all) and "Exchange" (bearing one another's burdens) to which he refers so often and so gnomically in his religious essays beginning in 1938 resonate through *Descent into Hell* in a profound display of power.

Also published in 1937 was "The New Milton" (collected in *The Image of the City*, 1958), pointing out the "element of comedy" in *Paradise Lost*. In a touching subtext Williams discusses Milton's blindness in terms clearly based on his own father's experience. The 1938 essay "Religious Drama" (*The Image of the City*), says trenchantly that plays dealing with dogmas are "almost all bad." A lecture given in Paris, "On Byron and Byronism," was also published in 1938, as were the biographical essays "Queen Victoria" and "H. M. P." (on Helen M. Peacock). Another whimsical essay on music, "Sound and Variations" (*The Image of the City*), appeared the same year. Even this minor piece contains a significant aphorism: art "provokes true emotions, and consequently does not represent them."

In 1938 Williams published the first of his two major volumes of Arthurian poetry, *Taliessin through Logres*, in which all he had learned about verse was applied in works of powerful originality. He also published his first volume of explicitly theological speculation, *He Came Down from Heaven*.

With the outbreak of World War II in 1939, Oxford University Press moved to Southfield House, Oxford. Although Williams's wife remained in London, she had forgiven his infatuation with Phyllis Jones. At Oxford, Williams lectured on Milton, and Lewis reports that he held the undergraduate audience spellbound as he spoke on chastity in *Comus*. His seminal essay "Sensuality and Substance" (*The Image of the City*), appeared in the journal *Theology* in 1939. Although theology was not a new theme for him, here it takes the central position as he discusses the sacrality of matter and of the human body; the "Affirmation of Images" (related to the "Affirmative Way" as opposed to the more commonly used "Negative Way" of mysticism); the holiness of the intellect; and the concept of "Romantic Theology." Blake and D. H. Lawrence are compared, and their heresies against these concepts are corrected. "Poetry," Williams says, "is sensual and intellectual, like sex."

Also in 1939 Williams published his second volume of theological speculation, *The Descent of the Dove*. A related essay, "The Church Looks For-

ward" (1940; collected in *The Image of the City*), contains the pronouncement that theologians have worked out "the doctrine of our Lord as God" but that "The doctrine of His Manhood . . . has still to be worked out and put into action." Continuing the theme expressed in his earliest essays, he derives the subject of "The Image of the City in English Verse" (1940; in *The Image of the City*) from the vision of "the New Jerusalem" in Revelation and sees its most perfect literary expression in a line from *Henry V*: "The singing masons building roofs of gold." An interview, "Taste in Literature" (1940), offers a rare example of his speaking style. In "The Recovery of Spiritual Initiative" (1940), an address to a group of sociologists, he says acerbically that the church is served by people "who blanket their messages by making heroic efforts to talk in a way nobody listens to."

The introduction to *The English Poems of John Milton* (1940) includes a comment which probably contributed to C. S. Lewis's *Perelandra* (1943): "Obedience . . . is the proper order of the universe in relating to a universal law," and an analysis of Satan's sense of "injured merit" which certainly contributed to Lewis's *A Preface to Paradise Lost* (1942). This essay contains Williams's most-quoted aphorism, "Hell is always inaccurate." Hell, as Williams personifies it, is unable to understand not only Heaven but ordinary human life.

Williams's second introduction of 1940, to Søren Kierkegaard's *The Present Age*, reports that this prophet attacked his "Age" for "its mediocrity, its insignificance, its solemn and imbecile hypocrisy." To Kierkegaard, " 'The Crowd' meant . . . number, quantity, multiplication," whereas, Williams says, "there is only the individual and necessity. There and there only is Authority."

Nine essays–the longest series published by Williams in any one year–appeared in 1941. Later included in *The Image of the City* are: "Charles Williams on *Taliessin through Logres*," "Blake and Wordsworth," "The Redeemed City," and "Natural Goodness." "Charles Williams on *Taliessin through Logres*" sets forth the major symbols he added to the Arthurian canon: "the identification of the Empire of Byzantium . . . with the human organism" and the magical, disciplinary, and measuring properties of the hazel rod (which have caused some observers to see a sadistic element in the poems). "Blake and Wordsworth" returns to Williams's study of "the feeling intellect"; comparing Blake's "prophetic books"

Williams in 1935 (photograph by Elliott & Fry)

with Wordsworth's *The Prelude* (1850), he defines his doctrine of "Co-inherence" as "the exchange of pardon between all men and women." In "The War for Compassion" he sees World War II as being fought for "the restoration . . . of the natural rights of man" already existing before the church and calls on the church to search for "what remains of freedom in the most abandoned or the most oppressed." In "Notes on the Way," after commenting on words the war has coined (*quisling*) or debased (*appeasement*), he gives his only published reference to his exile in Oxford. Mourning "by Isis for my lovelier Thames," he laments that while unlike the Psalmist, "It is no Babylon that receives us, but friends and comfortable houses," even so, like Dante, he eats "the salt bread" and "climbs the steep stairs of others." In "The Redeemed City," a major theological essay, he says of Britain: "There is no final idea for us but the glory of God in the redeemed and universal union–call it Man or the Church or the City." In "Natural Goodness" he argues that the natural and the supernatural are not actually opposed and that "Matter and 'nature' have not, in themselves sinned; what has

sinned is spirit." The essay *Religion and Love in Dante: The Theology of Romantic Love* contains the heart of Williams's thought, which influenced his friend Dorothy L. Sayers in her translation for Penguin of *The Divine Comedy*. Dante's work begins with "nightmare" and culminates in "the supernatural validity of that 'falling-in-love' experience" of Dante with Beatrice, he says, discussing an idea he later developed most fully in *The Figure of Beatrice* (1943). *The Way of Exchange* declares that "exchange and substitution fills the phrase 'bear ye one another's burdens' with a much fuller meaning than is usually ascribed to it." For Williams, "Compacts can be made for the taking over of the suffering of troubles, and worries, and distresses, as simply and as effectively as an assent is given to the carriage of a parcel." Williams's *Witchcraft* (1941) is still one of the best studies of its subject.

"Notes on the Way" (28 February 1942) comments that in Williams's Arthurian myth "there was imagined a union of geography, physiology, and metaphysics," and adds: "philosophic truths depend for the Church on the body. Torture and concentration camps and slavery are against the body." The body was for Williams a measure of the real and was intrinsically innocent.

Williams had defined the Affirmation of Images in "The Church Looks Forward" as "Justice, Charity, Union." These, he said there, "are the three degrees of the Affirmation of the Images, and all of us are to be the images affirmed." In a rare discussion of the Rejection of Images in "St. John of the Cross" (1942) he calls it one of the "darker metaphors," but an image nonetheless. He adds that "even the images must be loved only because God loves them." In "The Index of the Body" (1942; in *The Image of the City*) he reviews the uses in astrological and religious symbolism of the body as a figure for the cosmos, and "not merely the old spatial macrocosmic heavens, but the deep heavens of our inner being," in other words, of the Unconscious. C. S. Lewis used the phrase "deep heaven" with this meaning in *That Hideous Strength* (1945). Williams had joined Lewis's circle, "The Inklings," a group that met weekly for drink, conversation, and reading aloud from their works in progress.

By 1943 he was lecturing regularly at Oxford University, which gave him an honorary M.A. in that year. In "A Dialogue on Mr. Eliot's Poem" (1943) he imagines a conversation between Nicobar, Eugenio (evidently himself), Sophronisba, and Celia on *Little Gidding* (1942), pronouncing these verses in Celia's voice "soliloquies from the heart's cloister." The chidden Eugenio laments of his earlier, lower estimation of Eliot, "I have said so much that I do not clearly remember." A second conversation between the four voices, "A Dialogue on Hierarchy" (1943; collected in *The Image of the City*), concludes that "we are not to suppose that the hierarchy of one moment is likely to be that of the next," and that "Equality is the name we give to the whole sum of such exchanges." This idea also anticipates Lewis's *That Hideous Strength*.

Williams's introduction to *The Letters of Evelyn Underhill* (1943) remains essential to the understanding of Underhill. Expecting more because of their shared membership in an offshoot of the Golden Dawn, Williams finds her occult novels disappointing. From his own experience of "Impossibility," in which what is becomes what ought not to be, he understands her shock when Pius X condemned Modernism: "It is the details of the Impossibility that press home—the sordid, the cosmic, the agonizing," he says feelingly, echoing his painful encounter with "Celia." He finds that Underhill's *Mysticism* (1911), which he "must

Williams in Oxford, 1939 (photograph by Anne Spalding)

have read . . . within a year or two of its appearance," still has for him the "immediate sense of authority."

Of all his theological essays, "What the Cross Means to Me" (1943; collected as "The Cross" in *The Image of the City*) is the most accessible and the most profound: "It is credible that the Almighty God should . . . create beings to share His Joy . . . but it is not credible that a finite choice ought to result in an infinite distress." The Cross demonstrates that "alone among the gods, He deigned to endure the justice He decreed," Williams says, and adds of the Cross that "This is what Almighty God, as well as we, found human life to be." Writing in the depths of World War II, he says, "It is finished; we too do but play out the necessary ceremony. As in bombings from the air, cancer, or starvation, for instance? Yes, I suppose so; if at all, certainly in those examples." He concludes: "Not the least gift of the Gospel is that our experience of good need not be separated from our experience of evil."

Williams's second volume of Arthurian poetry, *The Region of the Summer Stars*, was published in 1944, as was an essay related to his poetry, "Malory and the Grail Legend" (*The Image of the City*). Neither Tennyson nor William Morris "had the full capacity of the mythical imagination," he says, and he praises Malory's figure of Galahad as "that in the human soul which finds Christ." The last year of his life saw the publication of his superb supernatural novel *All Hallows' Eve* and his final introductory essay, "On the Poetry of *The Duchess of Malfi*," a dark opinion of a darker work. In this triumphant novel and this dystopic essay the extremes of his extraordinary personality are encompassed. Williams died on 15 May 1945 from complications of surgery to correct a recurrent intestinal disorder. His death shocked his friends: Lewis wrote that when Williams died, it was the idea of death which had to change.

In his lifetime, Charles Williams enjoyed the approval of some distinguished peers. His earliest posthumous appreciation came from Lewis in *Arthurian Torso* (1948). Anne Ridler edited anthologies of his essays in 1958 and 1961; in her commentary on the first she wrote that his "literary criticism is 'creative criticism' of a kind that has been somewhat out of fashion since the analytical critics were in the ascendant." In *Charles Williams* (1966) Mary McDermott Shideler comments that his "non-fiction is more explosive and illuminative than his imaginative writings . . . because expository writings cannot be brushed off by alluding to fantasies or figures of speech."

During the 1980s several books on Williams appeared, including Alice Mary Hadfield's second and indispensable biography. In *Charles Williams: Poet of Theology* (1983) Glen Cavaliero perceives that in the "critical books one can see Williams moving towards an equation between literary method and personal apprehension. The 'why' of poetry was implicit in its 'how.' The discovery, which must have come naturally to one who was steeped in an incarnational theology, was to have a lasting impact on his development both as theologian and as artist."

At this distance, Williams's critical works emerge as vivid cultural artifacts, revealing a mind original, individual, personal, and intuitive, through which is refracted, as through a prism, the uncertain sunlight of his era.

Bibliographies:

Lawrence R. Dawson, Jr., "A Checklist of Reviews by Charles Williams," *Papers of the Bibliographical Society of America*, 55 (Second Quarter 1961): 100-117;

Lois Glenn, *Charles W. S. Williams—A Checklist* (Kent, Ohio: Kent State University Press, 1975).

Biographies:

Alice Mary Hadfield, *An Introduction to Charles Williams* (London: Hale, 1959);

Hadfield, *Charles Williams: An Exploration of His Life and Work* (London: Oxford University Press, 1983).

References:

Humphrey Carpenter, *The Inklings* (London: Allen & Unwin, 1978);

Glen Cavaliero, *Charles Williams: Poet of Theology* (Grand Rapids, Mich.: Eerdmans, 1983);

Lawrence R. Dawson, Jr., "Reflections of Charles Williams in Literature," *Ball State Teachers College Forum*, V (Winter 1964): 23-29;

John Heath-Stubbs, *Charles Williams* (London: Longmans, Green, 1955);

Mary McDermott Shideler, *Charles Williams* (Grand Rapids, Mich.: Eerdmans, 1966);

Shideler, *The Theology of Romantic Love: A Study in the Writings of Charles Williams* (New York: Harper, 1962);

Agnes Sibley, *Charles Williams* (Boston: Twayne, 1982).

Papers:

Many of Williams's papers and publications are held by the Wade Collection, Wheaton College, Wheaton, Illinois.

Leonard Woolf

(25 November 1880 - 14 August 1969)

R. D. Schell
Laurentian University

BOOKS: *The Village in the Jungle* (London: Arnold, 1913; New York: Longmans, Green, 1913);

The Wise Virgins: A Story of Words, Opinions and a Few Emotions (London: Arnold, 1914);

International Government: Two Reports (London: Allen & Unwin, 1916; New York: Brentano's, 1916);

The Future of Constantinople (London: Allen & Unwin, 1917; New York: Macmillan, 1917);

Co-operation and the Future of Industry (London: Allen & Unwin, 1918);

International Economic Policy (London: Labour Party, 1919);

Economic Imperialism (London: Swarthmore / New York: Harcourt, Brace & Howe, 1920);

Mandates and Empire (London: British Periodicals, 1920);

Empire and Commerce in Africa: A Study in Economic Imperialism (London: Allen & Unwin / New York: Macmillan, 1920);

Socialism and Co-operation (London & Manchester: National Labour, 1921);

Stories of the East (Richmond, Surrey, U.K.: Hogarth, 1921);

International Co-operative Trade (London: Fabian Society, 1922);

Fear and Politics: A Debate at the Zoo (London: Hogarth, 1925);

Essays on Literature, History, Politics, Etc. (London: Hogarth, 1927; New York: Harcourt, Brace, 1927);

Hunting the Highbrow (London: Hogarth, 1927);

Imperialism and Civilization (London: Hogarth, 1928; New York: Harcourt, Brace, 1928);

The Way of Peace (London: Benn, 1928);

After the Deluge: a Study in Communal Psychology, 2 volumes (London: Hogarth, 1931, 1939; New York: Harcourt, Brace, 1931, 1939);

Quack, Quack! (London: Hogarth, 1935; New York: Harcourt, Brace, 1935);

The League and Abyssinia (London: Hogarth, 1936);

Leonard Woolf with Sally, the Woolfs' dog (courtesy of Hogarth Press)

Barbarians at the Gate (London: Gollancz, 1939); republished as *Barbarians Within and Without* (New York: Harcourt, Brace, 1939);

The Hotel (London: Hogarth, 1939);

The War for Peace (London: Routledge, 1940);

The International Post-War Settlement (London: Fabian Publications/Gollancz, 1944);

Foreign Policy: The Labour Party's Dilemma (London: Fabian Publications/Gollancz, 1947);

Principia Politica: A Study of Communal Psychology (London: Hogarth, 1953; New York: Harcourt, Brace, 1953);

Sowing: An Autobiography of the Years 1880-1904 (London: Hogarth, 1960; New York: Harcourt, Brace, 1960);

Growing: An Autobiography of the Years 1904-1911 (London: Hogarth, 1961; New York: Harcourt, Brace & World, 1961);

Diaries in Ceylon, 1908-1911: Records of a Colonial Administrator (Dehiwala: Ceylon Historical Journal, 1962; London: Hogarth, 1963);

Beginning Again: An Autobiography of the Years 1911-1918 (London: Hogarth, 1964; New York: Harcourt, Brace & World, 1964);

Downhill All the Way: An Autobiography of the Years 1919-1939 (London: Hogarth, 1967; New York: Harcourt, Brace & World, 1967);

The Journey Not the Arrival Matters: An Autobiography of the Years 1939-1969 (London: Hogarth, 1969; New York: Harcourt, Brace & World, 1970).

Collection: *In Savage Times: Leonard Woolf on Peace and War*, selected by Stephen J. Stearns (New York: Garland, 1973).

OTHER: "Three Jews," in *Two Stories*, by Leonard and Virginia Woolf (Richmond, Surrey, U.K.: Hogarth, 1917);

The Framework of a Lasting Peace, edited, with an introduction, by Woolf (London: Allen & Unwin, 1917);

The Intelligent Man's Way to Prevent War, edited, with an introduction, by Woolf (London: Gollancz, 1933);

"Can Democracy Survive?," in *The Modern State*, edited by Mary Adams (London: Allen & Unwin, 1933);

Labour's Foreign Policy, edited by Woolf (London: Gollancz/New Fabian Research Bureau, 1934);

Revision of Treaties and Changes in International Law, edited by Woolf (London: Gollancz/New Fabian Research Bureau, 1934);

"The Early Fabians and British Socialism," in *Shaw and Society: An Anthology and a Symposium*, edited by C. E. M. Joad (London: Oldham's, 1947);

"Political Thought and the Webbs," in *The Webbs and Their Work*, edited by Margaret Cole (London: Meuller, 1949);

A Calendar of Consolation, compiled by Woolf (London: Hogarth, 1967; New York: Funk & Wagnalls, 1968).

TRANSLATIONS: Maksim Gorky, *Reminiscences of Leo Nicolayevitch Tolstoi*, translated by Woolf and S. S. Koteliansky (Richmond, Surrey, U.K.: Hogarth, 1920; New York: Huebsch, 1920);

The Note-Books of Anton Tchekhov, translated by Woolf and Koteliansky (Richmond, Surrey, U.K.: Hogarth, 1921; New York: Huebsch, 1921);

The Autobiography of Countess Sophie Tolstoi, translated by Woolf and Koteliansky (Richmond, Surrey, U.K.: Hogarth, 1922; New York: Huebsch, 1922);

I. A. Bunin, *The Gentleman from San Francisco, and Other Stories*, translated by Woolf, Koteliansky, and D. H. Lawrence (Richmond, Surrey, U.K.: Hogarth, 1922; New York: Seltzer, 1923);

Gorky, *Reminiscences of Tolstoy, Chekhov and Andreev*, translated by Woolf, Koteliansky, and Katherine Mansfield (London: Hogarth, 1934).

Though less well known than his wife, Virginia, Leonard Woolf also had a remarkable career. His political education was multifaceted and complete, and despite success in the Ceylon civil service, he became a forceful critic of imperialism and an outstanding champion of the self-determination of third-world peoples. Contact with hideous London slums, totally alien to his boyhood, and with the desperate plight of working-class women led him to be a lifelong socialist and an early advocate of women's rights. World War I, which destroyed forever the old secure civilization he knew as a child, made him a proponent of the League of Nations, a hater of tyranny, and a student of the roots of war and the inadequacies of the human psyche that failed to match his own unflinching rationalism. Becoming a novelist before his wife, he soon abandoned fiction for literary journalism and political comment, producing some forty books and thousands of essays, only to turn his hand in old age to writing a classic autobiography (in five volumes beginning in 1960).

Leonard Sidney Woolf was born on 25 November 1880 in Kensington, Middlesex, the second child (of ten) of Sidney Woolf, Q.C., a barrister, and Marie de Jongh Woolf, of Dutch birth. Members of a reformed synagogue, the senior Woolfs had left the more traditional Hebrew culture of their ancestors. Fiercely admiring of his father, Leonard was likewise intended for the bar and also showed an early bent for journalism in

The Woolfs in 1914, two years after their marriage

two childhood productions assembled for family consumption, "The Leonard Paper" and "Zoological News." Sidney Woolf died young in 1892 (when Leonard was twelve), leaving a large, young family and an estate of £6,120, equal to the lifetime earnings at that time of, say, a police inspector or a teacher in a better school, but barely a year's earnings for Woolf at the bar. Leonard's lifelong habit of carefulness with money was thus born of a painful forced adjustment, not to poverty, but to acquiring an upper-middle-class education on lower-middle-class means. Woolf was educated at St. Paul's School, a Tudor foundation where the curriculum was still the almost total diet of Latin and Greek it had been in John Milton's day, and at Trinity College, Cambridge, where he read for the Classical Tripos and was inducted into the secret Cambridge

Conversazione Society ("The Apostles"). Contemporary fellow members included philosopher G. E. Moore, John Maynard Keynes, and Lytton Strachey.

Failing to gain first-class honors on the second part of the Tripos and doing poorly on the civil service examination, Woolf entered the Ceylon Service, a less-sought-after branch, and left England for seven years in 1904, taking with him a fox terrier and seventy volumes of Voltaire. Efficient, hardworking, and ultra-organized, he rose quickly, becoming an assistant government agent, responsible on his own for Hambantota Province, at the age of twenty-eight. Woolf became increasingly disaffected, however, with both his country's role and his own in Ceylon. This attitude, coupled with his developing relationship with Virginia Stephen, led to his resignation from the service in 1912, toward the end of a year's furlough in England.

Married later that year to Virginia, who had just enough income to support them both, Woolf first sought a living from writing fiction. *The Village in the Jungle* (1913), his first novel, remains a genuine original, an account of small-village life that re-creates plausibly and powerfully, yet somewhat vicariously, the natives' fears and vulnerabilities in the face of a hostile environment and an alien administration that fails to understand them even when it seeks to provide care and justice. *The Wise Virgins* (1914), drawing on another aspect of Woolf's experience, treats fictionally a young Jew who falls in love, like Woolf, with the daughter of a well-established Victorian intellectual. Much of the detail successfully combines class satire with psychological insight, but the identity of the central characters as artists is given no real vitality.

It soon became apparent that fiction did not pay well enough and that Virginia Woolf's otherwise adequate income would not support the medical and nursing expenses incurred in connection with her major mental breakdown in 1913. Meanwhile, however, Leonard Woolf's considerable sense of social duty, refined and developed by his service in Ceylon, took new directions, facilitated in part by the activities of friends. Madge Vaughan's sister Marny, working among the poor of Hoxton with the Care Committee, arranged encounters with the horrors of urban poverty that helped make him a socialist. Even more decisive was Margaret Llewelyn Davies, who led him into the Co-operative Movement, a working-class organization. The movement provided an elaborate alternative to the capitalist economy, maintaining its own network of factories, distribution arrangements, and shops. As he says in *Beginning Again* (1964), Woolf saw in the movement "a means of applying some of the principles of democracy to the economic system." A June 1913 article for the liberal-leaning *Manchester Guardian* brought him to the attention of Beatrice and Sidney Webb, who were the founders and leaders of the Fabian Movement, the inventors, more or less, of the science of political economy, especially as applied to local government, and the instigators of the London School of Economics. They were also patrons of promising young men suitable to their purposes. Woolf was put to work writing two reports that were published as *International Government* in 1916, and a new career was begun. (The reports first appeared as two supplements to the *New Statesman*, another Webb initiative.)

Guided by a conviction that the problem of war can (and must) be analyzed on scientific lines, Woolf wrote that it was imperative for hostile nations, like criminal individuals, to be restrained by subjecting pernicious national wills to the control of international law. A whole range of necessary enabling institutions is envisioned in *International Government*, including arbitration boards and judicial tribunals with binding international authority. Prewar entanglements of secret diplomacy must be replaced by open internationalization of law, information, society, and standards. Specific organizations are needed to oversee public health, industry and commerce, crime control, maritime law, labor legislation, copyright enforcement, and so on.

A passionate belief in the power of reason pervades Leonard Woolf's nonfiction writings, especially those on international affairs. World War I, the "Deluge" in the title of *After the Deluge* (1931, 1939), destroyed the kind of privileged Victorian society that Woolf emerged from and, although a nervous tremor and Virginia Woolf's precarious health gained Woolf himself exemption from military service, left his generation decimated and emotionally scarred. A sense of the war's horror and an almost evangelical conviction that it must be prevented from happening again figure in much of Woolf's subsequent writing career.

Other books on the same internationalist lines followed quickly. *The Framework of a Lasting Peace* (1917), edited and introduced by Woolf, reiterates the call for the substitution of law for force and presents the itemized peace proposals of five groups, including the Fabians. *The Future of Constantinople* (1917) argues that the various nationalistic aspirations to power centered on that city were perhaps the real cause of World War I (and of earlier wars since 1453). Settling the city's future in international terms, in keeping with its cosmopolitan population and its strategic position, both military and economic, is seen as "a test case of the success of the Allies' aims in the war." *Mandates and Empire* (1920), one of six League of Nations Study Circle booklets (G. Lowes Dickinson and Arnold Toynbee wrote others), advocates that the control and development of African and Asian territories be "mandated" on a stewardship basis for the well-being of the inhabitants, instead of for the imperialist expansion of European interests. Similar concerns are explored with encyclopedic thoroughness in a spe-

The Woolfs' residence in Rodmell, where they often retreated from London to relax and write

cific context in *Empire and Commerce in Africa* (1920).

Woolf's interests again turned to the Co-operative Movement in 1921, as seen in *Socialism and Co-operation*, in which he envisions the fulfillment of socialist aspirations in an extension of the principles of cooperation, covering all phases from production, through distribution, to retailing of goods. *International Co-operative Trade* (1922), written as a Fabian tract, represents the culmination of Woolf's interest in the movement and a point of intersection with his internationalism. Hitherto, the Co-operative Wholesale Society, a part of the movement, had to import from capitalists abroad, through capitalist channels. Woolf sees investments by the movement in a tea estate in Ceylon or a wheat farm in Canada as obvious further steps needed to complete the cycle. Along with new extension of the organization, he envisions an international information bureau or clearinghouse, an international buying agency, and an international bank to finance trade, production, and cooperative credit. A fully articu-

lated system would thus provide an international cooperative exchange operating in all countries independently of capitalist channels. Such a system would also provide working relationships between consumer movements and agricultural movements. It would constitute, in fact, the establishment of a fully international movement on the same basis as existing national ones.

Woolf's assimilation into the inner circles of socialist politics was swift, helped by extensive publishing in several journals, among them *New Weekly*, *Co-operative News*, the *Times Literary Supplement* (to which his wife contributed long before him and contributed much more frequently), the *Contemporary Review*, the *International Review* (edited by Woolf from 1919 to 1920), the *New Statesman*, and the *Nation and Athenaeum*. Woolf served as literary editor of the *Nation and Athenaeum* from 1923, when Keynes bought an interest in it, until it amalgamated in 1931 with the *New Statesman*. This was to be Woolf's last salaried position. It had first been offered to T. S. Eliot, who found its six-month guarantee of tenure insufficient security compared to his lifetime position at Lloyds Bank. After Woolf's *International Government* was used to draft Britain's League of Nations proposals, he became honorary (unpaid) secretary of the Labour party's Advisory Committee on Imperial Questions–a position he held for many years–and was a somewhat reluctant (and unsuccessful) candidate for one of the anachronistic and long-since-abolished Combined University parliamentary seats.

After their marriage in 1912, the Woolfs had soon moved out of London to Richmond for the sake of Virginia's precarious health, and there, as a therapeutic exercise, they had acquired a modest handpress and an assortment of type. Beginning with their own *Two Stories* (1917), they published with their own hands several modest booklets, often written by friends, and including an early collection of Eliot's poetry. As success came, the press expanded rapidly, soon contracting printing out to jobbing printers. James Joyce's *Ulysses* (1922) was reluctantly turned down in spite of their admiration for it when, because of fear of prosecution for publishing obscenities, no willing printer could be found. The Hogarth Press, so named after their house in Richmond, became at a later date the first publisher in England of the collected works of Sigmund Freud.

Subscription selling began early, and with the Woolfs' expansion various series of books were launched. One of these, the Hogarth Essays, included Leonard Woolf's *Fear and Politics: A Debate at the Zoo* (1925), a proto-Orwellian animal fable in which roles are reversed and the zoo's inhabitants debate about the outside world only to decide in the end that they are much better off with the humans locked securely out. A second monograph essay, *Hunting the Highbrow* (1927), is less successful in transcending the schoolmasterly device that organizes it, a taxonomy of true and phony versions of "highbrows," complete with Latin species and subspecies. The message, however, remains pure Woolf: that true highbrows are civilization's essential and saving element.

The Hogarth Press also occasioned Woolf's forays into the field of translation, with some Russian items of classic interest appearing in the early 1920s. The real translation was, however, done by S. S. Koteliansky and others; Woolf's contribution was to translate Koteliansky's erratic phrasing into standard English.

The Woolfs with Sally at Rodmell in 1938 (photograph by John Lehmann)

Most of Woolf's early journalism for the *Nation and Athenaeum* and the *New Statesman* was literary in character, and much of it was collected in *Essays on Literature, History, Politics, Etc.* (1927). Some of the earliest *New Statesman* writings use character sketches as a mode of sociological exploration, fragments perhaps of Woolf's abandoned career aspirations as a fiction writer. Much of the *Nation and Athenaeum* writing deals with poets, novelists, and belles lettres. Although his critiques have not generally contributed anything of significance to the present understanding of the writers under examination, they nevertheless seem hardly to have become dated. This is perhaps due to a liveliness of style and a gift for drawing anecdotal interrelationships between writer and work. He is at his best when writing of those who, like Ben Jonson, were interesting characters with interesting lives. (Woolf later praised Winston Chur-

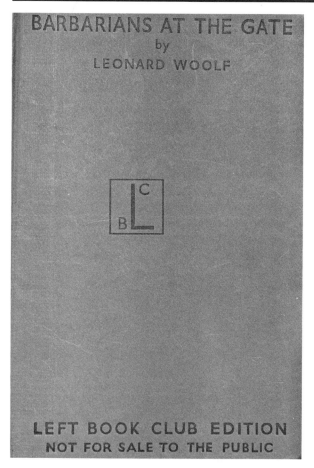

*Cover for the book-club edition of Woolf's 1939 book decry-
ing the excesses of social, economic, and political elitism*

foundation of civilized life which was at stake in
the [Alfred] Dreyfus case" (23 November 1935).
In one place this stridency hints publicly at the private desperation that led the Woolfs to lay in a
stock of gasoline for the purpose of asphyxiating
themselves in the event of Adolf Hitler's expected success at invading England: "The only individual right which the state will leave to its citizen will be the legal right to escape from it by
suicide. The frequency with which that right is
used will then be the measure of the people's civilization" (15 August 1936). Some of Woolf's most
scathing observations came at the expense of public figures whose biographies he reviewed. Arthur, Lord Balfour became one such target and
seems to focus many of Woolf's concerns (14
November 1936): "The blindness with which
aristocracies—another name for vested interests—
encompass their own and other people's ruin is a
commonplace of history and is illustrated once
more in the life of Balfour. The Marxist sees in
it a proof of materialist determination, but it may
equally be explained as part of the psychological
determination of history." This kind of note
reaches a peak of both bitterness and devastation
in a 1 May 1943 review of a silly account by Neville Henderson (Chamberlain's Berlin ambassador) of his dog Hippy. Hippy's mindless blood-
sporting savagery is made to reflect both on his
ineffectual master and on Hitler as another "mongrel Austrian"; Hippy (Woolf says) would have
been the better ambassador.

Woolf's *New Statesman* review essays, several
a year, continued unabated after the personal tragedy of Virginia's suicide in 1941, and on through
the war and after. In 1955 he was trying to apply
to the nuclear bomb menace the same rational
and analytic approach used forty years earlier to
deal with the international government problems
of those simpler days. Another late piece (12 November 1955) uses autobiographical reflections in
an impassioned plea against capital punishment:
"But not primarily because of the unfortunate
'criminal' and his agony in the condemned cell or
in the garden and upon the cross; no, the argument against capital punishment was its effect
upon, its meaning for, the miserable young Dep-
uty Fiscal from Kensington and Cambridge, the
too jaunty and fidgety superintendent from
Wormwood Scrubs, the young clergyman praying
hysterically for the soul of the condemned man,
the frightened Sinhalese warder from a Kenyan
village, the uncomfortable hangman—and behind
those the lawyers and the court, the Crown Prose-

chill, whom he generally regarded as something
of a Victorian relic, for producing writing that
gives life to its subjects.) Woolf seems particularly
adept as an early critical sponsor of Eliot's *Waste
Land* (1922). The Hogarth Press had been one of
Eliot's early publishers, and Eliot was a close
friend of the Woolfs.

In the 1920s and thereafter most of Woolf's
journalism was in the form of review essays, but
the center of his concerns became gradually
much more historical and political. The note he
sounds is often negative, especially when perceived abuses of class, privilege, and colonial imperialism are involved, as seen in many essays for
the *New Statesman*. Of the British in India he
writes (30 June 1934): "One can but marvel at
the astonishing capacity of patriotism for finding
food for self-glorification in that revolting record." He becomes progressively more strident
about the decay of civilization, finding something
of current relevance in the dubious honor of an
earlier age: "They [the dictators] destroyed that

cutor and the self-righteous judge, the legislators in Columbo and Westminster—and behind these again the anonymous multitude and what we call civilization."

Woolf's most sustained series of political essays, some two dozen, appeared over the course of a quarter century in the *Political Quarterly*, which he founded with William Robson in 1930 and edited jointly with him for many years. The originally intended audience was the Labour party M.P. and his like, perhaps properly motivated, but in need of more educated, intellectual guidance. The enlightened liberal's keynote concerns are all there, especially disenchantment with a world that has failed to make the League of Nations the instrument for preventing war that less spineless political leaders might have made it, and early insight into the catastrophic and inhuman nature of the German misadventure into Fascism and Nazism. After World War II (in 1946) there is an examination of the problem of controlling nuclear power, and some perspicuous comments on the role of a socialist England in postwar European occupation. (Woolf prescribes avoiding the identification with capitalist America that would vitiate Labour party goals.) An early essay (1931) looks at radio broadcasting as a potent tool for creating the kind of educated public that a true democracy needs, and sees in the autocratic management by John Reith and the aged and unrepresentative board the major problems of the British Broadcasting Corporation state monopoly: education for democracy must itself be democratically organized.

Woolf's introduction to *The Intelligent Man's Way to Prevent War* (1933; with essays by Norman Angell, Gilbert Murray, Harold Laski, and others) began a spate of writings by him that announced with increasing clarity the inevitability of war and discussed a characteristic and recurrent Woolf theme: Europe "on the road back to Barbarism." With a premonition of its true significance unusual for the time, he quotes *Mein Kampf* (1925, 1927; translated in 1933) on Hitler's intentions and speaks of how "we are now witnessing . . . a rebellion [based on] all that is savage in us. . . ." Symptoms cited include economic crisis, political instability, tension between nations, glorification of Fascist mass murders, suppression of liberty and all freedom of thought, and barbarous persecution and torture of liberals, socialists, pacifists, and Jews. More coolly philosophical, "Can Democracy Survive?" (included in *The Modern State*, 1933) contrasts free-

dom with "disciplined obedient order" and brings a socialist dimension to the question by inquiring into human happiness and fulfillment, especially the happiness of ordinary people.

Labour's Foreign Policy (1934), edited by Woolf, essentially adapts ideas already central to Woolf's repertoire of themes. The League of Nations is seen as absolutely pivotal to Labour's policy: there can be no alternative to collective security. A new foreign policy should provide for the submission of all disputes to arbitration by compulsory judicial decision, as well as giving precise definitions of aggression to help establish when fundamental obligations have been violated, and must establish aid for victims of aggression. The league is seen to be headed on a path of failure with concomitant effects on the psychology of league supporters. And although there is an ominous emergence of dictatorships, Woolf sees a majority still wishing to work for peace, especially in England, France, and Russia, and he sees Fascist governments as having at least put the "cards on the table." The Labour party should seek changes in the league to make pooled security effective and, failing that, should invite willing states to join a "pooled security block." *The League and Abyssinia* (1936) sees the problem of that country as a touchstone for proving the seriousness of commitment to League of Nations diplomacy.

The War for Peace (1940) lies in a direct line of descent from *International Government*: "The object is to see whether one can draw the broad outline of an international system of law, cooperation, and peace, using for the purpose simply common sense and our experience of human government." For a rationalist like Woolf the elimination of war should in theory be simple: "Economically we live international lives. Yet we have consistently refused to recognize the fact in the international system, the political and economic organization of international relations." *The International Post-War Settlement* (1944) was published by the Fabian Society in cooperation with all-purpose left-wing publisher Victor Gollancz. Written on the eve of the Allies' Dumbarton Oaks meetings, it offers some recurrent left-wing suggestions aimed at extending interwar Labour party positions on international policy, including the calls for an international economic and political authority, a system of security guarantees, and an alternative to power politics.

Woolf also wrote three large, theoretical volumes that share the subtitle "A Study of Commu-

Charlotte Evans's bust of Woolf, located on the grounds of Monk's House

nal Psychology." The first two were published as *After the Deluge*. The fact that wars begin in the minds of men provides the impetus for this massive treatment of the interactions between communal beliefs and communal actions, a study seen by Woolf as without serious academic precedent. As elsewhere in Woolf the essential contest of history is seen to be between civilization and democracy on one hand and nationalist interests on the other. Volume 1 deals with methodology and considers the implications of the American Revolution; volume 2 concerns the French July Revolution of 1830 and the English Reform Bill of 1832. The third volume appeared in 1953 with the somewhat pretentious title *Principia Politica*. There Woolf found it necessary to foreshorten his overambitious scheme and to limit himself to a consideration of the modern totalitarian state, as exemplified by the Germany of Hitler and the Russia of Joseph Stalin.

Back in the later 1930s, in the face of mounting fear of another war and of the end of civilization, Woolf had aired the same themes in two other studies, aimed at a more general audience.

Quack, Quack! (1935), despite its inelegantly dismissive title, brings considerable sophistication to its task, a shrill proclamation of the betrayal of reason by the Western world and by the Fascist regimes in particular. For Woolf civilization is more or less equivalent to the ability and will to bring reason to bear on man's fundamental and lightly masked savagery. Such a quasi-Freudian understanding of human psychology is also evident in Woolf's sense that Fascists of Hitler's ilk (like primitive shamans) are both users of fear to control others and are themselves animated by deep irrational terrors and inadequacies. Woolf's most scathing criticism, however, is reserved for the antirational tendency in Western philosophy ("Intellectual Quack, Quack," with Henri Bergson as chief culprit, and with Immanuel Kant, Thomas Carlyle, and Friedrich Nietzsche as progenitors), which he sees as a concomitant and facilitating energy for the atrocities of the dictators. *Barbarians at the Gate* (1939), published in one of Gollancz's distinctive and prolific series of "Left Book Club Editions," is also something of a jeremiad about the decline of civilization, although this time the prime focus is on the internal barbarism of social, economic, and political privilege.

Two late essays in collections, written after the 1946 Labour party landslide victory, chart the contributions of Sidney and Beatrice Webb to the subsequent history of British Labour politics. "The Early Fabians and British Socialism" argues that George Bernard Shaw, the Webbs, and other early Fabians "cut off British Socialism from the continental stream of Marxist revolution and turned it into a highly respectable and constitutional movement." Sidney Webb's "gas and water socialism" is seen as the "economic side of the democratic ideal," a "gradual extension of collective ownership and control and a gradual extinction of private, individual, and class privileges and monopolies." The essay is in a 1947 collection commemorating Shaw, whose passion for destructive criticism is seen by Woolf as leaving him with no urge or patience for construction in socialism and politics; the Webbs, on the other hand, "by their writings, their sedulous penetration of trade unions, co-operative societies, local government, and preeminently the Labour Party" are seen as the true founders of modern British socialism. In "Political Thought and the Webbs" Woolf looks at their "utterly selfless" character and presents them as the near-single-handed inventors of the scientific study of social organisms.

Leonard Woolf ended his long and varied career as a writer with five volumes of autobiography. These will in all likelihood be his most lasting literary achievement, and for other reasons than their details about his well-known wife, or the fact that the best of his other nonfiction writings have not had the anthologizing they deserve. Not just mines of the merely factual, the autobiographies are themselves essays on a series of themes of considerable moment: the art of administration as applied to colonial government and to publishing, the lessons of a life in politics, the vanity of human endeavor–presented in the tradition of the preacher in Ecclesiastes–the thoughtful savoring of the lost world before the "deluge," and, most importantly, the affectionate celebration of a series of remarkable friendships.

Woolf died on 14 August 1969 shortly after completing the final volume of his autobiography. Noel Annan, Leslie Stephen's biographer, assessed Woolf's achievement thus (in the *Political*

Quarterly, vol. 41, 1970): "If Britain today is vastly more skeptical than it was of the necessity of hanging all murderers, enforcing monogamous sexual relationships, and imprisoning homosexuals, blasting colonial people with cordite, proclaiming as offensively as possible the superiority of the white to all other races, and, therefore its indisputable right to treat them as second-class citizens, some of the credit goes to [Bertrand] Russell and Woolf and their friends." Woolf's autobiographical volumes are tinged with a note of self-effacement that often modulates into a nostalgic pessimism about his achievements having any lasting effectiveness at all. However, Annan continues, "in the ninth decade of their lives, they saw their own countrymen, at last accepting in principle the kind of behavior they had urged them to adopt in the nineteen twenties. . . ."

Letters:

Letters of Leonard Woolf, edited by Frederic Spotts (San Diego: Harcourt Brace Jovanovich, 1989).

Bibliography:

Virginia Woolf Quarterly, 1 (Fall 1972): 120-140;

Leila M. J. Luedeking, "Bibliography of Works by Leonard Sydney Woolf (1880-1969),"

Biographies:

George Spater and Ian Parsons, *A Marriage of True Minds* (New York & London: Harcourt Brace Jovanovich, 1977);

Duncan Wilson, *Leonard Woolf: A Political Biography* (New York: St. Martin's, 1978).

References:

Quentin Bell, *Virginia Woolf: a Biography*, 2 volumes (London: Hogarth, 1972);

Catalogue of Books from the Library of Leonard and Virginia Woolf (Brighton, U.K.: Holleyman & Treacher, 1975);

Selma S. Meyerowitz, *Leonard Woolf* (Boston: Twayne, 1982).

Papers:

Leonard Woolf's papers (Sx. Ms. 13) are housed at the University of Sussex and were cataloged by Elizabeth Ingles and George Spater as *Leonard Woolf Papers c1885-1969* (1980).

Virginia Woolf

(25 January 1882 - 28 March 1941)

Alan Kennedy

Carnegie-Mellon University

BOOKS: *The Voyage Out* (London: Duckworth, 1915; revised edition, New York: Doran, 1920; London: Duckworth, 1920);

Two Stories Written and Printed by Virginia Woolf and L. S. Woolf (Richmond, Surrey, U.K.: Hogarth Press, 1917); Virginia Woolf's story republished as *The Mark on the Wall* (Richmond, Surrey, U.K.: Hogarth Press, 1919);

Kew Gardens (Richmond, Surrey, U.K.: Hogarth Press, 1919; Folcroft, Pa.: Folcroft, 1969);

Night and Day (London: Duckworth, 1919; New York: Doran, 1920);

Monday or Tuesday (Richmond, Surrey, U.K.: Leonard & Virginia Woolf at the Hogarth Press, 1921; New York: Harcourt, Brace, 1921);

Jacob's Room (Richmond, Surrey, U.K.: Leonard & Virginia Woolf at the Hogarth Press, 1922; New York: Harcourt, Brace, 1923);

Mr. Bennett and Mrs. Brown (London: Leonard & Virginia Woolf at the Hogarth Press, 1924; Folcroft, Pa.: Folcroft, 1977);

The Common Reader (London: Leonard & Virginia Woolf at the Hogarth Press, 1925; New York: Harcourt, Brace, 1925);

Mrs. Dalloway (London: Leonard & Virginia Woolf at the Hogarth Press, 1925; New York: Harcourt, Brace, 1925);

To the Lighthouse (London: Leonard & Virginia Woolf at the Hogarth Press, 1927; New York: Harcourt, Brace, 1927);

Orlando: A Biography (New York: Gaige, 1928; London: Leonard & Virginia Woolf at the Hogarth Press, 1928);

A Room of One's Own (New York: Fountain Press / London: Hogarth Press, 1929; New York: Harcourt, Brace, 1929);

Street Haunting (San Francisco: Westgate Press, 1930);

On Being Ill (London: Leonard & Virginia Woolf at the Hogarth Press, 1930);

Beau Brummell (New York: Rimington & Hooper, 1930);

The Waves (London: Leonard & Virginia Woolf at the Hogarth Press, 1931; New York: Harcourt, Brace, 1931);

A Letter to a Young Poet (London: Leonard & Virginia Woolf at the Hogarth Press, 1932; Folcroft, Pa.: Folcroft, 1975);

The Common Reader: Second Series (London: Leonard & Virginia Woolf at the Hogarth Press, 1932); republished as *The Second Common Reader* (New York: Harcourt, Brace, 1932);

Flush: A Biography (London: Leonard & Virginia Woolf at the Hogarth Press, 1933; New York: Harcourt, Brace, 1933);

Walter Sickert: A Conversation (London: Leonard & Virginia Woolf at the Hogarth Press, 1934; Folcroft, Pa.: Folcroft, 1970);

The Roger Fry Memorial Exhibition: An Address (Bristol: Bristol Museum and Art Gallery, 1935);

The Years (London: Leonard & Virginia Woolf at the Hogarth Press, 1937; New York: Harcourt, Brace, 1937);

Three Guineas (London: Hogarth Press, 1938; New York: Harcourt, Brace, 1938);

Reviewing (London: Hogarth Press, 1939; Folcroft, Pa.: Folcroft, 1969);

Roger Fry: A Biography (London: Hogarth Press, 1940; New York: Harcourt, Brace, 1940);

Between the Acts (London: Hogarth Press, 1941; New York: Harcourt, Brace, 1941);

The Death of the Moth and Other Essays (London: Hogarth Press, 1942; New York: Harcourt, Brace, 1942);

A Haunted House and Other Short Stories (London: Hogarth Press, 1943; New York: Harcourt, Brace, 1944);

The Moment and Other Essays (London: Hogarth Press, 1947; New York: Harcourt, Brace, 1948);

The Captain's Death Bed and Other Essays (New York: Harcourt, Brace, 1950; London: Hogarth Press, 1950);

A Writer's Diary: Being Extracts from the Diary of Virginia Woolf, edited by Leonard Woolf (Lon-

Virginia Woolf

don: Hogarth Press, 1953; New York: Harcourt, Brace, 1954);

Hours in a Library (New York: Harcourt, Brace, 1957);

Granite and Rainbow (London: Hogarth Press, 1958; New York: Harcourt, Brace, 1958);

Contemporary Writers (London: Hogarth Press, 1965; New York: Harcourt, Brace & World, 1966);

Nurse Lugton's Golden Thimble (London: Hogarth Press, 1966);

Collected Essays, 4 volumes (London: Hogarth Press, 1966-1967; New York: Harcourt, Brace & World, 1967);

Stephen versus Gladstone (Headington Quarry, U.K., 1967);

A Cockney's Farming Experiences, edited by Suzanne Henig (San Diego: San Diego State University Press, 1972);

Mrs. Dalloway's Party: A Short Story Sequence, edited

by Stella McNichol (London: Hogarth Press, 1973; New York: Harcourt Brace Jovanovich, 1975);

The London Scene: Five Essays (New York: Hallman, 1975);

The Waves: The Two Holograph Drafts, transcribed and edited by John W. Graham (Toronto & Buffalo: University of Toronto Press, 1976);

Moments of Being: Unpublished Autobiographical Writings, edited by Jeanne Schulkind (London: Chatto & Windus for University Press, 1976; New York & London: Harcourt Brace Jovanovich, 1977);

Freshwater: A Comedy, edited by Lucio P. Ruotolo (London: Hogarth Press, 1976; New York & London: Harcourt Brace Jovanovich, 1976);

The Diary of Virginia Woolf, edited by Anne Olivier Bell, 4 volumes (London: Hogarth Press, 1977-1982; New York: Harcourt Brace Jovanovich, 1977-1982);

Books and Portraits, edited by Mary Lyon (London: Hogarth Press, 1977; New York: Harcourt Brace Jovanovich, 1978);

The Pargiters, edited by Mitchell A. Leaska (New York: New York Public Library, 1977; London: Hogarth Press, 1978);

Virginia Woolf's Reading Notebooks, edited by Brenda R. Silver (Princeton, N.J. & Guildford, Surrey: Princeton University Press, 1982);

Melymbrosia: An Early Version of The Voyage Out, edited by Louise A. DeSalvo (New York: New York Public Library, 1982);

A Passionate Apprentice [early journals] (London: Hogarth Press, 1990).

Virginia Woolf is known primarily as a novelist rather than as an essayist, although she was a prolific writer of essays. Indeed, one of her advocates has gone so far as to say that her reputation as a novelist has led to her neglect as an essayist, especially as a writer of literary critical essays. If literary critical essays are to be counted as personal essays (and they are, of course, as personal as any other essay), then by sheer volume of output Woolf is a major essayist of the twentieth or of any other century. Her own definition of the personal essay is qualitative rather than quantitative, claiming that the essay is designed to give pleasure to the reader.

Adeline Virginia Stephen was born in London on 25 January 1882 to Leslie Stephen, editor of the *Cornhill* magazine and the *Dictionary of National Biography*, and his second wife, Julia Prinsep Jackson Duckworth Stephen. She was educated at home, where she was given the run of her father's extensive library. Her mother died in 1895, precipitating Virginia's first nervous breakdown. After Leslie Stephen died in 1904, Virginia and her sister and brothers—Vanessa, Thoby, and Adrian—moved to the Bloomsbury section of London. In 1912 she married Leonard Woolf, who had just resigned from the civil service after spending seven years in Ceylon. She suffered another nervous breakdown in 1913. Her first novel, *The Voyage Out*, was published in 1915. In 1917 the Woolfs, as a hobby, began printing their own works and those of friends on an old handpress set up on the dining room table of their home, Hogarth House, in Richmond; the Hogarth Press soon developed into a full-fledged publisher of experimental writings, including all of Virginia Woolf's books. Moving to Tavistock Square in Bloomsbury, the Woolfs became the cen-

ter of the "Bloomsbury group," an assemblage of intellectuals that included E. M. Forster, Lytton Strachey, John Maynard Keynes, and Vita Sackville-West. On 28 March 1941 Virginia Woolf drowned herself in a pond near Monks House, the Woolfs' home in Sussex.

Woolf's essays are available in the uniform edition put together by her husband as *Collected Essays* (1966-1967). This work is now the standard reference collection. The four volumes of this edition reprint the essays that had appeared earlier in six volumes, two of them published during Virginia Woolf's lifetime: *The Common Reader* (1925), *The Common Reader: Second Series* (1932), *The Death of the Moth and Other Essays* (1942), *The Moment and Other Essays* (1947), *The Captain's Death Bed and Other Essays* (1950), and *Granite and Rainbow* (1958). As editor, Leonard Woolf made the somewhat arbitrary decision to divide the content of the four-volume collection so that "the essays in Vols. I and II are mainly literary and critical, those in Vols. III and IV are mainly biographical." This decision is equaled in oddity by his arranging the essays chronologically by topic rather than by date of composition, so that "a critical essay on a writer born in, say, 1659 precedes one on a writer born in, say, 1672, and a biographical essay on Chaucer precedes one on Sir Walter Raleigh."

The wisdom or otherwise of his practice can be tested by a contextual reading of the essay "The Death of the Moth." In *Collected Essays* it is the final essay of the first volume. The clinical observation of the natural death of a moth (not in a flame but on a windowsill) seems designed not so much to produce pleasure in a reader as to register strangeness (the word *strange* is a key word here and in many of Woolf's other essays): "The struggle was over. The insignificant little creature now knew death. As I looked at the dead moth, this minute wayside triumph of so great a force over so mean an antagonist filled me with wonder. Just as life had been strange a few minutes before, so death was now as strange. The moth having righted himself now lay most decently and uncomplainingly composed. O yes, he seemed to say, death is stronger than I am." The last sentence is likely to strike one as odd, even as almost laughable. But it is an accurate register of the strangeness that is the object of the meditation. Since the essay is placed just after one on Katherine Mansfield ("A Terribly Sensitive Mind"), one might think that Leonard Woolf's chronological principle has served some acciden-

Virginia Stephen in 1903; she married Leonard Woolf in 1912.

tal aesthetic end–the essay makes a lyric comment on the pathetic death of Mansfield. Considered, however, in the context of the volume to which it gave the title, it has even more force. There, it is the lead essay; it is followed, apparently inconsequently, by "Evening Over Sussex: Reflections in a Motor Car." The roaming structure of the second piece does not produce a good essay, but nevertheless the piece ends with a connected thread of recollection of the "bodiliness" of human existence. This essay is followed by "Three Pictures," a coyly melodramatic piece about the death of a sailor. Then comes "Old Mrs. Grey," about a woman all of whose reasons for living are gone but, as she says: " 'I don't seem able to die.' " The comment seems to echo the theme of the opening essay, the romance of the heroic struggle of life against the mastery of death. What is potentially naively romantic in that essay, however, is countered here by the closing comments on Mrs. Grey: "So we–humanity–insist that the body shall still cling to the wire. We put out the eyes and the ears; but we pinion it there, with a bottle of medicine, a cup of tea, a dying fire, a rook on a barn door; but a rook that still lives, even with a nail through it."

This passage achieves a quality which one might as well call strangeness, or indeterminability. It radiates possibilities of reflection, use, force. It avoids both the mastery and the impotence of saying anything whose meaning can be fixed in the reader's mind. Like its subject it hovers between life and death, yet on the side of life. *The Death of the Moth and Other Essays* ends with "Thoughts on Peace in an Air Raid," which presents a picture of the body of Virginia Woolf curled up in her bed under the rain of bombs over London, opining that we are the victims of "unconscious Hitlerism" and of a "desire for aggression, the desire to dominate and enslave." One need not claim that the whole of *The Death of the Moth and Other Essays* is organically unified. One can see, however, that the volume has more apparent intelligence in its organization than has the later *Collected Essays*. (Leonard Woolf 's note to the earlier volume leaves tantalizingly vague just who was responsible for the principle of ordering, himself or Virginia.)

In a review of Rudyard Kipling's *Notebooks*, originally written for the *Athenaeum*, Woolf ex-

become excited as the lights of
Truro appeared (his sister explained,
as he grinned at her) Happily
he took to running in the corridor,
& chewing people the moon. His
sister said that she often feared for
his life, especially on moonlight
nights – did he take the stairs for the
lights of Truro? – but was heavenly
sailing for South Africa, where a
brother kept an Inn. Then there
was a woman with eyes like those
bunches of frosted grapes one sees
in grocers shops – who divides
her time between Spain & Penzance,
thinking that they have much in
common, owing to the Armada.
Then there was a virgin, who only
brought of her own hat, which, with
its dead sea salt, would lop sideways –
& in the midst of them all sat an
aged couple, growing colder &
colder, on a polytechnic tour.
          But I must now go to bed
                    VS

Last page of a letter from Virginia Stephen to Clive Bell, her sister Vanessa's husband, dated 26 December 1909
(Sotheby's, 15 December 1982)

plains that "Between the ages of sixteen and twenty-one, speaking roughly, every writer keeps a large note book devoted entirely to landscape." (The autobiographical sketches in *Moments of Being* [1976] suggest the truth of this statement, in her own case at least.) Every apprentice writer, she contends, tries for a correspondence between word and natural object until at last, with maturity, the writer turns his or her attention to "the usual thing–the human being." So that the reader will not take her rough way of generalizing as bespeaking an unjustified authoritarianism, she quotes the following lines from Kipling: "A fat carp in a pond sucks at a fallen leaf with just the sound of a wicked little worldly kiss. Then the earth steams and steams in silence, and a gorgeous butterfly, full six inches from wing to wing, cuts through the steam in a zigzag of colour and flickers up to the forehead of the god." This piece of apparently amateur realism is given full praise: "That is a perfect note. Every note of it has been matched with the object with such amazing skill that no one could be expected to bury it in a notebook." But on finding so many perfect notes "buried" in Kipling's book, one is fatigued, irritated: "One has to shut the eyes, shut the book, and do the writing over again." The writing has to be done over because Kipling has not answered the question: "who, after all, is seeing this temple, or God, or desert?" One has to rewrite Kipling to introduce "the usual thing": the point of view, the personalized element, the sensibility in which the landscape is rendered.

To turn a "literary" review into a personal essay, Woolf "shuts the eyes" to let her imagination have free run. The arbitrary constrictions of such a method are evident as soon as one reflects on the naive assumption that "description" is meant in Kipling's note to have an iconic relation to some "object." It takes a great deal of shutting of the eyes, to the extent of deliberate insensibility, not to note the sucking, wicked, little worldly kiss of the carp; the "fallen" leaf; the steaming earth; and the six inches of aerial beauty raising itself to the forehead of the god. The "note" of Kipling is a self-contained prose poem, and as she does elsewhere (for example, in the essay "A Letter to a Young Poet"), Woolf shows herself insensitive to poetry. She says that "all notebook literature produces the same effect of fatigue and obstacles . . . some block of alien matter which must be removed or assimilated before one can go on with the true process of reading."

An attempt to read through the collection of Woolf's essays offers the same difficulties that she found in Kipling's notes. One is led to ask what the importance of these little personal pieces is, and how one is to respond to them. Their range is wide, and includes reviews of writers contemporary or near contemporary: Kipling, Forster, Strachey, Henry James, Rupert Brooke, George Gissing, Marie Corelli, Thomas Hardy; essays on the great Victorian and Romantic poets and novelists, the major Elizabethans, and eighteenth-century figures: Raleigh, Montaigne, Swift, Lord Chesterfield, Sterne, Walpole, White, Dr. Johnson, Fanny Burney and her family, Mrs. Thrale, Jane Austen, Coleridge, Shelley, Donne, Defoe, Dorothy Wordsworth, William Hazlitt, De Quincey, Gibbon; essays on a host of minor figures from the past: Jack Mytton, James Woodforde, John Skinner, Emily Davies, Lady Augusta Stanley, Anne Thackeray, Lady Dorothy Nevill, Archbishop Thomson, Laetitia Pilkington, Dr. Wilkinson, and Captain Jones; essays on general subjects: the imagination, war and peace, the nature of the human mind and the question of identity, the art of biography, relations of the sexes, class in Britain and in British writing, the nature of reading and writing, illness, aging, the ideal, the promises of the body, death, feminism, and the need for a steady income of about five hundred pounds per year. One reads these essays not because one expects them to provide the critical truth on literary and historical matters. One reads them because they are "personal essays"; and Woolf's own essay on Montaigne reminds one that the essay is an *attempt* at something, an attempt likely to be characterized by failure and incompleteness. The essay experiments with life, with the mind, and with writing. It reaches out, builds up, declares that time is too short or space does not allow (a common rhetorical device of Woolf's), withdraws, closes the window, and begins again on the following page to take the risk again, to build up and attempt to escape neatly, aesthetically.

One of the best of all of Woolf's essays is "Mr. Bennett and Mrs. Brown." It is a defense of the new modes of fiction writing which she stands for and a critique of the limits of naturalist/realist fiction of the sort produced by Wells, Galsworthy, and Bennett. She creates in a short space a character on the subway, Mrs. Brown, and by her own methods effectively gives a sense of Mrs. Brown's life. She then constructs parodic and insightful versions of how her trio of realists would see Mrs. Brown, or fail to see her because of their need to make some kind of polemic point instead of rendering sensibility. It is an effective sustained piece.

Similarly, other essays on literary figures, while not of great value as literary criticism, are interesting and valuable. In the essay on Montaigne she asks, with him, why one should not draw one's own portrait with a pen. She decides that Montaigne, Pepys, and Rousseau succeeded in self-portraiture. The topic makes one think that her essays are part of her attempt to draw her own portrait, obliquely. A recurrent note in many of the essays, one that seems to be an important element in her self-portrait, is a certain view of the soul; as she puts it in the Montaigne essay: "observe, too, her duplicity, her complexity.... She believes; at the same time she does not believe." This characteristic of the soul can be called flexibility of identity, paradox, or skepticism. The Montaigne essay concludes with a note of total skepticism: she asks if beauty is enough, or if there is not "some explanation of the mystery." "To this what answer can there be? There is none. There is only one more question: 'Que scais-je?'" An almost Nietzschean dialectic emerges in some of her work: a will to power struggles with a counterforce of impotence. "Dr. Burney's Evening Party" is a pleasant anecdote of how Dr. Johnson came to dinner at the Burneys' and encountered Fulke-Greville, "one of those tortured and unhappy souls who find themselves torn asunder by opposite desires." One of those, perhaps, whose feminine soul in her duplicity is complex, paradoxical? Someone who might have the author's sympathy? Hardly. The story is one of masterful one-upmanship in which Dr. Johnson crushes Fulke-Greville with a studied silence followed by an open hint that the fellow is monopolizing the fireplace. The essay is a strange paean to the power of the literary lion. It bespeaks a dream of power, of mastery, to be realized by becoming a writer.

The essay "Jack Mytton" sympathetically traces Mytton's brief career. Mytton had "a body hewn from the solid rock, a fortune of almost indestructible immensity." No moth he. But death finds out strange ways for those with power, with mastery. Mytton is mysteriously (there is no psychological analysis in the essay) given to "heroic" excesses of gambling, drinking, and physical feats; he is one who for some reason "leapt at every obstacle." It does not take much Freud to lead one to speculate that one who leaps unnecessarily at obstacles is one who is not fully master of himself.

Similarly, the oscillation between mastery and impotence informs the essay "Swift's Journal to Stella." Swift's worldly power is the force of his writing: "For the time being Swift was omnipotent. Nobody could buy his services; everybody feared his pen." This power is enjoyed in a secret exchange, which one must think of as in some way sexual, with Stella: "He scribbled all this down to Stella without exultation or vanity. That he should command and dictate, prove himself the peer of great men and make rank abase itself before him, called for no comment on his part or on hers." Woolf inevitably finds evidence of the soul's duplicity here: the split between Swift the man of affairs and the private correspondent, between "Presto" and "t'other I." Like the moth, though, all ends in a strangeness beyond knowledge. Swift extends the sexual power of words to Vanessa. Vanessa insists that Swift marry her, and Swift rejects her with what she describes as "killing words." So deadly are the master's words that pitiful Vanessa dies three weeks after their utterance. So the openness of the power of the word can kill the secret sexual contact. So too, however, can the secret language of the journal itself kill: Stella eventually wears out from the "strain" and "concealment" and dies. Not informed about the nature of Ménière's disease, Woolf fictionalizes and thematizes Swift's long illness and death, and the reader is left to speculate on the strange and inexplicable mad end of the writer's power.

Swift is one emblem of the dialectic of mastery and impotence; Sterne is another. Sterne's exotic style in *Tristram Shandy* (1759-1767) is not exactly an achievement, it seems, since "The jerky, disconnected sentences are as rapid and it would seem as little under control as the phrases that fall from the lips of a brilliant talker." In this lack of control he is nevertheless "on far more intimate terms with us to-day than his great contemporaries the Richardsons and the Fieldings." But Sterne, although "far more nimble," is "less profound than the masters of this somewhat sedentary school...." Lacking this tame mastery, agilely impotent in the face of his own sentences, Sterne nevertheless nimbly rescues himself by means of his very art of vertigo: "For Sterne was a master of the art of contrast...."

There is at least one other focus of Woolf's essays: her concern with the questions of women and literature. Here the picture of the febrile

Drawing of Woolf in 1912 by her sister, Vanessa (courtesy of Mrs. Trekkie Parsons; by permission of Angelica Garnett)

spokesperson of the split mind, the neurasthenic sensibility, must be put aside. When she speaks of the position of women, she speaks clearly, with force. The force, it should be noted, clearly delineates the impotence of women under present conditions.

The most effective extended presentation of her social views is in *A Room of One's Own* (1929). Her solution to the social question seems absurd: just give every woman (and man) a guaranteed income of about five hundred pounds per year, and it will all work out. On the other hand, in the absence of any other method to end the injustice, a demand for a modest five hundred pounds is hard to fault. It is little enough to ask. And although the fictional persona she creates for herself in this work may seem silly at times, one can only regard with admiration and wonder the lightness of touch with which she dissects male power and injustice. She performs the perfect stylistic trick here: impotence speaking in

just the right voice is force, and does the bit that writing can to undo an unjust and traditional dispensation of power and wealth.

In "Professions for Women" in *Collected Essays* she recounts her personal encounter with the "Victorian Angel" that haunts every ambitious woman: "I turned upon her and caught her by the throat." "Though I flatter myself that I killed her in the end, the struggle was severe. . . ." She solved the problem of the Angel, "But the second, telling the truth about my experiences as a body, I do not think I solved. I doubt that any woman has solved it yet." Perhaps some women are now solving that problem, building on the efforts of earlier writers such as Virginia Woolf.

Letters:
The Flight of the Mind: The Letters of Virginia Woolf, Volume I, 1888-1912, edited by Nigel Nicolson and Joanne Trautmann (London: Hogarth Press, 1975); republished as *The Let-*

Woolf, circa 1925

ters of Virginia Woolf, Volume I: 1888-1912 (New York & London: Harcourt Brace Jovanovich, 1975);

The Question of Things Happening: The Letters of Virginia Woolf, Volume II, 1912-1922, edited by Nicolson and Trautmann (London: Hogarth Press, 1976); republished as *The Letters of Virginia Woolf, Volume II: 1912-1922* (New York & London: Harcourt Brace Jovanovich, 1976);

A Change of Perspective: The Letters of Virginia Woolf, Volume III, 1923-1928, edited by Nicolson and Trautmann (London: Hogarth Press, 1978); republished as *The Letters of Virginia Woolf, Volume III: 1923-1928* (New York & London: Harcourt Brace Jovanovich, 1978);

A Reflection of the Other Person: The Letters of Virginia Woolf, Volume IV, 1929-1931, edited by Nicolson and Trautmann (London: Hogarth Press, 1978); republished as *The Letters of Vir-*

ginia Woolf, Volume IV: 1929-1931 (New York & London: Harcourt Brace Jovanovich, 1979);

The Sickle Side of the Moon: The Letters of Virginia Woolf, Volume V, 1932-1935, edited by Nicolson and Trautmann (London: Hogarth Press, 1979); republished as *The Letters of Virginia Woolf, Volume V: 1932-1935* (New York & London: Harcourt Brace Jovanovich, 1979);

Leave the Letters Till We're Dead: The Letters of Virginia Woolf, Volume VI, 1936-1941, edited by Nicolson and Trautmann (London: Hogarth Press, 1980); republished as *The Letters of Virginia Woolf, Volume VI: 1936-1941* (New York & London: Harcourt Brace Jovanovich, 1980).

Bibliographies:
Robin Majumdar, *Virginia Woolf: An Annotated Bibliography of Criticism, 1915-1974* (New York & London: Garland, 1976);

B. J. Kirkpatrick, *A Bibliography of Virginia Woolf*, third edition (Oxford: Clarendon Press, 1980).

Biographies:

Quentin Bell, *Virginia Woolf: A Biography*, 2 volumes (New York: Harcourt Brace Jovanovich, 1972);

John Lehmann, *Virginia Woolf and Her World* (New York: Harcourt Brace Jovanovich, 1975);

George Spater and Ian Parsons, *A Marriage of True Minds: An Intimate Portrait of Leonard and Virginia Woolf* (New York: Harcourt Brace Jovanovich, 1977; London: Cape/Hogarth Press, 1977);

Phyllis Rose, *Woman of Letters: A Life of Virginia Woolf* (New York: Oxford University Press, 1978; London: Routledge & Kegan Paul, 1978);

Lyndall Gordon, *Virginia Woolf: A Writer's Life* (Oxford: Oxford University Press, 1984).

References:

Noel Annan, "Virginia Woolf Fever," *New York Review of Books*, 25 (20 April 1978): 16-28;

Nancy Topping Bazin, *Virginia Woolf and the Androgynous Vision* (New Brunswick, N.J.: Rutgers University Press, 1973);

Bulletin of the New York Public Library, special Virginia Woolf issue, 80 (Winter 1977);

Leon Edel, *Bloomsbury: A House of Lions* (Philadelphia & New York: Lippincott, 1979);

Avrom Fleishman, *Virginia Woolf: A Critical Reading* (Baltimore: Johns Hopkins University Press, 1975);

Ralph Freedman, ed., *Virginia Woolf: Revaluation and Continuity* (Berkeley & London: University of California Press, 1980);

Mary Gaither, "A Short History of the Press," in *A Checklist of the Hogarth Press*, by J. Howard Woolmer (Andes, N.Y.: Woolmer/Brotherson, 1976);

Elaine K. Ginsberg and Laura Moss Gottlieb, eds., *Virginia Woolf: Centennial Papers* (Troy, N.Y.: Whitston, 1983);

Mark Goldman, *The Reader's Art: Virginia Woolf as Literary Critic* (The Hague: Mouton, 1976);

Susan Rubinow Gorsky, *Virginia Woolf* (Boston: Twayne, 1978);

Jean Guiguet, *Virginia Woolf and Her Works*, translated by Jean Stewart (New York: Harcourt, Brace & World, 1965);

Carolyn G. Heilbrun, *Toward a Recognition of Androgyny* (New York: Knopf, 1973);

Katherine C. Hill, "Virginia Woolf and Leslie Stephen: History and Literary Revolution," *PMLA*, 96 (May 1981);

Manly Johnson, *Virginia Woolf* (New York: Ungar, 1973);

Richard Kennedy, *A Boy at the Hogarth Press* (Harmondsworth, U.K.: Penguin, 1972);

Jacqueline E. M. Latham, ed., *Critics on Virginia Woolf* (London: Allen & Unwin, 1970);

John Lehmann, *Thrown to the Woolfs* (New York: Holt, Rinehart & Winston, 1978);

Thomas S. W. Lewis, ed., *Virginia Woolf: A Collection of Criticism* (New York: McGraw-Hill, 1975);

Jean O. Love, *Virginia Woolf: Sources of Madness and Art* (Berkeley & London: University of California Press, 1977);

Robin Majumdar and Allen McLaurin, *Virginia Woolf: The Critical Heritage* (London: Routledge & Kegan Paul, 1975);

Jane Marcus, ed., *New Feminist Essays on Virginia Woolf* (Lincoln: University of Nebraska Press, 1981; London: Macmillan, 1981);

Herbert Marder, *Feminism and Art: A Study of Virginia Woolf* (Chicago: University of Chicago Press, 1968);

Allen McLaurin, *Virginia Woolf: The Echoes Enslaved* (Cambridge: Cambridge University Press, 1973);

Perry Meisel, *The Absent Father: Virginia Woolf and Walter Pater* (New Haven & London: Yale University Press, 1980);

Modern Fiction Studies, special Virginia Woolf issue, 18 (Autumn 1972);

Monique Nathan, *Virginia Woolf*, translated by Herma Briffault (New York: Evergreen Books, 1961);

Joan Russell Noble, ed., *Recollections of Virginia Woolf by Her Contemporaries* (New York: Morrow, 1972);

Jane Novak, *The Razor Edge of Balance: A Study of Virginia Woolf* (Coral Gables: University of Miami Press, 1975);

Roger Poole, *The Unknown Virginia Woolf* (Cambridge: Cambridge University Press, 1978);

Thomas Jackson Rice, *Virginia Woolf: A Guide to Research* (New York & London: Garland, 1984);

Harvena Richter, *Virginia Woolf: The Inward Voyage* (Princeton: Princeton University Press, 1970);

S. P. Rosenbaum, *The Bloomsbury Group: A Collection of Memoirs, Commentary and Criticism* (Toronto: University of Toronto Press, 1975);

Michael Rosenthal, *Virginia Woolf* (London: Routledge & Kegan Paul, 1978);

Sonya Rudikoff, "How Many Lovers Had Virginia Woolf?," *Hudson Review*, 32 (Winter 1979-1980);

Beverly Ann Schlack, *Continuing Presences: Virginia Woolf's Use of Literary Allusion* (University Park: The Pennsylvania State University Press, 1979);

Stephen Spender, *The Struggle of the Modern* (Berkeley: University of California Press, 1963);

Mark Spilka, *Virginia Woolf's Quarrel with Grieving* (Lincoln & London: University of Nebraska Press, 1980);

Claire Sprague, ed., *Virginia Woolf: A Collection of Critical Essays* (Englewood Cliffs, N.J.: Prentice-Hall, 1971);

Elizabeth Steele, *Virginia Woolf's Literary Sources and Allusions: A Guide to the Essays* (New York & London: Garland, 1983);

Stephen Trombley, *All That Summer She Was Mad* (New York: Continuum, 1982);

Twentieth Century Literature, special Virginia Woolf issue, 25 (Fall/Winter 1979);

Virginia Woolf: A Centenary Perspective (London: Macmillan, 1984);

Virginia Woolf: A Feminist Slant (Lincoln & London: University of Nebraska Press, 1983);

Virginia Woolf: New Critical Essays (London: Vision, 1983);

Virginia Woolf Quarterly (San Diego: Aeolian Press, 1972-);

René Wellek, "Virginia Woolf as Critic," *Southern Review*, 13 (July 1977);

Leonard Woolf, *Beginning Again: An Autobiography of the Years 1911 to 1918* (New York: Harcourt, Brace & World, 1964);

Woolf, *Downhill All the Way: An Autobiography of the Years 1919 to 1939* (New York: Harcourt, Brace & World, 1967);

Woolf, *The Journey Not the Arrival Matters: An Autobiography of the Years 1939 to 1969* (New York: Harcourt, Brace & World, 1970).

Papers:

The three major collections of Virginia Woolf's papers are: The Henry W. and Albert A. Berg Collection of English and American Literature, New York Public Library; The Charleston Papers, King's College, Cambridge; and the Monk's House Papers, University of Sussex Library. The Washington State University Library at Pullman, Washington, has an extensive collection of books from Virginia and Leonard Woolf's libraries and other relevant materials. The University of Texas at Austin has material by Woolf in its manuscript collection.

Checklist of Further Readings

Agate, James. *Agate's Folly*. London: Chapman & Hall, 1925.

Agate. *Fantasies and Impromptus*. London: Collins, 1923.

Agate. *White Horse and Red Lion*. London: Collins, 1924.

Barron, Oswald. *Day In and Day Out*. London & New York: Cassell, 1924.

Bensusan, S. L. *Fireside Papers*. London: Epworth Press, 1946.

Bowen, Elizabeth. *Collected Impressions*. London & New York: Longmans, Green, 1950.

Bowen, Marjorie (Gabrielle Margaret Vere Campbell). *World's Wonder and Other Essays*. London: Hutchinson, 1938.

Brown, Ivor. *Masques and Phases*. London: Cobden-Sanderson, 1926.

Butchart, Isabel. *Other People's Fires*. London: Sidgwick & Jackson, 1924.

Church, Richard. *Calling for a Spade*. London: Dent, 1939.

Church. *Calm October*. London: Heinemann, 1961.

Church. *A Country Window*. London: Heinemann, 1958.

Collins, V. H., ed. *Three Centuries of English Essays*. Freeport, N.Y.: Books for Libraries Press, 1967; London: Oxford University Press, 1981.

Darwin, Francis. *Springtime and Other Essays*. London: John Murray, 1920.

Davidson, John. *The Man Forbid, and Other Essays*. Boston: Ball, 1910.

Delafield, E. M. (Edmee Elizabeth Monica De La Pasture). *General Impressions*. London: Macmillan, 1933.

De La Mare, Walter. *Pleasures and Speculations*. London: Faber & Faber, 1940.

Dent, J. C., ed. *Ten Modern Essays*. London: Heinemann, 1930.

English Essays of To-day. London & New York: Published for The English Association by Oxford University Press, 1936.

Feldberg, Katherine, ed. *Of Men and Manners: The Englishman and His World*. Miami: University of Miami Press, 1970.

Fleming, Peter ("Moth"). *Variety: Essays, Sketches and Stories*. London & Toronto: Cape, 1933.

Freeman, John. *English Portraits and Essays*. London: Hodder & Stoughton, 1924.

Gardiner, A. G. ("Alpha of the Plough"). *Selected Essays*. London & Toronto: Dent / New York: Dutton, 1920.

Gardiner. *Many Furrows*. London & Toronto: Dent / New York: Dutton, 1924.

Garvin, Viola Taylor ("V"). *As You See It*. London: Methuen, 1922.

Gosse, Edmund. "Essay," in *Encyclopædia Britannica*, eleventh edition. New York: Encyclopædia Britannica, 1910.

Gould, Gerald. *Refuge from Nightmare and Other Essays*. London: Methuen, 1933.

Gregory, Alyse. *Wheels on Gravel*. London: John Lane, 1938.

Hamilton, Hamish, ed. *Majority, 1931-1952*. London: Hamilton, 1952.

Harrison, Frederic. *Memories and Thoughts*. London & New York: Macmillan, 1906.

Hastings, William Thomson, ed. *Contemporary Essays*. Boston & New York: Houghton Mifflin, 1928.

Hewlett, Maurice. *In a Green Shade*. London: Bell, 1920.

Hewlett. *Last Essays*. London: Heinemann, 1924; New York: Scribners, 1924.

Hewlett. *Wiltshire Essays*. London & New York: Oxford University Press, 1921.

Inge, W. R. *Labels & Libels*. New York & London: Harper, 1929.

Inge. *A Rustic Moralist*. London: Putnam's, 1937.

Inge, ed. *The Post Victorians*. London: Nicholson & Watson, 1933.

Jepson, R. W., ed. *Essays by Modern Writers*. London & New York: Longmans, Green, 1935.

Joad, C. E. M. *Opinions*. London: Westhouse, 1945.

Joad. *More Opinions*. London: Westhouse, 1946.

Koestler, Arthur. *Drinkers of Infinity: Essays, 1955-1967*. London: Hutchinson, 1968.

Macaulay, Rose. *A Casual Commentary*. London: Methuen, 1925; New York: Boni & Liveright, 1926.

Macaulay. *Personal Pleasures*. London: Gollancz, 1935; New York: Macmillan, 1936.

Machen, Arthur. *Dog and Duck*. New York: Knopf, 1924.

Marriott, J. W., ed. *Modern Essays and Sketches*. London, Edinburgh & New York: Nelson, 1935.

Massingham, H. J. *Untrodden Ways*. London: Unwin, 1923.

McDowall, Arthur. *A Detached Observer*, edited by Mary McDowall. London: Oxford University Press, 1934.

McDowall. *Ruminations*. London: Heinemann, 1925; Boston & New York: Houghton Mifflin, 1925.

Middleton, Richard. *Monologues*. London: Unwin, 1913.

Milne, James. *A London Book Window*. London: John Lane, 1924; Freeport, N.Y.: Books for Libraries Press, 1968.

Montague, C. E. *The Right Place*. London: Chatto & Windus, 1924.

Murray, D. L. *Scenes & Silhouettes*. London: Cape, 1926.

Nevinson, H. W. *Words and Deeds*. Harmondsworth & New York: Penguin, 1942.

Norman, Sylva, ed. *Contemporary Essays 1933*. London: Mathews & Marrot, 1933.

Norwood, Gilbert. *Spoken in Jest*. Toronto: Macmillan, 1938.

Partridge, Eric. *Journey to the Edge of Morning*. London: Müller, 1946.

Ponsonby, Arthur. *Casual Observations*. London: Allen & Unwin, 1930.

Priestley, J. B., ed. *Essayists Past and Present*. New York: Dial, 1925; London: Jenkins, 1925.

Pritchard, F. H., ed. *Essays of To-Day*. London: Harrap, 1923; Boston: Little, Brown, 1924.

Pritchard, ed. *Essays of To-Day and Yesterday*. London: Harrap, 1926.

Pritchard, ed. *More Essays of To-Day*. London: Harrap, 1928.

Read, Herbert. *A Coat of Many Colours*. London: Routledge & Kegan Paul, 1956.

Rhondda, Margaret Haig (Thomas) Mackworth, Second Viscountess. *Notes on the Way*. London: Macmillan, 1937; Freeport, N.Y.: Books for Libraries Press, 1968.

Rhys, E., ed. *Modern English Essays*, 5 volumes. London & Toronto: Dent / New York: Dutton, 1922.

Rhys, and Vaughan, Lloyd, eds. *A Century of English Essays*. London: Everyman's Library, 1913; New York: Dutton, 1913.

Runciman, James. *Side Lights*, edited by John F. Runciman. London: Unwin, 1893.

Saintsbury, George. *The Collected Essays and Papers of George Saintsbury*, 4 volumes. London & Toronto: Dent / New York: Dutton, 1923-1924.

Sharp, William ("Fiona MacLeod"). *At the Turn of the Year*. Edinburgh: Turnbull & Spears, 1913.

Sharp. *Where the Forest Murmurs*. New York: Scribners, 1906.

Spectator Harvest, with a foreword by Wilson Harris. London: Hamilton, 1952.

Squire, J. C. *Essays at Large, by Solomon Eagle*. London & New York: Hodder & Stoughton, 1922.

Squire. *Life and Letters; Essays by J. C. Squire*. New York: Doran, 1921.

Street, G. S. *A Book of Essays*. Westminster: Constable, 1902; New York: Dutton, 1903.

Street. *People and Questions*. London: Secker, 1910.

Swinnerton, Frank. *The Georgian Scene: A Literary Panorama*. New York: Farrar & Rinehart, 1934. Republished as *The Georgian Literary Scene: A Panorama*. London & Toronto: Heinemann, 1935.

Tanner, W. M., and D. Barrett, eds. *Modern Familiar Essays*. Boston: Little, Brown, 1930.

Thomas, Gilbert Oliver. *Calm Weather*. London: Chapman & Hall, 1930.

Walker, Hugh. *The English Essay and Essayist*. London & Toronto: Dent / New York: Dutton, 1915.

Waugh, Evelyn. *A Little Order*, edited by Donat Gallagher. London: Methuen, 1977; Boston: Little, Brown, 1981.

West, Rebecca. *The Strange Necessity: Essays and Reviews*. London: Cape, 1928; Garden City, N.Y.: Doubleday, Doran, 1928.

Woolf, Leonard S. and Virginia, eds. *The Hogarth Essays*. Freeport, N.Y.: Books for Libraries Press, 1970.

Contributors

Ronald Ayling...*University of Alberta*
Robert Beum ....*St. John's, Newfoundland*
William Blissett ....*University of Toronto*
Robert L. Calder...*University of Saskatchewan*
Nils Clausson ....*University of Regina*
W. Glenn Clever...*University of Ottawa*
Charles Doyle ....*University of Victoria*
Jonathan D. Evans...*University of Georgia*
Joyce T. Forbes...*Lakehead University*
J. P. Greenwood...*Waterloo, Ontario*
R. C. Johnson...*University of British Columbia*
J. Kieran Kealy ....*University of British Columbia*
Patrick J. Kelly..*St. Thomas More College*
Alan Kennedy ....*Carnegie-Mellon University*
Christopher Kent...*University of Saskatchewan*
Laurence Kitzan ....*University of Saskatchewan*
Thomas A. Kuhlman..*Creighton University*
John Lingard...*University of Western Ontario*
Charles E. May...*California State University, Long Beach*
Nancy-Lou Patterson ....*University of Waterloo*
Ian Ross..*University of British Columbia*
R. D. Schell...*Laurentian University*
Angus Somerville ....*Brock University*
Ralph Stewart ....*Acadia University*
R. D. Stock ....*University of Nebraska at Lincoln*
Bruce Stovel..*University of Alberta*
Frank M. Tierney..*University of Ottawa*
George Woodcock...*Vancouver, British Columbia*

Cumulative Index

Dictionary of Literary Biography, Volumes 1-100
Dictionary of Literary Biography Yearbook, 1980-1989
Dictionary of Literary Biography Documentary Series, Volumes 1-7

Cumulative Index

DLB before number: *Dictionary of Literary Biography*, Volumes 1-100
Y before number: *Dictionary of Literary Biography Yearbook*, 1980-1989
DS before number: *Dictionary of Literary Biography Documentary Series*, Volumes 1-7

A

D

F

G

L

S

T

U

8411

(Continued from front endsheets)

71: *American Literary Critics and Scholars, 1880-1900*, edited by John W. Rathbun and Monica M. Grecu (1988)

72: *French Novelists, 1930-1960*, edited by Catharine Savage Brosman (1988)

73: *American Magazine Journalists, 1741-1850*, edited by Sam G. Riley (1988)

74: *American Short-Story Writers Before 1880*, edited by Bobby Ellen Kimbel, with the assistance of William E. Grant (1988)

75: *Contemporary German Fiction Writers*, Second Series, edited by Wolfgang D. Elfe and James Hardin (1988)

76: *Afro-American Writers, 1940-1955*, edited by Trudier Harris (1988)

77: *British Mystery Writers, 1920-1939*, edited by Bernard Benstock and Thomas F. Staley (1988)

78: *American Short-Story Writers, 1880-1910*, edited by Bobby Ellen Kimbel, with the assistance of William E. Grant (1988)

79: *American Magazine Journalists, 1850-1900*, edited by Sam G. Riley (1988)

80: *Restoration and Eighteenth-Century Dramatists*, First Series, edited by Paula R. Backscheider (1989)

81: *Austrian Fiction Writers, 1875-1913*, edited by James Hardin and Donald G. Daviau (1989)

82: *Chicano Writers*, First Series, edited by Francisco A. Lomelí and Carl R. Shirley (1989)

83: *French Novelists Since 1960*, edited by Catharine Savage Brosman (1989)

84: *Restoration and Eighteenth-Century Dramatists*, Second Series, edited by Paula R. Backscheider (1989)

85: *Austrian Fiction Writers After 1914*, edited by James Hardin and Donald G. Daviau (1989)

86: *American Short-Story Writers, 1910-1945*, First Series, edited by Bobby Ellen Kimbel (1989)

87: *British Mystery and Thriller Writers Since 1940*, First Series, edited by Bernard Benstock and Thomas F. Staley (1989)

88: *Canadian Writers, 1920-1959*, Second Series, edited by W. H. New (1989)

89: *Restoration and Eighteenth-Century Dramatists*, Third Series, edited by Paula R. Backscheider (1989)

90: *German Writers in the Age of Goethe, 1789-1832*, edited by James Hardin and Christoph E. Schweitzer (1989)

91: *American Magazine Journalists, 1900-1960*, First Series, edited by Sam G. Riley (1990)

92: *Canadian Writers, 1890-1920*, edited by W. H. New (1990)

93: *British Romantic Poets, 1789-1832*, First Series, edited by John R. Greenfield (1990)

94: *German Writers in the Age of Goethe: Sturm und Drang to Classicism*, edited by James Hardin and Christoph E. Schweitzer (1990)

95: *Eighteenth-Century British Poets*, First Series, edited by John Sitter (1990)

96: *British Romantic Poets, 1789-1832*, Second Series, edited by John R. Greenfield (1990)

97: *German Writers from the Enlightenment to Sturm und Drang, 1720-1764*, edited by James Hardin and Christoph E. Schweitzer (1990)

98: *Modern British Essayists*, First Series, edited by Robert Beum (1990)

99: *Canadian Writers Before 1890*, edited by W. H. New (1990)

100: *Modern British Essayists*, Second Series, edited by Robert Beum (1990)

ST. MICHAEL'S PREP SCHOOL LIBRARY
1042 STAR RT. - ORANGE, CA 92667